Arctic Fever

Anastasia Likhacheva
Editor

Arctic Fever

Political, Economic & Environmental Aspects

Editor
Anastasia Likhacheva
Faculty of World Economy
and International Affairs
National Research University Higher
School of Economics
Moscow, Russia

ISBN 978-981-16-9615-2 ISBN 978-981-16-9616-9 (eBook)
https://doi.org/10.1007/978-981-16-9616-9

© The Editor(s) (if applicable) and The Author(s), under exclusive license to Springer
Nature Singapore Pte Ltd. 2022
This work is subject to copyright. All rights are solely and exclusively licensed by the
Publisher, whether the whole or part of the material is concerned, specifically the rights of
reprinting, reuse of illustrations, recitation, broadcasting, reproduction on microfilms or in
any other physical way, and transmission or information storage and retrieval, electronic
adaptation, computer software, or by similar or dissimilar methodology now known or
hereafter developed.
The use of general descriptive names, registered names, trademarks, service marks, etc.
in this publication does not imply, even in the absence of a specific statement, that such
names are exempt from the relevant protective laws and regulations and therefore free for
general use.
The publisher, the authors, and the editors are safe to assume that the advice and information in this book are believed to be true and accurate at the date of publication. Neither
the publisher nor the authors or the editors give a warranty, expressed or implied, with
respect to the material contained herein or for any errors or omissions that may have been
made. The publisher remains neutral with regard to jurisdictional claims in published maps
and institutional affiliations.

This Palgrave Macmillan imprint is published by the registered company Springer Nature
Singapore Pte Ltd.
The registered company address is: 152 Beach Road, #21-01/04 Gateway East, Singapore
189721, Singapore

A Melting Jackpot: General Overview of Rising Ambitions in more and more Vulnerable Arctic Region

This book represents an attempt of comprehensive analysis of the Arctic as a rapidly evolving phenomenon in international affairs—for a rising number of stakeholders. The book unites scholars from 11 countries, involved in Arctic, law, energy and climate studies. And all of them focus on evolving routines of the Arctic region, emergence of new factors, and their implications for international relations in the region, national Arctic strategies and existing joint institutions and projects. The book provides various views on the present and the future of the *Arctic as an international region with strong state actors*: some authors stay on rather alarmist positions, the others concentrate on rising opportunities for cooperation "due to" climate threats—a pretty new challenge for international system, where a threat is objective while a particular enemy doesn't exist.

The table of content reflects new roles of the Arctic region: as a playground for the old-school nation state competition and even confrontation on one hand, and a new source for international cooperation in energy, logistics and natural sciences—on the other. Climate change, political tensions and economic competition make Arctic a heating up venue of international relations. New Arctic fever, studied through a comparative analysis of different regional agendas, especially within the focus on United States–China–Russia triangle, represents the main subject of our book.

The basic research hypothesis behind this book states that *a period when the Arctic region was called the territory of cooperation, free of existing*

v

intense tensions, typical for international relations, had passed. Militarization is proceeding rapidly, which, given the Arctic geography, is capable of changing fundamentally the strategic position of the opposing sides. The growing role of the Arctic in the global economy attracts the attention of new players, including China. An "Arctic triangle" is being formed, consisting of the United States, Russia and China, whose capabilities, ambitions and diplomatic potential are about to determine the future development of the Arctic region. At the same time, an institutional design of Arctic cooperation, established around the Arctic Council, does not fit to a set of modern challenges that the region faces. As a result, the institution fails to play its crucial role of mediator for member states.

This dualism of state-centric and problem-centric approaches will accompany the reader across the whole book. The most recent "intro" in Arctic affairs—a spillover of contradictions and conflict between the United States and Russia, as well as the United States and China, attracts attention of the authors from the Centre for Comprehensive European and International studies of the HSE, Dmitry Suslov and Vassily Kashin. Their triangular point of view is further developed by Ilya Kramnik from IMEMO RAS with the military analysis of the Arctic agenda and partially shared by the scholars from the US (George Soroka from Harvard University draws a dynamic portrait of the US Arctic policy) and China (Dr. Long ZHAO presents an alternative view on the Arctic affairs from the position of a non-Arctic state, brilliantly illustrating differences of the Chinese approach compared to a Russian one and challenges of Sino-American relations in the Arctic region).

However not all the authors share the importance of a triangular framework, focusing more in their analysis on traditional Arctic challenges of the environmental character or institutional limitations for fruitful cooperation. We can find this focus both in the chapters of the scholars from Arctic states, like Norway (chapter by Andreas Østhagen from Fridtjof Nansen Institute and High North Center) or Canada (P. Whitney Lackenbauer, Canada Research Chair (Tier 1) in the Study of the Canadian North and Professor in the School for the Study of Canada at Trent University co-authors with Peter Kikkert, Irving Shipbuilding Chair in Arctic Policy in the Brian Mulroney Institute of Government), and Asian-observers of the Arctic Council, like Japan (see a chapter by Juha Saunavaara and Marina Lomaeva from Arctic Research Center of the Hokkaido University.). These chapters are more state-centric and also illustrate various lenses that arctic stakeholders "wear" these days.

Some topical priorities of the book are determined by the most dynamic changes of Arctic status quo of the post-Cold war period.

First, Russian Chairmanship in the Arctic council of 2021–2023 coincides with an extensive domestic Arctic reform: Ru*ssia actively reassess its role in the Arctic balance of power, responsibility, economy and energy*—and we invited several authors to highlight different aspects of this transformation—the most intense of the last 30 years. Professors Boris Porfiriev and Vladislav Leksin from Russian Academy of Science (RAS) focus on economic aspects of a new Arctic strategy, while professors Valery Kryukov and Vladimir Nefedkin from the Institute of Economics and Industrial Engineering, Siberian Branch of the RAS in Novosibirsk, as well as Alexander Pilyasov from Lomonosov Moscow State University and Elena Putilova (ANO "Institute of Regional Consulting") represent more of critical analysis of innovative and inclusive challenges for the Arctic region respectively.

Similarly rising ambitions of non-Arctic states both in Asia and Europe multiplied by their rising role as green regulators for Arctic energy projects, call for more detailed representation of their strategies than before: the readers can find it both in Chinese and Japanese chapters, mentioned above, or in the very special puzzle—the European chapter that unites scholars from France, Great Britain, Norway in their attempts to balance European and national Arctic ambitions of the European states—to check the results just read the chapter by Emilie Canova, from University of Cambridge (UK), Camille Escudé-Joffres from Sciences Po (France), Andreas Raspotnik from Nord University (Norway) and Florian Vidal, from University of Paris.

Second, the book clearly focuses on climate change and attempts to re-evaluate environmental agenda of the Arctic. First, from theoretical point of view, like in the chapters of Lassi Heininen, Professor of Arctic Politics at the University of Lapland and Chairman of the Steering Committee of Northern Research Forum (Finland), or Andrey Skriba and Arina Sapogova (HSE Lab for Research of Political Geography and Modern Geopolitics) with the focus on the phenomena of Environmental geopolitics in the Arctic. Second, from the prospective of the energy–climate nexus, like Ilya Stepanov, deputy head of the HSE Lab of Economics of Climate Change, or Dr. Morena Scalamera from Leiden University, who dedicates her chapter to EU Green deal and its implications for Russian Arctic energy projects.

Third, we provide a space for scholars who study Arctic as a complex international region, still united by joint projects and formats, to share their views on the evolution of these common goods of the Arctic region. First, they do study it from institutional point of view, like Pavel Gudev from RAS and Dmitriy Tulipov from Saint-Petersburg University do in their chapter, dedicated to the Arctic Council, or Daria Boklan from the HSE International Law Department with the pioneer analysis of the navigation regimes in the melting, but more fragile Arctic. Second framework is project oriented. It is represented by various chapters: the assessments of the shelf-projects in the modern Arctic by Alexey Fadeev, Chief Researcher of the G.P. Luzin Institute of Economic Problems of Integrated Scientific Institution of RAS and Marina Fadeeva from Peter the Great St. Petersburg Polytechnic University. Also, readers will find the analysis of the Northern sea route as an energy bridge in a chapter prepared by Vitaly Ermakov from the HSE and Oxford Energy Institute and Anna Ermakova from University of Denver, and representation of Arctic research cooperation in a chapter of the group of scholars from the leading Russian Arctic research consortium with Konstantin Zaikov ahead (from NArFU named after M.V. Lomonosov in Arkhangelsk).

As an editor I express my profound gratitude to all the authors for their efforts to present a fresh and non-biased analysis of the most recent developments in the Arctic region. This book won't be possible without the generous support of the Faculty of World Economy and International affairs of the HSE, and enthusiastic work of many research assistants of the Centre for Comprehensive European and International Studies who had been carefully dealing with 20 chapters from three continents—especially to Vladislav Semenov, who bridged our authors and publishing house deadlines so carefully. I also would like to express my profound gratitude to Dr. Alexander Lukin, Head of the Department of International Relations of the HSE—for his initial inspiring introduction of the idea. Hope that this book will open new discussions and policy advice research initiatives aimed at the provision of safer, prosperous and more sustainable Arctic in the very nearest future.

Anastasia Likhacheva
Dean, Faculty of World Economy
and International Affairs
Higher School of Economics
Moscow, Russia

CONTENTS

Why Arctic and Why Now?

Arctic as a New Playground for Great Power Competition: The Russia–China–United States Triangle — 3
Dmitry Suslov and Vassily Kashin

The Cold War in the Cold Region: A Return — 31
Ilya Kramnik

The Age of Climate Change, as a Challenge for States, and IR Theories — 45
Lassi Heininen

Climate Change and Energy Transition: Controversial Implications for the Arctic Region — 67
Ilya A. Stepanov

Environment, Geopolitics and Environmental Geopolitics in the Arctic: Is There a Logic of Conflict Among Institutions of Cooperation? — 85
Andrei Skriba and Arina Sapogova

Kaleidoscope of Independent Agendas for the Arctic: Russia

Risks and Socioeconomic Priorities for Sustainable
Development of the Russian Arctic ... 115
Vladimir N. Leksin and Boris N. Porfiriev

Corporations in the Russian Arctic—From Dominance
to Leadership ... 137
Valeriy A. Kryukov and Vladimir I. Nefedkin

Peripheral Innovation System and Its Place
in the Development of the Russian Arctic Resources ... 155
Alexander Pilyasov and Elena Putilova

Kaleidoscope of Independent Agendas for the Arctic: North America

A Reluctant Arctic Power No More? The United States'
Evolving Engagement with the High North ... 193
George Soroka

A "Profound Change of Direction?" Canada's Northern
Strategy and the Co-Development of a "New" Arctic
and Northern Policy Framework ... 241
P. Whitney Lackenbauer and Peter Kikkert

Kaleidoscope of Independent Agendas for the Arctic: Scandinavia and Europe

Norway's Arctic Policy: High North, Low Tension? ... 277
Andreas Østhagen

European Policies in the Arctic: National Strategies
or a Common Vision? ... 305
Emilie Canova, Camille Escudé-Joffres, Andreas Raspotnik,
and Florian Vidal

The EU's Low-Carbon Policies and Implications for Arctic
Energy Projects: The Russian Case ... 333
Morena Skalamera

Kaleidoscope of Independent Agendas for the Arctic: Asia

Challenges and Common Agenda for Arctic Cooperation in the Post-pandemic Era: A Chinese Perspective   357
Long ZHAO

Japan Facing the Arctic and North: Interplay Between the National and Regional Interests   393
Marina Lomaeva and Juha Saunavaara

Cooperative and Multilateral Agenda of the Arctic Region: Despite All Odds. International Law, Institutions and Regimes for the Arctic Region

Institutional Framework for Arctic Governance: Do We Need Reforms?   431
Pavel Gudev and Dmitriy Tulupov

Channeling of Liability: Shall Arctic States Be Liable for Environmental Harm in the Arctic Caused by Navigation or Polluter Pays Principle Should Prevail?   451
Daria Boklan

Cooperative and Multilateral Agenda of the Arctic Region: Despite All Odds. Development Projects and Initiatives in the Arctic Region: Infrastructure, Natural Resources, Research and Innovation

Northern Sea Route as Energy Bridge   473
Vitaly Yermakov and Ana Yermakova

Arctic Shelf Projects as a Driver for Social and Economic Development of the High North Territories: International Experience and Potential for Russian Practice   497
Alexey Fadeev and Marina Fadeeva

Innovative Scientific and Educational Projects of the Barents Euro-Arctic Region as a Resource for the Development of Interregional Cooperation in the Arctic   529
Konstantin S. Zaikov, Lyubov A. Zarubina, Svetlana V. Popkova, Nikita M. Kuprikov, Mikhail Yu. Kuprikov, and Denis O. Doronin

Index   555

LIST OF CONTRIBUTORS

Boklan Daria Department of International Law, Faculty of Law, National Research University Higher School of Economics, Moscow, Russia

Canova Emilie Scott Polar Research Institute, University of Cambridge, Cambridge, UK

Doronin Denis O. ANO Research Center "Polar Initiative", Moscow, Russia

Escudé-Joffres Camille Center for International Studies (CERI), Sciences Po Paris, Paris, France

Fadeev Alexey G. P. Luzin Institute of Economic Problems of Kola Science Centre, Russian Academy of Science, Apatity, Murmansk region, Russia;
Higher School of Industrial Management, Peter the Great St. Petersburg Polytechnic University, St. Petersburg, Russia;
Russian Gas Society, Moscow, Russia

Fadeeva Marina Higher School of Industrial Management, Peter the Great St. Petersburg Polytechnic University, St. Petersburg, Russia

Gudev Pavel Center for North American Studies, Primakov Institute of World Economy and International Relations Russian Academy of Sciences (IMEMO RAS), Moscow, Russia

Heininen Lassi University of Lapland, Rovaniemi, Finland; Arctic Yearbook, Akureyri, Iceland

Kashin Vassily Center for Comprehensive European and International Studies, National Research University Higher School of Economics, Moscow, Russia

Kikkert Peter Brian Mulroney Institute of Government, St. Francis Xavier University (StFX), Antigonish, NS, Canada

Kramnik Ilya Institute of World Economy and International Relations, Russian Academy of Sciences, Moscow, Russia

Kryukov Valeriy A. Institute of Economics and Industrial Engineering, Siberian Branch of the Russian Academy of Sciences, Novosibirsk, Russia; Higher School of Economics, Moscow, Russia

Kuprikov Mikhail Yu. Moscow Aviation Institute, National Research University, Moscow, Russia

Kuprikov Nikita M. Moscow Aviation Institute, National Research University, Moscow, Russia

Lackenbauer P. Whitney Trent University, Peterborough, ON, Canada

Leksin Vladimir N. Federal Research Center "Computer Science and Control", Russian Academy of Sciences, Moscow, Russia

Lomaeva Marina Arctic Research Center, Hokkaido University, Sapporo, Japan

Nefedkin Vladimir I. Institute of Economics and Industrial Engineering, Siberian Branch of the Russian Academy of Sciences, Novosibirsk, Russia

Østhagen Andreas Fridtjof Nansen Institute, Lysaker, Norway

Pilyasov Alexander Lomonosov Moscow State University, Moscow, Russia

Popkova Svetlana V. International Cooperation Department, NArFU named after M.V. Lomonosov, Arkhangelsk, Russia

Porfiriev Boris N. Institute of Economic Forecasting, Russian Academy of Sciences, Moscow, Russia

Putilova Elena ANO "Institute of Regional Consulting", Moscow, Russia

Raspotnik Andreas Fridtjof Nansen Institute, Oslo, Norway

Sapogova Arina Laboratory for Research of Political Geography and Modern Geopolitics, Higher School of Economics, Moscow, Russia

Saunavaara Juha Arctic Research Center, Hokkaido University, Sapporo, Japan

Skalamera Morena Institute for History, University Lecturer in Russian and International Studies, Leiden University, Leiden, Netherlands

Skriba Andrei Laboratory for Research of Political Geography and Modern Geopolitics, Higher School of Economics, Moscow, Russia

Soroka George Harvard University, Cambridge, MA, USA

Stepanov Ilya A. Laboratory for Climate Change Economics, National Research University Higher School of Economics, Moscow, Russia

Suslov Dmitry Center for Comprehensive European and International Studies, National Research University Higher School of Economics, RIAC Member, Moscow, Russia

Tulupov Dmitriy St. Petersburg State University, Saint Petersburg, Russia

Vidal Florian Paris Interdisciplinary Energy Research Institute (LIED), Paris Cité University, Paris, France

Yermakov Vitaly Oxford Institute of Energy, Higher School of Economics, Oxford, UK

Yermakova Ana University of Denver, Denver, CO, USA

Zaikov Konstantin S. Department of Regional Studies, International Relations and Political Science, NArFU named after M.V. Lomonosov, Arkhangelsk, Russia

Zarubina Lyubov A. International Cooperation Department, NArFU named after M.V. Lomonosov, Arkhangelsk, Russia

ZHAO Long Institute for Global Governance Studies, Shanghai Institutes for International Studies, Shanghai, China

LIST OF FIGURES

Climate Change and Energy Transition: Controversial Implications for the Arctic Region

Fig. 1   Dynamics of the price of Brent crude oil, quarterly, USD per barrel (*Source* Euromonitor International)   76

Corporations in the Russian Arctic—From Dominance to Leadership

Fig. 1   Dividends to consolidated proceeds from sales for the entire Norilsk Nickel Group of companies in 2006–2019 (*Source* The authors' calculations and Norilsk Nickel annual statements https://www.nornickel.ru/investors/disclo sure/annual-reports/. Accessed 20 June 2021)   147

Peripheral Innovation System and Its Place in the Development of the Russian Arctic Resources

Fig. 1   Patent activity of three Arctic corporations: NovaTEK (a), Nrolisk Nickel (b) and Gazpromneft (c)   174

A "Profound Change of Direction?" Canada's Northern Strategy and the Co-Development of a "New" Arctic and Northern Policy Framework

Fig. 1   Mary Simon's principles of partnership (*Source* Simon, 2017)   256

Norway's Arctic Policy: High North, Low Tension?

Fig. 1   Map of Norway, with the Arctic Circle highlighted   281

European Policies in the Arctic: National Strategies or a Common Vision?

Fig. 1   Institutional intricateness between the EU and the Arctic (Canova, 2020)   312

Northern Sea Route as Energy Bridge

Fig. 1   Northern Sea Corridor and Northern Sea Route (*The Economist*, 2014)   475
Fig. 2   Volume of shipments via NSR by type of cargo, 2014–2020   478
Fig. 3   Shipments via NSR by Arctic class of vessels, 2014–2020   479
Fig. 4   Number of Yamal LNG carriers navigating NSR per month   481
Fig. 5   The split in shipments via NSR between Europe and Asia in 2020   481
Fig. 6   International transit via NSR   482
Fig. 7   International transit via NSR by direction of shipment   483
Fig. 8   Average winter (left graph) and summer (right graph) temperatures in the vicinity of the Northern Sea Route   486
Fig. 9   Extent of minimum ice coverage (recorded in September) of seas along the NSR—Kara sea, Laptev sea, East Siberian sea, Chukchi sea   487
Fig. 10   Chronology of major events in the history of Soviet and Russian nuclear icebreaker fleet   488
Fig. 11   Novatek's LNG production and evacuation plans   491
Fig. 12   LNG comparative logistics and costs on shipments to Asia in 2020   492
Fig. 13   Vostok oil project   493

Arctic Shelf Projects as a Driver for Social and Economic Development of the High North Territories: International Experience and Potential for Russian Practice

Fig. 1	History of Russian Arctic development (PJSC Gazprom Neft. Access mode: www.gazprom-neft.ru)	499
Fig. 2	Contribution of enterprises located in the Arctic zone to GDP and Russian exports	509
Fig. 3	Inter-sectoral management framework	522

List of Tables

Climate Change and Energy Transition: Controversial Implications for the Arctic Region

Table 1	Changes in the volume and structure of primary energy consumption in key markets according to the IEA 2020 forecast	74

Peripheral Innovation System and Its Place in the Development of the Russian Arctic Resources

Table 1	Comparative analysis of patent activity	173
Table 2	Geography of citations and references of patents of "NovaTEK" on the main stages of the production process	175
Table 3	Geography of citations and references of patents of "Norilsk Nickel" for the main stages of the production process	176

Norway's Arctic Policy: High North, Low Tension?

Table 1	Arctic policy documents released since 2003	287

xxiii

xxiv LIST OF TABLES

European Policies in the Arctic: National Strategies or a Common Vision?

Table 1	List of European Union policy documents relating to the Arctic	306
Table 2	Profiles of French Ambassadors for Polar Affairs (2009–2021)	316

Challenges and Common Agenda for Arctic Cooperation in the Post-pandemic Era: A Chinese Perspective

Table 1	Shipping statistics of COSCO shipping via NSR/Northeast Passage from 2013 to 2019	372

Japan Facing the Arctic and North: Interplay Between the National and Regional Interests

Table 1	Timeline of Japan's Arctic engagement and establishment of the related institutions	397
Table 2	Japan's principal actors involved in the North/Arctic-related projects	398
Table 3	Japan/Hokkaido's participation in the Arctic/North-related forums	403
Table 4	Japan's representative Arctic/North-related projects	405
Table 5	Timeline of Hokkaido and Sapporo's Northern/Arctic engagement (Babin & Saunavaara, 2021; Kossa et al., 2020; WWCAM, 2020a)	414

Arctic Shelf Projects as a Driver for Social and Economic Development of the High North Territories: International Experience and Potential for Russian Practice

Table 1	Major accidents and incidents on offshore platforms and facilities (Fadeev et al., 2019)	513
Table 2	Objective positive and negative consequences for the region of the development of oil and gas fields on its territory (Kryukov & Tokarev, 2007)	525

Why Arctic and Why Now?

Arctic as a New Playground for Great Power Competition: The Russia–China–United States Triangle

Dmitry Suslov and Vassily Kashin

INTRODUCTION

The role and place of the Arctic in the international relations agenda is changing and growing rapidly. From the periphery of international relations and an area of low politics, it is becoming one of the central regions of great power competition, where the three major powers of contemporary international system—the United States, China and Russia—face

---

This chapter draws some ideas from Report of the HSE University "Russian Policy in the Arctic: International Aspects".—Karaganov, S. A., Likhacheva, A. B., Stepanov, I. A., Suslov, D. V., et al. (2021, April 13–30). Russian Policy in the Arctic: International Aspects: rep. at XXII Apr. International Academic Conference on Economic and Social Development, Moscow. Moscow: Higher School of Economics Publishing House. https://cceis.hse.ru/data/2021/05/20/1434678670/Russian_Policy_in_the_Arctic_report.pdf.

D. Suslov (✉)
Center for Comprehensive European and International Studies, National Research University Higher School of Economics, RIAC Member, Moscow, Russia
e-mail: dvsuslov@hse.ru

© The Author(s), under exclusive license to Springer Nature Singapore Pte Ltd. 2022
A. Likhacheva (ed.), *Arctic Fever*,
https://doi.org/10.1007/978-981-16-9616-9_1

each other. The US relations with both Russia and China are in a state of systemic, comprehensive and long-term confrontation, whereas Moscow and Beijing, although major partners for each other in general and in the Arctic in particular, fundamentally disagree about the region's governance. In 2019, 2020 and 2021 the United States published three military Arctic strategies in a row—Arctic Strategy of the Department of Defense (2019), the Department of the Air Force (2020) and the Department of the United States Army (2021), respectively, in which it claimed that the period when the Arctic remained primarily a region of international cooperation is now in the past, and that the region was one of the most preferential for building up its military presence. The US State Secretary under Trump Administration described the new role of the Arctic in 2019 as a terrain of "power and competition" (Sengupta, 2019).

The basic reason behind the Arctic's growing international centrality is the coincidence of its profound transformation, caused by the climate change, with the recent shift of US–Russia and US–China relations toward systemic confrontation. This differs the current developments in the Arctic from the previous Cold war: at that time the region, firmly covered by ice, was considered unchangeable. Despite it was one of the areas where the USSR was bordering NATO and where the Soviet strategic nuclear force was deployed, it was peripheral for the Cold war confrontation. The latter centered in Europe and was much more significant in other regions. Now, on the contrary, the Arctic might become one of the central regions of a much less orderly new great power confrontation.

Due to the peculiarities of the northern ecosystems[1] (Goosse et al., 2018), the rise in surface temperature in the Arctic in the past few decades has been twice as fast as the world average, and climate change processes

---

[1] The peculiarities of the Arctic climate are due to the presence of a number of positive feedback mechanisms. For example, snow and ice reflect about 80% of the in-coming solar radiation, while the open ocean surface—only 20%. The gradual melting of ice leads to a decrease in the reflectivity of the earth's surface, which increases its temperature faster than usual.

V. Kashin
Center for Comprehensive European and International Studies, National Research University Higher School of Economics, Moscow, Russia
e-mail: vkashin@hse.ru

in the Arctic will continue to progress at an accelerated pace (Pörtner et al., 2019). On the one hand, the climate dynamics leads to greater accessibility of the Arctic territories in terms of resource development and transport development, thus increasing the region's importance and attractiveness for both Arctic and non-Arctic countries, who are interested in using these development and transport opportunities. On the other hand, the warming of the region leads to a rapid increase in risks and challenges of multiple nature—socio-economic, ecological and geopolitical ones, the manifestations of which are not limited to the Arctic region (Whiteman et al., 2013; Yumashev et al., 2019).

Among the non-political challenges the effects of the permafrost thawing should be mentioned, which include destruction of the infrastructure, and increased risks of man-made disasters, coastal erosions, floods, as well as threats to life for the indigenous population. Management of these risks already requires huge investments of the Arctic states, and especially Russia, whose Arctic coast is the longest and whose economic dependence on the Arctic is the most among the regional states.

Whereas the geopolitical challenge is that against the background of the US confrontation with Russia and China, as well as a more active foreign policy of Beijing, "opening" of the Arctic from ice and in terms of economic and transport opportunities result in a "spillover" of great power rivalry into the region. This spillover, in its turn, triggers new militarization of the region and a more intense international competition in the Arctic as a whole, which increases the risks of inadvertent military conflict and jeopardizes economic development. Thus, negative political consequences of the climate change in the Arctic impede or at best limit utilization its positive effects in terms of economic development.

Three major aspects of this challenge could be identified, and all three are likely to aggravate in the near and middle-term future. First, the "opening" of the Arctic from ice, its increasing accessibility, as well as the dependence of the whole world on climatic processes in the region, accelerate the penetration of the non-Arctic countries into the region and their attempts to get involved into the Arctic agenda and start participating in the Arctic governance. This strengthens contradictions between the Arctic and non-Arctic nations, weakens the established system of the Arctic governance, which centers around the Arctic Council. Besides, since China is one of the non-regional states demanding greater role and say in the Arctic affairs, this adds the Arctic dimension to the US–China confrontation and strengthens a disagreement between Beijing and Moscow.

Second, the melting of the Arctic ice intensifies the "spillover" of overall rivalry between the United States and Russia and the United States and China to the Arctic. On the one hand, the Arctic Ocean becomes more accessible for military activities and starts to be perceived, at least by the United States, as a corridor for power projection, rather than as a natural buffer. On the other hand, the great power confrontation incentivizes the parties to interpret intensified activities of the other side in the Arctic (which are natural provided the greater chances to conduct economic operations in the region) in a zero-sum game, thus creating the security dilemma pattern and an arms race. For instance, it is natural for Russia to increase its military presence in the Arctic provided the role the region plays in its economic development (about 10% of Russian GDP originates in the region) and the increased interest of the others toward it. Whereas due to the overall US–Russia confrontation the United States interprets this increase as a threat or at least as an unfriendly move, and reacts with the military increase of its own, triggering, in its own turn, as a new wave to reaction from Russia. The same confrontational logic also makes the United States perceiving China's presence in and interest toward the Arctic as an unfavorable development or even a security risk.

Third, the melting of the Arctic ice challenges the current regional international legal regime of navigation in the Arctic, exemplified by the Article 234 of the UN Convention of the Law of the Sea (UNCLOS), which is called "Ice-covered areas", and which provides the Arctic coastal nations with an inclusive right to exercise non-discriminatory control over their Arctic waters within the 200-mile Exclusive economic zones beyond the 12-mile territorial waters. As the Arctic ice melts and the Arctic Ocean is progressively becoming "a normal sea", this Article and the according privilege of the coastal states might become negligible, and the legal restrictions on the presence of any vessels—military and non-military beyond the 12-mile territorial waters of the Arctic states would disappear. Russia, which considers control over its Arctic waters and the Northern Sear Route as vital for economic and military security provided the length of its Arctic border and the role the region plays in its development, would consider it as a national security threat.

Moreover, these three challenges are interrelated and reinforce each other. For instance, greater penetration of the non-Arctic actors, including

China, into the region, strengthen the spillover of the US–China confrontation into the area and triggers additional rivalry between the United States and Russia, as the latter reacts to the increase of the US confrontational policies in a zero-sum way. Similarly, destruction of the Article 234 regime and the prospects of unlimited numbers of foreign vessels increased presence in proximity to the Russian Arctic shores, as well as of Russia losing legal tools to control the Northern Sear Route, which will play increasingly important role in its own domestic trade and economic development, would create incentives for Moscow to try to maintain its control over the area and security by unilateral military means, resulting in further militarization of the region. In the context of the US–Russia confrontation this would trigger counter military buildup on the part of the United States, thus sparking another arms race cycle. The United States is already depicting Russian commitment to controlling its 200-mile zone in the Arctic, fully congruent with the existing UNCLOS regime, as a challenge to international law and security. Finally, the US–China confrontation and resultative American pressure on China in the Pacific strengthens Beijing's interest in the Arctic as an alternative communication route to Europe, which, in its turn, increases the spillover of the US–China competition to the Arctic.

It is worth analyzing these three challenges of the Arctic geopolitics in more detail.

To Whom Does the Arctic Belong? China and Other Non-Arctic Players in the Region

Climate change and the resultative "opening of the Arctic" strengthen interest toward the region from many non-Arctic players in Europe and Asia, who question the traditional model of the Arctic governance, which is based on the 8-party Arctic Council, and insist that the region should be perceived as a "heritage of humanity" and thus belong to the international community as a whole (and its major centers of power), not just to the Arctic states. The most powerful among these non-regional players is China, which plays the most active role in the Arctic of all the non-regional countries. China positions itself as a Near-Arctic State (近北极国家), justifying its interest in the management of the region by the impact of the ongoing climate change on China.

At the moment, there is no reason to consider the Arctic as a priority of the Chinese foreign policy. China allocates very limited resources to its presence in the Arctic region. In terms of significance for the PRC, the Arctic direction is not comparable to Africa, the Middle East and even Latin America. However, the economic and technological rise of China in the twenty-first century has led to the intensification of its policies in almost all spheres and in all regions of the world. The Arctic is not an exception. It is a separate significant area of the Chinese diplomacy, which was shown by the White Paper on China's Arctic policy issued by the State Council of the PRC in 2018. Since the 2000s, China has started actively investing in Arctic projects in various countries of the region. At the same time, the scope of the research on the Arctic carried out by the PRC and the interest in participation in global governance issues on the Arctic have been growing. Against the backdrop of a relatively rapid recovery of the Chinese economy, the protracted recovery from the crisis in several regions of the world creates an opportunity for Beijing to expand its global influence by increasing its presence in or near the Arctic, as well as through strengthening cooperation with the northern countries.

China's interest in the region has three critical components: *the climate agenda, maritime communications, and resources.*

The essential role of the Arctic in the global climate change induces the PRC, on the one hand, to build up its scientific presence in the region, relying on several partners, and on the other hand, to take an active part in its governance. China is developing its fleet of research Arctic vessels, permanent scientific facilities in Norway, Sweden and Iceland. Chinese scientists regularly conduct joint expeditions with Russian colleagues in the Russian sector of the Arctic.

The PRC's interest in the Northern Sea Route (NSR) relates to the desire to diversify the logistics of the Chinese foreign trade by reducing dependence on sea lines of communication passing through the South China Sea and the Malacca Strait. At the same time, in the future, with a further reduction in ice cover, the Northern Sea Route will become more and more promising and attractive not only from a strategic, but also from a commercial point of view. In any case, the Arctic maritime routes are for China mainly of a potential importance: they may begin to play a crucial role for the Chinese economy in case of a sharp warming in the Arctic, or in case of military-political crisis in the South China Sea or in the Indian Ocean, where the main routes connecting China with economic partners in Europe lie.

China's attention to the Arctic resources is largely due to the peculiarities of the Chinese policy to ensure economic security, which dictates the need to diversify the sources of imports of strategic raw materials. The Chinese economic presence in the region is currently highly diversified. In addition to participating in the largest Yamal LNG project in the Russian territory, Chinese companies have their own projects in Norway, Iceland, Greenland, the Arctic regions of Finland and Canada.

China emphasizes that the resources of the Arctic region are the heritage of mankind, and it is important to defend the freedom of navigation, flight, construction of infrastructure facilities and exploitation of natural resources in the Arctic in accordance with international law. Herewith, the key accent is placed on the legal framework created by the UN Convention on the Law of the Sea and the Svalbard Treaty, which give a wide range of states an opportunity to be present in the Arctic.

Finally, in the future, the issue of China's military presence in the region may also appear. Contacts with Chinese experts indicate the interest of the Chinese side in exploring the possibilities for the advancement of the Chinese Navy through the Arctic waters, including through the Northern Sea Route. China is going through a period of rapid naval expansion, and, to date, it is known that the Chinese industry has projects of ice-class nuclear ships.

The main tool for promoting Chinese interests in the Arctic is building a network of bi-lateral economic partnerships with Iceland (Embassy, 2019), Norway (Xinhua, 2019), Greenland and Denmark (Clingendael, 2020) and of course Russia (Kalyukov & Dzyadko, 2019). Although today Russia is not the only or an uncontested partner of China in the Arctic, China's economic expansion in other Arctic countries (Iceland, Denmark, Canada) is under growing political pressure amid the conflict with the United States. It can be expected that as this conflict deepens, the value of Russia as a partner of the PRC in the Arctic will increase.

At the moment, China's economic, scientific and infrastructural presence in the Arctic region is rather diversified. China has resource and infrastructure projects not only in Russia (Yamal-LNG and related facilities), but also in Norway, Iceland, Greenland. Permanently operating Chinese scientific bases are located in Svalbard (Norwegian Government Security & Service Organisation, 2010) and Iceland (InterAct, n.d.). In the north of Sweden, in Kiruna, there is a Chinese station for communication and tracking of space objects (Sina, 2004). Despite the ongoing recurrent joint scientific expeditions to the Arctic with the participation of the Shirshov Institute of Oceanology of Russian Academy of Sciences, there are no permanent Chinese scientific bases in Russia.

The 2017 White Paper "Vision for Maritime Cooperation under the Belt and Road Initiative" released by the Chinese government represents the Arctic Ocean as a possible "blue economic passage" (蓝色经济通道) (Xinhua, 2017). Since then, the concept of the Chinese presence in the Arctic has begun to develop and to take new forms. The 2018 White Paper dedicated to China's Arctic policy has defined the Chinese interest in cooperation in the Arctic specifically: China has put forward the Polar Silk Road initiative (The State Council, 2018). In particular, the Paper indicates that the PRC would encourage investments of Chinese enterprises in the infrastructure of the region and organize test passes of commercial ships through the Arctic routes. It also expressed the hope for multilateral cooperation in the development of merchant shipping in the Arctic.

The main purpose of the White Paper publication (The State Council, 2018) was the desire to outline China's position on the Arctic, as well as the desire to convey China's commitment to working with all parties to maintain peace, stability and sustainable development of the Arctic. It is emphasized that China does not intend to interfere in the affairs of the Arctic in any form in matters that are the sovereign prerogative of the Arctic countries, but it will use the tools available in international law to actively participate in the management of the region and its development (two principles: "不越位"—do not overplay; "不缺位"—do not miss the opportunity). The PRC's position on the joint management of the Arctic is described in three terms: maintenance (the legal framework), respect (to international cooperation) and development (of the international governance mechanisms).

In the Arctic, the PRC officially sets itself the following aims: (1) to protect the common interests of all countries of the international community; (2) to preserve Arctic's peculiarities by deepening scientific research in the region, using modern technologies to protect the environment, and more actively responding to the challenges of global warming. At the same time, *respect, cooperation, non-zero-sum game (referred as "win–win" in Chinese documents), and sustainability* are considered as basic principles, on the basis of which multilateral and bilateral issues of regional development should be discussed. China is ready to cooperate with different levels of government bodies both of states that have direct access to the Arctic space, and of all other interested parties, including international and non-governmental organizations.

Declared Goals of China's Policy in the Region

China declares the following goals and principles of its Arctic policy:

- Deepening research and understanding of the Arctic: participation in the monitoring and assessment of local climatic and environmental changes, as well as the implementation of multi-level continuous observations of the atmosphere, sea, sea ice, glaciers, soil, bioecological character and environmental quality through the creation of Arctic observation systems, construction of joint research (observative) stations, as well as the development of the Arctic observation network and participation in it. China will allocate investments for research and development of safe equipment in the field of depth exploration, drilling, exploitation of Arctic oil and gas fields.
- Protecting the Arctic environment and tackling the climate change problem: the PRC is working with other states to strengthen control over sources of marine pollution, such as ship discharges, sea dumping and air pollution; protects endangered flora and fauna; studies the mechanisms of global warming in order to respond to its threats.
- Legal and rational use of the Arctic's resources: Northeast, Northwest and Central passages may soon become important shipping routes, and China intends to build the Polar Silk Road, relying on these shipping zones; China respects the sovereign rights of the Arctic countries to deposits of mineral resources in the region, nevertheless, calls for cooperation in matters of their extraction; the region may become an important fishing destination in the near future, and China calls for the conservation and rational use of fish resources in the Arctic; the region is becoming an attractive destination for tourism, and the government encourages Chinese companies to develop this type of activity, focusing on ecotourism.

In the future, China's interests and policy in the Arctic may undergo certain changes. The guidelines for reducing carbon dioxide emissions announced in the country's 14th Five-Year Plan for National Economic and Social Development (2021–2025) adopted in March 2021 suggest that China will reach a peak around 2030 and become a carbon–neutral country by 2060. Combined with similar measures in other major economies, this may lead to a reduction in demand for oil and, to a lesser extent, for natural gas. On the other hand, the development of new industries, including those related to the production of electric vehicles, may increase China's demand for other Arctic resources, such as non-ferrous and rare earth metals. As stated above, interest in using the Northern Sea Route for civil and military purposes may grow sharply in case of reduction of the ice cap and an increase in military and political tensions in the South China Sea. Finally, the importance of scientific presence in the Arctic and active participation in the discussion on the Arctic climate agenda will inevitably increase along with the aggravation of the problem of global warming.

Other non-Arctic states increasingly proclaim their interest in the region as well. The European Union and individual European countries (including France and Great Britain) have issued a number of documents in recent years aimed at promoting their interests in the Arctic, while France periodically (albeit unsuccessfully) tries to obtain the status of an Arctic country, using the rights to the archipelago Saint Pierre and Miquelon. In January 2021 India published its own official document on its policy in the Arctic, titled "India's Arctic policy, Roadmap for Sustainable Engagement" (Ghosh & Aggarwal, 2021), in which it emphasized the region's growing importance for New Delhi as a rising great power. Back in 2013, China, Japan, the Republic of Korea, India, and Singapore became observers to the Arctic Council.

The increased activism of the non-Arctic states in the region challenges the established model of the Arctic governance, centered around the Arctic Council, and strengthens geopolitical competition in the region, accelerating the spillover of great power rivalry into the Arctic. The latter, in its turn, also undermines effectiveness of the Arctic Council and the established model of the Arctic governance as a whole. A vicious circle emerges.

First, the non-Arctic states openly question the principle, according to which the region must be governed by the Arctic nations only with the Arctic Council being the major governance institution. In particular, China, while trying to intensify its role in the Arctic governance, opposes the exclusive role of the Arctic Council countries and claims that the Arctic is the "heritage of mankind", rather than only of the Arctic states. This position is fundamentally different from the Russian one, as well as the position of other Arctic states, and is one of the few cases of divergence of Russia's and China's positions on the international agenda (so far this contradiction has not affected their practical cooperation in the Arctic and elsewhere).

Second, with the increased presence and activism of non-regional states the Arctic Council is less and less able to act as the sole platform for coordinating actions and cooperation in the region. A new system of institutions of international interaction is being formed around the Arctic, which is less and less connected with the Arctic Council and equally encompasses both the Arctic and non-Arctic states. Among them, for example, are the Polar Code adopted in 2017 by the International Maritime Organization to regulate shipping in the Arctic, International Governmental Scientific Forum of 20 Countries Interested in Arctic Research (held since 2016) and the Agreement on the Prevention of Unregulated Fishing on the High Seas in the Central Arctic Ocean signed by Russia, the United States, Canada, Norway, Denmark, Iceland, Japan, the Republic of Korea, China and the EU in 2018. It is increasingly clear, that without greater flexibility in the decision-making process, which means addressing the greater role of non-regional actors in the Arctic agenda, while maintaining the central role of the Arctic states, effectiveness of the Arctic Council as an international institution will inevitably decrease further.

Third, increased presence of the non-Arctic nations accelerates the spillover of the overall geopolitical competition into the Arctic, which, in its turn, aggravates the crisis of the Arctic Council even further. For instance, geopolitical rivals of China perceive its greater involvement of China into the Arctic—even rhetorical and symbolic—in a zero-sum way and rush to take "compensatory" measures. The increased role of China in the Arctic is one of major the reasons why the Trump Administration rejected the tradition of resisting the "high politics" and hard security issues from penetration into the Arctic agenda and made its overall Arctic policy much more security-centric and openly confrontational against China and Russia. The China factor also seems to be one of the reasons behind India's increased interest in the region (Ramesh, 2021).

This increased geopolitical competition, in its turn, accelerates the crisis of the Arctic Council. The reason behind its ability to function despite tense political relations among member-states (primarily Russia and NATO Arctic counties) was its exclusive focus on "low politics" issues (environment, economic development, transport, science and research, maritime safety, indigenous peoples, etc.) and resistance to involve into "high politics". Military security has of course been an important part and parcel of the overall international affairs in the Arctic, but it was discussed and addressed outside of the Arctic Council framework. Today the geopolitical agenda is intruding the Arctic Council and the Arctic agenda, curtailing the potential for cooperation in the traditional for the Council activities areas (Balton & Zagorskiy, 2020). The outcome of the 2019 ministerial meeting of the Arctic Council was indicative, when the parties, for the first time in the entire history of its existence, were unable to adopt a final declaration. The formal reason for this was the disagreement over the mention of the climate change problem in the final version of the declaration, which the US delegation insisted on deleting. Whereas the fundamental one was the confrontational approach the United States started to manifest toward Russia and China in the Arctic. Vivid indication of the latter was the speech delivered at the meeting by the then US Secretary of State Mike Pompeo, who, in addition to traditional criticism of Russian Arctic policy, accused China of expansion and aggression in the Arctic.

Spillover of the Confrontation and Militarization of the Arctic

The US confrontation with Russia and China is systemic and global, covering the majority of regions and domains, where the sides face each other. Due to geographic proximity between Russia and the United States and NATO it would have spread to the Arctic anyway. However, climate change and the melting of the Arctic ice intensifies this "spillover". First, as outlined above, it creases a sense of "opening" of the Arctic and increases the region's attractiveness and importance for both Arctic and non-Arctic countries. In conditions of this new "Arctic hype", those countries, who can afford it, try to increase their posture in the region—military and non-military, usually following the logic, that if the new "vacuum" is not filled by themselves, it will be filled by someone else. In these circumstances and provided the strategic role the Arctic plays in Russian economic development and security, it is hardly surprising, that Russia increases its military presence in the region as well. It is also quite normal, that Russian military buildup in the Arctic exceeds the ones of the others: the region plays much more vital role for Russia, than it does for any other country.

Second, as Russia and China intensify their activities in the region and raise its importance in their official strategic documents, the logic of the confrontation compels the United States to regard it as a challenge if not a threat. Russia is officially declared an adversary of the United States in the Arctic in all the three US military Arctic strategies, and Russian policy in the region is considered as a threat to US national security and a challenge to the international order. As the Arctic Strategy of the US Army states, "America's great power competitors – Russia and China – have developed Arctic strategies with geopolitical goals contrary to U.S. interests" (Department of the Army, 2021).

Russia, on its part, also tries to strengthen defense of this strategically important region in conditions of the overall confrontation with the United States and considers increase of American military presence in the Arctic as a military challenge. Russian military posture in the Arctic since 2014 has significantly grown. For instance, in December 2014 the Northern Fleet Joint Strategic Command was established. This is fully understandable: the length of the Russian Arctic coast and the country's dependence on the Arctic resources and transport routes makes a hypothetical US military presence in adjacent areas a much greater threat for Moscow, than an emergence of Russian military presence in the Arctic areas close to the United States. Whereas the United States regards the Russian military buildup in the Arctic in a strictly confrontational way and increases the military presence of its own. Similarly, even the hypothetical possibility of a real Chinese military presence in the region also causes serious concern in the West. Such a threat is mentioned in several American military planning documents and statements made by American leaders, even though it may still be years before the first Chinese warship appears in the Arctic waters.

Third, the melting of the Arctic ice makes the region more accessible for military presence and operations. The US Department of Defense Arctic Strategy, followed by the relevant strategies adopted by the US Air Force and the US Army, claim that the opening of the Arctic from the ice turns it into a "corridor of rivalry between great powers", providing rival powers (that is, Russia and China) with quick access to American territory and critical infrastructure. The DoD Arctic Strategy defines the region as "a potential avenue for expanded great power competition and aggression spanning between two key regions of ongoing competition identified in the NDS [National Defense Strategy] — the Indo-Pacific and Europe — and the U.S. homeland" (Department of Defense, 2019). The Arctic Strategy of the US Army points out, that "Beyond traditional functions in ballistic missile defense, the Arctic, especially Alaska, as an operational space presents unique opportunities for power projection to enhance U.S. Army competition activities and our ability to respond in crisis and/or conflict" (Department of the Army, 2021).

All three factors result in a new wave of militarization of the Arctic. Russia so far leads in this process, which is, again, normal provided the lengths of the Russian Arctic territory and coast and the region's significance for its economic development and security. The United States, as stated in its three military Arctic strategies, considers buildup of its military presence in the region as an important priority.

The leading role is played by the Air Force, which accounts for 80% of all the US military expenses in the Arctic. In 2020 the Pentagon started to deploy the fifth-generation fighters F-35 "Lightning" at Eielson base at Alaska. 54 jets are supposed to be deployed there by the end of 2021, which would make Alaska the place of largest concentration of the US 5th generation fighters. The Arctic Strategy of the US Air Force states, that from this base the F-35 fighters could conduct military operations both at the Pacific and at the European theaters (Department of the Air Force, 2020).

The major priorities of the US Army in the Arctic, according to its Arctic Strategy, are: to "be able to project power from, within, and into the Arctic to conduct and sustain extended operations in competition, crisis, and conflict from a position of advantage; to employ calibrated force posture and multi-domain formations to defend the homeland and pose dilemmas for great power competitors; to engage with and strengthen allies and partners to maintain regional stability; and to generate Arctic-capable forces ready to compete and win in extended operations in extreme cold weather and high-altitude environments" (Department of the Army, 2021).

The Arctic also remains a region of strategic military importance, where the marine component of Russian strategic nuclear force (strategic nuclear submarines) is deployed, as well as a lion share of the Russian navy in general (the Northern Fleet). It is not a coincidence, that the flagship of the whole Russian navy—"Admiral Kuznetsov" aircraft carrier cruiser—is also the flagship of the Northern fleet. The famous (for its cruises all over the world) "Peter the Great" heavy nuclear missile cruiser also belongs to this fleet. The role as the hub for marine component of the Russian strategic nuclear Triad explains the high activity of the United States and some of its NATO allies' navy in the region. Furthermore, as the trajectory of nuclear-armed ICBMs in the case of a US–Russian strategic nuclear conflict also passes through the Arctic, the region holds major elements of Russian and the US early warning systems. Finally, Fort Greely at Alaska is the main military site of the US strategic missile defense system, where GBI strategic military interceptors are deployed in 2000s.

The military dynamics in the Arctic is determined not only by the actions of Russia and individual NATO countries, but also by the direction of the US-Chinese rivalry. The Chinese fleet is gradually expanding the geographic scope of its operations and has already visited the North Atlantic several times.

To date, China's military presence in the Arctic on a permanent basis is a hypothetical perspective. Current China's scientific research in the Arctic is carried out by civil governmental institutions. The Chinese navy does not possess ice-class ships adapted for use in the Arctic and does not have experience of operating in the region, even in the framework of joint exercises with Russia. At the same time, there are certain prerequisites that allow to expect an increase in the Chinese military activity in the region in the future. These prerequisites are related to growing China's interest in the Northern Sea Route, the growth of its economic activity in the Arctic and the rapid increase in the size of the PLA Navy and the expansion of the geography of its activity.

As of today, Chinese programs for the study of the Arctic are entirely in the hands of civilian structures. Polar Research Institute of China located in Shanghai (China-Nordic Arctic Research Centre), which is currently subordinate to the Ministry of Natural Resources of the People's Republic of China, is responsible for research programs both in the Arctic and in the Antarctic. The Institute owns both Chinese polar icebreakers (The Arctic Institute, n.d.)—the first one was purchased in Ukraine in the 1990s and converted into Xue Long (MarineTraffic, n.d.) (originally—Soviet Project 10621s icebreaker-transport vessel), the second one was built in Shanghai according to the Finnish Aker Arctic Company's project called Xue Long-2 (Aker Arctic, n.d.). Thus, both Chinese polar icebreakers are entirely designed abroad and contain a large amount of imported equipment. In addition to the icebreakers of the Polar Research Institute of China, the PLA Navy has a small number of icebreakers of its own design and construction. However, they are focused on working in the freezing areas of the Yellow Sea, primarily in the Bohai Bay, and are not adapted for use in polar regions (Song & Jia, 2021).

At the same time, the need for a naval presence in the Arctic is widely discussed in Chinese publications and interviews on naval topics (*Global Times*, 2013). In particular, a number of publications note that the Chinese naval strategy, currently formulated as "near seas defense and far seas protection" (近海防御, 远海防卫) will be expanded in the future and will include, in particular, "expansion into the two poles" (两极拓展) (Huang, 2019). In 2018, the PRC launched the schematic design of a nuclear icebreaker (Xinhua, 2018), although the decision to build that kind of a ship probably has not been made. The increasing of polar research is one of priorities declared in the 14th Five-Year Plan for National Economic and Social Development of the PRC.

Although the Chinese Navy has not been in the Arctic waters, it has been expanding its presence in the Atlantic Ocean for a long time, including in the North Atlantic Ocean. In 2015 and 2017, the Chinese Navy ships entered the Baltic Sea, and besides, conducted joint exercises with the Russian Baltic Fleet in 2017 (Weitz, 2021). The exercises caused concerns on the part of a number of NATO members. One possible interpretation was that in doing so China responded to the European countries' navies growing activity in the Pacific Ocean. The Chinese naval theorists consider the Navy presence in the North Atlantic Ocean as a necessary condition to successfully confront the United States at sea, including to counter the US efforts to establish a naval blockade of China. On their part, the US and British naval specialists consider the possible appearance of the Chinse Navy in this area as a real threat, which requires to take preventive measures.

At the moment, the PLA has significant technical groundwork to prepare its military to act in the Arctic. This groundwork has been created as a result of long-standing efforts to prepare military to fight in the extreme conditions of the Tibetan plateau, where extremely low temperature and permafrost in some areas are accompanied by thin air. To date, the Chinese have conducted testing of a range of major weapons, military and special equipment in service with the PLA's Air Force, Ground Force and Rocket Force in the conditions of the high-mountainous and cold Tibetan plateau. There have been developed instructions for use of various types of equipment, created special equipment for the operation in the extreme conditions, mastered the construction of facilities for the deployment and logistics of troops.

China produces various types of special vehicles for areas with extreme climate (including all terrain tracked carriers based on Russian and Swedish models) (NORINCO, n.d.), as well as special equipment for military personnel to operate in such conditions. Combined with the experience gained during the scientific expeditions of the Polar Research Institute, this gives China the technical capabilities for the future use of its armed forces in the Arctic (Sina, 2004). As shown above, China has limited experience in the independent construction of icebreaking vessels and seeks to develop and build up the existing technical groundwork in this direction—up to the study of the issue of building its own nuclear icebreaker.

Anyway, China's intentions regarding military presence in the region remain unclear. As of today, the mention of China as one of the main military opponents in the Arctic in the US and British documents seems to be a clear exaggeration and is probably pursuing political goals related to limiting Chinese economic activity and overall political presence in the region.

ARCTIC OCEAN AS A "NORMAL SEA"? EROSION OF THE UNCLOS ARTICLE 234 REGIME

Regulation of the Arctic navigation is another crucial aspect of international relations in the region, involving economic, transport and security aspects. Whereas contradictions over this regulation and over the legal status of the Arctic Ocean as such are an essential element of growing great power rivalry in the region. Today Arctic navigation is regulated by the legal regime, established by Article 234 of the UN Convention on the Law of the Sea "On Ice-Covered Areas", which gives the Arctic countries exclusive control not only over 12-mile territorial waters, but also over a 200-mile exclusive economic zone. This provides the full legal basis for Russia and Canada to demand control over the Northern Sea Rout and the North-West Passage accordingly. Moscow considers this control an essential prerequisite for national security. It allows Russia, first, to limit the number of foreign vessels and supervise their navigation in the region of strategic importance; second, to maintain sovereignty over its Arctic shores as it tries to multiply the number of foreign partners in the economic exploration of the region; and third, to preserve the principle, according to which Arctic governance is conducted by the Arctic states only, despite the growing involvement of the non-Arctic states into the region. Potentially, as the Northern Sea Route becomes an important international trade avenue, control over it could bring Russia lots of financial and economic profits.

The United States, some of its Arctic NATO allies, and non-Arctic nations, on the contrary, have been challenging this rule and Russian ambitions to control the 200-mile piece of its Arctic waters for years. Washington, who has never ratified the UNCLOS and has traditionally used the freedom of navigation principle as a tool to promote its global presence and to limit the postures of its adversaries, has always been its the most vocal critic. However, as the ice coverage of the Arctic Ocean has been preventing free navigation anyway, while US–Russian relations were non-adversarial since 1991 and till 2014, this contradiction was peripheral for both US–Russian relations and the Arctic agendas. And the uncontested status of the Article 234 of the UNCLOS provided firm legal justification and legitimization of the Russian position.

Today the situation is rapidly changing in both dimensions in a way unfavorable for Russia. The US-Russia confrontation and the melting of the Arctic ice strengthen this contradiction and risk making it one of the major ones on the Arctic agenda, aggravating other negative trends as well. As the current Article 234 legal regime is linked to the ice coverage, the melting of the ice creates the prospects for its evaporation and raises the question of the gradual transformation of the Arctic Ocean from a zone of exclusive interests of the Arctic countries into "ordinary" international sea waters. This would destroy the main and only legal instrument for Russia to exercise control over its Arctic waters within the 200-mile distance, including the Northern Sea Route, provide additional argumentation to the United States, and create the prospects for qualitative increase of the presence of foreign vessels—military and non-military, of Arctic and non-Arctic states, in proximity of the Russian Arctic shores on a permanent or at least regular basis. Expert discussions on revising the status of Article 234 are already underway in the United States both within the framework of government commissions and at think tanks, incl. Wilson Center (Schreiber, 2019).

The erosion of the current legal regime in the Arctic based on Article 234 of the UN Convention and its transformation into an "ordinary sea" is fraught, first of all, with the spread of practices of interstate relations and competition typical for other contested maritime regions into the Arctic. In particular, situation in the Arctic would resemble the one existing in the South China Sea, where the United States emphasizes its disagreement with the Chinese ambitions to dominate the majority of the sea with regular and demonstrative passages of American naval vessels through the waters that Beijing considers a part of Chinese sovereign territory. One needs to remember, that South China Sea is the region, where US–China confrontation is mostly intensive, and the risk of direct military clash between them is highest. Whereas for Russia strategic importance of the Arctic is no less at all, and perhaps is even higher, than is importance of the South China Sea for Beijing.

The risk of the situation in the South China Sea becoming a model for great power relation in the Arctic is hardly hypothetical. The United States openly declares in its official military Arctic strategies that it does not recognize Moscow's claims to exclusive control over its Arctic waters and intends to challenge these claims by regularly identifying its presence under the slogan of "protecting freedom of navigation". As the 2019 Arctic Strategy of the US Department of Defense claims, "DoD will continue to fly, sail, and operate wherever international law allows. When necessary and appropriate, the United States will challenge excessive maritime claims in the Arctic to preserve the rules-based international order and the rights and freedoms of the international community in navigation and overflight, as well as for other, related high seas uses" (Department of Defense, 2019). A more active Chinese presence in the Arctic waters will give this US policy a special dynamic.

Due to the strategic importance of the Arctic for military security and economic development, Russia cannot but react to such a development by building up its own military presence in the region further, transforming it into a "military fortress". This would create the risk of further militarization of the Arctic, the arms race and military incidents, and the overall development of the situation in the region in a similar way to the model of the South China Sea. Namely, the regular presence in the Arctic seas of warships, and in the airspace—the aviation of the United States and NATO countries, as well as China, under the pretext of ensuring freedom of navigation. The general military and political tension in the Arctic will qualitatively increase, whereas its economic development would be jeopardized. Indeed, international community, both Arctic and non-Arctic countries, would strongly criticize and reject Russian attempts to maintain control of the 200-mile Arctic waters beyond the UNCLOS framework, especially though unilateral military means, and the United States and the European Union would quite likely react with further anti-Russian sanctions.

Another vicious circle emerges: Russia needs control over its Arctic waters and the Northern Sea Route for its economic development, but the means to impose and maintain it beyond the UNCLOS framework undermine the prospects for this very development. Moreover, further militarization of the region on the Russian part would probably fail to prevent the presence of foreign vessels in proximity to the Russian Arctic shores: on the contrary, the United States would accelerate demonstrative operations for the sake of "freedom of navigation", thus strengthening the arms race spiral and increasing the risks of inadvertent military clashes.

Last but not least, the erosion of the Article 234 regime and the uncontrolled and unlimited presence of anyone in the Arctic would lead to a critical increase in the pressure on the fragile Arctic ecosystems. Freeing Arctic ecosystems from ice does not make them less vulnerable in the face of increasing economic activity in the region and requires the development of new preventive solutions, aimed at avoiding an environmental crisis in the region that would have global consequences. In this situation, Article 234 of the UN Convention on the Law of the Sea seems the most important instrument for protecting marine ecosystems in the waters lying along the coastline of the Arctic countries within their exclusive economic zone.

What to Do? Policy Prescriptions for Russia

Since the US confrontation with China and Russia is systemic and long-term, while the climate change in the Arctic is irreversible, it is hardly possible to roll the above-mentioned tendencies of the Arctic becoming an area of great power rivalry back. Still, some measures could be taken in order to mitigate and slow them down. Russia, which presides in the Arctic Council in 2021–2023, should lead in this process.

First, Russia should cooperate with the European Arctic states and Canada on preservation of the UNCLOS Article 234 regime despite the gradual shrinking of the ice cover. If it succeeds, the principle, according to which overall governance of the Arctic belongs to the Arctic states, and centrality of the Arctic Council would be strengthened, non-Arctic states would not get unrestricted access to the regional waters, and the militarization of the area would also be restrained, as well as the growth of political confrontation between Washington and Moscow. Indeed, unlimited freedom of navigation in close proximity to Russian and some other Arctic states' shores could be one of the most powerful triggers of confrontation and militarization.

In order to preserve the Article 234 regime, its new interpretation should be suggested within the Arctic Council and eventually accepted by at least majority of its member-states, not linked with the ice cover of the Arctic Ocean. Fragility of the Arctic ecosystems should be at the center of the new interpretation. Indeed, in the context of the growing international importance of the Arctic region and the acceleration of climatic changes, the freeing of its water areas from ice not only does not reduce, but increases the susceptibility of Arctic ecosystems to negative economic impact. The lack of legal arguments in Russia and other Arctic states for non-discriminatory control over navigation in the Arctic waters is fraught with a critical aggravation of environmental problems in the region.

Thus, the new interpretation of the Article 234 should claim, that unrestricted navigation in the Arctic waters is too dangerous for its environment (especially since the risk of accidents will be remaining high for a very long time, and the overwhelming majority of states lack the necessary technologies and equipment to navigate the Arctic waters safely), so the coastal states should exercise responsible control over the Arctic navigation for the sake of protecting environment. The suggested formula is "exclusive rights of the Arctic states in exchange for their increased responsibility for the protection of the Arctic marine ecosystems". The Arctic nations, including Russia, should profoundly increase environmental responsibility of their own behavior in the Arctic, and raise the importance of environmental protection in their national and international Arctic policies.

Russia, in particular, should attach much greater importance to the environmental problems in the Arctic, consider it a vital priority of its chairmanship in the Arctic Council, intensify relevant cooperation with the other Arctic states, increase investments into research and science on climate and environmental issues in the Arctic and strengthen environmental aspect of its economic and social policy in the region. Due to the length of the Russian Arctic, Russia should diplomatically insist on the role of a leader in protecting the environment and a "fighter on the front line", which will consolidate the status of an Arctic country that, like no one else, understands the scale of threats in the region and bears effective responsibility for its future.

Despite the suggested interpretation does not require a re-writing of the Article 234 and is fully congruent with the UNCLOS spirit and letter, which emphasizes the need to protect rare and vulnerable ecosystems, such as the Arctic one, it will certainly face resistance from the United States and non-Arctic states, including China. The former considers refusing Russia of the control over Northern Sea Route as an effective tool of containment and pays much less attention to ecological considerations. Still, the chances for support of the suggested interpretation by the majority of the Arctic states exist. First and foremost, Russia should intensify diplomatic engagement of the Scandinavian states and Canada, building stronger cooperation with them on protection of the Arctic environment.

Greater flexibility of the US position is also not impossible in the middle-term prospect. Three positive preconditions for such change exist. First, containing China has become a far more strategic priority for the United States, than containing Russia, and preservation of the Article 234 regime limits China's presence and role in the Arctic, which is a US neighborhood as well. Second, environmental and climate agenda has become one of the major priorities of the Biden Administration, which has clearly stated its interest to cooperate with Russia on climate issues, including the Arctic. The latter, for instance, was part of the US–Russian climate negotiations during the visit of the US Special Presidential Envoy for Climate John Kerry to Moscow in July 2021. A strong US–Russia cooperation on If Russia environmental and climate processes in the Arctic coupled with Moscow proving with particular action, that it is seriously concerned about the state of the Arctic environment, and altering its domestic policy in the region accordingly, would create greater prerequisites for the US support of the suggested principle of "exclusive rights for exclusive responsibility". Third, if Russia convinces Arctic NATO allies of the United States (Norway, Denmark), as well as EU members Sweden and Finland, it would be harder for Washington to continue the struggle against the Article 234 rights and its suggested new interpretation.

The second measure to mitigate the spillover of the great power rivalry into the Arctic is strengthening the Arctic Council and resisting penetration of the hard security problems into its agenda, preserving the traditional compartmentalization of the overall Arctic agenda. It is vital to discuss and address the military issues in the Arctic in order to avoid uncontrollable arms race and inadvertent military clashes and incidents, keep the rivalry at least manageable. In particular, strengthening de-confliction mechanisms and lines of communication, discussing military doctrines and postures, strengthening confidence-building measures and rules of military conduct in the Arctic seem essential. In order to build confidence in the region, it is advisable to consider the possibility of regular meetings on military security in the Arctic with the participation of representatives of the foreign policy and military departments of the Arctic states. To ensure operational interaction, the possibility of creating a hotline for the exchange of information between the military departments of the Arctic countries, whose units are deployed in the northern latitudes should be worked out. But such actions must be taken outside of the Arctic Council framework—within the OSCE, NATO-Russia Council and at bilateral levels between Russia and the Arctic NATO countries—the United States, Canada and Norway, Iceland and Denmark.

As for strengthening of the Arctic Council and the major institution of cooperation and governance in the region, it could be done by intensifying cooperation over its traditional "low politics" agenda: environmental protection, struggle against and adaptation to climate change, sustainable and responsible economic development of the region, management of navigation and development of transport communications, subregional and cross-border cooperation, protecting indigenous peoples of the North, etc. Moreover, the suggested way to preserve exclusive rights of the Arctic states in terms of navigation regulation also seems to be an effective tool to strengthen the Arctic Council and its role in governing the region. Evaporation of this rule would accelerate transformation of the Arctic into a "heritage of humanity" and the "emasculation" of the Arctic Council.

The third measure to mitigate and compensate for the great power rivalry in the Arctic is simply strengthening cooperation between Russia and the Western Arctic states whenever possible. Compartmentalization should be the governing principle: despite the spillover of confrontational logic, the Arctic must remain an area of intensive (ideally—prevailing) cooperation. Great power confrontation and "low politics" cooperation should coexist in parallel dimensions. In case of US–Russia relations, the Arctic does have potential to be one of the areas of their selective cooperation. The above-mentioned issues of environmental protection and other elements of traditional Arctic agenda are the most suitable ones to build a positive agenda.

Finally, managing Moscow–Beijing cooperation in the Arctic is an important element of the US–Russia–China great power triangle in the region. Despite their disagreements over the status of the Arctic and navigation regime, China is the major Russian partner in developmental projects in the Russian Arctic (such as Yamal LNG Gas Project between the Russian Novatec and Chinese National Petroleum Corporation).

Whereas Russia is the major Chinese partner in developing new transport corridors between Asia and Europe, which Beijing considers vital in conditions of its deepening confrontation with the United States.

On the one hand, Russia–China partnership provides the United States with further argumentation for its strategy of dual simultaneous containment of and confrontation with Russia and China, with the Arctic being one of the regions, where Washington faces Moscow and Beijing at the same time and their close cooperation. The Arctic Strategy of the US Army "Regaining Arctic Dominance" talks about "Russian and Chinese Confluence" (Department of the Army, 2021). According to the document, "Moscow has turned to Beijing as a source of long-term financing and technology to aid the energy and infrastructure development in the High North. This has emboldened China's pursuit of its Arctic economic ambitions under the auspices of its Polar Silk Road Fund at the exact moment when Beijing's global economic ambitions under the banner of its Belt Road Initiative are gaining momentum".

On the other hand, the systemic nature of US–Russia and US–China confrontation and sanctions the United States continues to impose against Russia, which are very unlikely to be repealed or diminished in the observable future, leave no alternative to this cooperation. Both sides need it: Russia—for considerations of economic development, China—for considerations of security and diversification of maritime routes. In order to avoid additional risks, Russia–China partnership in the Arctic should be properly managed.

First, both sides should regard it as a symmetrical win–win interdependence, which should not be exploited for the sake of unilateral advantages. For Russia, China will remain to be the main promising market for resources extracted in the Arctic, a source of capital and a supplier of several types of equipment used for Arctic development. For China, Russia may turn out to be the PRC's uncontested partner in the region. Since all the Arctic states, except for Russia, are close allies of the United States, the Chinese presence in the region is experiencing increasing political pressure. Already at this stage, there is a growing suspicion of Chinese investments and scientific activities in the region. Arctic NATO members are already experiencing the negative impact of the US–China confrontation. To date, relations between the PRC and Canada have already been seriously undermined, and this has resulted in informal sanctions against certain items of Canadian export to China. Other countries are under growing pressure from the United States to abandon new and to wind down existing Chinese projects in the region. It creates obstacles for new projects. Consequently, in the foreseeable future Chinese policy in the Arctic will increasingly depend on cooperation with Russia. This also applies to the military area: a permanent presence of the Chinese fleet in the Arctic will only be possible with the Russian consent (which is unlikely unless a serious further intensification of Russia's confrontation with the United States) and will rely on the Russian bases.

Second, in conditions of this symmetrical and mutually beneficial interdependence, Russia should firmly promote the "manageable openness" principle in its relations with China in the Arctic: welcome cooperation on concrete economic, transport and environmental projects, but insist that this project-based cooperation does not translate into China obtaining a role in the Arctic governance. Major projects of strategic significance must be firmly controlled by Russia without any passing of decision-making to the Chinese counterparts.

Third, Russia should diversify the list of non-Western partners in the region and intensify cooperation with the other Asian states—India, Japan, Republic of Korea and ASEAN countries. As with the Russian "Turn to the East" as a whole, it is vital, that cooperation with Asian countries in the Arctic does not end with China only.

REFERENCES

Aker Arctic. (n.d.). *Xue Long 2*. https://akerarctic.fi/en/reference/xue-long-2/. Accessed Aug 7.

Balton, D., & Zagorskiy, A. (2020). Управление морскими ресурсами в Северном Ледовитом океане [Marine resource management in the Arctic Ocean]. *Российский совет по международным делам (РСМД)* [Russian Council on International Affairs (RIAC)], 56. https://russiancouncil.ru/pap ers/Arctic-Marine-Report56.pdf. Accessed Aug 7.

China-Nordic Arctic Research Centre. (n.d.). *Polar Research Institute of China*. https://www.cnarc.info/members/21-polar-research-institute-of-china. Accessed Aug 7.

Clingendael Report. (2020, June). *Presence before power*. https://www.clinge ndael.org/pub/2020/presence-before-power/4-greenland-what-is-china-doing-there-and-why/. Accessed Aug 7.

Department of Defense Arctic Strategy. (2019, June). *Report to Congress*. https://media.defense.gov/2019/Jun/06/2002141657/-1/-1/1/2019-DOD-ARCTIC-STRATEGY.PDF. Accessed Aug 7.

Department of the Air Force of the U.S. (2020, July 21). *Arctic Strategy.* https://www.af.mil/Portals/1/documents/2020SAF/July/Arctic Strategy.pdf. Accessed Aug 7.

Department of the Army of the U.S. (2021, January 19). *Regaining Arctic dominance: The U.S. army in the Arctic.* https://api.army.mil/e2/c/downlo ads/2021/03/15/9944046e/regaining-arctic-dominance-us-army-in-the-arc tic-19-january-2021-unclassified.pdf. Accessed Aug 7.

Embassy of the People's Republic of China in the Republic of Iceland. (2019, October 4). *Sino-Icelandic economic and trade relationship.* http://is.china-embassy.org/eng/zbgx/jmgx/t1653166.htm. Accessed Aug 7.

Ghosh, S., & Aggarwal, M. (2021, January 22). Research and resources are two pillars of India's draft Arctic policy. *Mongabay.* https://india.mongabay. com/2021/01/research-and-resources-are-two-pillars-of-indias-draft-arctic-policy/. Accessed Aug 7.

Global Times. (2013, July 15). *Zhongguo haijun jiang shezu bianyuan haiyu yinggai zhongdian guanzhu beibingyang* [The Chinese navy to set foot in the marginal seas, it should focus on the Arctic Ocean]. https://mil.huanqiu. com/article/9CaKrnJBkOd. Accessed Aug 7.

Goosse, H., Kay, J. E, Armor, K. C., Bodas-Salcedo, A., Chepfer, H., Docquier, D., Jonko, A., Kushner, P. J., Lecomte, O., Massonnet, F., & Park, H. S. (2018). Quantifying climate feedbacks in polar regions. *Nature communications, 9*(1), 1–13. https://www.nature.com/articles/s41467-018-04173-0. Accessed Aug 7.

Huang, J. (2019, August 16). Xin shidai woguo haijun de xan zhanlve [The new strategy of the Chinese Navy in the new era]. *FX361.com.* https://m.fx361. com/news/2019/0816/5427432.html. Accessed Aug 7.

InterAct. (n.d.). *China Iceland arctic research observatory.* https://eu-interact. org/field-sites/karholl-research-station/. Accessed Aug 7.

Kalyukov, E., & Dzyadko, T. (2019, April 25). НОВАТЭК договорился о продаже 20% «Арктик СПГ 2» китайским компаниям [NOVATEK agreed to sell 20% of Arctic LNG-2 to Chinese companies]. *РБК [RBC].* https:// www.rbc.ru/business/25/04/2019/5cc176b99a79473082e419f9. Accessed Aug 7.

MarineTraffic. (n.d.). *Xue Long.* https://www.marinetraffic.com/en/ais/det ails/ships/shipid:551884/mmsi:412863000/imo:8877899/vessel:XUE_ LONG. Accessed Aug 7.

NORINCO. (n.d.). *Chanpin zhanshi* [Products presented]. http://hyj.norinc ogroup.com.cn/col/col5721/index.html. Accessed Aug 7.

Norwegian Government Security and Service Organisation. (2010). *Agreement between The Polar Research Institute of China (PRIC), the People's Republic of China and The Norwegian Polar Institute (NPI), Norway on*

Polar research cooperation. https://www.regjeringen.no/globalassets/upload/kd/vedlegg/forskning/pric_agreement.pdf. Accessed Aug 7.

Pörtner, H. O., Roberts, D. C., Masson-Delmotte, V., Zhai, P., Tignor, M., Poloczanska, E., Mintenbeck, K., Alegría, A., Nicolai, M., Okem, A., & Petzold, J. (2019). *IPCC Special Report on the Ocean and Cryosphere in a Changing Climate.* The Intergovernmental Panel on Climate Change (IPCC). https://www.ipcc.ch/site/assets/uploads/sites/3/2019/12/SROCC_Citations.pdf. Accessed Aug 7.

Ramesh, R. (2021, May 19). *India's role in the Arctic: Reviving the momentum through a policy.* The Arctic Institute. https://www.thearcticinstitute.org/india-role-arctic-reviving-momentum-through-policy/. Accessed Aug 7.

Schreiber, M. (2019, April 4). Russia and Canada may lose their legal claim to Arctic seaways as ice melts, experts say. *Arctic-Today.* https://www.arctictoday.com/russia-and-canada-may-lose-their-legal-claim-to-arctic-seaways-as-ice-melts-experts-say/. Accessed Aug 7.

Sengupta, S. (2019, May 6). United States rattles arctic talks with a sharp warning to China and Russia. *The New York Times.* https://www.nytimes.com/2019/05/06/climate/pompeo-arctic-china-russia.html. Accessed Aug 7.

Sina. (2004, April 2). Zhongguo xin gaoyuan fanghan micai fu pei fa xizang junqu budui (zutu) [China's new plateau cold-proof camouflage uniforms distributed to the Tibet Military Region troops (photo)]. http://mil.news.sina.com.cn/2004-04-02/0957190854.html. Accessed Aug 7.

Song, L., & Jia, H. (2021, February 1). Haijun pobingchuan wancheng di 84 ci huang bohai bing qing diaocha renwu [The Navy icebreaker completes the 84th Yellow Sea and Bohai Sea ice survey mission]. *China Military.* http://www.81.cn/hj/2021-02/01/content_9978094.htm. Accessed Aug 7.

The Arctic Institute. (n.d.). *China.* https://www.thearcticinstitute.org/countries/china/. Accessed Aug 7.

The State Council. (2018, January 26). *Full text: China's Arctic policy.* http://english.www.gov.cn/archive/white_paper/2018/01/26/content_281476026660336.htm. Accessed Aug 7.

Weitz, R. (2021, July 9). *Assessing Chinese–Russian military exercises: Past progress and future trends.* Center for Strategic and International Studies. https://www.csis.org/analysis/assessing-chinese-russian-military-exercises-past-progress-and-future-trends. Accessed Aug 7.

Whiteman, G., Hope, C., & Wadhams, P. (2013). Vast costs of Arctic change. *Nature News and Comment, 499*(7459), 401–403.

Xinhua. (2017, June 20). *Full text: Vision for maritime cooperation under the Belt and Road Initiative.* http://www.xinhuanet.com/english/2017-06/20/c_136380414.htm

Xinhua. (2018, June 27). *Woguo shou sou he dongli pobingchuan jie kai miansha——jiang wei haishang fudong hedianzhan dongli zhichi pu ping daolu* [China's first nuclear-powered icebreaker unveiled—To pave the way for power support for offshore floating nuclear power plants]. http://www.xinhuanet.com/politics/2018-06/27/c_1123041028.htm. Accessed Aug 7.

Xinhua. (2019, May 17). *Companies from China, Norway voice hope for more economic, trade cooperation.* http://www.xinhuanet.com/english/2019-05/17/c_138066300.htm. Accessed Aug 7.

Yumashev, D., Hope, C., Schaefer, K., Riemann-Campe, K., Iglesias-Suarez, F., Jafarov, E., Burke, E. J., Young, P. J., Elshorbany, Y., & Whiteman, G. (2019). Climate policy implications of nonlinear decline of Arctic land permafrost and other cryosphere elements. *Nature Communications, 10*(1900). https://doi.org/10.1038/s41467-019-09863-x

The Cold War in the Cold Region: A Return

Ilya Kramnik

INTRODUCTION

An increase in Great Powers activity in the Arctic, including military, economy and other spheres, is becoming a key factor shaping the outlook for the region, which is gradually shifting from being an area of peace and cooperation to becoming an arena of rivalry. Russia and NATO, the two main military powers in the Arctic, are stepping up their efforts in the region, which will radically change the security architecture there in the post-Soviet period.

THE CONTOURS OF RIVALRY

The end of the first Cold War and the consequent collapse of the USSR brought a sharp decline of military activity in the Arctic from both sides: both Russia and the United States no longer saw the region as a likely battleground.

I. Kramnik (✉)
Institute of World Economy and International Relations,
Russian Academy of Sciences, Moscow, Russia
e-mail: ikramnik@imemo.ru

© The Author(s), under exclusive license to Springer Nature
Singapore Pte Ltd. 2022
A. Likhacheva (ed.), *Arctic Fever*,
https://doi.org/10.1007/978-981-16-9616-9_2

Many military installations were closed during this period. In the Russian North, the civilian population, which had grown during the Soviet period upon the active development of Arctic resources and the military presence in the region, was also significantly reduced. By the second half of the 1990s, this presence decreased to sporadic air force exercises and limited Northern Fleet activity, primarily in the Barents and Kara Seas.

The first hints of a possible new increase in military activity in the region began in the 2000s, when the US Navy begin conducting regular ICEX (Kramnik, 2018a) drills, with combat training beneath the ice, including target search and tracking, torpedo firing, and ice base equipment testing. During the same period, Russian aviation will intensify its presence in the North by resuming regular long-range flights (Strokan & Reutov, 2007).

During the first phase until the end of the 2000s, this presence remained somewhat sporadic, not changing the situation in the region as a whole. The Arctic continued to be quiet and sparsely populated—economic activity beyond the polar circle also remained at a minimum level.

In 2010s, Russia began the large-scale restoration of long-term military presence in the Arctic. In 2014, a separate military structure in Arctic was formed—Joint Strategic Command North. The Russian Navy's Northern Fleet formed the backbone of the new structure's forces (Ramm et al., 2019). During the same period, the construction of new military bases and the renovation of some of the old installations began in earnest. Work has begun in almost the entire Russian sector of the Arctic: on the islands of the Franz Josef Land, Novaya Zemlya, Severnaya Zemlya, Novosibirsk Islands, Wrangel Island, as well as on the mainland from the Kola Peninsula to Chukotka (Grischenko, 2017).

The target of a military reactivation was a ensure control over its waters and airspace, given their growing economic importance. In 2013, oil production began at the Prirazlomnoye field, and the construction of the Sabetta port as part of the Yamal-LNG project also began. So, in 2013, the lead nuclear-powered icebreaker Arktika of the new project 22,220 was laid down in St. Petersburg (Kogtev, 2015).

By now, the situation in the Arctic is relatively favorable for the Russian Federation in terms of the Great Powers balance. Because of its geographical position, Russia controls a large part of the Arctic Ocean, the most navigationally accessible part—Norway is the only major Arctic country with better conditions, whose entire coastline faces ice-free seas. Compared to Canada and the United States, the Russian Arctic has the longest navigation period, a smaller area and thickness of ice cover, and numerous bases and ports on the coast and islands. Both developments of the resources of the Russian North and transit shipping contribute to this. Of course, the NSR is still a long way from the performance of the southern seas, but the prospects for the development of this route are significant.

At the same time, due to deteriorating relations between Russia and NATO, largely (but not only) due to the events in Ukraine in 2014, Western powers are also stepping up their activities in the region. In 2015, the first major NATO Air Force exercise, Arctic Challenge (SLDinfo, 2015), involving neutral partner nations (Finland, Sweden and Switzerland), took place in the Arctic. In autumn 2018, in Norway and surrounding waters, was held Trident Juncture 2018 (NATO, 2018)— the largest exercise since the collapse of the Soviet Union. The exercise aimed to test the capabilities of NATO's rapid reaction forces and the participant's ability to manage the support they receive from allies.

Even before the Ukrainian crisis, the Alliance had begun to re-establish its military presence in Iceland. Earlier this presence was wiped out after the withdrawal of American planes from the Keflavik AFB in 2006. A NATO air patrol was announced as a purely unarmed mission with observation goals started in 2007. In 2013, the readiness level was increased, and since 2014, aircrafts have regularly carried weapons during intercept missions (NATO, 2014).

In the early spring of 2020, NATO planned to hold Cold Response 2020 exercises in the Arctic. The exercise aimed to train troops in low and extreme cold temperatures. The COVID 19 has changed these plans, forcing a cancellation of the drills (Interfax, 2020).

The entry of a group of NATO ships comprising the HMS Kent and three destroyers from the US Navy Sixth Fleet—DDG-75 Donald Cook, DDG-78 Porter and DDG-80 Roosevelt from the DESRON 60, permanently based in Rota, Spain—into the Barents Sea in May 2020 was a logical continuation of the general trend of increasing NATO activity in the region (Larter, 2020). From this point onwards, the permanent presence of the US Navy and its allies in the region, backed up by Norwegian bases, could be said to be a permanent presence. On 20 October, another ship of the DESRON 60, the DDG-71 Ross, arrived in the Barents Sea and was soon joined by the fleet tanker T-AO-203 Laramie. The task force practiced navigating in Arctic conditions, including transferring fuel and cargo on the move, in addition to the usual combat service tasks of monitoring the airspace, sea surface and searching for Russian submarines. A month earlier, USS Ross had participated in NATO maneuvers as part of a multinational anti-submarine force. In addition to the US Navy destroyer, the task force also included HMS Sutherland, HNoMS Thor Heyerdahl and the RFA Tidespring. US Naval aviation P-8A Poseidonanti-submarine aircraft provided air support to the NATO ships. At the same time, the French frigate Aquitaine was operating in the Norwegian Sea.

In 2020, the United States also increased the activities of its submarine force in the region. During this year, nuclear-powered submarines, including the SSN-21 Seawolf, were twice announced to enter Norway, with the submarine activities usually are strictly classified. According to the US media, these missions, like the flights of strategic bombers, are demonstrative, "sending a clear signal to Russia about the American presence in the region" (Mcleary, 2020). This activity relies on Norwegian infrastructure: in September 2020, a media reported the work completed on the new Grøtsund naval base near Tromsø. The new installation will allow US ships and submarines more frequent visits and forward deployment if necessary.

In spring 2021, the United States and Norway signed a supplementary agreement on the use of military infrastructure. After parliamentary approval of the agreement, the United States will be able to start building at Rygge airfield in the southern part of the country on the coast of Oslo-fjord, Sola airfield near Stavanger in south-western Norway, Evenes airfield near Narvik and Ramsund naval base near Narvik on the opposite side of Ofotfjord, on Hjelløya island. Now Ramsund is the main base of the Norwegian Navy's Special Operations Forces (Mcleary, 2021).

The new airfields will be used as the forward operating base of P-8A maritime patrol aircrafts and B-1B bombers. The main task of the P-8A will be "to monitor Russian submarines sailing from Northern Fleet's main base on Kola peninsula, hard up against the Norwegian border" (Mcleary, 2021).

The B-1B bombers were first deployed to Norway at Ørland Air Base in late February 2021. During the visit to Europe, they also performed a training and demonstration flight over the Baltics while being escorted by Italian and German Air Force Typhoon fighters based in the Baltic states as part of NATO's Baltic Air Policing mission (NATO, 2021). However, being based in Norway could allow US aircraft to perform more significant missions than demonstration flights. According to Jeffrey Harrigian, commander of the US Air Force in Europe and Africa, bombers trained interactions with various forces in the air and on the ground, including special operations forces, during the Norway deployment. Special operations forces are supposed to be used behind enemy lines to transmit information to combat aircrafts about the most important targets that require an immediate attack (Trevithick, 2021). "During any future contingency, including a high-end conflict with a near-peer adversary, such as Russia, the Air Force could still potentially commit B-1Bs to close air support missions, in addition to long-range strike sorties",—US military commentator Joseph Trevithick said. He also highlights that the bombers deployment in northern Norway gives them quick access into the Norwegian and Barents Seas airspace, and in the High North too. According to Trevithick, the B-1Bs would provide a "new challenge" for Russian operations in these regions, foremost for the Northern and Baltic Fleets, and would support NATO forces in countering Russian Navy attempts to break through the North Atlantic via the GIUK border in a hypothetical conflict (Trevithick, 2021).

A significant step to strengthening NATO's naval capabilities in the North region was the reactivating of the US Navy's 2nd Fleet in 2018. At the beginning of 2020, it will reach the operating capability (Stars & Stripes, 2020). During the first Cold War, it was the 2nd Fleet that was the strongest of the US Navy's operational fleets. In the autumn of 2020, there was talk of the possibility of re-establishing an independent Atlantic Fleet Command to deal with current threats (Eckstein, 2020b). "The Atlantic Fleet will confront the assertive Russian Navy, which has been deployed closer and closer to our East Coast, with a tailored maritime presence capability and lethality",—Secretary of the Navy Kenneth Braithwaite said.

At the same time, naval cooperation between the United States and Great Britain continues to get stronger. In October 2020, US Navy Chief of Naval Operations Admiral Mike Gilday and Britain's First Sea Lord Tony Radakin reached an agreement to work towards the interchangeability of aircraft carriers in naval operations. The arrangement was announced after a NATO exercise in the Atlantic, during which from the British aircraft carrier Queen Elizabeth both British and the US Marine Corps F-35B operated (Eckstein, 2020a). Radakin noted the interaction between the United States, Britain and NATO allies in anti-submarine actions in the Atlantic. The parties intend to enhance cooperation by organizing "tech bridges"—online dialogues between the armed forces, industry and academia representatives.

US-Canadian cooperation continues to develop within the North American air defense system, NORAD. NORAD activity remains mostly unchanged, but strain to air defense system growing as general tensions in the region increase. This includes the US Arctic territories: in the Alaska Air Defense Identification Zone (ADIZ), for example, more than 60 Russian aircraft were intercepted in 2020, according to Lieutenant General David Krumm, commander of the US Air Force in Alaska, the highest number since 1991 (Cohen, 2021). In the mid-2010s, this number was around 10 aircraft per year.

In May 2021, NORAD forces were involved in a major exercise Northern Edge 2021 (Olson, 2021). The novelty of this activity lies in the active engagement of the US Navy's Air Force and the practice of inter-theater force redeployment. In particular, B-52 strategic bombers from INDOPACOM bases flew to Alaska in the NORTHCOM zone. In addition, a number of methods of command and control were tested. The aim of the exercise was in practice interoperability between the US Air Force, Navy and Marine Corps aviation, using F-22A, F-35B, upgraded F-15EX fighters, which will eventually replace the F-15s of older versions in the NORAD system, and F/A-18E/F naval aircrafts, with the active participation of reconnaissance, AWACS, electronic warfare and other special mission aircrafts. During the exercise, new communication and data exchange tools were used, SpaceX's Starlink satellite network in particular.

According to US sources, Northern Edge 2021 will not be the largest of the drills in the series, but it will be the most distributed, with active use of network-centric systems and a battle network. In addition, this is the first exercise in the Northern Edge series that will involve an aircraft carrier and a Marine Expeditionary Unit (USS Theodore Roosevelt Public Affairs, 2021).

In the Alaska area, the United States is also considering reactivating several closed and renovating existing airfields (Axe, 2021). "By operating from forward operating locations such a King Salmon, we are proving our strategic flexibility, freedom of movement and our ability to develop and to execute proactive and scalable options for future missions", said Brig. Gen. William Radiff, deputy commander of North American Aerospace Defense Command Alaska Region.

Overall, we can state that NATO military activity has now reached a sufficiently high level, which may increase in the future as new military installations develop and the number of ice-class ships and vessels increases.

Plans and Strategies

Of significant interest are documents that allow forecasting of further developments, on both sides, including military planning documents. In particular, the US Army's Arctic Strategy, adopted in 2021. The strategy text considers the strengthening of Russia's position in the region and China's desire to gain reliable access to Arctic resources as a threat. US Army will field a new division, including specially trained brigade combat teams, whose command-and-control system will allow for multi-domain operations involving different branches of the armed forces.

The US Navy's Arctic Strategy (Bye, 2021), for its part, notes that the importance of the Arctic is growing as the ice melts. "Despite containing the world's smallest ocean, the Arctic Region has the potential to connect nearly 75% of the worlds population – as metlting sea ice increases access to shorter maritime trade routes linking Asia, Europe and North America",—notes the strategy.

The strategy assesses as a threat the development of the Northern Sea Route for both military and commercial purposes, investments in the construction of new and the reorganization of existing military bases, the improvement of command and control systems, communications and in general the development of means to project military power. According to the United States, Russia seeks "unlawful" traffic regulation along the Northern Sea Route. The strategy authors believe these actions "undermine global interests, promote instability and ultimately degrade security in the region".

A similar document was issued last year by the US Air Force (Secretary of the Air Force Public Affairs, 2021). The priority of the Air Force and the newly created space forces in 2020 is the protection of the country, including timely warning of a nuclear attack. Overall, the U.S. Air Force strategy is most concerned with strategic stability issues while addressing current political and climatic topics weakly.

The US Department of Defense's Arctic Strategy (Humpert, 2019a), released in 2019, also mentions the issue of climate change. "Diminishing Arctic Sea ice is opening new shipping lanes and increasing access to natural resources during the summer months. If the warming trends continue at the current rate, Arctic Sea ice loss may result in nearly ice-free late summers by the 2040s",—states the text. The strategy points to increased Russian and Chinese activity and highlights the Russian military buildup in the region as a threat.

The UK's new Arctic defense strategy, released in 2018, is also interesting (Defense.Info, 2018). According to the London strategists, the Arctic is a region whose openness and importance are growing as the ice melts and the navigation season expands, leading to increased military activity. Russia's activity in the region highlights as the main threat, with extensive use of the submarine fleet and increased military buildup. The strategy includes, among other things, increased training for personnel in severe cold weather conditions and RoyalAir Force fighter patrols in Iceland.

The main Russian document defining Moscow's policy goals and objectives in the region is the strategy for developing the Arctic zone of the Russian Federation and ensuring national security for the period until 2035, approved by President Vladimir Putin's decree in October 2020 (Government of Russia, 2020).

The Strategy states the critical importance of the Arctic zone for the Russian economy, due to its production of more than 80% of natural gas and 17% of oil and gas condensate in Russia, and the demand for high-tech domestic products generated by Arctic investment projects. Also highlights the role of the Arctic as a strategic reserve for the development of the mineral resource base, the value of the Northern Sea Route as a transport corridor of global importance, and the prospects of this role increasing because of climate change.

There is also an increase in the conflict potential in the Arctic, which requires a constant increase in the combat capabilities of the armed forces and other Russian military formations and structures in the Arctic zone.

Chinese Impact

The Russia-NATO rivalry, while fascinating to outside observers, does not exhaust the Arctic picture. The activity of China, which is interested in the Arctic resource and transit potential, becomes a factor that could have a significant influence on the balance of power in the region in the medium term.

Russian researchers, Dmitri Trenin (2020) in particular, point out that China's interest in the Arctic is different than that of Russia. However, with its vaster economic, financial and technological resources, the PRC has significant capabilities to change the game rules and the positions of the major players. They may have higher ability than Russia's to maintain the status quo. At the same time, Trenin observes that, despite significant contradictions between Russia and many NATO countries, Moscow's position on the status of the Northern Sea Route is close to that of Canada on the Northwest Passage. Furthermore, Russia, like other Arctic states, seeks to guarantee its rights in Spitsbergen, where Norway has recently tended to impose unilateral restrictions. However, Trenin argues that China's position on Arctic status is more similar to that of the United States and other non-Arctic maritime powers, even though China's desire to gain a foothold in the Arctic is seen in the United States as a threat, as we have argued above.

China's 2018 Arctic Strategy (The State Council Information Office of the People's Republic of China, 2018) defines Beijing's status as "an active participant, builder and contributor in Arctic affairs who has spared no efforts to contribute its wisdom to the development of the Arctic region". China declares its interest in Arctic research, environmental protection, use of natural resources, cooperation in managing the region and promoting peace and stability. Although the wording is emphatically friendly, it masks the possibility of future tensions with other Arctic powers, including Russia, by signaling Beijing's claim to a major role in the Arctic and its "wish to play one of the leading roles among them in formulating the Arctic agenda" (Gudev, 2019).

China's potential in the region could be significantly affected by its icebreaker program, which envisages the acquisition of heavy icebreakers, including possibly nuclear-powered (Humpert, 2019b) China's first heavy icebreaker, designated Xue Long 3, would be expected to enable passage through the Northern Sea Route, including through areas of heavy ice, except during the most severe winter period, which is expected to be shorter.

It is still difficult to talk about China's military plans in the Arctic, given that such plans need a basis in the form of bases, which China does not have in the region. In these circumstances, it can be assumed that Chinese military activity in the Arctic can only become realistic if Beijing manages to reach an agreement with Moscow on the use of one or more Russian bases. So far, this seems unlikely without a further major deterioration in

Russia's position, which would force it to make such an acknowledgment of China's role and capabilities in a region that Russia has perceived as its own for centuries.

Conclusion

A key feature of the Arctic as a theater of operations is the inaccessibility of the region, which has not changed much even in the face of climate change. The region is only being developed around a small number of more or less major population centers, which are reached by roads of limited capacity. The main modes of transport in the Arctic are by the sea and by air. But maritime transport, even though the climate has softened considerably in recent years, is still hampered by the ice cover.

This means a sharp "increase of the weight" of each military facility in the Arctic—the destruction of an individual depot, base, airfield or other military facilities can cause more serious damage to the military potential of its possessor than the destruction of the same facility in temperate latitudes. At the same time, Russia's ability to build up its forces in the Arctic beyond those already deployed there at present is rather limited. The main limiting factors are insufficient capabilities of cargo and other military aviation, including shortage of special mission aircrafts, such as tankers and AWACS; critical shortage of Russian Navy warships and slow speed of their construction (Kramnik, 2018b).

Against this background, NATO's decisive superiority in economic power and industrial capability threatens to upset the balance of power when this superiority translates into numerical superiority of NATO forces in the region. Under such circumstances, the ability to produce the many types of armaments and military equipment acquires special weight: warplanes, primarily special aircrafts, warships, and several others, in particular air and missile defense equipment. So far, Russia can boast of a rhythmic and stable production volume enabling it to fully and timely meet the needs of its Armed Forces only with respect to the last item out of the above-mentioned ones.

This situation also contains a threat for NATO: the potential deterioration of Moscow's position in the Arctic could accelerate the decision to cooperate with China.

REFERENCES

Axe, D. (2021, May 7). A cold, foggy U.S. Air force base waits just 200 miles from Russia. *Forbes.* https://www.forbes.com/sites/davidaxe/2021/05/07/a-cold-foggy-us-air-force-base-waits-just-200-miles-from-russia/?sh=1a3e226b5e52. Accessed 28 July 2021.

Bye, H.-G. (2021, January 6). US Navy arctic strategy: New challenges in a "blue" Arctic. *High North News.* https://www.highnorthnews.com/en/us-navy-arctic-strategy-new-challenges-blue-arctic. Accessed 28 July 2021.

Cohen, R. (2021, April 28). Spike in Russian aircraft intercepts straining Air Force crews in Alaska, three-star says. *AirForce Times.* https://www.airforcetimes.com/news/your-air-force/2021/04/28/spike-in-russian-aircraft-intercepts-straining-air-force-crews-in-alaska-three-star-says/. Accessed 28 July 2021.

Defense.Info. (2018, October 2). UK announces New Arctic strategy. *Defense.Info.* https://defense.info/re-thinking-strategy/2018/10/uk-announces-new-arctic-strategy/. Accessed 28 July 2021.

Eckstein, M. (2020a, December 2). SECNAV announces the return of the U.S. Atlantic fleet, focus will be on Russian threat. *USNI News.* https://news.usni.org/2020/12/02/secnav-announces-the-return-of-the-u-s-atlantic-fleet-focus-will-be-on-russian-threat. Accessed 28 July 2021.

Eckstein, M. (2020b, October 20). U.S., U.K. Navies working to achieve 'interchangeability' in carrier forces, collaboration on unmanned and AI. *USNI News.* https://news.usni.org/2020/10/20/u-s-u-k-navies-working-to-achieve-interchangeability-in-carrier-forces-collaboration-on-unmanned-and-ai. Accessed 28 July 2021.

Government of Russia. (2020). *Стратегия развития Арктической зоны Российской Федерации и обеспечения национальной безопасности на период до 2035 года* [Strategy of development of the Arctic Zone of the Russian Federation and the provision of national security for the period to 2035]. E-Fund of Law and Regulatory-Technical Documents. https://docs.cntd.ru/document/566091182. Accessed 28 July 2021.

Grischenko, N. (2017, January 26). Россия построит в Арктике более 100 военных объектов [Russia to build over 100 military facilities in the Arctic]. *RG.ru.* https://rg.ru/2017/01/26/reg-szfo/rossiia-postroit-v-arktike-bolee-100-voennyh-obektov.html. Accessed 28 July 2021.

Gudev, P. A. (2019). New risks and opportunities for interstate cooperation in the Arctic. *Arktika i Sever* [Arctic and North], *36*, 57–83. https://doi.org/10.17238/issn2221-2698.2019.36.5

Humpert, M. (2019a, June 7). New U.S. department of defense Arctic strategy sees growing uncertainty and tension in region. *High North News.* https://www.highnorthnews.com/en/new-us-department-defense-arctic-strategy-sees-growing-uncertainty-and-tension-region. Accessed 28 July 2021.

Humpert, M. (2019b, December 16). China reveals details of newly designed heavy icebreaker. *High North News*. https://www.highnorthnews.com/en/china-reveals-details-newly-designed-heavy-icebreaker. Accessed 28 July 2021.

Interfax. (2020, March 11). Норвегия отменила совместные с НАТО учения Cold Response [Norway cancels joint cold response exercise with NATO]. *Interfax*. https://www.interfax.ru/world/698624. Accessed 28 July 2021.

Kogtev, Yu. (2015, April 16). Три метра льда под килем [Three meters of ice under the keel]. *Kommersant*. https://www.kommersant.ru/doc/2704192. Accessed 28 July 2021.

Kramnik, I. (2018a, March 18). Арктическое всплытие: почему в Северных морях растет активность подлодок НАТО [Arctic ascent: Why NATO submarines are on the rise in the North Seas]. *Izvestiya*. https://iz.ru/720909/ilia-kramnik/arkticheskoe-vsplytie. Accessed 28 July 2021.

Kramnik, I. (2018b, September 12). Поближе к берегу: как изменится состав ВМФ России [Closer to the shore: How the composition of the Russian Navy will change]. *Izvestiya*. https://iz.ru/787950/ilia-kramnik/poblizhe-k-beregu-kak-izmenitsia-sostav-vmf-rossii. Accessed 28 July 2021.

Larter, D. B. (2020, March 12). The US Navy returns to an increasingly militarized Arctic. *DefenseNews*. https://www.defensenews.com/naval/2020/05/11/the-us-navy-returns-to-an-increasingly-militarized-arctic/. Accessed 28 July 2021.

Mcleary, P. (2020, September 3). Norway expands key Arctic port for more US Nuke sub visits. *Breaking Defense*. https://breakingdefense.com/2020/09/norway-expands-key-arctic-port-for-more-us-nuke-sub-visits/. Accessed 28 July 2021.

Mcleary, P. (2021, April 19). Norway, US Bolster Russian sub watching with new bases. *Breaking Defense*. https://breakingdefense.com/2021/04/norway-us-bolster-russian-sub-watching-with-new-bases/. Accessed 28 July 2021.

NATO. (2014, February 3). *NATO flies with partners over Iceland for first time*. NATO. https://www.nato.int/cps/en/natohq/news_106841.htm. Accessed 28 July 2021.

NATO. (2018, October 31). *Trident juncture 18*. NATO Media resources. https://www.nato.int/cps/en/natohq/news_158620.htm. Accessed 28 July 2021.

NATO. (2021, March 5). *US B-1B lancer bombers arrive in Europe and fly over the Baltic states*. NATO Multimedia. https://www.natomultimedia.tv/portal/Asset.html?id=646022. Accessed 28 July 2021.

Olson, W. (2021, May 4). Joint exercise of US forces in Alaska mimics 'what future conflict could feel like'. *Stars and Stripes*. https://www.stripes.com/theaters/us/joint-exercise-of-us-forces-in-alaska-mimics-what-future-conflict-could-feel-like-1.672168. Accessed 28 July 2021.

Ramm, A., Kozachenko, A., & Stepovoy, B. (2019, April 19). Полярное влияние: Северный флот получит статус военного округа [Polar influence: The Northern fleet will receive the status of a Military district]. *Izvestiya*. https://iz.ru/869512/aleksei-ramm-aleksei-kozachenko-bogdan-stepovoi/poliarnoe-vliianie-severnyi-flot-poluchit-status-voennogo-okruga. Accessed 28 July 2021.

Secretary of the Air Force Public Affairs. (2021, July 21). *Department of the Air Force introduces Arctic strategy*. U.S. Air Force. https://www.af.mil/News/Article-Display/Article/2281305/department-of-the-air-force-introduces-arctic-strategy/. Accessed 28 July 2021.

SLDinfo. (2015, April 11). Arctic challenge exercise 2015: Norway as the lead nation. *SLDinfo*. https://sldinfo.com/2015/04/arctic-challenge-exercise-2015-norway-as-the-lead-nation/. Accessed 28 July 2021.

Stars & Stripes. (2020, January 2). *Navy's Atlantic-based 2nd Fleet command now fully operational*. Stars and Stripes. https://www.stripes.com/theaters/us/navy-s-atlantic-based-2nd-fleet-command-now-fully-operational-1.613273. Accessed 28 July 2021.

Strokan, S., & Reutov, A. (2007, Aug 20). Далеко идущие вылеты: Россия нашла адекватный ответ США в воздухе [Long-range missions: Russia found an adequate response to the US in the air]. *Kommersant*. https://www.kommersant.ru/doc/796621. Accessed 28 July 2021.

The State Council Information Office of the People's Republic of China. (2018). *China's Arctic policy*. http://english.gov.cn/archive/white_paper/2018/01/26/content_281476026660336.htm. Accessed 27 July 2021.

Trenin, D. (2020, March 31). *Russia and China in the Arctic: Cooperation, competition, and consequences*. Carnegie Moscow Center. https://carnegie.ru/commentary/81407. Accessed 28 July 2021.

Trevithick, J. (2021, March 9). B-1B bomber makes Arctic pit stop for the first time. *The Drive*. https://www.thedrive.com/the-war-zone/39675/b-1b-bomber-makes-arctic-pit-stop-for-the-first-time. Accessed 28 July 2021.

USS Theodore Roosevelt Public Affairs. (2021, May 4). *Theodore Roosevelt CSG begins exercise Northern edge 2021*. Commander, U.S. Pacific Fleet. https://www.cpf.navy.mil/news.aspx/140169. Accessed 28 July 2021.

The Age of Climate Change, as a Challenge for States, and IR Theories

Lassi Heininen

INTRODUCTION

Five years after the Paris Summit the world was hit by another non-military threat and global crisis, the COVID-19 pandemic as "an invisible enemy causing terror among citizens and threatening our modern societies". Economic, traffic and other human activities were decreased, energy was saved by lockdowns and other strict regulations, as well as CO_2 emissions (in 2020) were cut by a few percent (Heininen, 2020, p. 309–310). These cuts were soon compensated by the boom & boost of the exit strategies of recovering supported by huge investment packages to infrastructure, business & companies to grow. The post-COVID-19 investment plans are said to be allocated to "New Green Deal" projects for climate change mitigation, and for a shift in energy production from conventional energy sources to alternative and renewable sources (though there is no guarantee that the investments will be allocated as planned).

L. Heininen (✉)
University of Lapland, Rovaniemi, Finland
e-mail: lassi.heininen@ulapland.fi

Arctic Yearbook, Akureyri, Iceland

© The Author(s), under exclusive license to Springer Nature
Singapore Pte Ltd. 2022
A. Likhacheva (ed.), *Arctic Fever*,
https://doi.org/10.1007/978-981-16-9616-9_3

Though those markets are growing fast, much thanks to advanced technology, there are a few hindrances or obstacles, such as shortages in supply chains (of minerals), that of land, as well as lack of capital. The advanced and cheaper technology for alternative energy is being accelerated by business and companies, and the new green deal investments are being financed by States, which are in charge of the post-COVID-19 exit strategy.

Following from this, and in order to cause an economic recovering of the global economy as quickly as possible, the G7 Summit in June 2021 agreed on huge infrastructure investments, "COVID-19, Climate Change and Recovering" proposed by US President Joe Biden. As, these investments were also meant to challenge China and its huge and ongoing infrastructure investments and projects, also called One Belt—One Road, you might wonder if there is a competition on infrastructure investments: "One Belt – One Road" vs. "US Global Infrastructure Plans". And further, which is the most important priority in global crisis: to interpret tackling against climate change as a common goal by all Paris Agreement signatories or have a hegemony competition on mega-projects and investments.

The co-chair of the IPCC Valerie Masson-Delmotte and UN General Secretary Antonio Guterres put it bluntly as they stated that the report's message is an awakening call to the reality and means "code red for humanity". Buzan and Hansen (2011, p. 268) put it bluntly ten years ago, when they foresaw and warned that "the two most likely environmental wild cards are global warming... and the possibility of a rampant and virulent epidemic". Indeed, both are there (or here when writing this article in August 2021): The latest UN Climate Change Report by IPCC, as the most holistic scientific report on global impacts of climate change, states that the goal of 1.5 degrees Celsius requires to cut the emissions to a half by the end of 2020s and reach the neutrality of CO_2 emissions by 2050. The COVID-19 pandemic continues and is far from over, as there are new waves and mutations of the virus, as well as shortage and slowness in vaccinations (*The Economist*, 2021c).

The ambitious goals of the Agreement are said to be taken as a given and determined mission, and there are numerous statements based on the Agreement and its goals, such as "Governments have said that they want to cut greenhouse gas emissions dramatically. Decades of subsidy and support have made available a range of technologies ready to do so. The time is ripe to push those technologies as hard as possibl—both to battle rising temperatures and, governments hope, advance their countries' role in a green economy... [however] Rich countries have failed to provide the $100bn a year in climate finance that they promised developing countries in Paris" (*The Economist*, 2021b, pp. 16–18).

Following this, there is a question whether the Paris Agreement will make a difference as such, and would mitigation be still possible (to be implemented), and would it solve the problem? Or is it too late and too little to mitigate, and should concentrate on adaptation? Or, when taking into consideration these investments, and the related boost in utilization, production and economy, are States seriously trying to reach the targets, and if States, as the signatories of the Agreement are able and capable to reach the goals, meaning that average temperatures will not rise more than +1.5 degrees Celsius, and further carbon neutrality by 2050? Or is the same kind of lost opportunity happening with the mitigation of climate change what is with the global vaccination of the COVID-19 pandemic, as the G7 failed to act fast to inoculate the entire world population, especially people in developing countries, against the pandemic entering into "a moral failure and a diplomatic disaster" of the international community (*The Economist*, 2021b, p. 10).

From the point of view of climate change mitigation and biodiversity the situation does not look promising that in a global crisis states behave like this. Though climate change is well known today, it is surprising that extreme weather conditions we experienced in summer 2021 all over the world—record high temperatures in the Northern Hemisphere (e.g. 48 degrees Celsius in Verkhoyanks, Siberia), wildfires (e.g. in Western coast of North America, Mediterranean, Siberia), floods (e.g. in Central Europe, Turkey, Asia), droughts (e.g. in Turkey, Middle East, California) and that floods and wildfires exist at the same time in a limited geographical area—are still taken as surprises, and not necessarily connected to climate change as consequences of rapid global warming. Further, that there is neither more holistic understanding of the dynamics of the combination of climate change, pollution and loss of biodiversity, nor state policies or coordinated international programs and activities for these dynamics, although a global crisis has put the existence of human life and humankind into a danger.

Behind this are, of course, several multidimensional reasons. Among them is the above question if the States are seriously trying to reach the Paris Agreement's goals, and if they are capable to make the hard decisions of mitigation, or is there political inability in the implementation? Another reason might be that environmental issues, in particular climate change and biodiversity, are neither explicitly much discussed in main IR theories, nor examined and analyzed enough in political sciences. The environment and environmental issues, as well as environmental politics, are included in a light of critical research within, and alternatives theories of, IR (e.g. Critical environmental studies, Development theories, Marxism, Feminism). An environmental approach is also narrowly discussed in grand theories of social and political sciences, such as in Idealism, Development theories, and, in particular, in Geopolitics, less so in mainstream IR theories.

The focus of this article is to discuss environmental issues, including climate change, in IR and political sciences theories, and based on that what kind of challenge it is for states and state policies. Firstly, it is briefly described how environmental issues were brought onto political agenda of States. Secondly, the paper discussed environmental issues in IR/Political sciences theories and research based on a review of twelve textbooks. Finally, there are conclusions and brief discussion on environmental issues, in particular climate change mitigation, as challenge to States.

ENVIRONMENTAL ISSUES ONTO POLITICAL AGENDA OF STATES

Though environmental issues, in particular climate change (mitigation), have become heavily politicized, this development is rather recent, as they used to be among the fields of low politics. During the 1960s, people and civil societies started to become concern on a state of their lands, waters and fauna and flora due to two things: radioactivity in nature (due to nuclear tests), and distribution of manmade chemical compounds (e.g. Heininen, 2013).

In particular, air pollution, including "anthropogenic pollutants originating in the heavily industrialized, mid-latitude regions of Eurasia which are transported in the Arctic region by the wind currents" (Soroos, 1990), was defined as a problem by residents and local societies. On the global agenda of environmental problems and challenges a concern on atmospheric (long-range) pollution was growing "as scientific evidence mounted on the scope and consequences of acid rain,... and a trend toward global warming". In addition of international regimes to address acid rain and ozone depletion, "negotiations began on a regime to limit climate change", in particular the Arctic haze (including soot), as a distinctively Arctic phenomenon in 1990s (Soroos, 1990).

This served as a trigger for an "environment awakening" phenomenon and the related movement in North America and Europe. Following this, the first UN Conference on the Human Environment, bringing together representatives of member states, took place in 1972 in Stockholm, though interestingly there was no mention of global warming at the Conference (Myers, 1993, p. 212). In the early 1990s, there was a considerable enthusiasm toward "greening" of the world at the end of the Cold War, and that political ecology would be promoted, though for example, Shevardnadze (1991) (the former foreign minister of the Soviet Union) was skeptical about States' ability, alone, and leaned for (international) NGOs for assistance. However, the creation of the United Nations Human Development Programme (1994), including the concept of "Human security", was an important step toward bringing environmental issues onto international political agenda of States.

The environmental awakening was strengthened in the early 2000s due to global warming, which created larger and stronger activities and new movements. As an outcome, the environment was transferred from a field of low politics to that of high politics, and now the current global crisis could and should be even a bigger reason for, not only to study, but try to find solutions to the problem. Also, the COVID-19 pandemic surprised the world and international community when it started in early 2020. It is possible to say that both were the so-called "unknowns", though not "unknown unknowns", as the Earth has always faced climate change, and COVID-19 was not the first coronavirus.

Interestingly, the impacts of global warming have been known, scientifically and partly secretly, at least for 70 years or so, as "climate change became a U.S. national security concern even before the Cold War became hot" (Doel, 2009, p. 17). Correspondingly, in the Soviet Union research and studies on anthropogenic climatic change were started in the 1970s, before most other countries, including conclusions that "future warming will probably reduce precipitation over some regions with insufficient moisture in the middle latitudes and that the higher temperature will diminish the area of polar sea ice" (Anthropogenic Climatic Change,

1991, p. 319). Unlike, no articles on the ecological modernization[1] of Russia was found in a review in the domestic Russian academic journals on economics and sociology, and only a few studies on the subject in the English-language literature (Tokunaga, 2010).

The mainstream international politics by States, as the Special Edition/Issues 2008 of Newsweek (e.g. pp. 8–11, 22–23, 26–27) well shows, even demonstrates, concentrates on states, alliance and power (both military, economic and power), in particular, the United States as the leading and "most frightened nation" and "an unlikely ally" to China. Concerning the environment and climate the Edition briefly mentions carbon emissions, low-carbon economy and the Kyoto Protocol, and discussed on energy by asking "How to fuel the country, while saving the world" (Newsweek, 2008, pp. 36–37, 44–47).

Finally, the Paris Agreement, which is interpreted and manifested as being a success, was negotiated and adopted by 196 States under the auspices of the United Nations Framework Convention on Climate Change at COP21 in December 2015 and entered into force a year later. According to the agreement the signatories agreed to "holding the increase in the global average temperature to well below 2 degrees C above pre-industrial levels and pursuing efforts to limit the temperature increase to 1.5 [degrees] C above pre-industrial levels", as well as to achieve this goal greenhouse gas emission neutrality (net-zero) should be achieved globally by 2050 (Rogelj, 2016; United Nations, 2015).

In spite of all this, in 2021 the humankind is living in the middle of global crises, great power rivalry, in particular stiff competition between China and the United States, meaning that continuing regional warfare in Middle East and Middle Asia dominates world politics. Therefore, although there are promises and principal agreements of the States, it is not clear if the rivals continue cooperation on tackling problems, such as climate change, or concentrate on hegemony competition.

---

[1] Here considered as industrial restructuring leading into environmentally sound economy, as well as the development of institutional capacity for an effective environmental policy.

Environmental Issues in IR/Political Sciences Theories and Research

A hypothesis of this paper is that Climate Change is a challenge to a State, as well as state politics defined in a traditional way. This is no surprise, as it threatens national security, which is the core of state sovereignty and the most ultimate aim of a state; national security does not have a price. Further, mainstream IR theories, such as Political realism, Classical geopolitics, are stuck with a State as the main, if not the only, and dominating international actor in international/world politics, and IR was founded to support a state and the unified state system.

Political realism does not have much to say on the environment and the environmental issues. Except that power, as well as hegemony, of a state is interpreted as a natural state—a model comes from nature—and therefore "anarchy" is a natural state of the international system, as it is the competition on natural resources, as Hobbes was writing in Leviathan. Unlike Political Realism, there is a direct interrelation between the environment and Classical geopolitics, though less so with discourses of new and critical geopolitics. Among those discourse/sub-theories of Classical geopolitics which include the environment are:

1. Firstly, Teleology on space defining a state like a living organism which needs space and resources to grow (e.g. Kjellen, Ratzel);
2. Secondly, the Resource models of geopolitics, among the Explanative geopolitical theories, emphasizing flows of natural resources and raw materials (e.g. theses by Malthus on limits of natural resources; Ehrlich's on the Population Bomb);
3. Thirdly, the Technology models of geopolitics (e.g. Mackinder's Heartland theory) emphasizing a keen relationship between the environment and security, and environmental impacts by the military, also in peace time (e.g. Galtung, Heininen, 1991).

Classical idealism, represented by Immanuel Kant, recognizes a nature, as well as nature conservation and traditional knowledge, and defines a harmony between a man and a nature as an important objective. Marxism includes the dialect of a nature by Engels, and the idea of a transfer from "Biosphere" to "Noosphere" (=sphere of intellect) (e.g. Laptev). Unlike Liberalism/Neoliberalism, Marxism prefers economics over a nature.

52   L. HEININEN

Even the new versions of IR theories, such as New Realism, New Geopolitics, which are based on redefinitions and reinterpretations, do not make big differences as they are stuck with the unified state system, too. New realism (for example, by Kenneth Waltz) recognizes intergovernmental organizations (legal, economic) and international cooperation, including cooperation on climate change by states. New Geopolitics, emphasizing an importance of geoeconomics, has a little to say here, though the environment is taken as a geopolitical threat, where states collapse due to the explosion of demographic and environmental forces, the degradation of natural environment has caused migration and growth of urban areas, and consequently, disintegration and ethnic conflicts.

Instead of New Geopolitics, Critical geopolitics recognizes new non-state actors and more factors, such as identity, knowledge as a power, the environment, as well as politicization of a (physical) space.

Environmental issues have been explicitly discussed in modern theories of social sciences, in particular Development theories. Modernization, Dependence and Alternative development theories (e.g. Hettne), including the dilemma between a center and a periphery, examine and analyze dependence of peripheries on centers, including the dilemma between a center and a periphery (like for example, the exploitation of natural resources for the benefit of centers). Maybe the best known is the concept of Sustainable development, which was defined for the first time by the Brundtland Commission in the 1980s, and which has been since then heavily politicized and became a powerful discourse.

The concept of the Epistemic community, emphasizing the role of knowledge-based, or epistemic, communities "in articulating state policies under conditions of technical uncertainty" (Haas, 1990), is a lively example of Critical environmental studies. As in nature, there are always changes, as well as in international politics, also in Environmental Politics you have changes and challenges, such as first, the globalization and its features (e.g. climate change and other global environmental threats and risks, populations growth, urbanization as more people live in cities, new kind of relations between developed and developing countries) require global environmental politics; second, the Growth-oriented economy versus the limits of the globe, including on the one hand, an economic growth in developing countries, in particular in China and India, and on the other hand, declining economic growth causing less welfare and more poverty in poor countries, and scarcity of resources and pollution; third, collapse of failed/fragile states (e.g. Somalia). A special and increasing danger is an "irreversible collapse" of an industrial civilization, and the entire political-economic system, based on the "most salient interrelated factors which explain civilisational decline, and which may help determine the risk of collapse today: namely, Population, Climate, Water, Agriculture, and Energy" (see Ahmed, 2014).

Thirty years ago Haas (1990, p. xviii) wrote in the introduction of his environmental studies that "Social Sciences have done relatively well at developing theories to explain periods of order and stability, but have done much less well at explaining the dynamics of periods of change.. and have not been very good at analyzing complex, nonlinear systems such as international environmental issues seem to involve". Instead, "Environmental Science", as a field of research, has existed since the late 1960s, though it was interpreted as "a science on everything", which, even as a thought, is impossible.

What about the last 30 years? An environmental point of view, including biodiversity and climate change, is still a bit odd and little studied in political sciences, as I have argued. For this article, I made a short review on IR and Political sciences textbooks (of the last 30 years) to examine if this is the case. I selected 12 books (nine on IR theories, one on Peace studies and two IR and the Arctic) as textbooks, not based on keywords or algorithms on the internet, how environmental issues are discussed (see the list of references). By using the following six indicators/variables: biodiversity, climate change/global warming, ecology/green politics, the environment, pollution, and sustainable development—I studied if, and measured how, environmental issues are explicitly mentioned (in an index) and/or explicitly discussed in (the contents of) a book.

Biodiversity

Burchill and Linklater (1996, pp. 255, 266) briefly mention biodiversity and the Biodiversity Convention of 1992 in the chapter of "Green Politics". Buzan and Hansen (2011, p. 128) only mention the term. As a counter-argument to the belief of "significant numbers of people [in the USA]… that 'global warming' is a hoax", Masker (2021, pp. 390–391) includes a short article (originally in BBC News) on animal and plant species under the threat of extinction. Including biodiversity as a part of environmental issues Lamy et al. (2013, pp. 445–446) introduces and discusses the "Doomsday" Seed Vault in Svalbard as an interesting case to store two billion seeds which represent almost 4.5 million species of food plants as a "response to fears about the long-term effects global warming might have on biodiversity and crop output".

Murray and Nuttall (2014, p. 461) briefly mention the Arctic Biodiversity Assessment and its aims to evaluate changes in the Arctic due to economic activities, climate change and ultra-violet radiation. Durfee and Johnstone (2019, pp. 32, 232–236) explicitly discuss biodiversity in the Arctic, and conservation of biological diversity in the context of international environmental law, including the Agreement of Polar Bears as an example.

Climate Change/Global Warming/Greenhouse Effect

Climate, or "climatic factors", not explicitly climate change, is briefly discussed by Dougherty and Pfaltzgraff (1990, pp. 56–57), as a part of Environmental theories. Interestingly, Barash (1991, p. 366) mentions the Environmental Modification Convention (Enmod) which prohibits "the alteration of the environment, including the climate, of an adversary" for military purposes. Focusing on great powers and strategic stability in the twenty-first century, not surprisingly Herd (2010, pp. 82–97, 129–130, 149–150, 165–167, 181–184) includes a chapter on "How energy and climate change may pose a threat to sustainable security", as well as short analyses of how Russia, China, India and the EU interpret or respond to climate change, and in general environmental and energy security. Interestingly, Herd (2010, pp. 93–95) is one of the very few, if not the only, in this review explicitly mentioning "mitigation" as "climate change is becoming more severe… [and] the decarbonization of the world's energy sources" is the only sustainable long-term solution. Correspondingly, Buzan and Hansen (2011, p. 268) puts it bluntly in the conclusions that "the two most likely environmental wild cards are global warming… and the possibility of a rampant and virulent epidemic".

Masker (2021, pp. 390–393) briefly deals with climate change including two short articles, one on the threat of extinction of animal and plant species, and another on losses of Greenlandic glaciers. Climate change and greenhouse gases, as a global factor, is wildly discussed in Lamy et al. (2013, pp. 133, 454–460), and how the issue is shaping foreign policy priorities (e.g. of island states in the Pacific and Indian

Ocean), and Kyoto Protocol is an example of international (environmental) cooperation and environmental regime. Lamy et al. (2013, p. 443) argue that climate change shows that the question of "to understand the circumstances under which potentially effective international cooperation can occur" is still important.

Not surprising that climate change is explicitly discussed in the two books on IR and the Arctic: Murray and Nuttall (2014) discuss it mostly in the context of Arctic policies of the Arctic states and the Arctic Council observer states. Durfee and Johnstone (2019, pp. 126–132, 237–240) discuss the topic through the entire book, including the impacts of climate change on Arctic resources and livelihoods (e.g. whaling, fisheries), especially on the Indigenous peoples, and define the related black carbon and methane as challenges.

Ecology/Green Politics

Barash (1991, pp. 493–523) devotes a whole chapter, "Ecological Wholeness", to the environmental issues, where the environment, awareness and activism, and greenhouse effect, and problems of energy are broadly discussed. The book also briefly mentions ecology in the context of environmental organizations, in particular Greenpeace (Barash, 1991, pp. 66, 547). When discussing about international relations theory versus the future, Booth and Smith (1995, p. 344) note with hesitation, among others, that "[I]t is extremely doubtful whether the planet can endlessly sustain the expanding wants of Western appetites and the expanding needs of the rest. Of the two, the former is the greater threat to the planet". In a chapter of "Green Politics", Burchill and Linklater (1996, pp. 252–270) broadly discuss green political theory, including ecocentrism and the "limits to growth" argument and sustainable development, and global ecology, including arguments against development and reclaiming the commons, as well as briefly mention the ecological crisis (Burchill & Linklater, 1996, p. 220). When introducing "Culture, ideology and the myth function in IR theory", Weber (2005, p. 4) briefly mentions "ecologism" as an example of "conscious ideologies", though nothing about biodiversity, climate, the environment, pollution or sustainable development.

Masker (2021, pp. 371–381) includes a comprehensive and interesting article (by Peter Christoff) on typology of different kinds of states based on the environment and green politics, in particular how "ecomodern-ization" will be done, toward an "Environmental State". According to the typology, "Green states", "were they to exist, would be characterized by the predominance of types of state activity" aimed at strong ecological modernization, and with "[S]ignificant state capacity for ecologically sustainable development would be evident" in the areas of consensus formation, strategic planning, policy coordination and integration, and implementation (Masker, 2021, p. 377). In addition, in the chapter on environmental issues, Lamy et al. (2013, pp. 219, 227, 419, 429, 436) mention ecological footprint, green revolution, Green Movement and the environmental NGOs, such as Greenpeace, but does not explicitly discuss about ecology or green politics.

Murray and Nuttall (2014, pp. 105–128) have a chapter on ecological sovereignty and Arctic politics, including discussion on "greening sovereignty" and "ecological politics" in the Arctic, as well as an interpretation of the Arctic "as a human/non-human collective". The textbook by Durfee and Johnstone (2019) does not explicitly discuss ecology or green politics.

The Environment

Dougherty and Pfaltzgraff's textbook (1990, pp. 53–80, 441) has a chapter "Environmental Theories", including theories on the environment and its role in IR, critiques of environmental theories and environmental monitoring—all this is mostly about theories of (Classical) geopolitics and their critiques. Williams (1992, pp. 17, 68–71, 83) does explicitly discuss the "nature" (though nothing about the environment), mostly meaning that "[T]he world order seems to be *natural* and appears equally natural for us to accept it as such", and about the nature of humankind or "humankind's natural state". Nature and law are also combined by referring to Hobbes that "the laws of nature are identical with the laws of international society", and to Kant "that even wars may be seen as a positive light as 'nature's' way of encouraging states to live in peace with each other" (Williams, 1992, pp. 40–43, 62, 84).

Booth and Smith (1995, pp. 129–152) dedicate a chapter to the environment, titled "International Political Theory and the Global Environment". It includes discussion on traditional and new agendas of the theme, the environment and the global economy, the emergence of "transnational civil society", and the state system versus the global environment, strongly arguing that the environment is an issue on political agenda of states after it became global. Here, Hurrell's interpretation that "the fragmented system of sovereign states has become a fundamental obstacle to the effective and equitable management of an interdependent world in general and the global environment in particular" (Booth & Smith, 1995, p. 147) is interesting, even striking. Behind this observation is "the concern for sovereignty remains a fundamental factor in global environmental politics in both North and South and the political acceptance of the erosion of sovereignty is less apparent than legal declarations would tend to suggest" (Booth & Smith, 1995, p. 138).

In addition of the broad discussion on green political theory, ecocentrism and global ecology Burchill and Linklater (1996, pp. 220–221) explicitly mention global environmental crises in the context of "Feminism". Among the Cold War challenges to national security, Buzan and Hansen (2011, pp. 123–129) recognize "Structural violence, economics and the environment", though the environment plays a minor role here, and the study is more about widening and deepening security including human security. Interestingly, they note that environmental security is "threatened through climatic changes or through the degradation of land, biodiversity, the atmosphere, water, forests, coastal area and rivers", and "[I]n terms of the driving forces, this happened mainly as a response to *events* in the slow-moving sense: a generally rising concern about the (in)stability of the ecosphere" (Buzan & Hansen, 2011, pp. 128–129). Masker's textbook, "Introduction to Global Politics" is consisted of several short reading selections, which makes it fragmented, but also allows to discuss on several points of view, including the environment as a part of global issues (Masker, 2021, pp. 185–186, 323). Lamy et al. (2013, pp. 434–464) dedicate a whole chapter on environmental issues on the international agenda, including a brief history with chronology, discussion on the environment in IR theories, functions of international (environmental) cooperation and regimes and climate change.

A bit surprising that the environment is explicitly briefly discussed in Murray and Nuttall (2014, pp. 447–456, 494, 599–621): on the one hand, in the context of the Arctic Environmental Protection Strategy (AEPS), and on the other hand, in that of the Antarctic and its significance for the Arctic, due to the strong environmental protection aspect of the Antarctic Treaty System. Durfee and Johnstone (2019, pp. 218–227, 228–248) dedicate a chapter on environmental protection in the

Arctic, which is understandable and was even required in late 2010s, combining environmental and human security, human rights and the environment, and describing principles of international environmental law and environmental impact assessment, including requests of UNCLOS.

It is also relevant to know if, and how, the interrelationship between the environment and security is discussed. Herd (2010, pp. 129–130, 149–150, 165–167) explicitly discusses on "Environmental security", and "Energy security" in the contexts of China's, India's and Russia's responses to climate change. Buzan and Hansen explicitly discuss on "Environmental security" and "Human security" (Buzan & Hansen, 2011, pp. 57–58, 128–129, 187–191, 202–205, 212–213, 268–270). Masker (2021, p. 402) only briefly defines "Human security". Lamy et al. (2013, e.g. pp. 318–321, 330–333) explicitly discuss the "Human security". Durfee and Johnstone do so as well, even including "Food security" (Durfee & Johnstone, 2019, pp. 87–94, 254–255).

Pollution

Environmental pollution is briefly mentioned by Dougherty and Pfaltzgraff (1990, pp. 75, 103), who mention it as a cause of an "enduring concern for the late twentieth century", and, according to George Kennan, "the most serious problems... [which] the leading industrial and maritime nations" have created. Barash (1991, pp. 497–501) has a comprehensive discussion on the importance of clean air and water, solid waste disposal and environmental problems, such as nuclear waste. As a part of studying global ecology, Burchill and Linklater (1996, pp. 263–264) briefly deal with pollution mentioning oil spills and nuclear accidents. Understandably, pollution is briefly discussed in Masker's textbook (2021, pp. 186, 363) as a part of environmental issues, and also in the context of the "Tragedy of the Commons". Pollution and pollution control, including international agreements, such as the 1979 Convention on Long-Range Transboundary Air Pollution, is explicitly discussed in Lamy et al. (2013, pp. 438–442, 448–450).

Murray and Nuttall (2014) do not explicitly mention pollution. Durfee and Johnstone (2019, pp. 218–227, 241–243) wildly discuss pollution, starting from vessel-source pollution and maritime safety, including the Polar Code, and finishing with the long-range contaminants.

Sustainable Development

Barash (1991, pp. 534–540) discusses development and development theories (meaning "modernization" or "growth theory", the "Dependencia" theory) in the contexts of the Third World, new international economic order, the debt problems, and hunger, without explicitly mentioning environmental issues. Booth and Smith (1995, p. 131) make a note that the linkage between poverty, population pressure and environmental degradation is widely recognized, and that sustainable development is "an inherently global issue both because of the high levels of economic interdependence that exist within many parts of the world economy and because it raises fundamental questions concerning the distribution of wealth, power and resources between North and South". Interestingly, the authors argue that Brazil and India have moved away "from the rigid dichotomy between environment and development by laying greater weight on the importance of protecting the environment and on moving towards more sustainable patterns of economic development" (Booth & Smith, 1995, p. 137).

As mentioned earlier, Burchill and Linklater (1996, pp. 256–258, 264–266) discuss sustainable development under the titles of "Limits to growth" and "Against development". Instead of sustainable development, Herd (2010, p. 83) discusses and prefers "sustainable security" rather than "climate security" and "collective security". The term "Development" is several times mentioned in Buzan and Hansen (2011), for example, in the context of "Common security" and "Human security" (Buzan & Hansen, 2011, pp. 137–138, 202–205), but not explicitly the term "Sustainable development". A short article on "Needs versus Greed" and the European Union's "ability to implement sustainable policies at home" could be taken as an example of sustainable development in Masker (2021, pp. 171–172, 359–361). Sustainable development is defined and wildly discussed, together with democracy and empowerment, in Lamy et al. (2013, pp. 421, 439–443, 450–452).

Again, a bit surprising that the two books on IR and the Arctic do not explicitly discuss sustainable development. It is mentioned in the context of the Arctic Council, as its other pillar of the Council (environmental protection being another), and its Sustainable Development Working Group (SDWG). Murray and Nuttall (2014, p. 461) do it very briefly, and Durfee and Johnstone (2019, pp. 236–237, 241–243, 254)

60 L. HEININEN

describe the concept and links it to the Arctic Environmental Protection Strategy (AEPS).

Conclusions and Discussion

Based on the review of the twelve IR and Political sciences textbooks, there are a few (tentative) conclusions. Firstly, not surprisingly the most recent books (of 2010s) explicitly discuss climate change and global warming, and biodiversity, and correspondingly, the books of 1990s explicitly discuss more on pollution and sustainable development. Actually, there is a gap about 20 years between 1991 (Barash) and 2010 (Herd) that climate change is not explicitly discussed. When Dougherty and Pfaltzgraff (1990) introduce "Environmental Theories", it mostly refers to theories of Geopolitics, and Lamy et al. (2013) include a whole chapter on environmental issues on the international agenda of global politics, and takes the Doomsday Seed Vault as an example of biodiversity.

Secondly, biodiversity was on the agenda of the 1992 Rio de Janeiro at UN Environmental Summit, where the party states signed an agreement with three goals: to protect the biodiversity of a nature, use resources by sustainable way and share the benefits of gene resources. Thus, it should be on the political agenda of states, in particular on that of the Arctic states, but those goals of the 1992 Summit have mostly failed (Viljanen, 2021, p. 20). This partly explains why biodiversity is barely discussed, and loss of biodiversity is not even mentioned in the IR textbooks, though it is a surprise as it has become an important political issue.

Thirdly, more surprising is, however, that ecology and green politics are not more explicitly discussed. Though ecology is mainly about philosophy and values, it also deals with politics, power and a State (e.g. "Green state"), economics (e.g. "limits of growth"), as well as civil society and activism (e.g. environmental movements, Greenpeace).

Fourthly, from the point of view of the environment vis-a-vis a state, the most interesting and politically striking is the interpretation by Hurrell (1995) that the system of sovereign states has become a "fundamental obstacle to the effective and equitable management of an interdependent world in general and the global environment in particular". This supports the thesis of political inability of States to make the hard decisions, mitigate or adapt to climate change. This inability is revealed by the ambivalence of Arctic development, when "the Arctic states are searching for a balance between environmental protection and economic activities, and proclaim that there must be such a balance,… when it comes to environmental protection versus economic development" (Heininen et al., 2020, p. 251).

Fifthly, the interrelationship between the environment and security is related to the obstacle of sovereign States to tackle climate change, as the keen interrelationship is a rather new approach and still partly debated. There are, however, a few alternative discourses on security—for example "Environmental security", and that of "Human security"—directly connected to the environment, and "Human security" also to climate change. As noted earlier, only a couple IR textbooks (Buzan & Hansen, 2011; Herd, 2010) explicitly discuss "Environmental security", and a few ones (Buzan & Hansen, 2011; Durfee & Johnstone, 2019; Lamy et al., 2013; Masker, 2021) explicitly discuss "Human security". Based on the recent extreme weather conditions, and taken into consideration risks and uncertainties caused by global warming, the approaches of environmental and human security are relevant and timely. Here, sovereign states have failed in their most important task, i.e. to secure the everyday life of their citizens, as there is no safe place due to floods, droughts, wildfires, hot weather and the COVID-19 pandemic, as well as the related uncertainties of rapid climate change—all non-military new kind of threats and risks, which cannot be defended by the military. Following from this, maybe another concept, comprehensive security can be interpreted to be a part of climate change mitigation and sustainable development, globally and locally, as well as bringing in an ultimate precondition that people and civil societies should be recognized as actors, and owners, of security.

Sixthly, pollution is also explicitly, though narrowly, discussed in the textbooks, in particular in those on the IR and the Arctic. Here, air and water pollution is closely tied with modernization and industrialization, and long-range pollution is a global issue of international law and politics. However, as discussed earlier, (long-range) air and water pollution, namely chemicals, other manmade toxics, and radioactive wastes, were the main reasons for concern on the environment by the people, and interpreted as the first trigger to cause protests and an environmental awakening during the 1960s. This new kind of (environmental) activism pushed governments to act, as well as the scientific community and other experts to launch alternative discourses on security, such as UN reports. It was "nuclear safety", due to radioactive wastes in the Arctic region and Northern seas, that started peoples' protests and pushed governments (of Russia, the United States and the Nordic countries, as well as the European Union) to act and take this environmental problem onto their political agendas, as the Arctic military environmental cooperation (AMEC) well shows (Heininen, 2013).

Seventhly and finally, it seems to be that a solution for problems is searched separately, like, for example, first how to tackle, or adapt to, climate change, and then for other challenges. This is a problem, as these issues are interrelated and cannot be separated from each other, or briefly saying "the environment cannot be isolated as a specific policy field, as it is within a society" (Haila & Heininen, 1995). Thus, it is not only about climate change per se, as there are also other environmental challenges causing global crises—pollution, loss of biodiversity, pandemics—which also pose a great risk to humanity. For example, the loss of biodiversity—we face now the sixth mass extinction, as an outcome of a combination of pollution, human exploitation of resources, water and land, climate change, and bioinvaders—which is as great, maybe even bigger, a risk to humanity as the climate change, as we are depending on a nature and its resources. Instead, a holistic approach is much needed, which could be achieved for example, by interpreting and adopting Comprehensive security.

All in all, States are hesitating in mitigation of climate change, and seem to have applied political inability to act, though we face more than a wicked problem, a global crisis of rapid global warming and the related uncertainties, pollution and mass extinction of a nature, and environmental degradation combined, as well as a global pandemic. The summer 2021 has shown that there is no safe place on the earth where to go. Following from this, Hurrell's (1995) thesis that the state system is an obstacle to managing the global environment, including climate change and loss of biodiversity, is very relevant notion. States have also failed in their most important task, to secure the everyday life of their citizens and societies, even state sovereignty is in a danger. If they would have political capability, they would prioritize the mitigation by allocating financial resources for that—we already have scientific understanding and readiness, and advanced technologies—instead of continuing arms race and allocating money for warfare. For example, it would make a difference in climate change tackling having the $2 trillion which the US government has used on the unsuccessful war in Afghanistan within the last 20 years.

This is not surprising, when taken into consideration the original nature and main aim of a State, and the idea and structure of the unified state system, which is much supported by the mainstream IR theories emphasizing a unified state as the most important international actor, and the determined nature of international system with "anarchy". The importance of (geo)economics is emphasized, where States have a minor role in taking care of infrastructure, defense of borders and territories, and minimum well-being of citizens, and having a low level of regulation. As a result of this kind of faith of capitalism States should give a big part or their mandate and power to economic actors, mostly multinational companies (in particular big technology giants, financial companies), and are been allowed to operate globally without regulations, and thus keep their profits without taxation in the heavens (in average $1 trillion of global profits in 2016 were booked in investment hubs, such as the Cayman Islands, Ireland and Singapore [*The Economist*, 2021a, p. 68]), even to create a global system for taxing has been a slow and painful process.

The faith of technology is there as an aim of advanced development, as well as the final way to survive. One of the most recent innovations to respond to climate change is geoengineering. Yes, technology has meant progress and implemented development making possible many things, but it also has some severe and destructive consequences for the environment and societies, such as pollution, over-use of resources, land and waters, armed conflicts and global warming (Niiniluoto, 2020).

Climate change and the related uncertainties, in particular climate change mitigation, are challenges to the State and state politics, defined by traditional way, and national (universal, competitive military) security, guaranteed by the military, as the most ultimate aim of a State. Behind are the political and economic, in particular security-political, elites (of a State), who have adopted an idea of superior, even exclusive, expertise, quality and the consequent authority on national defense and security-policy; most of them have been trained in special (defense) courses for elites run by armies and other military organizations.

References

Ahmed, N. (2014, March 14). Nasa-funded study: Industrial civilisation headed for 'irreversible collapse'? *The Guardian*. https://www.theguardian.com/env

ironment/earth-insight/2014/mar/14/nasa-civilisation-irreversible-collapse-study-scientists. Accessed 14 Aug 2021.

Barash, D. P. (1991). *Introduction to peace studies*. Wadsworth Publishing Company.

Booth, K., & Smith, S. (Eds.). (1995). *International relations theory today*. The Pennsylvania State University Press.

Budyko, M. I., & Yu, I. (Eds.). (1991). *Anthropogenic climatic change*. The University of Arizona Press.

Burchill, S., & Linklater, A. (1996). *Theories of international relations*. St. Martins Press.

Buzan, B., & Hansen, L. (2011). *The evolution of international security studies*. Cambridge University Press.

Doel, R. E. (2009). What's the place of the physical environmental sciences in environmental history? *Revue D'histoire Modern Et Contemporaine [english Language Version]*, *56*(4), 137–164.

Doughery, J. E., & Pfaltzgraff, R. L. (1990). *Contending theories of international relations*. HarperCollins Publishers.

Durfee, M., & Johnstone, R. L. (2019). *Arctic governance in a changing world*. London: Rowman & Littlefield.

Haas, P. M. (1990). *Saving the Mediterranean: The politics of international environmental cooperation*. Columbia University Press.

Haila, Y., & Heininen, L. (1995). Ecology: A new discipline for disciplining? *Social Text, 42*, 153–171.

Heininen, L. (1991). Sotilaallisen läsnäolon ympäristöriskit Arktiksessa - Kohti Arktiksen säätelyjärjestelmää [Environmental risks of military presence in the Arctic: Towards a regime]. *Tampere Peace Research Institute. Research Report No. 43*. Tampereen Pikakopio Oy.

Heininen, L. (2013). 'Politicization' of the environment: Environmental politics and security in the Circumpolar North. In B. S. Zellen (Ed.), *The fast-changing Arctic: Rethinking Arctic security for a warmer world* (pp. 35–55). University of Calgary Press.

Heininen, L. (2019). Ympäristönäkökulma politiikkatieteissä – outo tutkimusalue? *Kosmopolis, 50*(3/2020), 67–78.

Heininen, L. (2020). The 'Regime' nature of the Arctic: implications for world order. In K. Spohr & D. S. Hamilton (Eds.), *The Arctic and world order* (pp. 309–325). Johns Hopkins University Press.

Heininen, L., Everett, K., Padrtova, B., & Reissell, A. (2020). Arctic policies and strategies—Analysis, synthesis, and trends. *Polar Geography, 43*(2–3), 240–242.

Herd, G. P. (Ed.). (2010). *Great powers and strategic stability in the 21st century: Competing visions of world order*. Routledge.

Hurrell, A. (1995). International political theory and the global environment. In. K. Booth, & S. Smith (Eds.), *International relations theory today* (pp. 129–153). The Pennsylvania State University Press.

Lamy, S., Baylis, J., Smith, S., & Owens, P. (Eds.). (2013). *Introduction to global studies* (2nd ed.). Oxford University Press.

Masker, J. S. (2021). *Introduction to global politics. A reader*. New York: Oxford University Press.

Murray, R., & Nuttall, A. (Eds.). (2014). *International relations and the Arctic: Understanding policy and governance*. Cambria Press.

Myers, N. (1993). *Ultimate security: The environmental basis of political stability*. W.W. Norton & Company.

Newsweek. (2008). *Newsweek: Special Edition/Issues 2008*.

Niiniluoto, I. (2020). *Tekniikan filosofia*. Gaudeamus.

Rogelj, J. (2016, November). Between 1.5 C and 2 C—Analyzing the global warming targets. *International Institute for Applied Systems Analysis* (IIASA). IIASA Policy Brief, November 2016 (#14). https://iiasa.ac.at/web/home/resources/publications/IIASAPolicyBriefs/pb-14temp-WEB.pdf. Accessed 18 Jul 2021.

Shevardnadze, E. (1991, August 31). Governments alone won't turn the world green. *New Scientist*. https://www.newscientist.com/article/mg13117846-300-forum-governments-alone-wont-turn-the-world-green-eduard-shevardna dze-looks-at-ways-of-ensuring-the-triumph-of-political-ecology/. Accessed 19 Jul 2021.

Soroos, M. S. (1990). *Arctic haze: A case study in regime formation*. Prepared for the Arctic Cooperation Project directed by G. Osherenko & O. Young, Dartmouth College. August (mimeo).

The Economist. (2021a, May 15). Corporate tax: The big carve-up. *The Economist*, 68–69.

The Economist. (2021b, June 12). "The G7 Summit: Inoculation, inoculation, inoculation"; "Missing ingredients.". *The Economist*, 10, 16–18.

The Economist. (2021c, July 3). "The long goodbye."; "Coats of many colours." *The Economist*, 11, 19–22.

The Economist. (2021d, July 24). "No safe place.", "Burning down the house.", "After the floods." *The Economist*, 7, 13–17.

Tokunaga, M. (2010). Environmental governance in Russia: The 'closed' pathway to ecological modernization. *Environment and Planning A, 42*(7), 1686–1704.

United Nations. (2015). *Paris Agreement*. http://unfccc.int/files/essential_bac kground/convention/application/pdf/english_paris_agreement.pdf. Accessed 19 Jul 2021.

United Nations Development Programme. (1994). *United Nations Human Development Programme*. Oxford University Press.

Viljanen, M. (2021, August). Rikas luonto suojelee elämää. *Tiede*, 14–21. https://lehdet.digilehdet.fi/4ad9637a-8ede-450a-ae4b-794c0ddd601d/14?lang=fi. Accessed 19 Jul 2021.

Weber, C. (2005). *International relations theory: A critical introduction* (2nd ed.). Routledge.

Williams, H. (1992). *International relations political theory*. Open University Press.

Climate Change and Energy Transition: Controversial Implications for the Arctic Region

Ilya A. Stepanov

CHALLENGES AND OPPORTUNITIES IN THE ARCTIC UNDER THE CHANGING CLIMATE

Upside of the Warming Arctic

Due to the specifics of northern ecosystems,[1] in the past few decades, the rise of the Arctic surface temperature has been twice as fast as the world

---

[1] The specifics of the Arctic climate change are determined by a number of positive feedback mechanisms. For example, snow and ice reflect about 80% of the incoming solar radiation, while the open ocean surface reflects only 20%. The continuous ice melting leads to a decreased reflectance of the earth's surface, which increases its temperature faster than usual.

The research leading to these results has received funding from the Basic Research Program at the National Research University Higher School of Economics. Partial financial support was received from the Faculty of World Economy and International Affairs of the National Research University Higher School of Economics.

I. A. Stepanov (✉)
Laboratory for Climate Change Economics, National Research University Higher School of Economics, Moscow, Russia
e-mail: iastepanov@hse.ru

© The Author(s), under exclusive license to Springer Nature Singapore Pte Ltd. 2022
A. Likhacheva (ed.), *Arctic Fever*,
https://doi.org/10.1007/978-981-16-9616-9_4

average. Today, the Arctic has become the main natural laboratory for studying the effects and processes of global climate change (Goosse et al., 2018). In the twenty-first century, temperature records have been broken almost every year (IPCC, 2013; Overland et al., 2015). Global warming leads to the thawing of permafrost and shrinking of the ocean ice cover. In recent decades, the area of the September ice cover (i.e., during the period of its minimum) has been decreasing at a rate of 13% per decade and has decreased by almost half compared with the 1980s (IPCC, 2013).

The accelerated ice melting leads to the increased transport potential of the Arctic and draws attention of the international community to the Northern Sea Route (NSR) as a promising alternative to the longer southern route through the Suez Canal and the Malacca Strait. Reduction of the ice cover and the development of navigation technologies extend the navigation period in the Arctic Ocean. While in 1980 it was limited to August and September, now it includes July and October. During especially warm years, it can start in June and end in November. On average, the duration of the NSR navigation period is growing at a rate more than half a month per decade (Mohov & Hon, 2015). As far as the navigation gets easier, the speed of vessels passing through the NSR also increases. It has doubled since 1990 (Aksenov et al., 2017).

Ice melting increases accessibility of the Arctic resources. The region is rich in non-ferrous and rare earth metals, gold, diamonds and hydrocarbons. So far, the most authoritative assessment of the Arctic resource base is the study by the US Geological Survey of 2008. According to the Survey, the Arctic contains 13% (90 bn barrels) of unexplored oil resources and 30% (47.3 bn cubic meters) of undiscovered natural gas (Bird et al., 2008). In total, there are 61 large hydrocarbon fields in the region, 43 of which are in Russia, 11—in Canada, 6—in Alaska and 1 is in Norway. Most of the Arctic resources are located on the continental shelf at a depth of at least 500 meters and require special exploration and extraction technologies.

Estimations of the Arctic resource and transport potential demonstrate that the most promising areas for economic development are the Barents Sea and its coastal areas and, to a lesser extent, the Beaufort, and Kara Sea. Among other things, the significant potential of the Barents Sea region is largely due to the rich reserves of hydrocarbons, the already well-developed port and navigation infrastructure, and geographical proximity to the NSR. Within the North Atlantic, promising areas are the eastern and western coasts of Greenland, particularly due to large oil and gas fields and well-established fishing industries (Kjartan et al., 2017).

Downside of the Warming Arctic

In the next decades, the climate change in the Arctic will continue at an accelerated pace (Pörtner et al., 2019). On the one hand, warming leads to greater accessibility of the Arctic territories in terms of resource exploitation and transport development. On the other hand, it provokes significant climatic and environmental risks, which fall well beyond the Arctic region.

The most serious climate-related security risks within the Arctic are forest fires, adverse changes in the habitat of animals and plants, coastal erosion and thawing of permafrost. The latter results in the destruction of housing, transport and energy infrastructure accompanied by critical damage to ecosystems (Higuera et al., 2008; Hovelsrud et al., 2011; Melvin et al., 2017; Roshydromet, 2014). Rapid climate changes do not give Arctic flora and fauna sufficient time to adapt. Climate change and the ice melt raise the issue of the polar bear population survival and threaten the existence of seals and walruses (Leksin & Porfir'ev, 2017; Pagano et al., 2018).

Outside the Arctic, a number of regions lying below sea level become victims of changes happening in the North. The melting of Arctic glaciers, especially the Greenland ice sheet, leads to an increase in the world Ocean level and poses a threat to the livelihood of millions of people across the globe (Lee & Asuncion, 2020; Tedesco et al., 2011). Accelerated temperature rise and permafrost thawing result in the formation of methane funnels and natural emissions of the methane; increasing concentration of methane further boosts global climate change (Anisimov, 2007).

With the expansion of economic activity along with the growing accessibility of the Arctic region, local environmental risks also increase critically. Economic activity in the northern latitudes is associated with a range of environmental risks—from pollution of soils, groundwater, rivers and seas with heavy metals, petroleum hydrocarbons and other toxic substances to the disruption of the habitat and migration of birds and ungulates, which also have adverse effects for the Arctic indigenous population. The development of the shelf and shipping in northern waters, in turn, may disrupt the marine animals' habitat, invoke additional risks of liquid hydrocarbon spills, and is accompanied by emissions of toxic pollutants from the fossil fuels combustion (Makarov & Stepanov, 2015).

The Arctic has one of the most fragile ecosystems on the planet. At low temperatures, the processes of assimilation of any waste and pollution are extremely slow; the negative consequences of human activity remain here for hundreds of years. Poor biodiversity in the Arctic ecosystems results in the high risks of the food chain disruption for animals and plants. When there is a lack in biodiversity, the loss of one of the chain links might lead to the death of a range of dependent species.

Climate-related risks are not only limited to non-traditional security threats, but also bring purely traditional security challenges. Growing accessibility of the Arctic draws attention of the international community to the region as a playing field for superpower states (for more details, see chapter "Arctic as a New Playground for Great Power Competition: The Russia–China–United States Triangle"). The risk of military strategic rivalry is increasing while the degree of this risk is to a large extent determined by the rate of Arctic warming.

Energy Transition and Low-Carbon Development of the Global Economy

Low-Carbon Trends of the Global Economic Development

The role of the energy complex in the world economy was steadily growing during the twentieth century. This was largely due to the two world wars, which boosted the development of fossil fuel technologies, the rapid industrialization of Western countries, and then Asia-Pacific countries, especially China. Energy consumption was growing in line with the global GDP. In the twenty-first century, global energy markets are undergoing dramatical transformations because of the technological shifts and the new role of environmental and climate agenda.

Today, the decarbonization and national green development plans determine the way the global energy landscape is changing. The Paris Agreement, adopted in 2015 and ratified by 193 countries, reflects the commitment of the global community to reduce greenhouse gas emissions and implement climate change adaptation programs, especially in the most vulnerable and poorest countries and regions of the world (Apparicio & Sauer, 2020; Makarov & Stepanov, 2018).

During the last decade, costs of renewable energy generation have been decreasing rapidly while renewable energy capacities have expanded dramatically (IEA, 2020b). The "greening" of national economies becomes an increasingly popular policy decision. The greenhouse gas emissions reduction becomes a tool for increasing energy efficiency, strengthening energy security, and ensuring economic growth for a growing number of countries (Dolata-Kreutzkamp, 2008; European Commission, 2008; Schmitz, 2017). The ambitious European Green Deal program adopted in the EU, which sets the goal to achieve carbon neutrality by 2050, is intertwined with the socio-economic recovery plan on the way out of the COVID-19 crisis.

Every year the problem of climate change becomes even more acute. The decarbonization of the world economy becomes self-replicating, and government climate policies are complemented by a growing number of corporate climate change mitigation initiatives. Financial markets are rapidly being transformed. Green financial markets capitalization is growing every year: in 2019, the issue of green bonds increased by more than one and a half times and reached \$259 bn (CBI, 2020). Finally, divestments (withdrawal of capital investments) from assets in "dirty" industries become more widespread. An increasing number of large investment funds, pension funds, insurance companies, and other institutional investors announce plans to divest from carbon-intensive projects (Arabella Advisors, 2018).

Leading countries pursued an active climate policy long before the Paris Agreement adoption. In the United States, the decarbonization was closely related to the shale revolution in the late 2000s, which made it possible to increase the production and consumption of natural gas significantly and reduce the share of coal in the energy balance, which in turn has led to a considerable emissions reduction. In Europe, the green processes began even earlier. Since the mid-2000s measures to support renewable energy expanded dramatically in European countries (Stepanov & Albrecht, 2019). In 2007 the "20–20–20" program was approved, which set the goals to reduce greenhouse gas emissions by 20% (compared to the 1990 level), increase energy efficiency by 20%, and increase the share of renewable energy in the energy balance to 20% (European Commission, 2019).

Since the 11th Five-Year Plan (2006–2010), the issues of environmental protection and emissions reduction have become especially important in China. Promotion of the environmental agenda became a result of critical levels of air pollution in large industrial cities of the eastern provinces and the rising demand of Chinese citizens for better environment. In recent years, China has been rapidly strengthening the environmental legislation, shutting down the dirtiest coal power plants, extending the requirements for industrial efficiency and expanding the shares of renewable energy sources and natural gas in the energy balance.

In most developed countries, emissions reduction has long become a mainstream of the economic policy which brings rapid changes in energy, transport, industrial sectors, agriculture, finance, etc. Back in the 2000s, one could say that climate policy is mostly the policy for developed countries importing fossil fuel (i.e. the EU). Today, climate policies, including carbon pricing, also become widespread in the developing countries of Asia, Latin America, and Africa.

Targets to achieve carbon neutrality by 2050 have already been outlined by such largest economies as the EU, United States, United Kingdom, Japan, Republic of Korea, Canada, Mexico, and South Africa. China is planning to achieve carbon neutrality by 2060. Altogether, 60 countries have already announced their goals to achieve carbon neutrality, and about the same number of states are considering such a possibility at the highest political level.

Changes in the Global Energy Mix

The decarbonization of the world economy results in slowing growth of demand for fossil energy sources (and the reduction of the energy demand in developed countries) given growing competitiveness of carbon-free or low-carbon energy sources. In the 2000s the global demand for fossil fuels grew at an average rate of 2.4% per year, in the 2010s, it already accounted for 1.3%.[2]

The last forecast by the International Energy Agency (IEA) includes two main scenarios—the Stated Policies Scenario and the Sustainable Development Scenario. The Stated Policies Scenario is based on current energy and climate policy plans and strives to implement both the 2020 post-crisis recovery plans and nationally determined contributions submitted to the Paris Agreement. The Sustainable Development

---

[2] Author's calculation based on IEA, World Energy Statistics and Balances.

Scenario is based on the trajectory required to achieve the UN Sustainable Development Goals, including targets to reduce local air pollution, provide an access to affordable and clean energy, and effectively address climate change.

Regardless of the speed of changes in the conditions of inter-fuel competition, tightening climate policy and green technologies development will have the most detrimental effect on coal consumption. Its share in the global energy balance will continue to decline rapidly. According to the International Energy Organization (IEA, 2020a), in the Stated Policies Scenario, the share of coal in the global energy balance is going to fall from 26% in 2019 to 19% by 2040 and to 10% in the Sustainable Development Scenario (Table 1).

The future of coal depends largely on two competing trends. On the one hand, every year coal will come under an increasing pressure from less carbon intensive and cleaner energy sources such as natural gas and renewable energy sources. On the other hand, the pace of coal being crowded out of the global energy balance will be largely determined by the ability to solve basic socio-economic problems in developing countries, for which coal has been and remains a key source of affordable energy. At the same time, in relatively wealthy countries, the demand for coal will depend on the pace of improvement of cleaning, capturing, and storing emissions technologies. With proper government support, these technologies can significantly slow down the process of decarbonization.

Nowadays, there are two opposite trends in the oil market. On the one hand, the development of new extraction technologies and the growing accessibility of unconventional oil underlie market growth. On the other hand, the development of new more energy-efficient consumption technologies, combined with the rapid development of the electric car market and the escalation of the inter-fuel competition in the industry restrain oil consumption. In general, a slowdown in oil consumption growth should be expected in the medium term.

Unlike coal, the dynamics of oil demand is less sensitive to the tightening climate policy. The oil demand is less elastic in price compared to the demand for other types of fossil fuels and is mainly determined by volumes of oil use in the transport sector. In this regard, in the State Policies Scenario, oil demand will continue to grow in absolute terms in line with a gradual reduction of its share in global energy consumption from 31% in 2019 to 28% in 2040. At the same time, the Sustainable Development Scenario envisions that oil consumption will peak soon and

Table 1 Changes in the volume and structure of primary energy consumption in key markets according to the IEA 2020 forecast

Mtoe (% in total consumtion)	World			Europe		
	2019	2040: scenarios		2019	2040: scenarios	
		Stated policies	Sustainable development		Stated policies	Sustainable development
Coal	3775 (26%)	3314 (19%)	1295 (10%)	271 (14%)	114 (7%)	51 (4%)
Oil	4525(31%)	4832 (28%)	3006 (23%)	617 (32%)	406 (25%)	218 (15%)
Natural Gas	3340 (23%)	4321 (25%)	2943 (23%)	495 (26%)	438 (26%)	271 (19%)
Nuclear	727 (5%)	896 (5%)	1126 (9%)	241 (12%)	182 (11%)	219 (15%)
Renewable	2039 (22%)	3721 (22%)	4649 (36%)	315 (16%)	534 (32%)	682 (47%)
Total	14,406 (100%)	17,085 (100%)	13,020 (100%)	1939 (100%)	1674 (100%)	1441 (100%)
Mtoe (% in total consumtion)	**North America**			**Asia Pacific**		
	2019	2040: scenarios		2019	2040: scenarios	
		Stated Policies	Sustainable Development		Stated Policies	Sustainable Development
Coal	302 (11%)	88 (3%)	29 (1%)	2894 (47%)	2824 (36%)	1095 (18%)
Oil	992 (37%)	855 (33%)	465 (24%)	1542 (25%)	1781 (23%)	1157 (19%)
Natural Gas	905 (33%)	967 (38%)	518 (27%)	702 (11%)	1252 (16%)	1056 (18%)
Nuclear	251 (9%)	179 (7)	215 (11%)	172 (3%)	416 (5%)	533 (9%)
Renewable	254 (9%)	483 (19%)	722 (37%)	813 (13%)	1598 (20%)	2149 (36%)
Total	2704 (100%)	2571 (100%)	1949 (100%)	6123 (100%)	7872 (100%)	5989 (100%)

Source Calculated on the basis of International Energy Agency. World Energy Outlook 2020. https://www.iea.org/reports/world-energy-outlook-2020. Accessed 15 June 2021

will go down both in absolute and relative terms—to the level of 23% of total energy consumption in 2040 (Table 1).

Over the next twenty years, natural gas will be in the most favorable position among three types of fossil fuels—primarily due to the increase in its consumption in developing countries. Natural gas is more environmentally friendly and less harmful to the climate than oil and coal; natural gas is used in the electric power industry as a bridge between coal and renewable energy sources, which can significantly reduce the volume of greenhouse gas emissions. While some developed countries have the technology and resources to switch to renewable energy, gas will likely remain the only acceptable option for an energy transition in developing countries.

The IEA's short-term forecast 2030 suggests that total gas demand will quickly recover from the pandemic period and will be 15% higher than in 2019 by the end of the decade (IEA, 2020a). The global gas demand growth will be by half triggered by the demand growth in the Asia-Pacific region, which is caused by China's policy of abandoning coal in favor of gas. The main driver for the gas market development is the growth of liquified natural gas (LNG) trade, which allows to increase total market efficiency (through increased competition, price convergence in major markets, increased supply response to demand, etc.) (McKinsey & Company, 2021).

In the State Policies scenario, the IEA forecasts an increase of the natural gas share in total global consumption from 23% in 2019 to 25% by 2040, and in the Asian market from 11 to 16% respectively. It seems unlikely that developed countries, even the ones which have a growing share of renewable energy in the energy mix, will fully stop the consumption of natural gas in the foreseeable future. However, the EU consumption is likely to be rather stable, while North America will increase production and become one of the largest LNG exporters. Even in the IEA Sustainable Development scenario the share of natural gas in global consumption will remain approximately at the same level, even if there will be an overall reduction in the absolute volumes (Table 1).

CLIMATE-ENERGY TRENDS' NEXUS AND ITS IMPLICATIONS FOR THE ARCTIC STATES

Global climate change does not turn the Arctic into a promising region for the extraction of energy resources and international transit contrary to the point of view that prevailed in the 2000s. The Arctic is indeed becoming more accessible. But the global energy transition and growing environmental risks increase the requirements for expensive Arctic projects, the implementation of which is less profitable because of low energy prices.

Apparently, we are now at the beginning of another cycle of rising energy prices. At the beginning of 2016, the daily spot price of Brent crude oil fell to $30—the lowest in the last ten years. Last year, this minimum was updated due to the global crisis caused by the COVID-19 pandemic: the spot price fell below $10 per barrel on some days in April 2020. Now, in the period of recovery from the crisis and demand recovery, we are witnessing a gradual increase in prices (Fig. 1). Nevertheless, considering the new role of the decarbonization of global energy as a structural factor in the development of energy markets, which restrains the growth in the energy demand, the price level is unlikely to return to the values of the late 2010s.

A number of estimates suggest that "fears (or dreams) of high oil, gas, and coal prices are a thing of the past. The world has entered an era of

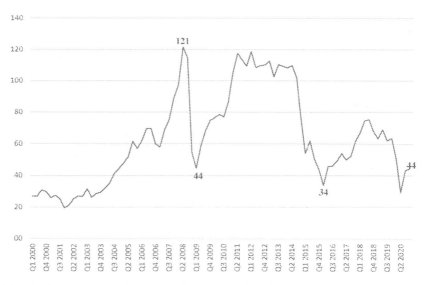

Fig. 1 Dynamics of the price of Brent crude oil, quarterly, USD per barrel (*Source* Euromonitor International)

broad technological and inter-fuel competition. For all areas of consumption, there are many promising competing solutions that are ready to offer an alternative promptly and win back the market when the prices of the dominant fuel increase" (Makarov et al., 2019).

Even if the Arctic resources are significantly more accessible (due to warming and new technologies), the dynamics of energy demand on a global scale will not be the same. While in the 2000s the global demand for fossil fuels grew at an average rate of 2.4% per year, in 2010–2018 1.3% per year, in the period 2019–2040 it will grow at a rate of 0.5–0.9% per year (IEA, 2020a). Demand for energy resources will continue to grow the fastest in Asia, but even there, energy consumption is to peak in the coming decades (CNPC Economics & Technology Institute, 2018). While some opportunities to increase natural gas export still remain - primarily due to the growing Chinese import, the plans of implementing new oil and especially coal projects in the Arctic are barely viable since they require significant investments in infrastructure, logistics, and administrative and tax support.

The transformation of global energy markets increasingly calls into question the feasibility of developing hydrocarbons at the Arctic continental shelf. In the coming decades, the demand for gas in both Europe and Asia will be fully covered by extraction from traditional, primarily gas, continental fields, developed, for example, within the framework of the Russian Yamal LNG and Arctic LNG-2 projects and may be few additional ones.

The period of development of the Arctic projects (especially the most capital-intensive offshore projects) from exploration to product sales lasts on average a decade. Therefore, the strategy of large-scale long-term development of the energy resources of the Arctic shelf is fraught with a decrease in the profitability and investment attractiveness of the economic processes associated with it.

Despite the declared interest in the development of the shelf often expressed by some officials of Arctic and Asian states, development of oil and gas fields in the Arctic seas goes at a low pace. Only a modest segment of the Arctic economy still accounts for offshore hydrocarbon production. The main added value in the Arctic oil and gas industry is generated by continental fields.

Some geological explorations of the Arctic shelf is still in progress, but apart from Norway (the Snøhvit and Goliath fields), where the whole oil and gas production is conducted at sea, and one project in Russia (the Prirazlomnoye field), oil and gas production on the shelf of the Arctic Ocean is barely carried out. Another Russian offshore project for the development of one of the world's largest Shtokman gas condensate fields in the Barents Sea was frozen in the early 2010s due to unexpected changes at the natural gas market conditions (caused by the shale revolution in the United States).

The governments of Canada, the United States, and Norway built a support system for resource companies thoroughly. The production of Arctic hydrocarbons is not their main and even not the only opportunity for the development of the northern territories. In 2021, Denmark abandoned plans to develop new oil and gas fields on the continental shelf in order to achieve climate goals (Ambrose, 2020). The energy policy of the developed Arctic countries implies not so much the development of the resource base and expansion in the Arctic, but the use of the fuel deposits to launch innovative processes in the economy and society and to stimulate the development of new technologies (Kryukov et al., 2020).

Russia is gradually moving toward a similar model of implementing Arctic projects. But so far, Russian energy companies mainly use foreign technologies in the oil and gas sector, while their own technological solutions are created rarely (Shafranik & Kryukov, 2016). At the state level, large-scale plans for the development of the Arctic have been announced, which, however, do not fully consider economic, technological, and environmental risks (Likhacheva et al., 2021). This was clearly demonstrated by the manmade disaster in May 2020 in Norilsk. Western sanctions and the overall market conditions restrict the possibility of attracting large-scale investment and technological transfer to the Russian Arctic from abroad. Therefore, plans for further economic development of the region, especially by extensive methods, i.e. increasing hydrocarbon production, hardly meet the objectives of sustainable development of the region.

The prospects for the development of international shipping in the Arctic—through the Northern Sea Route that runs along the Russian coast—are also directly dependent on the ongoing transformations in the global energy markets. Despite more favorable ice conditions and the expansion of the navigation period, the conditions for transit shipping in the Arctic, in fact, do not change for the better.

They are determined by the possible cost savings in the transportation of goods from Asia to Europe and backwards compared to alternative southern routes. Bunker fuel costs are one of the largest components of the total transportation costs. According to various estimates, the share of bunker fuel costs lies in the range from 36 to 57% of total transportation costs (Makarov et al., 2015).

It is the opportunity to save on transportation operational costs which is often highlighted as the main competitive advantage of the Northern Sea Route. It is by a third shorter than the southern route, which passes through the Strait of Malacca, the Indian Ocean, and the Suez Canal. The higher the price level for bunker fuel, which is directly related to oil prices, the higher is the commercial attractiveness of the northern short transport routes compared to the longer southern ones.

But so far, relatively low prices for bunker fuel (together with the lack of icebreaking support, port infrastructure, and an insufficient quality navigation and rescue systems) do not allow to achieve sufficient savings. This does not encourage transporters to switch from long southern routes from Southeast Asia to Europe to a relatively shorter route passing through the NSR. The peak of transit traffic on the NSR was in 2013, when 71 vessels passed through the NSR during the whole year (Nazarov, 2019). As a comparison, this is less than the number of ships passing through the Suez Canal daily.

The prospects for the development of international transit in the Russian Arctic are also limited by other structural factors. Structural changes in the Chinese economy result in a transformation of the system of international relations in the Asia-Pacific region. It is now more often described as the "Asia for Asia" model, in which the Asia–Pacific countries[3] orient their foreign economic specialization toward the needs of the Chinese market (Bordachev et al., 2015). While in the late 1990s and early 2000s, 40% of the foreign trade of Asian countries took place within the region, now it is about 50%.[4] The slowdown and transformation of China's economy is holding back the growth of global trade, in particular trade between Europe and Asia. While in the period 2001–2009 it grew by 125%, in the period 2011–2019 it grew by only 15%.[5]

These circumstances might also be a part of the long-term economic downturn in European countries (in particular, against the background of

---

[3] Asia-Pacific countries include China, Japan, the Republic of Korea, the ASEAN countries, and India. Although India is not geographically part of the Pacific Basin, it is considered by many to be part of this macro region.

[4] Author's calculations based on Trade Statistics for International Business Development: https://www.trademap.org.

[5] Ibid.

the COVID-19 pandemic) which could make the development of international shipping in the Arctic, with all its advantages (including potential savings in costs and time of transportation), not as optimistic as previously seen. Moreover, the already existing sea routes are being developed (including the expansion of the Suez Canal in 2015) simultaneously with the gradual development of the competing land routes (including the Western China—Eastern Europe railway).

In the aftermath of the COVID-19 pandemic, we are to take a fresh look at the prospects for the development of the Arctic region. With the global economy and energy demand growth slowdown, the attractiveness of the Arctic hydrocarbons, expensive in extraction and transportation, is falling. Even if the price level and the volume of demand for energy resources return to pre-crisis levels, it is hardly possible to expect that the Arctic shelf will become a new global resource base, playing a comparable role with the fields of the Persian Gulf. Moreover, it is even dangerous to strive for this.

Despite the recent emergence of several international agreements aimed at controlling and eliminating spills in the Arctic seas, limiting local air pollution, preserving marine ecosystems, etc., the growth rate of environmental risks is outstripping the growth of the capabilities of the Arctic countries and other actors involved in their adequate management. Now, on the way out of the crisis, under critical environmental risks, which cannot be managed by existing technologies, is perhaps the best time to shift the focus of Arctic policy from the tasks of exploration and expansionist development toward strengthening the socio-environmental agenda.

References

Aksenov, Y., Popova, E. E., Yool, A., Nurser, A. G., Williams, T. D., & Bertino, L. (2017). On the future navigability of Arctic sea routes: High-resolution projections of the Arctic Ocean and sea ice. *Marine Policy, 75*, 300–317.

Ambrose, J. (2020). Denmark to end new oil and gas exploration in North Sea. *The Guardian.* https://www.theguardian.com/business/2020/dec/04/denmark-to-end-new-oil-and-gas-exploration-in-north-sea. Accessed 14 Mar 2021.

Anisimov, O. A. (2007). Potential feedback of thawing permafrost to the global climate system through methane emission. *Environmental Research Letters, 2*(4). https://doi.org/10.1088/1748-9326/2/4/045016

Apparicio, S., & Sauer, N. (2020, August 13). Which countries have not ratified the Paris climate agreement? *Climate Home News.* https://www.climatechangenews.com/2020/08/13/countries-yet-ratify-paris-agreement/. Accessed 20 June 2021.

Arabella Advisors. (2018). *The global fossil fuel divestment and clean energy investment movement.* https://www.arabellaadvisors.com/wp-content/uploads/2018/09/Global-Divestment-Report-2018.pdf. Accessed 20 June 2021.

Bird, K. J., Charpentier, R. R., Gautier, D. L., Houseknecht, D. W., Klett, T. R., Pitman, J. K., Schenk, C. J., Tennyson, M. E., & Wandrey, C. J. (2008). Circum-Arctic resource appraisal: Estimates of undiscovered oil and gas north of the Arctic Circle. *US Geological Survey, 2008–3049.*

Bordachev, T. V., Likhacheva, A. B., & Zhang, S. (2015). Chego khochet Asia: potreblenie, vsaimosavisimost, kapital I kreativnost [What does Asia wants? Consumption, interdependence, capital and creativity]. *Russia in Global Affairs, 13*(1), 82–96.

CBI. (2020). *Green bonds global state of the market 2019.* https://www.climatebonds.net/resources/reports/green-bonds-global-state-market-2019. Accessed 20 June 2021.

CNPC Economics and Technology Institute. (2018). *Clean China energy outlook 2050.* https://eneken.ieej.or.jp/data/8192.pdf. Accessed 14 Mar 2021.

European Commission. (2008). *Climate strategies & targets.* https://ec.europa.eu/clima/policies/strategies_en. Accessed 20 June 2021.

European Commission. (2019). *2020 climate & energy package.* https://ec.europa.eu/clima/policies/strategies/2020_en. Accessed 25 Nov 2019.

Dolata-Kreutzkamp, P. (2008). Canada-Germany-EU: Energy security and climate change. *International Journal, 63*(3), 665–681.

Goosse, H., Kay, J. E., Armour, K. C., Bodas-Salcedo, A., Chepfer, H., & Docquier, D., Alex, J., Kushner, P., Olivier, L., François, M., Hyo-Seok, P., Felix, P., Gunilla, S., Vancoppenolle, M. (2018). Quantifying climate feedbacks in polar regions. *Nature Communications, 9*(1), 1–13. https://www.nature.com/articles/s41467-018-04173-0. Accessed 20 June 2021.

Higuera, P. E., Brubaker, L. B., Anderson, P. M., Brown, T. A., Kennedy, A. T., & Hu, F. S. (2008). Frequent fires in ancient shrub Tundra: Implications of paleorecords for Arctic environmental change. *PLoS ONE, 3*(3). https://doi.org/10.1371/journal.pone.0001744

Hovelsrud, G. K., Poppel, B., van Oort, B., & Reist, J. (2011). Arctic societies, cultures and peoples in a changing Cryosphere. *Ambio, 40*, 100–110. https://doi.org/10.1007/s13280-011-0219-4

IEA. (2020a). *World Energy Outlook 2020—Analysis*. https://www.iea.org/rep orts/world-energy-outlook-2020. Accessed 14 Mar 2021.

IEA. (2020b). *Global energy review 2020*. https://www.iea.org/reports/global-energy-review-2020. Accessed 20 June 2021.

IPCC. (2013). Climate change 2013: *The physical science basis*. Contribution of Working Group I to the Fifth Assessment Report of the IPCC. Cambridge University Press.

Kjartan, E., Ulfarsson, G. F., Valsson, T., & Gardarsson, S. M. (2017). Identification of development areas in a warming Arctic with respect to natural resources, transportation, protected areas, and geography. *Futures, 85*, 14–29. https://doi.org/10.1016/j.futures.2016.11.005

Kryukov, V. A., Skufina, T. P., & Korch, E. A. (2020). *Economika sovremennoi Arktiki: v osnove uspeshnosti effektivnoye vsaimodeistvie i upravlenie integralnimi riskami* [The economy of the modern Arctic: Effective interaction and integrated risk management are at the heart of success]. FRC KRC of RAS.

Lee, M., & Asuncion, R. C. (2020). Impacts of sea level rise on economic growth in developing Asia. *Resources and Environmental Economics, 2*(1), 102–111.

Leksin, V. N., & Porfir'ev, B.N. (2017). Specifika transformacii prostranstvennoj sistemy i strategii pereosvoeniya rossijskoj Arktiki v usloviyah izmenenij klimata [Transformation specifics of the spatial system and the strategy of the Russian Arctic redevelopment in the context of climate change]. *Ekonomika regiona*. https://cyberleninka.ru/article/n/spetsifika-transformatsii-prostrans tvennoy-sistemy-i-strategii-pereosvoeniya-rossiyskoy-arktiki-v-usloviyah-izm eneniy-klimata. Accessed 14 Mar 2021.

Likhacheva, A. B., Makarov, I. A., Stepanov, I. A., Suslov, D. V., Kashin, V. B., & Boklan, D. S. (2021). *Russian policy in the Arctic: International aspects*. Higher School of Economics Publishing House.

Makarov, A. A., Mitrova, T. A., & Kulagin, V. A. (2019). *Global and Russian energy outlook 2019*. The Energy Research Institute of the Russian Academy of Sciences, Moscow School of Management SKOLKOVO. https://www.eri ras.ru/files/forecast_2019_en.pdf. Accessed 14 Mar 2021.

Makarov, I. A., Sokolova, A., & Stepanov, I. A. (2015). Prospects for the Northern sea route development. *International Journal of Transport Economics, 42*(4), 431–460.

Makarov, I. A., & Stepanov, I. A. (2015). Ekologichesckiy faktor economicheskogo razvitiya Rossiyskoy Arktiki [Environmental factor of economic development of the Russian Arctic]. *ECO, 45*(11), 120–138. https://doi.org/10. 30680/ECO0131-7652-2015-11-120-138

Makarov, I. A., & Stepanov, I. A. (2018). Parizhskoe klimaticheskoe soglashenie: vliyanie na mirovuyu energetiku i vyzovy dlya Rossii [Paris climate agreement: Impact on global energy and challenges for Russia]. *Aktual'nye problemy Evropy, 1*, 77–100.

McKinsey & Company. (2021). *Global gas outlook to 2050*. https://www.mck insey.com/industries/oil-and-gas/our-insights/global-gas-outlook-to-2050#: ~:text=LNG%20demand%20grew%20by%201,declining%20pipeline%20and% 20domestic%20gas.&text=Approximately%20200%20MT%20of%20additio nal%20liquefaction%20capacity%20is%20needed%20by%202050. Accessed 14 Mar 2021.

Melvin, A. M., Larsen, P., Boehlert, B., Neumann, J. E., Chinowsky, P., Espinet, X., Martinich, J., Baumann, M. S., Rennels, L., Bothner, A., Nicolsky, D. J., & Marchenko, S. S. (2017). Climate change damages to Alaska public infrastructure and the economics of proactive adaptation. *Proceedings of the National Academy of Sciences of the United States of America, 114*(2), E122–E131. https://doi.org/10.1073/pnas.1611056113

Mohov, I. I., & Hon, V. C. (2015). Prodolzhitel'nost' navigacionnogo perioda i ee izmeneniya dlya Severnogo morskogo puti: model'nye ocenki [The duration of the navigation period and its changes for the Northern Sea Route: Model estimates]. *Arktika: ekologiya i ekonomika, 2*, 88.

Nazarov, D. (2019, February 20). *Transit statistics 2018*. Northern Sea Route Information Office. https://arctic-lio.com/transit-statistics-2018/. Accessed 14 Mar 2021.

Overland, J., Hanna, E., Hanssen-Bauer, I., Kim, S.-J., Walsh, J. E. & Wang, M., Bhatt, U. S., & Thoman, R. L. (2015). Surface air temperature. *Arctic Report Card 2015*. https://www.researchgate.net/publication/299442816_ Arctic_Report_Card_2015. Accessed 14 Mar 2021.

Pagano, A. M., Durner, G. M., Rode, K. D., Atwood, T. C., Atkinson, S. N., Peacock, E., Costa, D. P., Owen, M. A., & Williams, T. M. (2018). High-energy, high-fat lifestyle challenges an Arctic apex predator, the polar bear. *Science, 359*(6375), 568–572. https://doi.org/10.1126/science.aan8677

Pörtner, H. O., Roberts, D. C., Masson-Delmotte, V., Zhai, P., Tignor, M., Poloczanska, E., Mintenbeck, K., Alegría, A., Nicolai, M., Okem, A., Petzold, J., Rama, B., & Weyer, N. M. (2019). *IPCC special report on the ocean and Cryosphere in a Changing Climate (SROCC)*. https://www.ipcc.ch/srocc/. Accessed 14 Mar 2021.

Roshydromet. (2014). *Vtoroj ocenochnyj doklad Rosgidrometa ob izmeneniyah klimata i ih posledstviyah na territorii Rossijskoj Federacii* [Second assessment Report of Roshydromet on climate changes and their consequences on the territory of the Russian federation]. https://cc.voeikovmgo.ru/ru/publik atsii/2016-03-21-16-23-52. Accessed 20 June 2021.

Schmitz, H. (2017). Who drives climate-relevant policies in the rising powers? *New Political Economy, 22*(5), 521–540. https://doi.org/10.1080/135 63467.2017.1257597. Accessed 20 June 2021.

Shafranik, Yu. K., & Kryukov, V. A. (2016). *Nevtegasoviy sector Rossii: trudniy put k mnogoobraziyu* [Russia's oil and gas sector: The hard road to diversity]. Higher School of Economics Publishing House.

Stepanov, I. A., & Albrecht, J. (2019). Decarbonization and energy policy instruments in the EU: Does Carbon pricing prevail? *NRU Higher School of Economics*, Series EC "Economics", 211.

Tedesco, M., Fettweis, X., van den Broeke, M. R., van de Wal, R. S. W., Smeets, C. J. P. P., van de Berg, W. J., Serreze, M. C., & Box, J. E. (2011). Record summer melt in Greenland in 2010. *Eos Trans, AGU, 92,* 126.

Environment, Geopolitics and Environmental Geopolitics in the Arctic: Is There a Logic of Conflict Among Institutions of Cooperation?

Andrei Skriba and Arina Sapogova

INTRODUCTION

As the northmost polar region of the Earth, the Arctic includes ice waters of the Arctic Ocean and continental landmasses of Eurasia, North America and islands and archipelagoes lying to the north of the so-called Arctic Circle. From a geographical perspective, all these characteristics denote the "High North" which refers collectively to the northern areas or "everything north of the Arctic Circle" (Østhagen, 2021). If one looks at the region from a political point of view, then the concept of "the Arctic" refers to the eight coastal states (the Arctic states)—Canada, Denmark, Finland, Iceland, Norway, Russia, Sweden and the United States—which

---

A. Skriba (✉) · A. Sapogova
Laboratory for Research of Political Geography and Modern Geopolitics,
Higher School of Economics, Moscow, Russia
e-mail: askriba@hse.ru

A. Sapogova
e-mail: aisapogova@edu.hse.ru; asapogova@hse.ru

© The Author(s), under exclusive license to Springer Nature
Singapore Pte Ltd. 2022
A. Likhacheva (ed.), *Arctic Fever*,
https://doi.org/10.1007/978-981-16-9616-9_5

own both land areas and the body of water. But, despite some semantical differences, these and some other concepts ("Circumpolar North", "Circumpolar Arctic") are mutually overlapping and are more often than not employed interchangeably in regards to the Arctic, or the Arctic region.

There are two main ways to approach the Arctic region when it is placed within the context of international relations. If international relations are understood in a broader sense as the interaction between states and other actors on extended areas of concerns, then the Arctic could be said to constitute a complex region composed of both land and sea parts. A range of questions related to the Arctic region essentially exceed the limits of the national agenda and require an inclusive dialogue (e.g., environmental protection, global warming and climate change, socio-economic conditions of indigenous peoples inhabiting the region, etc.).

When deliberately positioned in the context of international *competition* between states, a wider interpretation of the Arctic geographic configurations begins to narrow down. The terrestrial part is not a constituent of this competition, being part of the sovereignty of the Arctic countries. Consequently, it is the maritime Arctic in particular which played and continues to play a pivotal role in the power relations across a range of issues such as access to vital resources, security concerns, control over trade routes, etc. In this sense, the notion of competition in the region applies primarily to the maritime Arctic as space.

The "emptiness" of the Arctic space has been one of the reasons behind the limited attention drawn to the region in the earlier centuries upon its discovery. In recent decades, however, there is growing international attention to the Arctic region. With the natural transformations of the sea ice landscape, the Arctic region has become increasingly accessible for human activity, including shipping, resource exploration, tourism, other types of economic and commercial activity, as well as a political endeavor. As a consequence of these changes, a concept of "New Arctic" was developed to illuminate "how, and in what parts, the natural and political system is being transformed" (Evengård et al., 2015) and to disclose potential implications of the changing Arctic. As Zellen (2009) enunciates, "the arrival of the long-awaited Age of the Arctic now appears to be just around the corner". In addition, some representatives of the geopolitical tradition even refer to the region as a "new geopolitical pivot" (Antrim, 2010).

In these changing (political) conditions, some scholars and policy-makers consider the New Arctic as a zone of cooperation.[1] An enhanced focus on the environmental discourse prompted the reassessment of foreign policy strategies of the eight Arctic nations, which opened up the opportunity for turning the New Arctic into a zone of peace. These observations are confirmed by the rapid dynamics of institutional building in the post-Cold War era, which saw the establishment of high-level multilateral forums and the gradual development of the Arctic conference system.

On the contrary, other scholars hold that not only is the Arctic not completely devoid of power competition, but this competition will only continue to grow. As Huebert (2019) highlights, although "there is a growing discussion over whether or not the security environment of the Arctic is re-entering a 'new' Cold War... [T]he crux of the argument is that the era of Arctic exceptionalism is coming to an end". It is believed that the Arctic region is gradually transforming into an arena of inter-state conflict, with the existing frictions between national governments epitomizing the struggle for access to natural resources and control over space. In the words of Zellen (2009), "the climate is rapidly warming, threatening to bring an end to the Arctic as we know it, creating much uncertainty about its future—and ours".

However, at the moment a conflict-centered interpretation of the New Arctic essentially lacks profound empirical data to corroborate the main conclusion and draws instead on circumstantial evidence. Firstly, the conclusion about interstate competition in the High North seems to have been erroneously extrapolated from the broader conflictual dynamics between states in other regions of the world. In this sense, the uninformed projection of the global political dynamics onto the Arctic ignores the region's specific geographic characteristic. Secondly, the likelihood of full-scale interstate tensions in the Arctic as compared to interstate frictions in other regions has been exaggerated and derived from the false premise about the so-called "Arctic hype" (Tunsjø, 2020). Finally, the proposed

---

[1] The exceptional status of the Arctic region has been reflected in the idea of "negotiated exceptionalism", which refers to the intrinsically consensual nature of the Arctic regional order (Exner-Pirot & Murray, 2017). One more interpretation—that the Arctic has been generally referred to as a distinctive and exceptional territory of peaceful cooperation and dialogue, which has been notably detached from and unaffected by the global political dynamics (Käpylä & Mikkola, 2015).

thesis about competition in the Arctic fundamentally ignores the existing multilateral institutions as well as the prevailing ecological agenda, which serves to bring the Arctic states together rather than yield disunity and conflict in the circumpolar relations.

Geographic and climate-related conditions, which account for the special status of the Arctic, coupled with the recent transformations of the region's environment as a result of climate change, make the region unique, indeed. And behind this feature (so far) it is really difficult to discern the Hobbesian war of all against all. Hence the question: is there competition in the Arctic today, and if so, how does this compare to a rich and intense natural agenda?

To answer these questions, this article consists of the following parts. In the first section, we examine the history of relations in the Arctic to see whether the region indeed has always been free of competition. The second section is devoted to the more modern Arctic, in the period after the end of the Cold War, when the region saw the development of institutions of peace and cooperation. This, as well as environmental changes and the struggle to alleviate their consequences, complicated the application of several theories such as geopolitics, despite their relatively good adaptability to exploring the relationships between politics and the environment. Therefore, in the fourth section, we propose to look at the Arctic through the prism of environmental geopolitics, which allows us to comprehensively incorporate both environmental changes and the logic of conflict in the analysis. We are going to examine this through the prism of three approaches to study interstate relations in the Arctic further to confirm this relationship and to better understand the specifics of competition among states in this region.

The Path from the Geographic Periphery to the Political Significance

The longer the Age of Discovery went, the clearer a peripheral status of the Arctic in international relations became. Earlier discovery attempts—including overland and maritime expeditions—were significantly curtailed owing to the severe climate in the High North and limited technological development. Whereas some scholars point out that "during the nineteenth and twentieth century, the High Arctic was an area for exploration, fantasy, and geopolitical competition" (Keskitalo, 2012) the political dynamics here was particularly slow. Firstly, even the simplest application of sovereignty through effective occupation was practically impossible owing to the remoteness from the colonial capitals and severe climate conditions. Secondly, it was rather challenging to determine the object of competition because most of the Arctic unexplored by that time (as opposed to the Antarctic) was located not on land, but the ocean area covered by the perennial sea ice.

Yet even in the case of the few islands not yet occupied, the struggle of the Arctic countries for their possession was not so acute. The case of Spitsbergen (Svalbard)[2] is a perfect illustration. By the early twentieth century, sovereignty over Spitsbergen remained one of the unresolved uncertainties, with several European powers expressing their claims over the archipelago's coal deposits. An increased commercial activity, including fishery and resource extraction, so, it laid the foundation for competition, which resulted in the 1920 Spitsbergen Treaty. On the one hand, it legally granted "full and absolute sovereignty" over the archipelago to Norway. On the other hand, Norwegian sovereignty was limited in the questions about demilitarization of the Spitsbergen and peaceful exploration of its resources by all the parties of the treaty.

However, even despite the "frozen" in every sense of the policy in the Arctic up to the mid-twentieth century, it would be inaccurate to claim that the region remained aside global competition, at least in theory. For instance, British geographer and "father" of geopolitics Halford Mackinder highlighted the unique security setting of the High North for Russia, saying that "a hostile invasion across the vast area of circumpolar ice and over the Tundra mosses and Taiga forests of Northern Siberia seems almost impossible" (Mackinder, 1942). One could draw a similar conclusion concerning other states, where the Arctic became a "new military frontier" that made any aggressive invasion difficult or inexpedient (Honderich, 1987).

The role of the Arctic that remained "frozen" began to dramatically change during the Cold War years, when technological advancements enhanced the strategic military standing of the two major actors—the United States and the USSR. With the arrival of strategic bombers and intercontinental ballistic missiles, the Arctic region represented the

---

[2] Spitsbergen refers to the largest island which constutes a part of of the Svalbard Archipelago and falls under the sovereign jurisdiction of Norway. Both concepts are often used interchangeably to describe the same group of islands north of Norway.

shortest distance between the Western and Eastern blocs, making the circumpolar Arctic a perfect "staging location for strikes against each other" (Huebert, 2019). As Østreng (1977) showcases, "[t]he Ballistic Missile Early Warning System (BMEW) in the Arctic gives the retaliatory forces of the United States a warning time of 15–20 minutes" which provides sufficient time to launch a counter-attack against the Soviet adversary. In the same way, Soviet SS-N-8 Delta-class submarines in the Murmansk area notably "enhanced the strategic significance of their Arctic deployment" (Østreng, 1977). Hence, it was 75 years ago when technological and military advancements in the High North, rather than climate change, prompted the development of the Arctic region as an international arena.

Apart from the military and strategic dimension, the significance of the Arctic concerned the civil side—aviation. Since 1944 in line with the Chicago Convention, countries of the world agreed upon the principle of mutual open skies. The fact that the Soviet Union did not join the Convention turned the Arctic into an "under-used" space and extended the distance of commercial flights from Western Europe to the Far East. For instance, to travel from Tokyo from London in the 1950s, one would need to fly across the south of Eurasia and make several stops before reaching the destination. Conversely, in the 1970s, the partial overflight over the Arctic enabled to reduce the travel time by redirecting the flying route to Alaska, with only one stop in Anchorage.

In the 1970s–80s, when the balance of power between the United States and USSR was generally established across all the regions (including the Arctic), the two superpowers began to seek new regimes to manage their competition. These included the 1991 Strategic Arms Reduction Treaty (START I) which led to a reduction of strategic and tactical weapons, and the 1996 Arctic Military Environmental Cooperation (AMEC) program which enabled to decrease in the number of Soviet nuclear submarines in the Arctic Ocean (Huebert, 2019). Another significant outcome was the 1983 United Nations Convention on the Law of the Sea. Although not specifically designed to address the ambiguities related to managing Arctic space, this legal regime became one of the key points in the development of circumpolar relations. It established universal rules for relations in the maritime Arctic and thereby helped to avoid any transition of competition in the air to the sea surface.

In particular, as specified under Article 3 of UNCLOS, each of the Arctic coastal states possesses full sovereignty only over the 12-nautical-mile territorial sea. Article 56 underlines an exclusive sovereign right to an exclusive economic zone (EEZ) within the 200-nautical-mile limit from the baseline, which includes continental shelf and its natural resources. At the same time, Article 76 allows for the expansion of the limits of the continental shelf through the submission of scientific proof by the coastal State to the Commission on the Limits of the Continental Shelf. Other maritime areas either beyond the 200-nautical-mile delimitation or exceeding the limits of extended continental shelf fall within a category of "high seas", which underpins special legal conditions granting all states the freedom of navigation, overflight, scientific research and other freedoms specified by Article 87. It is further notable that a legal regime underpinned by UNCLOS included several provisions pertaining to "ice-covered areas" where "severe climatic conditions and the presence of ice covering" enables coastal states to introduce specific laws and regulations (Article 234).

Although the established Law of the Sea regime did not eliminate competition in the Arctic, legal provisions included in the Convention facilitated an orderly and rule-based settlement of the overlapping sovereign claims in the Arctic Ocean and other maritime disputes between the Arctic states. The same can be said about the overall competition in the Arctic, which became more orderly by the end of the Cold War.

In general, it was during the Cold War that the Arctic began to "unfreeze" politically. And although competition here was largely limited by the structure of international relations, which reduced the number of actors to two superpowers, these events showed that in a political sense, the Arctic region was no exception for competing centers of power and that the past lack of attention to the High North was due to the lack of an object of competition here as well as the harsh climate and the lack of technology that could allow one to pass through the ice-covered region and project strength. The Cold War period was characterized by technological development and thus contributed to growing competition. The post-Cold War period presented an additional, but equally important factor—the changing environment of the Arctic.

Competition in the Arctic: Geopolitics or Regimes?

After the Cold War, competition in the Arctic declined as it did in the rest of the world. At the same time, in the 1990s, there was a growing concern about environmental issues and the augmentation of climate-related uncertainties, which essentially laid the foundation for the emergence of the "new" Arctic. The notion of the New Arctic referred to the changing geophysical landscape of the region as a result of global climate change and thawing of the Arctic Sea ice. On the one hand, this opened up new opportunities for navigation and commercial activities in the resource-rich Arctic basin and therefore created more opportunities to advance national interests. On the other hand, such changes threatened the stability of Arctic nature (both in its marine part and in national territories). As a result, one more emerging concern was related to the problems of indigenous peoples and local communities, who faced the risk of losing their natural living environment.

All these unconventional threats became the basis for the political activity of a new type when the traditional logic of conflict and zero-sum game competition was gradually superseded by more cooperative relations between the Arctic nations. As a result, there emerged a range of intergovernmental institutions and several multilateral agreements underpinning a peaceful and orderly regime in the Arctic region. As such, the signing of the Arctic Environmental Protection Strategy (AEPS) by the governments of Canada, Denmark, Finland, Iceland, Norway, Sweden, the Soviet Union and the United States in 1991 marked the pioneer stage in the conjoined aspirations of the Arctic states to establish a stable regional order in the High North. Following the 1996 Ottawa Declaration, the creation of the Arctic Council represented a formalization of multilateral cooperation efforts of the circumpolar nations aimed at "sustainable development and environmental protection in the Arctic" (Ottawa Declaration, 1996).

As a formal and hierarchically organized intergovernmental body, the Arctic Council—in addition to the eight Member States which hold the monopoly on decision-making—includes Permanent Participants and Observers. The former comprises six organizations representing the interests of the Arctic indigenous peoples (e.g., Aleut International Association) which reserve consultation rights regarding negotiated and implemented Arctic policies. The latter is composed of non-Arctic states,[3] international organizations and NGOs which granted a right to participate in meetings and workshops within the institutional framework of the Arctic Council.

While the Arctic Council deals with environmental problems, there has never been an organization(s) in the region to deal with political issues. Although there was an attempt to create a community of the five Arctic littoral states (Canada, Denmark, Norway, Russia and the United States of America), or the so-called Arctic Five, it never developed into a full-fledged organization with its agenda and institutions to advance the interests of its members. Perhaps the most important result of her work to date was the Ilulissat Declaration of 2008, in which the five recognized the Arctic Ocean as a unique ecosystem, "which the five coastal states have a stewardship role in protecting" (The Ilulissat Declaration, 2008). But at the same time, concerning any potential disputes, the Arctic Five has declared a commitment to the law of the sea and "to the orderly settlement of any possible overlapping claims" (The Ilulissat Declaration, 2008). In essence, this became especially significant for the United States, which formally is still not a signatory of the Law of the Sea.

All these events and processes meant two things. The first is that the security agenda in the Arctic is not only expanding but also goes far from military issues, thereby broadening the political corridor for new actors, including non-governmental ones. Depledge and Dodds (2017) coined such a variety of formats as the "bazaar of Arctic governance". Second, regime theory and intergovernmentalism are better suited for studying relations in the Arctic and such a phenomenon as Arctic politics. Of course, this situation did not suit realistic thinkers and supporters of hard power, who believed that the military threat did not disappear and remained somewhere out there, among the melting ice. This cohort includes Antrim (2010) and many other scientists who have turned to the explanatory power of geopolitics to show competition in the New Arctic.

At first glance, geopolitical approaches are especially applicable to the Arctic, where new military threats and opportunities are associated precisely with the geographical changes in the region. First, geopolitics deals with the compression of space–time, such as in the Arctic due to

---

[3] Germany, Netherlands, Poland, United Kingdom, France, Spain, China, India, Italy, Japan, South Korea, Singapore, Switzerland.

melting ice, which opened up new opportunities for the power projection through the High North or the use of the region as a transit corridor.

Secondly, geopolitics takes into account technical advances (both past and ongoing), which similarly facilitate more efficient use of the Arctic space. This could include both the aforementioned means of transport, as well as the advances in resource mining technologies over the recent decades, in particular—advancement in the petroleum drilling industry.

Hence, thirdly, geopolitics can show the economic side of interstate competition—what the founder of geo-economics Luttwak referred to as the "logic of conflict, grammar of commerce" (Luttwak, 1990). The geographic location of the Arctic littoral states provides them with the possibilities for economic empowerment through greater accessibility of the resources, development of shipping routes and shipbuilding industry, and exploitation of fishing resources which are almost exclusively found within their EEZ (Wegge & Keil, 2018). Private companies, whose work is beneficial for the state, can also be involved in this case. One of the notable examples is Russian hydrocarbon production in the Prirazlomnoye field which belongs to Gazprom Neft Shelf.[4] Another highly debated topic in recent decades has been the expansion of the EEZ and the spread of sovereign rights to the continental shelf claimed by Norway, Canada, Denmark and Russia. The latter has made the most noticeable progress having submitted scientific evidence to extend outer limits of the continental shelf to the Commission on the Limits of the Continental Shelf in 2001 and issuing the revised Submission in 2015.

Finally, fourthly, critical geopolitics is another good method to show the origins of the national interests of the Arctic and non-Arctic states in this region. For example, what meaning does the Arctic states give to the Arctic in their statements or strategic documents, and what national interests are behind this? Or why do circumpolar states pay different attention to the Arctic: Why does Russia seem to be more concerned about investing resources in its Arctic meanings than, say, the United States,

---

[4] According to Gazprom Website, estimated oil reserves in the Gazprom-owned Prirazlomnoye filed amounts up to more than 70 million tons. The field produce 3.14 million tons of oil in 2019, with a potential production level of hydrocarbons is equal to approximately 5.5 million tons per year.

which also has access to the Arctic Ocean? Also, how do near-Arctic countries, such as China or even India, construct their status and their rights to be present in the High North? These questions are heard not only among the scholars but also in the expert and political environment of the highest level. For example, they were voiced by the President of the Republic of Iceland at the "The Future of the Arctic" session organized by the Council on Foreign Relations:

> *It will, for example, be a testing ground where South Korea can justify, why is it so interested in the Arctic? Why does the leadership of South Korea visit Greenland? Why does the prime minister of China talk about the Arctic when he comes to Iceland? What is the agenda? I was in India a few weeks ago. The first item on the meeting with the foreign minister of India was India's desire to be a member of the Arctic Council. It's kind of crazy, paradoxical, that now I have to discuss in Delhi their membership in the Arctic Council.* (Council on Foreign Relations, 2013)

Thus, on the one hand, competition in the Arctic has declined since the end of the Cold War and was replaced by institutions of cooperation. On the other hand, the environment in the Arctic is changing, which forces many scientists to describe international relations in the Arctic through the prism of different geopolitical approaches. While the first view took all the processes in the New Arctic seriously, geopolitics, however, treated them selectively by taking only those variables that concern power competition and thereby leaving the environmental agenda out of the scope.

ENVIRONMENTAL GEOPOLITICS: THEORY AND ARCTIC PRACTICE

Geopolitical approaches, with their undoubted merits, have a weak point. All of them, in one way or another, deal with the old Arctic or with the global Arctic,[5] or with the possible Arctic, talking about promising power rivalries and conflicts between states. The only exception, perhaps, is critical geopolitics, which is not geopolitics but critical theory. However, in it,

---

[5] The term "global Arctic" reflects a "more global outlook on the Arctic" and the understanding the region is increasingly affected by the global environmental and economic transformations" (Dodds, 2018). In the context of competition, this means the presence in the Arctic of countries from any part of the world.

the state and politics, and therefore the conventional aspects of strength and security, are also the first thing we look at.

In the New Arctic, however, the security agenda has already expanded to include environmental changes and challenges. Ignoring these new aspects of security and focusing only on hard power leaves Arctic high politics not fully addressed, especially when compared to other regions. According to Tunsjø (2020), this should take us away from the Arctic to other parts of the world, since any possible conflict can only "spill over into the High North from somewhere else". Thus, the key point here is not to compare the levels of competition in the Arctic with other places (where the Arctic surely gives way), but to include a broader security agenda in the competition. In other words, to make Arctic geopolitics not intense, but complex due to the additional role of environmental problems.

The first attempt to integrate the environmental agenda into geopolitics was made at the turn of the century. Then it was referred to as "green geopolitics", the main idea of which consisted in the perception of the Earth as a common home, where there were new geographies of danger, e.g., anthropogenic and/or natural environmental threats discussed by Dalby (2007). However, this understanding of threats contradicted the division of the world into states and their conflicting interests—the very historical essence of geopolitics. Therefore, the further development of these ideas proceeded away from classical geopolitics—in a global context and regarding the Anthropocene phenomenon.[6] Thus, scholars believed that "deterministic arguments about climate shaping human destiny are no longer relevant to the geopolitics of the twenty-first century" because "climate change is a production problem, not an environmental one" (Dalby, 2013). And since, in their understanding, these are not countries, but humanity as a whole which "is making its future", this approach had little contribution to the study of international relations in any region.

The second and a bit more successful attempt to fit the environment into geopolitics was made by Shannon O'Lear, who introduced the term "environmental geopolitics". She defined environmental geopolitics

---

[6] The Anthropocene refers to the new geologic era which was brought about as a product of human activity that dramatically transformed the Earth's environment. The "Anthropocene geopolitics" recognizes the possibility to re-evaluative the traditional understanding of the relationship that defines the interaction between state and external environments (Dalby, 2007).

as "an approach to examining how environmental themes are used to support geopolitical arguments and realities" by asking "how the environment is brought into narratives, practices, and physical realities of power and place" (O'Lear, 2018). An important addition to understanding the relationship between the environment and geopolitics (in its more classical interpretation) has been a broader interpretation of security beyond the state and beyond the military sector. In other words, it was the securitization of the environment where a range of issues was considered as threats to security across various spheres of life and different actors. In her research, O'Lear identified four main topics on which themes of security and risk are constructed: human population, resource conflicts, climate change and "science and imagery as ways of understanding and responding to environmental issues". Also, in contrast to Simon Dalby's "green geopolitics", environmental problems as a threat to security were believed to be not only global but also domestic, which therefore implied that their influence (i.e., through perception) on public policy might not be universal and global.

At the same time, the second attempt to marry together environment and geopolitics similarly lacked an international dimension. In her book, O'Lear (2018) focused more on internal politics as a response to environmental threats to security, or, as she puts it, "how environmental features are described, promoted, bounded, and attached to human values and concerns or portrayed as threats requiring action".

The same approach, however, can be applied to the behavior of countries with each other in those places where the environmental agenda is perceived by them as important. This method is close to critical geopolitics, but its understanding of threats is somewhat broader than traditional military threats. The environment can challenge people, cities, industries, companies, etc. Moreover, the source of this threat in environmental geopolitics, being not a rival state actor, can be located both close to the border and in a wider space (like the Arctic). In general, in this approach, a dynamic environment meets a dynamic perception of its problems on the part of states, where the second dynamic takes place both in space (each state adopts a specific view on issues which are accorded the highest significance) and time (views of different issues could vary from government to government).

This approach seems to be perfectly suited for today's Arctic. It provides a detailed clarification of interstate competition at the expense of the natural agenda where it exists and has an impact. In the Arctic, the environmental agenda is not only present (which is equal to the concept of "New Arctic"), but also its influence manifested itself when institutions of cooperation and development were created. As a result, one gets the opportunity—by means of applying environmental geopolitics—to integrate this seemingly peaceful agenda into the logic of conflict and competition.

Environmental Geopolitics Beyond Domestic Politics

The changing environment, as Shannon O'Lear has shown, is forcing countries to look at security issues more broadly and respond to them within domestic politics. Each of the Arctic countries includes the factor of the environmental change in their domestic policies. The response measures could be divided into two related groups. The first group incorporates measures directed at the prevention of environmental problems, which most often boil down to restrictions on human activity. The second group deals with the struggle against the consequences of environmental changes that have already occurred. In this case, security is understood not as the ability to protect oneself from natural disasters (especially those that have already happened), but the ability to adapt to a new environment and prevent future threats (not necessarily natural) that this new environment potentially conceals.

All Arctic states combine these approaches to one degree or another. For instance, Canada regards its North as national heritage, while the "Northern Strategy" issued by the Canadian government highlights not only challenges but also opportunities in regard to the ongoing transformations in the North (Government of Canada, 2009). In the "Norwegian High North Strategy", much attention is simultaneously paid to environmental protection and resource extraction, especially in Svalbard (Norwegian Ministry of Foreign Affairs, 2006). A similar broader approach is utilized by Iceland, with its Arctic policy aimed at "securing Icelandic interests concerning the effects of climate change, environmental issues, natural resources, navigation and social development" (Norwegian Ministry of Foreign Affairs, 2006). Recognizing the priority of the environmental agenda, "National Strategy for The Arctic Region" identified the following key interests: "to evolve infrastructure, to preserve Arctic region freedom of the seas, to provide for future the United States energy security" (The White House, 2013).

Russia, where state activity is regulated by the presidential decree "Foundations of State Policy of the Russian Federation in the Arctic"[7] and National Security Strategy,[8] achieved both significant theoretical and practical results in these matters. According to the decree, the main threats to Russia caused by environmental changes in the Arctic include, among the first, a decrease in the local population and a low level of infrastructure development, as well as low rates of geological exploration of potentially lucrative mineral resource deposits (President of the Russian Federation, 2020). Hence, Russia's Arctic policy included not only cleanup programs, but also the development of coastal territories. Among the main achievements was the construction of an icebreaker fleet (including the world's only nuclear-powered icebreakers), floating nuclear power plants to supply cities with electricity, the restoration of old and the creation of new military facilities.[9] Similarly, the new National Security Strategy (2021) indicates environmental problems and rational use of natural resources of the Russian Arctic zone.

At first glance, such a policy does not automatically equal geopolitical competition since it is oriented inward. However, it must be admitted that the measures taken to respond to environmental changes make the country stronger and safer, which creates imbalances at the international level and geopolitical risks for other countries in the Arctic. Hence, other Arctic countries sometimes react negatively to the internal policy

---

[7] The 2008 decree formalised Russian state policy in the Arctic up to 2020, while the 2020 revision of the earlier document—up to 2035.

[8] A new Strategy of National Security was published on July 2, 2021. It highlights the continuing Western hegemony and "crisis of modern models and instruments of economic development" in the face of the "increasing instability in the world" and signals a gradual decline of the 2015 cooperative approach to managing newly emerging security concerns in the Arctic region (President of the Russian Federation, 2021).

[9] With a gradual expansion in the post-Cold War years, Russia has intensified its military build-up in the Arctic through the development of infrastructure, defence technology and construction of nuclear icebreakers. The sheer scope and size of militarisation in the Russian Arctic generated an increasing concern among other Arctic states. For further information on Russia's Arctic expansion see: https://www.businessinsider.com/r-putins-russia-in-biggest-arctic-military-push-since-soviet-fall-2017-1.

of Russia.[10] In that, other Arctic nations attributed to Russia geopolitical motives as Russia purportedly seeks external continuation of its Arctic policy. This was especially true in regards to the planting of the Russian flag during the "Arktika 2007" expedition headed by the Russian polar explorer Artur Chilingarov, whose purpose was to support the Russian claim to extend its EEZ. Although this went beyond the limits of domestic policy, the request was submitted to Commission on the Limits of the Continental Shelf (CLCS) in line with the provisions of international law and did not constitute an attempt of forcible takeover. Nonetheless, this symbolic gesture provoked widespread, international attention. In Canada, for instance, the minister of foreign affairs at the time, Peter MacKay, rejected the perceived goal of the act—to strengthen the Russian claim to the shelf (Lomonosov Ridge) below the North Pole: "This isn't the fifteenth century. You can't go around the world and just plant flags and say 'We're claiming this territory" (Parfitt, 2007).

Such preoccupation also worked in an opposite direction. That is, in the abovementioned "Foundations of State Policy of the Russian Federation in the Arctic", the following aspects are named among the main challenges to Russia's presence in the Arctic: obstruction of Russia's economic or other activities by foreign states, intensification of their military presence in the Arctic region and increasing potential for conflict in the High North, incomplete international legal delimitation of maritime spaces, etc. (President of the Russian Federation, 2020). Thus, one could say that the peaceful and domestic environmental geopolitics discussed by Shannon O'Lear is not an end-point and continues internationally, where governments monitor both the foreign policy actions of rival states and their domestic policies. In a sense, we are dealing with the geopolitics of environmental geopolitics, when a broad interpretation of security and responses to environmental threats within a country entails (and therefore cannot always be separated from) traditional interstate competition.

Moreover, if we go back to the example of shelf claims, we can find the element of environmental geopolitics here as well. Although

---

[10] At the official meeting with Icelandic foreign minister in May 2021, U.S. Secretary of State Antony Blinken denounced Russia's actions in the Arctic as "unlawful maritime claims" and criticised Russia's recent advances in the region as being "inconsistent with international law", especially in regard to the prohibition of foreign vessels transit in the Northern Sea Route (Skydsgaard & Pamuk, 2021).

the struggle for resources relates more to classical geopolitics or geo-economics, various reports on estimated resource deposits in the Arctic indicate large volumes of oil, gas and other minerals in comparison to the existing reserves or production/consumption rates (e.g., Bird et al., 2008; National Petroleum Council, 2015). This directly correlates with the themes of resource conflicts and the problem of resource supply for the population of different countries and fits the topics of environmental geopolitics. In other words, the possession of Arctic resources is both a competitive advantage, but also part of a policy directed at preventing environmental threats in the future.

Environmental Geopolitics and Arctic Identity

The previous examples were more concerned with domestic politics and through it influenced the relations between countries. However, the environmental agenda could have not only an indirect contribution to the geopolitical competition, but it also directly impacts the latter. As part of critical approaches, environmental geopolitics is concerned with deconstructing images and discourses that can be created to reinforce prudent geopolitical interests rather than pure environmental concerns. In this section, we will show how environmental factors in the Arctic are involved in the discourses related to competition, projection of dominance and various means to keep opponents at distance, as well as how these discourses work toward geopolitical inclusion or exclusion from the region.

From the perspective of critical geopolitics, access to the Arctic is closely associated with the process of how the country positions itself as an Arctic state, or in other words, with the formation of an Arctic identity. The most successful in this effort were the five coastal states that have access to the Arctic Ocean, as well as those three countries that are inside the Arctic Circle (i.e., Sweden, Finland and Iceland). As a case in point, Canada's Northern Strategy explicitly underlines that Canada "is a Northern nation" and the North constitutes a "fundamental part of national identity" (Government of Canada, 2009). This works in a similar way for Denmark: it is stated in the preamble to the "Kingdom of Denmark Strategy for the Arctic 2011–2020" document signed by the governments of Denmark, Greenland and the Faroe Islands that the "the Kingdom of Denmark is centrally located in the Arctic" and that all its three parts "share common values and interests and all have a responsibility in and for the Arctic region" (Government of Denmark, Greenland and the Faroe Islands, 2011). It turned out to be more difficult for other countries that are interested in having their presence in the Arctic but had to invent their "belonging" to the High North. To illustrate, Great Britain justifies its interests by accentuating "proximity to the Arctic" in the "Beyond the Ice" national approach to the Arctic (Government of the United Kingdom, 2018), while China has constructed the idea of a "near-Arctic state" articulated in China's Arctic Policy (State Council of the People's Republic of China, 2018)—both due to their geographical proximity to (although not the inclusion as such) the Arctic Circle.[11]

However, behind such rhetoric, it is not always possible to discern that today it is the environmental factor that is crucial for the way Arctic identity is implemented in practice. First, one could mention the fact that many treaties and institutions which have become an important part of the actors' involvement in Arctic policy and cooperation, started with an environmental agenda. As such, the Arctic Council (1996) had a prototype in the form of the AEPS (1991). In other words, the environmental factor became the first mechanism to enable the Arctic states to institutionalize their status in the region. Secondly, it is the environmental agenda that remains at the center of attention of meetings and forums at various levels. The operation of the Arctic Council is still focused on two main areas: environmental protection and sustainable development, which is equally linked to climate change in the region. In the Arctic Circle (non-governmental organization), the environment is also one of the three main themes along with cooperation for development and polar/ice identity.

Accordingly, on the one hand, the environmental agenda has been historically associated with the formation of the Arctic identity due to its connection to the North and the climate changes taking place there. This connection persists today: it gives those states which are most concerned with environmental problems and fully involved in their resolution a higher status. In support of this thesis, one could cite excerpts from the Ilulissat Declaration, where five coastal states emphasized their special

---

[11] With the Arcttic Circle located at a latitude of 66°30′ N, the northernmost parts of United Kingdom, Shetland Islands, lies approximately above a latitude of 600 N as well as Manchuria in the Northeast China stretches up to 50–550 N (Young, 2019).

place in the protection of the Arctic environment and their special vulnerability because of the growing international activity in the region: "The Arctic Ocean is a unique ecosystem, which the five coastal states have a stewardship role in protecting", "The increased use of Arctic waters for tourism, shipping, research and resource development also increases the risk of accidents" (The Ilulissat Declaration, 2008). On the other hand, the same criterion serves as an additional filter for other countries with interests in the Arctic but is not directly related to its natural problems and the struggle to alleviate them. This applies among other things to Arctic Council Permanent Observers that "observe" the environmental issue from afar.

Environmental factor affects the presence and status in the Arctic not only of external countries but also intrapolar ones. Thus, Denmark's participation in the Arctic Council and the Arctic Five is justified by the fact that the Danish government maintains control over Greenland. But the further good relations between Denmark and Greenland seem to depend on the assistance provided by the Danish government. Especially in a situation where, in Greenland itself, there exists support for the course of independence among the island's local (i.e., Inuit, therefore the Arctic) population. It is no coincidence that Danish security policy in Greenland is gradually moving away from a one-sided rigid understanding of threats and is focusing more on a wider range of "services". As Ackrén and Jakobsen (2015) note,

> Denmark's current military presence [...] is seen more as a symbolic than a realistic military defense of the territory. On the other hand, the Danish military has many real societal and civil tasks in Greenland such as surveillance, search and rescue operations, fishery inspections, ice observation, transport etc. Military tools may thus be seen as not only covering traditional 'hard' purposes of national security but also contributing to human security.

Thus, although the Arctic is formally a region open to everyone, the Arctic countries declare their privilege due to their proximity to the Arctic and its opportunities as well as problems, where the environmental agenda has become an important part of such identity and belonging. Therefore, the entrance to this "club" today is associated not only with the geographic location (e.g., proximity to the Arctic Circle), the willingness to invest in the region and develop commercial projects (e.g., the Chinese Polar Silk Road) or introduce a comprehensive strategy underlining the daunting environmental concerns justifying the deepened involvement in the rapidly changing region.

An equally important criterion is a practical contribution to the sustainable (i.e., directed at environmental protection) development of the Arctic region. From this point of view, one could draw on the efforts of China, which invests in scientific research in the Arctic (Bowman & Xu, 2020), as well as the European Union and its funding of the Arctic-related projects as part of the Horizon 2020 Programme (European Union, 2014). Notably, the formal political and financial involvement of non-Arctic interests proceeds within the limits of their observer status, which significantly confines the range of legal instruments utilized by the European Union or Asian countries to expand their presence in the Arctic. While the Arctic governance framework continues to rely on the multilateral cooperation between the member-states of the Arctic Council, in face of the thawing Arctic ice and rising sea ice level even these eight Arctic nations recognized the fundamental nature of the international implications of the changing Arctic.

The Logic of Conflict, the Grammar of Environmental Protection

Environmental geopolitics has been set up as part of a critical approach. Accordingly, in the first two cases, we looked at how the environmental agenda influenced geopolitical perception or became an element of the geopolitical discourse in its international dimension, i.e., with regard to competition between states. At the same time, one can look at environmental geopolitics more traditionally—as an instrument of power standoff. In this case, environmental geopolitics will be close to geo-economics and geopolitics. From geo-economics, environmental geopolitics will borrow non-political instruments of influence (where geopolitical motives could not be immediately discernible), and from geopolitics—priorities of the state aimed at strengthening of its relative standing and creating for itself (or its companies) better working conditions and additional advantages, both nationally and at the regional level.

As a case in point, one could analyze the carbon tax which the European Union plans to charge for products (including imported ones) with a high carbon footprint.[12] On the one hand, the imposition of a carbon tax similarly constitutes an element of environmental geopolitics in its critical understanding: the European authorities (and the authorities of the EU countries) have expanded their understanding of security threats to include the factor environment, which has been reflected in the new legislation. On the other hand, the outward orientation of the new carbon regulations provides the European governments with a powerful tool for creating preferential conditions for national companies (which have prepared for the transition to the new rules of the game in advance) than for their foreign competitors. Furthermore, the European Union could potentially abuse this legal instrument by deliberately freezing access to the European market for companies from rival countries, which will be temporarily denied approval until any disputes are settled down. Although the recent proposal on the European Green Deal (The European Commission, 2021) remains rather restrained in this matter, the possibility of such geopolitics is dictated by the very trend of the European political discourse concerning both the green agenda in general and in relation to the Arctic competitors in particular, such as Russia and China.

Similarly, the environmental agenda is used in regard to Arctic issues as far as new legislation is created or existing international treaties are interpreted in a new way. The first example concerns the case of Norway. On one hand, in line with the 1920 Svalbard Treaty, Norway is obliged to provide all signatories with equal rights to conduct commercial activity in the archipelago. On the other hand, Article 2 of the Treaty contains a remark which stipulates that "Norway shall be free to maintain, take or decree suitable measures to ensure the preservation and, if necessary, the re-constitution of the fauna and flora of the said regions, and their territorial waters" (cited in Schönfeldt, 2017). Consequently, today, protected areas cover about 2/3 of the total land area of the archipelago и about 86.5% of its territorial waters (Lier et al., 2010), which obstructs the presence of foreign interests in this part of the Arctic.

---

[12] In recent years, a growing number of European countries have developed new fiscal policies to limit the amount of carbon emissions. Within the framework of the EU Emissions Trading System, member-states have indicated their commitment to achieve carbon neutrality by imposing higher carbon tax rates and other restrictions on power, manufacturing and industrial sectors. The EU's 2021 carbon border tax will first of all apply to the most polluting industries (e.g., electricity and steel production) and is anticipated to be increasing by 10 billion euro annually (Financial Times, 2021).

The third example is sea trade routes, the use of which has become more convenient and cheaper for goods transportation between continents. Concerning the Northwest Passage, the Canadian government has been claiming since the 1970s and 1980s that the baselines around its archipelagos in the North "define the outer limit of Canada's historical internal waters" (cited in Pharand, 2007) in the 1985 statement by Secretary of State for External Affairs Joe Clark, which caused discontent among Canadian allies (i.e., US and European countries). Discussions on this issue continue, although they remain extremely rare owing to the relatively insignificant volume of maritime traffic in the Northwest Passage (due to the complicated navigation conditions which make this sea route to a large extent closed for the full-scale international transit).

Things are moving more intensively in regards to the Northern Sea Route (NSR) which remains a fully operational sea route today and, the construction of Leader-class icebreakers has a chance to become year-round maritime passage. Here, Russia went further than other Arctic states in its efforts to promote "environmental" interpretation of international laws. According to Article 234 of UNCLOS,

> *The Coastal States have the right to adopt and enforce non-discriminatory laws and regulations for the prevention, reduction and control of marine pollution from vessels in ice-covered areas within the limits of the exclusive economic zone, where particularly severe climatic conditions and the presence of ice covering such areas for most of the year create obstructions or exceptional hazards to navigation, and pollution of the marine environment could cause major harm to or irreversible disturbance of the ecological balance. Such laws and regulations shall have due regard to navigation and the protection and preservation of the marine environment based on the best available scientific evidence.* (Convention on the Law of the Sea, 1982)

This broad formulation allowed Moscow to declare additional requirements for ships that pass along the Northern Sea Route (NSR). In 2020, the Russian Government announced the Navigation Rules for the Northern Sea Route, which introduced additional obligations for foreign vessels, both commercial and military (which are formally excluded from the provisions of Article 234 by Article 236 of UNCLOS). Contrary to the backlash received from some Arctic countries (especially, the United States), some scholars claim that this does not contradict the existing law of the sea (Chircop et al., 2014). This notwithstanding, it is notable that Russian politicians and scholars (as well as some of their Canadian colleagues) who argue in support of these additional rules specifically refer to environmental issues, such as severe weather conditions due to climate change in the Arctic and other risks of shipping for the vessels, which are not suitable for such a transit because of the specific national criteria required by the countries they travel from (Kotlyar, 2015; Mikheev, 2017).

The third and final example concerns the so-called Polar Code, which was adopted by the International Maritime Organization in 2014. The Code specifies the technical requirements for ships sailing in polar waters. In particular, the Preamble underlines "the relationship between the additional safety measures and the protection of the environment" (International Maritime Organization, 2014). Formally, these are additional measures that apply to all countries. Nevertheless, the very fact of the existence of this code points out the peculiarities of the Arctic as a region (no other region has special rules of navigation), as well as of the Arctic states, which, when developing this code, had the opportunity to influence its formulations and requirements. Thus, the technical advantages that vessels of these countries might have were legalized with a particular reference to the importance of environmental protection.

Conclusion

The emerging competition between states in the Arctic is notably different from international relations in other regions. In the High North, neither harsh military confrontation nor large-scale military exercises take place. Moreover, due to the absence of disputed land territories in the Arctic where people would live, there exist no other forms of regional disputes and conflicts. This specificity of the Arctic has been preserved over the past decades, despite profound environmental transformations that profoundly impacted the material landscape of the region. While these changes have created a new geopolitical environment, at the same time they led to the erosion of fierce competition between a range of additional security threats.

Nevertheless, one could not unequivocally conclude that the uniqueness of the region consists in the absence of competition and traditional geopolitics. After all, the region harbors the same countries that until recently, during the Cold War, viewed the Arctic in the context of military confrontation. It is possible to argue that geopolitically neutral actors— such as Sweden and Finland (not NATO members) as well as Iceland

and Denmark (Greenland)—equally remain part of the regional dynamics while being more concerned with the protection of their sovereignty rather than active competition with others within a broader scope of the Arctic. At the same time, more ambitious actors including Russia, the United States and Canada are still present in the region and could be followed by the United Kingdom, China as well as other states similarly interested in expanding their involvement in and development of the Arctic. Thus, since the Arctic still includes the same states that compete with each other in other parts of the world, there is no evidence to suggest that the region is capable of changing the fundamental motives of human and state behavior and ultimately eradicating the struggle for power as an element of its nature.

An exclusive characteristic of the Arctic region is reflected not in the absence of competition per se, but the unique nature of this competition as well. Similar to security issues which are understood more broadly than military ones in the face of climate change, competition has also gone far beyond the limits of hard power. Environmental geopolitics as a relatively new theoretical strand has been employed to describe this logic. On the one hand, this is a critical view on how the environmental agenda is perceived by the Arctic states and employed by Arctic governments in domestic and foreign policy, which subsequently affects interstate competition. On the other hand, this approach shows how environmental problems could create new environmental instruments that are utilized by state actors (among others) in the pursuit of geopolitical and geo-economic imperatives.

The aforementioned dynamics captures the essence of environmental geopolitics in the Arctic. It might be argued that the Arctic region is probably closer to competition than environmentalists would prefer. Such geopolitics goes beyond national boundaries and enters the realm of power geopolitics. Although it is also true that the logic of the conflict remains intact only in the most general terms and that the environmental agenda, as a new instrument of competition, begins to influence its content. In other words, the understanding of security, state interests and the traditional competition continues to be ingrained in the behavior of any state (especially in regard to powerful and ambitious states), but they gradually transform in the sense of the meaning that they convey to become increasingly complex.

At first glance, these changes are positive since they remind that tough military confrontation constitutes only part of international relations and that countries need to find opportunities for cooperation, even when they remain competitors. However, for the sake of keeping the Arctic balanced and free of conflicts, it is important to remember that competition continues and that one should not neglect this particular aspect in Arctic politics amid melting ice and emerging institutions of cooperation. Furthermore, the unique geophysical configuration of the region implies that the adverse consequences of competition-related disruptions would have a significantly more profound effect on the Arctic than other parts of the world.

REFERENCES

Ackrén, M., & Jakobsen, U. (2015). Greenland as a self-governing sub-national territory in international relations: Past, current and future perspectives. *Polar Record, 51*(4), 404–412.

Antrim, C. L. (2010). The next geographical pivot: The Russian Arctic in the twenty-first century. *Naval War College Review, 63*(3), 14–38.

Bird, K. J., Charpentier, R. R., Gautier, D. L., Houseknecht, D. W., Klett, T. R., Pitman, J. K., Moore, T. E., Schenk, C. J., Tennyson, M. E., & Wandrey, C. R. (2008). *Circum-Arctic resource appraisal: Estimates of undiscovered oil and gas north of the Arctic Circle* (No. 2008–3049). US Geological Survey.

Bowman, L., & Xu, Q. (2020). *China in the Arctic: Policies, strategies, and opportunities for Alaska.* Center for Arctic Policy Studies.

Chircop, A., Bunik, I., McConnell, M. L., & Svendsen, K. (2014). Course convergence? Comparative perspectives on the governance of navigation and shipping in Canadian and Russian Arctic waters. *Ocean Yearbook Online, 28*(1), 291–327.

Council on Foreign Relations. (2013). *The future of the Arctic: A new global playing field.* https://www.cfr.org/event/future-arctic-new-global-playing-field-0

Dalby, S. (2007). Ecology, security, and change in the Anthropocene. *The Brown Journal of World Affairs, 13*(2), 155–164.

Dalby, S. (2013). The geopolitics of climate change. *Political Geography, 37,* 38–47.

Depledge, D., & Dodds, K. (2017). Bazaar governance: Situating the Arctic circle. In *Governing Arctic change* (pp. 141–160). Palgrave Macmillan.

Dodds, K. (2018). Global Arctic. *Journal of Borderlands Studies, 33*(2), 191–194.

European Union. (2014). *Communication from the Commission to the European Parliament, the Council, the European Economic and Social Committee and the Committee of the Regions: A new skills agenda for Europe.* https://op.europa.eu/en/publication-detail/-/publication/ae5 ada03-0dc3-48f8-9a32-0460e65ba7ed/language-en

Evengård, B., Larsen, J. N., & Paasche, Ø. (Eds.). (2015). *The New Arctic.* Springer.

Exner-Pirot, H., & Murray, R. W. (2017). Regional order in the Arctic: Negotiated exceptionalism. *Politik, 20*(3).

Financial Times. (2021). *EU carbon border tax will raise nearly €10bn annually.* https://www.ft.com/content/7a812f4d-a093-4f1a-9a2f-877c41811486

Gazprom. (n.d.) *Prirazlomnoye field: The only Russian hydrocarbon production project implemented on the Arctic shelf.* https://www.gazprom.com/projects/prirazlomnoye/

Government of Canada. (2009). *Canada's Northern strategy: Our North, our heritage, our future.* https://publications.gc.ca/site/eng/9.674653/public ation.html?wbdisable=true

Government of Denmark, Greenland and the Faroe Islands. (2011). *Kingdom of Denmark strategy for the Arctic 2011–2020.* Ministry of Foreign Affairs of Denmark. https://um.dk/en/foreign-policy/the-arctic/

Government of the United Kingdom. (2018). *Beyond the ice: UK policy towards the Arctic.* https://assets.publishing.service.gov.uk/government/uploads/sys tem/uploads/attachment_data/file/697251/beyond-the-ice-uk-policy-tow ards-the-arctic.pdf

Honderich, J. (1987). *Arctic imperative: Is Canada losing the North?* University of Toronto Press.

Huebert, R. (2019). A new Cold War in the Arctic?! The old one never ended!. *Arctic Yearbook,* 1–4.

International Maritime Organization. (2014). *International code for ships operating in polar waters (Polar Code).* https://www.liscr.com/sites/default/files/liscr_imo_resolutions/MSC.385%2894%29.pdf

Käpylä, J., & Mikkola, H. (2015). *On Arctic exceptionalism: Critical reflections in the light of the Arctic sunrise case and the crisis in Ukraine* (Working paper 85) (pp. 1–22). The Finnish Institute of International Affairs.

Keskitalo, E. C. (2012). Setting the agenda on the Arctic: Whose policy frames the region? *The Brown Journal of World Affairs, 19*(1), 155–164.

Kotlyar, V. (2015). *Ispol'zovanie ledokolov v akvatorii Severnogo morskogo puti dlya obespecheniya bezopasnosti moreplavaniya sudov pod inostrannym flagom: pravovye osnovy i slozhivshayasya praktika* [The use of icebreakers in the water area of the Northern sea route to ensure the safety of navigation of ships under a foreign flag: Legal framework and established practice]. Rossijskij sovet po mezhdunarodnym delam [The Russian International Affairs Council]. https://russiancouncil.ru/sevmorput#kotlyar

Lier, M., Aarvik, S., Fossum, K., Von Quillfeldt, C., Barr, S., Hansen, P. H., & Ekker, M. (2010). *Protected areas in Svalbard-Securing internationally*

ENVIRONMENT, GEOPOLITICS AND ENVIRONMENTAL GEOPOLITICS ...   111

valuable cultural and natural heritage. Norwegian Directorate for Nature Management. https://en.visitsvalbard.com/dbimgs/Eng_brosj_SvalbardProt ectedareas.pdf

Luttwak, E. N. (1990). From geopolitics to geo-economics: Logic of conflict, the grammar of commerce. *The National Interest, 20*, 17–23.

Mackinder, H. (1942). *Democratic ideals and reality a study in the politics of reconstruction*. Constable Publishers.

Mikheev, V. (2017). *Severnyj morskoj put'. Ispol'zovanie ledokolov. Pravovye osnovy i slozhivshayasya praktika* [Northern sea route. Use of icebreakers. Legal basis and established practice]. Rossijskij sovet po mezhdunarodnym delam [The Russian International Affairs Council]. https://russiancouncil.ru/sevmorput miheev

National Petroleum Council. (2015) *Realizing the promise of US Arctic oil and gas resources: Part one*. https://www.npcarcticreport.org

Norwegian Ministry of Foreign Affairs. (2006). *The Norwegian high North strategy*. https://www.regjeringen.no/globalassets/upload/ud/ved legg/strategien.pdf

O'Lear, S. (2018). *Environmental geopolitics*. Rowman & Littlefield.

Østhagen, A. (2021). Norway's arctic policy: Still high North, low tension? *The Polar Journal*, 1–20.

Østreng, W. (1977). The strategic balance and the Arctic ocean: Soviet options. *Cooperation and Conflict, 12*(1), 41–62.

Parfitt, T. (2007). Russia plants flag on North Pole seabed. *The Guardian, 2*(8). https://www.theguardian.com/world/2007/aug/02/russia.arctic

Pharand, D. (2007). The Arctic waters and the Northwest passage: A final revisit. *Ocean Development & International Law, 38*(1–2), 3–69.

President of the Russian Federation. (2020). *Foundations of the Russian Federation State Policy in the Arctic for the period up to 2035* (A Davis & R Vest, Trans.). Moscow, Kremlin. https://dnnlgwick.blob.core.windows.net/por tals/0/NWCDepartments/Russia%20Maritime%20Studies%20Institute/Arc ticPolicyFoundations2035_English_FINAL_21July2020.pdf?sr=b&si=DNN FileManagerPolicy&sig=DSkBpDNhHsgjOAvPILTRoxIfV%2FO02gR81NJS okwx2EM%3D

President of the Russian Federation. (2021). *Ukaz Prezidenta Rossijskoj Federacii O Strategii Nacional'noj Bezopasnosti Rossijskoj Federacii* [Decree of the President of the Russian Federationon on the national security strategy of the Russian Federation]. http://publication.pravo.gov.ru/Document/View/000 1202107030001

Schönfeldt, K. (Ed.). (2017). *The Arctic in international law and policy*. Bloomsbury.

Skydsgaard, N., & Pamuk, H. (2021). Blinken says Russia has advanced unlawful maritime claims in the Arctic. *Reuters*. https://www.reuters.com/world/

europe/russia-has-advanced-unlawful-maritime-claims-arctic-blinken-2021-05-18/

State Council of the People's Republic of China. (2018). *China's Arctic policy*. The State Council Information Office of the People's Republic of China. http://english.www.gov.cn/archive/white_paper/2018/01/26/content_281476026660336.htm

The Arctic Council. (1996). *Declaration on the establishment of the Arctic Council 1996—Ottawa declaration*. http://library.arcticportal.org/1270/1/ottawa_decl_1996-3..pdf

The European Commission. (2021). *European Green Deal: Commission proposes transformation of EU economy and society to meet climate ambitions*. https://ec.europa.eu/commission/presscorner/detail/en/ip_21_3541

The Ilulissat Declaration. (2008). *Arctic Ocean Conference* (pp. 27–29). https://arcticportal.org/images/stories/pdf/Ilulissat-declaration.pdf

The White House (2013). *National strategy for The Arctic Region*. https://obamawhitehouse.archives.gov/sites/default/files/docs/nat_arctic_strategy.pdf

Tunsjø, Ø. (2020). The great hype: False visions of conflict and opportunity in the Arctic. *Survival, 62*(5), 139–156.

UN General Assembly. (1982). *Convention on the Law of the sea*. https://www.un.org/depts/los/convention_agreements/texts/unclos/unclos_e.pdf

Wegge, N., & Keil, K. (2018). Between classical and critical geopolitics in the changing Arctic. *Polar Geography, 41*(2), 87–106.

Young, O. R. (2019). Constructing the "new" Arctic: The future of the circumpolar North in changing global order. *Outlines of Global Transformations: Politics, Economics, Law, 12*(5), 6–24.

Zellen, B. S. (2009). *Arctic doom, Arctic boom: The geopolitics of climate Change in the Arctic* (p. 93).

Kaleidoscope of Independent Agendas for the Arctic: Russia

Risks and Socioeconomic Priorities for Sustainable Development of the Russian Arctic

Vladimir N. Leksin and Boris N. Porfiriev

SUSTAINABILITY AS A CHARACTERISTIC OF THE STATE AND POTENTIAL OF SOCIOECONOMIC SYSTEMS

The concepts of "sustainable development" and "sustainable growth" are among the most frequently used terms in fundamental strategic documents of different states and the world community as a whole. At the same time, the term "*sustainability*" is *invariably* interpreted as the ability to maintain one's state or (in relation to the process, system) one's essence when internal and external conditions change, *resist* external influences and return to the initial state, as well as *long-term* and stable operation

---

V. N. Leksin (✉)
Federal Research Center "Computer Science and Control", Russian Academy of Sciences, Moscow, Russia
e-mail: vnleksin@hse.ru; leksinvn@yandex.ru

B. N. Porfiriev
Institute of Economic Forecasting, Russian Academy of Sciences, Moscow, Russia
e-mail: b_porfiriev@mail.ru

© The Author(s), under exclusive license to Springer Nature Singapore Pte Ltd. 2022
A. Likhacheva (ed.), *Arctic Fever*,
https://doi.org/10.1007/978-981-16-9616-9_6

of a system. In contrast, the term "sustainable development" in relation to socioeconomic systems, processes and phenomena is not construed so unequivocally.

This term began to be applied by scholars, politicians, and the media after the report "Our Common Future" issued in 1987 by the UN Commission on Environment and Development (Brundtland, 1987). It defined sustainable development as development that meets the needs of the present without compromising the ability of future generations to meet their own needs. The ambiguous term "needs" was used in the report mainly in relation to natural resources, which limited the significance of the key factor—human capital, the quantitative and qualitative growth of which determines the dynamics and sustainability of the development of the modern economy and society as a whole.

Focused on the needs of society, this approach to defining sustainable development has been reflected, and to a large extent remains relevant, in national research works on the sustainable development of socioeconomic systems. One of the overview reports on this issue contains a list of interpretations of the concept of "sustainable development" found in a number of domestic publications (Porohin et al., 2014). Summarizing these interpretations, the authors of the report define the sustainability of a socioeconomic system (region) as the ability of such a system to maintain balance, function steadily in the long term and develop in the changing external and internal environment. The same publication also contains various (differing in substance) interpretations of the concept of "sustainable development." Summarizing them, the authors conclude: "In our opinion, the most justified is the point of view that defines sustainable development as a continuous process of satisfying the needs of society." The continuity of the process means, "constant or increasingly growing opportunities for meeting needs in the long term, which is possible if a balance of interests and harmonious interaction between all subsystems of the socioeconomic system are achieved" (Porohin et al., 2014, p. 819). Such a definition, acceptable as an abstract and ambitious target for achieving a certain ideal state of society, is extremely difficult to use for determining specific goals and objectives for public management of complex socioeconomic systems.

In view of this, an updated concept of sustainable development has been prepared. Without giving up its original meaning, it balances the economic, social and environmental components of sustainability and the very process of societal development, gearing long-term economic growth

RISKS AND SOCIOECONOMIC PRIORITIES FOR SUSTAINABLE ... 117

toward achieving social and environmental goals that ensure better living standards and quality of life. It is this concept of sustainable development that has become the ideological basis for modern international and national strategic documents and practical actions of states, social movements and, in part, businesses in this sphere.

When using this concept as a basis for substantiating *socioeconomic priorities for the sustainable development of the Russian Arctic zone (RAZ), it seems necessary to make a number of important clarifications.* The stability of the RAZ as a spatial (macro-regional) system should be understood as the possibilities and realities of its functioning (performance of social, economic, infrastructure, environmental and other functions by the population, businesses and the government) in a way that preserves and reproduces basic elements and connections within this system and ensures non-destructive integration of new elements and connections into it. The proposed interpretation of sustainability is based on the existing preconditions for enhancing the capacity of self-organization, self-development and adaptation of this system to internal and external factors, including the global and regional climate. In our opinion, this regime of RAZ functioning in the twenty-first century should become a fundamental principle and a practical task of public and administrative regulation.

However, the RAZ operates and will continue to operate amid increasingly growing disturbances and with naturally limited administrative and financial (including investment) management capabilities. This emphasizes the significance of determining priorities and substantiating indicators for the sustainable development of the RAZ and its various components. In this regard, it is advisable to use the experience of such adaptation that was acquired in relation to the UN Millennium Development Goals system in 2000–2015 and which was analyzed in detail in the Reports of the UN Human Development Report for the Russian Federation.[1]

Finally, managing the sustainable development of the RAZ spatial system, by definition, implies minimizing (or, if there is a regulatory framework, bringing to an acceptable level) risks for the operation of various components of this system and the integral risk for the system as a

---

[1] See, for example, Bobylev (2010). As for the RAZ development priorities, they are discussed in detail below, in section "RAZ Sustainable Functioning Priorities" of this chapter.

whole. Sustainability becomes yet another synonym for security. Ensuring both implies additional stringent requirements concerning the management of risks, particularly strategic ones, such as geopolitical and climate change.

Stability and Safety in the Integral Characteristic of RAZ Functioning

The RAZ contains the largest (of all Russian macro-regions) part of the geopolitical, spatial, natural resource and economic potential of the country, as well as risks associated with the realization of this potential. Conceptually significant for substantiating the structure of priorities for public management of RAZ development, the connection between the broadly interpreted notion of national security (in economic, social, environmental terms, etc.) and sustainable development has been stated in government strategic documents for several years.

For example, the National Security Strategy of the Russian Federation for the Period up to 2020 (Decree of the President of the Russian Federation of May 12, 2009) adopted in 2009 emphasized that "along with achieving the main *national security priorities*, the Russian Federation focuses its efforts and resources on… *sustainable development priorities*" (hereinafter italicized by the authors V.L., B.P.). The new National Security Strategy of the Russian Federation (Decree of the President of the Russian Federation of December 31, 2015), adopted in its place at the end of 2015, has strengthened the organic connection between security and sustainability. Its first paragraph emphasizes that "the national interests and strategic national priorities of the Russian Federation, the goals, tasks and measures in the field of domestic and foreign policy are aimed at strengthening the national security of the Russian Federation and ensuring the *sustainable development* of the country in the long term." In addition, it says that "favorable conditions for the long-term sustainable development of the Russian Federation shall be created by ensuring strategic stability" (another synonym for sustainability). The National Security Strategy of the Russian Federation names the following as national security threats: "a set of conditions and factors that create a direct or indirect possibility for damaging national interests," including the *effects of climate change*. Among the main threats, it names "natural calamities, accidents and disasters, including those related to global climate change, deteriorating infrastructure and fires." All this should be expressly stated in updated strategic documents defining directions for the sustainable development of the Russian Arctic zone.

In the context of this chapter, the Economic Security Strategy of the Russian Federation for the Period up to 2030 (Decree of the President of the Russian Federation of May 13, 2017), adopted in May 2017, is of particular interest, since it proposes not only doctrinal provisions of economic security as such, but also the structure of relevant indicators correlated with RAZ sustainable development objectives. An analysis of this document indicates that it would be legitimate to consider it a strategy for ensuring sustainable development "at the federal, regional, municipal, and sectoral levels," including the Arctic macro-region. A number of provisions in the Economic Security Strategy of the Russian Federation for the Period up to 2030, concerning national security at the regional level in the medium term, directly appeal to the key parameters of RAZ stability. These include reducing the level of interregional differentiation in the socioeconomic development of Russian regions (this is one of the main reasons for the outflow of people from the Russian Arctic zone) through balanced territory development; coordinating the deployment of transport, engineering and social infrastructures at all levels (nodal problem in the RAZ); improving resettlement patterns and deployment of productive forces (one of the major topics in all strategic documents for the development of the RAZ).

The list of the strongest impacts on the state of and prospects for the economy, called "challenges and threats" and presented in section II of the Economic Security Strategy of the Russian Federation for the Period up to 2030, is fully consistent with the RAZ security to sustainability ratio. Thus, the main strategic national security threats in the economic field are the most characteristic of the Russian Arctic: "the raw-material export model of development and high dependence on external economic conditions, lag in the development and introduction of advanced technologies, deterioration and depletion of the raw-material base, decreasing production and dwindling reserves of strategically important minerals, increasing shortages of labor resources, uneven development of regions, and diminishing stability of the national resettlement system."

Existing and Emerging (Expected) Problems and Risks for Sustainable Development of the Russian Arctic Zone

An analysis of the existing and a forecast of expected threats to the sustainable functioning of Russia's Arctic macro-region is the subject of many special studies and, moreover, an almost mandatory component of any work related to the problems of the Russian Arctic zone.[2] We identify three main groups of such threats: (1) natural and climatic, (2) ecological, technological, and social, and (3) political, legal, and strategic.

Natural and climate risks for the sustainable functioning of the RAZ are well known and have been described many times.[3] A harsh climate, long winters with the lowest temperatures on the planet and short summers, strong winds, especially on the coast of the Arctic Ocean, thick ice cover and permafrost are the best known, but not all features of this region. Arctic territories are still characterized by significantly lower population density and predominantly focal development patterns, which, however, has helped preserve a relatively clean environment in the Arctic compared to most other parts of the world and is the reason for relatively local ecological problems in areas with high levels of industrial and radiation pollution (Morgunov, 2011, p. 55).[4]

The combination of the spatial and geographical factors with extreme natural and climatic conditions determines the increased sensitivity and vulnerability of the natural and human-created Arctic environment to technological impacts, as well as climate change. In recent decades, the

---

[2] Summarized materials of leading think tanks and results of the authors' own research are offered in the monograph (Leksin & Porfir'ev, 2016). See also a number of foreign scientific publications on this issue: Carson and Peterson (2016), Emery (1981), Folke (2006), Forbes (2008), Hinzman et al. (2013), Rammel et al. (2007).

[3] See, for example, Pachauri and Meyer (2014), Larsen et al. (2014), ACIA (2005), Barber et al. (2008), The Economist (2012), Derocher et al. (2004), Drinkwater (2011), Drinkwater et al. (2010), Forbes (2011), Hof et al. (2015), Kaplan et al. (2003), Kattsov et al. (2010), Post et al. (2009), Schaefer et al. (2012), Swann et al. (2010).

[4] A well-known example of such trouble spots is the city of Norilsk, which has repeatedly been included in the list of the most polluted cities in Russia and the world. Its already unfortunate reputation was further damaged by an environmental emergency on May 29, 2020, as a result of which more than 20,000 tons of diesel fuel flowed out of a reserve fuel tank at a thermal power plant owned by the Norilsk-Taimyr Energy Company (which is part of the Norilsk Nickel group of companies), seriously polluting the river Daldykan.

above-listed features of the Arctic have changed significantly due to climate variations, primarily global warming which occurs much faster in this part of the world than elsewhere. This creates numerous new impacts (both negative and positive) on all activities in the Russian Arctic zone, which necessitates additional requirements for state regulation of Arctic redevelopment.[5]

When characterizing natural and climatic threats to the sustainable functioning of the Russian Arctic macro-region, it is necessary to emphasize the increasing systemic (synergetic) effect produced by a *combination* of such impacts, especially on the health of people in the Russian Arctic. Climate change leads to additional mortality (from heat waves and cold waves); increased morbidity, especially from natural focal infectious diseases, due to the spread of pathogens and their carriers to new geographic areas, and bird migration; deteriorating health and quality of life of indigenous small-numbered peoples of the North as hunting and fishing conditions worsen and the number of injuries increases, for example, because of earlier breakup of sea ice (Curtis et al., 2005; McMichael et al., 2003; Revich, 2017; Revich et al., 2016).

The vulnerability of the Russian Arctic's population to the effects of climate change is exacerbated by factors specific to this region as compared to Alaska, northern Canada, Greenland, or Arctic territories of the Scandinavian countries. These factors are associated with a much larger population, the scale of economic activities in this region and their environmental consequences. For example, the Russian Arctic zone is home to 46 cities and towns with a population of 5000 or more people, the world's largest metallurgical plants, mines, mining and processing facilities, collieries, closed nuclear weapons testing grounds, radioactive waste disposal sites and other facilities characterized by a high (or increased) level of environmental pollution (Porfir'ev & Terent'ev, 2016).

The next group of threats to the safe and sustainable development of the Russian Arctic is the *environmental, technological and social risks for its economic development and redevelopment*. They are caused, firstly, by general factors found in other regions of Russia as well (primarily, outdated industrial technologies and obsolete organizational and administrative techniques and resource management systems that fall

---

[5] A detailed description of these processes is presented in the authors' publication: Leksin and Porfir'ev (2017).

behind advanced international standards); secondly, by the peculiarities of economic activities in the Arctic, namely the focal development of the territory and its resources, the wide use of the rotational team method (closely linked with the time-server mentality), excessive concentration of economic and social facilities in a limited area, large distances and insufficient transport accessibility.

However, as Siberian economists rightly emphasize, these "known risks... do not compare with those we will face in the future due to large-scale industrial development of oil and gas resources in the Arctic seas and the growth of transit transport flows" (Silkin et al., 2013). First of all, these are high environmental risks associated with oil and gas field operations in extreme natural and climatic conditions of the Arctic, including accidents and oil spills during offshore production or sea transportation. Such large-scale manmade emergencies during oil and gas production in the Arctic's extreme climate are very likely. This may entail not only financial losses and reputational damage to companies, but also reputational and political risks for countries participating in such oil and gas projects. However, threats to the sustainable development of the RAZ are not limited solely to hydrocarbon production and transportation. Significant geological (given low reliability of the resource base), technological, ecologic, financial, and economic risks also come from the development of rich solid mineral fields in the Russian Arctic, a significant amount of which is concentrated in large deposits of the Norilsk ore region (as evidenced by a large-scale accident at a thermal power plant in Norilsk in May 2020).

Another group of threats to the safe and sustainable development of the RAZ includes *political, legal, and strategic risks* associated with Russia's limited and/or not fully determined rights and jurisdictions in the relevant territories. The main subject of legal discussions is the Arctic shelf, primarily its significant part located between the eastern meridional border and the boundaries of the 200-mile economic zone [this topic is considered separately in another chapter by Daria Boklan "*Channeling of Liability: Shall Arctic States be Liable for Environmental Harm in the Arctic Caused by Navigation or Polluter Pays Principle Should Prevail?*"— ed.]. As for strategic risks, their comparative analysis, carried out in a pioneer work written in the early 2000s jointly by experts from the Russian Academy of Sciences and the Ministry of Emergencies (Vorob'ev, 2005), and later in its updated version (Porfir'ev, 2010), showed that the main problem is an insufficiently justified and/or erroneous choice of priorities for the socioeconomic development of the country. This is directly related to the Arctic. Choosing a proper redevelopment strategy for the Russian Arctic is of paramount importance not only for this macro-region itself, but, given its importance for the country, also for the sustainable development and, in general, for the future of the whole of Russia.

Finally, the same group of risks to the safe and sustainable functioning of the RAZ also includes potential military conflicts. Foreign policy, including military, threats to the security and sustainable functioning of the RAZ are very serious. Nevertheless, in our opinion, priority belongs to the growing "peaceful" challenges and risks associated with Russia's incorporation into the global economic and competitive environment and with budget possibilities to finance the Russian Arctic development program.

RAZ Sustainable Functioning Priorities

The list of priorities for the sustainable functioning of the Russian Arctic zone, adopted in 2013 by the Strategy for the Development of the Arctic Zone of the Russian Federation and National Security for the Period up to 2020, and largely duplicated the following year in the state program Socioeconomic Development of the Arctic Zone of the Russian Federation for the Period up to 2020, determines general directions for RAZ development with a view to addressing its key social, economic, environmental, and ethnonational problems. These priorities are in line with the aforementioned UN 17 sustainable development goals for the period of 2016–2030, adapted to the conditions of the Russian Arctic.

Piling up unresolved and new problems and threats to the safe and sustainable functioning of the RAZ with limited budgetary resources, volatile hydrocarbon prices, ongoing interstate confrontation, climate change and other external and internal restrictions hindering the fulfillment of the tasks set in the adopted strategic documents on the development of the Russian Arctic zone make it necessary to rank and clarify development priorities. These priorities are as follows: in the *social (socioeconomic) sphere*—preserving and improving people's health, including the most vulnerable groups (high-risk groups, such as indigenous small-numbered peoples of the North); in the *economic sphere*—improving the connectivity and reliability of the transport system; efficient power supply to dispersed energy users; facilitating (promoting) investment and production activities of large corporations. Below is the rationale for the listed key tasks to ensure the sustainable functioning of the Russian Arctic zone.

The priority task of *preserving and improving people's health* hardly requires any special arguments. It becomes particularly relevant due to the accelerated (compared to the rest of Russia) climate warming and, accordingly, more serious consequences of this process for the Arctic macro-region. Therefore, the main efforts in solving this task should be focused on a strategy for adapting people to changing natural and climatic conditions. This strategy is implemented in different parts of the Arctic through special regional plans of action.

Such a plan has been developed for the Russian Arctic and is being implemented in the Arkhangelsk Region with the assistance of the WHO Regional Office for Europe (Revich et al., 2016). It contains a set of measures to adapt the health system to the changing climate, taking into account the specific health risks for different age, social and ethnic groups of the population (especially the indigenous small-numbered peoples of the North), a particular area or locality. At the local level, the plan implies developing a set of recommendations for assessing the costs and effects of specific methods for adapting vulnerable populations to different climate change scenarios. For the region as a whole, it calls for improving laboratory facilities of the sanitary service, developing health services in remote areas of the Nenets Autonomous Region, and creating mobile medical units. With regard to heat waves, the plan suggests changing the work schedule of healthcare institutions, temporarily suspending scheduled operations, informing people about the danger of heat waves, paying more attention to certain high-risk groups, such as the elderly and children, and a number of other measures.

Taking into account the recommendations of international experts, particular attention should be paid to small settlements and places of compact residence of indigenous small-numbered peoples of the North, for which the following stages of adaptation are envisaged: (1) assessing known and potential risks associated with environmental changes through traditional environmental knowledge; (2) prioritizing existing and potential threats, including infectious diseases of humans and animals, changes in the state of permafrost, and extreme weather events through monitoring; (3) planning and implementing adaptation measures for certain high-risk population groups, including nomadic families, children, pregnant women, as well as measures to reduce health risks in each of the professional, age and other high-risk categories (Revich et al., 2016).

Among the sustainable economic development priorities, the special importance of *transportation services* for the sustainable functioning of the RAZ is underscored by three factors. Firstly, this territory is mainly an exporting macro-region (the largest supplier of products for export and domestic consumption outside the region), while its internal needs (for equipment, construction materials, food) are met, much more so than in the rest of the country, through deliveries from other Russian regions. Secondly, the connectivity of regions, towns and economic facilities within the RAZ is the lowest in Russia. Thirdly, all available means of transportation and its infrastructure in the RAZ is extremely dependent on unstable and often extreme weather and climatic conditions, which becomes critical due to accelerated climate change.

All policy documents on the development of the RAZ name the *Northern Sea Route (NSR)* as the most important waterway, which already has necessary infrastructure for servicing large-capacity vessels (11 sea and several river ports). This is undoubtedly one of the main guarantees of the sustainable functioning of the RAZ, although the NSR itself is not yet sufficiently connected with the rest of the transport systems in the region and has a number of other problems we considered above.

Restoring the integrated *polar aviation* structure should be considered an undisputed priority in ensuring the sustainable development of the RAZ. Its demolition began more than forty years ago with the abolition of the relevant centralized department and the creation in its place of the Arkhangelsk, Krasnoyarsk, Yakutsk, and Magadan civil aviation administrations. In the 1990s, this process was further exacerbated by the closure of airfields, as a result of which only 10 out of 40 airfields remained in the Murmansk region, 10 out of 33 in the Chukotka Autonomous Region, 11 out of 19 in the Yamalo-Nenets Autonomous Region, etc. Currently, there are just about 70 airfields, heliports and landing sites, mainly unpaved, in the Russian Arctic zone, and the general condition of the fleet is worse than in the rest of Russia. Currently, the hubs in Moscow, St. Petersburg Yekaterinburg, Novosibirsk, Krasnoyarsk, Yakutsk, Salekhard, and Tyumen provide aviation services in the RAZ. The interests of agency (intermediary) organizations play the main role in determining the cost of flights.

Studies indicate that in order to ensure sustainable transportation services in the entire Arctic region, it will be necessary, "to successively connect the largest airport complexes with additional service capacities in the Arctic territories that have the highest industrial potential:

Murmansk—Naryan-Mar—Novy-Urengoy—Norilsk. This corridor could then be extended to Anadyr and Arkhangelsk, because of which six largest Arctic airfields will directly handle 62% of air passengers and 58.3% of freight traffic in the Arctic, bypassing transit facilities in Moscow and the capitals of federal districts... Subsequently, the main advantage of this form of air traffic will become a natural 'Arctic priority,' that is, the delivery of Arctic cargos to Arctic locations using optimal transportation legs. This will minimize dependence on distance, time of cargo handling and connections in 'traditional' transit hubs. As a result, the Arctic will gain greater autonomy" (Nalimov, 2016).

An important task in the safe and sustainable functioning of the RAZ is to ensure *comfortable (technically reliable and economically affordable for all consumers) power supplies*. This is a problem not only of the RAZ, but also of the entire Russian North, which occupies more than 60% of the country's territory and where consumers receive electricity mainly from diesel power plants working on fuel brought in from other regions. In recent years, fuel supplies for these plants (excluding defense facilities) have reached about one million tons per year. The wear and tear and low efficiency of such power plants increase the cost of electricity they produce (15–150 rubles for 1 kWh; in some northern settlements the cost is as high as 300–400 rubles/kWh), which is one of the factors that raise the cost of living in the Russian Arctic and increase budget expenses for subsidies to numerous and diverse consumers of such expensive electricity.

One of the ways to avoid using and replace diesel fuel and coal for power generation is to convert power plants to local "Arctic" fuel—liquefied natural gas (including the construction of standard storage facilities and means of delivery by sea, river, and road). In any case, this will be environmentally and economically more efficient than burning coal and fuel oil. Another option is to use local renewable energy—wind, sun, water (small hydropower solutions), as well as biomass (wood). Many territories of the RAZ (especially on the coast of the Kara Sea) have high wind energy potential. There are many calculations proving its efficiency, especially in the form of wind/diesel power plants. The combined socioeconomic effect of such power supply systems is ensured not only by improved energy security of remote consumers, a 15–20% reduction of energy losses during transportation and distribution by bringing power production facilities closer to consumers, more reliable power supplies, a lower cost of power for the end user, smaller amounts of fuel brought in from other regions, but also by better environmental safety as the amount of harmful emissions and waste (in the form of barrels of fuel) from diesel power plants will decrease (Elistratov & Konishchev, 2014). Wind power plants combined with other renewable energy sources in the RAZ are already under construction. One such example is the Yurta power plant built in the village of Mys Kamenny (Yamal Peninsula). All equipment for it was manufactured in Russia, designed specifically for operation in extreme conditions of the Far North, and is able to withstand temperatures as low as minus 60 °C.

Russia's largest corporations play an extremely important role in ensuring the sustainable functioning and development of the Russian Arctic zone. This is due, firstly, to their substantial financial possibilities, which is particularly important in the absence of sufficient federal budget resources; and secondly, to their high scientific and technological potential, which is a prerequisite for maintaining their competitiveness in the world market. The contribution of the largest Russian companies to ensuring the sustainability of this macro-region will be determined both by broader traditional activities (new projects) and the modernization of existing industries (among other things, in order to reduce negative impacts on the environment and population). This applies primarily to leading national (in some cases, international) companies, such as Gazprom, Rosneft, MMC Norilsk Nickel, NOVATEK, AK Alrosa, and PhosAgro.

Understanding the sustainable development of spatial systems as their sustainable functioning, the characteristics and parameters of such functioning proposed in this chapter, and the rationale for a close connection between security and sustainability in relation to the specific conditions of the Russian Arctic allow making substantial adjustments to the MBO priorities for the integrated development of this macro-region, formulated in the Strategy for the Development of the Arctic Zone of the Russian Federation and National Security for the Period up to 2020 and in the state program Socioeconomic Development of the Arctic Zone of the Russian Federation for the Period up to 2020. The need for such adjustments is long overdue,[6] but it took time to substantiate the grounds for them. In particular, it has become clear that the Arctic policy should

---

[6] The authors presented the rationale and specific proposals for such adjustments in their publications over the past three years, including those listed in the references section of this chapter.

necessarily specify management activities for adaptation to the current and expected large-scale effects of climate change.[7]

In this regard, reducing additional risks to people's health (primarily that of indigenous peoples) from climate change becomes particularly relevant and strategically important as a social priority for the sustainable functioning and development of the RAZ. In addition, without questioning the need for further efforts to build infrastructure and new ships for the Northern Sea Route, the total modernization of inland river routes and polar aviation seems equally important in order to ensure the sustainable functioning of the entire Russian Arctic zone. Another imperative is major improvements ensuring efficient supplies of electric and thermal energy to all consumers without exception, shifting from the use of diesel fuel and coal for these purposes to liquefied natural gas and renewable energy that reduces environmental impacts and climate-related risks. According to specialists from the Center for Energy Efficiency, better energy efficiency and the development of renewable energy production in the RAZ could save up to 100 billion rubles annually and ensure the energy and economic security of these territories.[8]

It must be emphasized that all the above clarifications and adjustments to the RAZ operation priorities are designed to simultaneously ensure safety and enhance stable development of the entire Arctic spatial system. Given budget shortages at all levels and limited access to foreign capital, it seems necessary to accord the most favored treatment status to large national corporations and other commercial structures in order to build new and modernize existing production facilities, transport, and other infrastructure in the RAZ. Similar conditions should be created for enterprises and organizations located in other parts of the country but fulfilling important orders for the needs of the Russian Arctic.

[7] The detailed justification of this provision is given in our paper: Leksin and Porfir'ev (2017).

[8] Analysis of the current situation of isolated power supply systems with high energy costs. Report for discussion: CENEF (2017).

Novelties of State Policy in 2020 and Prospects for Sustainable Development of the RAZ

The most significant steps in the Russian Arctic policy ensuring the sustainable operation of this territory were taken in 2020, when its basic principles (Decree of the President of the Russian Federation of March 5, 2020) (hereinafter referred to as the Fundamental Principles 2020–2035) and the RAZ development strategy for the period up to 2035 (Decree of the President of the Russian Federation of October 26, 2020) (hereinafter referred to as the Strategy 2020–2035) were fundamentally updated. They not so much summed up the results of the previous stage of the state Arctic policy[9] as for the first time outlined a specific program of action for the period up to 2035 for each constituent entity of the Russian Federation and municipality within the RAZ. It is also important that, according to paragraph 26 of the Fundamental Principles 2020–2035, the priority efficiency indicators for the new Arctic policy also include such socially significant parameters as life expectancy at birth in the RAZ, the migration growth rate and unemployment in this territory (calculated in accordance with the ILO methodology), the number of jobs at enterprises in the RAZ and the average salary of their employees, etc., along with such indisputably important indicators as the share of gross regional product (GRP) produced in the RAZ in Russia's total GRP or the share of value added of high-tech and knowledge-intensive sectors in GRP produced in the RAZ.

The Strategy 2020–2035 contains numerical values of these indicators for each stage of the strategy. The increased role of the Russian Arctic in the federal administrative system is emphasized by the fact that according to Article 23 of Fundamental Principles 2020–2035, the overall supervision of Russia's state policy in the Arctic is carried out by the President of the Russian Federation, and, according to Article 38 of the Strategy

---

[9] Article 6 of the Strategy 2020–2035 indicated that life expectancy at birth in the RAZ increased from 70.65 years in 2014 to 72.39 years in 2018; migration from the Arctic zone over the same period decreased by 53%; unemployment (calculated by the ILO methodology) dropped from 5.6% in 2017 to 4.6% in 2019; the share of GRP produced in the RAZ in Russia's total GRP increased from 5% in 2014 to 6.2% in 2018; the volume of cargo transportation in the Northern Sea Route water area grew from 4 million tons in 2014 to 31.5 million tons in 2019; and the share of modern weapons, military and special equipment in the RAZ increased from 41% in 2014 to 59% in 2019.

2020–2035, he also oversees the implementation of this strategic document (earlier, Article 37 of the previous Strategy 2013–2020 just stated that its implementation is overseen by the Government of the Russian Federation). No other macro-region of Russia has so far been under direct presidential supervision.

In the summer of 2020, a federal law was adopted, offering unprecedented state support for entrepreneurial activity in the RAZ (#193-FZ). Its goal was formulated as "economic development, stimulation and reinvigoration of investment and entrepreneurial activity, and the creation of an economic basis for advanced social development and higher quality of life in the RAZ," and its subject in Article 1 is defined as "determining the legal regime of the zone." The law applies free customs zone procedures to the entire RAZ and proclaims it "equated to a special economic zone." The main actor is a RAZ "resident," that is, an individual entrepreneur or a legal entity which is a commercial organization registered in the RAZ and which has concluded an agreement on investment activities in this zone and has been included in the register of its residents.[10] The law introduces an "authorized federal executive body that develops state policy and regulates the development of the RAZ."[11] The law on territories of advanced socioeconomic development in the Russian Federation creates the institution of "Management Company" and its "subsidiaries." Both this body and the management company have been granted broad administrative powers. The law has also established such a new institution as the "public council of the Arctic zone" with various tasks, including the monitoring of interaction between RAZ residents and indigenous small-numbered peoples living in this zone and participating in the development of environmental protection measures.

The same law also provides for numerous economically significant measures of state support for entrepreneurial activity in the RAZ. These include, for example, tax benefits for residents of the zone, reimbursement of part of insurance premiums paid to state extra-budgetary funds and other measures to support these residents, special terms for the provision of land plots and real estate in state or municipal ownership located on

[10] A person who has lost the status of RAZ resident has the right to carry out entrepreneurial activity and dispose at his own discretion of movable and immovable property belonging to him in this zone.

[11] These functions, in principle, should be carried out by the designated federal Ministry for the Development of the Far East and the Arctic.

them, etc. No other macro-region of Russia has ever seen such attention to corporate entities engaged in the redevelopment of the Arctic.

$$* \quad * \quad *$$

Conclusion

Sustainable functioning of the Russian Arctic as a unique spatial system of the highest geostrategic, geoecologic (including geoclimatic), and geoeconomic significance has in recent years been in the focus of Russia's top-level decision-makers. As Russian President Vladimir Putin emphasized in his speech at the International Arctic Forum (Arkhangelsk, March 2017), "We aim to ensure its sustainable development, create a modern infrastructure, develop natural resources, strengthen the industrial potential, improve the quality of life for the indigenous Northern people, maintain their unique culture and traditions and provide government assistance toward these goals. However, these goals must not be viewed separately from the task of preserving the biological diversity and the fragile ecosystems of the Arctic" (Kremnlin.ru).

References

#193-FZ, Federal Law of 13.07.2020. *On state support for entrepreneurial activity in the Arctic zone of the Russian federation*. http://kremlin.ru/acts/bank/45677. Accessed 12 July 2017.

ACIA. (2005). *Arctic climate impact assessment*. Cambridge University Press.

Barber, D. G., Lukovich, J. V., Keogak, J., Baryluk, S., Fortier, L., & Henry, G. H. R. (2008). The changing climate of the Arctic. *Arctic, 61*(1), 7–26.

Bobylev, S. N. (Ed.). (2010). *Doklad o razvitii chelovecheskogo potenciala v Rossijskoj Federacii 2010 Celi razvitiya tysyacheletiya v Rossii: vzglyad v budushchee* [Russian federation human development report 2010 millennium development goals in Russia: A look into the future]. PROON.

Brundtland, G. H. (Ed.). (1987). *Our common future: Report of the World Commission on environment and development*. Oxford University Press.

Carson, M., & Peterson, G. (Eds.). (2016). *Arctic resilience report*. Arctic Council.

CENEF. (2017). *Discussion paper*. TSENEF. http://www.cenef.ru/file/Discussion_paper1.pdf. Accessed 1 July 2017.

Curtis, T., Kvernmo, S., & Bjerregaard, P. (2005). Changing living conditions, life style and health. *International Journal of Circumpolar Health, 64*(5), 442–450.

Decree of the President of the Russian Federation of December 31. (2015). *#683 "On the national security strategy of the Russian federation"*. http://base.gar ant.ru/71296054/#ixzz4k3hldXk7. Accessed 12 July 2017.

Decree of the President of the Russian Federation of March 5. (2020). *#164 "On the basic principles of state policy of the Russian federation in the Arctic for the period up to 2035"*. https://garant.ru/products/ipo/prime/doc/736 06526/. Accessed 12 July 2017.

Decree of the President of the Russian Federation of May 12. (2009). *#537 "On the national security strategy of the Russian federation up to 2020"*. /Sobraniye zakonodatelstva rossiiskoi federatsii, 2009, # 20, Article 2444.

Decree of the President of the Russian Federation of May 13. (2017). *#208 "On the national security strategy of the Russian federation."*/ Sobraniye zakonodatelstva rossiiskoi federatsii, 2009, # 20, Article 2902.

Decree of the President of the Russian Federation of October 26. (2020). *#645 "On the strategy for the development of the Arctic zone of the Russian federation and national security for the period up to 2035"*. https://garant.ru/products/ipo/prime/doc/74710556/. Accessed 12 July 2017.

Derocher, A. E., Lunn, N. J., & Stirling, I. (2004). Polar bears in a warming climate. *Integrative and Comparative Biology, 44*(2), 163–176.

Drinkwater, K. F. (2011). The influence of climate variability and change on the ecosystems of the Barents sea and adjacent waters: Review and synthesis of recent studies from the NESSAS project. *Progress in Oceanography, 90*, 47–61.

Drinkwater, K. F., Beaugrand, G., Kaeriyama, M., Kim, S., Ottersen, G., Perry, R. I., Pörtner, H. O., Polovina, J. J., & Takasuka, A. (2010). On the processes linking climate to ecosystem changes. *Journal of Marine Systems, 79*(3–4), 374–388.

Elistratov, V. V., & Konishchev, M. A. (2014). Vetro-dizel'nye elektrostancii dlya avtonomnogo energosnabzheniya severnyh territorij Rossii [Wind-diesel power plants for autonomous power supply to the northern territories of Russia]. *Al'ternativnaya energetika i ekologiya, 11*(151), 62–70.

Emery, F. E. (1981). *Systems thinking: Selected readings* (Revised ed.). Penguin Modern Management Readings.

Folke, C. (2006). Resilience: The emergence of a perspective for social–ecological systems analyses. *Global Environmental Change, 15* (3), 253–267.

Forbes, B. C. (2008). Equity, vulnerability and resilience in social-ecological systems: A contemporary example from the Russian Arctic. *Research in Social Problems and Public Policy, 15*, 203–236.

Forbes, D. L. (Ed.). (2011). *State of the Arctic coast 2010: Scientific review and outlook.* International Arctic Science Committee, Land-Ocean Interactions in the Coastal Zone, Arctic Monitoring and Assessment Programme, International Permafrost Association, Helmholtz-Zentrum

Hinzman, L. D., Deal, C. J., McGuire, A. D., Mernild, S. H., Polyakov, I. V., & Walsh, J. E. (2013). Traectory of the Arctic as an integrated system. *Ecological Applications, 23*(8), 1837–1868. https://doi.org/10.1890/11-1498.1

Hof, A. R., Jansson, R., & Nilsson, C. (2015). *Future of biodiversity in the Barents region.* TemaNord.

Kaplan, J. O., Bigelow, N. H., Prentice, I. C., Harrison, S. P., Bartlein, P. J., Christensen, T. R., Cramer, W., Matveyeva, N. V., McGuire, A. D., Murray, D. F., Razzhivin, V. Y., Smith, B., Walker, D. A., Anderson, P. M., Andreev, A. A., Brubaker, L. B., Edwards, M. E., & Lozhkin, A. V. (2003). Climate change and Arctic ecosystems: Modeling, paleodata-model comparisons, and future projections. Journal of Geophysical Research 108, D19:8171.

Kattsov, V., Ryabinin, V., Overland, J., Serreze, M., Visbeck, M., Walsh, J., Meier, W., & Zhang, X. (2010). Arctic sea ice change: A grand challenge of climate science. *Journal of Glaciology, 56*(200), 1115–1121.

Kremlin.ru. *Vladimir Putin took part in the plenary meeting of the IV International Arctic Forum "The Arctic: Territory of dialogue".* http://kremlin.ru/events/president/news/54149. Accessed 12 July 2017.

Larsen, J. N., Anisimov, O. A., Constable, A., Hollowed, A. B., Maynard, N., Prestrud, P., Prowse, T. D., & Stone, J. M. R. (2014). Polar regions. In V. R. Barros, C. B. Field, D. J. Dokken, M. D. Mastrandrea, K. J. Mach, T. E. Bilir, M. Chatterjee, K. L. Ebi, Y. O. Estrada, R. C. Genova, B. Girma, E. S. Kissel, A. N. Levy, S. MacCracken, P. R. Mastrandrea, & L. L. White (Eds.), *Climate change 2014: Impacts, adaptation, and vulnerability.* Part B: Regional aspects. Contribution of working group II to the fifth assessment report of the intergovernmental panel on climate change (pp 1567–1612). Cambridge University Press.

Leksin, V. N., & Porfir'ev, B. N. (2016). *Gosudarstvennoe upravlenie razvitiem Arkticheskoj zony Rossijskoj Federacii* [State management of the development of the Arctic zone of the Russian federation]. Nauchnyj konsul'tant.

Leksin, V. N., & Porfir'ev, B. N. (2017). Specifika transformacii prostranstvennoj sistemy i strategii pereosvoeniya rossijskoj Arktiki v usloviyah izmeneniya klimata [Specificity of the transformation of the spatial system and the strategy of redevelopment of the Russian Arctic in the context of climate change]. *Ekonomika regiona, 3,* 641–657.

McMichael, A. J. Campbell-Lendrum, D. H., Corvalán, C. F., Ebi, K. L., Githeko, A. K., Scheraga, J. D., & Woodward, A. (Eds.). (2003). *Climate change and human health: Risks and responses.* WHO.

Morgunov, B. A. (Ed.). (2011). *Diagnosticheskij analiz sostoyaniya okruzhayushchej sredy Arkticheskoj zony Rossijskoj Federacii (Rasshirennoe rezyume)* [Diagnostic analysis of the state of the environment in the Arctic zone of the Russian Federation (Extended summary)]. Nauchnyj mir.

Nalimov, P. A. (2016). Perspektivy edinoj Arkticheskoj transportnoj sistemy [Prospects for a unified Arctic transport system]. In V. V. Ivanter (Ed.), *Arkticheskoe prostranstvo Rossii v XXI veke: faktory razvitiya, organizaciya upravleniya* [Arctic space of Russia in the XXI century: Factors of development, management organization] (pp. 953–977). Nauka.

Pachauri, R. K., & Meyer, L. A. (Eds.). (2014). *Climate change 2014: Synthesis report*. Contribution of Working Groups I, II and III to the Fifth Assessment Report of the Intergovernmental Panel on Climate Change Core Writing Team. IPCC.

Porfir'ev, B. N. (Ed.). (2010). *Strategicheskie riski razvitiya Rossii: ocenka i prognoz. Sb. nauchnyh trudov*. Institut ekonomiki RAN.

Porfir'ev, B. N., & Terent'ev, N. E. (2016). *Ekologo-klimaticheskie riski social'no-ekonomicheskogo razvitiya Arkticheskoj zon Rossijskoj Federacii* [Ecological and climatic risks of socio-economic development of the Arctic zones of the Russian Federation]. *Ekologicheskij vestnik Rossii, 1*, 44–51.

Porohin, A. V., Porohina, E. V., Soina-Kutishcheva, Y. U. N., & Baryl'nikov, V. V. (2014). Ustojchivost' kak opredelyayushchaya harakteristika sostoyaniya social'no-ekonomicheskoj sistemy [Stability as a defining characteristic of the state of the socio-economic system]. *Fundamental'nye issledovaniya, 12*(4), 816–821.

Post E., Forchhammer, M. C., Bret-Harte, M. S., Callaghan, T. V., Christensen, T. R., Elberling, B., Fox, A., & Gilg, O., David, H., Toke, H., & Rolf, I. M. S., Erik, J., David, K., Jesper, M., McGuire, A., Søren, R., Schindler, D., Stirling, I., Tamstorf, M., Aastrup, P. (2009). Ecological Dynamics Across the Arctic Associated with Recent Climate Change. *Science*, 325 (5946), 1355–1358. https://doi.org/10.1126/science.1173113

Rammel, C., Stagl, S., & Wilfing, H. (2007). Managing complex adaptive systems—A co-evolutionary perspective on natural resource management. *Ecological Economics, 63*(1), 9–21. https://doi.org/10.1016/j.eco lecon.2006.12.014

Revich, B. A. (2017). Determinants of public health in Arctic and Subarctic territories of Russia. *Studies on Russian Economic Development, 1*, 39–47.

Revich, B. A., Har'kova, T. L., Kvasha, E .A., Bogoyavlenskij, D. D., Korovkin, A. G., & Korolev, I. B. (2016). *Demograficheskie processy, dinamika trudovyh resursov i riski zdorov'yu naseleniya Evropejskoj chasti Arkticheskoj zony Rossii* [Demographic processes, dynamics of labor resources and health risks of the population of the European part of the Arctic zone of Russia]. LENAND.

Schaefer, K., Lantuit, H., Romanovsky, V., & Schuur, E. A. G. (2012). *Policy implications of Warming Permafrost*. United Nations Environment Programme Special Report.

Silkin, V. Y. U., Tokarev, A. N., & Shmat, V. V. (2013). Osvoenie Arktiki: vremya riskovat'? [Arctic exploration: Time to take risks?]. *EKO, 4*, 27–55.

Swann, A. L., Fung, I. Y., Levis, S., Bonan, G., & Doney, S. (2010). Changes in Arctic vegetation induce high-latitude warming through the greenhouse effect. *Proceedings of the National Academy of Sciences of the United States of America, 107*(4), 1295–1300.

The Economist. (2012, June 16). *Cold comfort: Special report: The Arctic*.

Vorob'ev, Y. U. L. (Ed.). (2005). *Strategicheskie riski Rossii: ocenka i prognoz* [Strategic risks of Russia: Assessment and forecast]. Delovoj ekspress.

Corporations in the Russian Arctic—From Dominance to Leadership

Valeriy A. Kryukov and Vladimir I. Nefedkin

INTRODUCTION

Russia and other countries have been developing Arctic resources for several decades; they have gained practical experience of implementing large-scale projects and established fairly stable research approaches toward assessing their economic effectiveness, social and environmental impacts. At the same time, the practice of developing Arctic resources in Russia is largely based on stereotypes that date back to the 1930s and the 1950s, a period of forced industrialization and focal development of natural resources. The unconditional priority of that time was the development of unique mineral resources (hydrocarbons, precious metals, polymetallic ores, and diamonds)—from extraction to transportation—as quickly as possible and at almost any cost. Economic effects and social and environmental impacts of such projects were largely overlooked by the "organizers of Soviet industry." Changes in post-Soviet Russia

V. A. Kryukov (✉) · V. I. Nefedkin
Institute of Economics and Industrial Engineering, Siberian Branch of the Russian Academy of Sciences, Novosibirsk, Russia

V. A. Kryukov
Higher School of Economics, Moscow, Russia

© The Author(s), under exclusive license to Springer Nature Singapore Pte Ltd. 2022
A. Likhacheva (ed.), *Arctic Fever*,
https://doi.org/10.1007/978-981-16-9616-9_7

after the privatization of major resource development facilities shifted the emphasis but did not change the paradigm. A new generation of "effective managers" is concerned primarily with the current task of maximizing financial results and with super-intensive use of assets, a significant part of which was created in Soviet times. As a result, sustainable development tasks are solved for the most part "virtually" in the form of colorful but insipid corporate reports, containing generalized indicators that have little in common with the real state of affairs in concrete localities.

Increased attention to the place and role of the Arctic both in the economy and in the current geopolitical situation, in our opinion, requires a critical reevaluation of previous and existing approaches in order to develop new methods based on best foreign practices and international standards for sustainable development, as well as best domestic practices.

In our study, large companies engaged in the extraction and processing of natural resources are considered as key actors (players) in the development of the Arctic. Their interaction among themselves and with other project participants is analyzed in the context of different approaches to the development of Arctic natural resources. We have put emphasis on the contours of a new organizational and economic mechanism that could ensure effective interaction and coordination of the interests of key actors with other participants, which are directly or indirectly involved in developing new resource territories or utilizing existing extractive capacities, and which have reached the stage of maturity and are beginning to cut their production volumes. An organizational and economic mechanism in this case will mean the established formal and informal rules of interaction between participants (players), their mutual obligations, and special conditions for the distribution of costs and benefits generated by projects.

LARGE COMPANIES AS KEY PLAYERS IN THE ARCTIC

In the new institutional economic theory, pooling of resources within one organization is seen as an alternative to market coordination through the price mechanism. Therefore, the participation of a large company in a project limits the market, that is, the price mechanism of resource allocation. According to R. Kouz, "all segments of the economy where the allocation of resources does not depend directly on the price mechanism could be brought together into one firm" (Kouz, 1995, p. 23).

How justified is the replacement of the market mechanism (external transactions) with intra-company coordination in Arctic conditions? The latter include remoteness from the main centers of economic activity (places where goods and services are provided for the implementation of projects, as well as places where the obtained raw materials and semi-products are sold); a closed (localized) nature of the economic systems within which projects are implemented; seasonality and significant time gaps during the implementation of individual stages of projects; unique natural and geocryological conditions; a significant period of the anthropogenic "aftermath" of previous projects for the environment and living conditions of the indigenous small-numbered peoples of the North, etc.

In general, the existence of companies and their growing ambitions are based on the possibility of reducing transaction costs and minimizing uncertainty by planning future transactions. According to Kouz, all other things being equal, firstly, the lower a company's costs and the slower these costs increase as transactions multiply, the bigger the company will be. This condition ensures the possibility of achieving economy of scale. Obviously, in the Arctic, this possibility can be realized through participation in large and/or unique natural resource development projects attractive for business. Secondly, the fewer mistakes an entrepreneur makes and the slower the number of such mistakes grows as transactions multiply, the bigger the company will be. Due to the above circumstances, the price of mistakes (environmental and socioeconomic) in the Arctic is significantly higher than in projects implemented in regions with a high level of business activity. But at the same time, according to Kouz, "an organization's costs and losses due to erroneous decisions will increase as transactions expand and diversify, and the likelihood of relevant price changes grows" (Kouz, 1995, p. 23). "Expansion of transactions" means in this case greater transaction costs, which may override other benefits from participation in a large project. In the Arctic, the probability that market costs (transaction costs) will exceed corporate expenses (internal coordination costs) is significantly higher than anywhere else. This theoretical conclusion explains the desire of companies to internalize external transactions and use internal coordination in projects implemented in the Arctic and in similar conditions. It is this factor that is the cause of and the reason for the relatively high degree of isolation of Arctic projects. This results in the expansion of companies. It should also be borne in mind that technological advances promoting spatial convergence of factors of production spur companies to grow in size. For example, the development of communication technologies reduces management costs, which also contributes to the growth of companies.

We can conclude, therefore, that large businesses have certain advantages in the implementation of large-scale resource development projects in the Arctic in comparison with small and medium-sized businesses. This is true not only of the "pinpoint" effect determined by the possibility of reducing specific costs (saving on semi-fixed costs), but also of the spatial (agglomeration) effect. Since such projects are usually implemented in compact areas (focal development) remote from business centers, they also involve the creation of necessary life support systems. Large companies in this case can benefit further from the concentration of factors of production by using the engineering and social infrastructure they create.

The listed advantages of large companies and their natural desire to create vertically integrated production structures for economic activities in the Arctic do not mean that the results of their operation will satisfy other players that are also project participants and beneficiaries. There are many examples where the economic success of large corporations leads to devastating environmental and social consequences (externalities) for third parties. The attractiveness of ambitious Arctic projects for large companies and their ability to use existing factors of production more effectively do not guarantee that the creation of large, vertically integrated industries in the Arctic will unconditionally benefit all interested parties. What is good for large corporations is not always good for other participants. As O. Williamson notes, "there is no reason to conclude that the observed development of vertical integration is not excessive in terms of social well-being" (Williamson, 1995, p. 52). This largely explains the emergence and evolvement of discourse on the imperative of sustainable economic development as an alternative to the "irresponsible" behavior of natural resources companies.

Sustainable Development and Arctic Projects

The term "sustainable development," which had originally emerged from a rather narrow environmental agenda, eventually acquired a broader economic and social meaning. This can be seen from how the list of so-called sustainable development goals (SDGs) expanded over time. The current list of SDGs (UN SDG Indicator) achievement indicators includes indicators characterizing not only the state of the global ecosystem, but also the safety of people, youth employment, poverty reduction, mitigation of various types of discrimination, and overcoming of social and economic inequalities. After the UN conference in Rio de Janeiro (1992), active work began to devise sustainable development indicators for assessing the degree of development sustainability in time for the whole world, individual countries, and companies. Similar indicators are proposed in the World Bank's annual World Development Indicators report (World Bank, 2020).

The term "sustainable development" is increasingly applied not only to global and national ecosystems, but also to inland regions within the same national jurisdictions. Methods and indicators have been developed for calculating environmental and economic indices for Russian regions (Bobylev et al., 2012).

Large companies also act as sustainable development agents, primarily companies operating in the resource sector and creating the greatest risks to the eco-social environment. The UN Report on Sustainable Development Goals for 2020 says, "Since 2017, the overall quality of sustainability reports has improved around the world. The share of reporting in the environmental, social, and institutional and governance dimensions that is aligned with the minimum requirements outlined in SDG indicator 12.6.1 (the number of companies publishing sustainability reports) has almost doubled. However, in many of the companies' reports, certain critical aspects of environmental, social and governance domains were hardly mentioned" (SDGs Report, 2020, p. 49).

With regard to Arctic territories, sustainable development, in our view, should be interpreted not only in the context of preserving the natural environment, sensitive to anthropogenic impacts, and the traditional way of life and economic activity of local peoples in the territories of traditional exploitation of natural resources, but also from the point of view of overcoming territorial inequality through both an equitable distribution of value added (rent) derived from the use of unique Arctic resources, and spatial accessibility of social services. The sustainable development of the Arctic should be considered in connection with the need to continuously increase the social value of economic results in the near and distant future. In this sense, future generations are also engaged in Arctic projects. One cannot fail to note, for example, the position assumed on these issues by Walter Hickel, Governor of Alaska in the 1960s and the 1990s, and how he defended it (Hickel, 2002).

Awareness of the common and distinctive characteristics of the Arctic economy was the result of efforts by many researchers and practitioners from various countries. For example, the first official report on the Arctic human dimension noted the following key features (AHDR, 2004, pp. 69–80):

- While the development of natural resources creates considerable wealth, these resources are mainly supplied to markets outside the Arctic region;
- Extracted resources generally belong to external owners of capital (corporations) which control daily operations and profits.
- Corporations' activities ruin the traditional way of natural resource management, leaving the costs for the territories concerned to deal with.

The aforementioned features create spatial asymmetries between costs and benefits. A relatively small part of the income and profits from projects implemented by these corporations in the Arctic stays in the region, while the bulk goes to the main beneficiaries outside it. At the same time, costs (environmental and social) remain in the Arctic.

Due to the remoteness of most Arctic regions, the total production and transport costs are much higher compared to those outside the Arctic. As a result, high costs do not allow Arctic manufacturers to compete with non-Arctic producers for whom economic factors are more accessible and less expensive. This causes the Arctic's asymmetry in the global economy: the export of raw materials in large volumes to highly developed regions and the import of most finished products for domestic needs. General peculiarities of the Arctic economy are fully applicable to projects implemented in the Russian Arctic. However, institutional and economic mechanisms vary considerably from country to country. What makes Russia distinct in this regard is primarily high inertia and numerous approaches that were adopted in the 1930s and the 1950s.

Combines

Industrial trust companies and syndicates created during the NEP period—relatively independent production and marketing enterprises— could not solve mobilization production tasks related to the development of natural resources and large-scale industrialization in the 1930s–1939. Soviet researcher of the North and head of the Commission on the Problems of the North S.V. Slavin noted that "oasitic development in a natural and economic environment characteristic of northern regions has brought to life special forms and methods of development management, which earlier, before the national economic councils were created in 1957, were in stark contrast to the established methods and forms of national economic management in the habitable southern regions of the country. These are territorial transport-industrial and industrial-transport combines" (Slavin, 1961, p. 46).

The concept of combines is based on N.N. Kolosovsky's theory proclaiming the efficiency of energy production cycles (EPC) as a basis for cooperative operation of different industries. The EPC was understood as "a set of production processes consistently deployed in an economic region of the USSR by combining this type of energy with resources, from primary forms—extraction and refinement of raw materials—to the production of all types of finished products, which can be made locally by bringing production to the sources of raw materials and energy and the rational use of all of their components" (Kolosovskij, 1958, p. 144).

In 1931, the XVI Congress of the All-Union Communist Party (Bolsheviks) set the task of creating the Ural-Kuznetsk Combine, which became the largest coal and metallurgical base in the east of the country and played an important strategic role during the Great Patriotic War. Starting in 1932, several organizations responsible for infrastructure development and construction in the Arctic were created during the following few years: GlavSevMorput, Dalstroy, SevVostLag, and PechoraLag. In 1935, the Council of People's Commissars of the USSR adopted the Decree "On the Construction of the Norilsk Combine" and on the re-subordination of Norilskstroy to the NKVD. The plant was built by Norillag prisoners transferred to Norilsk from Solovetsky prison camps (GULAG: Jekonomika prinuditel'nogo truda, 2008).

The efficiency of combines in a mobilization economy was determined by the possibility of combining significant resources and powers with an integrated approach to solving infrastructure problems, by "attachment" to a certain territory and the use of almost free forced labor with minimal expenses on social infrastructure. The combines ensured the integration of the Arctic economy at all stages of its operation into the "generally accepted industrial mode" (from engineering solutions to resettlement schemes), while ignoring the economic conditions of the indigenous small-numbered peoples of the North.

The historical limitations and low social efficiency (with complete disregard for environmental requirements) of combines geared toward obtaining necessary resources for the country at any cost were obvious to certain scholars and practitioners. For example, in his works, afore-mentioned Slavin S.V. called for reforming the management system in the northern territories. According to historian Kalemeneva E.A., "while formerly economists described the Far North exclusively through the lens of its resource potential, starting in the mid-1950s, Slavin rethought the idea of the North's peculiarity to speak of the need for increased attention to the local population and an appropriate level of comfort in the region" (Kalemeneva, 2018, p. 194).

In a broader sense, the main negative consequence of socialist combines was the lack of conditions for the subsequent development of the Arctic economy when the exploitation of its unique resources would move into more advanced stages. These stages are characterized not only by a high degree of reserve depletion at the best mining and geological deposits, but also by the need to employ other mining technologies and, most importantly, other forms of coordination and cooperation among all interested stakeholders. In the absence of such "tuning," previously created production facilities and transport infrastructure can no longer serve as development drivers and bases for the implementation of ongoing and new projects for the development of resources in the Arctic.

From Combines to Private Corporations

Since the early 1990s, key players in the Arctic have been making a transition, largely spontaneously, from Soviet combines to transregional and transnational corporations (Korostelev, 2008).

This transition has the following features:

- privatization of combines on general principles with uncertain long-term obligations regarding previous environmental damage;
- lack of procedures and mechanisms ensuring real participation of regions and local communities in solving Arctic development problems;

- financial and economic policy of "key players" that prioritize current marginal efficiency and maximize dividends rather than solving long-overdue environmental and social problems;
- high payoffs from the sale of extracted primary resources, preparation and simple refining (processing) of raw materials;
- focus on the acquisition and use of cutting-edge knowledge, imported technologies, and equipment. Low connectivity with other sectors and economic activities both nationally and in regions that used to be key territories for the development of the North and the Arctic;
- extremely small expenditures on science and domestic advanced technologies and solutions;
- regions and municipalities have no real rights and powers to grant licenses for the use of natural resources.

Nowadays, two main models of organizing interaction between Arctic project participants exist in Russia. The first one is the paternalistic model, dating back to the era of socialist combines, which is based on the dominance of the state represented by the federal authorities and on the so-called cooperation agreements. Although the monitoring of these agreements was included in the Unified Action Plan for the Implementation of the Fundamental Principles of State Policy of the Russian Federation in the Arctic for the Period up to 2035 and the Strategy for the Development of the Arctic Zone of the Russian Federation and National Security for the Period up to 2035 (Resolution #996-r, 2021), their legal force is more than conditional. The second model is based on the principles of co-participation and, taking into account foreign and domestic experiences, seems to be more progressive. It implies co-participation of regions and local communities in the implementation of projects through the supply of various goods and services, including as part of auxiliary and complementary economic activities.

However, the current Russian practice leans more on the first approach and focuses on making key decisions at the federal level. Its imperative is "efficiency." The quotation marks in this case emphasize the predominantly narrow understanding of this term, which means current marginal efficiency; transparency relates only to the production segment, and manageability refers to the simplicity and visibility of the processes that are implemented as part of such projects.

The current Russian model historically gravitates toward the paternalistic approach that implies the adoption of key decisions at the federal level. Its peculiarities are genetically determined and inherited from the socialist period. These include a short investment phase of projects, a constant shortage of all factors and conditions for the implementation of projects and, as a result, delayed resolution of problems to ensure the sustainable socio-ecologic and economic functioning of pioneer development territories. This model is also characterized by the absence of economic and legal mechanisms for the abolition of previous production facilities and the reclamation of territories under them. Other countries use so-called liquidation funds for this purpose. Russia, as is known, has no such mechanism. In 2015, the Russian government debated the bill "On the Liquidation Funds of Subsoil Users," but the Ministry of the Environment decided to postpone the decision on this issue until 2019 (Neftegaz.ru., 2019). Meanwhile, the need for the decommissioning of previous capacities becomes increasingly urgent in a number of Arctic regions, including the Norilsk industrial region, the Timan-Pechora region, Yamal, and northeastern Russia. Arctic clean-up activities have so far been relatively small in scale and deal only with the visible damage that can be remedied through the traditional collection and disposal of recyclables and debris from previous business activities. Therefore, it can be stated that the paternalistic model of socialist combines, even in its modernized form, obviously does not correspond to sustainable development goals. The Arctic requires different approaches to organizing interaction between stakeholders, taking into account, above all, the peculiarities of Arctic projects and the Arctic economy.

High revenues from the export of primary products and the absence of mechanisms and procedures for repairing previous damage inflicted by project activities ensure the sustainability of this model despite loose integration with other industries and economic activities. While previous combines were designed to address national priorities, the current mechanism aims to address fiscal challenges and maximize the benefits of private shareholders. For example, the Yamal LNG projects, as well as projects related to the development of the Norilsk region and the northeast of the country are almost not connected via production and technological cooperation with central and southern Siberia and the east of Russia as a whole. Combined with the extremely low expenditures on science and domestic advanced technologies in the field of resource extraction and processing, this greatly undermines possibilities for the sustainable operation of the

Russian economy as a whole. Norilsk Nickel and Yamal LNG mainly use the services of equipment suppliers from the Republic of Korea, Germany, and Norway. Russian contractors for the most part perform civil works and supply auxiliary and supporting equipment.

Corporate policies are largely determined by dividend payments. For example, Norilsk Nickel allocates a significant and increasingly large part of its proceeds from sales for the payment of dividends (see Fig. 1).

Excessively large dividends mean, in fact, deferred payments related to the environment and "historical costs" which should be included in these companies' expenses. Restoring justice in this matter through hands-on management, such as the fine paid by Norilsk Nickel as compensation for the damage caused by a diesel fuel spill in the summer of 2020, is quite spectacular, but is hardly effective for the affected region. Of 146.2 billion rubles paid by the company in fine by court order, an unprecedented amount for Russia, 145.4 billion rubles were paid as compensation for the damage to water bodies and went to the federal budget, and 684.9 million rubles, i.e., less than 0.5%, went to the municipal budget of Norilsk as "compensation for the damage to the soil" (RBC, 2021).

At the same time, some of the companies operating in the Russian Arctic can be considered sustainable development leaders. These include the Canadian company Kinross Gold, operating in Russia since 1995. The

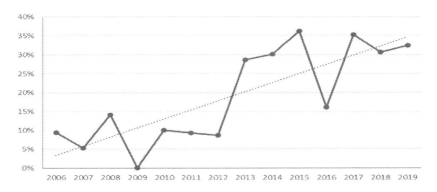

Fig. 1 Dividends to consolidated proceeds from sales for the entire Norilsk Nickel Group of companies in 2006–2019 (*Source* The authors' calculations and Norilsk Nickel annual statements https://www.nornickel.ru/investors/disclosure/annual-reports/. Accessed 20 June 2021)

company has been consistently and proactively applying the principles of sustainable development from the very start of the Dome gold mining project (Chukotka Autonomous Region). Its total accumulated investments are estimated at $3.5 billion. The company uses state-of-the-art technologies for mining, territory development, and environmental safety approaches. Kinross Gold is one of the largest employers in the region. Most of its workers are residents of the Magadan Region and Chukotka. The Dome mine employs about 1500 people in two four-week shifts. The company also provides indirect employment and the opportunity to conduct business as part of auxiliary and related economic activities.

Embeddedness vs Social Responsibility

The Russian and international experience of large projects is replete with examples when the interests of key players contradicted the interests of the local population and caused serious social and environmental problems. The priority of narrow corporate and, above all, financial and economic goals, combined with the possibility of obtaining significant rental income, leads to well-known consequences, thoroughly described in the literature, that are barely consistent with the sustainable development goals in the relevant territories. In this case, the economic power of large corporations should be limited by institutional mechanisms such as corporate social responsibility (CSR) as an institutional alternative to government regulation that implements Kouz-type transactions between corporations and their stakeholders (Polishchuk). However, the CSR mechanism has not yet yielded the expected results in Russia. As noted above, agreements signed by and between large companies and the authorities do not have the force of law and therefore often are not fully implemented or not implemented at all.

Direct coercion by the government toward participation in the development of territories in many cases discourages businesses and cannot be considered a solution. In our opinion, it would be more reasonable to follow the principle of corporate inclusion or embeddedness. According to M. Heidenreich, the potential for the embeddedness of transnational corporations is determined by the fact that they combine the benefits of global strategies with inclusion in heterogeneous social and, most importantly, national contexts. This integration contributes to the innovation of transnational corporations by facilitating their access to external resources and competencies and coordinates their actions with internal and external actors (Heidenreich, 2012). In social sciences, embeddedness is associated with the names of K. Polan'i (2002) and M. Granovetter (2002) and characterized by the dependence of a phenomenon (individual, organization, a set of relations, or a sphere of activity) on its environment and social ties (Jozsa, 2016). Therefore, corporate embeddedness in this context is not social responsibility (through Kouz-type voluntary transactions) or coercion toward localization through government regulation. Embeddedness may imply the integration of a division (subsidiary) of a corporation into the local environment and inspire actions aimed both at creating and redistributing value added (Belyavskiy, 2020, p. 168). In our opinion, the concept of embeddedness can be extended not only to transnational, but also to Russian (transregional) corporations engaged in Arctic projects.

Pitfalls and Success Formula

What needs to be done in order to adopt modern principles and approaches facilitating interaction among all participants? Firstly, regions should participate in determining conditions for the development and use of natural resources. Russia has a constitutional rule or principle—Article 72 of the Constitution—which allows this. Secondly, regulators should determine adequate deductions to regional budgets for the use of subsoil and natural resources. Thirdly, it is necessary to adopt a set of conditions for the use of domestically manufactured equipment, as well as the development of technologies and acquisition of new knowledge. Indigenous communities should have an opportunity to participate in discussing, determining, and developing forms of co-participation in various auxiliary and supporting activities under resource development projects. This participation should not be limited to some form of financial support only.

From the point of view of modern approaches, it is absurd when one company is fully responsible for the entire field. The world practice is to create consortia or alliances of companies that jointly participate in development, thus reducing risks and ensuring the search for technologies and transfer of knowledge. Unfortunately, one of such agreements between Norilsk Nickel and Russian Platinum did not take place, although it was initiated and supported by the President of Russia, and the two companies signed a letter of intent in his presence, stating their willingness to conclude such an agreement. These practices and approaches should be pursued more actively. This will require amendments to the relevant legislation governing the provision and development of a wide range of technical, scientific, and industrial services.

There are many "pitfalls" in building potential leader companies. Excessive fascination with the possibilities of digitalization also poses great dangers. Recently adopted amendments to the Russian Law "On Subsoil" provide for holding electronic auctions for the right to use subsoil areas (Federal Law #123-FZ, 2021). However, granting the right to use subsoil resources is not the same as selling movable property, securities, or other financial assets. It means handing over national resources for long-term use, which is usually stipulated by a whole range of non-financial conditions and obligations. Such a method of "digital" administration undermines the very foundations of resource exploitation on the basis of sustainable development.

Unfortunately, at present, a narrow fiscal understanding of the role of foreign companies in Russian resource development projects prevails. There are examples of effective and responsible participation of foreign companies in joint projects with Russia, including those based on production sharing agreements. One such example is the Sakhalin-2: due to this project, the region's budget has increased several-fold, and Russia (Gazprom) has obtained access to new technologies, thus commissioning its first-ever offshore gas production platform. It is important that the project operator Sakhalin Energy has established a regular dialogue with the interested parties. In particular, during the preparation of the Sustainable Development Report for 2019, two rounds of interactive meetings were held, during which representatives of stakeholders could address questions to company officials and get answers, as well as express their opinion on the importance of a particular aspect of the company's activities. In addition, when preparing the report, the company took into account the results of regular media monitoring, annual public opinion surveys, and the analysis of messages sent to the company (Sakhalin Energy, 2019).

Nevertheless, there are also negative examples. The Singapore trading company Trafigura Group, which does not have oil production competencies, has been declared a foreign partner of the large-scale Vostok-Oil project, but its share in the project was acquired through borrowing in the Russian market (Farchy & Hoffman, 2021). As a result, Russia has not received either funding, or technology, or new practices that could be used for the sustainable development of the territories involved in the project.

In Lieu of Conclusion

Companies focused on social and eco-economic sustainability do not come into being all by themselves. Corporate sustainable development reports do not yet prove that businesses are really making great efforts and ready to invest. Such a line of socially responsible behavior in the Russian Arctic can be formed only through interaction between the government, society and the business community. Designating a certain company as a leader is not so much a statement of its compliance with some metrics that characterize the scale of activity and financial and economic results, as an indicator of its success in creating approaches and procedures that provide advanced solutions to the problems described above. The creation of such companies will require major changes to institutional rules, including the drafting and implementation of new regulatory acts at the federal and regional levels.

References

AHDR. (2004). *Arctic human development report*. Stefansson Arctic Institute.

Belyavskiy, B. (2020). Social embeddedness as a business goal: New theoretical implications from the case of a global value chain. *Journal of Economic Sociology, 21*(3), 151–172.

Bobylev, S. N., Minakov, V. S., Solovyeva, S. V., & Tretyakov, V. V. (2012). *Ekologo-ekonomicheskiy index regionov Rossii* [Eco-economical index of Russian regions]. https://wwf.ru/upload/iblock/dc8/index.pdf. Accessed 28 July 2021.

Farchy, J., & Hoffman, A. (2021). Trafigura got $7 billion Russian loan for Arctic oil deal. *Bloomberg*. https://www.bloomberg.com/news/articles/2021-01-05/trafigura-s-arctic-oil-bet-is-backed-by-7-billion-russian-loan?sref=5sK6q3I6. Accessed 28 July 2021.

Federal Law #123-FZ. (2021). On Amendments to the RF Law 'Subsoil Resources,' Article 1 of the Federal Law 'On Licensing Certain Types of Activity' and the Annulment of the Decree of the Supreme Soviet of the Russian Federation 'On the Procedure for Enacting the Regulations on the Licensing of the Use of Subsoil Resources' and Certain Provisions of Legislative Acts of the Russian Federation.

Granovetter, M. (2002). Jekonomicheskoe dejstvie i social'naja struktura: problema ukorenennosti. *Jekonomicheskaja sociologija, 3*(3), 44–58.

GULAG: Jekonomika prinuditel'nogo truda. (2008). Moscow: Rossijskaja politicheskaja jenciklopedija (ROSSPJeN); Fond Pervogo Prezidenta Rossii B.N. El'cina.

Heidenreich, M. (2012). The social embeddedness of multinational companies: A literature review. *Socio-Economic Review, 10*, 549–579. https://doi.org/10.1093/ser/mws010

Hickel, W. J. (2002). *Crisis in the commons: The Alaska solution.* Alaska Pacific University.

Jozsa, V. (2016). Corporate embeddedness from a new perspective. *CROMA, 4*, 15–29.

Kalemeneva, E. A. (2018). Smena modelej osvoenija sovetskogo Severa v 1950-e gg. Sluchaj Komissii po problemam Severa. *Sibirskie istoricheskie issledovanija, 2*, 181–200. https://doi.org/10.17223/2312461X/20/10

Kolosovskij, N. N. (1958). *Osnovy jekonomicheskogo rajonirovanija.* Gos.izdatel'stvo politicheskoj literatury.

Korostelev, A. (2008). *Delo 'Norilsky Nikel'* [Norilsk Nickel Case]. Algoritm.

Kouz, R. G. (1995). Priroda firmy. In V. M. Gal'perina (Ed.), *Sbornik statej «Teorija firmy», serija «Vehi jekonomicheskoj mysli»* (pp. 11–32). Jekonomicheskaja Shkola.

Neftegaz.ru. (2019). https://neftegaz.ru/news/gosreg/227368-minprirody-otkladyvaet-pravila-formirovaniya-likvidatsionnykh-fondov-do-2019-g/. Accessed 17 June 2021.

Polan'i, K. (2002). *Velikaja transformacija: Politicheskie i jekonomicheskie istoki nashego vremeni.* Aletejja.

Polishchuk, L. *Corporate social responsibility vs. government regulation: Institutional analysis with an application to Russia.* https://www.hse.ru/data/393/364/1237/CSR_paper_revised.pdf. Accessed 28 July 2021.

RBC. (2021). Nornikel' vyplatil rekordniy shtraf RUB 146 mlrd za razliv topliva. https://www.rbc.ru/business/10/03/2021/6048a2309a794732bec10c5d. Accessed 28 July 2021.

Resolution #996-r. (2021). Resolution of the RF Government of April 15, 2021, "On the Approval of a Single Action Plan for the Implementation of the Fundamental Principles of State Policy of the Russian Federation in the Arctic for the Period up to 2035 and the Strategy for Developing the Arctic Zone of the Russian Federation and Ensuring National Security for the Period up to 2035".

Sakhalin Energy. (2019). http://www.sakhalinenergy.ru/upload/iblock/10f/GRI-2019_RUSSIAN_FINAL.pdf. Accessed 10 June 2021.

SDGs Report. (2020). Doklad o celjah v oblasti ustojchivogo razvitija. Organizacija ob#edinennyh nacij. https://unstats.un.org/sdgs/report/2020/The-Sustainable-Development-Goals-Report-2020_Russian.pdf. Accessed 10 May 2021.

Slavin, S. V. (1961). *Promyshlennoe i transportnoe osvoenie Severa SSSR.* Izdatel'stvo jekonomicheskoj literatury.

UN SDG Indicator. https://www.un.org/ga/search/view_doc.asp?symbol=A/RES/70/1&Lang=R. Accessed 17 June 2021.

Williamson, O. I. (1995). Vertikal'naja integracija proizvodstva: soobrazhenija po povodu neudach rynka. In V. M. Gal'perina (Ed.), *Sbornik statej «Teorija firmy», serija «Vehi jekonomicheskoj mysli»* (pp. 33–54). Jekonomicheskaja Shkola.

World Bank. (2020). https://data.worldbank.org/indicator. Accessed 17 June 2021.

Peripheral Innovation System and Its Place in the Development of the Russian Arctic Resources

Alexander Pilyasov and Elena Putilova

INTRODUCTION

The object of our study is the peripheral innovation system of the regions of the Russian Arctic—we first identified this type as a separate one when conducting a general typology of innovation systems in Russia (Pilyasov, 2012). We look at it with strong integration with production of natural resources. This is the main difference between our approach and the work of foreign colleagues on regional innovation systems.

The aim of the study was to theoretically conceptualize and empirically generalize the main features and essential characteristics of the peripheral innovation system. This goal envisaged the solution of three tasks: characterization of the basic innovation process in the regions of the Russian Arctic in the context of resource development; identification of key actors,

---

A. Pilyasov (✉)
Lomonosov Moscow State University, Moscow, Russia
e-mail: pelyasov@mail.ru

E. Putilova
ANO "Institute of Regional Consulting", Moscow, Russia
e-mail: es_putilova@mail.ru

© The Author(s), under exclusive license to Springer Nature
Singapore Pte Ltd. 2022
A. Likhacheva (ed.), *Arctic Fever*,
https://doi.org/10.1007/978-981-16-9616-9_8

networks and institutions of the peripheral innovation system of the Arctic using specific examples and analytical materials; description of two spatial forms of the peripheral innovation system—urban and district.

Innovation and Modern Arctic Development

Modern economic development is based on an innovative process—and in full agreement with the best achievements of regional science, it is obvious that the process of developing the Arctic also has an innovative nature. It is innovations—technological, organizational and institutional—that provide powerful breakthroughs, "splashes" of development in new areas. This was the case, for instance, with the Varandey terminal, which, in fact, uncorked the development of an entire network of oil fields in the northern part of the Nenets Autonomous Okrug (NAO), the development of which had been constrained for decades by the lack of oil transportation infrastructure. Besides, the "unclogging" of oil production in the NAO was associated with institutional innovations—the development of legislative principles for production sharing agreements, which, in turn, allowed a number of environmental technologies to "enter" the territory of Russian Arctic.

The innovative nature of the modern economy—including the resource-based one—makes it precisely from this angle to reconsider the theory of the Arctic development (colonization). The Soviet theory of the Northern development assumed a system of development bases—organized in a rigid hierarchy: there were rear, outpost, and local bases; together with the development routes (*trassas*) they constituted the supporting framework for the development. The entire structure appeared to be rigid, based on a hierarchy of mainly material flows—and oriented, at the limit, towards the gradual transformation of a developing territory into a developed one. It is advisable to preserve such a systematic approach to a general, comprehensive coverage of the entire territory of new development with a single gaze now, but it is necessary to revise the fundamental approaches to the structure of the system itself.

First of all, obviously, the elements of the development system itself should be revised, reassembled. These are no longer settlements of the first builders, conceived mainly as future "stationary" cities (shift camps existed in Soviet times, but were thought of as an exception rather than a rule)—these are shift camps. At the same time, such an "unthinkable" phenomenon as shift towns appears—perhaps this is how the port of

Sabetta should be called, which already numbers about three tens of thousands of shift "population". The role of winter, seasonal tracks has significantly increased, and the whole territorial structure of colonization is becoming more mobile and lightweight.

In accordance with the innovation imperative, a new hierarchy of individual elements of the development network is emerging. If earlier we were talking about bases mainly as centers of material production, now it is necessary to talk about bases—centers of knowledge production. Along with the unconditional priority of large research centers as bases for innovative developments "for the North" (analogous to the rear bases of the Soviet era), a very specific type of "innovative pilot" stands out in new development areas, where an intensive development of a new model under new conditions is underway.

The examples of the Ardalinskoye field, Kharyaga and Varandey show that in order to achieve innovative breakthroughs, here, at the forefront of development, the efforts of many companies, many players are concentrated—and, as already mentioned, a specific "Arctic" version of the well-known "triple helix" model (Etzkowitz, 2008) is being implemented, providing a well-coordinated interaction between business, science and the state.

It is known from classical works on the geography of innovations that production facilities with different innovative "load" have different principles of placement. Enterprises of intensive innovative search, venture capital companies are located in a concentrated manner; the agglomeration effect, positive externalities from each other's activities are important to them. Mass production enterprises that use innovative developments of the past, specializing in the production of goods at the end of their life cycle, tend to economize on scale, these are large enterprises scattered over a vast area.

Similarly, specific patterns can be observed in the development process. Not only innovative, scientific bases but also enterprises directly in the mining areas can be differentiated both by their innovative role and by the principles of location. The example of the NAO already shows how joint ventures (a form of pooling the efforts of many players) concentrate "at the entrance" to new development areas, form the "vanguards" of development here—these are the Kharyaga and Ardalinsky projects at the entrance to the NAO from the south, and Varandey—at the entrance/exit to the NAO from the north, from the sea. At these vanguard points, fundamentally new models of territory development with specific properties are formed—and then these models are already broadcast, cloned both territorially (deep into the developed territory) and organizationally (once developed technological solutions, becoming routine, sooner or later can be duplicated by individual companies).

In this example, we see the activity of the frontier factors, and, first of all, the impulsive nature of the advancement of development inland. In Soviet times, the smooth, progressive nature of the development of the Soviet economy was proclaimed, which was politically important to oppose the spontaneous cyclical nature of the Western market economy. And all this had been fully applied to the development process.

However, in reality, in a more or less pronounced form, frontier cyclicality was characteristic (but unnoticed!) in the Soviet realities of development. Innovative breakthroughs were ensured by the desperately bold explorations of geologists like Bilibin, Salmanov and many others, the ability to organize new powerful structures—from the Northern Sea Route to Tyumennefegaz, the ability to mobilize, motivate and inspire millions of first builders.

Inspirational breakthroughs were followed by periods of inertia—however, important from the point of view of arranging the life of new areas, stabilizing the entire system. The Soviet theory of development did not see the "post-frontier" realities, the possibility of curtailing projects—which occurred precipitously in many areas with a change in the government model of the Northern development.

The Phenomenon of the Peripheral Innovation System of the Arctic

The concept of a regional innovation system (RIS) appeared in the early 1990s, primarily through the efforts of the English scientist F. Cooke (1992), who had "projected" onto the region for several years by that time the existing concept of national innovation systems developed by C. Freeman (1982, 1995), R. Nelson (1993) and B.-A. Lundvall (1992). The key idea of the RIS concept is that not only technological issues but also the spatial context and institutional environment are important for the innovation process unfolding in a specific space. That is why the "actors-networks-institutions" triad has become the main one for this concept: it deals well with the questions of the local "atmosphere" posed by specific players; external and internal connections and communication channels through which knowledge enters the system and is redistributed inside; institutions that concentrate stocks of knowledge and contribute to its renewal.

In classical works on regional innovation systems, a special type of peripheral innovation systems is rarely distinguished. The main attention of researchers is paid to the innovation process of densely developed regions and large urban agglomerations, global cities—traditional centers of diversified creative service and manufacturing industry. And this is natural: the mainstream of innovations, patents and new knowledge is generated here.

However, for Russia, in which the resource-extracting regions of the Arctic and the North make up most of the country's territory, another research turn is extremely relevant: to make the object of study not large agglomerations and a zone of main settlement, but transport-remote and climatically uncomfortable territories of the country, rich in natural resources. A generalization of the few works that have appeared in the last ten years on innovations at the periphery, on peripheral innovation systems (Asheim et al., 2019; Dawley, 2014; Ferrucci & Porcheddu, 2006; Isaksen & Karlsson, 2016; Karlsen et al., 2011; Petrov, 2011; Virkkala, 2007), allows us to identify their key features.

First of all, it is the small number of knowledge organizations of all types. In these conditions, the knowledge potential of the often-operating global resource corporation—the local branch of TNCs (Iammarino & McCann, 2013), with which local small businesses contract—gains unprecedented importance. Resource corporations become conductors of new technologies to remote areas, production innovations and determine, in general, the technological trajectory (Dosi, 1982) of the development of the territory of their presence.

The projects they are implementing for new resource development through subcontracting procedures, close interaction with local small businesses, if realized, can have a profound impact on the formation of a local innovation system. This role can be compared with the role of universities and other institutions of higher and professional education in the developed regions.

The traditional dichotomy of fundamental and applied science, academic and engineering innovations, characteristic for developed regions, here, in a sparse periphery, with a small variety of competencies, technologies and knowledge, is replaced by complex innovations that integrate academic and experienced engineering knowledge (Asheim et al., 2019).

Within peripheral innovation systems, spatial knowledge flows are usually very weak, for the simple reason that there is a lack of diverse knowledge and necessary competencies in local labor markets. Under these conditions, many resource corporations working in the Arctic and in the North (for example, Norilsk Nickel, Surgutneftegaz, etc.) are forced to "internalize" various types of knowledge: to reach a high level of self-sufficiency in technical, engineering, geological and other knowledge. This causes the desire of Arctic firms to ensure the stability of the work of their qualified and competent personnel, who have developed unique local competencies, and to create their own research centers in the external rear and internal outpost development bases (for example, St. Petersburg, Murmansk, Tyumen, etc.).

Another clearly manifested strategy of obtaining knowledge by resource corporations of the Arctic and the North is their entry into geographically wide networks of cooperation with external, domestic and foreign partners, carriers of unique knowledge and competencies in the exploration of natural resources, including on the shelf, in mining technologies, complex resource fields, etc. But even for those resource corporations of the Arctic periphery, which habitually rely on their internal knowledge, to overcome path-dependency and the inevitable intellectual blindness, it is critically important to have a network of external partners—suppliers of new knowledge. Foreign studies show that, all other things being equal, large and small firms in the periphery are more likely to enter into contractual relations with distant (global) partners and, in general, are more inclined to cooperate than firms in developed areas (Isaksen & Karlsson, 2016). Thus, it can be expected that resource corporations in the Russian Arctic are more communicatively active than corporations in the manufacturing industry in the zone of Russia's main settlement.

A thin layer of structures that generate new knowledge (academic and corporate research and design institutes, universities and colleges, retraining centers, etc.) naturally leads in the peripheral innovation system to well-known and many times described problems. First of all, this is informational blindness in the already created resource specialization of the territory, which leads to negative lock-in of development along a given trajectory, the extraction of natural resources in already well-known geological structures and areas, to the timidity of attempts to break inertia and try to enter a new cycle of resource development, with new natural resources, in new geological structures and in new areas.

Another common problem is associated with the implementation of achievements and developments by the local research subsystem in a more conservative operational subsystem, when new knowledge is really there, but due to the conservatism and inflexibility of mining structures, it is not used. The situation can be resolved by creating spin-offs of large parent corporate structures and start-ups that are more ready to commercialize the analytical knowledge of research units.

Another typical problem is related to the lack of synergy between the few local structures carrying knowledge, the fragmentation of the key actors of the peripheral innovation system, the lack of internal flows of knowledge and collective learning (researchers call this phenomenon communication failures (Todtling & Trippl, 2005)). Often this is due to the insufficient "absorptive capacity" (or innovation capacity) of the main actors of the local innovation system, i.e. their lack of readiness in terms of education and qualifications to evaluate and implement the proposed new knowledge (to combine it with the already existing and familiar). The problem is being solved by hiring new qualified and competent personnel. The lack of synergy of actors for "gluing" pieces of different knowledge into a new integrity can also be a consequence of the huge distances of the peripheral resource territories, which make it impossible for regular personal communication and exchanges of knowledge between professionals.

Instead of permanent, stationary urban and economic agglomerations characteristic of developed areas, here, in the remote territories of the Arctic and the North, temporary agglomerations (for example, in the form of shift camps), mobile economic associations of economic entities arise. These temporary concentrations of economic entities, which are extremely characteristic of the Arctic, are based on the effects of temporal proximity—a concept that has been developed in recent years by the French school of proximity theory headed by A. Torre (2008)— in the form of business trips, periodic conferences, industrial exhibitions, etc.

The small number of organizations carrying new knowledge is combined in peripheral innovation systems with the enormous importance of state institutions for support, activation of the innovation process, few scientific structures, higher and secondary vocational education. Comparatively, the role of such support and such structures is much higher here than in the developed central regions.

The whole process of economic development and modern existence of the Arctic territories, the tone of their socio-economic development is associated with the involvement of natural resources in the turnover. Resource-based is an essential feature of these territories of Russia.

But this means that the peripheral innovation system is inextricably linked with the development of natural resources. This is especially true at the stages of pioneering development, but further, as the resource province ages and the local economy diversifies (unless the "unpromising territory" is closed), this "resources-development-innovation" relationship persists but takes on other forms. The nerve of the Arctic peripheral innovation system is the extension of the life cycle of the resource development of the territory. Exploration (geological exploration), engineering and technological (mining) and institutional (organizational) innovations work for this super-task.

This does not mean that the innovation process cannot unfold in the housing and communal services of Arctic cities, in the systems of daily life support, food, energy and transport security of local communities in the Arctic. It is in recent decades that we have seen colossal breakthroughs here—from the snowmobile revolution to alternative energy. However, it is in the resources, in the use of natural resources, that the innovation process acquires here systemic integrity. Since the entire economy here is built around resources and is simply created, took place because resource development has begun, it is logical to build a local innovation system around the phenomenon of resource development. In addition, already on the core of resource development, life-supporting and social innovations are gradually being threaded.

But the peripheral innovation system is not just linked to resource development—it is a spatio-temporal phenomenon that develops in conjunction with the dynamics of the development and depletion of the resource province. The innovation process is sensitive in its intensity (depth) and diversification (spatial and sectoral breadth), general tension, to the challenges of each age of the resource area. And this is the essential difference between our ideas and the Soviet era, when the innovation process was "allowed" mainly only at the stage of information study, exploration and search in the area of new development. By default, it was assumed that at the stage of development, extraction and processing of a natural resource, it seems to be no longer there (Mosunov et al., 1990). In the most pioneering stage of resource development, enterprising people and firms are the main generators of innovation: at the stage of recovery and stabilization of production—large super organizations-corporations and at the stage of decaying production—small business structures.

Its own institutions and structures of the innovation system characterize the exploration phase of development (without a starting breakthrough in innovative search, there will be no subsequent development). The stage of pioneering development is characterized by the geographical expansion of prospecting operations and the active introduction of technical production innovations.

At the stage of maturity, the intensity of the search process usually weakens. After the breakthrough geological discovery, the exponential growth in the intensity of exploration and the dynamics of technological renewal is weakening. This period of innovation sluggishness for the territory and key actors involved in the subsoil use process, depending on the situation, can last from several years to decades. The open reserves are too high and the content of the natural component in the initial mixture (ore) is too high. It takes time to "digest" them, and this time is unfavorable for radical manufacturing innovations.

However, then, under the influence of a sharp imbalance of redemption and an increase in reserves at the stage of depletion or intense competition between actors within the innovation system of the territory, the innovation process is again sharply radicalized: fundamentally new ideas about the geological structure of the territory and potentially attractive geological structures by age and depth, fundamentally new technologies for the extraction of natural resources and their transportation appear. This allows to postpone (sometimes for a long time) the inevitable depletion of the natural resources of the territory.

The previous cycle is repeated: at the stage of production reaching a new plateau, the intensity of innovation activity in terms of coverage area and the revolutionary nature of the technologies used and geological concepts decreases. Then, at the stage of recession, again the need for an innovation process in both subsystems increases.

But this phase cannot be called a direct repetition of the previous one: firstly, the need for local knowledge about the natural assets of the depleted province increases significantly, it becomes not enough just general conceptual ideas about the geological structure, details are required that are tuned to take into account the characteristics of a particular production facility (field); secondly, innovative search is expanding (democratized) in the structures that conduct it, the privilege of only large resource corporations is being lost. This often happens against the background of a radical change of the main actors themselves—from large companies to their spin-offs or non-integrated small and medium-sized mining enterprises. During this period, due to the gradual diversification of the local economy in large Arctic settlements, the main center of the innovation system is gradually moving from fishing grounds, from the field of exploration and prospecting, mining technologies, here, to scientific and educational institutions, to the sphere of transport, energy and service facilities. These innovations were necessarily present at the stage of pioneering development, but then they were dependent, derivative in nature and now they are autonomized, concentrated in the former large bases of economic development, they acquire independent character.

At the stage of pioneering development (greenfield project), the peripheral innovation system is a single fused core—a generator of complex "development" innovations, in which production search, engineering, institutional and all social and life-supporting innovations are closely merged. Then a fork arises: if the development proceeds according to a temporary scheme, then the innovation system is extremely non-stationary and ready to roll up and relocate to a new location; if the development process acquires duration and social-production stationarity, then the search and operational subsystem gains autonomy within the innovation system.

Further, the innovation system is reborn from a narrow sectoral one, in which the main role is played by two intersecting, interacting with each other subsystems (the generation of new knowledge and its use) to a wide territorial one, in which the local social context and the already equipped settlement space of urban agglomerations, single-industry cities and rotational settlements, not only industrial but also life support, social, managerial and other innovations are generated. They are gradually breaking away from the production core and becoming more autonomous. The system is no longer connected to the integrity of the type of resource and resource development, but a place—a specific city or region. There is a regeneration of a previously corporate, sectoral innovation system into a territorial one, confined to an urban agglomeration or a municipal district, which is necessarily accompanied by a territorial relocation of centers of competence—first closer to production sites, then to research and educational centers—outpost and rear development bases. Thus, depending on the age of development, the peripheral innovation system takes the form of a sectoral or territorial.

However, at the same time, this means that the phenomenon of the territorial innovation system is approaching the well-described situations for the old and developed territories of the world. Always present in the Arctic, an alternative to this evolutionary path of development of the innovation system is the termination of its existence in case of refusal to further develop the territory.

Within a typical peripheral innovation system of the Arctic, two interacting subsystems play an important role: accumulation of knowledge about natural resources (in the form of two components of general formalized knowledge and local tacit knowledge); exploitation of natural resources. They are in a dialectical contradiction—due to the effect of diminishing returns, the extinguishing of natural resource reserves during their extraction constantly threatens to outstrip their growth in the course of exploration and prospecting. The need to constantly balance the work of these two subsystems determines the acute drama of their interaction.

These two blocks differ significantly in the nature of anchor knowledge, its localization (concentration in space), structural envelope, mode and type of dynamics of the innovation process. A common regularity of both subsystems is the increasing role and significance of local knowledge as the process of resource development deepens. The process of localization of both geological and mining knowledge during the long-term exploitation of a resource province is absolutely natural and gives a chance for the emergence of small businesses both in exploration and production, because it is no longer possible to get the effect of the development on a scale of vast "regional" areas at once. Another regularity is associated with the fact that with a significant duration of the stabilization phase or slow extinction of production within the system, resistance to any radical exploration, engineering or institutional (organizational and structural) innovations increases. Only an extreme, simply desperate necessity compels its key actors to make revolutionary changes.

The research subsystem is based on analytical knowledge about the geological structure of the territory, geological structures, their age and spatial occurrence. The operational subsystem is based on synthetic, engineering knowledge of the technological foundations of the mining process.

After the initial breakthrough in the form of a geological discovery in the first subsystem, a weakening of the intensity of efforts naturally follows, while it is at this time that the second subsystem acquires an accelerated development, introduces technological innovations on a large scale (both others and ours). Then "fatigue" accumulates in it—radical innovations are replaced by gradual ones: both subsystems inertially generate "rationalization proposals" instead of revolutionary breakthroughs. The situation persists until a landslide drop in production, which leads either to a complete reformatting of the work of the innovation system in the direction of the key resource, forms of its search and production or to the curtailment of the process of economic development.

The two main blocks of the innovation system can be located either within the same structural circuit or be in different production circuits. It depends on the phase and model of economic development. In the state-controlled Soviet model of the 1930s–1950s, initially, both subsystems were usually located within one economic structure—the superorganization of development (for example, the state-owned trust "*Dalstroy*"). Similarly, in the corporate development of Arctic resources in the modern period, both subsystems are located together within the contour of a large resource company. This provides the necessary synergy to the innovation process.

After the transition to a departmental model of economic development in the late Soviet era (1970–1980s), both subsystems were located in different structural envelopes of geological departments and mining associations, central administrations, which, along with the outputs of specialization, increased the conflict of interests and strengthened the contradictions in their interaction.

Due to the significant expeditionary mobility in the accumulation of knowledge about the resources of a new territory, the territorial structure of the search subsystem is usually more changeable than the operational one, although the specific ratio depends on the type of natural resource. For example, for alluvial gold, both exploration and production territorial structures are highly non-stationary. On the other hand, for the resources of ore gold, diamonds, oil, the exploratory territorial structure of centers of knowledge accumulation is usually more mobile than the territorial structure of the centers of competence of the extractive industry. The spatial area of prospecting activity is always wider than mining (and it itself is more mobile) simply because many discoveries of geologists have not been picked up by miners for a long time.

The law of diminishing returns from resource deposits and previously discovered resource provinces makes it increasingly difficult to balance the growth and redemption of reserves over the years. Therefore, it is natural that over the years the load on the new knowledge generation subsystem, which must respond to this challenge, increases. New inventions, technical innovations, engineering solutions, geological discoveries, structural transformations are designed to delay the inevitable moment of total depletion of the resource province and to ensure a soft "landing" of actors on a neighboring flank territory or water area or in conjugated natural resources (from gas to condensate, from gold to polymetals, etc.). The specific possibilities (supply) of exploratory, technological and institutional innovations for the peripheral innovation system depend on the current technical and economic structure (pickaxe-shovel or bulldozer-excavator or digital platform with remote control) and the leading economic structures and institutions that dominate the economy (for example, integrated combines, sectoral departments or resource companies).

As the development process deepens, new resource discoveries and pioneer development sites are localized. A dichotomy between green-field and brownfield development projects, that is, projects "from scratch" and projects for the modernization of previously created mining and processing production facilities, arises, which is unusual for the initial pioneering development of new vast areas of the North and the Arctic.

The nature of the innovation process and the type of knowledge involved in each type of project are radically different. In the first case of a greenfield project, scientific and technical, academic knowledge, sometimes a fundamental scientific discovery, is actualized. Such, for example, are the transition from the development of "pipe" gas fields on the Yamal Peninsula to LNG projects in the north of the Yamal Peninsula and on Gydan. Here the innovation system is present in a "narrow", production sense, with its inherent contradictory dialectic of relations between the search and production subsystems.

On the other hand, engineering and technological knowledge of how to improve the previous production process is the most important for projects for the modernization of old mining areas. Very different effects of knowledge accumulation and commercialization work here in comparison with the first case: copying the best practices of other foreign and domestic industries, rationalization proposals of employees of production branches of companies, corporate and local centers for retraining and retraining of personnel in urban outpost development bases play a huge role. And in general, the innovation system here has a broad, diversified nature, it is confined not to the branch of specialization, but to the place of deployment—large Arctic and northern scientific and educational centers for the generation of new knowledge. The most important and simple differentiating marker of the innovative system of greenfield and brownfield projects is the system of "renewal"/reproduction of personnel: in the first case, located in the nearest outpost development base, it is intended only for shift workers and technicians, in the second case, located in large rear and outpost bases development—for highly qualified personnel (engineers, geologists, miners, etc.).

The question arises about the boundaries of the peripheral innovation system, about the area of its functioning in the regions of the Arctic and the North. It directly depends on the implemented model of the economic development process. In the nationalized model of pioneering development, we are talking about a large area regional innovation system. The active coordinating role of the state forms a single exploration area over a vast territory and a network of infrastructurally interconnected production facilities. A state-owned peripheral innovation system usually has an extensive regional contour (outline).

On the other hand, with the corporate model of economic development by the efforts of large resource companies, the outline of the innovation system is more modest, confined to the area of the company's licensed areas, linked into a unity by year-round or seasonal infrastructure and communication systems. Here, as in the NAO or YaNAO, a set of enclave-localized corporate non-stationary innovation systems takes place within a large area of new pioneering development, with sometimes duplication of search efforts. In exceptional cases of intercorporate alliances, coordination of companies' innovation systems is also possible.

There is also an intermediate case of state-corporate development, when the main burden of infrastructure development falls on the state, and all mining activities on corporate structures. Here, it is possible to partially consolidate the innovative efforts of various actors on the common state transport and innovation infrastructure (for example, in the form of an experimental testing ground for collective training of skills in experimental production from deep-lying oil-bearing strata). Here, semi-autonomous local corporate innovation systems are integrated into the general regional state-corporate system. Typically, such integration is carried out through the docking of corporate mining subsystems, and not exploratory ones: the companies usually conduct the search stage separately.

Actors of the Peripheral Innovation System

It is natural that the key actors in the economic development of the Arctic are also the main players in the peripheral innovation system. The short first period, as a rule, they are single entrepreneurs and small venture capital firms, which subsequently give way to large companies—they for a long period, in phases of rapid growth and stabilization, then a decrease in the production of a natural resource, retain their hegemony among economic structures, only for the stage of decay of the resource province, yielding it again to small businesses.

Therefore, it is natural to pay special attention to the resource-corporate structure of the territory (the type of the extracted resource and the age of its development, the mining company and the location of its headquarters and production branches). In the modern Russian Arctic, four types of regions can be distinguished with their own specifics of interaction between the territory and the company in the process of resource development. Each type forms its own characteristic innovation system.

The first type is when one large resource company, in fact, contains a vast corporate territory, that is, a single district social and production complex—structures of the extractive industry, transport, energy, construction, trade and other divisions. We are talking about Norilsk Nickel and the Norilsk industrial region. It is unprecedented in the global Arctic that this has been happening for over 80 years. Over the decades, a self-sufficient regional corporate innovation system has been created here, with its own design institutes, a system of training and retraining of personnel, and centers of unique competencies.

The second type is when several "headquarters" corporations are adjacent to each other when developing relatively young oil and gas assets. The importance of the reserves of the resource province is emphasized by the presence here, not of branches, but of the headquarters of large oil and gas companies in Russia. In this case, there is a coexistence of several only weakly interacting local corporate innovation systems, each of which is characterized by its own characteristics and relies on its own basic single-industry city or district. We are talking about the Yamal-Nenets Autonomous Okrug.

The third type is when in the territory of a young oil and gas province there are branches of large resource companies that do not have a stationary support base here, and all development is carried out on a rotational, mobile, "volatile" basis. In Ann Markusen's (1996) terms, it is a "branch office (satellite) platform". It is impossible to talk about an innovation system in the traditional sense here, we are talking about a rotational quasi-system, which is part of the "mainland" systems of corporations—Rosneft, Lukoil, Tatneft, etc. This is the Nenets Autonomous Okrug.

The fourth type is when branches of large resource companies in Russia are working on projects in the old industrial relatively densely populated areas of the Arctic. Here, a contradiction arises between the filiality of the status of development actors and the local innovation system and the established local scientific and educational structures of universities, academic institutes, and professional colleges. In the positive case, it is possible to integrate the local systems of individual companies into the regional innovation system, and use a common innovation, educational and engineering infrastructure. We are talking about the mining development of the Murmansk region and the coal-mining development of the Vorkuta basin of the Komi Republic.

The fifth type is the island centers of industrial innovations, timed to the pioneering mining development of individual resource enclaves of the Chukotka Autonomous Okrug, Arctic Yakutia, Taimyr, etc. Branches of large resource companies operate here, and the innovation process is reduced to ongoing improvements in mining. It cannot rely on either local intellectual development bases, or on the created innovation infrastructure and centers of competence. The situation is similar to the third type, but in an even weaker form: there are even fewer available elements of the innovation system, and the layer of innovative actors and institutions is thinner.

In the Russian Arctic, there are examples of powerful centers of engineering products, for which their own scientific and technical support has been created (for example, the Sevmash enterprise of the Arkhangelsk region). We do not consider them for reasons of similarity with "mainland" innovation systems. For us, the criterion for the Arctic character of the innovation system is the fact that the key actor in it is a large resource corporation. This is a feature of the current stage of the development of the Russian Arctic.

Our linking of the modern innovation system of the Arctic territories to the area of activity of key actors represented by resource corporations has strengths and weaknesses. The strengths include the fact that all the tools for analyzing transnational corporations developed in the world science (including the famous paradigm "asset control scheme—placement—organizational structure" by J. Dunning [2001]) can be used for a substantive study of the corporate innovation system. Headquarters, social embeddedness, and responsibility in the territory of presence, relations with local subcontractors, the degree of decentralization of power within the company and other well-known and repeatedly described parameters of the corporation's behavior, directly affect the nature of the local innovation process and corporate innovation system (primarily in the choice the main sources of new knowledge—from within or from the outside?). The weakness is that this approach inevitably creates a narrowing associated with the underestimation of the role of non-production, not related to core mining activities, innovations, which are especially important and significant for the old industrial territories of the Arctic.

To assess the sources of new knowledge for the classic resource corporation of the Arctic (whose main production assets are located in the Arctic), a comparative analysis of the patent activity of "NovaTEK", "Norilsk Nickel" and "Gaspromneft" had been carried out. We were primarily interested in the question of whether the company relies on its own or borrowed sources of new technical knowledge.

The database of the Federal Institute of Industrial Property FIPS-Rospatent[1] was used, which contains the most complete information about Russian registered patents and published applications, as well as archives of USSR patents: for "NovaTEK" since 2004, for "Norilsk Nickel" since 1990, for "Gazpromneft" from the year 2000.

Patent details include the patent number, filing dates, filing and registration dates and the starting date of the patent validity period, patent authors and patentee, a description of the invention, and a list of documents cited in the search report. Information about the documents cited in the search report, its authorship and copyright holder make it possible to determine which sources of scientific knowledge, developments and technological solutions rely on the Russian Arctic companies-patent holders in the conduct of research and development and their application.

The list of documents cited in the report contains references to literary sources, most often scientific publications on the topic of development, as well as individual patents on the basis of which the development is presented. The references to the cited patents include both Russian and

[1] FIPS Patent Search Database URL: https://www1.fips.ru/iiss/.

foreign patent documents. Google Patents,[2] a search engine that indexes over 87 million patents and patent applications from 17 patent offices, including the United States Patent and Trademark Office (USPTO), European Patent Office (EPO), China National Intellectual Property Office (CNIPA), Japan Patent Office (JPO), World Intellectual Property Organization (WIPO) and Canadian Intellectual Property Office (CIPO). The Google Patents service made it possible to determine the copyright holder of both Russian and foreign patents referred to in the patent applications of "NovaTEK", "Norilsk Nickel" and "Gazpromneft".

To search for patent applications by FIPS, carried out for Russian Arctic companies, we used a search by the line "(73) Patentee", as keywords for the query were used the full names of the companies-patent holders of interest—"NovaTEK", "Norilsk Nickel" and "Gazpromneft". After the elimination of duplicated information, 49 patents of NovaTEK, 75 patents of Norilsk Nickel and 291 patents of Gazpromneft remained.

To determine the source (geographic referencing) of the new knowledge underlying the submitted patents, information about the authors of the patent and the organization in which the authors are employed was used. As an alternative method, it is possible to use the specified address for correspondence in the patent abstract, but it more often reflects the location of the company's head office or the scientific and technical department of the company responsible for organizing the filing of the patent application. Information about the authors of the patent made it possible to identify the parent organization—a company, scientific institute or university, within which the research work was carried out and the development patented as a result. In some cases, it was not possible to find information about the place of employment of the author-inventor of some patents. In this case, the correspondence address indicated in the patent abstract was used.

Comparison of the patent activity of three corporations reveals the fact that "Norilsk Nickel" relies more on its own innovation system than that of "NovaTEK" (Table 1): the former purchases less than 3% of patents from outside organizations, the latter—more than a quarter. The middle position is occupied by "Gazpromneft", which buys about 11% of all patents on the side. Over 80 years of its existence, "Norilsk Nickel" has created a highly diversified socio-economic system in the industrial region

---

[2] https://patents.google.com/.

Table 1 Comparative analysis of patent activity

	Norilsk Nickel	NovaTEK	Gazpromneft
Total patents	75	49	291
Including developed by ourselves	50 + 4 Gipronickel Institute (72%)	34 (69.4%)	252 (86.6%)
Together	19	2	8
Purchased from third parties	2 (2.7%)	13 (26.5%)	31 (10.7%)
Patents without references	11 (14.7%)	15 (30.6%)	34 (11.7%)
Cited patents	64	34	257

of its presence, while the much younger "NovaTEK" (25 years+) and "Gazpromneft" rely on the knowledge of an older partner, "Gazprom".

A comparative analysis of the intensity of patenting activity by year (Fig. 1) reveals a sharp unevenness: 55% of all patents at NovaTEK fall on two fruitful years—2010 and 2012; 41% of all patents of Norilsk Nickel fall on three years—1993, 2003 and 2006; 30% of all patents of Gazpromneft fall on the two peak years 2008 and 2019.

Typically, the acceleration of production activities and economic development occurs with a small-time lag, several years after the peaks of patent activity.

Against the background of the general trend towards self-sufficiency in knowledge of Arctic corporations, which manifests itself in a high proportion of their own patents, the geographical and institutional analysis of references to other inventions is of particular interest. At NovaTEK, the main patent activity is confined to the stage of gas processing and liquefaction (Table 2). And these stages are characterized by the most extensive geography of cities and structures to which the inventors refer. Moscow, Tyumen, Ufa, St. Petersburg and Orenburg are among the most frequently cited cities in Russia, according to several technological stages. They can be recognized as intellectual rear bases for NovaTEK's projects. Among the most frequently cited foreign cities, in which the structures–developers of inventions used in NovaTEK's patents are located, are Paris, Houston, Munich, Tokyo and Shell's headquarters in the Netherlands.

In the geographical structure of patent references of "Norilsk Nickel", the first lines are occupied by the cities in which the corporation's structures of design institutes, branches and headquarters are located: Moscow, St. Petersburg, Monchegorsk, Norilsk and Krasnoyarsk (Table 3). We can

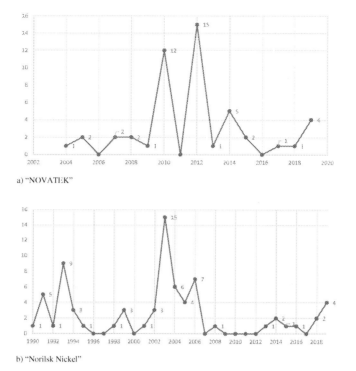

a) "NOVATEK"

b) "Norilsk Nickel"

c) «Gazpromneft»

Fig. 1 Patent activity of three Arctic corporations: NovaTEK (a), Nrolisk Nickel (b) and Gazpromneft (c)

Table 2 Geography of citations and references of patents of "NovaTEK" on the main stages of the production process

	Production, preparation of field units	Processing of associated and other	Gas liquefaction	Transport	Production service, management, etc. LNG engines
Total patents	9	15	11	5	9
Cities of patent citation	18	19	20	10	6
including	Moscow (6)	Moscow (8)	Moscow (6)	Moscow (2)	Moscow (2)
	Tyumen (4)	Tyumen (3)	Tyumen (1)	Tyumen (1)	Tyumen (1)
	Ufa (3)		Ufa (2)		
	St Petersburg (1)		St Petersburg (2)		
	Orenburg (1)	Orenburg (1)		Orenburg (1)	
		Yekaterinburg (1)	Yekaterinburg (1)		
	Novii Urengoi (1)	Novii Urengoi (1)		Novii Urengoi (1)	
	Paris (1)	Paris (1)	Paris (5)		Paris (1)
	Huston (1)		Huston (3)	Huston (1)	
		Munich (2)	Munich (3)		
		Tokio (4)	Tokio (1)		
	Headquarter of Shell (2)	Headquarter of Shell (1)			
	Tashkent (1)	Tashkent (2)			
	Rotterdam (1)				Rotterdam (1)

Notes The number of references in patents for organizations in these cities is given in brackets

Table 3 Geography of citations and references of patents of "Norilsk Nickel" for the main stages of the production process

	Technological stages of the resource chain						
	Mining	Ore beneficiation	Extraction	Processing	Electrolysis	Flotation	Complex metallurgical processing of specific metals (cobalt, palladium), etc
Number of patents	2	3	8	22	10	7	23
Total number of cities in patent references	4	4	15	31	18	11	16
	Lyubertsy (1)		Moscow (6)	Moscow (8)	Moscow (2)	Moscow (5)	Moscow (2)
	St. Petersburg (1)	St. Petersburg (2)		St. Petersburg (5)	St. Petersburg (2)	St. Petersburg (1)	
		Krasnoyarsk (1)	Krasnoyarsk (1)	Krasnoyarsk (1)		Krasnoyarsk (4)	Krasnoyarsk (3)
			Yekaterinburg (3)	Yekaterinburg (1)	Yekaterinburg (1)		Yekaterinburg 1
			Monchegorsk (1)	Monchegorsk (8)	Monchegorsk (1)	Monchegorsk (1)	

Technological stages of the resource chain

Mining	Ore beneficiation	Extraction	Processing	Electrolysis	Flotation	Complex metallurgical processing of specific metals (cobalt, palladium), etc
			Norilsk (1)	Norilsk (1)		
			V. Pyshma (1)			V. Pyshma (1)
		Tokyo (3)	Tokyo (4)	Tokyo (1)		Tokyo (1)
			Toronto (7)	Toronto (1)		
			Catlettsburg (2)	Catlettsburg (4)		
			Espoo (4)			Espoo (1)
	Butte (2)		Butte (1)		Butte (1)	
		Salt Lake City(2)	Salt Lake City(1)	Salt Lake City(1)		
		Johannesburg (1)	Johannesburg (1)	Johannesburg (1)		
		Quebec (1)		Quebec (1)		Quebec (1)
		London (1)	London (1)	London (1)		

Notes The number of references in patents for organizations in these cities is given in brackets

say that patent citations give away the "city network" of the company. Of those actively presented in patent references in several technological stages, only Yekaterinburg and Verkhnyaya Pyshma are exceptions: there are no Norilsk Nickel divisions here, but intellectual influence on the company's patents exists.

The list of foreign cities in which the structures are located, which are actively referenced in the company's patents, is headed by Tokyo, Toronto, Catlettsberg (Kentucky) and Espoo (the satellite city of Helsinki). They are followed by cities whose intellectual footprint is slightly weaker in Norilsk Nickel's patent references—Butte (Montana), Provo and Salt Lake City (Utah), Johannesburg, Quebec and London. It can be hypothesized that the better "self-sufficiency" of Norilsk Nickel with its own patent developments in comparison with NovaTEK is combined with more active use of external knowledge networks in the form of patent links to external organizations.

Against the background of other Arctic companies in Russia and the world, "Norilsk Nickel" is an absolutely unique phenomenon due to the fact that its corporate innovation system is extremely diversified in the sectoral, territorial and structural terms: there are research, design and educational institutions located in several large Russian cities-intellectual bases of mining development of the Norilsk industrial area. The innovation system of many other companies, as the analysis of patent statistics of NovaTEK shows, is simpler. In the future, it remains to be seen whether this is primarily due to the considerable age of the company's work in the Arctic territory or reflects the type of natural resources that Norilsk Nickel mines, the unique properties of ore and specific methods of its processing into metals. Compared to hydrocarbons, these natural assets seem to have a higher processing specificity. And this specificity puts a special strain on innovation and new knowledge.

Networks—Communication Permeability of Space Inside and Outside

Networks play an important role in the innovation process—communication channels through which knowledge flows to the main actors of innovation in the Arctic (resource corporations, small and medium-sized businesses, management structures, etc.). Since there are few transport and communication channels in the Arctic, it is relatively easy during expeditionary surveys and opinion polls, to trace the main ways of migration of new knowledge inward, into the local innovation system.

The efficiency and activity of knowledge flows inside, into the innovation system, in the rarefied environment of the Arctic is very much dependent on the prevailing year-round and seasonal, land, water and air transport channels, the availability of stable high-speed Internet,[3] the configuration of stationary and temporary elements of the settlement system (centro-peripheral or polycentric, presence or absence of large urban agglomerations, etc.) and their interaction with the nearest internal, Arctic and external, mainland, outpost and rear intellectual development bases (centers of knowledge and competence). The integral result of the interaction of these forces can be called the communication permeability of a specific area of the Arctic space.

The realities of the Russian Arctic show that this property of its spaces is radically different from each other. At one pole, there is the westernmost Murmansk region, permeated with information flows, which has the best transport and telecommunications facilities in the Arctic. It is not surprising that according to the composite innovation index (Rating...2020) and according to a number of formal indicators, for example, the number of R&D personnel, it breaks away not only from the Arctic but even from its southern neighboring regions.

At the other pole is the easternmost "island" and roadless Chukotka Autonomous Okrug, where even the issues of stable high-speed Internet communication have not yet been resolved (no telecommunications cable has yet been laid). Compared to another Arctic island, the Nenets Autonomous Okrug, it is much more "exposed" to external information flows due to active labor migration and traditional vacation trips from the North to the "mainland" and vice versa, which is confirmed by a comparison of the statistics of the ratio of external and internal migration turnover in ChAO and NAO (Pilyasov et al., 2017).

In addition to the communication permeability of the Arctic space, for the success of the innovation process, the absorption capacity to accept and implement innovations, the desire and readiness to conduct innovative activities, which, in turn, depend on the needs of the economy, on the

---

[3] A feature of the Arctic community of people is that, with the insufficient development of the Internet in comparison with large urban agglomerations of Russia, they use it more actively for self-learning and obtaining new knowledge: (Pilyasov, 2018). This is due not so much to the desire to overcome information and physical remoteness, but also on average with a higher proportion of people with higher education in the Arctic compared to the rest of Russia.

challenges of new economic development, are very important. And here the champion in the Arctic is the Yamal-Nenets Autonomous Okrug: with average indicators in terms of the number of people employed in the innovation system, the region has been the champion in the Arctic since 2017 in terms of the number of patents issued for inventions, since 2015—in developed advanced production technologies. R&D expenditures of corporate structures that are conducting new development of Yamal have grown almost 45 times since 2010.[4] On the other hand, in the Murmansk region, against the background of brilliant communication permeability, the main actors of economic development in the form of branches of large companies, until recently, showed weak demand for local innovations and, with good development of the local state R&D sector in the local scientific center Apatity, the level of innovativeness of corporate mining the industry was weak or average.

When characterizing the communication permeability of specific Arctic spaces, it is important to take into account its specific administrative status: (a) the entire region belongs to the Arctic zone; (b) part of the region belongs to the Arctic zone, the rest is included in the regions of the Far North and equivalent areas; (c) part of the region belongs to the Arctic zone, the rest—to the northern and temperate zone. In the latter case, it is easier to form effective south–north communication links between the rear intellectual bases of the south located within the same region and areas of the new corporate development of the Arctic: for example, the Krasnoyarsk Territory or the Republic of Sakha (Yakutia).

The main actors of the local innovation system obtain new knowledge through various internal and external communication networks, using well-known and described forms of social interaction: labor migration of qualified personnel to development projects in the Arctic; cooperation of corporations with consumers, suppliers, scientific and educational structures in the implementation of mining projects; internships and business trips for corporate employees; invitations of world-class experts, etc. (Of course, there are also non-communication forms of acquiring new knowledge in the form of purchasing patents, licenses, high-tech equipment, etc.). The peculiarity of the Arctic is that temporary proximity plays a huge role in gaining new knowledge in the form of expeditions, business trips, production meetings and meetings of production

---

[4] Statistics on innovations in Russia: https://rosstat.gov.ru/folder/14477.

leaders. When distances to the utmost separate specialists from each other, building bridges of temporary communication between them plays an unprecedented role and is comparatively more important than on the "mainland".

Institutions—Specific Arctic Institutions for Development Innovation

Institutions play an important role in the operation of the peripheral innovation system in the Arctic. Their basic feature, in comparison with similar institutions for the innovation process in old developed regions, is their remoteness from the main centers of strategic decision-making, both state and corporate. The institutional remoteness of the Russian Arctic means its dependence on federal norms and rules that determine key decisions in the field of economic development of its resources. Tying the periphery to federal norms and rules of economic activity inevitably lagging behind it, in the event of its rapid, dynamic development (especially characteristic of the stages of pioneer development) is counterproductive.

Overcoming this contradiction built into the peripheral innovation system between inertial unified federal institutions and very specific and dynamically changing local conditions for development activities is possible through a significant decentralization of power and authority from the central command headquarters to the Arctic branches, from federal ministries and departments to places of pioneering economic development.

The best solution is to allow and recognize the right of the periphery to experiment, which inevitably violates or goes beyond the scope of federal regulations. Here it is more important than the usual provision of budget incentives for innovation. The conditions for the development of the resources of the Arctic differ to such an extent from the average statistical conditions of ordinary production activities in the country that this also affects the special nature of the accumulation of knowledge and competencies. Therefore, the encouragement of expeditionary forms of obtaining new knowledge in the search subsystem and pilot experiments in the operational subsystem is the most effective solution from the side (on the part) of state and business managers.

Many institutional experiments and innovations in the Arctic innovation system relate to land and resources, which are the backbone of the local economy and the main priority of the innovation process. For example, these are experimental environmental management regimes applied here for the first time in the country (production sharing agreements), training grounds for collective production training in unconventional geological formations (for example, a testing ground for developing the resources of the deep-lying Bazhenov formation). They always sharply intensify the processes of accumulating new knowledge for the operation of the operational and search subsystem of the innovation system.

"Point" and Areal Peripheral Innovation System

The interaction of actors, networks and institutions within the Arctic innovation system in the development of natural resources can take place in the extremely localized format of a single-industry city or in the areal format of a regional corporate contour (a regional cluster of production sites of a company/companies). In both cases, the actors may be the same, but the nature of communication and knowledge flows, institutions of the innovation process differ significantly.

The development of an innovation system in a single-industry town is closely related to the activities of the city-forming mining enterprise. There are different options:

a. the city-headquarters of the resource company (for example, the city of Kogalym as the center of Lukoil-Western Siberia)—in this case, the independence of economic decisions and the innovation process is significantly higher;

b. a dependent city from a larger mono-resource and administrative center (for example, the city of Muravlenko in the Yamal-Nenets Autonomous Okrug, which is in the orbit of influence of the larger neighboring Noyabrsk);

c. an island mono-resource city with high autonomy of the local branch of the resource corporation (the city of Gubkinsky in Yamal-Nenets Autonomous Okrug).

An innovative system built into the urban economy during the pioneer development phase is responsible for the rapid adjustment of exploration and operational subsystems in closely located new production projects. The city naturally turns into the nearest intellectual center, a local development base.

Later, at the stage of rapid growth and then stabilization of production volumes, the imperative of industrial innovation dies out, the "degree" of innovation moves to other spheres of the urban economy (social, life support, recreational, etc.). A narrowly sectoral production sharpened innovation system is being reborn into a territorial one.

At the stage of production decline, the imperative of industrial innovation intensifies again. City-forming production enterprises face challenges to mitigate the negative effects of declining returns from natural depletion of natural assets and extend the life cycle of a field due to new technologies and methods of exploration and production, for example, enhanced oil recovery technologies, utilization of associated petroleum gas, processing condensate fractions of local hydrocarbons, etc.

The innovation process in these conditions is directed either at giving the former development a second wind (for example, by working off the man-made dumps of the previous years of development); or to update the development process by switching it, for example, from gas production to gas condensate, from placer to ore gold, etc.; or the formation of a completely new trajectory of resource development. The first and second options can be accompanied either by the preservation of the previous key corporate actors, which in this case themselves carry out innovative modernization of their production assets, or by the emergence of small and medium-sized actors who are included in the production and innovation system in order to give it new dynamics. In this case, completely new effects start to work here.

In the third option, a new large corporate player, new entrepreneurs may appear and leaving/crushing, crumbling of the former city-forming enterprise is highly probable. Here a strong contradiction arises between the urgent need for the innovation process and the weak interest of the previous actor to carry it out. The functions of the driver of the innovation system must be taken up by someone from the local economy or a newly arrived corporate structure (which is less likely).

This is the general scheme, the implementation of which is fraught with colossal difficulties. Peripheral economic and geographic position of single-industry cities in the Arctic; cognitive and other blockages of new trajectories of development due to the long-term blindness of corporate generals and leaders of local authorities on one path, chosen in Soviet times; the massive outflow of talented youth over the past decades and a very weak inflow of new qualified personnel due to the chronic shortage of housing, which is stronger here than in the average Russian city, sharply limit the set of ideas for the development of a city-forming enterprise and new trajectories of development. And if we add to this the not infrequent intellectual monopoly on solving urban problems on the part of the leadership of the city-forming enterprise, then the field of opportunities for the promotion and discussion of new initiatives generally narrows down to a small window.

The strategies of "depressurization" of the city-forming mining enterprise, aimed at activating the impulses of production renewal, an intensified search for new trajectories of resource development, may include several main directions:

1. Transfer of production competencies from the branch of the corporation—the city-forming enterprise—to its spin-offs and start-ups, which are capable of giving radicality to the innovation process in mining.

2. Reducing the rigidity of the existing production chains in order to allow the coexistence of not one, but several technological chains focused on the production of qualitatively heterogeneous products aimed at different markets by small enterprises (spin-offs and spin-outs). This can naturally be facilitated by a change in the properties of natural assets—from qualitatively homogeneous to heterogeneous, mixed, condensate, which give rise to technological recombinations with obtaining a wide range of low-tonnage final products. Another way to reduce the rigidity of production chains was implemented in the Swedish Arctic monotown of Kiruna, where research laboratories AggloLab and MetLab were created within the city-forming enterprise itself, the state LKAB, working at the intersection of chemistry, metallurgy, engineering, electronics, information technology and the mine and LKAB enterprises have become natural testing grounds for laboratory achievements (Zamyatina & Pilyasov, 2015).

3. New industrial policy of local authorities, stimulating an innovative search for all subjects of the local production system, both large and small. Often, it is accompanied by the creation of innovative infrastructure facilities in the city or use for the purpose of industrial renewal of the infrastructure to support small businesses.

The regional innovation system of cluster corporate development can exist in stationary and mobile (rotational) form, relying on the mainland rear development bases. The areal space defines a completely different type of communication here than in a localized urban system. There, the city itself acts as the center of accumulation of borrowed and local information—in its structures, first of all, a city-forming enterprise, information flows are concentrated, which then "go" to the surrounding fields, and in the district system, independent extraction of new scattered information plays a significant role, including by expeditionary methods, and only then its concentration in mining points of growth or in the nearest production centers. In this sense, the regional innovation system is more tied to pioneering development, and the urban one—to the mature development and the formed territorial framework (the network of stationary settlement and infrastructure facilities) and the accumulated information base within the search and operational subsystem.

CONCLUSIONS

The concept of a peripheral innovation system significantly enriches our traditional ideas about the development of natural resources in the Arctic, expands the innovation process beyond the accepted framework of only the expeditionary, exploration stage to the next (stage of stabilization of production and depletion, aging of the resource province). A new understanding of knowledge as a true driver of the economic development of the Arctic territories of Russia is emerging. This view inherits the approaches of Friedrich List about the priority of creating new knowledge in the development process, the approaches of Karl Marx about science as a genuine productive force, Richard Nelson and other creators of the theory of innovation systems about the role of innovation in cultivating constructive diversity for development.

On the other hand, our linking the peripheral innovation system to natural resources, which are the basis of the Arctic economy, their search, extraction, processing, makes this very concept more substantive and adequate to the conditions of the Russian Arctic. At the stage of pioneering resource development, the peripheral innovation system has a production, sectoral nature. In the future, as the extraction of natural resources stabilizes and declines, it becomes more complex and transforms into a territorial one, which includes not only production but also social, life-supporting and service innovations.

The key actors in the peripheral innovation system of the Arctic are large resource companies. Only at the very first search stage and at the stage of depletion do small and medium-sized firms and individual entrepreneurs play a significant role. They convert the existing knowledge about the resources of the territory into a mining process, taking into account the technological capabilities and limitations of a particular historical era.

The success of the development of natural resources directly depends on the ability of key actors to "strain" internal and external channels for obtaining new knowledge. The frequent lack of local knowledge in the early stages of development forces corporations to actively "suck in" external knowledge and form temporary and permanent networks with external partners for this purpose. The efficiency of using the obtained external knowledge and its constructive "mixing" with the firm's own one depends on the "absorptive capacity" of resource companies, that is, the availability of educated and competent professional personnel.

An analysis of the patent activity of two Arctic corporations, "NovaTEK" and "Norilsk Nickel", revealed in both cases their sharp unevenness over the years and the presence of different strategies—more focused on the procurement of inventions on the side of the first company and the priority of own developments from the second company. Peak patenting activity in both cases anticipates the corporation's growing activity in the development of new resource projects in the Arctic.

Analysis of various factors that determine the intensity of the work of internal and external networks of knowledge flows led us to the concept of communication permeability of space. In the Arctic, it depends on settlement network configurations, major transport routes, broadband cable availability, and other factors. Among the Arctic territories of Russia, the Murmansk Region has the maximum communication permeability, and the Chukotka Autonomous District has the minimum. But for the successful deployment of the innovation process in the development of natural resources in the Arctic, in addition to communication permeability, a high innovation capacity (absorption capacity) of resource companies is also required as they are the key actors of the peripheral innovation system. It is influenced by various lock-ins—cognitive (narrow-mindedness of ideas), functional (established contracts, deeply rooted industrial relations) and political (relations between business and government in the territory of presence) (Todtling & Trippl, 2004).

The most important institutional contradiction in the work of the peripheral innovation system and in the entire process of economic development of the Arctic resources is the discrepancy between the unified federal norms and rules and the specific conditions of the Arctic. We call this, following the famous Alaskan economist Lee Huskey, the conditions of institutional remoteness of the Arctic. Overcoming its costs is associated with the delegation of powers in the innovation and development process from the center, from the headquarters of companies to the Arctic periphery, to branches. The full encouragement of experimentation and exploration in the work of the research and exploitation (mining) subsystem of the peripheral innovation system is a constructive response to this challenge.

Only in the last decade has the phenomenon of the peripheral innovation system been recognized in the world literature. However, it is still viewed as a single phenomenon. Meanwhile, our research and all practical experience confirm that the diversity of the peripheral systems of the Russian Arctic is not less, and possibly even more, than similar systems in densely populated territories of Russia and the world. The peripheral innovation system differs in the coverage of the area (urban or regional), in the degree of influence of the key actor (corporate, state-owned or state-corporate), in the stage of development to which it is confined (information, pioneer, stabilization and depletion), in the type of key natural resource and other factors.

It is the innovation system that determines the trajectory of the economic development process—whether it will be long-term or will it break off at the first stages. Its role in the old industrial Arctic territories is very prominent and relatively well studied. At this "bifurcation" stage, it sets the direction of future development. As Western researchers point out, here are possible:

a. renewal and deepening of the development path through revolutionary innovations;
b. diversification in the form of expanding the trajectory on the basis of previous competencies through gradual innovations (the so-called phenomenon of "related variety") or diversification without connection with previous competencies (the phenomenon of "unrelated variety");
c. creating a completely new trajectory of development through revolutionary innovations.

References

Asheim, B. T., Isaksen, A. A., & Trippl, M. (2019). *Advanced introduction to regional innovation systems.* Edward Elgar.

Cooke, P. (1992). Regional innovation systems: Competitive regulation in the new Europe. *Geoforum, 23*(3), 365–382.

Dawley, S. (2014). Creating new paths? Offshore wind, policy activism, and peripheral region development. *Economic Geography, 90*(1), 91–112.

Dosi, G. (1982). Technological paradigms and technological trajectories: A suggested interpretation of the determinants and directions of technical change. *Research Policy, 11*(3), 147–162.

Dunning, J. H. (2001). The eclectic (OLI) Paradigm Of International Production: Past, present and future. *International Journal of the Economics of Business, 8*(2), 173–190.

Etzkowitz, H. (2008). *The triple helix: University-industry-government innovation in action.* Routledge.

Ferrucci, L., & Porcheddu, D. (2006). An emerging ICT cluster in a marginal region. The Sardinian experience. In P. Cooke & A. Piccaluga (Eds.), *Regional development in knowledge economy* (pp. 203–226). Routledge.

Freeman, C. (1982). *The economics of industrial innovation.* Frances Pinter.

Freeman, C. (1995). The national system of innovation in historical perspective. *Cambridge Journal of Economics, 19*, 5–24.

Gokhberg, L. M. (2020). *Рейтинг инновационного развития субъектов Российской Федерации. Выпуск 6* [*Rating of innovative development of the constituent entities of the Russian Federation. Issue 6*]. National Research University Higher School of Economics.

Iammarino, S., & McCann, P. (2013). *Multinationals and economic geography. Location, technology and innovation.* Edward Elgar.

Isaksen, A., & Karlsson, J. (2016). Innovation in peripheral regions. In R. Shearmur, C. Carrincazeaux, & D. Doloreux (Eds.), *Handbook of the geographies of innovation* (pp. 277–285). Edward Elgar.

Karlsen, J., Isaksen, A., & Spilling, O. (2011). The challenge of constructing regional advantage in peripheral areas: The case of marine biotechnology in Thomson's Norway. *Entrepreneurship and Regional Development, 23*(3), 235–257.

Lundvall, B. -Å. (1992). *National innovation systems: Towards a theory of innovation and interactive learning.* Pinter.

Markusen, A. (1996). Sticky places in slippery space: A typology of industrial districts. *Economic Geography, 72*, 293–313.

Mosunov, V. P., Nikulnikov, Y. S., Sysoev, A. A. (1990). *Территориальные структуры районов нового освоения* [*Territorial structures of areas of new development*]. Nauka.

Nelson, R. (1993). *National innovation systems: A comparative analysis*. Oxford University Press.

Petrov, A. N. (2011). Beyond spillovers: Interrogating innovation and creativity in the peripheries. In H. Bathelt, M. Feldman, & D. Kogler (Eds.), *Beyond territory. dynamic geographies of knowledge creation, diffusion, and innovation* (pp. 168–190). Routledge.

Pilyasov, A. N. (2012). *Синергия пространства: региональные инновационные системы, кластеры и перетоки знания* [*Synergy of space: Regional innovation systems, clusters and knowledge flows*]. Oikumena.

Pilyasov, A. N. (2018). Арктическая диагностика: плох не метр - явление другое [Arctic diagnostics: The meter is not bad—The phenomenon is different]. *North and the Market: the Formation of the Economic Order, 61*(5), 35–56.

Pilyasov, A. N., Galtseva, N. V., & Atamanova, E. A. (2017). Economy of the Arctic "islands": The case of Nenets and Chukotka autonomous okrugs. *Journal of the Economy of the Region, 13*(1), 114–125.

Todtling, F., & Trippl, M. (2004). Like phoenix from the ashes? The renewal of clusters in old industrial areas. *Urban Studies, 41*(5/6), 1175–1195.

Todtling, F., & Trippl, M. (2005). One size fits all? Towards a differentiated regional innovation policy approach. *Research Policy, 34*(8), 1203–1219.

Torre, A. (2008). On the role played by temporary geographical proximity in knowledge transfer. *Regional Studies, 42*(6), 869–889.

Virkkala, S. (2007). Innovation and networking in peripheral areas—A case study of emergence and change in rural manufacturing. *European Planning Studies, 15*(4), 511–529.

Zamyatina, N. Y., & Pilyasov, A. N. (2015). *Инновационный поиск в монопрофильных городах. Блокировки развития, новая промышленная политика и план действий* [*Innovative search in single-industry cities: Development lock-ins, new industrial policy and a roadmap for change*]. URSS.

Kaleidoscope of Independent Agendas for the Arctic: North America

A Reluctant Arctic Power No More? The United States' Evolving Engagement with the High North

George Soroka

INTRODUCTION

Despite the United States having been an Arctic stakeholder for the better part of two centuries, for the majority of Americans the High North remains a distant afterthought, a vast expanse of white that sits, unknown and inscrutable, at the top of maps and globes. In contrast to Canadians, Russians, and Scandinavians, whose societal identities are notably shaped by their self-awareness of being Arctic nations, Americans living outside of Alaska rarely if ever think of themselves as citizens of an Arctic power. And while sparsely settled Alaska—geographically the largest state, at more than twice the size of Texas—accounts for an extremely meager 0.22% of the overall U.S. population (its total number of residents is just slightly higher than that of Boston),[1] only a miniscule percentage of Alaskans live

---

[1] Calculated on the basis of the latest available U.S. Census figures (https://www.census.gov/).

G. Soroka (✉)
Harvard University, Cambridge, MA, USA
e-mail: soroka@fas.harvard.edu

© The Author(s), under exclusive license to Springer Nature Singapore Pte Ltd. 2022
A. Likhacheva (ed.), *Arctic Fever*,
https://doi.org/10.1007/978-981-16-9616-9_9

in its northernmost reaches (Howell et al., 2020, p. 26). The Arctic is, in other words, far away for most Americans, both physically and mentally.

Moreover, how the United States officially defines this region is idiosyncratic. According to section 112 of the Arctic Research Policy Act of 1984, it encompasses "territory north of the Arctic Circle and all United States territory north and west of the boundary formed by the Porcupine, Yukon, and Kuskokwim Rivers; all contiguous seas, including the Arctic Ocean and the Beaufort, Bering and Chukchi Seas; and the Aleutian chain" (Arctic Research and Policy Act of 1984 [amended 1990]). Utilizing the three rivers to delineate the boundary "cuts off approximately two-thirds of Alaska," while including the Aleutian Islands, which extend down to 52°N, places the southern terminus of the U.S. Arctic on nearly the same latitude as London (Holm Olsen, 2020, p. 84).

Although the Arctic played a prominent role during the Cold War, its strategic relevance only subsiding after the dissolution of the Soviet Union in 1991, the region was always marginal in terms of domestic U.S. politics. Illustrating what an afterthought America's north has historically been for the Washington establishment, Warren Harding was the first sitting president to visit Alaska, which only achieved statehood in 1959. Harding traveled there in the summer of 1923, before dying on the return leg of his western tour (Eilperin, 2015). It was not until Barack Obama gave a speech in the northern Alaskan town of Kotzebue in 2015 that as an occupant of the White House finally visited the Arctic proper (White House, 2015).[2]

However, this previous lack of attention has today been replaced by a great deal of concern. The rapidity of climate change in the Arctic, which in relative terms is warming much faster than the rest of the world, is spurring this on. So too is Russia's rebuilding of its military infrastructure in the region, much of which was badly neglected in the years following the USSR's collapse. China's growing economic and scientific interest in the High North likewise plays a role, as exemplified by Beijing's efforts to integrate the "Polar Silk Road" into its larger Belt and Road Initiative. Taken together, these developments have caused some pundits to warn that a new "cold war" may be brewing in the Arctic, raising concerns that the United States is significantly behind other Arctic nations according to certain metrics, like the number of polar-class icebreakers it commands.

---

[2] Kotzebue, at slightly over 3000 inhabitants, is one of the largest settlements in the Alaskan Arctic.

The Arctic has traditionally been regarded as an "exceptional" region, one in which stakeholders have been able to compartmentalize their differences and cooperate even when tensions flared in other contexts. But as was illustrated by the incendiary speech delivered by then-U.S. Secretary of State Mike Pompeo at the May 7, 2019, Arctic Council ministerial meeting in Rovaniemi, Finland, this era may be coming to an end. In particular, Russia's actions in Syria and Ukraine, along with China's posturing in the South China Sea, have prompted the United States to focus renewed attention on this region.[3] Consequently, we have begun to witness spill-over effects from outside conflicts manifest in the Arctic; indicative of this, the U.S. Air Force, Army, Coast Guard, Navy, and Department of Homeland Security (DHS) have all released reports outlining their Arctic strategies in the last two years.[4]

Nonetheless, the main driver of change in the Arctic today is not geopolitical, but climatic. Unlike Antarctica, the Arctic is "fundamentally a maritime space" (Tallis, 2020). As such, the thawing cryosphere has led to the large-scale melting of sea ice, revealing "new" borders suddenly bereft of the natural defenses they had previously enjoyed. As will be discussed below, some of the anxieties and concerns this has generated are justified, others are overinflated, while still others are under-emphasized in the resultant discourses.[5]

In evaluating the present-day engagement of the United States with the High North, we can conceptually distinguish between Arctic-specific issues that are endogenous to the region and are thus unlikely to travel to other contexts, and Arctic-proximate issues that are exogenous to the region but nevertheless affect it. Increasingly, Arctic-proximate issues are taking center stage away from Arctic-specific issues. At the same time,

---

[3] Of the eight permanent members of the intergovernmental Artic Council only Finland, Russia, and Sweden are not NATO members (though Finland and Sweden work closely with the alliance on many initiatives). The other permanent Council members are Canada, Denmark (via Greenland), Iceland, Norway, and the United States.

[4] In the case of the Air Force, Army, and DHS, these were the first such documents to have ever been made public.

[5] The Arctic, however, remains a heterogenous space. Among other sub-regional distinctions, there are significant differences between weather patterns in North America and Europe that affect their respective Arctic zones; compared across similar latitudes, the former continent is much colder than the latter. The commonly held perception is that this disparity is related to the Gulf Stream and its offshoots warming northern Europe, though this explanation has been challenged (see Seager, 2006).

there are also other forces impacting the Arctic that need to be considered. In part, Arctic exceptionalism is finding itself threatened because this exceptionalism was meaningfully predicated on the climatic ferocity of the region and the attendant lack of access. While the latter still represents a formidable obstacle, it is less of one today than it was in the past.

However, when considering the role of the United States in the Arctic, it is imperative to not just look at the wider geophysical and geopolitical context but also analyze the changing domestic political landscape. This is especially so given that the United States just transitioned from one of the most iconoclastic administrations the American people have ever experienced (consider President Trump's apparently serious offer to buy Greenland from Denmark) to one led by a long-time Washington insider who has appointed a technocratic cabinet.

So, the question becomes: How much change can we expect in terms of Arctic policy from the Biden White House and Congress? Relatedly, how much consistency can the American people, along with their allies and adversaries, anticipate in Washington's approach to the region going forward? The latter, in particular, is a timely concern given the level of political polarization being evinced in the United States as the 2022 midterm elections loom and Donald Trump teases another presidential run in 2024. In November 2020, David Balton, former U.S. Ambassador for Oceans and Fisheries and currently a Senior Fellow at the Wilson Center's Polar Institute, participated in a panel discussion wherein he differentiated between policies that would change during the Biden administration, policies that might change, and policies that would not change. In the first category, Balton noted that there would be more emphasis on environmental concerns, working through multilateral institutions, and strengthening the international governance regime in the Arctic. In the second, more nebulous category, he placed United States –Russian relations and attitudes towards China. As regards the final category, Balton observed that when it came to Russia's military buildup in the Arctic, Washington will continue to try and contain Moscow in an effort to "reestablish a kind of equilibrium on security issues" (Balton, 2020).

Balton's prognoses were eminently reasonable and, in fact, reflect much of what we have already witnessed a year into Biden's tenure. Thus far, the new administration has proven more willing to cooperate multilaterally on climate change, and less interested in vilifying China or pursuing the sort of zero-sum international relations that the previous occupant of the White House was prone to engage in.[6] However, while recognizing that Trump's hawkish foreign policy rhetoric was intended to appease his domestic base and that much has changed since he left office, there is a conspicuous degree of continuity in how Washington perceives the main strategic challenges facing the United States in the Arctic. The political tone may have moderated, but concerns about China and Russia remain in the foreground.

Yet although climate change and human ingenuity are attenuating the Arctic's remoteness, this is still one of the most inaccessible regions in the world due to its extreme temperatures, lack of infrastructure, and sheer vastness. As such, it is critical to note that in the Arctic it is often difficult to disentangle strategic concerns from other domains. Militaries throughout the region, for example, are routinely utilized for search-and-rescue operations and to support scientific expeditions, and the development of northern ports and airfields may serve both commercial and strategic functions. Complicating matters further, whether out of necessity or preference, High North initiatives often cut across political boundaries and assume a trans-state character.

Therefore, with the proviso that all of the categories considered herein are to some extent interrelated and inter-dependent, discussion below begins by evaluating climate change in relation to the polar environment, as the majority of contemporary Arctic challenges proceed from this factor. Next assessed are security concerns and responses as they pertain to the U.S. presence in the Arctic, along with the degree to which Washington competes or cooperates with other actors in this region. Arctic economic matters are analyzed next, followed by a brief overview of the issues facing indigenous peoples living in northern Alaska and the scientific attention being paid to this ecosystem. The conclusion distills the most significant issues facing the Arctic today and ventures some recommendations for moving forward.

---

[6] Biden's predecessor appears to have focused on the Arctic in large measure because it played into a great-power competition narrative he was trying to deploy vis-à-vis China. And for all that Trump seemed oddly accommodating of Vladimir Putin in his public remarks concerning the Russian leader, with respect to the Arctic his administration pursued a decidedly confrontational policy with Moscow.

Climatic Change and the Arctic Environment

In August 2021, the Intergovernmental Panel on Climate Change (IPCC) released a startling report. Its authors, citing a "high degree" of confidence in their findings, claimed that in the last decade the Arctic's sea ice cover had reached its lowest point since at least 1850, and that means global sea levels had risen more rapidly since 1900 than during any other period in the preceding three millennia (at a minimum). As a result, they concluded that Arctic waters are likely to be free of ice at least once before 2050 during the annual September minima (IPCC, 2021). This publication followed on the heels of other dire reports. Indeed, one series of simulations predicted that the Arctic might be completely ice-free for three-to-four months annually by 2100, with the researchers involved cautioning that rising oceanic temperatures will portend "extreme consequences for Arctic communities and local ecosystems" (Landrum & Holland, 2020).

Empirical observations to date tend to bolster these crisis scenarios. September 2020 saw the second-lowest summer sea ice extent since satellite measurements began in 1979, the previous having occurred in September 2012. Winter sea ice cover has also been declining, but just as significantly, it has been thinning. We no longer encounter much two-, three-, and four-year-old sea ice in the Arctic. Most of it is now one-year ice, which behaves differently in terms of its physical properties and is easier for icebreakers and even ice-strengthened ships to navigate through. Less ice also means more unpredictability in aquatic systems. One consequence of this is that marine mammals and polar bears are moving away from their traditional ranges, making them more difficult and dangerous for humans to hunt (or avoid). Fisheries are likewise being affected; as valuable groundfish stocks move northward in response to warming waters, they are followed by the world's commercial fishing fleets. Not only does this have economic and political implications but it also disrupts marine ecosystems and the food chains they support (Huserbråten et al., 2019; Troell et al., 2017). Moreover, the ripples produced by such phenomena extend far beyond the Arctic, affecting far-flung ecological niches. The basic problem is that the earth's polar regions function as giant heat sinks, absorbing warmth from the atmosphere and oceanic currents. Even though the industrial footprint of the Arctic, and especially its U.S. sector, is minimal in comparison to other parts of the world, anthropogenic sources of greenhouse gases nonetheless affect it. What happens outside the Arctic does not stay outside the Arctic.

However, not only is the ice melting but land-based snow cover is also exhibiting a sustained decade-on-decade decline (Ballinger et al., 2020). Surface air temperatures in the Arctic are rising more than twice as fast as they are across the globe as a whole, with the second-highest average temperatures since measurements began in 1900 registered in the period between October 2019 and September 2020 (Ballinger et al., 2020; Scott, 2020).[7] This has led to the greening of the tundra and the thawing of its permafrost, which is releasing significant quantities of methane and carbon dioxide to the atmosphere, accelerating the process of global warming (Schaefer, n.d.). Although these trends are making the Arctic more accessible via maritime routes, they are simultaneously causing it to become more difficult to navigate overland, especially during the summer months. They are also altering wildlife habitats and the seasonal migration patterns of caribou and other species. Likewise, the feasibility of pursuing land-based extractive activities such as mining is closely tied to changing climatic conditions in the High North.

Similarly, a hotter Arctic is both triggering and worsening the effects of wildfires, most of which are caused by lightning strikes. Extreme weather conditions not only increase their number but allow them to burn longer and hotter due to drier conditions on the ground. Fires are particularly pernicious in this region because there is little that can be done to fight them, and because they are capable of releasing vast amounts of particulate pollution and combustion gases (York et al., 2020). Furthermore, so-called "zombie fires" can smolder for long periods of time in coal beds deep in the compressed organic matter that makes up the tundra, only to flare up again when conditions are suitable (Borunda, 2021).

Given that this chapter is being written in the midst of the Covid-19 pandemic, it seems particularly apt to note that Arctic warming also brings with it the potential to reanimate previously frozen bacteria and viruses that can threaten human and animal health. This is far from being only a theoretical concern, as a 2016 anthrax outbreak in northern Siberia is believed to have resulted from the thawing out of a decades-old reindeer carcass infected with *Bacillus anthracis* during a summer heatwave (Doucleff, 2016). Melting permafrost may likewise introduce novel

---

[7] The highest average temperatures were recorded just four years earlier.

diseases into Arctic wildlife, creating new vectors of dissemination and raising the chances for cross-species transmission (National Academies of Sciences, Engineering, and Medicine, 2020).

Not all environmental problems in the Arctic are directly related to climate change, however. There are also a number of legacy issues that continue to negatively affect residents of the High North. Among these is the common practice of using burn barrels to dispose of trash, which taints the air and soil with dioxins, furans, and other carcinogenic, mutagenic, and teratogenic compounds. Arctic denizens must also deal with the contamination of fish and marine mammals by persistent toxins such as methylmercury and PCBs. This is a particularly serious concern for indigenous coastal peoples for whom whale and walrus meat are staples, as these animals have the greatest propensity to bioaccumulate harmful substances due to their longevity and position at the top of the marine food chain. Similar concerns surround subsistence hunters who rely on terrestrial species such as caribou and muskox, especially given that lichens and mosses—key sources of nutrition for Arctic ungulates— are highly adept at absorbing the radionuclides that pollute the region from atmospheric weapons testing and nuclear accidents (e.g., Luedee, 2021; Saniewski et al., 2020). Additional environmental problems in the Alaskan Arctic include heritage pollution from previous mining activities and the deposition of air-borne mercury (mainly originating from coal-fired power plants, incinerators, and industries based in more southerly locales) in fragile tundra environments (Obrist et al., 2017).

Other issues are secondarily the result of climate change. Reductions in ice cover, for example, bring about greater utilization of Arctic sea lanes. "In the last decade," a 2019 U.S. government report notes, "the number of vessels operating in waters north of the Bering Strait around the Chukchi and Beaufort Seas has increased by 128% and is now 2.3 times larger than the number of ships passing through the region in 2008" (U.S. Committee on the Marine Transportation System, 2019, p. iv).[8] Growing marine traffic, in turn, increases underwater noise pollution and collisions with whales (Silber et al., 2021), as well as the level of black carbon emissions (and chances for oil or diesel spills). Additionally, the more Arctic waters are plied by fishing vessels, cruise ships,

---

[8] As the report points out, the duration of time vessels spend in Arctic waters has also increased in recent years.

and cargo vessels, the more need there will be to expand the region's search-and-rescue infrastructure.

Moreover, non-Arctic states are lured to the region by climate change and the opportunities it brings, whether these be strategic, economic, or scientific, and they are likely to play an expanding role therein moving forward. China is the most obvious of these actors. It justifies referring to itself as a "near-Arctic" state (despite the shortest distance between China and the Arctic being 1448 kilometers) and having permanent observer status in the Arctic Council, which it gained in 2013, in part because of the threat melting polar icecaps pose to its low-lying coastal areas.[9] On its face, this is a legitimate concern, as a warming Arctic contributes to raising sea levels, and it is certainly more convincing than landlocked Switzerland's tortured logic in claiming that it represents a "vertical Arctic" state due to its mountainous topography (Lanteigne, 2020, pp. 385–386).[10] Nonetheless, the interest China is expressing in the northern cryosphere reveals a profound lack of consensus among regional actors regarding how to react to Beijing's overtures.[11]

Climate change, however, is not just bringing outside states into the region. It is likewise exacerbating strife between the Arctic's uncontested stakeholders. For example, despite Canada being one of the United States' closest allies, Ottawa and Washington have engaged in a long-standing dispute over the Northwest Passage (NWP). The United States considers the NWP an international strait that should be freely passable, while Canada regards it to be part of its internal waters (Lalonde, 2020). Although this disagreement was largely hypothetical for many years, as the

---

[9] One estimate suggests China may have to relocate some 20 million people from low-lying coastal areas by mid-century (Nicholls et al., 2007, p. 5). However, this is partly a problem of China's own making. According to a recent study, in 2019 China was responsible for over 27% of global greenhouse gas emissions, far outpacing the U.S., which claimed second place with 11% (India was a distant third at just under 7%) (Larsen et al., 2021).

[10] In addition to China and Switzerland, the other permanent observers in the Arctic Council are France, Germany, Italy, Japan, the Netherlands, Poland, India, South Korea, Spain, and the United Kingdom.

[11] "Perhaps the biggest obstacle for the Arctic states," as Lackenbauer and Dean observe, "is that the unrealized promise of an internationalist 'Arctic exceptionalism' has left them ill-equipped to integrate China—a major, exogenous authoritarian power with substantial resources and growing global influence—into their mental map of an 'exceptional' region" (Lackenbauer & Dean, 2020, p. 346).

NWP becomes more readily accessible, it is turning into a point of pragmatic contention. A similar situation exists with the Northern Sea Route (NSR). Despite repeated complaints from the United States and other states that its actions violate international law, Russia has continued to increase its regulatory oversight of the NSR, which it is trying to fashion into a viable commercial thoroughfare.[12]

It is in the realm of addressing climate change and associated environmental challenges that we are likely to see the greatest divergence between Trump's administration and that of Biden. Trump was an unabashedly pro-fossil fuel politician, one who repeatedly touted the hydrocarbon potential of the Alaskan north and attempted to open up the Arctic National Wildlife Refuge (ANWR) for oil drilling, reversing six decades of protectionist precedent (Plumer & Fountain, 2020). In contrast, on his first day in office, Biden not only rejoined the Paris Climate Accords (from which Trump had withdrawn the United States from 2020) but also imposed a temporary moratorium on oil and gas leases in the ANWR (Stronski & Kier, 2021).[13] And while the previous administration had planned to make vast swaths Alaskan wilderness overseen by the Bureau of Land Management (BLM) available for resource extraction, in April 2021, the Department of the Interior postponed the scheduled opening of 28 million acres of BLM land to mineral exploration and mining (Hofstaedter, 2021).

During the Trump years, federal agencies seemed allergic to the terms "climate change" and "global warming." For example, when the Department of Defense presented its Arctic strategy report to Congress in June 2019, it utilized the euphemistic phrase "changing physical environment" (Department of Defense, 2019, p. 3). Contrariwise, before

---

[12] Moscow justifies its authority over the NSR by invoking the route's historical importance and citing article 234 of the United Nations Convention on the Law of the Sea (UNCLOS). Known as the "ice loophole," this article permits littoral states to regulate marine traffic in ice-covered waters that fall within their 370-kilometer exclusive economic zone (EEZ) in order to protect and preserve the environment (United Nations, 1982). However, the growing paucity of sea ice along the NSR is causing other countries to ever more intently question the degree of Russia's control.

[13] This new-found opposition to fossil fuels is not absolute. In August 2021 a federal judge blocked the construction of Willow, a multi-billion-dollar oil-drilling project ConocoPhillips was developing in Alaska's North Slope region that had been green-lighted by Trump but also had the support of the Biden White House (Davenport, 2021).

he was inaugurated, Biden pledged to create a new cabinet-level position tasked with addressing climate change, tapping former Secretary of State and one-time Arctic Council Chairman John Kerry to fill this post. As the Special Envoy for Climate Change, Kerry (who soon after Biden's inauguration reached out to his Russian counterpart Ruslan Edelgeriyev, signaling a desire to work together with Moscow on at least some matters [Stronski & Kier, 2021]) also sits on the National Security Council, elevating "the issue of climate change to the highest echelons of government" (Friedman, 2020).

Biden's Secretary of State, Antony Blinken, likewise represents a marked departure from his Trump-era predecessor, Mike Pompeo. During the May 2019 Arctic Council meeting in Rovaniemi, Pompeo blasted both China's growing northern presence and Russia's military buildup in the region, warning that the Arctic "has become an arena for power and competition" (Pompeo, 2019). He likewise called out both countries for their environmental records in the High North (while praising that of the United States), yet refused to sign a multilateral declaration on the environment and sustainable mineral development in the Arctic due to the inclusion of language referencing the serious threat posed by climate change.[14] In contrast, Blinken set a very different tone during the May 2021 Arctic Council ministerial in Reykjavik, Iceland, during which chairmanship of the Council was handed over to Russia. He not only met with his Russian counterpart Sergei Lavrov on the sidelines of this event (representing the first cabinet-level contact between the two countries since Biden assumed office [Kramer, 2021]), but also expressed no qualms about signing the Reykjavik Declaration, which does mention climate change and establishes the Council's first ten-year strategic plan for the region (Arctic Council, 2021). In his remarks, Blinken furthermore stressed that the "climate crisis" was a priority for the United States, specifically singling out the need to reduce methane and black carbon emissions in the Arctic (Blinken, 2021).

Meanwhile, the new administration kept James DeHart, a career diplomat, on as the U.S.'s Coordinator for the Arctic, a position to which

---

[14] This was the first time that the signing of such an agreement has had to be cancelled since the Arctic Council was founded in 1996 (Johnson, 2019).

DeHart was appointed in July 2020.[15] Reflecting the changed tenor of the White House, DeHart characterized Blinken's Arctic Council appearance as "an opportunity to reset our leadership, and in particular on the issue of climate change" (Keleman, 2021).[16]

Arctic Security: Competition Increases

Many analyses of Arctic security begin by citing Mikhail Gorbachev's, 1987 Murmansk speech, in which the Soviet leader appealed for the region to become "a zone of peace" after enduring decades of Cold War militarization (Gorbachev, 1987). Indeed, the theme of peace and cooperation conspicuously undergird the adoption of the 1996 Ottawa Declaration, which established the intergovernmental Arctic Council. This organization has since come to play the leading role in regional affairs, but its remit has never included dealing with military and security matters (Arctic Council, 1996).[17]

However, the Arctic of the 1990s is not the Arctic of today. "The transformation of the Arctic is tightening the links between the region and the outside world," Oran Young wrote presciently almost a decade ago, "giving a variety of actors incentives to initiate new activities in the region and producing situations that may lead to rising tensions if nothing is done to devise rules of the game governing the behavior of participants in such activities" (Young, 2012, p. 81). Put differently, it is now necessary to "proactively reconcile the geopolitical with the geophysical" when it comes to discussing Arctic security (Burke, 2021).

At a macro level, we can categorize the main Arctic players in terms of norm-makers, norm-takers, and norm-breakers. The eight countries that have territorial claims in the High North all function, albeit to varying degrees, as norm-makers. Up until recently, these states have generally managed to cooperate on Arctic issues, obviating much of the need for

---

[15] Robert Papp, a former Coast Guard Admiral, had previously served as the State Department's Special Representative for the Arctic between 2014 and 2017, but the Coordinator role was only created in 2020.

[16] DeHart had already previously gone on record as stating that "with the new administration, we have a major focus on tackling the climate change crisis" (DeHart & Dorman, 2021).

[17] The Declaration's first footnote states: "The Artic Council should not deal with matters related to military security."

military posturing. Canada, Russia, and the United States are also the most prominent, if only occasional, norm-breakers.[18] Other state-level actors with an interest in the region, particularly the thirteen countries that hold permanent observer status in the Arctic Council, are on the whole norm-takers, accepting of the multilateral governance regime that has been established for the region and willing to work within it. China, however, is a wildcard.

In January 2018, Beijing released its first-ever white paper on the Arctic, which not only reiterated the controversial claim that China is a "near-Arctic" state, but also referred to it as an "important stakeholder in Arctic affairs." This document went on to emphasize that Beijing is committed to respecting "the existing framework of international law" in the Arctic and that it is pursuing its regional strategy "in accordance with the basic principles of 'respect, cooperation, win–win result and sustainability'" (Xinhua, 2018).[19] Prior to this, however, Chinese officials had made statements suggesting that the Arctic represented a "common heritage" of mankind and questioned the Arctic states' territorial claims (Rainwater, 2013). Consequently, more than a few U.S. observers regard this seemingly instrumental *volte-face* with suspicion, especially given that while China presents itself as a norm-taker in the Arctic, it acts as an unapologetic norm-breaker in the South China Sea.[20]

Beijing's strategic calculus in the Arctic appears predicated on guaranteeing access to natural resources and, secondarily, attaining a seat at the decision-making table, which becoming an established economic and scientific presence in the region would grant it. China is especially interested in diversifying its energy suppliers, including importing liquified

---

[18] For instance, the U.S. has still not ratified the 1982 UNCLOS treaty even though it expects other states to abide by it, while Canada and Russia insist on, respectively, treating the NWP and NSR as part of their territorial waters.

[19] In order to be granted permanent observer status in the Arctic Council, China was required to acknowledge the members states' sovereignty over their northern territories. (Note that in 2008 the five Arctic littoral states—Canada, Denmark [via Greenland], Norway, Russia and the United States—concluded the Ilulissat Declaration, the core tenets of which include blocking any attempt to make the Arctic Ocean an international commons and pledging to resolve conflicting territorial claims in an orderly fashion [Arctic Ocean Conference, 2008]).

[20] Distrust of Beijing's motives is furthered by the observation that Chinese leaders speak differently to domestic audiences about the Arctic than when they know their remarks will be scrutinized by the international community (Brady, 2017).

natural gas (LNG) produced in the Russian Arctic and shipped along the NSR. It has likewise explored utilizing the NSR for moving cargo from Asian manufacturers to Western markets.[21] But although transiting the NSR could save considerable time and fuel when compared to the Suez Canal, this Arctic sea lane also imposes a number of constraints that make it impractical for the large-scale movement of containerized cargo (Soroka, 2021).[22] As Anne-Marie Brady contends, "when China signals its interest in the Arctic routes, it should be understood as essentially reflecting geopolitical and geostrategic priorities rather than commercial ones" (Brady, 2017, p. 67).

However, when it comes to Arctic economics, China is a believer in diversification. Apart from the billions of dollars it has allocated to Russia energy producers, it has also made sizeable investments in a number of other states and territories, prominent among them are Iceland and Greenland (e.g., Auerswald, 2019; Volpe, 2020). (During the May 2019 Arctic Council meeting in Rovaniemi, Pompeo claimed that China's Arctic investments amounted to nearly 90 billion USD between 2012 and 2017, but this figure appears grossly overinflated.)[23]

In terms of scientific research, Beijing established its first permanent Arctic base, the Yellow River Station, on the island of Svalbard in 2004 (Polar Research Institute of China, 2019). Since then it has added a satellite receiving station in Kirkenes, Norway (2016), and the China–Iceland Arctic Science Observatory (2018). A third research station, a joint Chinese–Finnish collaboration, is currently being developed (Arctic Institute, n.d.). Having the ability to undertake Arctic science and support

---

[21] China is similarly eying the NWP, but due to its weather patterns, bathymetry, and almost total lack of infrastructure, the NWP is more difficult to traverse.

[22] In 2019, there were 37 full transits of the NSR, and 31.5 million metric tons of cargo moved along this waterway (Soroka, 2021). By way of comparison, in 2019 the Suez Canal recorded 2678 transits and slightly over 1.03 billion tons of cargo moved (Suez Canal, n.d.).

[23] Pompeo's figure was rounded up from the $89.2 billion of Chinese direct investment in the overall Arctic reported in a 2017 CNA report. However, the report's authors defined the Arctic as beginning at 60 degree north, whereas the Arctic Circle begins at approximately 66 degrees (meaning their assessment extended the conventional definition of this territory some 415 miles southward). Moreover, a CNA spokesperson acknowledged the data utilized were questionable (Lelyveld, 2019).

researchers in the region is a major reason Beijing cites for its development of an icebreaker fleet.[24]

From a security perspective, therefore, U.S. concerns over China's growing presence in the Arctic revolve around the belief that Beijing could be using economic investments and scientific inquiry as a pretext for achieving a strategic foothold in the region, for example, by building out infrastructure and then claiming the need to defend it or providing technology that could be repurposed for remote sensing or eavesdropping purposes. Reflective of these concerns is the controversy that erupted when the Chinese firm Huawei Marine entered into talks with Finland to link Europe to Asia through a 13,800 km undersea cable that was to be laid along Russia's Arctic coastline (Jüris, 2020).[25] Similar issues arose when it was revealed that Huawei wanted to build-out the Faroe Islands' 5G wireless infrastructure, with the United States objecting on security grounds and the Chinese Ambassador to Denmark (the Faroe Islands are an autonomous territory of the Kingdom of Denmark) allegedly threatening economic retaliation if Huawei were not granted the contract (Poulsen, 2020; Satariano, 2019). A recent proposal by the Chinese mining giant Shenghe Resources Holding to develop a large-scale rare earths mine in Greenland in conjunction with an Australian firm likewise raised the ire of the United States, which considers the region critical to its strategic interests (Meichtry & Hinshaw, 2021). DeHart summarized the current administration's position on such matters when he observed that the United States was "not saying no to all investment by China" in the Arctic, but that investments in critical infrastructure needed to be "looked at through a national security lens" (DeHart & Dorman, 2021).

The Russian Federation represents the other Arctic player that causes significant security concerns for the United States. According to 2019 Department of Defense (DoD) report, "competition with China and

---

[24] China has two polar-capable conventional icebreakers (its latest addition, the Xuelong 2, represents the first such domestically built vessel). A third, nuclear-powered icebreaker is currently under construction (Eiterjord, 2019).

[25] This project, along with a follow-up effort that relied on a non-Chinese consortium of foreign investors, was ultimately shelved, although in August 2021, a Russian initiative, dubbed Polar Express, began laying the 12,650 kilometer of cable that will ultimately connect Teriberka on the Barents Sea to Vladivostok on the Pacific Ocean (Stolyarov, 2021). Given that such cables "carry over 97% of all intercontinental electronic communications," it is clear why the United States is concerned over who controls them (Public–Private Analytic Exchange Program, 2017, p. i).

Russia" represents the "principal challenge to long-term U.S. security and prosperity" both within and outside the Arctic (Department of Defense, 2019, p. 2). Much like China, Russia has in recent years behaved as a norm-breaker in other parts of the world, notably Ukraine and Syria. However, we should be careful not to lump China and Russia together uncritically, as the relevant dynamics of how the United States understands and interacts with these two states are very different. The United States views China's presence in the Arctic at best warily,[26] whereas no one in Washington questions Moscow's legitimate strategic interests in the region. Boasting the most territory and coastline of any nation in the Arctic, Russia is seen as belonging in the Arctic, whereas China is not.

The apprehension surrounding Russia focuses on three main issues: its re-militarization of this region, its illegal—from the United States perspective—claims of jurisdiction over the NSR,[27] and the dual-use (i.e., economic and military) potential of this waterway and associated Arctic infrastructure. Alongside these specific concerns, Washington more generally perceives Russian foreign policy as increasingly aggressive and anti-Western, regarding Moscow's maneuvering abroad as a cynical attempt to regain lost great-power status on the world stage. Interpreting it in this manner provides a lens through which to understand events like the growing number and duration of Russian long-range air patrols off the Alaskan coast, which were resumed in 2007 but have in recent years become more confrontational (Cohen, 2021; Shelbourne, 2021), and the harassing behavior Russian naval forces in the Bering Sea have directed at American fishing vessels operating inside the United States' EEZ (Baker, 2020).

Russia has, over the course of the last decade, been quite active in refurbishing military installations in the High North, many of which were either abandoned or fell into disrepair after the dissolution of the

---

[26] Pompeo summarized the view of China as an Arctic interloper during in his May 2019 Arctic Council speech, in which he stated: "There are only Arctic states and non-Arctic states. No third category exists and claiming otherwise entitles China to exactly nothing" (Pompeo, 2019).

[27] Russia has long required vessels intending to transit the NSR to secure permits from the Northern Sea Route Administration and pay for Russian ice pilots and icebreaker support. As of 2019, it has also mandated that foreign governments whose warships wish to sail the NSR provide forty-five days' notice of this intent (Moscow reserves the right to deny such requests). Additionally, a December 2017 law restricts the loading of coal, oil, and natural gas at NSR ports to Russian-flagged vessels (Maritime Executive, 2019).

USSR, in addition to constructing new facilities and updating existing radar and air-defense systems. Estimates suggest that Russia has renovated or opened over 50 bases and other strategically important sites in the Arctic as part of this effort (Wicker & Sullivan, 2020). These range from smaller radar stations to the Nagurskoe air base, Russia's northernmost military outpost (located 965 kilometers from the North Pole, the latter is instantly recognizable due to its iconic "trefoil" structure painted in the colors of the Russian flag). Other key military bases that have been developed or upgraded include facilities on Cape Schmidt and the islands of Kotelny, Novaia Zemlia, Sredny, and Wrangel.[28] Moscow's ability to project power has also increased; for example, the lengthened runway at Nagurskoe can now support supersonic Tupolev Tu-160 strategic bombers (Sukhankin, 2020). Similarly, MiG-31BM interceptors have been deployed to the Rogachevo air base on Novaia Zemlia; with aerial refueling, these planes are capable of reaching the U.S. base in Thule, Greenland (Funaiole et al., 2021).

Meanwhile, administrative and operational changes have been made to the Northern Fleet, which is based in Severomorsk on the Kola peninsula. The largest of Russia's four geographic fleets,[29] it is home to approximately two-thirds of its nuclear navy (Åtland, 2017). These changes include a recent decision to redirect at least one of the *Borei*-class ballistic missile submarines being built for the Pacific Fleet to its Arctic counterpart, where it will join two others already in service (Kretsul & Cherepanova, 2021). The Northern Fleet is central to Moscow's regional security because Russian military planners have long relied on a bastion concept of defense, geared towards assuring access to the North Atlantic while preserving second-strike nuclear capabilities (Boulègue, 2019). Revealing the emphasis Moscow places on the High North, in January 2021 a new Northern Military District was formed, with the fleet at its center (Wade, 2014).[30] The establishment of this district, which encompasses the Russian Arctic, its coastline, and the NSR (Humpert, 2021), sends "a powerful signal to other actors of the importance of this region in Russian defense planning" (McDermott, 2021).

---

[28] Russia has also expanded the number of troops stationed in the region and improved the cold-weather combat training that they receive.

[29] The other fleets are the Baltic, Black Sea, and Pacific (there is also a Caspian Flotilla).

[30] Although as of December 2014, it had already been incorporated into the Joint Strategic Command North (OSK Sever).

Russia has also been expanding its polar icebreaking fleet, long the world's largest. Recent additions include the *Ivan Papanin* (launched October 2019), which represents a new class of armed, icebreaking patrol ships (Vavasseur, 2019), and the nuclear-powered *Arktika* (launched September 2020), currently the most powerful such vessel in the world (Nilsen, 2020c). By 2035, Moscow plans to have at least thirteen heavy icebreakers in service (more than doubling its current number), of which nine will be nuclear (Guardian, 2019).

The Russian military is likewise developing a new generation of futuristic weapons that are expected to be deployed in the Arctic, including the nuclear-powered Poseidon 2M39 torpedo and the hypersonic "Tsirkon" anti-ship cruise missile (Bergan, 2021; TASS, 2021). Moreover, it recently revealed plans to station MiG-31 fighter jets equipped with the hypersonic "Kinzhal" air-launched ballistic missile on the Kola peninsula and possibly elsewhere in the region (Lavrov & Kretsul, 2020; Nilsen, 2019).

However, advanced weaponry aside, the real-world impact of Russia's re-militarization campaign has often been overstated by Western analysts. Despite expending a great deal of effort to rebuild its presence in the Arctic, Russia has still not returned to Soviet-era levels of military capability there. The Northern fleet features fewer than 40 surface ships, of which only a dozen or so are major combatants (including its lone aircraft carrier, the *Admiral Kuznetsov*), and roughly the same number of submarines. Many of these vessels are of Cold War vintage and nearing the end of their service lives. Russia is also behind the NATO states in airpower—the Arctic bases it has built or refurbished predominantly support defensive rather than offensive capabilities, and Russian planes "mainly fly from the same distant airfields as 20 years ago because Russia's much-ballyhooed 'new Arctic bases' are too small—and lack the infrastructure—to house even a single fighter squadron much less a full air wing" (English, 2020). Meanwhile, Russia's newest submarines are technologically advanced, but endemic construction delays have hampered their deployment (Nilsen, 2021).

Nor does Russia's burgeoning icebreaker fleet necessarily represent cause for alarm, given that Russia has "ten times as much Arctic coastline as the United States and is roughly 50 times as economically dependent on the region" (English & Gardner, 2020). (Not to mention that its Arctic population is some 2.5 million people, far larger than that of any other northern country [Arctic Council, n.d.-a]). In addition, the frequently cited figure that Russia possesses nearly fifty polar-class icebreakers does not reflect the fact that a significant number of them are owned or operated by private companies and serve the needs of industry rather than the state (USCG Office of Waterways and Ocean Policy, n.d.). Moreover, armed icebreaking ships like the *Ivan Papanin*, which will be utilized mainly for routine coastal patrols and search-and-rescue operations, are not dissimilar to vessels already in service in Canada and throughout Scandinavia (English & Gardner, 2020).

What is of practical concern is the potential for downward-spiraling security dilemmas in the Arctic now that institutionalized avenues for bilateral and multilateral communication over military issues have been all but closed off, raising the level of tension and mistrust (Russia has not attended an Arctic Security Forces Roundtable meeting since the Ukrainian crisis in 2014, nor has the Arctic Chiefs of Defense Staff Conference taken place since then).[31] Moreover, NATO is increasingly being drawn into the Arctic but it has no clear mandate in the region, which it has traditionally avoided becoming involved in despite five of its member states being Arctic stakeholders (Breitenbauch et al., 2019).[32]

The increasing number and scale of military exercises involving the Arctic showcase the saber-rattling that has crept into the High North. These include Russia's Vostok 2018 exercise and the Russia Navy's August 2020 war-gaming simulation off of the Alaskan coast, the largest such undertaking in the area since the Soviet period (Isachenkov, 2020), as well as NATO's Trident Juncture 2018 and Formidable Shield 2021 exercises. Tactical deployments are also expanding in geographic scope.[33] For example, in 2020, four U.S. Navy vessels, accompanied by a Royal-Navy ship, sailed the Barents Sea for the first time since the 1980s.[34] Russia has also been moving further outside its traditional patrolling

---

[31] Russian officials recently called for reactivating contacts in both forums (Danilov, 2021; Reuters, 2021).

[32] Cooperation between the Arctic eight still takes place in the Arctic Coast Guard Forum (see Schreiber, 2021), but this body—which Russia is chairing between 2021 and 2023—does not deal with hard security issues.

[33] The Trump administration reportedly even considered having U.S. warships enter the NSR to assert their right of free passage, but the idea—which would have been regarded as a tremendous provocation by Moscow and could have turned into a major embarrassment for the U.S. if Russian icebreaker support or search-and-rescue assistance were needed—was ultimately abandoned (Nilsen, 2020c).

[34] Commenting on this display of force, U.S. Vice Admiral Lisa Francheti observed that during "these challenging times, it is more important than ever that we maintain our

range with its ships, submarines, and aircraft, increasingly probing the GIUK (Greenland-Iceland-United Kingdom) gap, the North Atlantic's most strategic transit point and one that has historically been controlled by NATO (Grove & Marson, 2020; Nilsen, 2020a).

Consequently, reactions to China and Russia in the Arctic are where we can expect the least change between the Trump and Biden administrations. Indicative of this, the Arctic strategy documents put out by the Air Force, Army, Coast Guard, Navy, and DHS are remarkably similar when it comes to identifying an emboldened Russia and an ambitious China as the main challenges facing the United States (Department of Air Force, 2020; Department of the Army, 2021; Department of the Navy, 2021; Department of Homeland Security, 2021; U.S. Coast Guard, 2019). However, the Arctic as a discrete region is less strategically central for the United States than the other four Arctic littoral states; what matters for Washington is how this region supports its abilities to project power in the Indo-Pacific and European theaters.[35] Russia has an Arctic strategy *qua* Arctic strategy, while the United States has an Arctic strategy only insofar as the Arctic is part of a broader geopolitical outlook. Indicative of this, Biden's *Interim National Security Strategic Guidance* makes no mention of the Arctic, though it does focus on the United States' "growing rivalry with China, Russia, and other authoritarian states" (White House, 2021a, p. 6). Neither is the region referenced in the *Summary of the 2018 National Defense Strategy* (Department of Defense, 2018), while the term "Arctic" only appears once in the *National Security Strategy* (White House, 2017).

In examining the positions adopted by the military branches and DHS, three things become immediately obvious. First, U.S. strategy in the region underscores a desire to return to the previous status quo. As the Navy report outlines, "[n]aval forces must operate more assertively across the Arctic ... to prevail in day-to-day competition as we protect the homeland, keep Arctic seas free and open, and deter coercive behavior and conventional aggression" (Department of the Navy, 2021, p. 4). Moreover, while emphasis is placed on working bilaterally or multilaterally with

---

steady drumbeat of operations across the European theater" (U.S. Naval Forces Europe-Africa/U.S. 6th Fleet Public Affairs, 2020).

[35] Responsibility for the Arctic is divided between the Northern Command (USNORTHCOM), Indo-Pacific Command (USINDOPACOM), and European Command (USEUCOM) (Department of the Army, 2021, p. 1).

regional partners, in terms of outside states zero-sum thinking continues to prevail, as reflected in the very title of the Army's report: *Regaining Arctic Dominance*.

Second, they do not conceptualize the Arctic in terms of exceptionalism. This is demonstrated by the surprising extent to which the strategic statements concerning this region, and military officials in general, argue by analogy. For example, the Coast Guard report notes that "China's attempts to expand its influence could impede U.S. access and freedom of navigation in the Arctic as similar attempts have been made to impede U.S. access to the South China Sea" (U.S. Coast Guard, 2019, p. 10). Likewise, Admiral James Foggo III, Commander of U.S. Naval Forces Europe, cautions that the United States "must pay particular attention to the improved capability of Russia to project power in the [Arctic] region, especially in light of Moscow's aggressive and destabilizing actions in the Black Sea and Eastern Mediterranean" (Foggo, 2019).

Finally, there is a normative subtext in these documents that relate to regime type, the implication being that non-democratic states are less trustworthy and predictable than are the United States' Arctic allies. This is witnessed by the almost moralistic language employed to characterize the regional activities, and purported priorities, of China and Russia. "Without sustained American naval presence and partnerships in the Arctic Region," reads the Navy report, "peace and prosperity will be increasingly challenged by Russia and China, whose interests and values differ dramatically from ours" (Department of the Navy, 2021, p. 2). For its part, the DHS strategy observes that Russia's and China's "malign behavior is at its most acute point since the Department's creation" (Department of Homeland Security, 2021, p. 4).[36] It goes on to accuse China of utilizing "nefarious methods to undermine international norms and institutions governing the Arctic to elevate its standing as a dominant global power" (Department of Homeland Security, 2021, p. 13).

Reflecting this increase in tensions with China and Russia, the Air Force has started to reinforce its presence in Alaska, where it flies mainly from Joint Base Elmendorf-Richardson in Anchorage and Eielson Air Force Base near Fairbanks, the latter located just 177 kilometers from the Arctic Circle. Currently, F-35 fighters are being transferred to Eielson,

---

[36] Specifically mentioned are their use of "non-kinetic instruments of power and influence, including cyber-attacks, disinformation campaigns, and exploitation of our immigration and trade systems."

which is expected to host 54 of them by December 2021 (Pawlyk, 2020). B-52 bombers have also recently deployed there (Ellis, 2020). Meanwhile, Elmendorf-Richardson is home to nearly 50 F-22 Raptors (Axe, 2020). Once all the F-35s are based at Eielson, "Alaska will be home to more advanced fighters than any other location in the world" (Department of Air Force, 2020). Indicative of the role air power plays in U.S. military planning, 79% of DoD resources allocated to the Arctic are earmarked for the Air Force (Department of Air Force, 2020, p. 4). In contrast, there is not a single Navy base in Alaska, where the United States' vital waterway interests focus on the Bering Strait, which connects the Chukchi and Bering Seas.[37] However, Alaska is important to the Air Force not so much because it is a gateway to the Arctic, but because basing planes there provides ready access to the Indo-Pacific and European theaters. It also represents "the shortest distance for adversaries to threaten the homeland with strategic air and missile attacks" (Department of Air Force, 2020), which explains why there has been considerable discussion in recent years about upgrading Alaska's early warning and air-defense systems (Wolfe, 2020).

The Army likewise forms a significant presence in Alaska, where, in addition to sharing facilities at Elmendorf-Richardson, it has two dedicated bases, Fort Wainwright and the much smaller Fort Greely, both located near Fairbanks in a sub-Arctic zone. All told, there are approximately 11,600 soldiers stationed at Elmendorf-Richardson and Wainwright under the command of the U.S. Army Alaska (USARAK) (Department of the Army, 2021, pp. 6–7).[38] In terms of assuring cold-weather warfare preparedness, the Army has for decades operated the Northern Warfare Training Center in Black Rapids, but in 2021, it added a new annual training event dubbed Arctic Warrior out of Fort Greely. Army units also participate with other branches of the military in the biennial Northern Edge exercise (Ellis, 2021).

---

[37] Whether coming or going, all trans-Arctic shipping moves through this strait, which is only 89 kilometer across at its narrowest point (the U.S. island of Little Diomede, located therein, lies just 3.5 kilometer from the Russian island of Big Diomede, despite falling on the opposite side of the international date line).

[38] As of early 2021, the Army was conducting a gap analysis of its cold weather capabilities, but at present there are no plans to station additional soldiers in Alaska (Kimmons, 2021).

As regards the Coast Guard, its three Alaskan bases (in Juneau, Valdez, and on Kodiak Island) are well removed from the Arctic. In fact, the Coast Guard only possesses two operational polar-class icebreakers, both of them based out of Seattle: the heavy *Polar Star* and medium *Healy*. However, the former (launched 1976) is tasked with running an annual resupply mission to McMurdo Station in the Antarctic, leaving the latter (launched 1999) as the only U.S. icebreaker that regularly operates in the Arctic.[39] Troubled by this, in 2020, the Trump administration decreed that the United States should have at least three "heavy polar-class security cutters" (i.e., armed icebreakers) in service by 2029 (Trump, 2020).[40] The total procurement cost for these vessels is estimated to be $2.6 billion (Congressional Research Service, 2020),[41] though there will be additional costs if the Coast Guard ends up expanding its Seattle berthing facilities (Bernton, 2021a). Nonetheless, the so-called "icebreaker gap" between the United States and Russia is over-hyped by politicians and media pundits. Such vessels are no doubt necessary for conducting search-and-rescue missions, provisioning remote bases, and supporting scientific research. They are also required for keeping sea lanes like the NSR open for military and commercial traffic (a situation that does not pertain to the U.S). However, at the end of the day Arctic security is not determined by icebreakers, but submarines, planes, and missiles.

Unlike in Alaska, where Arctic power projection is disproportionately reliant on the Air Force, on the Atlantic seaboard, where U.S. concerns center about Russia's ability to deny access to Arctic waters and project power beyond the Barents Sea and GIUK gap, the Navy reigns supreme. Attesting to this is the reestablishment of the Navy's 2nd

[39] For a time, the United States did not even have one polar-capable icebreaker operational, the Healy having been incapacitated by an electrical fire in 2020. However, it was eventually repaired, and in July 2021 the Healy began a voyage that will see it transit the Northwest Passage in the process of circumnavigating the North American continent (Bernton, 2021b).

[40] As the Coast Guard's Arctic strategy notes, while such allies as Canada, Denmark, and Norway have all invested in updated their regional patrol capacity in recent years, the United States. "is the only Arctic State that has not made similar investments in ice-capable surface maritime security assets" (U.S. Coast Guard, 2019, pp. 10–11).

[41] Prior to the release of this document, the Coast Guard had already taken the first step in this direction, announcing in April 2019 that VT Halter Marine in Mississippi was awarded a $746 million contract to design and begin fabrication of a heavy icebreaker (Larter et al., 2020).

Fleet in 2018 (Stars and Stripes, 2020). The 2nd Fleet is today again responsible for patrolling North Atlantic and Arctic waters, despite being based in Norfolk, Virginia (which lies some 3300 kilometers from the Arctic Circle). It is not yet clear how many vessels the fleet will eventually command, as it was only declared fully operational in December 2019 (Larter, 2019); if history is any guide, however, the number will be significant.[42] More generally, the U.S. Navy has for decades been the world's dominant sea power, and this is unlikely to change anytime soon. As Keith Patton of the Naval War College observes, while the Russian and Chinese navies enjoy an advantage when it comes to overall hull counts, the U.S. Navy features larger vessels optimized for distant deployments.[43] More concerning is the rough numerical parity between the United States, Russian, and Chinese attack submarines. However, Russia and China still field many conventionally powered subs, whereas the United States has for decades operated an entirely nuclear fleet designed for long-range operations and enjoys "a significant lead in subsurface firepower" (Patton, 2019). Nonetheless, Russia is increasingly challenging its underwater superiority. Russia's latest *Yasen*-class attack subs, comparable to the United States' *Virginia*-class, are highly advanced and capable performers (Mizokami, 2019). Moscow is also putting more of its technologically updated *Borei*-class ballistic missile submarines into service, while the United States has not yet started replacing its aging *Ohio*-class equivalents (Suciu, 2021).

In terms of Arctic and near-Arctic strategic infrastructure, the United States, as part of its effort to improve the early warning systems of the North American Aerospace Defense Command (NORAD), has in recent years upgraded the radar facilities at Thule Air Base in Greenland, which is primarily tasked with monitoring missile launches and providing space surveillance (Husseini, 2019; Newell, 2017). (At 1210 kilometers above the Arctic Circle, Thule is the United States' northernmost military installation.) It has also proposed to the Canadian government that further improvements be made to NORAD's surveillance capacity

---

[42] Before the 2nd Fleet was disestablished in 2011, it "oversaw approximately 126 ships, 4500 aircraft, and 90,000 personnel home-ported at U.S. Navy installations along the United States East Coast" (Naval Recognition, 2018).

[43] As one retired U.S. Navy captain writes, "[n]either Russia nor any other nation can use the surface of the world ocean except at the sufferance of the United States and its allies" (Dismukes, 2020, p. 13).

(Monga & Vieira, 2021). Additionally, portions of the naval air station in Keflavik, Iceland (originally deactivated in 2006) have been refurbished to accommodate P-8A Poseidon jets, which excel at anti-submarine warfare (Montgomery, 2018).

Cold, Hard Economics

A 2008 U.S. Geological Survey report estimated that the Arctic as a whole harbors "undiscovered, technically recoverable" hydrocarbons on the order of 90 billion barrels of oil, 1670 trillion cubic feet of natural gas, and 44 billion barrels of natural gas liquids, which at the time constituted roughly 22% of the globe's unexploited reserves (Stauffer, 2008). It also contains valuable mineral deposits, including copper, diamonds, gold, lead, nickel, rubies, platinum, zinc, and various rare-earth elements.[44] Consequently, while the United States is not nearly as economically dependent on the Arctic as Russia, the High North is still important for it, principally though not exclusively due to the oil industry.

The vast majority (roughly 95%) of Alaska's crude oil extraction takes place on the North Slope (U.S. Energy Information Administration, 2021).[45] This area produced an average of 496,106 barrels of oil daily in fiscal year 2019, with the hydrocarbon industry contributing more than \$3.1 billion in taxes and royalties to state and municipal coffers during that period (McDowell Group, 2020a, p. 4; Resource Development Council, n.d.-a). Indicative of how much hydrocarbons factor into its economy, Alaska is the only U.S. state that does not levy either sales or personal income taxes (McDowell Group, 2020a, p. 4).[46] In fact, before oil prices crashed in late 2014, over half of the annual state budget and more than 90% of its discretionary funds derived from hydrocarbons (Understanding Alaska's Budget, n.d.). And while the oil market's catastrophic collapse and relatively slow rebound has cut into this revenue

---

[44] The Arctic's estimated deposits of gold, nickel, platinum, and zinc alone are worth an estimated \$1 trillion (U.S. Government Accountability Office, n.d.).

[45] As of 2020, there were 17 primary companies involved in the discovery, production, refining, and transportation of hydrocarbons focused on the North Slope and Cook Inlet areas of Alaska (McDowell Group, 2020a, p. 1).

[46] The Permanent Fund, endowed by oil revenue, actually makes annual payments to all Alaskan residents.

stream,[47] state and local governments remain exceptionally reliant on the fossil fuel industry (see McDowell Group, 2020a, pp. 4–5). This holds true for the overall economy as well: in 2018 oil firms, in some way, shape, or form, employed around 77,600 individuals in Alaska (which translates to roughly one-quarter of all jobs in the state), accounting for an aggregate $4.8 billion in wages (McDowell Group, 2020a, p. 3; Resource Development Council, n.d.-a). Simply stated, "no other private sector comes close to generating more economic impact in Alaska than Alaska's oil and gas industry" (McDowell Group, 2020a, p. 6).

However, far from all the hydrocarbon potential of the Alaskan Arctic has been exploited; tremendous reserves still exist on the North Slope and in the ANWR. In addition, vast oil and gas fields lie offshore in the Beaufort and Chukchi Seas (Conley, 2013, p. 6). Nonetheless, the degree to which Arctic oil and gas will fund Alaska's future is uncertain. While energy prices have crept up off their previous lows, drilling in many parts of the Arctic, particularly offshore, remains cost-prohibitive. As the world begins to transition away from fossil fuels, it also becomes harder to justify engaging in upstream activities in remote wilderness areas. Infrastructure, or rather its absence, likewise plays a role. According to an industry association, Alaska sits atop an estimated 250 trillion cubic feet of natural gas, which could support the entire United States' needs, at current consumption levels, for over a decade. But it lacks a means by which to economically move even the gas that is already being produced as a by-product of oil drilling to market, leading most of it to be reinjected into the wells (American Gas Association, n.d.).

Similarly, mining is a big business in Alaska, including in its Arctic reaches. In 2019, mining activities in the state directly or indirectly supported some 9400 jobs and generated $740 million in wages (Resource Development Council, n.d.-b). (Nonfuel mineral production in the state of Alaska as a whole was valued at $3.69 billion in 2017 [Singh & Callaghan, 2017]). Looking at the Arctic portion of the state specifically, the Red Dog mine in the Northwest Arctic Borough is one of the world's top zinc producers (Teck, 2021). Moreover, there are still huge reserves of metals and other minerals that remain in the ground in the Alaskan Arctic. One of the most promising exploratory ventures in the region is the Upper Kobuk Mineral Project, which is

---

[47] From late 2014 to early 2016, oil prices fell from over $110/barrel to $30/barrel, resulting in the loss of thousands of jobs (McDowell Group, 2020a, p. 2).

seeking to develop the Arctic and Bornite deposits in Alaska's Ambler Mining District (McDowell Group, 2018, pp. 12–13; Wilson Center, n.d.). However, the future of mining in the north is clouded by the same environmental concerns that plague oil and gas development.

Another important economic sector in Alaska is commercial fishing, with its total seafood industry worth some $5.6 billion annually (McDowell Group, 2020b, p. 4). The financial impact of fishing is more limited in the northern reaches of the state, but the industry nonetheless employs some 3200 workers and injects around $42 million dollars into the Arctic-Yukon-Kuskokwim region (McDowell Group, 2020b, p. 14).

Alaskan tourism is similarly a huge industry, with an estimated economic benefit to the state of $4.5 billion in 2018 (Resource Development Council, n.d.-c). However, its contribution to the Alaskan Arctic is modest, mainly due to how remote and sparsely populated this territory is. Additionally, most visitors come to Alaska on cruise ships, which for financial and practical reasons (i.e., fuel cost, lack of docking facilities, and threat of sea ice) do not range far up the coast. Still, there exist possibilities for increasing the scale of cultural and ecological tourism in the north.

With the warming of the cryosphere, northern Alaska is also experiencing more shipping activity and general marine traffic. The United States does not have any deepwater Arctic ports at present, but in late December 2020 Congress authorized the construction of such a facility in near-Arctic Nome; estimates suggest its cost will exceed half-a-billion dollars (Rubano, 2021). Meanwhile, even the relatively southern city of Seward is seeking to recast itself as an Arctic access point (Rosen, 2016).

Indeed, the High North as a whole is today more economically accessible than ever, with formerly peripheral territories like Greenland becoming increasingly relevant to global trade. Reflecting this, in 2020 Washington announced that it was offering Greenland $12.1 million to promote economic development and reopening its consulate in Nuuk, the previous one having been shut down in 1953 (Bennett, 2020).[48]

Concurrently, parts of the United States have pursued localized business initiatives in the Arctic. For example, demonstrating how connections

---

[48] One year prior, the U.S. State Department and Greenland's Ministry of Mineral Resources and Labor signed a memorandum of understanding pledging to cooperatively develop the island's mineral resource sector as well as its governance (Naalakkersuisut, 2019).

between regions may be reimagined, the state of Maine has over the course of the last decade made a concerted effort to capitalize on the expansion of northern shipping, with lobbying by state officials resulting in the Icelandic shipping company Eimskip choosing the city of Portland to be their logistical hub for North America (Bell, 2016).[49]

Indigenous Peoples in the Alaskan Arctic

The High North has historically functioned as a *terra nullis* in the national imaginaries of Arctic countries, a great white wilderness to be explored, tamed, and ultimately exploited. But native peoples have lived there for untold generations, this "blank spot" on outsiders' maps serving as their pantry and bedroom. Today they continue to reside in the Arctic, often making up transborder populations given that their ancestors survived and even thrived in the region well before the tyranny of cartography was imposed on them.

According to the latest available figures, indigenous peoples in Alaska number roughly 114,400 individuals, comprising approximately 15.6% of the state's total population and constituting a particularly significant presence in Arctic and other rural areas (United States Census Bureau, n.d.).[50] It is difficult to precisely define the native groups that dwell in Alaska's northern territories, as identities are differently construed by academics, government officials, and natives themselves. Nonetheless, in this region, the main meta-division is between the various sub-groups that represent the Inuit and Athabaskan language families. Indigenous peoples are also organized around tribal affiliations, of which the federal Bureau of Indian Affairs recognizes some 200 in Alaska (Indian Affairs Bureau, 2019). Additionally, as the result of the 1971 Alaska Native Claims Settlement Act, indigenous Alaskans are divided into 13 regional corporations (and around 225 village-level corporations); these entities oversee their ancestral lands and support the community economically (Resource Development Council, n.d.-d).

---

[49] Both Maine's former governor, Paul LePage, and current governor, Janet Mills, have made appearances at Iceland's annual Arctic Circle Assembly to bolster the state's economic ties to the region.

[50] Calculated on the basis of reported census data; these figures only capture individuals identifying with one racial category.

The Arctic Council recognizes the unique socio-political positionality of native peoples in the High North, and as such accords certain of them extra-state representation as permanent members of this body. With regard to the inhabitants of Alaska, the two relevant groups are the Arctic Athabaskan Council and the Gwich'in Council International, both of which are constituent members of the Indigenous Peoples' Secretariat (Arctic Council, n.d.-b).

The issues facing native Alaskans in the Arctic today are manifold. Among its other effects, climate change has led to marked coastal erosion in parts of the region, forcing indigenous communities to relocate. Warming temperatures and diminishing ice cover are also having an impact on subsistence lifestyles (e.g., Schliess, 2016; Shallenberger, 2019). The alteration of animal migration patterns on land and in the water in response to unfolding environmental stressors has likewise aggravated the issue of food insecurity (Struzik, 2016). Moreover, there exist regional challenges that are not related to a warming globe but rather the remoteness of Arctic settlements. These have to do with a lack of roadways and other critical infrastructure (e.g., waste disposal, internet),[51] as well as persistent problems with access to basic services, healthcare prominent among them.

The latter observation is especially worth emphasizing in relation to Covid-19. In the United States, death rates early on in the coronavirus outbreak were nearly two times higher among American Indians and Alaskan Natives than the Caucasian population (Arrazola et al., 2020). Reasons for the pandemic's disproportionate impact on indigenous Arctic populations include lack of medical services, ineffective political representation, crowded/multigenerational living arrangements, and poor sanitary conditions, along with "higher rates of pre-existing health issues like diabetes, obesity, and respiratory infections" (Petrov et al., 2021, p. 1).

An Arctic Science

U.S. officials have often stressed scientific diplomacy as a way to promote the United States' soft power. Reflective of this, Barack Obama's administration organized the first science ministerial on the Arctic, which was held in Washington in 2016 (White House, 2016). The third such meeting

---

[51] Although in the case of internet access progress is being made (Federal Communications Commission, 2021).

222   G. SOROKA

took place in Tokyo in May 2021, during which "the U.S. delegation emphasized its resolve to strengthening our Arctic partnerships and to work to advance global research cooperation and collaboration to meet the challenges facing our climate and our planet for years to come" (White House, 2021b). It seems almost certain that the Biden administration, which has publicly recommitted the United States to fighting anthropogenic climate change, will continue pursuing policies that foster research on the warming cryosphere, as well as the Arctic more generally. Cross-border cooperation plays a key role in this context. (At present scientific research may be the only arena in which the United States can work effectively with Russia and China.) As James DeHart explains, "I don't know of any other region of the world, except maybe Antarctica, where international collaboration on science is so strong" (DeHart & Dorman, 2021).

Support for these endeavors comes from multiple sources, including federal and state governments (in the case of Alaska), public and private academic institutions, and various non-governmental funding bodies, all of which have begun paying more attention to the region in recent years. While aggregated funding figures do not exist for the latter two categories, we can get a sense of the federal government's spending on Arctic research as it pertains to the National Science Foundation (NSF). The Office of Polar Programs at the NSF, which is responsible for both Arctic and Antarctic research, oversees a variety of regional projects under the auspices of the Section for Arctic Science (National Science Foundation, n.d.-a). All told, for fiscal year 2021, the OPP's research budget is $101.32 million (National Science Foundation, 2021a). Regarding Arctic-specific activities, in 2016, the NSF created the Navigating the New Arctic (NNA) program as part of its "Big Ideas" initiative, intended to position the United States on the cutting-edge of the most significant and future-oriented domains in science and engineering (National Science Foundation, n.d.-b). In the 2021 grant cycle, the NNA anticipates funding up to 20 separate projects with a total estimated budget of $30 million (National Science Foundation, 2021b).[52] However, it is important to realize that these NSF programs represent only part of the United States' commitment to Arctic science. Even at the governmental

---

[52] There have been calls by scientists for the NSF to more overtly involve indigenous communities in this effort, in order to make Arctic research more relevant to their communities and responsive to their concerns (Early, 2021).

level, there are a number of other agencies that fund, and bodies that conduct, research relevant to the High North. A prominent example of the latter is the National Snow and Ice Data Center, which collects and analyzes polar climatic information (based in Boulder, Colorado, it is affiliated with the National Oceanic and Atmospheric Administration).

CONCLUSION

"Traditionally," write Kristina Spohr and Daniel Hamilton, "the Arctic has been a region where some big powers act small and some small powers act big" (Spohr & Hamilton, 2020, p. 2) Although showing signs of change, this observation well characterizes the United States' historical engagement with the High North. The Arctic certainly played a prominent role in the United States thinking during the Cold War, but it was mainly viewed as a component part of a wider geographic conflict rather than a discrete space important in its own right (the similarities to how the U.S. military today regards the Arctic are striking). This benign neglect has, in significant measure, resulted from the American people never really viewing themselves as an Arctic nation or conceiving of the region as one on which the United States' status and standing on the world stage depended. Thus, the Arctic serves a very different role for the United States than for Russia or even China.

However, while the Biden administration is less bellicose than its predecessor, in terms of hard-power contestation little has changed with the inauguration of a new president. The United States and its allies, both within NATO and outside of it, remain highly concerned about Russia's growing military presence in the Arctic and China's untransparent intentions towards the region (realistically, though, Beijing's northern focus remains modest in comparison to its involvement in other parts of the world).

Yet the ability to cooperate among the Arctic states has not fallen completely by the wayside. In addition to the 2021 signing of the Reykjavik Declaration, the Arctic Council has in recent years facilitated the negotiation of a regional search-and-rescue agreement (2011), an oil spill preparedness and response agreement (2013), and an agreement on scientific cooperation (2017) (Young, 2020, pp. 55–56). To this list of successes, we can add the adoption of the 2017 Polar Code, which regulates shipping in northern waters, and the 2018 Central Arctic Ocean Fisheries Agreement (Arctic Council, 2020). However, where dialogue and cooperation are most needed, namely in the strategic realm, they are not currently occurring. As a result, Arctic issues are becoming more difficult to compartmentalize away from non-proximate conflicts.

Mistrust and miscommunication of intentions is therefore the greatest security threat in the Arctic today. However, few expect a shooting war in the region anytime soon. We are much more likely to witness a continual skirmish of slights and provocations that, taken cumulatively, will impede cooperation on other important issues, chief among them climate change. This is most unfortunate, as the threat of a warming planet can only be addressed in a multilateral manner.

Given that the United States will remain the sole global superpower for the foreseeable future, it will have to balance between being a hegemon in the world system and interacting productively with other Arctic stakeholders, chief among them Russia (Lackenbauer & Dean, 2020, p. 347). "The real strategic choice," as English and Gardner write, "is whether to seek an accommodation that permits some measure of mutual security or to insist on continued U.S.-NATO dominance and risk escalating Arctic confrontation" (English & Gardner, 2020). So far, the latter option seems to be prevailing among United States decision-makers, which does not bode well for either the stability of regional security arrangements or the ability of Arctic states to address transborder issues.

What can be done to mitigate these problems? One intriguing proposal for defusing tensions in the region concerns creating a code of military conduct for the Arctic. Institutionalizing which practices will be tolerated as opposed to which will be deemed illegitimate would improve transparency and lessen the potential for non-threatening activities to be misconstrued (Boulègue, 2019). Another potential way forward is to "re-compartmentalize" the Arctic by allowing firms based in the United States and other Western countries to partner with Russia on infrastructure development and pollution abatement, activities currently impeded by the sanctions regime. Not only would this be in the interest of all involved, but "cooperation on environmental issues could help build the trust needed for Washington and Moscow to address more sensitive issues, including security arrangements for the region" (Graham & Jaffe, 2020). This latter approach holds particular promise, as while Russia has since 2014 looked towards China to help finance its ambitious Arctic projects (like Yamal LNG), neither country appears to be the other's preferred partner (Grove, 2021; Soroka, 2016).

In conclusion, writing about the High North in a time of Covid-19 takes on a special poignancy. Americans by this point in time have been admonished for months that masks and vaccinations are not just necessary to protect the individual but also to ensure the common good. The intentionality behind this rhetoric, which emphasizes our collective response to the pandemic, applies to a warming Arctic as well. For better or worse, we are all in this together.

REFERENCES

American Gas Association. (n.d.). *Alaskan natural gas*. https://www.aga.org/policy/economy/supply/alaskan-natural-gas/. Accessed 24 Aug 2021.

Arctic Council. (1996, September 19). *Declaration on the establishment of the Arctic Council*. https://oaarchive.arctic-council.org/bitstream/handle/11374/85/EDOCS-1752-v2ACMMCA00_Ottawa_1996_Founding_Declaration.PDF?sequence=5&isAllowed=y. Accessed 14 Aug 2021.

Arctic Council. (2020, October 28). *Exploring the Arctic Ocean: The agreement that protects an unknown ecosystem*. https://arctic-council.org/en/news/exploring-the-arctic-ocean-the-agreement-that-protects-an-unknown-ecosystem/. Accessed 25 Aug 2021.

Arctic Council. (2021, May 20). *Arctic Council foreign ministers sign the Reykjavik Declaration, adopt the Council's first strategic plan and pass the chairmanship from Iceland to the Russian Federation*. https://arctic-council.org/en/news/arctic-council-foreign-ministers-sign-the-reykjavik-declaration-adopt-councils-first-strategic-plan/. Accessed 14 Aug 2021.

Arctic Council. (n.d.-a). *The Russian Federation*. https://arctic-council.org/en/about/states/russian-federation/. Accessed 16 Aug 2021.

Arctic Council. (n.d.-b). *Indigenous peoples' secretariat*. https://arctic-council.org/en/about/indigenous-peoples-secretariat/. Accessed 19 Aug 2021.

Arctic Institute. (n.d.). *China*. https://www.thearcticinstitute.org/countries/china/. Accessed 20 Aug 2021.

Arctic Ocean Conference. (2008, May 28). *The Ilulissat Declaration*. https://arcticportal.org/images/stories/pdf/Ilulissat-declaration.pdf. Accessed 15 Aug 2021.

Arctic Research and Policy Act of 1984 (Amended 1990). (1990). National Science Foundation. https://www.nsf.gov/geo/opp/arctic/iarpc/arc_res_pol_act.jsp#112. Accessed 17 Aug 2021.

Arrazola, J., Masiello, M. M., Joshi, S., et al. (2020). COVID-19 mortality among American Indian and Alaska native persons—14 States, January—June

226   G. SOROKA

2020. *Morbidity and Mortality Weekly Report, 69*(49), 1853–1856. https://doi.org/10.15585/mmwr.mm6949a3

Åtland, K. (2017, June 12). *The building up of Russia's military potential in the Arctic region and possible elements of its deterrence.* Centre for Russian Studies. http://r-studies.org/cms/index.php?action=news/view_detaiIs&news_id=43590&lang=eng. Accessed 21 Aug 2021.

Auerswald, D. (2019, May 24). *China's multifaceted arctic strategy: War on the rocks.* https://warontherocks.com/2019/05/chinas-multifaceted-arctic-strategy/. Accessed 15 Aug 2021.

Axe, D. (2020, Jun 13). With F-22 Stealth Fighters running out, The U.S. Air Force got desperate. *Forbes.* https://www.forbes.com/sites/davidaxe/2020/06/13/with-f-22-stealth-fighters-running-out-the-us-air-force-got-desperate/?sh=3100c0e454fa. Accessed 25 Aug 2021.

Baker, M. (2020, November 12). 'Are We Getting Invaded?' U.S. boats faced Russian aggression near Alaska. *New York Times.* https://www.nytimes.com/2020/11/12/us/russia-military-alaska-arctic-fishing.html. Accessed 21 Aug 2021.

Ballinger, T. J., Overland, J. E., Wang, M., Bhatt, U. S., Hanna, E., Hanssen-Bauer, I., Kim, S. J., Thoman, R. L., & Walsh, J. E. (2020). *Surface air temperature. 2020* Arctic Report Card. https://doi.org/10.25923/gcw8-2z06

Balton, D. (2020, November 30). *The Arctic in a post-election world.* The Wilson Center. https://www.wilsoncenter.org/event/arctic-post-election-world. Accessed 17 Aug 2021.

Bell, T. (2016, October 6). How Maine is turning itself into an Arctic player. *Anchorage Daily News.* https://www.adn.com/arctic/2016/10/06/how-maine-is-turning-itself-into-an-arctic-player/. Accessed 21 Aug 2021.

Bennett, M. (2020, April 28). With a $12.1 million offer to Greenland, America is playing softball in the Arctic. *Arctic Today.* https://www.arctictoday.com/with-a-12-1-million-offer-to-greenland-america-is-playing-softball-in-the-arctic/. Accessed 17 Aug 2021.

Bergan, B. (2021, April 5). *A new Russian weapon can flood coastal cities with 'Radioactive Tsunamis'.* Interesting Engineering. https://interestingengineering.com/russian-weapon-flood-coastal-cities-radioactive-tsunamis. Accessed 21 Aug 2021.

Bernton, H. (2021a, May 12). Coast guard could triple base size on Seattle Waterfront as U.S. ramps up Arctic presence. *Seattle Times.* https://www.seattletimes.com/seattle-news/coast-guard-could-triple-base-size-on-seattle-waterfront-as-u-s-ramps-up-arctic-presence/. Accessed 25 Aug 2021.

Bernton, H. (2021b, July 21). Seattle-based icebreaker will make northwest passage transit in new Arctic mission. *Seattle Times.* https://www.seattleti

mes.com/seattle-news/seattle-based-icebreaker-will-make-northwest-passage-transit-in-new-arctic-mission/. Accessed 25 Aug 2021.

Blinken, A. J. (2021, May 20). *Secretary Antony J. Blinken intervention at Arctic Council Ministerial. U.S. Department of State*. https://www.state.gov/secret ary-antony-j-blinken-intervention-at-arctic-council-ministerial/. Accessed 14 Aug 2021.

Borunda, A. (2021, May 19). *'Zombie' fires in the Arctic are linked to climate change*. National Geographic. https://www.nationalgeographic.com/env ironment/article/zombie-fires-in-the-arctic-are-linked-to-climate-change. Accessed 17 Aug 2021.

Boulègue, M. (2019, June 28). *Russia's military posture in the Arctic: Managing hard power in a 'Low Tension' environment*. Chatham House. https://www.chathamhouse.org/2019/06/russias-military-posture-arctic. Accessed 21 Aug 2021.

Brady, A. M. (2017). *China as a Polar Power*. Cambridge University Press.

Breitenbauch, H., Søby, K., & Groesmeyer, J. (2019, November 28). *Military and environmental challenges in the Arctic*. Carnegie Europe. https://carneg ieeurope.eu/2019/11/28/military-and-environmental-challenges-in-arctic-pub-80424. Accessed 16 Aug 2021.

Burke, S. E. (2021, January 28). *The Arctic threat that must not be named: War on the rocks*. https://warontherocks.com/2021/01/the-arctic-threat-that-must-not-be-named/. Accessed 14 Aug 2021.

Cohen, R. (2021, April 28). Spike in Russian aircraft intercepts straining air force crews in Alaska, three-star says. *Air Force Times*. https://www.airfor cetimes.com/news/your-air-force/2021/04/28/spike-in-russian-aircraft-int ercepts-straining-air-force-crews-in-alaska-three-star-says/. Accessed 21 Aug 2021.

Congressional Research Service. (2020, December 9). *Coast guard polar security cutter (Polar icebreaker) program: Background and issues for Congress*. https://www.documentcloud.org/documents/20422285-coast-guard-polar-security-cutter-polar-icebreaker-program-background-and-issues-for-congress-dec-9-2020

Conley, H. A. (2013, July). *Arctic economics in the 21st century: The benefits and costs of cold*. Center for Strategic and International Studies. https://csis-web site-prod.s3.amazonaws.com/s3fs-public/legacy_files/files/publication/130 710_Conley_ArcticEconomics_WEB.pdf. Accessed 24 Aug 2021.

Danilov, P. B. (2021, January 19). *Russia wants to resume meetings between Arctic defense chiefs*. High North News. https://www.highnorthnews.com/ en/russia-wants-resume-meetings-between-arctic-defense-chiefs. Accessed 16 Aug 2021.

228   G. SOROKA

Davenport, C. (2021, August 18). Court blocks a vast Alaskan drilling project, citing climate dangers. *New York Times*. https://www.nytimes.com/2021/08/18/climate/alaska-willow-oil.html. Accessed 12 Aug 2021.

DeHart, J. P., & Dorman, S. (2021, March). *A balanced approach to the Arctic—A conversation with U.S. coordinator for the Arctic region James P. DeHart*. American Foreign Service Association. https://afsa.org/balanced-approach-arctic-conversation-us-coordinator-arctic-region-james-p-dehart. Accessed 14 Aug 2021.

Department of Air Force. (2020, July). *Arctic strategy*. https://www.af.mil/Portals/1/documents/2020SAF/July/ArcticStrategy.pdf. Accessed 16 Aug 2021.

Department of the Army. (2021, January 19). *Regaining Arctic dominance: The U.S. Army in the Arctic*. https://www.army.mil/e2/downloads/rv7/about/2021_army_arctic_strategy.pdf. Accessed 16 Aug 2021.

Department of Defense. (2018). *Summary of the 2018 National Defense Strategy of the United States of America*. https://dod.defense.gov/Portals/1/Documents/pubs/2018-National-Defense-Strategy-Summary.pdf. Accessed 25 Aug 2021.

Department of Defense. (2019, June). *Report to Congress: Arctic strategy*. https://media.defense.gov/2019/Jun/06/2002141657/-1/-1/1/2019-DOD-ARCTICSTRATEGY.PDF. Accessed 11 Aug 2021.

Department of Homeland Security. (2021, January). *Strategic approach for Arctic Homeland Security*. https://www.dhs.gov/sites/default/files/publications/21_0113_plcy_dhs-arctic-strategy_0.pdf. Accessed 16 Aug 2021.

Department of the Navy. (2021, January). *A Blue Arctic*. https://media.defense.gov/2021/Jan/05/2002560338/-1/-1/0/ARCTIC%2520BLUEPRINT%25202021%2520FINAL.PDF/ARCTIC%2520BLUEPRINT%252 02021%2520FINAL.PDF. Accessed 16 Aug 2021.

Dismukes, B. (2020). The return of great-power competition—Cold war lessons about strategic antisubmarine warfare and defense of sea lines of communication. *Naval War College Review, 13*(3), 2–27.

Doucleff, M. (2016, August 3). *Anthrax outbreak in Russia thought to be result of thawing permafrost*. NPR. https://www.npr.org/sections/goatsandsoda/2016/08/03/488400947/anthrax-outbreak-in-russia-thought-to-be-result-of-thawing-permafrost. Accessed 17 Aug 2021.

Early, W. (2021, February 5). *More indigenous knowledge needed to navigate 'New Arctic,' scientists say*. Alaska Public Media. https://www.alaskapublic.org/2021/02/05/researchers-ask-for-more-indigenous-input-in-national-arctic-science-initiative/. Accessed 25 Aug 2021.

Eilperin, J. (2015, August 15). The fascinating (and scenic) history of presidential visits to Alaska. *Washington Post*. https://www.washingtonpost.com/

news/the-fix/wp/2015/08/25/a-scenic-visual-history-of-presidential-visits-to-alaska/. Accessed 17 Aug 2021.

Eiterjord, T. A. (2019, September 5). Checking in on China's nuclear icebreaker. *The Diplomat.* https://thediplomat.com/2019/09/checking-in-on-chinas-nuclear-icebreaker/. Accessed 20 Aug 2021.

Ellis, T. (2020, June 17). *B-52s arrive at Eielson to prepare pilots to intercept Russian Aircraft.* Alaska Public Media. https://www.alaskapublic.org/2020/06/17/b-52s-arrive-at-eielson-to-prepare-pilots-to-intercept-russian-aircraft/. Accessed 25 Aug 2021.

Ellis, T. (2021, February 9). *As military concerns move to warming Arctic, army starts annual cold-weather training exercise.* Alaska Public Media. https://www.alaskapublic.org/2021/02/09/as-military-concerns-move-to-warming-arctic-army-starts-annual-cold-weather-training-exercise/. Accessed 25 Aug 2021.

English, R. D. (2020, June 18). Why an Arctic arms race would be a mistake. *Arctic Today.* https://www.arctictoday.com/why-an-arctic-arms-race-would-be-a-mistake/. Accessed 21 Aug 2021.

English, R. D., & Gardner, M. G. (2020, September 29). Phantom peril in the Arctic: Russia doesn't threaten the United States in the far north—But climate change does. *Foreign Affairs.* https://www.foreignaffairs.com/articles/united-states/2020-09-29/phantom-peril-arctic. Accessed 21 Aug 2021.

Federal Communications Commission. (2021, August 23). *FCC grants licenses for wireless services in Alaska tribal communities.* https://www.fcc.gov/document/fcc-grants-licenses-wireless-services-alaska-native-communities. Accessed 25 Aug 2021.

Foggo III, J. (2019, July 10). *Russia, China offer challenges in the Arctic.* Defense One. https://www.defenseone.com/ideas/2019/07/russia-china-offer-challenges-arctic/158303/. Accessed 25 Aug 2021.

Friedman, L. (2020, November 23). With John Kerry Pick, Biden selects a 'Climate Envoy' with stature. *New York Times.* https://www.nytimes.com/2020/11/23/climate/john-kerry-climate-change.html. Accessed 14 Aug 2021.

Funaiole, M. P., Bermudez Jr., J. S., & Wall, C. (2021, April 14). *Russia's northern fleet deploys long-range interceptors to remote Arctic base.* Center for Strategic & International Studies. https://www.csis.org/analysis/russias-northern-fleet-deploys-long-range-interceptors-remote-arctic-base?gclid=CjwKCAjw9uKIBhA8EiwAYPUS3P4a5eyj1aeR96LsF-gYm-vPOKHomptAoC3JfDikF5lJhMTKRfngshoCxGEQAvD_BwE. Accessed 21 Aug 2021.

Gorbachev, M. (1987, October 1). *Mikhail Gorbachev's speech in Murmansk at the ceremonial meeting on the occasion of the presentation of the order of Lenin and the Gold Star to the city of Murmansk.* Barentsinfo. https://www.barentsinfo.fi/docs/Gorbachev_speech.pdf. Accessed 14 Aug 2021.

230 G. SOROKA

Graham, T., & Jaffe, A. M. (2020, July 27). There is no scramble for the Arctic: Climate change demands cooperation, not competition, in the far north. *Foreign Affairs*. https://www.foreignaffairs.com/articles/russian-federation/2020-07-27/there-no-scramble-arctic. Accessed 25 Aug 2021.

Grove, T. (2021, May 25). Russian military seeks to outmuscle U.S. in Arctic. *Wall Street Journal*. https://www.wsj.com/articles/russian-military-seeks-to-outmuscle-u-s-in-arctic-11621935002?mod=searchresults_pos6&page=1. Accessed 25 Aug 2021.

Grove, T., & Marson, J. (2020, July 2). Russian submarines test NATO in icy North Atlantic. *Wall Street Journal*. https://www.wsj.com/articles/russian-submarines-test-nato-in-icy-north-atlantic-11593682201. Accessed 16 Aug 2021.

Guardian. (2019, May 26). *Russia launches new nuclear-powered icebreaker in bid to open up Arctic*. https://www.theguardian.com/world/2019/may/26/russia-launches-new-nuclear-powered-icebreaker-in-bid-to-open-up-arctic. Accessed 21 Aug 2021.

Hofstaedter, E. (2021, April 19). *Interior department delays plan to open 28 million acres of land in Alaska to mineral development*. KTOO. https://www.ktoo.org/2021/04/19/interior-department-delays-plan-to-open-28-million-acres-of-land-in-alaska-to-mineral-development/. Accessed 11 Aug 2021.

Holm Olsen, I. (2020). Greenland, the Arctic, and the issue of representation: What is the Arctic? Who has a say? In K. Spohr, D. S. Hamilton, & J. C. Moyer (Eds.), *The Arctic and world order* (pp. 77–97). Foreign Policy Institute/Henry Kissinger Center for Global Affairs, Johns Hopkins University SAIS.

Howell, D., Sandberg, E., & Brooks, L. (2020, April). *Alaska population projections: 2019–2045*. Alaska Department of Labor and Workforce Development. https://live.laborstats.alaska.gov//pop/projections/pub/popproj.pdf. Accessed 17 Aug 2021.

Humpert, M. (2021, January 13). *Russia elevates importance of northern fleet upgrading it to military district status*. High North News. https://www.highnorthnews.com/en/russia-elevates-importance-northern-fleet-upgrading-it-military-district-status. Accessed 21 Aug 2021.

Huserbråten, M. B.O., Eriksen, E., Gjøsæter, H., & Vikebø, F. (2019). Polar Cod in jeopardy under the retreating Arctic Sea ice. *Communications Biology, 407*(2). https://doi.org/10.1038/s42003-019-0649-2

Husseini, T. (2019, June 5). *Thule Air Base: Inside the US's northernmost military base in Greenland*. Airforce Technology. https://www.airforce-technology.com/features/thule-military-base-in-greenland/. Accessed 25 Aug 2021.

Indian Affairs Bureau. (2019, February 1). *Indian entities recognized by and eligible to receive services from the United States Bureau of Indian Affairs*. https://www.federalregister.gov/documents/2019/02/01/2019-00897/

indian-entities-recognized-by-and-eligible-to-receive-services-from-the-uni ted-states-bureau-of. Accessed 19 Aug 2021.

IPCC. (2021). Summary for policymakers. In V. Masson-Delmotte, P. Zhai, A. Pirani, S. L. Connors, C. Péan, S. Berger, N. Caud, Y. Chen, L. Goldfarb, M. I. Gomis, M. Huang, K. Leitzell, E. Lonnoy, J. B. R. Matthews, T. K. Maycock, T. Waterfield, O. Yelekçi, R. Yu, & B. Zhou (Eds.), *Climate change 2021: The physical science basis.* Contribution of Working Group I to the Sixth Assessment Report of the Intergovernmental Panel on Climate Change. Cambridge UP. In Press. https://www.ipcc.ch/report/ar6/wg1/ downloads/report/IPCC_AR6_WGI_SPM.pdf. Accessed 17 Aug 2021.

Isachenkov, V. (2020, August 30). Russian navy conducts major maneuvers near Alaska. *Military Times.* https://www.militarytimes.com/news/your-military/ 2020/08/30/russian-navy-conducts-major-maneuvers-near-alaska/. Accessed 16 Aug 2021.

Johnson, S. (2019, May 7). *U.S. sinks arctic accord due to climate change differences: Diplomats.* Reuters. https://www.reuters.com/article/us-finland-arctic-council/u-s-sinks-arctic-accord-due-to-climate-change-differences-dip lomats-idUSKCN1SD143. Accessed 14 Aug 2021.

Jüris, F. (2020, March 7). *Handing over infrastructure for China's strategic objectives: 'Arctic Connect' and the Digital Silk Road in the Arctic.* Policy brief presented at the conference "Beyond Huawei: Europe's adoption of PRC technology and its implications." https://sinopsis.cz/en/arctic-digital-silk-road/. Accessed 15 Aug 2021.

Keleman, M. (2021, May 15). *Blinken to head North on Arctic Trip.* NPR. https://www.npr.org/2021/05/15/997105721/blinken-to-head-north-on-arctic-trip. Accessed 14 Aug 2021.

Kimmons, S. (2021, March 19). *Army analyzing needs for Arctic operations.* Army News Service. https://www.army.mil/article/244456/army_anal yzing_needs_for_arctic_operations. Accessed 25 Aug 2021.

Kramer, A. E. (2021, May 22). In the Russian Arctic, the first stirrings of a very Cold War. *New York Times.* https://www.nytimes.com/2021/05/22/ world/russia-us-arctic-military.html. Accessed 14 Aug 2021.

Kretsul, R., & Cherepanova, A. (2021, May 11). За семь «Борей»: новую подлодку проекта 955 направят в Арктику [Over the seven "Borei": new project 955 submarine will be sent to the Arctic]. Izvestia. https://iz.ru/1162054/roman-kretcul-anna-cherepanova/za-sem-borei-novuiu-podlodku-proekta-955-napraviat-v-arktiku. Accessed 21 Aug 2021.

Lackenbauer, P. W., & Dean, R. (2020). Arctic exceptionalisms. In K. Spohr, D. S. Hamilton, & J. C. Moyer (Eds.), *The Arctic and world order* (pp. 327–357). Foreign Policy Institute/Henry Kissinger Center for Global Affairs, Johns Hopkins University SAIS.

Lalonde, S. (2020). The U.S.-Canada Northwest Passage Disagreement: Why agreeing to disagree is more important than ever. In K. Spohr, D. S. Hamilton, & J. C. Moyer (Eds.), *The Arctic and world order* (pp. 267–294). Foreign Policy Institute/Henry Kissinger Center for Global Affairs, Johns Hopkins University SAIS.

Landrum, L., & Holland, M. M. (2020, September 14). Extremes become routine in an emerging new Arctic. *Nature Climate Change, 10*, 1108–1115.https://doi.org/10.1038/s41558-020-0892-z

Lanteigne, M. (2020). Inside, outside, upside down? Non-Arctic states in emerging arctic security discourses. In K. Spohr, D. S. Hamilton, & J. C. Moyer (Eds.), *The Arctic and world order* (pp. 379–405). Foreign Policy Institute/Henry Kissinger Center for Global Affairs, Johns Hopkins University SAIS.

Larsen K., Pitt, H., Grant, M., & Houser, T. (2021, May 6). *China's greenhouse gas emissions exceeded the developed world for the first time in 2019.* Rhodium Group. https://rhg.com/research/chinas-emissions-surpass-developed-countries/. Accessed 16 Aug 2021.

Larter, D. B. (2019, December 31). *US navy declares new fleet created to confront Russia fully operational.* DefenseNews. https://www.defensenews.com/naval/2019/12/31/us-navy-declares-new-fleet-stood-up-to-confront-russia-fully-operational/. Accessed 25 Aug 2021.

Larter, D. B., Gould, J., & Mehta, A. (2020, June 9). *Trump memo demands new fleet of Arctic icebreakers be ready by 2029.* DefenseNews. https://www.defensenews.com/naval/2020/06/09/trump-memo-demands-new-fleet-of-arctic-icebreakers-to-be-ready-by-2029/. Accessed 25 Aug 2021.

Lavrov, A., & Kretsul, R. (2020, December 15). Холодный «Кинжал»: Северный флот получит стратегическое оружие [Cold "Dagger": the Northern Fleet will receive strategic weapons]. Izvestia. https://iz.ru/1099851/anton-lavrov-roman-kretcul/kholodnyi-kinzhal-severnyi-flot-pol uchit-strategicheskoe-oruzhie?utm_source=yxnews&utm_medium=desktop. Accessed 21 Aug 2021.

Lelyveld, M. (2019, May 24). *China's Arctic investments generate heat.* Radio Free Asia. https://www.rfa.org/english/commentaries/energy_watch/chi nas-arctic-investments-generate-heat-05242019113856.html?searchterm:utf8:ustring=%20china%5C%27s%20arctic. Accessed 15 Aug 2021.

Luedee, J. (2021). Locating the boundaries of the nuclear north: Arctic biology, contaminated caribou, and the problem of the threshold. *Journal of the History of Biology, 54*, 67–93.

Maritime Executive. (2019, March 8). *Russia tightens control over the Northern Sea Route*. https://www.maritime-executive.com/article/russia-tightens-control-over-northern-sea-route. Accessed 21 Aug 2021.

McDermott, R. (2021, January 6). *Russia's Northern Fleet upgraded to military district status*. Jamestown Foundation. https://jamestown.org/program/russias-northern-fleet-upgraded-to-military-district-status/. Accessed 21 Aug 2021.

McDowell Group. (2018, March). *The economic benefits of Alaska's mining industry*. https://www.mcdowellgroup.net/wp-content/uploads/2021/01/2017-ama-ei-final-report.pdf. Accessed 24 Aug 2021.

McDowell Group. (2020a, January). *The role of the oil & gas industry in Alaska's economy*. https://www.mcdowellgroup.net/wp-content/uploads/2020/01/mcdowell-group-aoga-report-final-1-24-2020.pdf. Accessed 24 Aug 2021.

McDowell Group. (2020b, January). *The economic value of Alaska's seafood industry*. https://uploads.alaskaseafood.org/2020/01/McDowell-Group_ASMI-Economic-Impacts-Report-JAN-2020.pdf. Accessed 24 Aug 2021.

Meichtry, S., & Hinshaw, D. (2021, April 8). China's Greenland ambitions run into local politics, U.S. influence. *Wall Street Journal*. https://www.wsj.com/articles/chinas-rare-earths-quest-upends-greenlands-government-11617807839. Accessed 15 Aug 2021.

Mizokami, K. (2019, September 20). Russia vs. America: Who has the world's best submarines? *National Interest*. https://nationalinterest.org/blog/buzz/russia-vs-america-who-has-worlds-best-submarines-82166. Accessed 25 Aug 2021.

Monga, V., & Vieira, P. (2021, February 27). Cold War-era defense system to get upgrade to counter Russia, China. *Wall Street Journal*. https://www.wsj.com/articles/cold-war-era-defense-system-to-get-upgrade-to-counter-russia-china-11614438048. Accessed 17 Aug 2021.

Montgomery, N. (2018, January 9). *No permanent basing for navy sub hunters in Iceland despite construction projects*. Stars and Stripes. https://www.stripes.com/news/no-permanent-basing-for-navy-sub-hunters-in-iceland-despite-construction-projects-1.505835. Accessed 25 Aug 2021.

Naalakkersuisut: Government of Greenland. (2019, June 4). *Memorandum of understanding between Greenland's Ministry of Mineral Resources and Labour and the U.S. Department of State*. https://govmin.gl/wp-content/uploads/2020/04/MoU_Govt_of_Greenland_USA_2019.pdf. Accessed 21 Aug 2021.

National Academies of Sciences, Engineering, and Medicine. (2020). *Understanding and responding to global health and security risks from microbial threats in the Arctic: Proceedings of a Workshop*. The National Academies Press. https://doi.org/10.17226/25887

234   G. SOROKA

National Science Foundation. (2021a). *Office of Polar Programs (OPP): NSF FY 2021 budget request to Congress*. https://nsf.gov/about/budget/fy2021/pdf/30_fy2021.pdf. Accessed 25 Aug 2021.

National Science Foundation. (2021b, March 5). *Navigating the new Arctic (NNA): Proposal*. https://www.nsf.gov/pubs/2021/nsf21524/nsf21524.htm. Accessed 25 Aug 2021.

National Science Foundation. (n.d.-a). *About Arctic sciences*. https://www.nsf.gov/geo/opp/arctic/index.jsp. Accessed 25 Aug 2021.

National Science Foundation. (n.d.-b). *Navigating the new Arctic*. https://www.nsf.gov/funding/pgm_summ.jsp?pims_id=505594. Accessed 25 Aug 2021.

Naval Recognition. (2018, August 25). *U.S. Navy reestablishes second fleet for North Atlantic area*. http://www.navyrecognition.com/index.php/naval-news/naval-news-archive/2018/august-2018-navy-naval-defense-news/6456-u-s-navy-reestablishes-second-fleet-for-north-atlantic-area.html. Accessed 25 Aug 2021.

Newell, B. (2017, May 2). *$40 million upgrade for Thule Radar unifies missile shield sites*. U.S. Air Forces in Europe & Air Forces Africa. https://www.usafe.af.mil/News/Article-Display/Article/1175567/40-million-upgrade-for-thule-radar-unifies-missile-shield-sites/. Accessed 25 Aug 2021.

Nicholls, R. J., Herweijer, C., & Hallegatte, S. (2007). *Ranking of the world's cities most exposed to coastal flooding today and in the future*. OECD.

Nilsen, T. (2019, December 19). Russia's top general indirectly confirms Arctic deployment of the unstoppable Kinzhal missile. *Barents Observer*. https://thebarentsobserver.com/en/security/2019/12/russias-top-general-indirectly-confirms-arctic-deployment-unstoppable-missile. Accessed 21 Aug 2021.

Nilsen, T. (2020a, February 29). Russian anti-sub aircraft on combat training further south in the GIUK gap than normal. *Barents Observer*. https://thebarentsobserver.com/en/security/2020/02/russian-anti-sub-aircraft-combat-training-further-south-normal-over-norwegian-sea. Accessed 16 Aug 2021.

Nilsen, T. (2020b, May 12). American flags in the Barents Sea are the 'New Normal,' a defense analyst says. *Arctic Today*. https://www.arctictoday.com/american-flags-in-the-barents-sea-are-the-new-normal-a-defense-analyst-says/. Accessed 16 Aug 2021.

Nilsen, T. (2020c, October 5). Russia's new giant icebreaker sailed straight to the North Pole. *Barents Observer*. https://thebarentsobserver.com/en/arctic/2020/10/russias-new-giant-icebreaker-sailed-straight-north-pole. Accessed 21 Aug 2021.

Nilsen, T. (2021, May 6). Northern fleet gets first Yasen-M class submarine. *Barents Observer*. https://thebarentsobserver.com/en/security/2021/05/northern-fleet-gets-first-yasen-m-class-submarine. Accessed 21 Aug 2021.

Obrist, D., Agnan, Y., Jiskra, M., Olson, C. L., Colegrove, D. P., Hueber, J., Moore, C. W., Sonke, J. E., & Helmig, D. (2017). Tundra uptake of atmospheric elemental mercury drives arctic mercury pollution. *Nature, 547*, 201–204. https://doi.org/10.1038/nature22997

Patton, K. (2019, April 24). *Battle force missiles: The measure of a fleet*. Center for International Maritime Security. https://cimsec.org/battle-force-missiles-the-measure-of-a-fleet/. Accessed 25 Aug 2021.

Pawlyk, O. (2020, April 23). *US intensifies advanced fighter buildup near Arctic as 1st F-35s arrive in Alaska*. Military.com. https://www.military.com/daily-news/2020/04/23/us-intensifies-advanced-fighter-buildup-near-arctic-1st-f-35s-arrive-alaska.html. Accessed 25 Aug 2021.

Petrov, A. N., Welford, M., Golosov, N., DeGroote, J., Devlin, M., Degai, T., & Savelyevd, A. (2021). The 'Second Wave' of the COVID-19 pandemic in the Arctic: Regional and temporal dynamics. *International Journal of Circumpolar Health, 80*(1), 1925446. https://doi.org/10.1080/22423982.2021.1925446

Plumer, B., & Fountain, H. (2020, August 17). Trump administration finalizes plan to open Arctic refuge to drilling. *New York Times*. https://www.nytimes.com/2020/08/17/climate/alaska-oil-drilling-anwr.html. Accessed 16 Aug 2021.

Polar Research Institute of China. (2019, February 18). *Arctic Yellow River Station*. https://www.pric.org.cn/EN/detail/content.aspx?id=3171277c-53b4-435b-b50a-b7588caeab55. Accessed 17 Aug 2021.

Pompeo, M. (2019, May 6). *Secretary of State Pompeo remarks on U.S.-Arctic policy*. C-SPAN. https://www.c-span.org/video/?460478-1/secretary-state-pompeo-warns-russia-china-arctic-policy-address-finland. Accessed 14 Aug 2021.

Poulsen, R. W. (2020, December 7). *Forget Greenland, there's a new strategic gateway to the Arctic*. Foreign Policy. https://foreignpolicy.com/2020/12/07/forget-greenland-faroe-islands-new-strategic-gateway-to-the-arctic/. Accessed 15 Aug 2021.

Public-Private Analytic Exchange Program. (2017, September 28). *Threats to undersea cable communications*. https://www.dni.gov/files/PE/Documents/1---2017-AEP-Threats-to-Undersea-Cable-Communications.pdf. Accessed 15 Aug 2021.

Rainwater, S. (2013). Race to the north: China's Arctic strategy and its implications. *Naval War College Review, 66*(2), 62–82.

Resource Development Council. (n.d.-a). *Alaska's oil & gas industry*. https://www.akrdc.org/oil-and-gas. Accessed 24 Aug 2021.

Resource Development Council. (n.d.-b). *Alaska's mining industry*. https://www.akrdc.org/mining. Accessed 24 Aug 2021.

Resource Development Council. (n.d.-c). *Alaska's tourism industry*. https://www.akrdc.org/tourism. Accessed 24 Aug 2021.

236 G. SOROKA

Resource Development Council. (n.d.-d). *Alaska native corporations.* https://www.akrdc.org/alaska-native-corporations. Accessed 19 Aug 2021.

Reuters. (2021, May 20). *Russia calls for military meetings between Arctic states as tensions rise.* https://www.reuters.com/world/russias-lavrov-calls-military-dialogue-between-arctic-states-2021-05-20/. Accessed 16 Aug 2021.

Rosen, Y. (2016, August 19). *The Arctic Circle may be more than 400 miles north, but Seward has become an Arctic port.* Anchorage Daily News. https://www.adn.com/arctic/2016/08/19/the-arctic-circle-may-be-more-than-400-miles-north-but-seward-has-become-an-arctic-port/. Accessed 21 Aug 2021.

Rubano, C. (2021, January 14). *Congress authorizes deepwater port in Nome.* Alaska Public Media. https://www.alaskapublic.org/2021/01/14/congress-authorizes-nome-deepwater-port-project/. Accessed 21 Aug 2021.

Saniewski, M., Wietrzyk-Pełka, P., Zalewska, T., Olech, M., & Węgrzyn, M. H. (2020). Bryophytes and lichens as fallout originated radionuclide indicators in the Svalbard Archipelago (High Arctic). *Polar Science, 25.* https://doi.org/10.1016/j.polar.2020.100536

Satariano, A. (2019, December 20). At the edge of the world, a new battleground for the U.S. and China. *New York Times.* https://www.nytimes.com/2019/12/20/technology/faroe-islands-huawei-china-us.html. Accessed 15 Aug 2021.

Schaefer, K. (n.d.). *All about frozen ground.* National Snow & Ice Data Center. https://nsidc.org/cryosphere/frozenground/methane.html. Accessed 17 Aug 2021.

Schliess, G. (2016, April 28). *Climate change: A village falls into the sea.* DW. https://www.dw.com/en/climate-change-a-village-falls-into-the-sea/a-18717942. Accessed 19 Aug 2021.

Schreiber, M. (2021, April 15). Arctic disaster responders train together in a first-of-its-kind joint exercise. *Arctic Today.* https://www.arctictoday.com/arctic-disaster-responders-train-together-in-a-first-of-its-kind-joint-exercise/. Accessed 16 Aug 2021.

Scott, M. (2020, December 8). *Arctic air temperatures continue a long-term warming streak.* Climate.gov. https://www.climate.gov/news-features/featured-images/2020-arctic-air-temperatures-continue-long-term-warming-streak. Accessed 17 Aug 2021.

Seager, R. (2006). The source of Europe's mild climate. *American Scientist, 94*(4), 334. https://www.americanscientist.org/article/the-source-of-europes-mild-climate. Accessed 17 Aug 2021.

Shallenberger, K. (2019, October 22). *Alaska: Climate change threatens indigenous traditions.* DW. https://www.dw.com/en/alaska-climate-change-threatens-indigenous-traditions/a-50722471.

Shelbourne, M. (2021, March 31). *NORAD: Russians stay in airspace 'For Hours' during flight operations near Alaska.* USNI News. https://news.

usni.org/2021/03/31/northcom-russians-stay-in-airspace-for-hours-during-flight-operations-near-alaska. Accessed 21 Aug 2021.

Silber, G. K., Weller, D. W., Reeves, R. R., Adams, J. D., & Moore, T. J. (2021). Co-occurrence of gray whales and vessel traffic in the North Pacific Ocean. *Endangered Species Research, 44*, 177–201. https://doi.org/10.3354/esr01093

Singh, M. M., & Callaghan, R. M. (2017). *The mineral industry of Alaska*. U.S. Geological Survey. https://www.usgs.gov/centers/nmic/mineral-industry-alaska. Accessed 24 Aug 2021.

Soroka, G. (2016). The political economy of Russia's reimagined arctic. In L. Heininen, H. Exner-Pirot, & J. Plouffe (Eds.), *The Arctic yearbook 2016* (pp. 359–389). Northern Research Forum. https://arcticyearbook.com/images/yearbook/2016/Scholarly_Papers/14.Soroka.pdf. Accessed 25 Aug 2021.

Soroka, G. (2021, June 21). *Russia and China in the Arctic: Cooperation or forbearance?* Paper presented at the annual meeting of the Council for European Studies.

Spohr, K., & Hamilton, D. (2020). Introduction: From last frontier to first frontier: The Arctic and world order. In K. Spohr, D. S. Hamilton, & J. C. Moyer (Eds.), *The Arctic and world order* (pp. 1–47). Foreign Policy Institute/Henry Kissinger Center for Global Affairs, Johns Hopkins University SAIS.

Stars and Stripes. (2020, January 2). *Navy's Atlantic-Based 2nd Fleet Command now fully operational.* https://www.stripes.com/theaters/us/navy-s-atlantic-based-2nd-fleet-command-now-fully-operational-1.613273. Accessed 17 Aug 2021.

Stauffer, P. (Ed.). (2008). *Circum-Arctic resource appraisal: estimates of undiscovered oil and gas north of the Arctic circle.* USGS Fact Sheet 2008-3049. https://pubs.usgs.gov/fs/2008/3049/fs2008-3049.pdf. Accessed 25 Aug 2021.

Stolyarov, G. (2021, August 6). *Russia starts operation to lay undersea fibre optic cable through Arctic.* Reuters. https://www.reuters.com/technology/russia-starts-operation-lay-undersea-fibre-optic-cable-through-arctic-2021-08-06/. Accessed 15 Aug 2021.

Stronski, P., & Kier, G. (2021, May 17). *A fresh start on U.S. arctic policy under Biden.* Carnegie Moscow Center. https://carnegie.ru/commentary/84543. Accessed 16 Aug 2021.

Struzik, E. (2016, March 17). *Food insecurity: Arctic heat is threatening indigenous life.* Yale Environment 360. https://e360.yale.edu/features/arctic_heat_threatens_indigenous_life_climate_change. Accessed 19 Aug 2021.

Suciu, P. (2021, March 7). Why the U.S. military fears Russia's New Borei-Class Submarine. *National Interest.* https://nationalinterest.org/blog/reboot/

238   G. SOROKA

why-us-military-fears-russias-new-borei-class-submarine-179567. Accessed 25 Aug 2021.

Suez Canal. (n.d.). *Navigation statistics*. https://www.suezcanal.gov.eg/English/Navigation/Pages/NavigationStatistics.aspx. Accessed 15 Aug 2021.

Sukhankin, S. (2020, March 16). 'The 'Military Pillar' of Russia's Arctic policy. Jamestown Foundation. https://jamestown.org/program/the-military-pillar-of-russias-arctic-policy/. Accessed 21 Aug 2021.

ТАСС [TASS]. (2021, March 25). "Циркон" успешно прошел испытания с надводного носителя ["Zircon" has successfully passed tests from a surface carrier]. https://tass.ru/armiya-i-opk/10997625?utm_medium=social&utm_campaign=smm_social_share. Accessed 21 Aug 2021.

Tallis, J. (2020, July 16). *Arctic East vs. West 2020*. CNA. https://vimeo.com/439249300. Accessed 17 Aug 2021.

Teck. (2021, August 26). *Red dog*. https://www.teck.com/operations/united-states/operations/red-dog/. Accessed 24 Aug 2021.

Troell, M., Eide, A., Isaksen, J., Hermansen, Ø., & Crépin, A. S. (2017). Seafood from a changing Arctic. *Ambio, 46*(3), 368–386. https://doi.org/10.1007/s13280-017-0954-2

Trump, D. J. (2020, Jun 9). *Memorandum on safeguarding U.S. national interest in the Arctic and Antarctic regions*. https://uaf.edu/caps/resources/policy-documents/us-memorandum-on-safeguarding-natl-interests-in-the-arctic-and-antarctic-regions-2020.pdf. Accessed 25 Aug 2021.

Understanding Alaska's Budget. (n.d.). *Understanding Alaska's revenue*. http://www.alaskabudget.com/revenue/. Accessed 24 Aug 2021.

United Nations. (1982, December 10). *United Nations convention on the law of the sea*. https://www.un.org/depts/los/convention_agreements/texts/unclos/unclos_e.pdf. Accessed 16 Aug 2021.

United States Census Bureau. (n.d.). *QuickFacts: Alaska*. https://www.census.gov/quickfacts/AK. Accessed 12 Sep 2021.

U.S. Coast Guard. (2019, April). *Arctic strategic outlook*. https://www.uscg.mil/Portals/0/Images/arctic/Arctic_Strategy_Book_APR_2019.pdf. Accessed 16 Aug 2021.

U.S. Committee on the Marine Transportation System. (2019, September). *A ten-year projection of maritime activity in the U.S. Arctic region, 2020–2030*. https://www.cmts.gov/downloads/CMTS_2019_Arctic_Vessel_Projection_Report.pdf. Accessed 17 Aug 2021.

U.S. Energy Information Administration. (2021, January 21). *Alaska: State profile and energy estimates*. https://www.eia.gov/state/analysis.php?sid=AK. Accessed 24 Aug 2021.

U.S. Government Accountability Office. (n.d.). *U.S. Arctic interests*. https://www.gao.gov/u.s.-arctic-interests. Accessed 24 Aug 2021.

U.S. Naval Forces Europe-Africa/U.S. 6th Fleet Public Affairs. (2020, May 4). *U.S., U.K. ships operate in the Barents Sea*. https://www.c6f.navy.mil/Press-Room/News/Article/2174342/us-uk-ships-operate-in-the-barents-sea/. Accessed 16 Aug 2021.

USCG Office of Waterways and Ocean Policy. (n.d.). *Major Icebreakers of the world*. https://www.dco.uscg.mil/Portals/9/DCO%20Documents/Office%20of%20Waterways%20and%20Ocean%20Policy/20170501%20major%20icebreaker%20chart.pdf?ver=2017-06-08-091723-907. Accessed 16 Aug 2021.

Vavasseur, X. (2019, October 31). *Russian navy icebreaker Ivan Papanin floated in St. Petersburg*. Naval News. https://www.navalnews.com/naval-news/2019/10/russian-navy-icebreaker-ivan-papanin-floated-in-st-petersburg/. Accessed 21 Aug 2021.

Volpe, M. (2020, March 24). *The tortuous path of China's win-win strategy in Greenland*. Arctic Institute. https://www.thearcticinstitute.org/tortuous-path-china-win-win-strategy-greenland/. Accessed 15 Aug 2021.

Wade, J. (2014, December 21). *Russia in the Arctic: OSK sever and Arctic security*. SOFREP. https://sofrep.com/news/russia-arctic-osk-sever-arctic-security/. Accessed 21 Aug 2021.

White House. (2015, August 31). *President Obama's trip to Alaska*. https://obamawhitehouse.archives.gov/2015-alaska-trip. Accessed 17 Aug 2021.

White House. (2016, September 28). *Arctic science ministerial*. https://obamawhitehouse.archives.gov/blog/2016/05/13/white-house-arctic-science-ministerial-september-28-2016. Accessed 25 Aug 2021.

White House. (2017, December). *National Security Strategy of the United States of America*. https://trumpwhitehouse.archives.gov/wp-content/uploads/2017/12/NSS-Final-12-18-2017-0905.pdf. Accessed 25 Aug 2021.

White House. (2021a, March). *Interim national security strategic guidance*. https://www.whitehouse.gov/wp-content/uploads/2021/03/NSC-1v2.pdf. Accessed 16 Aug 2021.

White House. (2021b, May 11). *Biden administration underscores commitment to combatting climate change, strengthening global partnerships at third Arctic science ministerial*. https://www.whitehouse.gov/ostp/news-updates/2021/05/11/biden-administration-underscores-commitment-to-combatting-climate-change-strengthening-global-partnerships-at-third-arctic-science-ministerial/. Accessed 25 Aug 2021.

Wicker, R., & Sullivan, D. (2020, October 19). *Polar icebreakers are key to America's national interest*. Defense News. https://www.defensenews.com/opinion/commentary/2020/10/19/polar-icebreakers-are-key-to-americas-national-interest/. Accessed 21 Aug 2021.

Wilson Center. (n.d.). *Upper Kobuk Mineral Project*. https://arcticinfrastructure.wilsoncenter.org/project/upper-kobuk-mineral-project. Accessed 24 Aug 2021.

Wolfe, F. (2020, November 23). Air force examining modernization of early warning radars. *Aviation Today*. https://www.aviationtoday.com/2020/11/23/air-force-examining-modernization-early-warning-radars/

Xinhua (2018, Jan 26). *Full text: China's Arctic policy*. http://english.www.gov.cn/archive/white_paper/2018/01/26/content_281476026660336.htm. Accessed 15 Aug 2021.

York, A., Bhatt, U. S., Gargulinski, E., Grabinski, Z., Jain, P., Soja, A., Thoman, R. L. & Ziel, R. (2020). *Wildland fire in high northern latitudes*. Arctic Report Card: Update for 2020. https://doi.org/10.25923/2gef-3964

Young, O. R. (2012). Arctic tipping points: Governance in turbulent times. *Ambio, 41*(81), 75–84. https://doi.org/10.1007/s13280-011-0227-4

Young, O. R. (2020). Shifting ground: Competing policy narratives and the future of the Arctic. In K. Spohr, D. S. Hamilton, & J. C. Moyer (Eds.), *The Arctic and world order* (pp. 47–63). Foreign Policy Institute/Henry Kissinger Center for Global Affairs, Johns Hopkins University SAIS.

A "Profound Change of Direction?" Canada's Northern Strategy and the Co-Development of a "New" Arctic and Northern Policy Framework

P. Whitney Lackenbauer and Peter Kikkert

INTRODUCTION

It came with a whimper, not a bang. After four years of development, Prime Minister Justin Trudeau's Liberal government released Canada's Arctic and Northern Policy Framework (ANPF) with little fanfare in September 2019. It appeared on the Crown-Indigenous Relations and Northern Affairs Canada (CIRNAC) website with no photos, maps, or even a downloadable pdf—just a wave of words, over 17,000 in the main chapter alone. The single infographic that accompanied the framework captured its main "highlights:" that a "whole-of-government,

---

P. W. Lackenbauer (✉)
Trent University, Peterborough, ON, Canada
e-mail: whitney.lackenbauer@uwaterloo.ca

P. Kikkert
Brian Mulroney Institute of Government, St. Francis Xavier University (StFX), Antigonish, NS, Canada
e-mail: pkikkert@stfx.ca

© The Author(s), under exclusive license to Springer Nature Singapore Pte Ltd. 2022
A. Likhacheva (ed.), *Arctic Fever*,
https://doi.org/10.1007/978-981-16-9616-9_10

co-development" process had involved the three territorial governments, over 25 Indigenous organizations, as well as three provincial governments.[1] Please check and confirm if the authors and their respective affiliations have been correctly identified. Amend if necessary.YES. Please confirm if the corresponding author is correctly identified. Amend if necessary.Yes, the corresponding author is correctly identified.

Despite grant proclamations from Ottawa, the policy itself does not represent the "profound change of direction" that the Trudeau government suggests. Instead, Canada's 2019 policy framework highlights well-known issues that Northern Canadians have identified for years, including climate change, food insecurity, poverty, health inequalities, and housing shortages. The collaborative process itself offers the most compelling justification for the Government of Canada's claim to a "profound change of direction" in the opening sentence of the ANPF (Government of Canada, 2019).

This chapter analyzes the benefits and limitations of the co-development approach that produced the ANPF, the expectations that it has set, and the persistent obstacles, competing ideas, and lingering questions that are likely to inhibit the enactment of this "shared vision." The government's emphasis on collaborative governance recognizes that when Ottawa has defined problems facing the North incorrectly or has set the wrong priorities, with little consultation from Northerners, policy responses have been short-sighted and ineffective. While critics lauded the process involved in co-developing the "new" framework, they ultimately questioned the hasty release of what seems to be an unperfected document, coming just a day before the federal government announced Canada's 2019 federal election. The ANPF appeared with no budget, timelines, or clear plan to address the wide array of challenges and issues identified. Critics quickly labelled the framework a "half-baked" and "chaotic mess" (Exner-Pirot, 2019) that simply lists well-known issues and gives "lip service to addressing the problems" (Greer, 2019) while providing no "concrete" plan for action (Weber, 2019).

The conspicuous lack of action on a strategic policy agenda since the release of the ANPF reveals a persistent Canadian challenge in setting practical priorities for federal policy implementation, particularly in the

---

[1] See CIRNAC (n.d.).

areas of economic development (given varied economies across the Canadian Arctic), promised investments in "transformative infrastructure," and addressing gaps in "access to the same services, opportunities, and standards of living as those enjoyed by other Canadians." In contrast to Russia, which released a series of Arctic strategies in 2020 and a transparent implementation plan in 2021, Canada has adopted a general Arctic policy and an ad hoc approach to prospective implementation. The Canadian approach avoids the stigma of centralized federal direction and empowers Northerners to discern policy priorities (at least in theory) by connecting their proposals to general policy framework language, guided by "principles of partnership" that emphasize community-based solutions and "flexible and adaptive policy." The challenge remains to achieve action on and coherence and synergy across programmes under this formula—with little indication that Canada has broken from its long-standing record of making strategic promises across the Arctic policy landscape and failing to enact them in practice.

MORE CONTINUITY THAN CHANGE: CANADA'S NORTHERN STRATEGY SINCE 1970

When Prime Minister Pierre Elliott Trudeau's Liberal government released its policy statement *Northern Canada in the 70's* in 1970, it marked a strong change in tone and emphasis from the federal Northern strategies that had preceded it. John Diefenbaker's famous "Northern Vision" unveiled in 1958 had offered a bold vision that sought to extend Canadian development into the Arctic and develop northern resources for the benefit of all Canadians. This political, ideological, and economic platform focussed on national development goals rather than the people of the North and lost momentum amidst the political turmoil that embroiled the Conservative government in the early 1960s (Isard, 2010). Twelve years later, Liberal minister of northern affairs Jean Chrétien focussed as much on the people of the North as he did on national economic outcomes. "In recent decades the native northerners have been offered new opportunities and facilities for strengthening their capacity to survive," his strategy explained. "But survival for them must be more than mere subsistence supplemented by Government subsidy. It must above all permit the people themselves to make their own choices as to the place they wish to occupy and the part they wish to play, in the evolving society of Canada, North and South of 60°" (Chrétien, 2020).

This has been a persistent theme ever since. Justice Thomas Berger's inquiry into the socio-economic and environmental impact of a proposed pipeline along the Mackenzie Valley elicited unprecedented public engagement, and its final report, *Northern Frontier, Northern Homeland*, highlighted competing visions of Canada's Northern future. "We look upon the North as our last frontier," he noted of the southern Canadian view. "It is natural for us to think of developing it, of subduing the land and extracting its resources to fuel Canada's industry and heat our homes. But the native people say the North is their homeland. They have lived there for thousands of years. They claim it is their land, and they believe they have a right to say what its future ought to be." Berger recommended a ten-year moratorium on any pipeline development so that Aboriginal land claims could be settled and appropriate conservation areas established beforehand (Berger, 1977, p. 1).[2] Thus, internal sovereignty claims by Canadian Indigenous groups changed the political dialogue, and Canada embarked upon a process of settling comprehensive land claims with Northern Indigenous peoples whose land rights had not been dealt with by treaty or other legal means—a process that has dramatically transformed Canada's political landscape and remains ongoing today.[3]

Canada's 1970 policy statement emphasized that "people, resources and environment are the main elements in any strategy for northern development." This trinity has remained remarkably consistent over the past half-century. The Trudeau government also noted that, "in the course of its policy review during the past year, the Government affirmed that the needs of the people in the North are more important than resource development and that the maintenance of ecological balance is essential. In the setting of objectives and priorities in the North, along with national policy goals, the essence of choice for the Government is to maintain an appropriate degree of balance among those three elements" (Chrétien, 2020). Striking the right balance across these three fundamental pillars remains the fundamental challenge of Canadian Arctic policymaking.

---

[2] See also CBC (n.d.) and O'Malley (1976).

[3] See, for example, Cameron and White (1995), Alcantara (2008), and Poelzer and Coates (2015).

While domestic drivers propelled the Canadian political agenda for most of the 1970s and early 1980s, sovereignty re-emerged as a catalyst for action following the August 1985 voyage of the US Coast Guard icebreaker *Polar Sea* through the Northwest Passage (NWP). In response, the Conservative government of Brian Mulroney announced that Canada was officially drawing straight baselines around its Arctic Archipelago effective 1 January 1986, thus confirming Canada's sovereignty over the NWP as "historic, internal waters." Concurrently, it outlined an aggressive plan to exercise control over its waters and assert its Arctic sovereignty[4] while simultaneously negotiating the 1988 Arctic Cooperation Agreement with the U.S. over icebreaker transits. By "agreeing to disagree" on the legal status of the passage, the two countries reached "a pragmatic solution based on our special bilateral relationship, our common interest in cooperating on Arctic matters, and the flora and fauna of the area"—one that did not prejudice either country's legal position or set a precedent for other areas of the world (Kirkey, 1995). With this understanding in place, Ottawa and Washington also collaborated to modernize North American Aerospace Defence Command (NORAD) assets in the Arctic to meet the common continental defence threat posed by the Soviet Union.[5] This was less about defending the Arctic than the approaches to North America, but affirmed the strategic importance of the region from a homeland security perspective.

After the end of the Cold War, Canada's official discourse on Arctic affairs shifted to emphasize circumpolar cooperation and broad definitions of security that prioritized human and environmental dimensions. Canada was an early champion of the Arctic Council and promoted the inclusion of Indigenous Permanent Participants with a seat at the table.[6] The Liberal government under Prime Minister Jean Chrétien (1993–2003) embraced this emphasis on international cooperation, and *The Northern Dimension of Canada's Foreign Policy* released in 2000 revealed how environmental and social challenges now predominated:

> Both the tradition of transnational co-operation and the new emphasis on human security are particularly applicable to the shaping of the

---

[4] See Huebert (2001a).

[5] For a strong overview, see Jockel (1991).

[6] See, for example, House of Commons Standing Committee on Foreign Affairs and International Trade (1997).

Northern Dimension of Canada's Foreign Policy. The circumpolar world that includes the northern territories and peoples of Canada, Russia, the United States, the Nordic countries plus the vast (and mostly ice-covered) waters in between was long a front line in the Cold War. Now it has become a front line in a different way—facing the challenges and opportunities brought on by new trends and developments. The challenges mostly take the shape of transboundary environmental threats—persistent organic pollutants, climate change, nuclear waste—that are having dangerously increasing impacts on the health and vitality of human beings, northern lands, waters and animal life. The opportunities are driven by increasingly confident northern societies who, drawing on their traditional values, stand poised to take up the challenges presented by globalization. Whereas the politics of the Cold War dictated that the Arctic region be treated as part of a broader strategy of exclusion and confrontation, now the politics of globalization and power diffusion highlight the importance of the circumpolar world as an area for inclusion and co-operation. (Department of Foreign Affairs and International Trade of Canada, 2000)

Framed by principles of Canadian leadership, partnership, and ongoing dialogue with Northerners, this new northern foreign policy was rooted in four overarching objectives: to enhance the security and prosperity of Canadians, especially Northerners and Aboriginal peoples; to assert and ensure the preservation of Canada's sovereignty in the North; to establish the Circumpolar region as a vibrant geopolitical entity integrated into a rules-based international system; and to promote the human security of Northerners and the sustainable development of the Arctic.

By the start of the new millennium, improvement in Indigenous self-government and devolution required new economic opportunities that promoted northern interests. "Defending" traditional state sovereignty slipped to the back burner, particularly as the environmental, societal, and economic sectors of security seemed more pressing without a superpower adversary threatening North America from across the pole. Instead, a rising tide of evidence about the pace and impacts of global warming in the Arctic led Canadian journalists and academic commentators to push for a more proactive Arctic strategy that anticipated emerging security challenges associated with climate change, boundary disputes, the contested status of the waters of the Northwest Passage for international transit shipping, resource development, and heightened international activity in the region more generally (Huebert, 2001b).[7] In December 2004, Paul Martin's Liberal Government announced an integrated Northern Strategy (devised in concert with the premiers of the Northern territories of Yukon, Northwest Territories, and Nunavut) built around seven main goals. First, the strategy promised to strengthen Northern governance, partnerships, and institutions to provide Northerners with greater control over decisions about their future. Second, it committed to establishing robust foundations for "strong, sustainable, diversified economies to allow northerners share in the benefits of northern development." Third, it proposed "to engage all partners in the North in the protection and stewardship of the environment." Fourth, it sought to promote "healthy, safe and sustainable northern communities" that would "promote self-reliance." Fifth, the document committed to ensuring that Canada would continue to play a "leading role" in promoting international cooperation, while taking Northerners' concerns into "consideration in national efforts to reinforce sovereignty, security and circumpolar cooperation." Sixth, the strategy promised to preserve, revitalize, and promote Indigenous cultures, recognizing and encouraging "the importance of language, traditional knowledge and way-of-life." Seventh, the government committed to ensuring that "Canada is a leader in northern science and technology, and to develop expertise in areas of particular importance and relevance to the North."[8] A 2005 International Policy Statement (IPS) also identified the Arctic as a priority area in light of "increased security threats, a changed distribution of global power, challenges to existing international institutions, and transformation of the global economy" that "reinforce the need for Canada to monitor and control events in its sovereign territory, through new funding and new tools."[9] Although the Liberal government fell before it could implement its vision, it had intertwined sovereignty and security in political rhetoric and strategic documents.

Stephen Harper's Conservatives embraced this agenda and made the Canadian North a key component of its 2005 election platform, accusing

---

[7] See, in particular, AMAP (2004).

[8] See Canadian Arctic Resources Committee (2006).

[9] The IPS focused on surveillance, such as infrared sensors for patrol aircraft, unmanned aerial vehicles, and satellites (Canada, 2005).

his Liberal predecessors of swinging the pendulum too far towards diplomacy and human development in the face of an alleged Arctic sovereignty "crisis." Harper asserted that "the single most important duty of the federal government is to protect our national sovereignty," requiring "forces on the ground, ships in the sea, and proper surveillance. And that will be the conservative approach" (Harper, 2005). His government's "use it or lose it" approach to Arctic policy dominated the agenda from 2006 to 2009, featuring a spate of commitments to invest in military capabilities to defend Canada's rights for the region.[10] This rhetoric frustrated and even offended Northerners, particularly Indigenous peoples who had lived in the region since "time immemorial" (and thus resented any intimation that it was not sufficiently "used") and continued to express concerns about their lack of substantive involvement in national and international decision-making. Inuit leaders insisted that "sovereignty begins at home" and that the primary challenges were domestic human security issues, requiring investments in infrastructure, education, and health care.[11] Furthermore, the Inuit Circumpolar Council's transnational *Circumpolar Inuit Declaration on Sovereignty in the Arctic* (2009) emphasized that "the inextricable linkages between issues of sovereignty and sovereign rights in the Arctic and Inuit self-determination and other rights require states to accept the presence and role of Inuit as partners in the conduct of international relations in the Arctic." The declaration envisions Inuit playing an active role in all deliberations on environmental security, sustainable development, militarization, shipping, and socio-economic development (ICC, 2009).[12]

The 2007 Speech from the Throne indicated that the Harper Government's broader vision for the Arctic went beyond traditional sovereignty and security frames. Arguing that "the North needs new attention," and

---

[10] See, for example, Harris (2007). On Harper's early vision, see Dodds (2011).

[11] See, for example, Kaludjak (2007) and Simon (2008); and the perspectives in Inuit Kanatami (2013).

[12] Inuit representatives have opposed state actions that they feel violate their interests, such as Canada's decision to host a meeting for the five Arctic coastal states in March 2010 without inviting Inuit and First Nations to the discussions, and even critiqued a bilateral Canada-Denmark Arctic defence and security cooperation agreement because they were not involved in negotiating it. As such, indigenous voices add to the complexity (and richness) of the Canadian message projected to the rest of the world.

that "new opportunities are emerging across the Arctic," the Conservatives promised to "bring forward an integrated northern strategy focussed on strengthening Canada's sovereignty, protecting our environmental heritage, promoting economic and social development, and improving and evolving governance, so that northerners have greater control over their destinies." This four-pillar strategy would be expanded to "improve living conditions in the North for First Nations and Inuit through better housing," as well as a pledge to "build a world-class arctic research station that will be on the cutting edge of arctic issues, including environmental science and resource development." While the government would proceed with its election promises to bolster Canada's security presence in the Arctic, its sovereignty assertion would include "complete comprehensive mapping of Canada's Arctic seabed." The following year, Prime Minister Harper reiterated his government's commitment to the "New North" during his fifth Northern tour, insisting that the four pillars constituted "a comprehensive vision for a new North, a Northern Strategy that will turn potential into prosperity for the benefit of all Northerners and all Canadians" (Government of Canada, 2008).

Northern leaders perceived the throne speech with a split feeling. On the one hand, Northerners applauded their inclusion in the Harper Government's expanded conceptualization of Arctic sovereignty. Similarly, territorial premiers were positive about the intentions for Northerners to have more control over their resource wealth, and their economies developed. Criticisms surrounding the Northern strategy generally fell into two categories. Mary Simon, the president of Inuit Tapiriit Kanatami (the national Inuit political organization), offered a common criticism of the strategy when she said that she wished "there would be a bit more detail" (Weber, 2007). Northwest Territories Premier Floyd Roland echoed Simon a couple of years later, expressing his hope that Conservatives would be "ready to release" a more substantive strategy document soon. "There are resources at stake here," he noted. "We need to have our policy or programme in place" (Weber, 2009). Another debate over the Northern Strategy orbited around the centrality of Inuit. Critics suggested that the strategy was too focussed on military dimensions of sovereignty and on foreign policy, and not sufficiently domestic-focussed on improving the lives of Northerners, particularly Inuit (Byers & Layton, 2007). "The bedrock of Canada's status as an Arctic nation is the history of use and occupation of Arctic lands and waters by Inuit for thousands of years," Simon explained. "This is helpful for Canada while defending claims of sovereignty against other nations" (Simon, 2007). Simon argued that any Canadian Northern strategy should be built on the twin pillars of "asserting Canada's sovereignty in the Arctic [by] establishing constructive partnerships with Inuit," and "urgent action by our government to get serious on a climate change strategy" (Simon, 2009).

When the Harper government unveiled its Northern Strategy in July 2009, it offered a message of partnership: between the federal government and Northern Canadians, and between Canada and its circumpolar neighbours. Critics suggested that the strategy simply reiterated previous government commitments, while supporters suggested that the official document outlined a more coherent framework that moved away from the sovereignty-obsessed "use it or lose it" message of previous years. The Conservatives now cast the United States as an "exceptionally valuable partner in the Arctic," noted opportunities for cooperation with Russia and "common interests" with European Arctic states, and emphasized domestic imperatives to improve the quality of life of Northerners. Filled with references to the central place of Northerners in decision-making related to the Arctic, the government's domestic emphasis shifted substantively after 2009 to emphasize economic development. By 2013 Rob Huebert asked: "when's the last time you hear anyone use the 'use it or lose it' analogy? ... It's very much focussed on improving the North for northerners now, rather than building up the security side."[13] Territorial premiers welcomed this change, but they also expressed concerns about what they saw as the Harper Government's "one-size-fits-all" policy of promoting private investment (Berthiaume, 2013).[14] "Mr. Harper's government obviously embraces a development model rooted in the idea that improved social indicators will follow economic development, particularly in sectors such as oil, gas and mining," Lackenbauer argued in August 2013. "Nevertheless, critics insist that the overall emphasis is

---

[13] Quoted in Wingrove (2013). As the documents in this volume show, however, the Harper Government continued to highlight military operations and training exercises—particularly the N-series (Nanook, Nunalivut, and Nunakput)—throughout its tenure in office.

[14] Internationally, the Harper Government also championed the creation of the Arctic Economic Council, "an independent organization that facilitates Arctic business-to-business activities and responsible economic development through the sharing of best practices, technological solutions, standards and other information" (Arctic Economic Council, 2015). For critiques, see Axworthy and Simon (2015) and Quinn (2016).

misplaced. Canadians should invest more in Northerners to improve social conditions and create healthier communities before priming the pump for resource developers" (Lackenbauer, 2013).

Pursuant to its third pillar, "Protecting the Arctic Environment," Canada committed to taking tangible action to protect and manage the unique and fragile ecosystems and wildlife of the Arctic which are being affected by global forces. Its "comprehensive approach" to environmental protection, built around the idea of sustainability, sought to balance the longstanding frontier-homeland equation, "ensuring [that] conservation keeps pace with development and that development decisions are based on sound science and careful assessment" (Government of Canada, 2009). In contrast to the positive image of support for science and environmental action promoted by official statements, critics chastised the Harper Government for its retreat from meaningful commitments to climate change mitigation efforts, reduced funding for climate research, "muzzling" of government scientists, and their prioritization of economic growth over environmental protection.[15]

The fourth pillar of the Northern Strategy committed to "Improving and Devolving Governance and Empowering the Peoples of the North." Domestically, this involved the ongoing negotiation and implementation of land claim and self-government agreements with Northern Indigenous peoples, as well as the negotiation of devolution agreements of federal responsibilities to the territorial governments. Successes included the 2014 devolution agreement with NWT, a land claim agreement with Inuit of Nunavik, and the start of land claim negotiations with the Acho Dene Koe First Nation and self-government discussions with the Inuvialuit, and preliminary steps to initiate devotion talks with Nunavut.[16] In its international dimension, improved governance initiatives included ongoing support for the Indigenous Permanent Participants in the Arctic Council and ensuring that the Northern governments and Indigenous organizations in Canada had opportunities to actively participate in shaping Canadian policy on Arctic issues.

The official *Statement on Canada's Arctic Foreign Policy*, released in August 2010, reiterated the importance of the Arctic in Canada's

[15] See, for example, Liberal Party of Canada (2015), Klinkenborg (2013), Gatehouse (2013), Munro (2015), and Hume (2015).

[16] See, for example, Alcantara (2013), Cameron and Campbell (2009), Rennie (2015), and INAC (2020).

national identity and its role as an "Arctic power." Its bottom-line message mirrored the Northern Strategy, outlining a vision for the Arctic as "a stable, rules-based region with clearly defined boundaries, dynamic economic growth and trade, vibrant Northern communities, and healthy and productive ecosystems." These themes bore striking resemblance to *The Northern Dimension of Canada's Foreign Policy* released by the Liberals in 2000. The first and foremost pillar of Canada's foreign policy remained "the exercise of our sovereignty over the Far North," but the "hard security" message of the 2006–2008 period was supplemented (if not supplanted) by the amplification in the tone of cooperation with circumpolar neighbours and Northerners. Reaffirming that Canada's Arctic sovereignty is longstanding, well-established and based on historic title (rooted, in part, on the presence of Canadian Inuit and other Indigenous peoples in the region since time immemorial), the statement projected a stable, secure circumpolar world—but one in which Canada would continue to uphold its rights as a sovereign, coastal state.[17]

Prime Minister Harper insisted that his nation-building efforts in the Arctic—one of his main legacy projects—were successful. "I think the overwhelming general perception in the North is that—and it is a fact—that no government has paid more attention and actually delivered more in the North than this government," Harper asserted in January 2014. "I mean, it isn't even a contest. We have done more and delivered more than several previous governments combined" (Chase, 2014). No federal government had invested more effort in raising the public profile of the Arctic in Canada since John Diefenbaker in the late 1950s; but the Conservatives' track record in implementing the Northern Strategy was spottier. This verdict fits with a general sense of academic frustration towards the Harper Government which, in terms of its Northern Strategy, tended to criticize its resource development and military focus at the expense of other socio-economic priorities.[18]

---

[17] Leading Canadian academic experts seemed to have reached a similar consensus around 2009, with the most strident proponents of the "sovereignty on thinning ice" school largely abandoning their earlier arguments that Canadian sovereignty will be a casualty of climate change and concomitant foreign challenges. Since then, academic narratives anticipating potential conflict tend to emphasize how other international events (such as Russian aggression in the Ukraine) could "spillover" into the Arctic or how new non-Arctic state and non-state actors might challenge or undermine Canadian sovereignty and security.

[18] See Griffiths et al. (2011), Lackenbauer, (2021) and Exner-Pirot (2016).

"Consultation Was Not Enough"

Liberal leader Justin Trudeau spent little time talking about the Arctic during the 2015 federal election campaign. His emphasis on the environment and reconciliation with Indigenous Peoples, however, indicated how his government would approach northern issues. "No relationship is more important to me and to Canada than the one with Indigenous Peoples," Trudeau highlighted in his mandate letter to each of his Cabinet ministers in November 2015. "It is time for a renewed, nation-to-nation relationship with Indigenous Peoples, based on recognition of rights, respect, cooperation, and partnership" (Prime Minister of Canada, n.d.). In May 2016, the Government of Canada announced its unqualified support for the United Nations Declaration on the Rights of Indigenous Peoples (UNDRIP), stressing that "meaningful engagement with Indigenous Peoples aims to secure their free, prior and informed consent when Canada proposes to take actions which impact them and their rights" (Coates & Favel, 2016).

Trudeau's focus on reconciliation framed the Joint Statement on Environment, Climate Change, and Arctic Leadership that he and President Obama released in March 2016. The two leaders articulated a shared vision for the Arctic that included close bilateral cooperation, working in partnership with Indigenous Peoples and Northerners, and science-based decision-making in conservation and economic development (Prime Minister of Canada, 2016a). Indigenous and environmental organizations in Canada applauded the statement, with national Inuit leader Natan Obed stating that "the final language in this document really spoke to Inuit" and heralding it "a tremendous breakthrough for Indigenous people who live in the Arctic" (Zerehi, 2016).

Trudeau and Obama followed up with a Joint Arctic Leaders' Statement on 20 December 2016 that sought to advance the objectives that they had outlined the previous March. This follow-up announcement launched concrete actions "ensuring a strong, sustainable and viable Arctic economy and ecosystem, with low-impact shipping, science based management of marine resources, and free from the risks of offshore oil and gas activity," that would "set the stage for deeper partnerships with other Arctic nations, including through the Arctic Council" (Prime Minister of Canada, 2016b). While framed in a bilateral and international context, the statement again provided strong insight into Canada's domestic Arctic policy goals. "The overall objective is to support Canada's commitments to reconciliation and renewed partnerships, strong Arctic communities, sustainable Arctic economies, acting within the realities of climate change, and ensuring a healthy Arctic environment," supplemental information from Indigenous and Northern Affairs Canada explained (INAC, 2016).

The United States–Canada Joint Arctic Leaders' Statement prioritized "soft security" and safety issues, environmental protection and conservation, the incorporation of Indigenous science and traditional knowledge into decision-making, supporting strong communities, and building a sustainable Arctic economy. The leaders also announced a moratorium on Arctic offshore oil and gas activity (The Liberal government failed to consult with the territorial governments or Northern Indigenous organizations about the moratorium, causing much indignation, particularly in the Northwest Territories) (Rogers, 2016; Van Dusen, 2016).

Prime Minister Trudeau also used the Joint Arctic Leaders' Statement to announce his plan to "co-develop a new Arctic Policy Framework, with Northerners, Territorial and Provincial governments, and First Nations, Inuit, and Métis People" that would replace his Conservative predecessor Stephen Harper's Northern Strategy. The Liberal government promised that a collaborative approach would ensure that the views and priorities of Arctic residents and governments would be at the "forefront of policy decisions affecting the future of the Canadian Arctic and Canada's role in the circumpolar Arctic." Through the framework's co-development process Ottawa promised that it would "reorganize and reprioritize federal activities in the Arctic" and "link existing federal government initiatives" (CIRNAC, 2019a).

Trudeau announced that his new framework would include an "Inuit-specific component, created in partnership with Inuit, as Inuit Nunangat [the Inuit homeland comprised of the Inuvialuit settlement region in the Northwest Territories, the entirety of Nunavut, the Nunavik region of Quebec, and the Nunatsiavut region of Newfoundland and Labrador] comprises over a third of Canada's land mass and over half of Canada's coast line, and as Inuit modern treaties govern the entirety of this jurisdictional space" (Prime Minister of Canada, 2016b). The government's focus on Inuit Nunangat throughout the process represented a significant departure from the approach utilized in Harper's Northern Strategy, which did not view the Inuit homeland as a cohesive space for policy-making and tended to examine priorities and interventions through the lens of Canada's three northern territories. The new process reflected the Trudeau government's distinctions-based approach that "respects the unique rights, interests and circumstances of Inuit, First Nations and Métis peoples" as well as the Inuit Nunangat Declaration on Inuit-Crown Partnership—a "bilateral partnership" to act on shared priorities (Prime Minister of Canada, 2017; CIRNAC, 2018). The adoption of Inuit Nunangat as a central policy framework also reflects the vision articulated a half-century ago by Inuit leaders at the July 1970 Coppermine Conference and by Inuit Tapirisat of Canada (now Inuit Tapiriit Kanatami) when it was created in 1971 (Bonesteel, 2008).

The appointment of Inuit leader Mary Simon as special representative to Minister of Indigenous and Northern Affairs Carolyn Bennett in July 2016 reflects the Trudeau's government's commitment to co-develop its Northern policy with Indigenous leaders. A longstanding champion of Inuit rights, Simon's formal role was to seek out the views of Northerners and provide advice to the federal government on future conservation and sustainable development goals that would support efforts to devise a new Shared Arctic Leadership Model. Given her mandate, as well as her previous critiques of "militaristic" Arctic strategies,[19] it is no surprise that her efforts emphasized environmental and human security considerations. Her *Interim Report on the Shared Arctic Leadership Model*, released in October 2016, identified marine conservation opportunities—and revealed how broadly she interpreted her mandate to tackle Northern (and particularly Inuit) cultural, socio-economic, and political challenges. "While conservation concerns inform many aspects of northern land claims agreements, Arctic peoples and their representative organizations and governments are far more preoccupied with issues related to supporting strong families, communities and building robust economies," Simon explained in her report. "Closing [the basic gaps between what exists in the Arctic and what other Canadians take for granted] is what northerners, across the Arctic, wanted to speak to me about as an urgent priority. Reconciliation is inextricably tied to this reality" (Simon, 2016). The *Pan-Territorial Vision*, released by the territorial governments in 2017, reiterated these governments' priorities and stressed the importance of resource development, economic diversification, innovation, and infrastructure to build stronger regional

---

[19] See, for example, Simon (1992, 2008).

economies (Governments of Northwest Territories, Nunavut & Yukon, 2017) (Fig. 1).

Simon's 2016 report highlighted that a "long history of visions, action plans, strategies and initiatives being devised 'for the North' and not 'with the North'" (Simon, 2017). The Liberal government sought to correct this tendency through extensive expert and public consultations with Indigenous people in Northern Canada. While Simon's Northern consultations focussed almost entirely on Inuit, the long co-development phase of the ANPF reflected a whole-of-government approach involving a wide range of departments and agencies in the region, the territorial governments, Quebec, Manitoba, and Newfoundland and Labrador. Regional roundtables, public submissions, and other face-to-face engagement initiatives solicited the input of Indigenous groups and other

1. Understanding and honouring the intent of Section 35 of the *Constitution Act of 1982:* All partners should understand and honour Canada's commitment to upholding Section 35 of the *Constitution* and strive to achieve forward momentum in defining how Section 35 can be applied to evolving policy and program initiatives.

2. Reconciliation: Reconciliation in partnerships and policy-making involves, at a minimum, a commitment to restoring relationships, seeing things differently than before, and making changes in power relationships.

3. Equality, trust, and mutual respect: A true partnership has to be built on equality, trust, transparency and respectful disagreement.

4. Flexible and adaptive policy: Nation-building in the Arctic will not be found in one-size-fits-all policy solutions. Policies need to adjust and adapt to circumstances.

5. Arctic leaders know their needs: Recognize that Arctic leaders know their priorities and what is required to achieve success.

6. Community-based solutions: Local leadership must be recognized and enabled to ensure community-based and community-driven solutions.

7. Confidence in capacity: An effective partnership has confidence in, and builds on, the capacities that are brought into the partnership, but also recognizes when capacity gaps need addressing.

8. Understanding and honouring agreements: The signing of an agreement is only the beginning of a partnership. Signatories need to routinely inform themselves of agreements, act on the spirit and intent, recognize capacity needs, respect their obligations, ensure substantive progress is made on implementation, expedite the resolution of disputes, and involve partners in any discussions that would lead to changes in agreements.

9. Respecting Indigenous knowledge: Indigenous and local knowledge must be valued and promoted equally to western science, in research, planning and decision-making.

Fig. 1 Mary Simon's principles of partnership (*Source* Simon, 2017)

stakeholders. This new approach to policymaking stressed that "consultation was not enough" and strived to involve stakeholders "in the drafting of the document" to place "the future into the hands of the people who live there" (CIRNAC, 2009).

A "Profound Change of Direction" or Incomplete Roadmap?

The Government of Canada released the Arctic and Northern Policy Framework (ANPF) on a website with little fanfare on 10 September 2019. Rushed onto the internet the day before the Trudeau Government called a new federal election and lacking the professional polish and glossy presentation characteristic of other Canadian policy statements, the Framework purported to represent a "profound direction change." Substantively, however, the main chapter of the ANPF lays out well-established issues, challenges, and opportunities facing Canada's Arctic and Northern regions, and indicates the federal government's primary goals and objectives. It details the impacts of climate change, particularly as it affects social and cultural norms, ways of knowing, and on-the-land activities. It also highlights the broad spectrum of socio-economic challenges facing the North, ranging from the lack of economic opportunity, to mental health challenges, to food insecurity, to gaps in infrastructure, health care, education, skills development, and income equality across the region. The framework notes the opportunities and challenges that stem from the North's youthful population, particularly in Nunavut where the median age is just over 26. In its effort to link existing federal initiatives to the ANPF, the government highlights specific examples of how the government is already addressing some of these issues in collaboration with its Indigenous and territorial partners throughout the document.

The ANPF's first and primary goal is to create conditions so that "Canadian Arctic and northern Indigenous peoples are resilient and healthy." This priority animates the entire document. To achieve this, the ANPF pledges to end poverty, eradicate hunger, reduce suicides, close the gap on education outcomes, provide greater access to skills developments, adopt culturally appropriate approaches to justice issues, and eliminate the housing crisis in the North. As examples of action already taken, the document notes the government's ongoing efforts to "support better, more relevant and accessible education," funding and skills training for community-led food production projects, updates to Nutrition North, and its investment in new addictions treatment facilities in Nunavut and Nunavik. This patchwork of government initiatives has not impressed critics who lamented that the framework failed to elucidate a coherent strategy or to establish clear metrics to address the dismal socio-economic and health indicators related to Canada's North. Despite few details about how the government actually plans to accomplish its overarching goal of "resilient and healthy" northern peoples and communities, this broad vision resonates with its strong commitment to reconciliation with Indigenous peoples, captured in the eighth goal: the promise of a future that "supports self-determination and nurtures mutually respectful relationships between Indigenous and non-Indigenous peoples."

Between these two pillars are a broad range of challenges, opportunities, and promises that form a tangled web of underdeveloped priorities. The second goal is strengthened infrastructure, including broadband connectivity, multi-modal transportation infrastructure, multi-purpose communications, energy, and transportation corridors, energy security and sustainability at the community-level, and social infrastructure. The ANPF points out that the government has already provided over $190 million in funding for improvements and expansion of existing local air and marine infrastructure. While these community-focussed initiatives are essential to the resilience and well-being of Northerners, the challenge remains how to justify the exorbitant costs associated with much larger "transformative investments in infrastructure." For example, the policy framework cites the federal government's investment of $71.7 million through the National Trade Corridors Fund for four Nunavut transportation projects. This funding included $21.5 million for preparatory work to the $500-million Grays Bay Port and Road Project, which, if completed, would create the first road connecting Nunavut to the rest of Canada. The ANPF mentions the project once and provides no detail on how the government plans to support this massive endeavour moving forward. Furthermore, it is silent on how decision-makers will approach opponents of the project who argue that the road will threaten the Bathurst caribou herd. More generally, how will the government decide which infrastructure projects get what funding when the ANPF and partner documents reiterate that so much investment is required across the North?

The framework highlights the need for "strong, sustainable, diversified, and inclusive local and regional economies," particularly through increased Indigenous ownership and participation, the reduction of income inequality, the optimization of resource development, economic diversification (including land-based, traditional economic activities), and the enhancement of trade and investment opportunities.[20] The framework also highlights the idea of a "conservation economy" (which makes conservation an important part of local economies) that the federal government is slowly growing in the Arctic in collaboration with northern Indigenous stakeholders. For instance, the creation of Tallurutiup Imanga Marine Conservation Area, co-developed with the Qikiqtani Inuit Association, has involved the establishment of the Guardians programme in Arctic Bay and funding to improve small craft harbours in the adjacent communities. Beyond these measures, however, the framework provides no roadmap or economic model for how to grow up and diversify the northern economy. How will the government approach the debate between those who want to heavily regulate resource development and those who believe regulations are strangling the northern economy—a conflict that the framework explicitly acknowledges? The consultations highlighted "co-management of renewable resources ... as a venue for collaborative management that can help integrate different viewpoints," but the ANPF does not indicate how this will work in practice.

The framework's fourth goal is to ensure that both Indigenous and scientific knowledge and understanding guide decision-making, and that Arctic and Northern peoples are included in the knowledge-creation process. While the government points to the funding it has already provided for the Polar Continental Shelf Program and the Eureka Weather Station, the framework includes no specifics on how it will support and fund its proposed expansion of domestic and international northern research. The same lack of detail on funding and execution is also reflected in discussion of the government's fifth goal, which focusses on ensuring healthy, resilient Arctic and northern ecosystems and promises action on a wide array of major objectives, ranging from mitigation and adaptation measures to climate change, to sustainable use of the ecosystems and species, and safe and environmentally responsible shipping.

---

[20] It cites existing federal efforts such as the Jobs and Tourism Initiative and Canadian Northern Economic Development Agency's Inclusive Diversification and Economic Advancement in the North (IDEANorth) programme, which "makes foundational investments in economic infrastructure, sector development and capacity building."

The sixth and seventh goals highlight measures to strengthen the rules-based international order in the Arctic. Emphasizing that the region is "well known for its high level of international cooperation on a broad range of issues," and "despite increased interest in the region from both Arctic and non-Arctic states," the ANPF commits to continued multilateral and bilateral cooperation in the Arctic. It confirms the Arctic Council as the "pre-eminent forum for Arctic cooperation" complemented by the "extensive international legal framework [that] applies to the Arctic Ocean." There is muscular language proclaiming how Canada "is firmly asserting its presence in the North" and pledges to "more clearly define Canada's Arctic boundaries"—a surprising statement given that Canada filed its Arctic continental shelf submission in May 2019, and one that seems to deviate from Canada's longstanding insistence that "Canada's Arctic sovereignty is longstanding, well-established and based on historic title, founded in part on the presence of Inuit and other Aboriginal peoples since time immemorial" (as written in Conservatives' 2009 Northern Strategy). There are also peculiar statements, such as the need to "regularize a bilateral dialogue with the United States on Arctic issues," with no clear explanation of where the bilateral relationship is deficient or what this means (CIRNAC, 2019c; Government of Canada, 2009).

The overall tenor, however, is generally optimistic. Canada's domestic priorities are being projected unabashedly into the international sphere, emphasizing the desire for regional peace and stability so that "Arctic and northern peoples thrive economically, socially and environmentally." Innovative elements include promises to "champion the integration of diversity and gender considerations into projects and initiatives, guided by Canada's feminist foreign policy," and increasing youth engagement in the circumpolar dialogue. Unfortunately, concrete examples of opportunities or new mechanisms to do so are not provided. Similarly, promises to help Arctic and northern businesses to pursue international opportunities "that are aligned with local interests and values" are welcome but vague, and the Trudeau government's vision for the Arctic Economic Council (AEC) is unclear. Well-established priorities, such as food security, improving health care services, and suicide prevention, are presented with no reference whatsoever to what has been done to forward these agendas internationally. There are some discernable policy changes, however. NATO is presented as a "key multilateral forum" in the Arctic—a clear shift from the reticence of previous governments who feared unnecessarily antagonizing Russia by having the alliance articulate an Arctic focus. Concurrently, the policy commits to "restart a regular bilateral dialogue on Arctic issues with Russia in key areas related to Indigenous issues, scientific cooperation, environmental protection, shipping and search and rescue"—a welcome acknowledgement that, despite resurgent strategic competition and divergent interests elsewhere in the world, both countries have many common interests in the Arctic. Furthermore, Canada commits to "enhance the reputation and participation of Arctic and northern Canadians, especially Indigenous peoples, in relevant international forums and negotiations," and to promote the "full inclusion of Indigenous knowledge" in polar research and decision-making. Specific examples relating to the marine environment, particularly the visionary work of the Pikialasorsuaq Commission, point to the benefits of this approach.

The priorities in the standalone "Safety, Security, and Defence" chapter (CIRNAC, 2019b) include Canada's continued demonstration of sovereignty, the strengthening of the military presence in the region, the defence of North America, improved domain awareness, reinforced whole-of-society emergency management, and continued engagement with local communities, Indigenous groups, and international partners. Much of the discussion reiterates policy elements in Canada's 2017 defence policy, *Strong, Secure, Engaged* (Department of National Defence of Canada, 2017). "While Canada sees no immediate threat in the Arctic and the North, as the region's physical environment changes, the circumpolar North is becoming an area of strategic international importance, with both Arctic and non-Arctic states expressing a variety of economic and military interests in the region," the policy framework emphasizes. "As the Arctic becomes more accessible, these states are poised to conduct research, transit through, and engage in more trade in the region. Given the growing international interest and competition in the Arctic, continued security and defence of Canada's Arctic requires effective safety and security frameworks, national defence, and deterrence." Priorities identified in the chapter include Canada's continued demonstration of sovereignty, the enhancement of the military presence in the region, the defence of North America, improved domain awareness, strengthened whole-of-society emergency management, and continued engagement with local communities, Indigenous groups, and international partners. It also points to the work around marine safety already accomplished by the *Oceans Protection Plan* (*OPP*) (Kikkert & Lackenbauer, 2021; Transport

Canada, 2020). Given the governmental action already taken through *SSE* and the *OPP*, this section of the ANPF provides the most detail on how the government aims to accomplish its objectives. It is also telling that this chapter was written with the least direct consultation and input from Northerners, thus offering the clearest vision of the federal government's priorities.

The Government of Canada has maintained that the Arctic and Northern Policy Framework represents a "profound change of direction." The seemingly random assortment of ongoing initiatives scattered throughout the framework's goals, however, highlight the lack of coherence in the federal government's approach to policy and programming in the North. While purporting to offer a "roadmap" to achieve a "shared vision" that identifies hazards, problems, and opportunities, the Government of Canada has not provided clear policy direction that sets a predictable route or establishes milestones to gauge progress. In tangible policy terms, the framework reflects and formalizes an ongoing process in which well-known policy challenges are addressed through ad hoc implementation by the federal government when its priorities align with those of key stakeholder partners at the territorial/provincial and Indigenous government/representative organization levels.

"A Shared Vision" or Muddling Through?

The partner chapters of the ANPG represent one of the most confusing parts of the entire framework and raise an important question: what happens when priorities do not align between key stakeholders? The Inuit Nunangat, NWT, Nunavut, and Pan-Territorial chapters that are included as appendices to the framework represent "the visions, aspirations and priorities of our co-development partners"—but they also highlight inability to reach "unanimous agreement" on key issues. At the beginning of the document, the government asserts that these partner chapters were "crucial" to the co-development process, that they "map out areas of present and future" collaboration between the Government of Canada and its partners, and that they will "provide guidance" on its implementation. At the tail end of the document, however, a caveat notes that these perspectives "do not necessarily reflect the views of either the federal government, or of the other partners." There is little indication throughout the framework on how exactly these chapters will inform federal policymaking, particularly in areas of disagreement. How will the framework reconcile some of the key differences in the partner chapters, particularly the NWT's call for a "lifting of the Beaufort Sea Moratorium" and the creation of a co-management agreement for the "responsible and sustainable development" of the region's offshore resources? (Government of the Northwest Territories, 2019). In April 2019, Inuit Tapiriit Kanatami president Natan Obed shed some light on the government's continued struggle to truly co-develop policies with Northerners. "After four years, this government is still not necessarily understanding how to transform the working relationship," he told a reporter. "… How the public service acts and the advice that it gives to any particular minister of the day has been entrenched for so long that we end up fighting that more than we fight the good intentions of ministers" (Wells, 2019).

Throughout the co-development of the ANPF, Trudeau emphasized its "Inuit-specific component, created in partnership with Inuit" that would take Inuit Nunangat as the primary lens through which to view policies focussed on Inuit. This represented a significant departure from previous governments in adopting an ethnic-based approach that seemed to place a higher political priority on relations with an Inuit advocacy organization rather than the territorial governments (including the Government of Nunavut responsible for a territory comprised of 85% Inuit). When asked whether the long-term goal for Inuit Nunangat was "a contiguous political space with similar jurisdiction to the provinces in the south," Obed replied: "Well, we'll see where our self-determination takes us" (Wells, 2019). By extension, the policy framework opened space to deliver services to Inuit through mechanisms parallel to (and in competition with) established Canadian federal-provincial/territorial channels. The Inuit Nunangat chapter, authored by ITK and included as an appendix to the ANPF, may or may not reflect the views of the federal government given its status as a "partner chapter," thus leaving lingering questions. How will Ottawa operationalize its focus on Inuit Nunangat moving forward? Will it support the re-drawing of Canada's political boundaries if self-determining Inuit decide that this is what they want? How will Inuit Nunangat, as a political jurisdiction, interact with the current roles and responsibilities of public territorial and provincial governments? The Trudeau government has offered little to no clarity on these fundamental questions with implications not only for the Arctic but for Canadian governance more generally.

The Government of Canada's emphasis on collaborative governance recognizes that where, in the past, Ottawa defined problems facing the

North incorrectly because of little consultation with Northerners, it set the wrong priorities and produced ineffective or unpopular policies. While many stakeholders have lauded the highly democratic consultative process involved in developing the ANPF, the actual product—with its comprehensive but thin main chapter published by the federal government and series of "partner chapters" offering distinct ideas—also speaks to the inability to achieve consensus and a retreat to general ideas rather than concrete implementation plans.

The ANPF concludes with a promise that the government will have ten years to "bring its goals and objectives into reality" and advises that federal-territorial-provincial and Indigenous partners will co-develop solutions and new governance mechanisms. As Minister of Crown-Indigenous Relations and Northern Affairs Carolyn Bennett noted after the ANPF's release, "you begin with the policy and then you work toward implementation … It's a matter of us now, as we move through each budget cycle of each government, having a road map for closing these gaps." Actual implementation of the ANPF remains opaque nearly two years later, with the minister's emphasis on "each budget cycle of each government" speaking to the absence of a long-term, publicly disclosed plan. A November 2020 press release, following a virtual meeting on ANPF implementation (the only one held as of June 2021), is a case in point. "Through the Arctic and Northern Policy Framework Canada will continue to work with our territorial, provincial and Indigenous partners to Build Back Better in a way that supports northern economies, as well as the social and political self-determination that underpins successful and long-lasting regional development," a cryptic press release offers. "These and other initiatives will continue to roll out in support of key priorities across Arctic and Northern regions thanks to collaboration with partners to the Framework and through the national and regional governance mechanisms discussed today" (CIRNAC, 2020).

In short, while Canada's "new" Arctic and Northern Policy Framework reiterates many complex challenges and opportunities facing the Arctic, and setting laudable goals such as ending poverty, eradicating hunger, and eliminating the housing crisis in the North, it offers few substantive approaches or mechanisms to meet them. With no budget, prioritization of investment plans, benchmarks, or consolidated plan to address the myriad challenges and issues identified in the ANPF, the Canadian framework stands in sharp control to the Russian strategic documents and implementation plans released in 2020 and 2021 that reflect a clear centralized plan, budgets, timelines, and measurable outcomes.[21]

The absence of a coherent strategy embedded in the ANPF speaks to the complicated process of co-developing policies across Canada's wide and disparate Arctic and Northern regions. Many different voices need to be taken into account, and the framework admits that the federal government and its partners could not reach a consensus on various issues. Rather than seeking to sell a particular vision, the Trudeau Government has instead offered general support for the broad spectrum of well-established Northern priorities without committing to specific objectives—and suggesting that this proves it is more responsive to Northerners' needs than preceding governments. This is revelatory of a policymaking ethos that avoids setting key immediate priorities and instead prefers to "discuss national and regional governance approaches going forward" (CIRNAC, 2020). Accordingly, over the past two year, there are little indications that the ANPF vision has secured widespread policy traction. While COVID-19-related travel restrictions and competitive policy priority associated with the pandemic partially explain limited progress, and various federal departments pursue ANPF investments identified in budget lines, actions to date show little evidence of a profoundly "new" direction.

When the ANPF was released publicly, Iqaluit Mayor Madeleine Redfern noted how "the framework speaks to the fact that we need to be more inclusive, more strategic. It's not a strategy per se, other than to say we need to actually be working together." Along similar lines, Nunavut Premier Joe Savikataaq called the policy a good beginning but noted, "We will be a lot happier when there is more tangible stuff that comes out" (Tømmerbakke, 2019). Will the Canadian federal government be able to co-develop initiatives in the face of differing opinions and priorities, especially around controversial issues such as resource and infrastructure development? More generally, it is unclear how the federal government intends to steer an increasingly expansive network of stakeholders as it works toward implementing a ten-year plan. Can it overcome disagreements and navigate the lack of consensus to move forward on the ANPF's strategic objectives? A clear and coherent governmental roadmap for action remains conspicuously absent so far. Instead, the framework

---

[21] On Russian strategies, see, for example: Sergunin and Konyshev (2019), Lagutina (2021), and Sukhankin et al. (2021).

continues to perpetuate a long history of ad hoc, reactive Arctic policymaking[22] that promotes incremental progress across a broad front of known issues. While delivering on Mary Simon's call for a "flexible and adaptive policy" that can "adjust and adapt to circumstances," it reiterates and consolidates longstanding needs without articulating a transparent action plan. Instead, in the Canadian policy space, "co-development" and "co-implementation" place the onus on Northerners to devise the practical strategies to close "gaps for the people of the North" and create "a lasting legacy of sustainable economic development." Whether this can produce material results that reduce "the basic gaps between what exists in the Arctic and what other Canadians take for granted"[23] remains to be seen.

Acknowledgements This work was supported by the Canadian Department of National Defence Mobilizing Insights in Defence and Security (MINDS) programme through the North American and Arctic Defence and Security Network (NAADSN); the Canada Research Chairs programme; and the Irving Shipbuilding Chair in Arctic Policy in the Brian Mulroney Institute of Government.

Parts of this chapter appeared previously as research notes: Canada's Arctic and Northern Policy Framework: A Roadmap for the Future? In L. Heininen, H. Exner-Pirot, J. Barnes (eds.), *Arctic Yearbook 2019* (pp. 332–339). Akureyri: Arctic Portal. https://arcticyearbook.com/images/yearbook/2019/Briefing-Notes/9_AY2019_BN_Kikkert_Lackenbauer.pdf; and A Better Road Map Needed for Arctic and Northern Policy Framework. *Policy Options* [online], Institute for Research on Public Policy, 17 September 2019, https://policyoptions.irpp.org/magazines/september-2019/a-better-road-map-needed-for-arctic-and-northern-policy-framework/.

References

Alcantara, C. (2008). To treaty or not to treaty? Aboriginal peoples and comprehensive land claims negotiations in Canada. *Publius, 38*(2), 343–369.

---

[22] See, for example, Huebert (1995), Coates et al. (2008), Griffiths et al. (2011), and Lackenbauer (2016, 2019).

[23] Simon quoted in CIRNAC (n.d.).

Alcantara, C. (2013). Preferences, perceptions, and veto players: Explaining devolution negotiation outcomes in the Canadian territorial north. *Polar Record, 249*(49), 167–179.

AMAP. (2004). *Arctic climate impact assessment 2004.* Arctic Monitoring and Assessment Programme (AMAP). https://www.amap.no/documents/doc/impacts-of-a-warming-arctic-2004/786. Accessed 31 July 2021.

Arctic Economic Council. (2015). *Backgrounder.* Arctic Economic Council. http://arcticeconomiccouncil.com/wp-content/uploads/2015/01/AEC-Backgrounder.pdf. Accessed 31 July 2021.

Axworthy, L., & Simon, M. (2015, March 4). Is Canada undermining the Arctic Council? *Globe and Mail.* https://www.theglobeandmail.com/opinion/is-canada-undermining-the-arctic-council/article23273276/. Accessed 31 July 2021.

Berger, T. R. (1977). *Northern frontier, northern homeland: The report of the Mackenzie Valley Pipeline Inquiry* (Vol. 1). Minister of Supply and Services Canada.

Berthiaume, L. (2013, August 30). *Questions raised on Harper government's approach to northern development.* Postmedia Breaking News.

Bonesteel, S. (2008). *Canada's relationship with Inuit: A history of policy and program development.* Indian and Northern Affairs Canada.

Byers, M., & Layton, J. (2007, September 6). How to strengthen our Arctic security: Keep our promises to the Inuit. *The Tyee.* https://thetyee.ca/Views/2007/09/06/ColdReality/. Accessed 31 July 2021.

Cameron, K., & Campbell, A. (2009). The devolution of natural resources and Nunavut's constitutional status. *Journal of Canadian Studies, 43*(2), 198–219.

Cameron, K., & White, G. (1995). *Northern governments in transition: Political and constitutional development in the Yukon, Nunavut and the Western Northwest Territories.* Institute for Research on Public Policy.

Canada. (2005). Canada's international policy statement, overview. Excerpted in Dean, R., Lackenbauer, P. W., & Lajeunesse, A. (2014). *Canadian Arctic defence and security policy: An overview of key documents, 1970–2012* (pp. 39–40). Centre for Military and Strategic Studies/Centre on Foreign Policy and Federalism.

Canadian Arctic Resources Committee. (2006). Renewing the Northern Strategy. *Northern Perspectives, 30*(1), 2.

CBC. (n.d.). *The Berger Pipeline Inquiry.* Canadian Broadcasting Corporation (CBC): Archives. https://www.cbc.ca/archives/topic/the-berger-pipeline-inquiry. Accessed 31 July 2021.

Chase, S. (2014, January 17). Q&A with Harper: No previous government has 'delivered more in the North'. *The Globe and Mail.* https://www.theglobeandmail.com/news/national/the-north/qa-with-harper-no-previous-govern ment-has-delivered-more-in-the-north/article16387286/. Accessed 31 July 2021.

Chrétien, J. (2020). *Northern Canada in the 70's: In Canada's Northern Strategies: From Trudeau to Trudeau, 1970–2020*. Arctic Institute of North America. http://pubs.aina.ucalgary.ca/dcass/85472.pdf. Accessed 31 July 2021.

CIRNAC. (2009, September). *Arctic and Northern policy framework*. Crown-Indigenous Relations and Northern Affairs Canada (CIRNAC). https://www.rcaanc-cirnac.gc.ca/eng/1560523306861/1560523330587. Accessed 31 July 2021.

CIRNAC. (2018, September 10). *Overview of a recognition and implementation of Indigenous rights framework*. Crown-Indigenous Relations and Northern Affairs Canada (CIRNAC). https://www.rcaanc-cirnac.gc.ca/eng/1536350959665/1539959903708?wbdisable=true. Accessed 31 July 2021.

CIRNAC. (2019a, May 14). *Toward a new Arctic Policy Framework*. Crown-Indigenous Relations and Northern Affairs Canada (CIRNAC). https://www.rcaanc-cirnac.gc.ca/eng/1499951681722/1537884604444. Accessed 31 July 2021.

CIRNAC. (2019b, September 10). *Arctic and Northern Policy Framework Safety, Security, and Defence chapter*. Crown-Indigenous Relations and Northern Affairs Canada (CIRNAC). https://www.rcaanc-cirnac.gc.ca/eng/1562939617400/1562939658000. Accessed 31 July 2021.

CIRNAC. (2019c, October 22). *Arctic and Northern Policy Framework: International chapter*. Crown-Indigenous Relations and Northern Affairs Canada (CIRNAC). https://www.rcaanc-cirnac.gc.ca/eng/1562867415721/1562867459588. Accessed 31 July 2021.

CIRNAC. (2020, November 24). *Minister Vandal, partners to the Arctic and Northern Policy Framework meet to discuss priorities for the North and Arctic*. Crown-Indigenous Relations and Northern Affairs Canada (CIRNAC). https://www.canada.ca/en/crown-indigenous-relations-northern-affairs/news/2020/11/minister-vandal-partners-to-the-arctic-and-northern-policy-framework-meet-to-discuss-priorities-for-the-north-and-arctic.html. Accessed 31 July 2021.

CIRNAC. (n.d.). *Highlights of Canada's Arctic and Northern Policy Framework*. Crown-Indigenous Relations and Northern Affairs Canada (CIRNAC). https://www.rcaanc-cirnac.gc.ca/DAM/DAM-CIRNAC-RCAANC/DAM-NTHAFF/STAGING/texte-text/nth-anpf_highlights_infograph_pdf_1567701943197_eng.pdf. Accessed 31 July 2021.

Coates, K., & Favel, B. (2016, May 19). *Embrace of UNDRIP can bring Aboriginal Canada and Ottawa closer together*. iPolitics. http://www.macdonaldlaurier.ca/embrace-of-undrip-can-bring-aboriginal-canada-and-ottawa-closer-together-ken-coates-and-blaine-favel-for-ipolitics/. Accessed 31 July 2021.

Coates, K. C., Lackenbauer, P. W., Morrion, W. R., & Poelzer, G. (2008). *Arctic front: Defending Canada in the Far North*. Thomas Allen.

Department of Foreign Affairs and International Trade of Canada. (2000). *The Northern dimension of Canada's foreign policy*. Arctic Portal Library. http://library.arcticportal.org/1255/1/The_Northern_Dimension_Canada.pdf. Accessed 31 July 2021.

Department of National Defence of Canada. (2017). *Strong, secure, engaged: Canada's defence policy*. http://dgpaapp.forces.gc.ca/en/canada-defence-pol icy/docs/canada-defence-policy-report.pdf. Accessed 31 July 2021.

Dodds, K. (2011). We are a northern country: Stephen Harper and the Canadian Arctic. *Polar Record, 47*(4), 371–374.

Exner-Pirot, H. (2016). Canada's Arctic Council chairmanship (2013–2015): A post-mortem. *Canadian Foreign Policy Journal, 22*(1), 84–96.

Exner-Pirot, H. (2019, September 12). *Canada's new Arctic policy doesn't stick the landing*. RCI: Eye on the Arctic. https://www.rcinet.ca/eye-on-the-arc tic/2019/09/12/canada-arctic-northern-policy-trudeau-analysis/. Accessed 31 July 2021.

Gatehouse, J. (2013, May 3). When science goes silent. *Maclean's*. https://www.macleans.ca/news/canada/when-science-goes-silent/. Accessed 31 July 2021.

Government of Canada. (2008, March 10). *Prime Minister Harper delivers on commitment to the "New North"*. Government of Canada: News release. https://www.canada.ca/en/news/archive/2008/03/prime-minister-harper-delivers-commitment-new-north-.html. Accessed 31 July 2021.

Government of Canada. (2009). *Canada's Northern Strategy: Our North, Our heritage, Our future*. Government of Canada.

Government of Canada. (2019). *Arctic and Northern Policy Framework*. Crown-Indigenous Relations and Northern Affairs Canada (CIRNAC). https://www.rcaanc-cirnac.gc.ca/eng/1560523306861/1560523330587. Accessed 31 July 2021.

Government of the Northwest Territories. (2019). *Arctic and Northern Policy Framework*. https://www.eia.gov.nt.ca/sites/eia/files/arcticnorthernp olicyframework_-_final-web.pdf. Accessed 31 Jul 2021.

Governments of Northwest Territories, Nunavut, and Yukon. (2017). *Pan-territorial vision for sustainable development*. The Government of Nunavut. https://www.gov.nu.ca/executive-and-intergovernmental-affairs/inform ation/arctic-and-northern-policy-framework-pan. Accessed 31 July 2021.

Greer, D. (2019, September 18). Arctic framework same old, same old. *Kivalliq News*. https://nunavutnews.com/nunavut-news/arctic-framework-same-old-same-old/. Accessed 31 July 2021.

Griffiths, F., Huebert, R., & Lackenbauer, P. W. (2011). *Canada and the changing Arctic: Sovereignty, security, and stewardship*. Wilfrid Laurier University Press.

Harper, S. (2005, December 22). *Harper stands up for Arctic sovereignty*. Address in Ottawa.

Harris, K. (2007, February 23). Laying claim to Canada's internal waters. *Toronto Sun*.

House of Commons Standing Committee on Foreign Affairs and International Trade. (1997). *Canada and the circumpolar world: Meeting the challenges of cooperation into the twenty-first century*. Public Works and Government Services.

Huebert, R. (1995). Polar vision or tunnel vision the making of Canadian Arctic waters policy: The making of Canadian Arctic waters policy. *Marine Policy, 19*(4), 343–363.

Huebert, R. (2001a). A Northern foreign policy: The politics of Ad Hocery. In K. Nossal & N. Michaud (Eds.), *Diplomatic departures: The conservative era in Canadian foreign policy, 1984–1993* (pp. 84–99). UBC Press.

Huebert, R. (2001b). Climate change and Canadian sovereignty in the Northwest passage. *Isuma: Canadian Journal of Policy Research, 2*(4), 86–94.

Hume, M. (2015, November 8). Federal scientists eager to share their research now that muzzles are off. *Globe and Mail*. https://www.theglobeandmail.com/news/british-columbia/federal-scientists-eager-to-share-their-research-now-that-muzzles-are-off/article27171269/. Accessed 31 July 2021.

ICC. (2009). *A circumpolar declaration on sovereignty in the Arctic*. Inuit Circumpolar Council (ICC). https://www.itk.ca/publication/circumpolar-declaration-sovereignty-arctic. Accessed 31 July 2021.

INAC. (2016, December 20). *FAQs on actions being taken under the Canada-US Joint Arctic statement*. Indigenous and Northern Affairs Canada (INAC). https://www.rcaanc-cirnac.gc.ca/eng/1482262705012/1594738557219. Accessed 31 Jul 2021.

INAC. (2020, November 10). *Nunavut devolution*. Indigenous and Northern Affairs Canada (INAC). https://www.rcaanc-cirnac.gc.ca/eng/1352471770723/1537900871295. Accessed 31 July 2021.

Isard, P. (2010). *Northern vision: Northern development during the Diefenbaker era*. Unpublished M.A. thesis, University of Waterloo.

Jockel, J. (1991). *Security to the North: Canada-US defense relations in the 1990s*. Michigan State University Press.

Kaludjak, P. (2007, July 18). *The Inuit are here, use us*. Ottawa Citizen. https://www.pressreader.com/canada/ottawa-citizen/20070718/281891588870676. Accessed 31 July 2021.

Kanatami, T. (2013). *Nilliajut: Inuit perspectives on security, patriotism and sovereignty*. Inuit Qaujisarvingat.

Kikkert, P., & Lackenbauer, P. W. (2021, July). Search and rescue, climate change, and the expansion of the coast guard auxiliary in Inuit Nunangat/the Canadian Arctic. *Canadian Journal of Emergency Management*, 1(2), 26–62.

Kirkey, C. (1995). Smoothing troubled waters: The 1988 Canada-United States Arctic co-operation agreement. *International Journal*, 50(2), 401–426.

Klinkenborg, V. (2013, September 21). Silencing scientists. *New York Times*. https://www.nytimes.com/2013/09/22/opinion/sunday/silencing-scientists.html. Accessed 31 July 2021.

Lackenbauer, P. W. (2013, August 20). Harper's Arctic evolution. *Globe and Mail*. https://www.theglobeandmail.com/opinion/harpers-arctic-evolution/article13852195/. Accessed 31 July 2021.

Lackenbuaer, P. W. (2016). Canada's Northern Strategy: A Comprehensive Approach to Defence, Security, and Safety. In J. Higginbotham & J. Spence (Ed.), *North of 60: Toward a Renewed Canadian Arctic Agenda*, Waterloo: Centre for International Governance Innovation. 43–48.

Lackenbauer, P. W. (2019). Canada's Emerging Arctic and Northern Policy Framework: Confirming a Longstanding Northern Strategy. In *Breaking the Ice Curtain? Russia, Canada, and Arctic Security in a Changing Circumpolar World*, eds. P. W. Lackenbauer and S. Lalonde. Calgary: Canadian Global Affairs Institute. 13–42.

Lackenbauer, P. W. (2021). Toward a Comprehensive Approach to Canadian Security and Safety in the Arctic. In *Understanding Sovereignty and Security in the Circumpolar Arctic*, ed. W. Greaves and P. W. Lackenbauer. Toronto: University of Toronto Press, 137–167.

Lagutina, M. (2021). Russia's Arctic policies: Concepts, domestic and international priorities. *Polar Journal*, 11(1), 118–135.

Liberal Party of Canada. (2015, August). *A new plan for Canada's environment and economy*. Liberal Party of Canada. https://www.liberal.ca/files/2015/08/A-new-plan-for-Canadas-environment-and-economy.pdf. Accessed 31 July 2021.

Munro, M. (2015, October 26). Unmuzzling government scientists is just the first step. *Globe and Mail*. https://www.theglobeandmail.com/opinion/unmuzzling-government-scientists-is-just-the-first-step/article26960757/. Accessed 31 July 2021.

O'Malley, M. (1976). *The past and future land: An account of the Berger inquiry into the Mackenzie Valley Pipeline*. P. Martin Associates.

Poelzer, G., & Coates, K. S. (2015). *From treaty peoples to treaty nation: A road map for all Canadians*. UBC Press.

Prime Minister of Canada. (2016a, March 10). *U.S.-Canada joint statement on climate, energy, and Arctic leadership*. http://www.pm.gc.ca/eng/news/2016/03/10/us-canada-joint-statement-climate-energy-and-arctic-leadership#sthash.XjRoT2R7.dpuf. Accessed 31 July 2021.

Prime Minister of Canada. (2016b, December 20). *United States-Canada Joint Arctic leaders' statement.* http://pm.gc.ca/eng/news/2016/12/20/united-states-canada-joint-arctic-leaders-statement. Accessed 31 July 2021.

Prime Minister of Canada. (2017). *Inuit Nunangat declaration on Inuit-Crown partnership.* Government of Canada. https://pm.gc.ca/en/news/statements/2017/02/09/inuit-nunangat-declaration-inuit-crown-partnership. Accessed 31 July 2021.

Prime Minister of Canada. (n.d.). *Ministerial Mandate Letters.* http://pm.gc.ca/eng/ministerial-mandate-letters. Accessed 31 July 2021.

Quinn, E. (2016, January 26). How an Arctic initiative by Canada has gone from being blasted by critics to praised by international politicians. *Eye on the Arctic.* http://www.rcinet.ca/eye-on-the-arctic/2016/01/26/how-will-arctic-economic-council-shape-business-future-of-the-north/. Accessed 31 July 2021.

Rennie, S. (2015, February 3). Nunavut Premier seeks devolution pact, eyes control over land, resources. *The Globe and Mail.* https://www.theglobeandmail.com/news/national/nunavut-premier-seeks-devolution-pact-eyes-control-over-land-resources/article22777248/. Accessed 31 July 2021.

Rogers, S. (2016, December 21). Nunavut disappointed in Trudeau's 'spur of the moment' plans for Arctic. *Nunatsiaq News.* http://www.nunatsiaqonline.ca/stories/article/65674nunavut_disappointed_in_trudeaus_spur_of_the_moment_plans_for_arctic/. Accessed 31 July 2021.

Sergunin, A., & Konyshev, V. (2019). Forging Russia's Arctic strategy: Actors and decision-making. *Polar Journal, 9*(1), 75–93.

Simon, M. (1992). Militarization and the aboriginal peoples. In F. Griffiths (Ed.), *Arctic alternatives: Civility or militarism in the circumpolar north* (pp. 55–57). Science for Peace/Samuel Stevens.

Simon, M. (2007, July 26). Inuit: The bedrock of Canadian sovereignty. *Globe and Mail.* https://www.theglobeandmail.com/opinion/inuit-the-bedrock-of-arctic-sovereignty/article724371/. Accessed 31 July 2021.

Simon, M. (2008, April 11). Does Ottawa's Northern focus look backwards? *Nunatsiaq News.*

Simon, M. (2009). Inuit and the Canadian Arctic: Sovereignty begins at home. *Journal of Canadian Studies, 43*(2), 251.

Simon, M. (2016, October 31). *Interim report on the shared Arctic leadership model.* Crown-Indigenous Relations and Northern Affairs Canada (CIRNAC). https://www.rcaanc-cirnac.gc.ca/eng/1481656672979/1537886690726. Accessed 31 July 2021.

Simon, M. (2017, March). *A new shared Arctic leadership model.* Crown-Indigenous Relations and Northern Affairs Canada (CIRNAC). https://www.rcaanc-cirnac.gc.ca/eng/1492708558500/1537886544718#sec4. Accessed 31 July 2021.

Sukhankin, S., Bouffard, T., & Lackenbauer, P. W. (2021). Strategy, competition, and legitimization: Development of the Arctic Zone of the Russian Federation. *Arctic Yearbook*. https://arcticyearbook.com/images/yearbook/2021/Scholarly-Papers/12_AY2021_Sukhankin.pdf. Access 15 November 2021.

Tømmerbakke, S. G. (2019, September 12). Why the Canadians are provoked by the new and ambitious Arctic policy document. *High North News*. https://www.highnorthnews.com/en/why-canadians-are-provoked-new-and-ambitious-arctic-policy-document. Accessed 31 July 2021.

Transport Canada. (2020). *Oceans Protection Plan initiatives map*. Government of Canada. https://www.tc.gc.ca/en/campaigns/oceans-protection-plan-initiatives-map.html. Accessed 31 July 2021.

Van Dusen, J. (2016, December 22). *Nunavut, N.W.T. premiers slam Arctic drilling moratorium*. CBC News North. http://www.cbc.ca/news/canada/north/nunavut-premier-slams-arctic-drilling-moratorium-1.3908037. Accessed 31 July 2021.

Weber, B. (2007, October 16). *Northern leaders like that Harper has expanded view of Arctic sovereignty*. Canadian Press.

Weber, B. (2009, January 13). *Arctic sovereignty not under threat despite U.S., European policies*. Canadian Press.

Weber, B. (2019, September 11). New federal Arctic policy focuses on human health, environment, infrastructure. *National Post*. https://nationalpost.com/pmn/news-pmn/canada-news-pmn/new-federal-arctic-policy-focusses-on-human-health-environment-infrastructure. Accessed 31 July 2021.

Wells, P. (2019, April 3). Inuit leader Natan Obed on working with the liberals—And his vision for the future. *Maclean's*. https://www.macleans.ca/politics/natan-obed-inuit-snc-lavalin-tuberculosis/. Accessed 31 Jul 2021.

Wingrove, J. (2013, July 26). Harper's focus for North shifts from sovereignty to development. *The Globe and Mail*. https://www.theglobeandmail.com/news/politics/harpers-focus-for-north-shifts-to-development/article13470372/. Accessed 31 July 2021.

Zerehi, S. S. (2016, March 11). *Trudeau-Obama shared Arctic leadership model a hit with Inuit and environmental groups*. CBC News. http://www.cbc.ca/news/canada/north/trudeau-obama-washington-visit-arctic-promises-1.3486076. Accessed 31 July 2021.

Kaleidoscope of Independent Agendas for the Arctic: Scandinavia and Europe

Norway's Arctic Policy: High North, Low Tension?

Andreas Østhagen

INTRODUCTION[1]

In 2005, the then Norwegian foreign minister Jonas Gahr Støre urged the people to "Look north."[2] Speaking in Tromsø, the self-proclaimed Arctic capital of Norway, he launched what was to become Norway's new foreign policy flagship: the High North policy (*nordområdepolitikken*).[3] With one-third of the landmass and 80% of its maritime domain located

[1] This chapter is a revised version of the article 'Norway's arctic policy: still high North, low tension?' by the author, published in *The Polar Journal*, 11(1), 75–94 (2021).

[2] Quoting a poem by Norwegian poet Roy Jacobsen.

[3] Note that a distinction is made between the High North and the Arctic here. The High North (nordområdene in Norwegian) has in many contexts been used to denote the immediate areas in the North that are part of, or are adjacent to, Norway. This includes the Barents Sea and the archipelago of Svalbard but not the entire polar region. The Arctic, on the other hand, refers to the entire circumpolar region (i.e., the entire area north of the Arctic Circle). However, it should be noted that such a separation is not necessarily unequivocally accepted, as the terms are often used interchangeably. See Skagestad 2009 for a longer discussion on the use of these terms.

A. Østhagen (✉)
Fridtjof Nansen Institute, Lysaker, Norway
e-mail: ao@fni.no

© The Author(s), under exclusive license to Springer Nature Singapore Pte Ltd. 2022
A. Likhacheva (ed.), *Arctic Fever*,
https://doi.org/10.1007/978-981-16-9616-9_11

278   A. ØSTHAGEN

north of the Arctic Circle, it is no wonder that Norwegian politicians have been quick to seize the opportunity to promote a hybrid mixture of foreign and regional policy tools as the world has turned its attention northwards. Other Arctic countries—like Denmark, Sweden and the USA—have been much slower to embrace the Arctic as a foreign policy priority, if at all.

In part, Norway's orientation towards the Arctic occurred as the result of a domestic initiative because economic opportunities were increasingly becoming apparent in the North. In part, international conditions were ripe as climate awareness, resource potential and Russian re-emergence started to appear on the agenda. Lastly, the new majority government in office beginning in the autumn of 2005 acted as policy entrepreneurs, building on the discrete Northern policy steps taken by the previous government.[4]

When the Norwegian High North policy saw the light of day 15 years ago, it was an optimistic promise of increased attention to the North, new economic opportunities and the strengthening of dialogue and cooperation with Russia (Medby, 2014). In the beginning, it looked hopeful: after the rather significant maritime boundary agreement with Russia regarding the Barents Sea was enacted in 2010, Russia's then President Medvedev declared a "new era" of relations between Norway and Russia (Aftenposten, 2010). A border regime was created in 2012 so that the inhabitants of northeastern Norway could travel visa free across the border to northwest Russia. The Arctic Council, created in 1996 to ensure cooperation on a range of issues in the Arctic, rose in stature and Norway managed to get the secretariat to Tromsø in 2011.

However, in 2014, the mood soured. First and foremost, the Russian annexation of Crimea contributed to changing the political climate in the North. Following, sanctions on Russia that targeted Arctic oil and gas development specifically were introduced by the European Union and the USA, which Norway also joined in on. Falling oil prices also led to the disappearance of many of the economic interests associated with the High North and to projects being placed on hold. Those who had expected (or

---

[4] The first policy documents concerning the "new" Arctic were written in 2003 and 2005 by the previous government.

hoped for) a Klondike in the North were disappointed, and the enthusiasm for the entire High North policy began to cool. It went from being a "priority" to a "responsibility."[5]

In late-2020 the government in Oslo, which has held office for almost eight years, released the third Arctic policy of Norway (the first came in 2005 and the second in 2011). In terms of foreign policy, this signalled a third phase of the Norwegian High North policy: a phase that has been characterised by great power rivalry and harsh rhetoric outside Norway's borders.[6] Of the various parts of the Arctic, challenges are the greatest in the European part—Norway's northern areas. Here, the military presence and provocative exercise activities have been increasing the most (Bruland & Bendixen, 2019; Norum, 2018). *Aftenposten*—Norway's largest printed newspaper—describes this development as a "power struggle on Norway's doorstep" (Moe, 2020). Although researchers have largely rejected the idea of a budding resource war in the North (Byers, 2017; Claes & Moe, 2018; Østhagen, 2015a), the view of and discourse about the Arctic has changed. More countries are now looking North and seem eager to use the Arctic as an arena for foreign policy influence and symbolic politics.

In the last decade, the Norwegian government has made use of the phrase "High North, low tension" to highlight that the Arctic, despite fantastical claims by some scholars and media outlets,[7] is a region characterised by amicable affairs. However, the question remains as to whether this is still an accurate portrayal of the current state of affairs and—crucially—Norway's Arctic approach. This chapter examines and reviews Norway's Arctic endeavours, not only limited to the official policy documents but also taking into consideration wider security concerns and interests.

The focus is on foreign policy dimensions, with an explicit emphasis on security policies. The chapter examines what defines Norway's Northern

---

[5] The Norwegian Ministry of Foreign Affairs changed its description in Norwegian from "satsning" to "ansvar."

[6] For example, in the autumn of 2019, the French Minister of Défense quoted a statement that referred to the Arctic as "the new Middle East": (French Ministry of Armed Forces, 2019).

[7] For an analysis, see Klimenko et al. (2019), Padrtova (2019), and Nilsson and Christensen (2019).

engagement and how that engagement has evolved since 2005. Furthermore, how priorities have shifted in terms of security policy in the North is examined. The discussion then turns to the challenges that Norway is currently facing in the domains of foreign and security policy in 2021 and that it may face in the future. These challenges are broadly categorised as relating to Russia's military posture—as is typical in Norwegian foreign and security policy outlooks—and the use of the Arctic as an arena for a China–US tug of war, which has emerged as an entirely new dimension of Arctic politics.

NORWAY AND THE HIGH NORTH (NORDOMRÅDENE)

The Norwegian definition of the Arctic includes everything north of the Arctic Circle (66°34 N). In Norway—a unitary state structure—this includes Nordland county, Troms and Finnmark county, the Svalbard archipelago and the island of Jan Mayen. The largest cities are Tromsø, Bodø and Harstad. The population of almost half a million in the Norwegian Arctic alone is relatively high compared to the North American Arctic, though it is sparsely populated by European standards. Of these, around 40,000 are Sami—the indigenous peoples of Norway that primarily resides in the two northern counties, albeit with some exceptions. The Sami have their own Parliament, located in Karasjok in Troms and Finnmark county, which has some political and administrative responsibilities.

In Norway, a distinction is generally made between the Arctic (referring essentially to the Arctic Ocean and the largely uninhabited territories of the High Arctic) and the High North (*nordområdene* in Norwegian). The High North is generally defined as the more hospitable and populated part of northern Norway and Svalbard as well as the adjacent maritime and land area in the European part of the Arctic (Fig. 1) (Skagestad, 2009; Støre, 2012).

Looking broadly at Norway's foreign and security approach to the Arctic, one-third of Norway's territory and 80 per cent of its maritime zones are found within the region; thus, the Arctic is clearly not isolated from larger national security and defence policies. Rather, the High North is central to Norway's security considerations, the primary concern being its shared land and sea border with Russia (Tamnes, 1997). Since the end of World War II, Norwegian security policy has concentrated on managing its relationship with its eastern neighbour. In what is generally

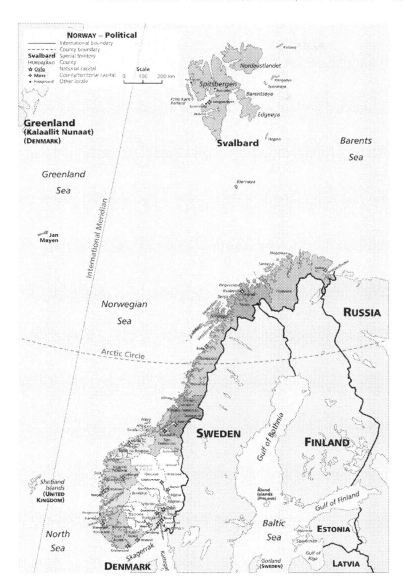

Fig. 1 Map of Norway, with the Arctic Circle highlighted

termed an asymmetric relationship, Norway has endeavoured to balance its military inferiority to Russia through its membership in NATO and a bilateral relationship with the US (Tamnes, 1997, 2011).

At the same time, Norway has been a strong supporter of multilateralism and cooperative solutions in its foreign policy (Neumann et al., 2008). This has created a situation in which, on the one hand, Norway has sought the active presence of and engagement with the US and its European allies, with the aim of deterring Russia. On the other hand, Norway has pursued multilateral cooperation with Russia through both international and regional organisations, including the UN, the Arctic Council and regional cooperation in the Barents area.

The Special Case of Svalbard

A special note on Svalbard is needed due to its rather unique status. In the early twentieth century, when promising discoveries of coal were being made and mines opened, specific steps were taken to establish an administration of this northern archipelago. Post-war negotiations resulted in a treaty that gave sovereignty over Svalbard (then called Spitsbergen) to Norway.[8] The treaty also aimed to secure the economic interests of nationals from other countries. This was done by including provisions on equal rights and non-discrimination in the most relevant economic activities; Norway could not treat other nationals less favourably than its own citizens, and taxes levied on Svalbard could be used solely for local purposes. Moreover, the islands could not be used for "warlike purposes."[9]

International economic interest in Svalbard plummeted before World War II, and soon only Norwegian and Soviet mining companies had activities there (Pedersen, 2017). Consecutive Norwegian governments in Oslo sought to maintain the Norwegian population on the islands, predominantly through subsidising coal mining and supporting the largest community, Longyearbyen.[10] Today, with the increased attention given to the Arctic region, the Svalbard archipelago has taken centre stage

---

[8] The Svalbard Treaty 1920.

[9] The Svalbard Treaty 1920, Art. 9.

[10] Named after the American John Longyear, whose Arctic Coal Company began coal mining there in 1906.

in regional relations. Although there is no dispute over the sovereignty of Svalbard, there is an ongoing disagreement over the status of the maritime zones around the archipelago (Østhagen, Jørgensen et al., 2020).

As coastal state rights expanded with the development of the Law of the Sea in the 1960s and 1970s, Norway—like most other states—declared an exclusive economic zone (EEZ) of 200 nm off its coast in 1976 (Norwegian Ministry of Trade Industry and Fisheries, 1976). According to the Norwegian government, Norway, as the coastal state of Svalbard, was entitled to establish an EEZ around the archipelago, as the non-discriminatory provision in the treaty referred only, and explicitly, to the islands themselves and their territorial waters (Pedersen & Henriksen, 2009; Ulfstein, 1995). Norway also considers the continental shelf to be under exclusive Norwegian jurisdiction. However, this view has been disputed by other states. To avoid further conflict, Norway established a Fisheries Protection Zone (FPZ) in 1977 (Norwegian Ministry of Trade Industry and Fisheries, 2014), which grants access to fisheries based on historic activity. Moreover, although there has been no oil or gas exploration in the area, the prospect of that activity, as well as the related dispute between Norway and the EU over rights to snow crab fisheries on the shelf (Østhagen & Raspotnik, 2018), has brought the status of the zones to the forefront of the Svalbard debates.

An Arctic Policy Emerges: 2005–2013

The Arctic moved to the forefront of Norwegian policymaking through a series of studies and parliamentary reports from 2003 to 2005 that highlighted the development potential of the region (Brunstad et al., 2004; ECON, 2005; Norwegian Ministry of Foreign Affairs, 2005; Orheim et al., 2003). This interest was particularly spurred by economic pursuits in the Barents Sea from the petroleum sector, as fields further south in the North Sea were depleting. The first Arctic policy document—*Opportunities and challenges in the North*—was released in 2005 by the conservative coalition government (Norwegian Ministry of Foreign Affairs, 2005). The "red-green" coalition government led by Jens Stoltenberg[11] took office a few months later and further emphasised Arctic affairs. Foreign

---

[11] Consisting of the Labour party (red), the Socialist Left party (red/green) and the Centre party (agrarian green).

Minister Jonas Gahr Støre in particular led the government's High North drive (Jensen & Hønneland, 2011).

During the Stoltenberg government, the elevation of the High North was part of the Norwegian Foreign Ministry's deliberate focus on circumpolar cooperation, which was designed to counterbalance the bellicose statements concerning the conflict potential in the North (Grindheim, 2009; Jensen & Hønneland, 2011). In both foreign and domestic media, Foreign Minister Støre and Prime Minister Stoltenberg frequently stressed the region's uniqueness as an area for cooperation (Moe et al., 2011; Støre, 2011, 2012). Notably, when the Russian scientist and parliamentarian Artur Chilingarov planted a flag on the North Pole seabed in 2007 and helped draw worldwide attention to the region, Støre used the opportunity to emphasise multilateral cooperation (Grindheim, 2009, pp. 6–10).

This culminated in a meeting between top-level political representatives of the five Arctic coastal states in Ilulissat, Greenland in 2008, where they publicly declared the Arctic to be a "region of cooperation" while also affirming the centrality of the Law of the Sea-regime more generally in the north (Arctic Council, 2008). The deterioration of relations between Russia and its Arctic neighbours since 2014 as a result of Russian actions in Eastern Ukraine and Ukraine's Crimean Peninsula did not change this.[12] Instead, the Norwegian Ministry of Foreign Affairs has continued to proactively emphasise the "peaceful" and "cooperative" nature of regional politics (Heininen et al., 2020; Wilson Rowe, 2020).

Moreover, Norway has actively pursued diplomatic and multilateral efforts to help ensure "low tension" in the High North (Stephen & Knecht, 2017). To this end, Norway has promoted the inclusion of other non-Arctic actors such as the EU and China in Arctic discussions (Offerdal, 2010), while also emphasising the primacy of Northern countries when dealing with Arctic issues. The emergence of the Arctic Council in the wake of the Cold War as the primary forum for regional affairs in the Arctic plays into this setting (Rottem, 2017), as Norway managed to get the secretariat permanently located in Tromsø (Graczyk & Rottem, 2020).

The renewed emphasis on the Arctic has also stressed the need to build a pragmatic bilateral relationship with Russia in order to manage

---

[12] See Byers (2017).

cross-border issues, ranging from migration and trade to fish stocks, and to improve people-to-people cooperation at the local and regional levels (Hønneland, 2012b). A highlight of this cooperative Arctic focus came in 2010, when Norway and Russia agreed to settle their boundary dispute in the Arctic (Norwegian Government, 2014b). After four decades of negotiation, both sides agreed to delineate a maritime boundary in the Barents Sea. Russia's Foreign Minister Lavrov and his Norwegian counterpart Støre subsequently co-authored an op-ed in the Canadian newspaper *Globe and Mail*, in which they asked Canada to take note: "if there is one lesson that the biting cold and the dark winters of the Arctic should teach us, it is that no one survives alone out there for long" (Lavrov & Støre, 2010).

This message could be considered equally applicable to Norway's efforts to keep its allies engaged in Northern affairs. Emphasis on cooperation with Russia has not diminished the overarching security concerns regarding its eastern neighbour. These concerns never entirely disappeared after the end of the Cold War but were seen as less pressing in the early to mid-2000s. Prior to 2005, and to a large degree from 2005 to 2007, traditional security aspects were almost absent from High North policy (Norwegian Foreign Ministry, 2009; Norwegian Ministry of Foreign Affairs, 2006). While cooperation continued to be highlighted in Norwegian foreign policy in general and the High North policy in particular, the years 2007 and 2008 witnessed a clear shift in Norwegian security and defence policy (and subsequently the High North policy to some extent). From 2007 to 2014, security was "enhanced" in High North policy in the sense that concerns about Russia were framed as "the changing security environment in the Arctic/High North" (Norwegian Government, 2017).

Thus, while continuing to emphasise the need for good neighbourly relations with Russia, the Stoltenberg government also made the decision to modernise the Norwegian military (e.g., Håkenstad & Bogen, 2015), which was clearly motivated by the potential for military challenge from Russia. Since 2008, securing NATO's and key allies' attention regarding Norwegian concerns in the North became the core effort of Norwegian security policy. Norwegian efforts to increase the relevance of Nordic Defence Cooperation (NORDEFCO) emerged around the same time, although these efforts have varied and at times floundered, as the Nordic countries have had diverging security approaches (Saxi, 2019). Russia was plainly the reason for Norwegian concerns, but Norwegian authorities rarely stated this explicitly, even in closed-door NATO settings (Østhagen et al., 2018). Only after the change of government in 2013 and the Ukraine crisis in 2014 did the Norwegian authorities start to refer openly to Russia as a potential threat to be deterred—a shift which in many ways was a return to normality in Norway–Russia relations (Rowe, 2015).

Arctic Shift: 2013–2014

After the new "blue-blue" (conservative) coalition government took over in 2013, a recalibration of Arctic expectations occurred.[13] The drop in the price of oil and natural gas, combined with the dramatic events in Ukraine in spring 2014, were key reasons for this shift. As NATO gradually returned to emphasising collective defence at home starting in 2014, Norwegian security and defence policy became more detached from its High North policy as it shifted towards more traditional Cold War issues and geography (Expert Commission, 2015). Instead of promoting NATO engagement in the Arctic, Norway placed new emphasis on maritime issues, particularly in the North Atlantic/Barents Sea (Søreide, 2016).

As a result, Norwegian High North policy—as a specific portfolio under the Norwegian Ministry of Foreign Affairs—became more concerned with soft security issues and regional development. Other engaged ministries, such as the Ministry of Local Government and Modernisation and the Ministry of Trade, Industry and Fisheries, have taken on a larger role in Norway's Arctic policy development. Norway's relationship to the Arctic at large, however, is inherently intertwined with its relationship with Russia and will be determined to a large extent by Russian actions and development (Norwegian Intelligence Service, 2016; Tamnes & Offerdal, 2014).

In November 2020, after seven years in office, the conservative coalition launched its first (and only the third in history) report to the Norwegian Parliament on Norway's High North policy. This document built on the previous mixing of regional and economic development priorities as well as rather general foreign policy aspirations. Even more explicitly stated than previous iterations, it focuses on how value creation

---

[13] The minority coalition consisted of the Conservative party (blue) and the Progress party (blue), which had the support of the Liberal party and the Christian Democratic Party in parliament.

and regional growth in the North is a target in itself, which would in turn support not only the local and national economy but also the foreign and security policy goals of Norway (Norwegian Ministries, 2020). The government also placed greater focus on some of the contentious issues that have arisen over the last three years concerning the role of China in the Arctic and the two-track relationship Norway has with Russia. These are addressed in more detail in the following section. Table 1 presents a summary of all the various Arctic policy and/or strategy documents released by the three different coalition governments since 2003.

Table 1 Arctic policy documents released since 2003

Year	Policy
2003	Mot Nord! Utfordringer og muligheter i Nordområdene [Towards North! Challenges and opportunities in the High North] (Norwegian Government, 2003)
2005	**Muligheter og utfordringer i Nord [Opportunities and challenges in the North] (Norwegian Government, 2005)**
2006	Barents 2020—Et virkemiddel for en fremtidsrettet nordområdepolitikk [Barents 2020—A tool for a forward-looking High North policy] (Norwegian Government, 2006a)
2006	Regjeringens nordområdestrategi [The Norwegian government's strategy for the High North] (Norwegian Government, 2006b)
2009	Nye byggesteiner i Nord [New building blocks in the North] (Norwegian Government, 2009)
2010	Nordområdesatsingen—Status Oktober 2010 [The High North initiative—Status October 2010] (Norwegian Government, 2010)
2011	**Nordområdene—Visjon og virkemidler [The High North—Visions and strategies] (Norwegian Government, 2011)**
2014	Nordkloden [Norway's Arctic policy] (Norwegian Government, 2014a)
2017	Nordområdestrategi—Mellom geopolitikk og samfunnsutvikling [Arctic Strategy] (Norwegian Government, 2017)
2020	**The Norwegian Government's Arctic Policy—People, opportunities and Norwegian interests in the Arctic (Norwegian Government, 2020)**

Notes Overview of the various policy and strategy documents released by the Norwegian Government between 2003 and 2021. Items in bold were reported to the Norwegian Parliament (Stortingsmelding)

Still High North, Low Tension?

Dancing with the Bear

In the confrontation between the two military blocs of the polar region during the Cold War, Norway was the only NATO country that shared a land border with the Soviet Union, which in turn defined Norway's Northern approach. From the mid-2000s onwards, the Arctic regained strategic importance. Echoing the dynamics of the Cold War, this occurred primarily because Russia under President Vladimir Putin began to strengthen its military (and nuclear) prowess in order to reassert Russia's position in world politics (Hilde, 2014, pp. 153–155). In addition to the changing political circumstances in the Arctic, the region's growing importance was also the result of Russia's naturally (i.e., geographically) dominant position in the North and its long history of a strong naval presence—the Northern Fleet—on the Kola Peninsula. This peninsula houses Russia's strategic submarines, which are essential to the county's status as a major global nuclear power (Sergunin & Konyshev, 2014, p. 75).

With Russia's re-establishment of its Northern Fleet primarily for strategic purposes (albeit with an eye towards regional development as well), Norway—with its defence posture defined by the situation in its northern areas to a large degree—faced a more challenging security environment. In general, western security analysts have interpreted Norway's northern areas to be covered by a so-called Russian "bastion concept"—a strategy developed during the Cold War in order to ensure access to and from the North Atlantic and to control access to the Northern Fleet's headquarters at Severomorsk (Kvam, 2018). Thus, military planning in Norway since the 1940s has been dominated by concerns over Russian military activity in the North—both as an extension of Russia's broader strategic plans and more recently in terms of other types of interference and destabilising measures vis-à-vis Norway's northernmost regions (Holtsmark, 2009; Rowe, 2015, 2018).

Since 2014, defence aspects have made relations increasingly tense, with bellicose rhetoric and increased military activity, including military exercises, on both sides (Friis, 2019; Norwegian Intelligence Service, 2020). The recent 2020-long-term plan for the Norwegian Armed Forces re-iterates Norwegian concerns over an increasingly tense great power rivalry in the High North, while adding plans to purchase new tanks, adding a new Army battalion in the north, acquiring new submarines and the phasing in of F-35 (replacing ageing F-16) aircrafts and P-8 (replacing ageing P-3) maritime surveillance aircrafts (Ministry of Defence of Norway, 2021).

One example of an Arctic-specific sensitive issue in Norway–Russia relations concerns the mentioned archipelago of Svalbard. The outlined FPZ arrangement satisfied several states that had voiced opposition to Norway's insistence on exclusive resource rights (Pedersen & Henriksen, 2009, p. 146), although the disagreement with Russia has continued to be a source of tension (Østhagen, 2018). The Russian position, expressed in diplomatic notes, has been that Norway had no right to unilaterally establish an FPZ and that fisheries in the waters around Svalbard should have been the subject of bilateral negotiations between Norway and Russia.[14] The argument is that the waters are international, and regulations—which can be set only by international fisheries organisations—can be enforced by the flag state alone, in this case Russia (Pedersen, 2009, p. 34).

With the strained Norway–Russia relations post-2014, further attention has been paid to the potential for conflict in the FPZ over fisheries (Østhagen, 2016). Both countries deem this to be a part of the Arctic that holds economic and strategic importance (Todorov, 2020). In February 2020, in connection with the centenary of the *Svalbard Treaty*, Russian Foreign Minister Lavrov sent a letter to his Norwegian counterpart listing Russia's complaints, including "the unlawfulness of Norway's fisheries protection zone" (Ministry of Foreign Affairs of the Russian Federation, 2020). Nevertheless, Norway and Russia, and earlier the Soviet Union, have a long history of cooperation in Arctic fisheries management. This has played a significant role in reducing tension in the Barents Sea and preventing small-scale incidents from escalating out of control (Hønneland, 2012a; Stokke, 2017).

Taming the Eagle

The Arctic does not play the same seminal role in security and defence considerations across all Arctic countries. For the Nordic countries and Russia, certain parts of the Arctic are central to their day-to-day security concerns. In North America, however, the Arctic's importance in

---

[14] Note from Russia to Norway, 18 August 1998, cited in Pedersen and Henriksen (2009, p. 146).

terms of national security has been lower, albeit increasing (Conley et al., 2020; Greaves & Lackenbauer, 2016). Security and—essentially—defence dynamics in the Arctic remain anchored at the sub-regional and bilateral level. Of these, the Barents Sea/European Arctic stands out. This has become apparent in the past decade as the number of military exercises in this part of the Arctic has increased, particularly with the engagement of the US.

For Norway, a close bilateral relationship with the US has been one of the pillars of Norwegian foreign and security policy in modern times. The US is seen as the ultimate guarantor of Norwegian sovereignty in balancing the security concerns regarding Russia (Rottem, 2007). However, Norway has always sought a balanced approach (albeit not neutral, as is the case with its neighbours Finland and Sweden) to US engagement in its northern domain, for example, by not allowing nuclear weapons to be stationed in its territory.[15] This approach has worked rather well, although concerns over too much US/NATO military activity were prevalent during the Cold War, with fears that Norway would get caught in between the two superpowers if conflict was to erupt (Hilde, 2019).

Although the same balancing act is still very much a cornerstone of Norway's security and defence posture in the North vis-à-vis Russia,[16] concerns over the US approach to Arctic or Northern European security have emerged as the Trump administration became more vocal about Arctic security issues from 2018 to 2019. On the one hand, Norway has long desired increased US and allied attention on the North (Hilde & Widerberg, 2010), starting with the Core Area Initiative launched by Norway through NATO in 2008 (Haraldstad, 2014; Søreide, 2014). On the other hand, 2019–2020 saw increasingly alarmist statements from US officials concerning the Arctic security environment,[17] and the US participated in multiple military exercises and "maritime security operations" in the Barents Sea (Nilsen, 2020; US Navy, 2020). As a result, some have argued that Norway risks getting too much of what it asked for in terms of US–Arctic engagement (Danilov, 2020a, 2020b). These concerns are

[15] See Skogrand and Tamnes (2001).

[16] In Norwegian, this policy is referred to as avskrekking og beroligelse (deterrence and reassurance). See Tamnes (1997).

[17] E.g., Office of the Under Secretary of Defense for Policy (2019) and Humpert (2020).

relevant not only to the discussion of traditional security and defence concerns in the High North/Barents Sea area but also in terms of the US' increasing obsession with China's Arctic interests.

Enter the Dragon

In the past decade, China has emerged as a new Arctic actor, proclaiming itself as a "near-Arctic state" (Kopra, 2013). The Arctic is just one arena where China's presence and interaction are components of an expansion of power in both soft and hard terms—be it through scientific research or investment in Russia's fossil fuel and mineral extraction industries across Arctic countries.[18] Beijing has used all the correct Arctic buzzwords about cooperation and restraint in tune with the preferences of the Arctic states, and it has emphasised interests in a "Polar Silk Route" and climate research (State Council of the People's Republic of China, 2018).

However, the US has explicitly rejected China's Arctic engagement. The US Secretary of State Richard Pompeo warned in 2019 that Beijing's Arctic activity risks creating a "new South China Sea" (The Guardian, 2019), which is related to how the Trump administration saw the Arctic as yet another arena of emerging systemic competition between the two countries (Tunsjø, 2018). Despite President Biden taking office in 2021, the Arctic is likely to continue to be relevant in the global power competition between China and the US.

Unlike its neighbourly relations with Russia, Norway's relationship with China is both more fragile and less immediately relevant. When the Nobel Committee—appointed by the Norwegian Parliament—awarded the Peace Price to human rights activist and Chinese dissident Liu Xiaobo in 2010, China punished Norway by limiting diplomatic contact and trade relations. Only in 2016 did relations between Norway and China normalise (Norwegian Government, 2016). Critics have since argued that Norway's kowtow to China to achieve resumption in relations went too far, especially as concerns over Chinese investments and intelligence gathering have increased post-2016 (Martinsen, 2020).

This feeds into fears across the Arctic concerned with the beginning of a more assertive Chinese presence where geo-economic actions[19] (i.e.,

---

[18] See Bennett (2017), Sun (2014), and Koivurova and Kopra (2020).

[19] See Lanteigne (2015) and Koivurova et al. (2020).

financial investments motivated by geopolitical goals) (Sparke, 1998) as part of a more ambitious political strategy aimed at challenging the hegemony of the "West" and also the balance of power in the north (Lanteigne, 2019; Willis & Depledge, 2014). North Norway is no exception, and debates in the country have emerged as regional and local actors grapple with China's more or less unfulfilled investment promises (Gåsemyr & Sverdrup-Thygeson, 2017; Lanteigne, 2019; Sverdrup-Thygeson & Mathy, 2020). Yet the exact details of *which* investments *where* are often not specified and the "China-fear" in the Arctic has for now been mostly rhetoric with few references to actual Chinese actions in the north.

Future Arctic Security Concerns for Norway

Starting with regional (intra-Arctic) dynamics, the central question for Norwegian decision-makers in Oslo is how northern relations can be insulated from events and relations elsewhere, while still standing "firm" vis-à-vis a resurgent Russian neighbour. Undoubtedly, the Arctic states—with Norway taking one of the leading roles—have managed to do a relatively good job at keeping relations civil in everything but military relations, despite setbacks due to the Russian annexation of Crimea in 2014. This political situation is underpinned by the Arctic states' shared economic interest in maintaining stable regional relations. Also, shifting global power balances and greater regional interest from Beijing need not lead to tension and conflict in the Arctic. On the contrary, they might spur efforts to find ways of including China in regional forums, alleviating the Arctic states' geo-economic concerns.

Moreover, we cannot discount the role of an Arctic community of experts, ranging from diplomats participating in forums such as the Arctic Council to academics and businesspersons who constitute the backbone of forums and networks that implicitly or explicitly promote Northern cooperation. Norway has been a proponent of this through venues such as the annual Arctic Frontier (in Tromsø) and High North Dialogue (in Bodø) conferences that have emerged in the past decade (Steinveg, 2017). Also noteworthy are new agreements and/or institutions that have been created to deal with specific issues in the Arctic as they arise, such as the 2018 "A5+5" (which includes China, Iceland, Japan, South Korea and the EU) agreement to prevent unregulated fishing in the Central Arctic Ocean as well as the Arctic Coast Guard Forum established in 2015 (Østhagen, 2015b; US Department of State, 2015). In these avenues of cooperation, Norway has been a rather proactive instigator and participant.

Other Arctic-related issues have been more difficult for Norway to manage. In the Norwegian Sea, a decade-long dispute between Iceland, the EU, the Faroe Islands and Norway over the distribution of the total allowable catch for mackerel has led to concerns over the stock being depleted (MSC, 2019). Climate change has led to shifts in the stock's distribution, and the ensuing disagreement over which principles should govern quota allocations has proven difficult to solve (Østhagen, Spijkers et al., 2020). In the FPZ around Svalbard, another dispute has emerged between the EU and Norway concerning whether or not the *Svalbard Treaty* applies to the shelf surrounding the archipelago (Østhagen & Raspotnik, 2018). The instigator of this dispute has been snow crab fisheries—a new and potentially highly profitable resource in the Norwegian Arctic (Hansen, 2015). These examples indicate that there are indeed issues in the Arctic that are cause for concern, although so far, they have been compartmentalised and kept from influencing pan-Arctic cooperation.

For Norwegian foreign and security policy in the North, however, the most pressing daily challenge is how to deal with and talk about Northern security concerns. The Arctic-wide debate on what mechanisms are best suited for further expanding security cooperation has been ongoing for a decade.[20] The Northern Chiefs of Defence Conference and the Arctic Security Forces Roundtable initiatives were established in 2011 and 2012 to address this issue, but they fell apart after 2014. The difficulties encountered while trying to establish an arena for security discussions indicate the high sensitivity to, and influence of, events and evolutions elsewhere (Depledge et al., 2019). Any Arctic security dialogue is fragile, and risks are being overshadowed by the increasingly tense NATO–Russia relationship in Europe at large.

Still, Norway maintains bilateral security dialogue with Russia through a direct channel between the Norwegian Armed Forces Headquarters outside of Bodø and the Northern Fleet at Severomorsk. Neighbours, after all, are forced to interact regardless of the positive or negative character of their relations. Nevertheless, bilateral relationships are impacted

---

[20] See Conley et al. (2012).

by regional relations (say, a new agreement signed under Arctic Council auspices), which can in turn have an impact on the same relations (deterioration in bilateral relations might, for example, make it more difficult to reach an agreement in the Arctic Council). In other words, bilateral relations, especially those as delicately balanced as Norway's relations with Russia, can easily become funnels for issues and dynamics at different levels of international politics.

Concluding Remarks

Norway has been one of the most Arctic-focused of all the circumpolar countries in the past two decades. This is partly due to Norway's geographic position—located at the relatively temperate nexus between the North Atlantic, the Barents Sea and the Arctic Ocean—and partly a result of its political handiwork starting in 2003–2005 to elevate the importance of the High North on both foreign and domestic policy agendas. Norway's Arctic policy endeavour has undergone several phases since its creation over 15 years ago. Excitement and euphoria[21] dominated the first phase, while security issues and economic disillusionment dominated the second. Now we are in the third phase, which has been dominated by geostrategic concerns and symbolic chest thumping by global actors.

Although the Norwegian High North (or Arctic if you will) policy is a unique hybrid mixture of regional and foreign policy tools, this article emphasises the broader security dimensions of Norway's Northern policy approach over the last decades. As Arctic "middle powers"[22] that are often free of broad international entanglements, countries like Norway, Canada and Denmark are likely to make use of their advantageous geographic positions to influence the near abroad. They are also concerned with upholding regional and global governance mechanisms (hereunder international law) that ensure stability and cooperation in the North and are eager to avoid the Arctic getting dragged into global rivalries or conflicts originating elsewhere.

[21] From Hønneland (2017).

[22] E.g. Crosby (1997).

In any case, it appears that Norway will continue to pursue an active role in the North, regardless of changes in government or further deterioration of Arctic regional relations. That prediction comes from the simple fact that almost 10% of Norway's population and much more of its economic and resource potential lie north of the Arctic Circle: the region is not a periphery the same way that Alaska or Greenland are vis-à-vis Washington DC or Copenhagen. The Arctic is integral to Norwegian economic and security concerns, which Norway's Arctic policy in recent decades has both contributed to and been a consequence of. Norway's entry into the UN Security Council (from 2021 until 2023) and its increased engagement with global ocean politics are also linked to its Arctic policy priorities (Østhagen, 2019).

The idiom "High North, low tension" still very much describes how Norway would *prefer* Arctic relations to be—especially vis-à-vis its Russian neighbour. Whether this description will continue to apply is up for debate. Military activity in the form of exercises and—at times—provocative manoeuvres in the Barents Sea is nothing new to that part of the world. What has changed is how that activity is being interpreted and how certain political leaders make symbolic statements about Arctic geopolitics. The worry, however, is that such hype might spur further increases in military activity and thus fuel the very race that leaders are fearful of. Due to its role as both a NATO member and Russia's neighbour, Norway in particular has a special responsibility to convey a cooler message while also continuing to encourage cooperative measures in the North, especially in the domain of security politics.

References

Aftenposten. (2010, September 15). *Grenselinjeavtalen Undertegnet*. https://www.aftenposten.no/verden/i/Vqojr/grenselinjeavtalen-undertegnet. Accessed 26 July 2021.

Arctic Council. (2008). *The Ilulissat declaration*. https://arcticportal.org/images/stories/pdf/Ilulissat-declaration.pdf. Accessed 26 July 2021.

Bennett, M. M. (2017). Arctic law and governance: The role of China and Finland (2017). *Jindal Global Law Review, 8*(1), 111–116. https://doi.org/10.1007/s41020-017-0038-y

Bruland, W., & Bendixen, A. (2019, March 29). *Amerikanske Bombefly i Øvelse Fire Steder Nær Russlands Grense* [American bombers in exercise four locations close to Russia's border]. NRK. https://www.nrk.no/tromsogfinnmark/amerikanske-bombefly-i-ovelse-fire-steder-naer-russlands-grense-1.14494969. Accessed 26 July 2021.

Brunstad, B., Magnus, E., Swanson, P., Hønneland, G., & Øverland, I. (2004). *Big oil playground, Russian bear preserve or European periphery?* Eburon Academic.

Byers, M. (2017). Crises and international cooperation: An Arctic case study. *International Relations, 31*(4), 375–402.

Claes, D. H., & Moe, A. (2018). Arctic offshore petroleum: Resources and political fundamentals. In S. V. Rottem, I. F. Soltvedt, & G. Hønneland (Eds.), *Arctic governance: Energy, living marine resources and shipping* (pp. 9–26f). I. B. Tauris.

Conley, H. A., Melino, M., Tsafos, N., & Williams, I. (2020). *America's Arctic moment: Great power competition in the Arctic to 2050.* Center for Strategic and International Studies (CSIS). https://csis-website-prod.s3.amazonaws.com/s3fs-public/publication/Conley_ArcticMoment_layout_WEBFINAL.pdf. Accessed 26 July 2021.

Conley, H. A., Toland, T., Kraut, J., & Østhagen, A. (2012). *A new security architecture for the Arctic: An American perspective* (Report). Center for Strategic & International Studies (CSIS).

Crosby, A. D. (1997). A middle-power military in alliance: Canada and NORAD. *Journal of Peace, 34*(1), 37–52.

Danilov, P. B. (2020a, May 27). Northern Norway may become piece in geopolitical game. *High North News.* https://www.highnorthnews.com/en/northern-norway-may-become-piece-geopolitical-game. Accessed 26 July 2021.

Danilov, P. B. (2020b, September 22). Researcher argues Norwegian participation in Barents Sea Military exercise was unfortunate. *High North News.* https://www.highnorthnews.com/en/researcher-argues-norwegian-participation-barents-sea-military-exercise-was-unfortunate. Accessed 26 July 2021.

Depledge, D., Boulègue, M., Foxall, A., & Tulupov, D. (2019). Why we need to talk about military activity in the Arctic: Towards an Arctic military code of conduct. In *Arctic Yearbook 2019.* https://arcticyearbook.com/arctic-yearbook/2019. Accessed 26 July 2021.

ECON. (2005). *2025 Ringer i Vannet.* http://www.aksjonsprogrammet.no/vedlegg/ECON_ringer06.pdf. Accessed 26 July 2021.

Expert Commission. (2015). *Unified effort.* https://www.regjeringen.no/globalassets/departementene/fd/dokumenter/rapporter-og-regelverk/unified-effort.pdf. Accessed 26 July 2021.

French Ministry of Armed Forces. (2019). *France and the new strategic challenges in the Arctic.* https://www.defense.gouv.fr/english/layout/set/print/content/download/565142/9742558/version/3/file/France+and+the+New+Strategic+Challenges+in+the+Arctic+-+DGRIS_2019.pdf. Accessed 26 July 2021.

Friis, K. (2019). Norway: NATO in the North? In N. Vanaga & T. Rostoks (Eds.), *Deterring Russia in Europe: Defence strategies for neighbouring states* (1st ed., pp. 128–145). Routledge.

Gåsemyr, H. J., & Sverdrup-Thygeson, B. (2017). Chinese investments in Norway: A typical case despite special circumstances. In J. Seaman, M. Huotari, & M. Otero-Iglesias (Eds.), *Chinese investment in Europe: A country-level approach* (pp. 101–109). IFRI.

Graczyk, P., & Rottem, S. V. (2020). The Arctic council: Soft actions, hard effects? In G. H. Gjørv, M. Lanteigne, & H. Sam-Aggrey (Eds.), *Routledge handbook of Arctic security* (pp. 221–234). Routledge.

Greaves, W., & Lackenbauer, W. P. (2016, March 23). Re-thinking sovereignty and security in the Arctic. *OpenCanada.* https://www.opencanada.org/fea tures/re-thinking-sovereignty-and-security-arctic/. Accessed 26 July 2021.

Grindheim, A. (2009). *The scramble for the Arctic? A discourse analysis of Norway and the EU's strategies towards the European Arctic.* Fridtjof Nansen Institute.

Håkenstad, M., & Bogen, O. (2015). *Balansegang: Forsvarets Omstilling Etter Den Kalde Krigen.* Dreyer.

Hansen, H. S. B. (2015). *Snow Crab (Chionoecetes Opilio) in the Barents Sea: Diet, biology and management.* The Arctic University of Norway.

Haraldstad, M. (2014). Embetsverkets Rolle i Utformingen Av Norsk Sikkerhet-spolitikk: Nærområdeinitiativet [The role of the bureaucracy in the shaping of Norway's security policy: The close area initiative]. *Internasjonal Politikk, 72*(4), 431–451.

Heininen, L., Everett, K., Padrtová, B., & Reissell, A. (2020). Arctic policies and strategies—Analysis, synthesis, and trends. http://pure.iiasa.ac.at/id/eprint/16175/1/ArticReport_WEB_new.pdf. Accessed 26 July 2021.

Hilde, P. S. (2014). Armed forces and security challenges in the Arctic. In R. Tamnes & K. Offerdal (Eds.), *Geopolitics and security in the Arctic: Regional dynamics in a global world* (pp. 147–165). Routledge.

Hilde, P. S. (2019). Forsvar Vår Dyd, Men Kom Oss Ikke for Nær. Norge Og Det Militære Samarbeidet i NATO [Defend our virtue, but do not get too close. Norway and the Military Cooperation in NATO]. *Internasjonal Politikk, 77*(1), 60–70. https://doi.org/10.23865/intpol.v77.1626

Hilde, P. S., & Widerberg, H. F. (2010). NATOs Nye Strategiske Konsept Og Norge [NATO's new strategic concept and Norway]. *Norsk Militært Tidsskrift, 4,* 10–20.

Holtsmark, S. G. (2009). Towards cooperation or confrontation? Security in the High North. *NATO Defence College, 45,* 1–12.

Hønneland, G. (2012a). *Making fishery agreements work: Post-agreement bargaining in the Barents Sea.* Edward Elgar.

Hønneland, G. (2012b). Norsk-Russisk Miljø- Og Ressursforvaltning i Nordom-rådene [Norwegian-Russian environmental and resource management in the

298 A. ØSTHAGEN

High North]. *Nordlit, 29.* http://septentrio.uit.no/index.php/nordlit/art icle/view/2303/2134. Accessed 26 July 2021.

Hønneland, G. (2017). *Arctic euphoria and international High North politics.* Palgrave Macmillan.

Humpert, M. (2020, May 25). U.S. warns of Russian Arctic military buildup: 'Who puts missiles on icebreakers?' *High North News.* https://www.highno rthnews.com/en/us-warns-russian-arctic-military-buildup-who-puts-missiles-icebreakers. Accessed 26 July 2021.

Jensen, L. C., & Hønneland, G. (2011). Framing the High North: Public discourses in Norway after 2000. *Acta Borealia, 28*(1), 37–54.

Klimenko, E., Nilsson, A., & Christensen, M. (2019). Narratives in the Russian media of conflict and cooperation in the Arctic. *SIPRI Insights on Peace and Security, 5,* 1–32.

Koivurova, T., & Kopra, S. (2020). *Chinese policy and presence in the Arctic.* Brill Nijhoff.

Koivurova, T., Kopra, S., Lanteigne, M., Nojonen, M., Smieszek, M., & Stepien, A. (2020). China's Arctic policy. In T. Koivurova & S. Kopra (Eds.), *Chinese policy and presence in the Arctic* (pp. 25–41). Brill Nijhoff.

Kopra, S. (2013). China's Arctic interests. *Arctic Yearbook, 2013,* 1–16. http://www.arcticyearbook.com/2013-articles/51-china-s-arctic-interests. Accessed 26 July 2021.

Kvam, I. H.-P. (2018). *'Strategic deterrence' in the North: Implications of Russian maritime defence planning and seapower to Norwegian maritime strategy.* University of Bergen. http://bora.uib.no/handle/1956/18770. Accessed 26 July 2021.

Lanteigne, M. (2015). The role of China in emerging Arctic security discourses. *S+F Security and Peace, 33*(3), 150–155.

Lanteigne, M. (2019, April 19). Snow fort or ice path? China's emerging strategies in the Arctic. *High North News.* https://www.highnorthnews.com/en/chinas-emerging-strategies-arctic. Accessed 26 July 2021.

Lavrov, S., & Støre, J. G. (2010, September 21). Canada, take note: Here's how to resolve maritime disputes. *The Globe and Mail.* http://www.theglo beandmail.com/opinion/canada-take-note-heres-how-to-resolve-maritime-dis putes/article4326372/. Accessed 26 July 2021.

Martinsen, K. D. (2020). Knefallet for Kina. *Nytt Norsk Tidsskrift, 37*(2), 179–189.

Medby, I. A. (2014). Arctic state, Arctic nation? Arctic national identity among the post-Cold War generation in Norway. *Polar Geography, 37*(3), 252–269. https://doi.org/10.1080/1088937X.2014.962643

Ministry of Defence of Norway. (2021). *Prop. 14 S. Evne til forsvar – vilje til beredskap. Langtidsplan for forsvarssektoren* [Ability to defend—Willingness to be prepared. Long-term plan for the defense sector]. https://www.regjer

ingen.no/contentassets/81506a8900cc4f16bf805b936e3bb041/no/pdfs/ prp202020210014000dddpdfs.pdf. Accessed 26 July 2021.

Ministry of Foreign Affairs of the Russian Federation. (2020). *Press release on Foreign Minister Sergey Lavrov's message to Norwegian Foreign Minister Ine Eriksen Soreide on the occasion of the 100th anniversary of the Spitsbergen Treaty.* https://www.mid.ru/en/web/guest/maps/no/-/asset_publis her/f4MKo6byouc4/content/id/4019093. Accessed 26 July 2021.

Moe, A., Fjærtoft, D., & Øverland, I. (2011). Space and timing: Why was the Barents Sea delimitation dispute resolved in 2010? *Polar Geography, 34*(3), 145–162.

Moe, I. (2020, February 22). *Arktis Smelter. Slik Bidrar Det Til Maktkamp På Norges Dørstokk* [Arctic melts. This is how it contributes to a power struggle on Norway's doorstep]. *Aftenposten.* https://www.aftenposten.no/verden/ i/awBvA5/arktis-smelter-slik-bidrar-det-til-maktkamp-paa-norges-doerstokk. Accessed 26 July 2021.

MSC. (2019). *MSC certificates suspended for all North East Atlantic Mackerel Fisheries.* Press Release. https://www.msc.org/media-centre/press-releases/ press-release/msc-certificates-suspended-for-all-north-east-atlantic-mackerel-fisheries. Accessed 26 July 2021.

Neumann, I. B., Carlsnaes, W., Skogan, J. K., Græger, N., Rieker, P., Haugevik, K. M., & Torjesen, S. (2008). *Norge Og Alliansene: Gamle Tradisjoner, Nytt Spillerom.* Norwegian Institute of International Affairs (NUPI).

Nilsen, T. (2020, June 4). B-52 on Arctic mission with Norwegian Fighter Jets. *The Barents Observer.* https://thebarentsobserver.com/en/security/2020/ 06/b-52-arctic-mission-norwegian-fighter-jets. Accessed 26 July 2021.

Nilsson, A. E., & Christensen, M. (2019). *Arctic geopolitics, media and power.* Routledge.

Norum, H. (2018, March 5). *Russland Simulerte Angrep På Vardø-Radar* [Russia Simulated Attack on Vardø-Radar]. NRK. https://www.nrk.no/ norge/_-russland-simulerte-angrep-pa-vardo-radar-1.13946450. Accessed 26 July 2021.

Norwegian Foreign Ministry. (2009). *Norway's High North strategy: Presence, activity and knowledge.* https://www.regjeringen.no/no/aktuelt/nor ways-high-north-strategy-presence-act/id544060/. Accessed 26 July 2021.

Norwegian Government. (2003). *Mot Nord! Utfordringer og muligheter i Nordområdene* [Towards North! Challenges and opportunities in the High North]. https://www.regjeringen.no/no/dokumenter/nou-2003-32/ id149022/. Accessed 26 July 2021.

Norwegian Government. (2005). *Muligheter og utfordringer i Nord* [Opportunities and challenges in the North]. https://www.regjeringen.no/no/dokume nter/stmeld-nr-30-2004-2005-/id407537/. Accessed 26 July 2021.

Norwegian Government. (2006a). *Barents 2020 – Et virkemiddel for en fremtidsrettet nordområdepolitikk* [Barents 2020—A tool for a forward-looking High North policy]. https://www.regjeringen.no/en/dokumenter/barents2020e/id514815/. Accessed 26 July 2021.

Norwegian Government. (2006b). *Regjeringens nordområdestrategi* [The Norwegian government's strategy for the High North]. https://www.regjeringen.no/en/dokumenter/strategy-for-the-high-north/id448697/. Accessed 26 July 2021.

Norwegian Government. (2009). *Nye byggesteiner i Nord* [New building blocks in the North]. https://www.regjeringen.no/en/dokumenter/north_blocks/id548803/. Accessed 26 July 2021.

Norwegian Government. (2010). *Nordområdesatsingen – Status Oktober 2010* [The High North initiative—Status October 2010]. https://www.regjeringen.no/no/dokumenter/nordomradesatsingen---status-oktober-201/id620374/. Accessed 26 July 2021.

Norwegian Government. (2011). *Nordområdene – Visjon og virkemidler* [The High North—Visions and strategies]. https://www.regjeringen.no/en/dokumenter/high_north_visions_strategies/id664906/.

Norwegian Government. (2014a). *Nordkloden* [Norway's Arctic policy]. https://www.regjeringen.no/en/dokumenter/nordkloden/id2076193/. Accessed 26 July 2021.

Norwegian Government. (2014b). *Delelinjeavtalen Med Russland* [Delimitation agreement with Russia]. https://www.regjeringen.no/no/tema/utenrikssaker/folkerett/delelinjeavtalen-med-russland/id2008645/. Accessed 26 July 2021.

Norwegian Government. (2016). *Statement on the government of the People's Republic of China and the Government of the Kingdom of Norway on normalization of bilateral relations.* https://www.regjeringen.no/globalassets/departementene/ud/vedlegg/statement_kina.pdf. Accessed 26 July 2021.

Norwegian Government. (2017). *Norway's Arctic strategy: Between geopolitics and social development.* https://www.regjeringen.no/contentassets/fad46f0404e14b2a9b551ca7359c1000/arctic-strategy.pdf. Accessed 26 July 2021.

Norwegian Government. (2020). *The Norwegian Government's Arctic Policy—People, opportunities and Norwegian interests in the Arctic.* https://www.regjeringen.no/en/dokumenter/arctic_policy/id2830120/. Accessed 26 July 2021.

Norwegian Intelligence Service. (2016). *Fokus 2016.* https://forsvaret.no/fakta_/ForsvaretDocuments/Fokus2016.pdf. Accessed 26 July 2021.

Norwegian Intelligence Service. (2020). *FOCUS 2020: The Norwegian Intelligence Service's assessment of current security challenges.* https://forsvaret.no/presse_/ForsvaretDocuments/Focus2020-web.pdf. Accessed 26 July 2021.

Norwegian Ministries. (2020). *The Norwegian Government's Arctic Policy: People, opportunities and Norwegian interests in the Arctic.* https://www.regjeringen. no/en/dokumenter/arctic_policy/id2830120/. Accessed 26 July 2021.

Norwegian Ministry of Foreign Affairs. (2005). *St.Meld. Nr. 30 (2004–2005): Muligheter Og Utfordringer i Nord.* https://www.regjeringen.no/conten tassets/30b734023f6649ee94a10b69d0586afa/no/pdfs/stm200420050030 000dddpdfs.pdf. Accessed 26 July 2021.

Norwegian Ministry of Foreign Affairs. (2006). *The Norwegian Government's High North strategy.* https://www.regjeringen.no/globalassets/upload/ud/ vedlegg/strategien.pdf. Accessed 26 July 2021.

Norwegian Ministry of Trade Industry and Fisheries. (1976). *Lov Om Norges Økonomiske Sone (Økonomiske Soneloven)* [Law on Norway's Economic Zone]. https://lovdata.no/dokument/NL/lov/1976-12-17-91. Accessed 26 July 2021.

Norwegian Ministry of Trade Industry and Fisheries. (2014). *Fiskevernsonen Ved Svalbard Og Fiskerisonen Ved Jan Mayen* [Fisheries protection zone around Svalbard and fisheries zone around Jan Mauen]. https://www.regjeringen. no/no/tema/mat-fiske-og-landbruk/fiskeri-og-havbruk/1/fiskeri/internasj onalt-fiskerisamarbeid/internasjonalt/fiskevernsonen-ved-svalbard-og-fisker iso/id445285/. Accessed 26 July 2021.

Offerdal, K. (2010). Arctic energy in EU policy: Arbitrary interest in the Norwegian High North. *Arctic, 63*(1), 30–42.

Office of the Under Secretary of Defense for Policy. (2019). *Report to Congress: Department of Defense Arctic Strategy.* https://media.defense.gov/2019/ Jun/06/2002141657/-1/-1/1/2019-DOD-ARCTIC-STRATEGY.PDF. Accessed 26 July 2021.

Orheim, O., Broch, I., Forsell, L., Kristoffersen, I., Stordal, V., Broderstad, E. G., Hansson, R., et al. (2003). *NOU 2003:32 Mot Nord! Utfordringer Og Muligheter i Nordområdene. Official Norwegian Report.* Vol. 32. Norwegian Ministry of Foreign Affaris. https://www.regjeringen.no/contentassets/ 28ed358f13704ed2bb3c2a7f13a02be9/no/pdfs/nou200320030032000ddd pdfs.pdf. Accessed 26 July 2021.

Østhagen, A. (2015a, May 27). *Arctic security: Hype, nuances and dilemmas.* The Arctic Institute. http://www.thearcticinstitute.org/2015a/05/052715- Arctic-Security-Hype-Nuances-Dilemmas-Russia.html. Accessed 26 July 2021.

Østhagen, A. (2015b, November 3). *The Arctic Coast Guard Forum: Big tasks, small solutions.* The Arctic Institute. http://www.thearcticinstit ute.org/2015b/11/the-arctic-coast-guard-forum-big-tasks.html. Accessed 26 July 2021.

Østhagen, A. (2016). High North, low politics maritime cooperation with Russia in the Arctic. *Arctic Review on Law and Politics, 7*(1), 83–100.

302   A. ØSTHAGEN

Østhagen, A. (2018). Managing conflict at Sea: The case of Norway and Russia in the Svalbard Zone. *Arctic Review on Law and Politics, 9*, 100–123.

Østhagen, A. (2019, September 19). Det Nye Havet [The New Ocean]. *Dagsavisen*. https://www.dagsavisen.no/debatt/det-nye-havet-1.1204572. Accessed 26 July 2021.

Østhagen, A., Jørgensen, A.-K., & Moe, A. (2020). The Svalbard fisheries protection zone: How Russia and Norway manage an Arctic dispute. *Арктика и Север* [Arctic and North], *40*, 183–205. https://doi.org/10.37482/issn2221-2698.2020.40.183

Østhagen, A., & Raspotnik, A. (2018). Crab! How a dispute over snow crab became a diplomatic headache between Norway and the EU. *Marine Policy, 98*, 58–64. https://doi.org/10.1016/j.marpol.2018.09.007

Østhagen, A., Sharp, G. L., & Hilde, P. S. (2018). At opposite poles: Canada's and Norway's approaches to security in the Arctic. *Polar Journal, 8*(1), 163–181.

Østhagen, A., Spijkers J., Totland, O. A. (2020). Collapse of cooperation? The North-Atlantic Mackerel dispute and lessons for international cooperation on transboundary fish stocks. *Maritime Studies, 19*(1), 155–165. https://doi.org/10.1007/s40152-020-00172-4

Padrtova, B. (2019). Frozen narratives: How media present security in the Arctic. *Polar Science, 21*(September), 37–46. https://doi.org/10.1016/j.polar.2019.05.006

Pedersen, T. (2009). Endringer i Internasjonal Svalbard Politikk [Changes in International Svalbard Policy]. *Internasjonal Politikk, 67*(1), 31–44.

Pedersen, T. (2017). The politics of presence: The Longyearbyen dilemma. *Arctic Review on Law and Politics, 8*, 95–108.

Pedersen, T., & Henriksen, T. (2009). Svalbard's maritime zones: The end of legal uncertainty? *The International Journal of Marine and Coastal Law, 24*(1), 141–161.

Rottem, S. V. (2007). The ambivalent ally: Norway in the new NATO. *Contemporary Security Policy, 28*(3), 619–637.

Rottem, S. V. (2017). The Arctic Council: Challenges and recommendations. In S. V. Rottem & I. F. Soltvedt (Eds.), *Arctic governance: Law and politics* (Vol. 1, pp. 231–251). I. B. Tauris.

Rowe, L. (2015). Fra Unntakstilstand Til En Ny Normal [From state of emergency to new normalcy]. In S. G. Holtsmark (Ed.), *Naboer i Frykt Og Forventning: Norge Og Russland 1917–2014 [Neighbors in fear and expectation: Norway and Russia 1917–2014]* (pp. 628–632). Pax Forlag.

Rowe, L. (2018). Fornuft Og Følelser: Norge Og Russland Etter Krim [Sense and sensibility: Norway and Russia after Crimea]. *Nordisk Østforum, 32*, 1–20.

Saxi, H. L. (2019). The rise, fall and resurgence of Nordic defence cooperation. *International Affairs, 95*(3), 659–680.

Sergunin, A., & Konyshev, V. (2014). Russia in search of Its Arctic strategy: Between hard and soft power? *Polar Journal, 4*(1), 69–87. https://doi.org/10.1080/2154896X.2014.913930

Skagestad, O. G. (2009). *Where is the 'High North'?—The High North—an elastic concept?* Norwegian Institute for Defence Studies (IFS). https://www.ogskag estad.net/HighNorthElasticConceptMay09.pdf. Accessed 26 July 2021.

Skogrand, K., & Tamnes, R. (2001). *Fryktens Likevekt. Atombomben, Norge Og Verden 1945–1970*. Tiden Norsk Forlag.

Søreide, I. E. (2014). *The security situation in Europe and the future of NATO—a Norwegian perspective*. YATA—NORSEC Conference. Speech/Statement—Norwegian Government. https://www.regjeringen.no/en/aktuelt/The-security-situation-in-Europe-and-the-future-of-NATO--a-Norwegian-perspe ctive/id757912/. Accessed 26 July 2021.

Søreide, I. E. (2016). *NATO and the North Atlantic: Revitalizing collective defense and the Maritime domain*. https://www.regjeringen.no/no/aktuelt/prism/id2508886/. Accessed 26 July 2021.

Sparke, M. (1998). From geopolitics to geoeconomics: Transnational state effects in the borderlands. *Geopolitics, 3*(2), 62–98.

State Council of the People's Republic of China (2018). *China's Arctic Policy*. http://english.gov.cn/archive/white_paper/2018/01/26/content_2 81476026660336.htm. Accessed 26 July 2021.

Steinveg, B. (2017). *The backdoor into Arctic governance?* UiT: The Arctic University of Norway. https://en.uit.no/nyheter/artikkel?p_document_id= 539701. Accessed 26 July 2021.

Stephen, K., & Knecht, S. (2017). *Governing Arctic change: Global perspectives*. Palgrave Macmillan.

Stokke, O. S. (2017). Geopolitics, governance, and Arctic fisheries politics. In E. Conde & S. S. Iglesias (Eds.), *Global challenges in the Arctic region: Sovereignty, environment and geopolitical balance* (pp. 170–195). Routledge.

Støre, J. G. (2011). Arctic state. *The Parliament Magazine*, April.

Støre, J. G. (2012). The High North and the Arctic: The Norwegian perspective. *The Arctic Herald, 2*(June), 8–15. https://www.regjeringen.no/no/aktuelt/nord_arktis/id685072/. Accessed 26 July 2021.

Sun, K. (2014). Beyond the Dragon and the Panda: Understanding China's engagement in the Arctic. *Asia Policy, 18*(1), 46–51. https://doi.org/10.1353/asp.2014.0023

Sverdrup-Thygeson, B., & Mathy, E. (2020). Norges Debatt Om Kinesiske Investeringer: Fra Velvillig Til Varsom [Norway's debate about Chinese investments: From willing to cautious]. *Internasjonal Politikk, 78*(1), 79–92.

Tamnes, R. (1997). *Oljealder 1965–1995: Norsk Utenrikspolitisk Historie*. Cappelen Damm.

Tamnes, R. (2011). Arctic security and Norway. In J. Kraska (Ed.), *Arctic security in an age of climate change* (pp. 47–64). Cambridge University Press.

Tamnes, R., & Offerdal, K. (2014). Conclusion. In R. Tamnes & K. Offerdal (Eds.), *Geopolitics and security in the Arctic: Regional dynamics in a global world* (pp. 166–177). Routledge.

The Guardian. (2019, May 6). US warns Beijing's Arctic activity risks creating 'New South China Sea.' *The Guardian.* https://www.theguardian.com/world/2019/may/06/pompeo-arctic-activity-new-south-china-sea. Accessed 26 July 2021.

The Svalbard Treaty. (1920). University of Oslo. https://www.jus.uio.no/english/services/library/treaties/01/1-11/svalbard-treaty.xml. Accessed 26 July 2021.

Todorov, A. (2020). Russia in maritime areas off Spitsbergen (Svalbard): Is it worth opening the Pandora's Box? *Marine Policy, 122*(December). https://doi.org/10.1016/j.marpol.2020.104264

Tunsjø, Ø. (2018). *The return of bipolarity in world politics: China, the United States, and geostructural realism.* Columbia University Press.

Ulfstein, G. (1995). *The Svalbard Treaty: From Terra Nullius to Norwegian Sovereignty.* Aschehoug.

US Department of State. (2015). *Arctic Nations sign declaration to prevent unregulated fishing in the central Arctic Ocean.* Press Releases: July 2015. https://www.state.gov/r/pa/prs/ps/2015/07/244969.htm. Accessed 26 July 2021.

US Navy. (2020). *U.S., U.K. ships operate in the Barents Sea.* News Articles. https://www.c6f.navy.mil/Press-Room/News/Article/2174342/us-uk-ships-operate-in-the-barents-sea/. Accessed 26 July 2021.

Willis, M., & Depledge, D. (2014, September 22). *How we learned to stop worrying about China's Arctic ambitions: Understanding China's admission to the Arctic Council, 2004–2013.* The Arctic Institute. https://www.thearcticinstitute.org/china-arctic-ambitions-arctic-council/. Accessed 26 July 2021.

Wilson Rowe, E. (2020). Analyzing frenemies: An Arctic repertoire of cooperation and rivalry. *Political Geography, 76.* https://doi.org/10.1016/j.polgeo.2019.102072

European Policies in the Arctic: National Strategies or a Common Vision?

Emilie Canova, Camille Escudé-Joffres, Andreas Raspotnik, and Florian Vidal

INTRODUCTION

Over the last decade, the European Union (EU) and its Member States have undertaken public policies in the Arctic region. However, the results appear uneven, with national strategies superimposed on that of the EU.

E. Canova
Scott Polar Research Institute, University of Cambridge, Cambridge, UK
e-mail: ejpc3@cam.ac.uk

C. Escudé-Joffres
Center for International Studies (CERI), Sciences Po Paris, Paris, France
e-mail: camille.escude@sciencespo.fr

A. Raspotnik
Fridtjof Nansen Institute, Oslo, Norway
e-mail: araspotnik@fni.no

F. Vidal (✉)
Paris Interdisciplinary Energy Research Institute (LIED), Paris Cité University, Paris, France
e-mail: florian.vidal@gmail.com

© The Author(s), under exclusive license to Springer Nature Singapore Pte Ltd. 2022
A. Likhacheva (ed.), *Arctic Fever*,
https://doi.org/10.1007/978-981-16-9616-9_12

306   E. CANOVA ET AL.

For the regional partners, the legibility and credibility of European action remain a difficult challenge.

This chapter will provide a historical overview of the EU's policy in the Arctic and give some indications of the future of European diplomatic action in the area. It will then turn to more specific case studies from the EU Member States. First of all, since 2016, French policy in the Arctic has shown deep limits and some inconsistencies. Some diplomatic postures have negatively affected France's potential role in this area. In contrast, the Italian and Spanish examples demonstrate coherent and structured policies, with limited means and institutional cohesion. This chapter will conclude with an assessment of the EU's short and medium-term perspective in the Arctic and its synergy with EU Member States Arctic policies.

THE EU'S ARCTIC POLICY IN MIDSTREAM

Ever since 2008, the EU and its main institutional actors—the European Commission, the Council of the European Union, and the European Parliament—have slowly but steadily developed a dedicated EU Arctic policy. To date, the list of EU Arctic policy documents includes thirtheen policy statements (see Table 1) with the EU's current Arctic orientations being largely defined by the 2021 Joint Communication on *A*

Table 1   List of European Union policy documents relating to the Arctic

2008	EP Resolution on Arctic governanceCommission Communication on The European Union and the Arctic region
2009	Council Conclusions on Arctic issues
2011	EP Resolution on A sustainable EU policy for the High North
2012	Commission and HR Joint Communication on Developing a European Union Policy towards the Arctic Region: progress since 2008 and next steps
2014	EP Resolution on the EU strategy for the Arctic Council Conclusions on Developing a European Union Policy towards the Arctic Region
2016	Commission and HR Joint Communication on An integrated European Union policy for the Arctic Council Conclusions on the Arctic
2017	EP Resolution on An integrated EU policy for the Arctic
2019	Council Conclusion on the EU Arctic Policy
2021	EP Resolution on The Arctic: opportunities, concerns and security challenges Commission and HR Joint Communication on A stronger EU engagement for a peaceful, sustainable and prosperous Arctic

Stronger EU Engagement for a Peaceful, Sustainable and Prosperous Arctic (European Commission, 2016, 2021).

The EU's renewed, yet still rather fractional, interest in the Arctic region does not come as a surprise given the Union's Arctic (policy) history, its regulatory regional influence, its economic and ecological footprint, and the increased global awareness on all Arctic matters—from climate change to international security (Raspotnik & Østhagen, 2021; Raspotnik & Stepień, 2020).

Yet, drafting a coherent and integrated Arctic policy has been a (institutional) challenge for the European Union (Raspotnik & Stepień, 2020). As such, the EU's Arctic policy is a composite one with a dual nature; always combining both domestic and foreign policies, not limited to a specific issue area but a cross-section of diverse departmental scopes (such as maritime affairs, climate change, energy, research or transportation) falling under the same geographic umbrella: the Arctic. Thus, for the EU the region is always—and simultaneously—internal and external, cross-border and regional, circumpolar and global. Moreover, the EU's Arctic policy is targeted at different audiences. These include EU citizens living in both Arctic and non-Arctic Member States, critical experts from the associated European Economic Area (EEA) states (Iceland and Norway) and Overseas Countries and Territories (Greenland), the general public from both well-disposed and more critical Arctic Ocean coastal states (Canada, the United States and Russia) as well as the entire Arctic-interested world beyond (Dolata, 2020; Raspotnik, 2021).

Today, the EU's Arcticness is defined by a "multifaceted and complex" presence and role in the Arctic which also explains the complexity of EU Arctic policy(-making) and its regulatory regional impact (Koivurova et al., 2021). Generally, many EU regulations and policies affect the Arctic—directly or indirectly. Being a sui generis political entity, the EU has a sophisticated institutional architecture and system of competences to guarantee a balance between Member States, the interests of its citizens and EU-ropean institutions, as determined by the Treaties. The role of the EU in the Arctic is thus constrained by the three types of competence in relation to the Member States: exclusive, shared, and complementary. As such, the EU has exclusive competence for the conservation of living marine resources under the Common Fisheries Policy (Art 3 TFEU) and thus negotiated the international agreement to prevent unregulated High Seas fisheries in the Central Arctic Ocean (CAO). Moreover, since only a small part of the Arctic regions—those of northern Finland and

Sweden—falls under the Union's jurisdiction, it is also through its foreign policy that the EU acts in the Arctic. Foreign policy, however, remains an intergovernmental area where Member States have to find a common position before acting. Therefore, the Member States have to agree on and approve the Union's Arctic policy, which contains external relations content, such as multilateral cooperation, or security issues, while various Member States are also working on their own Arctic policies (see the sections below on France; Italy, and Spain).

Thus, the EU, understood as a major global market, economy, and population, influences the Arctic environment and economy via pollution reaching the Arctic from Europe as well as owing to the EU's demand for Arctic resources. The EU can also influence the development of international norms that are of relevance for the Arctic. For instance, EU competences as regards maritime transport have made the Union an important stakeholder in international negotiations on Arctic maritime navigation, leading for example to the adoption of mandatory Polar Code standards within the framework of the International Maritime Organization (IMO). The European Commission is also one of the key players in international negotiations on the protection of biodiversity in the areas beyond national jurisdiction. This process can be of high importance for the future governance of the CAO. Other international regimes that should be mentioned are climate change related ones as well as instruments dedicated to long-range pollution, such as the Minamata Convention on Mercury and the Stockholm Convention on Persistent Organic Pollutants (POPs), where the EU can influence the placing of new POPs on the list of substances to be eliminated or restricted. Third, the EU may have a certain impact on entities operating in the Arctic. For instance, the EU can set rules for maritime traffic via its Member States' port state and flag state authorities—which rules are applicable to all vessels traveling via the Arctic and calling at European ports. Additionally, the EU can influence the European Arctic through its various funding schemes. EU structural programs are important for Finnish and Swedish regions. EU-supported cross-border cooperation programs such as the Northern Periphery and Arctic Programme operate across the region, including Greenland. Cooperation with Russia is facilitated by cross-border programs, especially the Kolarctic Programme and via four Northern Dimension partnerships (Raspotnik & Stepień, 2020, pp. 133–135).

The complex institutional structure of the EU and the multiple sectors relevant to Arctic policymaking make it difficult to align a cohesive and clear policy discourse and legal competences for straightforward actorness, which has also weakened the Union's credibility in the region.

Looking Back: A Retrospective Assessment of the EU Arctic Policy

Despite the EU's strong regulatory impact as well as its rather substantial Arctic policy history and its eleven documents since 2008, the EU has not yet developed a convincing regional narrative (Stepień & Raspotnik, 2019) on why and how the Union should be involved in Arctic matters; a narrative that goes beyond the usual suspects of climate change or bilateral crises that need EU-ropean management; a narrative that convinces both Arctic actors as well as reluctant or non-Arctic-interested Member States of the relevance of the EU's involvement in the area (Raspotnik, 2018).

The EU's Arctic story started in 2007–2008 with several events—the 2007 international polar year, the lowest summer sea-ice extent at that time, the now infamous Russian flag-planting at the seabed of the North pole or a US Geological survey on the potential of hydrocarbon in the Arctic—all revealing the importance of the region for the EU (Powell, 2011). Since, the EU has been engaged in the Arctic for environmental (protection of the fragile environment), climatic (fight against climate change and global warming), geopolitical (keeping the Arctic a low-tension area) and strategic reasons: hydrocarbon resources, new maritime routes and economic development. In an Arctic policy nutshell, the four (Joint) Communications of 2008, 2012, 2016 and 2021 put science, research, and innovation at the heart of EU action through three strategic priorities: combating the effects of climate change, fostering the sustainable development, particularly of the European Arctic, and enhancing international cooperation (*The European Union and the Arctic Region*, 2008; *Developing a European Union Policy Towards the Arctic Region: Progress Since 2008 and Next Steps*, 2012; *An Integrated European Union Policy for the Arctic*, 2016). However, the EU's engagement in the Arctic has not, yet, been perceived completely amicably by some Arctic actors who have rather considered the EU as an external actor trying to interfere in Arctic affairs and even impose its views on them. The 2008 proposition of the European Parliament to create an Arctic Treaty similar to the Antarctic Treaty (European Parliament, 2008), or ban on the trade of seal products have strained EU–Arctic relations and undermined the Union's overall credibility (Sellheim, 2016).

Also internally, the EU's regional commitment has fluctuated over the last decade as more pressing issues have arisen on the Union's agenda—from financial and migration crises to the United Kingdom leaving the European Union. Although more focused than its 2012 predecessor, the 2016 Joint Communication basically remained an overarching umbrella, bringing together a broad spectrum of Arctic relevant issues. As such, the policy does not include any specific targets but rather/only aimed to influence via focusing EU action, pinpointing activities that need to be continued, and highlighting aspects of EU policymaking that have relevance for the Arctic (Koivurova et al., 2021, pp. 42–43). Largely, the Arctic is only of peripheral concern for EU policymakers. This leaves the Arctic as a niche policy domain, dominated by special interests ranging from environmental protection to fisheries, from Indigenous Peoples' rights to regional development in Northern Fennoscandia (Raspotnik & Stepień, 2020).

Since 2018, EU's engagement in the Arctic has become slightly more visible with the following efforts to establish a clear(er) position in the region. In addition to negotiating and ratifying the CAO agreement, the European Commission organized the first EU Arctic Forum in Umeå (Northern Sweden) in October 2019 and co-funded (together with Germany) the 2nd Arctic Science Ministerial meeting in Berlin in October 2018. An important participation of high-ranked EU officials to the Arctic Frontiers Conference in February 2021 was also noticeable with the participation of HR/VP Borrell, Commissioner Sinkevicius, the EU's Arctic Ambassador Michael Mann and his predecessor Marie-Anne Coninxs. From April 2020 to May 2021, Ambassador Mann participated in more than 60 events/interviews related to the Arctic (according to his Twitter account).[1] The authors of the report *Overview of EU actions in the Arctic and their impacts* commissioned by the European Commission (Koivurova et al., 2021) observed that by being ready and willing to assess and publicize its impact on the Arctic the EU distinguishes itself among external actors active in the Arctic and thus promotes a responsible EU Arctic policy.

[1] https://twitter.com/MichaelMannEU.

Looking Forward: What Could Be Expected from the EU in the Near Future?

However, updating the policy in this context is not an easy task as there are many issues at stake for the EU to succeed in affirming its position as a coherent, constructive, and major geopolitical actor in the Arctic. There are hints that could lead to think that the policy update will not be a breakthrough but rather a continuation of its 2016 predecessor. Indeed, the public consultations had similar priorities as the previous framework (European Commission DG MARE & European External Action Service, 2021). But also faced with difficulties of being recognized as a legitimate actor in the Arctic as a unitary institution, the EU has recently been developing a more assertive stance based on geographical legitimacy and variegated connections (Canova et al., 2021).

As the EU is preparing a new Arctic policy it faces a paradoxical situation: it claims to be *in* the Arctic while also being considered as an *external* actor that is often viewed with suspicion by other Arctic actors for its efforts to interfere in Arctic affairs (Østhagen, 2013; Raspotnik, 2018). The EU's position—both inside and outside the Arctic region–thus raises crucial questions about how we understand the EU and its institutions as (a) geopolitical actor(s) and how it questions the current Arctic governance framework. Currently the Arctic Council only allows for two statuses—full member or Observer depending on the classification as "Arctic" or "non-Arctic"—, which makes it paradoxically easier for EU Member States to have a clear position on Arctic governance. Arguing that the EU is "in the Arctic" questions the current governance structure of the region.

The EU and the Arctic are linked through the European political structure and Arctic governance, in particular around the European Arctic (see Fig. 1). The Arctic Council has eight member states: the five coastal states—Canada, Denmark (Greenland), Norway, Russia, and the United States—and Iceland, Finland, and Sweden. Thus, from a state perspective, five of the eight Arctic states are linked to the European Union, either as Member States (Denmark, Finland and Sweden) or as members of the EEA and Schengen Area (Iceland, Norway). The Arctic Council welcomes non-Arctic states as observers. Thirteen non-Arctic states have been granted observer status at the Arctic Council, including eight European states, six of which are EU Member States. These states have all produced a document detailing their policy or strategy for the Arctic

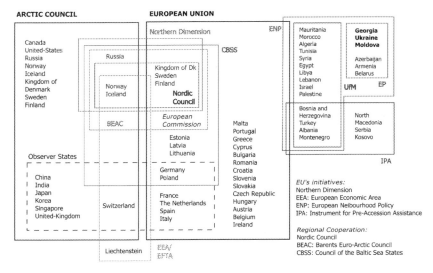

Fig. 1 Institutional intricateness between the EU and the Arctic (Canova, 2020)

region, indicating their geographical, scientific or geopolitical interest in the Arctic, but not necessarily linking their action in the Arctic to the actions of the EU.

Regarding the complexity of current Arctic realities in order to justify its Arctic engagement—both internally and externally—such simplification may not be enough. As of 2021, the EU has still not formally obtained Observer status at the Arctic Council and remains an ad hoc observer,[2] while six EU Member States have already obtained such status. Thus, in order for the EU to assert an Arctic policy that looks coherent and credible for both Member States and Arctic actors, it seems necessary for the EU to not only improve its institutional coherence, but also to articulate in a coherent manner the objectives of its Arctic policy with its legal competence (Koivurova et al., 2012), its capacity to act and the geographical location of its policy elements. The EU's interest would be

---

[2] First by Canada in reaction to the EU's ban on the trade of seal products, and later by Russia as a presumed response to the sanction's regime as part of the Ukraine crisis of 2014 (Raspotnik, 2018, pp. 91–92).

to articulate these different scales and to "show that at each scale there is a 'plus', an added value" (Foucher, 2018), compared to the sole action of Member States (Canova, 2020), who can thus also preserve their own (potentially different) justification of their engagement in the region.

The example of the EU's role in the CAO negotiations illustrates that when this articulation takes place, the EU is more easily perceived as a legitimate actor. However, this also requires the will from its Member States to acknowledge the Union's potential added value to their national policies and to accept more EU-ropean coordination when drafting their own Arctic statements. The example of France, as highlighted below, shows that it might be difficult when the country is proudly claiming its "polar" identity as sufficient to justify their engagement in the Arctic.

One key problem of creating an integrated EU policy for the Arctic is the different interests (if there even exists a particular Arctic interest) of the Member States. An effective EU Arctic approach requires that Member States collectively understand joint interests and regional sensitivities. Denmark, Finland, and Sweden share a particular position as Nordic EU-members at the Arctic Council. Advancing EU interests in the Arctic requires that all engaged Member States share a mutual understanding of the policy on the one hand, and of the means to implementing it, on the other. The examples of France, Spain, and Italy are investigated below as these countries developed sophisticated national strategies for the Arctic region over the past decade with yet uneven results. It shows the complexity as well of linking national interests with those of the European Union.

FRANCE'S INFLUENCE AND POLICY IN THE ARCTIC: THE SEARCH FOR A RENEWAL OF AMBITION

Among the most active EU Member States in the Arctic region, France is undoubtedly the most significant in its commitment. In a 2016 article, the French scientist Sebastien Gadal wrote that "Despite a long tradition of research in the Arctic region, French policy in the Arctic in appearance seems to be running backward" (Gadal, 2016). In the same year, the French Ministry of Foreign Affairs (MFA) released the French Arctic Roadmap ("Feuille de route"). In this landmark document, the MFA presented what it considers the "major challenges" of the Arctic in scientific cooperation, economy, security, environment, and governance. France asserted itself as a polar nation through scientific research, both in the Arctic and Antarctic. Besides recognizing that global warming offers new economic opportunities (the development of fishing, new maritime routes, etc.), France reaffirmed its high level of commitment to the region and its attachment to the challenges around environmental protection. The roadmap is a long (68 pages) descriptive and comprehensive document, beginning with research and scientific cooperation, economic opportunities, security, defense, and ending with "national interests and general interest in the Arctic". Each of the seven parts ends with recommendations.

Five years later, however, this ambitious plan never really materialized. We can identify a double problem: a lack of orientation at the beginning and a lack of follow-up afterward. The French Arctic Roadmap aimed to increase the French presence in the political, diplomatic, and scientific arenas of the Arctic. But it was never implemented because of its fuzzy approach, a lack of political will, and financial means. The gap between ambitions and actions is vast. For now, France's policy in the Arctic is spread out across a mosaic of institutions and actors. Even the definition of what we mean by "France" is complex, because of internal contradictions between the different Ministries' views.

At the time of writing, a new French polar strategy is also under preparation. Five years after the first statement of failure, we see a renewal of ambition for a new French Arctic policy. How is the French policy for the Arctic structured, what are its challenges, and what can we expect from this new Arctic statement?

France in the Arctic: A Stormy Road

French Arctic interest is justified by a long and permanent history of scientific activity and explorations in the polar regions, both Arctic and Antarctic: "The Arctic is also remote because of its difficult-to-access environment where extreme climatic conditions prevail; yet close because France has established itself over the past three centuries as a polar nation, with a strong tradition of expedition, exploration, and a permanent scientific presence at the poles" (Ministry for Europe and Foreign Affairs, 2016). Sustainable development and environmental protection are the second main drivers of the French policy in the Arctic. President François Hollande presented the Arctic Roadmap during the Arctic Circle Conference in November 2015 in Reykjavik as one of the bases of the 21st UN Climate Change Conference (COP 21) of December 2015 in Paris.

The economic interests related to oil, gas, and natural resource exploitation such as fisheries constitute the last aspect of the French policy. Even though there are few mentions of these in French policy reports on the Arctic, they are predominant in the background (Gadal, 2016).

Within the French MFA, the same diplomatic unit is managing both the Arctic and Antarctic. It is an important point that led to a lot of misunderstanding in the French Arctic policy, as, for example, the proposal for an Arctic Treaty. The idea that "France is a polar nation" is often hammered in official speeches and documents, such as the 2016 Roadmap. Indeed, France owns the subarctic territory of Saint Pierre et Miquelon, a remnant of the French empire off Newfoundland. Paris also has territorial claims in Antarctica. France avails itself of both a history and a geography that allows it to claim a greater influence in Arctic political decisions—without giving itself the means of its ambitions.

The Choice of High-Level Diplomacy: The Ambassador System

From 2009, France aims to engage an active diplomacy in the Arctic region. Since then, French policy in the Arctic is based on high-level diplomats and a fuzzy mosaic of science and policy actors. In 2007, the report of the French Senator Gaudin "French polar research on the eve of the international polar year" called for the establishment of an ambassador for the poles (Gaudin, 2007). France chose to use high-level diplomacy to define its Arctic Agenda: The President nominates well-known personalities to bring the Arctic issues to the highest level.

Appointed by former President Nicolas Sarkozy, Michel Rocard has been France's leading voice on Arctic foreign policy issues from 2009 up to his death in 2016. The official name of Michel Rocard's position was "Ambassador in charge of the International Negotiations for the Arctic and the Antarctic". This title gives a sense of how French policymakers seek to influence the governance structures: from a non-Arctic point of view but also as a potential user of the Arctic.

Ségolène Royal was the second Ambassador (2017–2020), nominated by President Emmanuel Macron. This nomination was perceived in France as a political move that gave the impression that polar issues in France were not considered such an important topic. After the departure of Ségolène Royal for political reasons (Méheut, 2020), the position was vacant for almost one year. It was urgent to appoint someone, only a few months away from the Antarctic Treaty Consultative Meetings (ATCM)

Table 2 Profiles of French Ambassadors for Polar Affairs (2009–2021)

Name	Mr. Michel Rocard	Mrs. Ségolène Royal	Mr. Olivier Poivre d'Arvor
Name of the position	Ambassador in charge of the International Negotiations for the Arctic and Antarctic	Ambassador in charge of the International Negotiations for the Arctic and Antarctic	Ambassador of the Poles and Maritime affairs
Dates of Office	March 2009–July 2016	September 2017–January 2020	November 2020–
Highest previous position	French Prime Minister (1988–1991)	Minister for the Environment, Energy, and Sea (2014–2017)	Ambassador in Tunisia (2016–2020) President of "France Culture", French Public Radio (2010–2015)

in Paris (June 2021). Emmanuel Macron nominated a more consensual personality, a diplomat, and a good connoisseur of the marine environment, Olivier Poivre d'Arvor. The name of the portfolio expanded to include maritime affairs, as a source of legitimacy for France which has the second largest Exclusive Economic Zone (EEZ) in the World (see Table 2).

The creation of ambassadors for Arctic issues highlights the growing interest of France in the Arctic region since the end of 2000. Indeed, France is the only non-Arctic state to have an Ambassador for the Polar regions. Besides this high-level diplomacy, French policy in this area is characterized by a mosaic of actors and institutions.

A Mosaic of Actors and Institutions: A Lack of Visibility, the Risk of Interference?

The French Polar Institute (Institut Paul Emile Victor, IPEV) structures polar research in France. It is a public consortium whose members are the MFA, the French National Center for Scientific Research (Centre national de la recherche scientifique, CNRS) or the National Center for Space Studies (Centre national d'études spatiales, CNES). The Ministry of Higher Education and Research is the main funding body of the French Polar Institute.

On the policy side, senators or deputies have a place in bridging the gap between scientists and politicians through public auditions. They are drawing political attention to Arctic issues. Senator Christian Gaudin (Gaudin, 2007, 2008) or André Gattolin have thus directed several voluminous reports on Arctic issues (Senate, 2013, 2014, 2017). It is the same for the National Assembly, where deputies have interviewed researchers to write a voluminous information report, warning about the lack of resources and calling for a stronger French voice in the Arctic (Foreign Affairs Committee from the National Assembly, 2021). Within the Ministry of the Armed Forces, the Directorate General of International Relations and Strategy contributes to the international policy coordinated by the MFA. Since 2016, it has been commissioning a consortium of researchers to take part in an "Arctic Observatory". The Canadian researcher Joël Plouffe considers this galaxy of scientists as a "knowledgeable Arctic elite" (Plouffe, 2012).

Outside of France, French research appears scattered and lacks visibility. For example, only one French university is taking part in UArctic (an international cooperative network based in the Circumpolar Arctic region, mainly consisting of universities), compared to ten in the United Kingdom: The University of Versailles Saint Quentin, with the CEARC research center (Cultures, Environment, Arctic, Representations, Climate). This lack of visibility in France and abroad is linked to the absence of a structure that brings together all the researchers, and to the lack of coordination between entities. For example, in 2019 the Ministry of the Armed Forces published a document including errors about the legal status of the Arctic (Directorate General of International Relations & Strategy, 2019) even though it is receiving analyses written by specialists within the "Arctic Observatory". In this document, the Ministry of Armed Forces signs a preface that contradicts the roadmap of the Ministry of Foreign Affairs (Canova et al., 2019). In this context, the overlap in ministerial discourse added confusion and provoked diplomatic outcry.

The Diplomacy of Arrogance? Navigating Between Lack of Means and Political Clumsiness

Indeed, it appears that the French policy and influence in the Arctic have two blocking points, which are quite paradoxical. First, France's influence has been undermined—and still is—by a determined, even arrogant posture. Secondly, France does not have the means of its declared determined ambitions.

First of all, France's influence in the Arctic has been undermined by what has been perceived as an arrogant posture. This arrogance goes together with a volunteerism posture in the Arctic since the nomination of Michel Rocard as Ambassador, in 2009. Joël Plouffe notes that Michel Rocard has embodied French Polar Policy (Plouffe, 2012).

Michel Rocard, former Prime Minister (1988–1991), was indeed known as the initiator of the Madrid Protocol (Protocol on Environmental Protection to the Antarctic Treaty, 1991) that led to the "sanctuarisation" of the Antarctic (Lasserre et al., 2021). The Madrid Protocol designates the Antarctic as a "natural reserve, devoted to peace and science" (Art. 2). Michel Rocard was dedicated to his work as Polar Ambassador, and he led the publication of the first French Arctic Roadmap. Nonetheless, Michel Rocard relied on his Antarctic "political success" to suggest to "improve" Arctic governance, confusing—or expressing confusion on (political) purpose—Arctic and Antarctic. Michel Rocard suggested making the Arctic a sanctuary on the model of the Antarctic, despite the clear differences between the two poles: "[My mission in the Arctic is about] establishing intergovernmental regulation to provide a protective international legal framework for the Arctic" (Denis, 2013).

This desire to strengthen the legal framework in the Arctic goes hand in hand with the criticism of the regional management within the Arctic Council, where France is an Observer (see Table 2). Michel Rocard criticized this "club diplomacy", considering that the Arctic is "managed like a syndicate of co-ownership" by the Arctic States (Denis, 2013). According to him, the Arctic States failed to integrate any binding regulations within its operating framework: the future of the Arctic is a matter for all its users, regardless of their territorial connections with the circumpolar space. Michel Rocard stood for the introduction of international management Arctic mode that would equalize the rights of the States of the Arctic Council with Observer countries.

Despite the legal regime existing in the Arctic, this idea of the Arctic as a "common good" has been used again in 2019 in the French Ministry of Armed Forces document (Directorate General of International Relations & Strategy, 2019). Florence Parly, the Minister of Armed Forces, wrote: "France wants to be a clear voice in the face of growing appetites: the Arctic does not belong to anyone". In law, the part of the Arctic that is not subject to the sovereignty of a state corresponds only to a marginal part of the central Arctic Ocean (Dodds, 2013). The rhetoric about the Arctic as a "global common" (Hardin, 1968), yet, serves political purposes for those who believe that the governance of Arctic space is "under pressure" and that riparian states should not be the only ones to have a voice in the region (Escudé-Joffres, 2020).

The document from the Ministry of Armed Forces is part of a series of diplomatic clumsiness that has tarnished France's reputation in the Arctic, making it appear like an arrogant power, unscrupulous toward international law. The chapter "The Arctic, an international challenge" of the French roadmap for the Arctic (Ministry for Europe and Foreign Affairs, 2016) is in line with this same offensive line, stating that "France calls for increased accountability of states outside the zone, potential users of the Arctic". Whether it is a vision of the Arctic as a common good to be protected or a questioning of the sovereignty of polar states, the message appears to be scrambled, depending on the year and the ministry (Canova et al., 2019). On top of that, the assumption that French policy is an assertion of sovereignty finds a limit: the 2016 Roadmap was merely a declaration of intentions with no concrete effects to follow.

Moreover, many researchers noted that France does not have the means to achieve its ambitions of polar research. "French polar research is at a turning point due to a lack of financial means" stated the Director of the French Polar Institute Jérôme Chappellaz (Valo, 2021). The Foreign Affairs Committee from the National Assembly also noted that the excellent rank of French research is a "miracle" given the lack of financial resources (Foreign Affairs Committee from the National Assembly, 2021).

2021: A New Ambassador and a New Start for a French Polar Policy?

After a year of vacancy, the appointment of a new French ambassador for the poles and maritime affairs in November 2020 provides renewed political impetus. Olivier Poivre d'Arvor has announced his intention to draft a new strategy, both for the Arctic and Antarctic, due to the synergy in research and polar history. This "polar" approach for the new strategy, which is intended to be published at the end of 2021 or beginning of 2022, is branded as new in France but has already been adopted by Spain for instance.

According to the information we have at the time of writing (summer 2021), it will no longer be a question of transposing to the North Pole what is done at the South Pole. The document is intended to be the opposite of the previous roadmap: a short strategy that will express ambition and a political vision of the French presence in the poles, in a spirit of European cooperation.

Three major orientations should appear. First, the fact that French legitimacy in the Poles rests above all on the researchers. Besides, France needs to structure and promote educational activities and the development of clusters in France. And finally, to highlight that France can contribute from an economic point of view in the field of services and infrastructures.

From National Polar Diplomacy to an Inclusive European Strategy: The Cases of Italy and Spain

While France relies on its new polar policy to revitalize its long-standing diplomatic action, some EU Member States demonstrate an increasing interest in the Arctic region since the beginning of the twenty-first century. The Arctic Council remains the best political platform to express this growing interest. Recently, the Czech Republic, Estonia, and Ireland officially applied to become observers. It can be seen as a continuation of a long-term trend set by Italy and Spain among others. Both are permanent observers; Italy joined the Arctic Council in 2013, while Spain accessed it in 2006. While Italy benefits from a relevant scientific background in the Arctic region, Spain intends to form reliable polar diplomacy. Although both countries use a thin line to maintain their national interests, they intend to shape their Arctic diplomacy in a European dimension.

Italy: A Long Experience and a Consistent Approach in the *Arctic*

When Italy obtained observer status in 2013, it marked the recognition of Italy's long tradition connected to this polar region. However, the same year, five other countries were also granted the status which somehow anonymized Italy's admission. In Rome, this accreditation is the best diplomatic conveyor to strengthen the country's long-standing scientific policy in the Arctic. Rome's participation as an observer consolidates national scientific and economic ambitions.

In their formal communication, Italian public authorities regularly remind the country's polar history with expeditions led by the Duke of Abruzzi in 1899 (Ministry of Foreign Affairs & International Cooperation, 2015; Robustelli, 2020). As a token marker, Italia led prominent scientific expeditions under the leadership of Umberto Nobile in 1926 and 1928 with the support of Mussolini's regime (Aas, 2005). In 1928, Nobile flew over the North Pole, which stands as the first scientific accomplishment for Italy's polar history—with Nobile, Italy discovered its "northern dimension" (Ministry of Foreign Affairs & International Cooperation, 2015). From this background, Italy has undertaken a shift in its science policy in the Arctic region in 1997 with the establishment of the research station *Dirigibile Italia* in Ny-Ålesund in Svalbard. This infrastructure is a strategic component to implement scientific activities in the area. That includes doing research on climatology and meteorology. The research station covers 170 square meters consisting of offices and laboratories, which gather seven persons on site. Since 2009, the research center has hosted three multidisciplinary missions: the Amundsen-Nobile *Climate Change Tower*, the aerosol and process laboratory at the Gruvebadet (GVB) interface, and a mooring of a research vessel in the inner part of Ny-Ålesund Fjord (Ministry of Foreign Affairs & International Cooperation, 2015). Under the supervision of the National Research Council (Consiglio Nazionale delle Ricerche, CNR), these Svalbard-based scientific programs prove the country's substantial activities in the region. Besides, Italy pursues polar research at sea through the polar research ship OGS Explora. This Italian ship sails both in the Arctic (off the coasts of Canada, Faroe Islands, Greenland, Iceland, and Norway) and the Antarctic areas and includes biological and oceanographic laboratories. All these measures give credit to the country's scientific activities in the area with other research communities.

Italy, however, has also relevant economic interests in the region, while global demand drives to run new oil and gas fields and mines. ENI, the Italian oil company, is the main stakeholder in the polar region, and is operating in Norway, Russia, and Alaska. The main ongoing project is the offshore exploitation of the Goliat platform in the Barents Sea, 100 km far from the Norwegian coasts. Launched in 2015, the Italian company manages the infrastructure but regularly deals with technical issues (Vidal,

2020). In the oil and gas sector, Italian companies are noteworthy active such as Saipem, which contracted a partnership with the French company Technip and the Russian NIPIgaspererabotka. This joint venture will participate in the Novatek project Arctic LNG 2 in the Yamal Peninsula (Saipem, 2019). Italian companies are, therefore, closely connected to Russia's energy projects in the region (Muro Pes, 2020; Parigi, 2020). This involvement extends to the renewable energy segment, particularly wind power infrastructures. The Italian group ENEL is building the largest wind power plant in the Murmansk Oblast. In that respect, the Kolskaya plant, which consists of 57 turbines, will generate about 750 GWh per year (Muro Pes, 2020).

To support Italian interests in the Arctic region, the government issued its first national strategy dedicated to this area. Under the supervision of the Ministry of Environment, the Ministry of Foreign Affairs, and the Ministry of Economic Development, the inter-ministerial coordination underlines the will and the necessity to efficiently articulate Italian priorities for the Arctic. Apart from the public authorities, the scientific community and private stakeholders also contribute to the design of Italian polar diplomacy. During a Parliamentary hearing held in 2017, the Chamber of Deputies welcomed a representative of the oil giant company ENI to outline their activities and highlight the growing interest in the Arctic region (Chambers of Deputies, 2018). On the one hand, the involvement of public institutions is fundamental in the definition of a long-term policy. On the other hand, scientific support aims to channel and evaluate the needs and relevance of Italian action. To this end, Italy is counting on its scientific research network to consolidate the national polar expertise. Among the scientific institutions, the CNR, the National Institute of Geophysics and Volcanology (INGV), and the Italian Institute of Oceanography and Applied Geophysics (OGS) are critical to operating scientific programs in the Arctic.

The Ministry of Foreign Affairs set up an Arctic Task Force (called "Tavolo Artico") to allow efficient governance on polar policy. This working body gathers 25 members from Ministries, research agencies, universities, and companies, while they meet on a regular basis. According to Robustelli (2020), the "Tavolo Artico" "represents an important moment of reflection and interaction among Italian stakeholders" (para.

7). The flexibility of the Italian approach to the Arctic allows it to undertake initiatives that should consolidate its scientific and economic interests while guaranteeing it access to international cooperation.

SPAIN: A SMART DIPLOMACY AND A QUEST FOR LEGITIMACY

Contrary to Italy, Spain did not benefit from the scientific background inherited from the last two centuries. Madrid's basis relating to its national Arctic policy relies on a thin line that dates to the early modern period. At the end of the sixteenth century, the Spanish captain Juan de Fuca tried to discover the Arctic Strait from the Pacific coast of America, but he failed (Almazova-Ilyana et al., 2020). This distant episode acts as the fanciful preamble to Spanish policy in the Arctic region. Spanish authorities embrace such a narrative emphasizing the significant contribution "to the early exploration of the polar regions, expanding the world's knowledge of their geography, botany, and navigation" (Ministry of Science & Innovation, 2016, p. 8). Such expeditions to the Arctic region remain the sole historical connection to Spain, at a time when the Empire had a hold on the Americas.

From the tenuous legitimacy in the Arctic, Spain has quietly built a substantial scientific reputation in polar science during the last three decades. However, before advancing Spain's scientific agenda in the Arctic, Spain managed in the first place to integrate polar diplomacy through the Antarctic. In 1988, Spain was granted the status of Consultative Party to the Antarctic Treaty. This incorporation was the first step of Spanish polar diplomacy, which led to a global political vision concerning the Earth's poles. Madrid used the scientific experience and knowledge gained in the South Pole to duplicate them in the Arctic.

In 2016, the Spanish government issued the country's first polar strategy, highlighting the scientific relevance to connect both polar regions. This document supports the overall vision of Spanish diplomacy in these parts of the world. From Spain's perspective, this national strategy is a statement of the impertinence of developing an independent strategy for the Arctic. Like the Antarctic, Spain's interests include a strong research focus consisting of scientific expeditions. Spanish scientists conduct a broad range of activities, including geological, biological, and atmospheric studies (Almazova-Ilyana et al., 2020). Spain, however, expressed its interest regarding three critical developments as Morera

Castro (2016) suggests: (1) oil and gas potential as well as critical raw materials; (2) the Northern Sea Route; and (3) fisheries. Fisheries are an important economic sector for this country. Indeed, Spain produces 1.2 million tons of fisheries per annum on average, more than any other EU country. In 1925, Madrid signed the Svalbard Treaty of 1920, which gives the right to the signatory countries to the exploitation of water and resources. Until today, the area of Svalbard is the unique spot in the polar region for the Spanish cod fleet. Indeed, to the fishing sector, Spain voices a clear interest in tourism and energy segments, but Madrid's leverage is not significant enough to influence local stakeholders for now.

Spain's major diplomatic success in the Arctic is to have been granted observer status in the Arctic Council since 2006. As Aguilera Aranda (2020) explains, Madrid accepted the rules, namely "to listen and learn" (para. 3). In support of Spain's growing activities in the Arctic region, the country participates in different forums available to echo their activity. Even if the Spanish government recognizes a low-profile attitude, a more visible and active policy aims to be developed. In order to ensure this, Spanish authorities underline that "the necessary measures must be taken to facilitate and promote the involvement of Spanish researchers in the Council's different working groups" (Ministry of Science & Innovation, 2016, p. 15).

Intending to structure Madrid's polar diplomacy, an "Arctic Constituency", an informal national task force, is supporting and sustaining the Arctic policy for the country. This working group is gathering experts and officials in charge of the follow-up of Arctic topics as well as interacting with Arctic stakeholders (Aguilera Aranda, 2020). As defined by the National Polar Strategy (Ministry of Science & Innovation, 2016), Madrid did not conceive a singular governance body for the Arctic policy. In a pragmatic way, their approach is globally addressed to both poles. Alongside this task force, the Spanish Polar Committee (Comité Polar Español, CPE) is responsible for formulating and coordinating the global polar strategy. This committee will be institutionalized in the near future, while the Ministry of Foreign Affairs and Ministry of Science and Innovation already sent their representatives (Ministry of Science & Innovation, 2020). The Spanish's global polar approach is pragmatically based on limited means with no permanent research base, for example.

In 2021, the Spanish government issued a policy paper on external actions until 2024, which highlights its commitment to the environmental protection of the Antarctic. It is worth noticing that the document does not mention the Arctic region, while science diplomacy stands as an instrument to foster Spain's "soft power". Instead of adopting a regional approach, the Ministry of Foreign Affairs and Ministry of Science and Innovation work together "to integrate the priorities of Spanish science policy into foreign policy objectives" (Ministry of Foreign Affairs, European Union & Cooperation, 2021, p. 85). At the operational level, the Spanish National Research Council (Consejo Superior de Investigaciones Científicas, CSIC) is leading the country's scientific activities, which are increasing with a positive trend in the Arctic. Among tangible results, we can mention Spanish activities within the Arctic Council. In 2020, Spain discussed with the AC about practical participation concerning the Arctic Migratory Birds Initiative (AMBI). The Conservation of Arctic Flora and Fauna (CAFF) established this initiative. Madrid offers "to host and provide financial support for the position of AMBI coordinator for the African-Eurasian Flyway" (Aguilera Aranda, 2020, para. 4). This example illustrates Madrid's ability to become a voice that matters in the bazaar of Arctic diplomacy.

Similar Drivers, Different Paths

Conde Pérez and Valerieva Yaneva (2016, p. 443) mention that "the international importance of the Arctic increases" while "many external actors are becoming interested in the region". Italy and Spain are among these external stakeholders as they demonstrate their respective ambitions and abilities to conduct a national Arctic policy. For both countries, the motives appear similar, while the means to accomplish their objectives differ. According to their respective national strategies, Italy and Spain are keen to get a role to play in the Arctic. The first concern in this area is connected to the ongoing environmental transformation. The effects of climate change in this region affect other regions of the world, including southern Europe. In light of these consequences, these countries recognize the necessity to implement reliable scientific research in the Arctic. This research overseas helps, in turn, to better understand the effects on their territory. This posture represents a catalyst for conducting their science diplomacy in the Arctic.

Although their relationship with the Arctic differs, the two countries converge these days in their political drive. Firstly, Italy "considers itself as 'conductor' of European interests in the region" (Lagutina, 2016, p. 138). Nonetheless, Norway and Russia are Italy's main partners, with common economic interests. Like other EU Member States, bilateral relations in the region induce the defense of the country's specific assets. On the other hand, Spain's Arctic strategy is in line with further European integration. Indeed, the European Union is seen as the most appropriate actor to influence the regional political process as its official polar strategy (2016) reminds us. All in all, Spain and Italy prove, on their own terms, a political and scientific coherence that makes their action in the Arctic viable in the long term.

Embraced in official statements and documents, the European dimension is the dominant vector in both countries' approaches in the area. After all, the political action of these countries, according to their public policy direction, is guided by EU principles.

Conclusion: From a Scattered Approach to the Implementation of a Coherent Block?

As discussed in this chapter, the EU is working to revive its diplomatic action in the Arctic region. For European policymakers and the EU's future Arctic policy, this means answering or, at least contemplating two open questions. First, what does the Arctic mean for a bloc of 27 Member States at the beginning of an era of global change? Second, what can the EU do to shape the future(s) of the Arctic in a European manner?

To achieve this, the European Union must overcome both internal and external challenges. On the internal side, the complexity of European governance hinders the development of an effective and coherent policy. On the external side, conflicts with certain states in the region— fisheries dispute around Svalbard with Norway, EU sanctions policy toward Russia—are limiting the policy options to influence regional decision-making.

In respect of its Member States, the national strategies relating to the Arctic show disparate results. After the failed 2016 Roadmap, France will introduce a broader national plan, including the Antarctic. In this way, it would come closer to the Spanish approach. From an operational and budgetary point of view, a global approach to the polar regions led by the EU Member States stands as the most appropriate diplomatic path diplomatic. Moreover, this yields a lasting solution to support effective diplomatic action.

As the Italian and Spanish cases reveal, these states continue being the public policy operators for political, scientific, and economic activities in the region. The implementation of these sparse policies questions about the ability of the European Union to align them with the Community's strategic objectives. Among these objectives, the necessity of finding a balance between the future-looking Green Deal and the current necessity of Arctic gas (and oil) for the Union's energy mix.

Under the aegis of EU Member States, scientific polar diplomacy must respond to the EU's global objectives. As operational actors, some EU Member States such as Italy and Spain unveil intentions in this direction. Looking forward, there is a wide range of resources of its Arctic policy so far underestimated on which the EU could focus, such as the EU's energy, space, and maritime policies. In turn, EU Member States like France and Germany can help shape these strategic guidelines into action. After all, it is a question of gaining the most effective response so that global European action can lead to a more coherent approach.

REFERENCES

Aas, S. (2005). New perspectives on the Italia tragedy and Umberto Nobile. *Polar Research, 24*(1–2), 5–15.

Aguilera Aranda, F. (2020, March 11). Interview with Arctic Council observer: Spain. *The Arctic Council.* https://arctic-council.org/en/news/interview-with-arctic-council-observer-spain/. Accessed 15 July 2021.

Almazova-Ilyana, A. B., Gabrielian, M. O., Kulik, S. V., & Yu Eidemiller, K. (2020). The "Arctic Vector" of Spanish foreign policy. *IOP Conference Series: Earth and Environmental Science, 539*(1), 012049. https://doi.org/10.1088/1755-1315/539/1/012049

Canova, E. (2020). Pour une prise en compte de la géographie dans la politique arctique de l'Union européenne [For a recognition of geography in the Arctic policy of the European Union]. *Etudes internationales, 51*(1), 89–116.

Canova, E., Escudé, C., Pic, P., Strouk, M., Verrier, N., & Vidal, F. (2019, November 5). L'Arctique, nouveau Moyen-Orient? 5 points pour déconstruire un mythe [The Arctic, a new Middle East? 5 takeways to deconstruct a myth]. *Le Grand Continent.* https://legrandcontinent.eu/fr/2019/11/05/arctique-moyen-orient-5-points-pour-deconstruire-un-mythe/. Accessed 10 Aug 2021.

Canova, E., Oreschnikoff, A., & Strouk, M. (2021, January 28). Exclusive interview with Michael Mann, EU's Ambassador at large for the Arctic/Special envoy for Arctic matters. *Le Grand Continent.* https://geopolitique.eu/en/2021/01/18/exclusive-interview-with-michael-mann-eus-ambassador-at-large-for-the-arctic-special-envoy-for-arctic-matters/. Accessed 10 Aug 2021.

Chambers of Deputies. (2018). La Strategia italiana per l'Artico [The Italian strategy for the Arctic]. *Chambers of Deputies*. https://www.camera.it/tem iap/documentazione/temi/pdf/1105156.pdf. Accessed 15 July 2021.

Communication of the Commission to the European Parliament and the Council—The European Union and the Arctic region. (2008). (testimony of European Commission). https://eur-lex.europa.eu/LexUriServ/LexUriServ. do?uri=COM:2008:0763:FIN:%20EN:PDF. Accessed 15 July 2021.

Conde Pérez, E., & Valerieva Yaneva, Z. (2016). The European Arctic policy in progress. *Polar Science, 10*(3), 441–449. https://doi.org/10.1016/j.polar. 2016.06.008

Denis, A. (2013, February 3). Michel Rocard: L'Arctique est géré comme un syndic de propriété [Michel Rocard: The Arctic is run like a property manager]. *Libération.* https://www.liberation.fr/futurs/2013/02/03/ michel-rocard-l-arctique-est-gere-comme-un-syndic-de-propriete_878996. Accessed 15 July 2021.

Directorate General of International Relations and Strategy. (2019). *La France et les nouveaux enjeux stratégiques en Arctique.* https://www.defense.gouv. fr/actualites/international/la-france-et-les-nouveaux-enjeux-strategiques-en-arctique. Accessed 15 July 2021.

Dolata, P. (2020). *A balanced Arctic policy for the EU* (p. 51) [In-depth analysis]. Policy Department for External Relations Directorate General for External Policies of the Union.

Dodds, K. (2013). The Ilulissat Declaration (2008): The Arctic States, «Law of the Sea,» and Arctic Ocean. *SAIS Review of International Affairs, 33*, 45–55. https://doi.org/10.1353/sais.2013.0018

Escudé-Joffres, C. (2020). *Coopération politique et intégration régionale en Arctique (1996–2019): Construction d'une région* [Theses, Institut d'Etudes Politiques de Paris]. https://hal.archives-ouvertes.fr/tel-02980869. Accessed 17 July 2021.

European Commission. (2012). *Developing a European Union Policy towards the Arctic Region: Progress since 2008 and next steps.* https://op.europa.eu/en/ publication-detail/-/publication/70245d63-201c-47e8-9091-d5c07b96d 964/language-en/format-PDF/source-112110791. Accessed 19 July 2021.

European Commission. (2016). *Joint Commission to the European: An integrated European Union policy for the Arctic* (testimony of European Commission & High Representative of the Union for Foreign Affairs and Security Policy). https://eur-lex.europa.eu/legal-content/EN/TXT/? uri=CELEX%3A52016JC0021. Accessed 19 July 2021.

European Commission. (2021). *A stronger EU engagement for a peaceful, sustainable and prosperous Arctic.* https://eur-lex.europa.eu/legal-content/ EN/TXT/PDF/?uri=CELEX:52021JC0027. Accessed 1 January 2022.

European Commission DG MARE & European External Action Service. (2021). *Summary of the results of the public consultation on the EU Arctic policy.* Publications Office. https://data.europa.eu/doi/10.2771/623044. Accessed 19 July 2021.

Foreign Affairs Committee from the National Assembly. (2021). *Rapport d'information déposé en conclusion des travaux d'une mission d'information sur la problématique des pôles: Arctique et Antarctique, présenté par MM. Éric Girardin et Meyer Habib* [Information report submitted at the end of the work of a fact-finding mission on the the poles issues: The Arctic and Antarctic, introduced by Mr Éric Girardin and Mr Meyer Habib] (N° 4082). https://www.assemblee-nationale.fr/dyn/15/rapports/cion_afetr/l15b4082_rapport-information. Accessed 15 July 2021.

Foucher, M. (2018). *Penser l'Union européenne à l'échelle mondiale, une conversation avec Michel Foucher.* https://legrandcontinent.eu/fr/2018/06/27/penser-lunion-europeenne-a-lechelle-mondiale/. Accessed 12 September 2020.

Gadal, S. (2016). Some fundamentals of the French policy in the Arctic. *Вестник СПбГУ, 2*, 110–117. https://doi.org/10.21638/11701/spbu06.2016.210. Accessed 19 July 2021.

Gaudin, C. (2007). *French polar research on the eve of the International Polar Year* (N° 230). https://www.senat.fr/opecst/english_report_polar_research/english_report_polar_research.html. Accessed 19 July 2021.

Gaudin, C. (2008). *Faut-il créer un observatoire de l'Arctique?* [Should an Arctic observatory be created?] https://www.senat.fr/rap/r07-503/r07-503.html. Accessed 19 July 2021.

Hardin, G. (1968). The tragedy of the commons. *Science, 162*(3859), 1243–1248. https://doi.org/10.1126/science.162.3859.1243

Koivurova, T., Hoel, A. H., Humpert, M., Kirchner, S., Raspotnik, A., Smieszek, M., & Stepień, A. (2021). *Overview of EU actions in the Arctic and their impacts.* https://eprd.pl/wp-content/uploads/2021/06/EU-Policy-Arctic-Impact-Overview-Final-Report.pdf. Accessed 19 July 2021.

Koivurova, T., Kokko, K., Duyck, S., Sellheim, N., & Stepień, A. (2012). The present and future competence of the European Union in the Arctic. *Polar Record, 48*(4), 361–371 (2012). https://doi.org/10.1017/S0032247411000295. Accessed 19 July 2021.

Lagutina, M. (2016). Strategy of the Italian Republic in the Arctic. *Arctic and North, 24*, 135–144. https://doi.org/10.17238/issn2221-2698.2016.24.155

Lasserre, F., Choquet, A., & Escudé-Joffres, C. (2021). *Géopolitique des pôles. Vers une appropriation des espaces polaires?* [Geopolitics of the poles: Towards an appropriation of polar areas?]. Le Cavalier Bleu.

Méheut, C. (2020, January 24). Macron Fires Ambassador who attacked his pension plan. *The New York Times*. https://www.nytimes.com/2020/01/24/world/europe/segolene-royal-macron.html. Accessed 19 July 2021.

Ministry for Europe and Foreign Affairs. (2016). *Le grand défi arctique — Feuille de route nationale sur l'Arctique* [The great Arctic challenge–National Arctic roadmap]. https://www.diplomatie.gouv.fr/fr/dossiers-pays/arctique/la-france-adopte-une-feuille-de-route-pour-l-arctique/. Accessed 19 July 2021.

Ministry of Foreign Affairs and International Cooperation. (2015). *Verso una Strategia italiana per l'Artico* [Towards an Italian strategy for the Arctic]. https://www.esteri.it/mae/resource/doc/2019/11/verso_una_strategia_italiana_per_lartico__linee_guida_nazionali.pdf. Accessed 15 July 2021.

Ministry of Foreign Affairs, European Union and Cooperation. (2021). *Estrategia de acción exterior 2021–2024* [External action strategy 2021–2024]. http://www.exteriores.gob.es/Portal/es/SalaDePrensa/ElMinisterioInforma/Documents/Proyecto%20Estrategia%20Accio%CC%81n%20Exterior%202021-2024.pdf. Accessed 16 July 2021.

Ministry of Science and Innovation. (2016). *Directrices para una estrategia polar española* [Guidelines for a Spanish polar strategy]. http://www.ciencia.gob.es/stfls/MICINN/Investigacion/FICHEROS/Comite_Polar_definitivo/Directrices_estrategia_polar_espanola.pdf. Accessed 15 July 2021.

Ministry of Science and Innovation. (2020). Real Decreto 852/2020, de 22 de septiembre, por el que se regula la composición y el funcionamiento del Comité Polar Español [Royal Decree 852/2020 of 22 September regulating the composition and operation of the Spanish Polar Committee]. *Boletín Official del Estado, 274*, 88746–88752.

Morera Castro, M. (2016, June 9). Los intereses de España en el Ártico [Spain's interests in the Arctic]. *Instituto Español de Estudios Estrategicos*. http://www.ieee.es/Galerias/fichero/docs_opinion/2016/DIEEEO58-2016_Espana_Artico_MariaMorera.pdf. Accessed 16 July 2021.

Muro Pes, A. (2020, November 10). Far but not so fast: Italy's role and interests in the Arctic. *The Arctic Institute*. https://www.thearcticinstitute.org/italy-role-interests-arctic/. Accessed 15 July 2021.

Østhagen, A. (2013). The European Union—An Arctic actor? *Journal of Military and Strategic Studies, 15*(2). https://jmss.org/article/view/58096. Accessed 19 July 2021.

Parigi, L. (2020, September 14). La strategia dell'Italia per l'Artico [Italy's strategy for the Arctic]. *Osservatorio Artico*. https://www.osservatorioartico.it/strategia-italia-artico/. Accessed 15 July 2021.

Plouffe, J. (2012). Thawing ice and French foreign policy: A preliminary assessment. In L. Heininen, H. Exner-Pirot, & J. Barnes (Eds.), *Arctic yearbook 2012.* https://arcticyearbook.com/arctic-yearbook/2012/2012-scholarly-papers/8-thawing-ice-and-french-foreign-policy-a-preliminary-assessment. Accessed 19 July 2021.

Powell, R. C. (2011). From the northern dimension to Arctic strategies? The European Union's envisioning of the high latitudes. In L. Bialasiewicz (Ed.), *Europe in the world: EU geopolitics and the making of European space* (pp. 105–126). Routledge.

Protocol on Environmental Protection to the Antarctic Treaty. (1991). *Secretariat of the Antarctic treaty.* https://www.ats.aq/e/protocol.html. Accessed 19 July 2021.

Raspotnik, A. (2018). *The European Union and the geopolitics of the Arctic.* Edward Elgar.

Raspotnik, A. (2021, March 16). The presence of the EU's Arctic future. *EURACTIV.* https://www.euractiv.com/section/arctic-agenda/opinion/the-presence-of-the-eus-arctic-future/. Accessed 19 July 2021.

Raspotnik, A., & Østhagen, A. (2021, March 10). *A global Arctic order under threat? An agenda for American leadership in the North.* Wilson Center: Polar Institute. https://www.wilsoncenter.org/blog-post/no-3-global-arctic-order-under-threat-agenda-american-leadership-north. Accessed 19 July 2021.

Raspotnik, J., & Stepień, A. (2020). The European Union and the Arctic: A decade into finding Its Arcticness. In J. Weber (Ed.), *Handbook on geopolitics and security in the Arctic: The high north between cooperation and confrontation* (pp. 131–146). Springer: Cham.

Robustelli, C. (2020, March 11). Interview with Arctic Council observer: Italy. *The Arctic Council.* https://arctic-council.org/en/news/interview-with-arctic-council-observer-italy/. Accessed 15 July 2021.

Saipem (2019, August 2). *Saipem joins the JV for the realization of the Arctic LNG2 project with a share worth approximately 2.2 billion Euro* [Press release]. https://www.saipem.com/en/media/press-releases/2019-08-02/saipem-joins-jv-realization-arctic-lng2-project-share-worth. Accessed 16 July 2021.

Sellheim, N. (2016). The voice of disapproval: The expressive function and paradox of the EU Seal Regime. *Polar Journal, 6*(2), 224–242.

Senate (France). (2013). *Arctique: Préoccupations européennes pour un enjeu global. Rapport d'information de M. André Gattolin, fait au nom de la commission des affaires européennes* [Arctic: European concerns for a global issue. Information report by Mr. André Gattolin, on behalf of the Committee for European Affairs]. (N° 684). https://www.senat.fr/notice-rapport/2013/r13-684-notice.html. Accessed 15 July 2021.

Senate (France). (2014). *Le Groenland, un carrefour entre l'Europe et l'Arctique? Rapport d'information de M. André Gattolin, fait au nom de la commission des affaires européennes* (N° 152). https://www.senat.fr/notice-rapport/2014/r14-152-notice.html. Accessed 15 July 2021.

Senate (France). (2017). *Union européenne et Arctique: Pour une politique ambitieuse et étoffée. Rapport d'information de M. André Gattolin, fait au nom de la commission des affaires européennes* (N° 499). https://www.senat.fr/notice-rapport/2016/r16-499-notice.html. Accessed 15 July 2021.

Stepień, A., & Raspotnik, A. (2019, August 19). The EU's Arctic policy: Between vision and reality. *CEPOB—College of Europe Policy Brief Series, #5.19.* https://www.coleurope.eu/research-paper/eus-arctic-policy-between-vision-and-reality

Valo, M. (2021, June 26). La recherche polaire française est à un tournant par manque de moyens [French polar research is at a turning point due to lack of resources]. *Le Monde.* https://www.lemonde.fr/sciences/article/2021/06/26/la-recherche-polaire-francaise-est-a-un-tournant-par-manque-de-moy ens_6085853_1650684.html. Accessed 15 July 2021.

Vidal, F. (2020). Les opérations extractives en Arctiques: les cas d'Equinor et de Norilsk Nickel [Extractive operations in the Arctic: The cases of Equinor and Norilsk Nickel]. In M. Vullierme (Ed.), *Réalités opérationnelles de l'environnement arctique. Approches transdisciplinaires et transsectorielles des impacts du changement climatique dans les sous-régions arctiques* (pp. 33–42). IRSEM.

The EU's Low-Carbon Policies and Implications for Arctic Energy Projects: The Russian Case

Morena Skalamera

INTRODUCTION

It was once a backwater, both bureaucratically and literally. Not anymore… *"the Arctic has become hot."* Enthusiasts say that under the melting ice of the Arctic, *"billions of tons of oil and billions of cubic meters of gas lie waiting*s." Some detractors reject the idea that big new oil and gas fields will be opened up under the Arctic, pointing to the extraction difficulties (and high costs in a current environment of low oil prices) that will be involved. Mainstream opinion, however, is cautiously sanguine, or at least has become so over the past few years following Russia's success in tapping the Arctic's gas resources. However, no one knows, almost by definition, how much there is in as yet unexplored fields or what the difficulties of recovering it may be.

Russia owns half the Arctic coastline and the lion's share of the region's resources. Almost 18% of Russia's territory (over three million

---

M. Skalamera (✉)
Institute for History, University Lecturer in Russian and International Studies, Leiden University, Leiden, Netherlands
e-mail: m.skalamera@hum.leidenuniv.nl

© The Author(s), under exclusive license to Springer Nature Singapore Pte Ltd. 2022
A. Likhacheva (ed.), *Arctic Fever*,
https://doi.org/10.1007/978-981-16-9616-9_13

square kilometers) is in the Arctic. Given its Arctic dominance, Russia is talking up the "potentially positive" changes and ways it could "use the advantages" of climate change, including (i) improving access to the abundant energy and mineral resources located there and (ii) beefing up the standing of the Northern Sea Route (NSR), thereby enhancing Russia's strategic, economic, and commercial importance.

On the energy front, despite enduring sanctions and the stagnation of the Russian economy, Moscow has kept up a steady pace in developing oil and gas reserves in its Arctic and sub-Arctic regions. Russian gas company Novatek, in particular, is in the process of succeeding in its bet on the Yamal Peninsula. In September 2020, it was reported that Novatek is on track to produce 57–70 million tons of liquefied natural gas (LNG) per year by 2030 despite the pandemic, around three times more than the current output. This would make Russia one of the world's top LNG producers, along with Qatar, Australia, and the United States. It would also boost its market share to 15% by 2025 from less than 10% in 2021 and enhance the country's position as the world's number one natural gas exporter (Reuters, 2020).

The remarkable success of Novatek's LNG gamble has meant that Russian LNG export strategy—and connected shift in government strategy—have both emerged as themes that are now discussed at the highest levels of Russian politics (Skalamera, 2021). In recognizing that Russia was late in entering the LNG game and is facing strong competition from a rising tide of global projects, the authorities have touted the expansion of Russia's global LNG market share as key to its grand strategy. For Novatek, this is a double boon. It will help it get Arctic resources to market faster and also, as the NSR becomes increasingly viable, diversify Russia's hydrocarbon-addicted economy. The Asia–Pacific region, indeed, is set to receive about 70% of hydrocarbon production, with shipments planned via the Northern Sea route.[1]

Sailing along the coast of Siberia by the north-east passage, or Northern Sea Route (NSR), cuts the distance between western Europe and east Asia by roughly a third. Despite Russia's excitement about

---

[1] The potential of the Northern Sea Route was already brought up in the Kremlin's 2008 Arctic Concept. President of the Russian Federation, "Basics of the state policy of the Russian Federation in the Arctic for the period until 2020 and beyond" (September 18, 2008). The same is reiterated in the "Foreign Policy Concept of the Russian Federation" (December 1, 2016).

cutting the journey time between Asia and Europe by one to two weeks, the NSR still requires nuclear icebreakers to accompany vessels, it is costlier than other trade routes, and only usable for six months a year at most. It is well-suited, however, as a shipping route for transporting oil and gas produced in the Arctic (Milne, 2018), which is where Russia's competitive advantage lies. In an attempt to make the route commercial, Russia has handed control of shipping to Rosatom, the state-run nuclear group, to pilot freighters along the route and allow year-round navigation (Astrasheuskaya, 2018). Russia hopes that a fleet of nuclear icebreakers will encourage investment across the NSR, increase commercial shipping through this emerging trade artery, and give more opportunities to Russian companies to supply LNG to east Asia (especially to China— already the world's second largest LNG market), and by doing so it hopes to undercut rivals including the United States and Australia. In July 2019, Novatek shipped its first ever LNG cargo through the NSR.[2] and while traffic is light today, it is reasonable to expect that it will grow as the polar ice recedes.

Explaining the *Timing* of Russia's Arctic LNG Shift

Periodization—using key dates to bracket distinct inflection points in world politics—is a common conceptual device in international relations scholarship. This section highlights the *timing* of Russia's aggressive expansion of Arctic LNG as a belated response to America's reshaping of the world markets for natural gas through the shale gas revolution. Some believed that the effects of America's shale abundance would force the Russian government to spur reform in its gas sector. In contrast to such expectations, the government did not rise to the occasion. Even after the shale gas revolution hit global gas markets in the early 2010s,

---

[2] The potential of the Northern Sea Route was already brought up in the Kremlin's 2008 Arctic Concept. President of the Russian Federation, "Basics of the state policy of the Russian Federation in the Arctic for the period until 2020 and beyond" (September 18, 2008). The same is reiterated in the "Foreign Policy Concept of the Russian Federation" (December 1, 2016).

undermining Russia's long-standing business model, Moscow worked to maximize income from oil and gas without the modernization that could have come about had the country permitted the introduction of outside investment and encouraged effective management (Vatansever, 2020). Instead, the disruptive effects of the "shale gale" were met by protectionism, the bolstering of massive state-owned energy enterprises, and an ever-assertive Russian posture on the international stage. The failure to reform the Russian economy, in turn, meant that new markets for Russia's prime export commodities—oil and gas—would become crucial to economic and political stability.

Several political factors explain why the Russian authorities have been averse to meaningful reform:

1. because Russia still operates in a universe where the sale of hydrocarbons will continue to guarantee Russia's international influence and status;
2. due to the oil and gas sector's importance as a source of rents for powerful vested interests
3. and given that oil and gas sales so thoroughly ensure domestic stability in Russia's "virtual economy".

Value creation in the economy is overwhelmingly concentrated in the energy sector. Most of the rest of the economy, including manufacturing, creates little added value. In some cases, it is even net-value-subtracting—heavily dependent on direct government subsidies and other handouts, including underpriced energy and other material inputs (Gaddy & Ickes, 1998). As a result, the twofold challenge for Russia's economic management is to ensure that value continues to be created by the oil and gas sectors and that enough of this value is shared with the rest of Russian industry for other sectors to be able to survive. The generosity of the government toward the hydrocarbon elite comes with strings attached: in return for their wealth, value-creating oil and gas elites should maximize performance, pay their taxes, and support the economically moribund but politically important sectors of the Russian economy, such as heavy manufacturing, where large numbers of jobs are concentrated (Szakonyi, 2017).

The US shale revolution, however, has created a ubiquitous market in LNG, leading to downward pressure on global gas prices. Russia's heavy dependence on energy and commodity exports makes it highly vulnerable to such strategic inflection points. The imposition of energy-related sanctions is another example of said vulnerability; since the onset of sanctions Russia has been unable to move away from Western high-tech energy technology (Shagina, 2020). Equipment for the industrial purification of natural gas, horizontal drilling units, offshore drilling rigs necessary in the Arctic permafrost, or software for hydraulic fracturing and a variety of other technologies are now on the banned list (Mitrova & Ladislaw, 2016, p. 10), while the government lacks the expertise as well the technologies to conduct hard-to-extract exploration of Arctic energy resources. In sum, in the face of the shale gas revolution and Western sanctions, Russia is aware of the need to diversify away from hydrocarbon and mineral exports and toward the knowledge economy while still cashing in on its bounteous resource endowment, but given the above structural challenges it struggles to do so. Russia remains a petrostate where oil and gas revenues comprise 37.4% of the federal budget revenue and account for 21% of the country's tax revenues (Ministry of Finance of Russian Federation, n.d.). This is less true of LNG (compared to pipeline gas or oil) because the government has granted substantial tax breaks to encourage development, but nevertheless over time LNG revenues could become important to the Russian state (Henderson & Yermakov, 2019, p. 4).

This is why, in light of an otherwise discouraging economic picture, Novatek's Yamal LNG development in the Russian Arctic is such a triumph. Beyond its obvious commercial-developmental goals, LNG also offers Russia the chance to enhance its geopolitical status and reclaim the mantle of the leading Arctic state. Boosting exports of LNG also involves developing international relations with a number of new and existing customers for Russian gas, encouraging the development of geopolitically important regions such as the Arctic and the Far East of Russia, and expanding Russia's commercial (and therefore political) reach to new areas such as North and South America and North-East Asia.

Novatek's Triumph

Taking advantage of the opportunities posed by the rapid melting of Arctic ice, Putin has made expanding Russia's position in the Arctic a top priority.[3] As argued by Henderson and Yermakov (2019, p. 14), the Yamal LNG project is as much a triumph for Russia and Novatek as it is for China. Novatek successfully brought together an international consortium comprising one international company with LNG expertise (Total), one major buyer of LNG (CNPC from China), and one major source of finance (the Silk Road Fund, whose investment opened the way for Chinese lenders to cooperate with the project).

The Role of China

Expanded use of Arctic gas is a strategic objective that China shares with Russia for three crucial reasons: Firstly, gas demand in China is growing rapidly. An increasing focus by the authorities on environmental issues and air quality from the mid-2010s points to a strategic goal of continuing to broaden China's gas import diversification options (Skalamera, 2018). Natural gas production has been growing at annual rates above 7% for more than a decade, yet imports provide about 40% of the rapidly rising demand (British Petroleum, 2020). Gas use, especially in power, will likely be boosted by China's recent carbon neutrality pledge as renewables are scaled up faster than would have otherwise been the plan, leading to greater demand for flexible capacity. The ongoing liberalization of the gas sector, in a context of lower natural gas prices, will further boost gas penetration (Meidan, 2020, p. 10). In this context, gas use is set to grow and play a role in China's energy transition at least until 2040–2045. As Beijing has committed to reducing greenhouse gas emissions by 25–30% by 2030, it joined the chorus of buyers demanding "Green LNG" and Novatek, indeed, has joined the race to make sales of the fastest growing fossil fuel as clean as possible (Shiryaevskaya & Khrennikova, 2021).

Secondly, the Chinese leaders have long emphasized avoiding excessive reliance both on the unstable regions of the Middle East and East

---

[3] In December 2017, with much fanfare, President Putin personally sent off Yamal LNG's first tanker to China, having been able to secure the project's financing from the French company Total (20%), China's state-owned energy company CNPC's (20%), and Beijing's state-owned Silk Road investment fund (9.9%), a $40 bn special financial mechanism to support China's ambitious aims with the Belt and Road Initiative (BRI).

Africa, and the Strait of Malacca,—a maritime chokepoint whose vulnerability to blockade by the US Navy has for years haunted Chinese leaders. Recent cooperation with Russia can be seen as an attempt to alleviate the "Malacca Dilemma" and reduce dependence on this sea route surrounded by Indonesia, Malaysia, and Singapore, America's Asian closest allies. The colossal Power of Siberia pipeline,[4] which is devoid of in-between transit countries will arguably service China with cheaper and reliable piped gas for decades to come. It is also a useful alternative to LNG deliveries that usually travel via vessel through the Strait of Malacca. Now LNG shipping, too, is possible while avoiding choke-points controlled by the US Navy. Use of the new trans-Arctic NSR—or "Polar Silk Road" (The State Council Information Office of the People's Republic of China, 2018), as it is called in Beijing—not only diversifies energy routes and lowers transport costs, but also offers China an opportunity to be an active Arctic stakeholder and, thus, to have a say on the questions of Arctic shipping, resource development and governance (Klimenko, 2019). China has been eager to invest in shipment through the Northern Sea route and has put out money on the development of the Arctic. Russia, for all the misgivings about not selling on the cheap, needs China if it wants to tap the Arctic's full commercial potential and set itself as the dominant Arctic shipping state.

Thirdly, there are also suggestions of an increasing security focus in China's Arctic policy. The strategic importance of Russian LNG is becoming increasingly apparent, both as a source of gas and as a source of geopolitical cooperation in the Arctic region. For China, investing in the "Polar Silk Road" is a golden opportunity to potentially gain greater access to Russia's natural resources that would have otherwise remained stranded at favorable prices, as well as to secure access to big infrastructure contracts that might have gone to Western competitors, and to provide financing for projects that will benefit Chinese firms.[5] China has,

---

[4] A pipeline that cost 55 bn and is long 4000 km.

[5] In 2018, China published an Arctic policy paper that explicitly linked the NSR to its ambitious BRI strategy, dubbing it the "Polar Silk Road." The paper mainly focuses on climate research and environmental protection, as well as identifying China as a "near-Arctic state." The paper is notably silent on China's interest in accessing the colossal oil and gas resources locked under the region's permafrost. More broadly, however, investment by Chinese state-controlled companies in the Russian Arctic can largely be interpreted as a way for Chinese oil and gas companies to cope with their growing import dependence.

indeed, taken advantage of Russia's geopolitical isolation, relative technological lag, and near-inability to obtain advanced technology from its traditional Western partners (Trenin, 2020). This underlines that for as long as western sanctions persist, Russia is going to need China more than the other way around and China's bilateral cooperation with Russia—in the Arctic and elsewhere—is seen as part of Xi's extensive Belt and Road diplomacy to realize China's broader aspirations in Eurasia.

The (Enduring) Role of Europe

Given the above, China is very interested in the development of Arctic shipping lanes. New freight opportunities interest China as ice recedes along the NSR. The geostrategic importance of a position in the Arctic is likely to encourage further offers of support from China that will help bolster Russia's LNG business in the region.

When possible, Yamal LNG would like to ship east, with the NSR serving as an important Arctic shortcut to reach premium Asian markets (China, Japan, and South Korea). However, for the foreseeable future the navigation window is likely to be limited to five to six months per year at best (July through November, with late June and early December as possibilities, depending on the weather). For the rest of the year, Yamal LNG has no other choice but to ship west, to European markets. As shown by Henderson and Yermakov (2019, p. 20), thus far Russian LNG exports have been quite diversified. While the majority of shipments went to Asia-Pacific, a significant share of sales also went to Europe, especially to markets such as Spain and the UK that are not reached by Russian pipeline gas.

In the short term, indeed, Russia's leverage as the leading supplier of piped gas to Europe, an increasingly important supplier of gas to China, and a rapidly rising global exporter of LNG could rise during the "low-carbon transition" period. Despite the uniquely toxic character of the EU–Russia gas relationship and the debates surrounding Nord Stream II, Russia has the largest available gas resource for Europe and is one of the cheapest sources of supply. As long as at least some fossil fuel power plants are needed to back up variable generation from wind and solar, and during the indeterminate period that will see homes and businesses switch to electricity for heating, there will still be demand for Russian gas in Europe (especially as domestic sources are rapidly depleting).

However, Europe's longer-term decarbonization plans call in question security of demand for Russian (and other) LNG and piped gas suppliers to the EU. In December 2019, the EU has unveiled the so-called Green Deal, aimed at creating the world's first carbon neutral continent by 2050. The Green Deal envisions a power sector based largely on renewable sources, the rapid phasing out of coal, decarbonization of gas and a focus on energy efficiency. These increasingly stringent carbon reduction targets create uncertainties for the medium-to-long-term prospects of the use of natural gas in the EU, as gas demand is foreseen to stabilize over the coming decade, and then fall abruptly as of 2040.

Roughly 65% of Russia's natural gas exports are still directed to Europe, a fuel that—for now—retains importance as a "bridge" to help the transition from a coal-burning past. Yet the world market for gas, too, has shrunk by more than 10% in the past decade and is liable to decline further as climate policies accelerate the switch to renewables. By 2040, EU-27's demand for gas is expected to sharply decline despite the depletion of indigenous sources (IEA, 2019). This casts increasing doubt about Russia's role in the EU's gas market from the 2030s onward, as 90% of Russia's current long-term gas contracts with European customers are due to expire around that date.

The Disruptive Effects of the Energy Transition

Many observers have argued that for oil and gas firms to survive, and even thrive in an energy transition, will require that they not only reduce their own emissions (such as from flaring and methane leaks), and invest in low-carbon technologies, but that they also advocate for stronger climate policy—and certainly do not stymie it (Bordoff, 2020; Losz & Elkind, 2019). In Europe, in particular, if the gas industry does not take decarbonization seriously and fails develop a convincing plan for its contribution to the achievement of the bloc's carbon reduction targets, it risks being significantly marginalized and ultimately removed from the European energy system (Stern, 2019). In a similar vein, without greater industry leadership and collaboration with the EU authorities, "green gas" may never become a commercial reality, and ultimately there may be little room left for natural gas in the European low-carbon energy systems.

As previously noted, Novatek is exploring investment opportunities to reduce emissions. This includes installing carbon capture and storage at one of its Arctic fields and exploring hydrogen opportunities (Shiryaevskaya & Khrennikova, 2021). While buyers from Singapore to Europe to China are increasingly demanding to know exactly how dirty the gas they are buying is, without further details on measurement, reporting, and verification some of these initiatives may amount to mere "greenwashing" of investments into strategic infrastructure. For instance, throughout 2020 there has been a cascade of new "net-zero" emission announcements by a broad variety of national and sub-national governments, businesses and (institutional) investors. Net-zero pledges have been welcomed by the UN as the most significant and encouraging climate policy development of the past year, while others see it as a form of "performative politics" to distract from more tangible climate actions that can help reduce emissions in the short-term. Some researchers now caution that "net-zero" narratives fit into a broader "normative turn" in global climate governance and its associated communicative techniques to galvanize international support for climate action. However, they will only have effect if concrete measures are rapidly put in place to achieve the objectives proposed by such norms (Blondeel et al., 2021).[6]

The introduction of increasingly stringent long-term emissions reduction targets in the EU—the world's most advanced climate bloc—nonetheless, will have great repercussions for Russia's grand strategy. As a result, Russian authorities seem to have reluctantly accepted that gas demand in Europe is going to decline after 2030 and have worked to re-focus on expanding other markets (particularly in Asia). Taking a positive step toward embracing and developing policies and technologies that would help the decarbonization of the natural gas supply chain (which would convince European politicians that gas should be taken seriously as a significant part of energy balances post-2030) does not seem to be part of Russia's export strategy as of yet.

[6] See also Blondeel et al. (2019).

The EU: World's Green Growth Champion or Protectionist Bloc

Europe wants to use the COVID-19 crisis to transition to a modern, resource-efficient and competitive digital and green economy. The so-called "carbon border tax" is a central theme in the European Commission's "green new deal" program; Russia has opposed Europe's call for an EU-wide carbon border tax and joined forces with other emerging economies, such as Brazil, in labeling it as a new form of "carbon protectionism" and a violation of World Trade Organization rules.

More recently, the EU has hoped that by coordinating with the United States and other innovation-oriented countries—such as Japan—the border carbon adjustment mechanism (BCA) could still become a powerful measure to achieve ambitious reductions in GHG emissions. In January 2019, and in line with its history of overt climate denial, the Trump administration threatened the EU with possible sanctions over plans for a BCA. The Biden presidency was expected to be far less critical and create more potential transatlantic synergies on this evolving issue.

Yet, while Europe hails the BCA as "an instrument … to level the playing field for European products if other countries do not go as far as us or refuse to go in the right direction […]" (Von der Burchard et al., 2019), there may be skepticism—if not outright retaliation from European trade partners, including from the US and China, regardless of whether the measure is WTO compliant. Trade partners—not least the Biden administration—may still see a border carbon adjustment mechanism as an "extraterritorial overreach." While climate and energy are likely to be key topics for a transatlantic reset during the Biden administration, a reappraisal of their relationship will likely not be a panacea for climate, mostly as a result of the domestic differences on important issues such as free trade. A March 2021 visit by John Kerry, currently Joe Biden's envoy on climate, showed the limits of what can be achieved at the transatlantic level. Reunited with his counterparts in Brussels for a trip that aimed to build a transatlantic climate alliance, Kerry warned that the BCA should be a "last resort" and expressed his concern about the trade implications of Brussels' plans (Hook, 2021).

Russia's Response

While Europe's energy transition has triggered a re-orientation in Russia's foreign policy and commercial strategy to the East, above all to China, the latter's recently declared carbon neutrality means that a gradual adaptation of Russia's obsolete business model may be inevitable. China, responsible for more than one-quarter of the world's carbon emissions, in October 2020 pledged to achieve carbon neutrality by 2060. It remains to be seen, however, whether China's rapid and ambitious adoption of net-zero targets presents a case of an emerging "standard of appropriate behavior," and the extent to which it will be followed by concrete implementation and regulation to achieve the policy's objectives (Blondeel et al., 2021). Either way, Russia should be more concerned about the advancement of decarbonization policies in Europe and around the world, as slowly but surely more regions are moving toward banning fossil fuels.

Meanwhile, as an economy based on hydrocarbons export, Russia is particularly skeptical about green solutions, both at home and abroad. At the moment, Moscow is still working to maximize income from oil and gas without recognizing the geopolitical dimensions of the low-carbon energy transition, and in particular the threats that it poses to its incumbent industries and economies reliant on fossil fuels. Some change, however, is visible from reading the country's official strategic planning documents. Russia's 2019 "Energy Security Doctrine" for the first time recognizes the introduction of the EU's ambitious long-term carbon reduction targets as a major political and economic challenge (Ministry of Energy of Russian Federation, 2019). Domestically, Moscow produces the so-called yellow and blue hydrogen (from nuclear and natural gas) and there is increasing talk about how Russia could, in principle, export hydrogen to the EU, therefore striving to remain relevant in Europe's new energy order. The potential details of these developments are peripheral to this chapter; what is of concern, however, is how the EU's accelerating decarbonization plans might become a flashpoint for new tensions with Russia in an increasingly multipolar international fabric (Scholten et al., 2020).

The Issue of Stranded Assets

An important concern is whether the energy transition may leave the Russian Arctic with large investment projects that are known as "stranded assets." The International Energy Agency defines stranded assets as "those investments which have already been made but which, at some time prior to the end of their economic life, are no longer able to earn an economic return" (Livsey, 2020). Vast swaths of oil and gas laying under the Arctic shelf may never be extracted because doing so would intensify global warming as foreign policy makers, fossil fuel companies, and leading thinkers come under increasing pressure to consider how the world will change in response to climate change.

Thanks to the combination of Chinese financing and European technology, Novatek managed to complete Yamal 1 on time and on budget, despite the harsh operating environment in the Yamal Peninsula and tough US sanctions against the company (Mitrova & Yermakov, 2019, p. 35). Yamal 2 now aims to emulate the success story of Yamal 1: first, by circumventing sanctions through the signing of an agreement with the British group TechnipFMC (Offshore Energy, 2019); and second, by finding alternative partners to Western investors, in this case the Japanese companies Mitsui & Co. and Mitsubishi Corporation, and Chinese money. In its search for investors for Yamal LNG 2, Novatek has looked to diversify the investment portfolio while retaining at least a 60% stake (Malte, 2019). Of course, the company has been forced to look for non-Western partners capable of providing cutting-edge technologies, and those partners mostly come from Asia.

The Russian state strongly supports the development of Arctic LNG production and provides tax breaks and other regulatory support to attract foreign investors. In 2016–2018, it was feared that the coming on stream of US LNG would create a global LNG glut. But as noted by Mitrova and Yermakov (2019, p. 36), extremely high LNG imports by China and other Asian economies in 2016–2018 cleared the glut and boosted prices. These positive price developments have helped Novatek's expansion plans.

But it remains to be seen whether Novatek's innovative policy will suffice in the face of several fundamental problems, such as the persistence of sanctions, the shale revolution (which has fundamentally eroded hydrocarbon industry profitability), and the renewables' revolution, which will continue to depress growth in demand for fossil fuels. The combined effect of these shocks has created a difficult business environment that may lead large foreign companies, including Chinese firms, to hesitate in developing expensive offshore fields (including on the Russian Arctic shelf). According to Tatiana Mitrova (2020), it is highly likely that the coronavirus pandemic will amplify and accelerate trends for decarbonization, especially in Europe, Russia's main export market. Some analysts go on to add that the instability of the oil market could hasten a structural shift toward renewable energy, by making traditional fossil fuel companies less attractive to investors. While renewable energy projects typically generate lower returns than oil and gas exploration, they also offer long-term price stability that would become more attractive in the current market. As Mitrova (2020) notes, there are already increasingly vocal calls from governments and international organizations to adopt a low-carbon approach to restarting the economy. In that sense, and not unlike other petrostates, Russia finds itself in a buyer's market that it cannot control.

Over the next few decades, mounting pressure to take action on the threat of climate change may be the single most important factor in deciding the fate of Russian LNG in the EU gas market. China is courted as a substitute, but its ability to supply the technology (including for seismic exploration in the Barents Sea) is limited. It is also questionable whether future oil (and gas) prices will justify the development of these remote reserves. A price of at least US$80 per barrel is required to make the Arctic offshore fields profitable; the current price is about US$48 (Kluge & Paul, 2020, p. 2). A more likely scenario is that a changing business climate—above all the volatility of oil prices—and climate geopolitics will prompt Russia to commit less effort to hard-to-extract Arctic resources.

As Mitrova and Ladislaw (2016, p. 7) note, low oil prices reduce the financial sustainability of the Russian oil and gas companies, result in investment cuts, and challenge implementation of large upstream megaprojects, such as offshore Arctic LNG. In the current price environment, many large projects—like the Shtokman field in the Barents Sea have either been frozen or implicitly postponed. This may result in a number of stranded assets in the Arctic shelf. It is this trend—along with Western sanctions—that explains lower appetite for big hydrocarbon investments in Russia among the world's oil majors. All this explains the gradual pivot to China and East Asia—in investments and in energy trade. Yet, it would be wrong to suggest that this creates a threat to European supplies: in an era of shale gas-induced abundance, global competition over the EU's gas market is fierce. Thus, even if Russia could actually get a short-term boost in geopolitical influence from climate action and use the Arctic's LNG in its quest to return to great power status, with LNG imports increasing there is no shortage of supply (and competition) in Europe's LNG market. This, in turn, entails a deepening of the Sino-Russian partnership in the Russian Arctic.

Prospects for a Pax Sinica?

Worries about Europe's "carbon protectionism" may reinforce a "Pax Sinica" in Eurasia. Alexander Gabuev (2020) has argued that the emergence of a Sino-Russian axis as the backbone of Beijing-centered order in Eurasia—a Pax Sinica—has profound security and economic implications for Europe. The implications of a growing Sino-Russian integration, are, indeed, of interest for Europe. The extent to which Sino-Russian [energy] cooperation will develop a military aspect in the Arctic detrimental to European security is one such uncertainty. In this sense, even though the EU lacks the required military capabilities to be a geostrategic player in the Arctic (Paul, 2021, pp. 3–4), using its broad expertise in scientific research and environmental projects might have positive spill-over effects on other areas of dispute.

Other observers argue that worries about an emerging Pax Sinica in the Arctic may be overblown. There could even be a paradox at play: Russia's essential security interests in the region to a degree stymie economic cooperation with external partners—including China—for the region's development (Aliyev, 2020, p. 6). Russia is well aware of China's markedly expanding commercial reach, in particular through the Belt and Road Initiative (BRI), and China's aspirations to significantly enhance its economic and political clout in Arctic governance. Precisely due to this expanding reach, the Russian government is known to deeply scrutinize its external partners, including Chinese companies willing to invest in the Arctic. Furthermore, Russia remains wary about forging any strategic alliance in a zone that it considers key to its own grand strategy despite Beijing's efforts to assert its broader regional agenda (Trenin, 2020). Cooperation between China and Russia in the Arctic is exclusively economic (i.e., *commercial realpolitik* is at the heart of their engagement (Buchanan, 2020)).

This creates an opening for the EU's Arctic diplomacy. Looking at the Arctic from the European perspective, harmonizing its ambitious climate

Russia's Arctic Paradox

The politics of climate change in the Arctic has to do with what has been called the "Arctic paradox." A decisive question for Russia will be how to resolve the "Arctic Paradox"—the trade-off between (i) pursuing economic opportunities through increasing commercialization of the Arctic region and (ii) preventing environmental degradation of its fragile ecologic system (Brzozowski, 2020). While the paradox is daunting for other Arctic countries as well,[7] Russia, as the largest Arctic state remains very ambivalent in its climate policy (Segurnin, 2021, p. 7).

Different countries do not look at the climate problem with the same urgency or in the same way and inevitably see even the most urgent global problems through the lens of their own interests. For Russia, the "Arctic paradox" is at the center of a range of other influences that tend to paralyze or inhibit meaningful climate action. Russia's official position is that climate change is real, anthropogenic, and negative, but Moscow will limit the impact of global warming through adaptation measures and continue, nonetheless, to give priority to its energy and extraction policies because it cannot afford to develop alternative economic strategies (Laruelle, 2020).

On the one hand, taking advantage of the opportunities posed by the rapid melting of Arctic ice, Putin has made expanding Russia's position in the Arctic a top priority. Valuable minerals and around a quarter of the world's still undiscovered reserves of oil and gas are thought to lie in the Arctic (Alexandra, 2020). The longest shoreline of the Arctic lies within the borders of Russia, so its presence in the region should not be immediately thought to be a military threat.

On the other hand, the Russian scientific community is in overwhelming agreement about the environmental hazard that human-driven climate change poses to Russia. The way Russia contributes to the work of the Arctic Council and other international organizations on Arctic environmental issues is indicative of its will to cooperate. The interests of

---

[7] For a paper that shows how growing oil and gas production is impeding Canada from meeting its climate commitments, too, and outlines how the federal government is supporting oil and gas production growth, see Carter and Dordi (2021).

Russia in the Arctic are complex and therefore these two approaches are interrelated.

What to do about the melting Arctic is a different question. Even if the November 2021 U.N. climate change conference in Glasgow accelerates action toward the goals of the Paris Agreement, the amount of carbon dioxide already in the atmosphere, together with that which will be added, looks bound eventually to make summer Arctic Sea ice a thing of the past. Unique ecosystems, and perhaps many species, will be lost in a tide of environmental change.

Climate-driven crises will upend traditional notions of political-military control. The looming catastrophe can be managed only cooperatively. Climate cooperation with Russia is thus somewhat like the need for nuclear arms control with the Soviet Union during the Cold War: in both cases, *realpolitik* means setting aside certain differences in order to cooperate on a dilemma that neither side can solve alone (Colgan, 2020; English & Gardner, 2020). Wise political leaders should see that the gains from careful cooperation on selected issues far outweigh the costs.

Conclusion

This chapter has made two key points. Firstly, the implications of the EU's "Green Deal' will be negative for Russia. As a result, mitigation of environmental damage rather than mere adaptation must follow (Lo, 2021, p. 22): this would entail projects for reducing emissions and mitigating environmental damage, such as carbon capture, utilization and storage, and policies and technologies that can help the decarbonization of the natural gas supply chain. The EU is opened to playing a larger role in enhancing the sustainability of the Russian Arctic as a provider of expert knowledge and technologies. Despite Russia's growing economic cooperation and ideological affinity for China, amidst enduring economic sanctions against Russia the latter is no alternative to Western technology in either renewable or hydrocarbon projects. As the energy transition gains momentum, some of Russia's Arctic hydrocarbon projects, may, thus, remain stranded.

Secondly, the larger challenge is how to find common ground on the issue of climate change, which may provide an opening in the fraught relationship with the United States. It remains to be seen how Russia is going to reconcile its participation in international climate negotiations (along with enhancing the role of renewable energy), with a "light" approach

350   M. SKALAMERA

to climate change; one that still features plans to increase hydrocarbon production in the Russian Arctic.

For US President Biden the climate crisis has become "existential"—in other words, it has moved to the center of US national security and foreign policy (Mead, 2021). Meanwhile, some other permanent members of the Security Council, notably Russia and China, have been reluctant to discuss climate change as a security risk, arguing that other venues, such as the U.N. climate meetings, are more appropriate (Busby et al., 2021).

Still, amidst currently very strained US–Russia relations, the climate crisis and governance of the Arctic may be present some of the very few openings for cooperation and warrant working together, as stressed during a summer 2021 visit by John Kerry to Moscow.[8] If the climate cautious as well as the climate ambitious are enlisted, and if a truly global effort is achieved, then there is the chance that international diplomacy on climate change can contribute more positively to a broader economic and ecological security agenda.

REFERENCES

Alexandra, B. (2020, January 28). New 'Arctic paradox' emerges, as economy and ecology seek balance. *Euractiv.*

Aliyev, N. (2020, September 5). Development in difficult times: Russia's Arctic policy through 2035. *Russian Analytical Digest*, n. 256.

Astrasheuskaya, A. (2018, December 13). Russia gives nuclear group control of Arctic sea route. *Financial Times.* https://www.ft.com/content/b5dc9c38-fd56-11e8-aebf-99e208d3e521. Accessed 27 July 2021.

Blondeel, M., Colgan, J., & Van de Graaf, T. (2019). What drives norm success? Evidence from anti–fossil fuel campaigns. *Global Environmental Politics, 19*(4), 63–84. https://doi.org/10.1162/glep_a_00528

Blondeel, M., Van Coppenolle, H., & Van de Graaf, T. (2021). *Dynamics of a 'net-zero' norm: Origins, diffusion and contestation.* Unpublished Manuscript. Presented at the ECPR General Conference.

Bordoff, J. (2020, January 29). How to broaden the coalition against climate change. *Foreign Policy.* https://foreignpolicy.com/2020/01/29/coalition-

---

[8] U.S. climate envoy John Kerry and Putin agreed that the United States and Russia should work together on climate issues. "The climate problem is one of the areas where Russia and the United States have common interests and similar approaches," Putin said during Kerry's visit as reported by *The Moscow Times* (2021).

against-climate-change-broaden-business-political-leaders/. Accessed 27 July 2021.

British Petroleum. (2020). *BP statistical review of world energy, 2020*. https://www.bp.com/content/dam/bp/business-sites/en/global/corporate/pdfs/energy-economics/statistical-review/bp-stats-review-2020-full-report.pdf. Accessed 27 July 2021.

Brzozowski, A. (2020, January 28). New 'Arctic paradox' emerges, as economy and ecology seek balance. *Euractiv*. https://www.euractiv.com/section/arctic-agenda/news/a-new-political-arctic-paradox-emerges-as-economy-ecology-seek-balance/. Accessed 27 July 2021.

Buchanan, E. (2020, July 21). There is no Arctic axis. *Foreign Policy*. https://foreignpolicy.com/2020/07/21/no-arctic-axis-china-russia-relationship-resources-natural-gas-northern-sea-route/. Accessed 27 July 2021.

Busby, J., Bazilian, M., & Krampe, F. (2021, March 2). Biden called climate change an 'existential threat.' Can the U.N. Security Council help? *The Washington Post*. https://www.washingtonpost.com/politics/2021/03/02/biden-called-climate-change-an-existential-threat-can-un-security-council-help/. Accessed 27 July 2021.

Carter, A. V., & Dordi T. (2021, April 14). Correcting Canada's 'one eye shut' climate policy. *Cascade Institute*. https://cascadeinstitute.org/technical-paper/correcting-canadas-one-eye-shut-climate-policy/. Accessed 27 July 2021.

Colgan, J. D. (2020, September 14). The climate case against decoupling. *Foreign Affairs*. https://www.foreignaffairs.com/articles/united-states/2020-09-14/climate-case-against-decoupling. Accessed 27 July 2021.

English, R. D., & Gardner, M. G. (2020, September 29). Phantom peril in the Arctic. *Foreign Affairs*. https://www.foreignaffairs.com/articles/united-states/2020-09-29/phantom-peril-arctic. Accessed 27 July 2021.

Gabuev, A. (2020, November 24). *Pax Sinica: Europe's dilemma in facing the Sino-Russian axis*. Carnegie Moscow Center. https://carnegie.ru/2020/11/24/pax-sinica-europe-s-dilemma-in-facing-sino-russian-axis-pub-83302. Accessed 27 July 2021.

Gaddy, C. G., & Ickes, B. W. (1998). Russia's virtual economy. *Foreign Affairs*. https://www.foreignaffairs.com/articles/russia-fsu/1998-09-01/russias-virtual-economy. Accessed 27 July 2021.

Henderson, J., & Yermakov, V. (2019). *Russian LNG: Becoming a global force* (The Oxford Institute for Energy Studies: OIES PAPER: NG 154). https://www.oxfordenergy.org/wpcms/wp-content/uploads/2019/11/Russian-LNG-Becoming-a-Global-Force-NG-154.pdf. Accessed 27 July 2021.

Hook, L. (2021, March 21). John Kerry warns EU against carbon border tax. *Financial Times*. https://www.ft.com/content/3d00d3c8-202d-4765-b0ae-e2b212bbca98. Accessed 27 July 2021.

IEA. (2019). *World Energy Outlook 2019: Flagship Report*. https://www.iea.org/reports/world-energy-outlook-2019. Accessed 27 July 2021.

Klimenko, E. (2019). *The geopolitics of a changing Arctic* (Background Paper). SIPRI. https://www.sipri.org/sites/default/files/2019-12/sipribp1912_geopolitics_in_the_arctic.pdf. Accessed 27 July 2021.

Kluge, J., & Paul, M. (2020). Russia's Arctic strategy through 2035. *SWP*. https://www.swp-berlin.org/10.18449/2020C57/. Accessed 27 July 2021.

Laruelle, M. (2020). Russia's Arctic policy: A power strategy and its limits. *IFRI*. https://www.ifri.org/en/publications/notes-de-lifri/russieneivisions/russias-arctic-policy-power-strategy-and-its-limits. Accessed 27 July 2021.

Livsey, A. (2020, February 4). Lex in depth: The \$900bn cost of 'stranded energy assets'. *Financial Times*. https://www.ft.com/content/95efca74-4299-11ea-a43a-c4b328d9061c. Accessed 27 July 2021.

Lo, B. (2021). The adaptation game—Russia and climate change. *IFRI*. https://www.ifri.org/en/publications/notes-de-lifri/russieneivisions/adaptation-game-russia-and-climate-change. Accessed 27 July 2021.

Losz, A., & Elkind, J. (2019, September). *The role of natural gas in the energy transition*. SIPA: Center for Energy Policy. https://www.energypolicy.columbia.edu/research/commentary/role-natural-gas-energy-transition. Accessed 27 July 2021.

Malte, H. (2019, June 6). Japan's Mitsui and Mitsubishi take 10 percent stake in Novatek's Arctic LNG 2. *High North News*. https://www.highnorthnews.com/en/japans-mitsui-and-mitsubishi-take-10-percent-stake-novateks-arctic-lng-2. Accessed 27 July 2021.

Mead, W. R. (2021, February 22). The polar bear paradox. *The Wall Street Journal*. https://www.wsj.com/articles/the-polar-bear-paradox-11614035542. Accessed 27 July 2021.

Meidan, M. (2020, December). Unpacking China's 2060 carbon neutrality pledge. *OIES: Oxford Energy Comment*. https://www.oxfordenergy.org/publications/unpacking-chinas-2060-carbon-neutrality-pledge/. Accessed 27 July 2021.

Milne, R. (2018, August 21). Maersk launches container ship on Arctic route. *Financial Times*. https://www.ft.com/content/fb38b6ac-a484-11e8-8ecf-a7ae1beff35b. Accessed 27 July 2021.

Ministry of Energy of Russian Federation. (2019). *Доктрина Энергетической Безопасности Российской Федерации* [Energy security doctrine of the Russian federation]. https://minenergo.gov.ru/system/download-pdf/14766/96941. Accessed 27 July 2021.

Ministry of Finance of Russian Federation. (n.d.). *Федеральный бюджет* [The federal budget]. https://minfin.gov.ru/ru/statistics/fedbud/. Accessed 27 July 2021.

Mitrova, T. (2020, July 8). The oil price crash: Will the Kremlin's policies change? *Russia Matters*. https://www.russiamatters.org/analysis/oil-price-crash-will-kremlins-policies-change. Accessed 27 July 2021.

Mitrova, T., & Ladislaw, S.O. (2016, March 16). *Shifting Political Economy of Russian Oil and Gas, Report*. CSIS: Center for Strategic and International Studies. https://www.csis.org/analysis/shifting-political-economy-russian-oil-and-gas-0. Accessed 27 July 2021.

Mitrova, T., & Yermakov, V. (2019, December 10). Russia's energy strategy-2035: Struggling to remain relevant. *IFRI*. https://www.ifri.org/en/publications/etudes-de-lifri/russieneireports/russias-energy-strategy-2035-struggling-remain. Accessed 27 July 2021.

Offshore Energy. (2019, May 21). Novatek brings in TechnipFMC for Arctic LNG 2 project. *Offshore Energy*. https://www.offshore-energy.biz/novatek-brings-in-technipfmc-for-arctic-lng-2-project/. Accessed 27 July 2021.

Paul, M. (2021, March 3). A new Arctic strategy for the EU. *SWP*. https://www.swp-berlin.org/publikation/a-new-arctic-strategy-for-the-eu. Accessed 27 July 2021.

Reuters. (2020 September 29). Russia's Novatek says on track for up to 70 million T/year of LNG by 2030. *Reuters*. https://www.reuters.com/article/us-novatek-lng/russias-novatek-says-on-track-for-up-to-70-million-t-year-of-lng-by-2030-idUSKBN26K125. Accessed 27 July 2021.

Scholten, D., Bazilian, M., Overland, I., & Westphal, K. (2020). The geopolitics of renewables: New board, new game. *Energy Policy, 138*, 111059. https://doi.org/10.1016/j.enpol.2019.111059

Segurnin, A. (2021, June 27). Upcoming Russian Arctic Council chairmanship: Priorities and implications for the High North. *Russian Analytical Digest, 269*, 5–8. https://css.ethz.ch/content/dam/ethz/special-interest/gess/cis/center-for-securities-studies/pdfs/RAD269.pdf. Accessed 27 July 2021.

Shagina, M. (2020, April). *Drifting East: Russia's import substitution and its pivot to Asia* (Working Paper No. 3). CEES: Center for Eastern European Studies. https://www.cees.uzh.ch/dam/jcr:19d4d0ec-ba85-490b-8909-a6b327c51f6e/CEES%20Working%20Paper%20No.3.pdf. Accessed 27 July 2021.

Shiryaevskaya, A., & Khrennikova, D. (2021, March 11). Russia's biggest LNG producer joins race to make fuel greener. *Bloomberg Green*. https://www.bloomberg.com/news/articles/2021-03-11/russia-s-biggest-lng-producer-joins-race-to-make-fuel-greener. Accessed 27 July 2021.

Skalamera, M. (2021). Russia's foray into Asia energy markets. In E. Buchanan (Ed.), *Russia energy strategy in Asia Pacific—Implications for Australia*. Australia University Press.

Skalamera, M. (2018). Explaining the 2014 Sino-Russian gas breakthrough: The primacy of domestic politics. *Europe-Asia Studies, 70*(1), 90–107.

Stern, J. (2019, February). *Narratives for natural gas in decarbonising European energy markets* (Paper: NG141). OIES. https://www.oxfordenergy.org/publications/narratives-natural-gas-decarbonising-european-energy-markets. Accessed 27 July 2021.

Szakonyi, D. (2017, November 29). Centrifugal forces: Why Russian oligarchs remain loyal to the Putin government. *Russia Matters*. https://www.russiamatters.org/analysis/centrifugal-forces-why-russian-oligarchs-remain-loyal-putin-government. Accessed 27 July 2021.

The Moscow Times. (2021, July 14). Putin says Russia, U.S. have 'common interests' on climate change. *The Moscow Times*. https://www.themoscowtimes.com/2021/07/14/putin-says-russia-us-have-common-interests-on-climate-change-a74518. Accessed 27 July 2021.

The State Council Information Office of the People's Republic of China. (2018). *China's Arctic policy*. http://english.gov.cn/archive/white_paper/2018/01/26/content_281476026660336.htm. Accessed 27 July 2021.

Trenin, D. (2020, March 31). *Russia and China in the Arctic: Cooperation, competition, and consequences*. Carnegie Moscow Center. https://carnegie.ru/commentary/81407. Accessed 27 July 2021.

Vatansever, A. (2020). Put over a barrel? "Smart" sanctions, petroleum and statecraft in Russia. *Energy Research & Social Science, 69*, 101607.

Von der Burchard, H., Barigazzi, J., & Oroschakoff, K. (2019, December 17). Here comes European protectionism. *POLITICO*. https://www.politico.eu/article/european-protectionism-trade-technology-defense-environment/. Accessed 27 July 2021.

Kaleidoscope of Independent Agendas for the Arctic: Asia

Challenges and Common Agenda for Arctic Cooperation in the Post-pandemic Era: A Chinese Perspective

Long ZHAO

INTRODUCTION

Climate change has dramatically transformed the Arctic over the past few decades. According to the latest research, even if global temperature rises by less than 2 degrees Celsius above pre-industrial levels, the Arctic could see a sea ice-free summer at least once a decade (IPCC, 2015). As a result of global warming, Arctic sea ice has been melting rapidly, potentially easing access to natural resources and opening up new maritime routes in the region. Decreased sea ice allows for additional human activity in the Arctic; this in turn exacerbates the damage to the Arctic ecosystem. Decreasing sea ice and permafrost—as a result of which more fresh water enters the Arctic Ocean—can change weather and climate conditions in other parts of the globe. The peace and stability of the Arctic, scientific research in the region, potential business opportunities, and international governance have sparked widespread attention and debates.

L. ZHAO (✉)
Institute for Global Governance Studies,
Shanghai Institutes for International Studies, Shanghai, China
e-mail: zhaolong@siis.org.cn

© The Author(s), under exclusive license to Springer Nature
Singapore Pte Ltd. 2022
A. Likhacheva (ed.), *Arctic Fever*,
https://doi.org/10.1007/978-981-16-9616-9_14

As states and nonstate actors explore different approaches to Arctic governance, a cohesive regime complex that integrates existing frameworks could help address the environmental, economic, anthropological, and geopolitical challenges this region faces. The changing Arctic environment could lead to an Arctic Gold Rush—states competing against one another to exploit oil and gas reserves and to claim the natural resources in sea areas by expanding the outer limits of their continental shelves. The Arctic has an estimated 90 billion barrels of oil and 1669 trillion cubic feet of natural gas, amounting to 22% of the world's oil and natural gas reserves (Kenneth et al., 2008). In addition, as the sea ice extent depletes, the Arctic could become an alternative corridor for international shipping. The Russian-governed Northern Sea Route (NSR) as the key section of the Northeast Passage (NEP), encompassing the maritime route along the Norwegian and Russian Arctic, has obvious advantages in maritime trade between ports in northwest Europe and northeast Asia, with shorter transport distance (30–50% less) and reduced sailing time (14–20 days) compared to the Suez route, assuming the same sailing speed (Gunnarsson, 2021, pp. 4–30). Meanwhile, Arctic shipping has also developed rapidly under the impetus of the energy industry, showing a good growth curve of shipping volume. According to the Northern Sea Route Administration, a total of 31.5 mln tons of goods were shipped on the route in 2019. Over the last three years, NSR volumes have hiked by more than 430% (Staalesen, 2020). In the first quarter of 2020, freight volume achieved year-on-year growth of 7.7%. The transportation of liquefied natural gas (LNG) constitutes the majority share of the volume; a total of 20.5 mln tons of LNG was sent out from the natural gas terminal Sabetta in Yamal. A vast majority of the marine traffic is destinational, via trans-Arctic voyages. The NSR seems gradually moving toward the goal of 80 mln tons of transportation by 2024 set by Russian President Vladimir Putin. However, before the natural resources can be extracted or the Arctic sea routes used, tremendous technical, environmental, and operational risks need to be addressed.

Political and security concerns are also associated with the changing Arctic. Eight Arctic countries (Canada, Denmark, Finland, Iceland, Norway, Russia, Sweden, and the U.S.) have sovereign rights and jurisdictions over their land territories, internal waters, territorial seas, exclusive economic zones, and continental shelves, the UN Convention on the Law of the Sea (UNCLOS) and general international law allow for all states to enjoy the rights of scientific investigation, navigation, overflight, fishing in the high seas and other relevant sea areas in the Arctic Ocean, and rights to resource exploration and exploitation. Although a basic legal framework exists, new issues could challenge peace and stability in the Arctic: opposing alliance structure between NATO and Russia inherited from the Cold War era; increasing Arctic military deployments; bilateral territorial disputes; legal claims concerning outer limits of continental shelves; disagreements on the legal status of Arctic shipping routes, including the Northeast Passage (NEP) and the Northwest Passage (NWP) through the Canadian Archipelago and North of Alaska; and nontraditional security issues such as catastrophic oil spills, environmental disasters, and maritime search and rescue responses. As the geoeconomic significance of the Arctic increases, even environmental protection issues that had been considered low politics—not concern the state's survival and strict national security—have come to involve national and international security.

To understand, protect, develop, and participate in the governance of the Arctic, so as to safeguard the common interests of all countries and the international community in the Arctic, and to promote sustainable development of the Arctic are China's policy goals with regard to the Arctic. China is defining itself as an important stakeholder in Arctic affairs and geographically a *Near-Arctic State*, one of the continental States that are closest to the Arctic Circle (State Council Information Office of China, 2018), which reflects the fact that China has many interlinks with the changing region. For instance, sitting downstream from the Arctic's climate system, northern China's climate, biological and environmental systems are directly affected by changes in the Arctic. In 2013, China became an accredited observer to the Arctic Council (AC), the main intergovernmental forum on issues regarding the environment and sustainable development of the Arctic, Chinese experts have been active in the research projects of several groups under the AC hereafter. In recent years, China has actively carried out multilateral and bilateral cooperation with Arctic countries and other stakeholders, which achieved remarkable results. For all stakeholders in Arctic affairs, including China, question how to respond to the current changes in the Arctic political, security, and economic landscape, and adapt to the new opportunities and challenges of Arctic international cooperation in the post-pandemic era, has become the most critical focus of discussion.

New Challenges for the Arctic Cooperation

In recent years, great power politics and competition in the Arctic affairs have increased significantly, the evolution of the regional political, security, and economic normal was synchronized with global power transition and structural adjustment. Under the impact of the COVID-19 pandemic, several new challenges have emerged to international interaction and cooperation in the Arctic.

The Reshaped Arctic Political Normal by Competition Between Major Powers

During the Trump administration of the U.S., the great power competition seems arrived in the Arctic. Due to its Arctic policy stagnation—mainly in the economic realm—the U.S. attempted to intensify competition among major powers as a response to the expanded military and economic footprints of Russia in the Arctic and the widening gap in Arctic activity capabilities between the U.S. and Russia. At the same time, despite the fact that China is one of the major contributors of international cooperation on Arctic climate and environmental management, science and technology development, and sustainable use, the relationship between the U.S. and China in the Arctic follows a trajectory of worldwide strategic competition between two countries. China's engagement with Russia on Arctic shipping and energy cooperation was interpreted by some scholars as building a spider web across the Arctic, along with the development of the Polar Silk Road, strategic deployment of scientists, possible military utilization, and exploring for oil and gas opportunities (McKay, 2019). Since the end of 2019, the U.S. Department of Defense, Coast Guard, and Air Force has, respectively, developed the *Arctic Strategy Report* (Department of Defense, 2019), *Arctic Strategic Outlook* (U.S. Coast Guard, 2019), and *Arctic Strategy* (Department of the NAVY, 2021), positioning China and Russia as a long-term threat to the U.S. Arctic security and challengers of the rule-based Arctic order, focuses on *day-to-day competition* (The Barents Observer, 2021). The U.S. government drew a direct connection between Chinese civilian research and a strengthened Chinese military presence in the Arctic Ocean, which could include deploying submarines. Furthermore, due to the Trump administration's neglect of climate change issues, the Arctic Council Ministerial meeting in 2019 has ended without a joint declaration for the first time ever.

The negative effects of great power competition are at risk of spreading, Nordic foreign ministers received the 2020 Nordic Foreign and Security Policy report, subtitled *Climate change, hybrid and cyber threats and challenges to the multilateral, rules-based world order*, which stated that China's presence and strategic interest in the Arctic will have security policy implications. The report also noted that the Chinese military has now begun to strengthen its knowledge of the Arctic, and China's broad interest in the Arctic underscores the importance of well-functioning, multilateral cooperation, where Arctic states must assume responsibility and play a key role in the interests of the Arctic environment and its societies. It expressed hope that Nordic countries will aim to formulate a common Nordic policy that facilitates partnerships with states that share similar views on the implications of increased Chinese Arctic involvement (Ministry of Foreign Affairs of Norway, 2020).

As some scholars pointed out, the U.S. has failed to sustain a national climate and economic policy in the Arctic for longer than four- or eight-year increments, and has largely failed to allocate adequate budgetary resources to enhance its physical presence in the region, whether for science, sustainable development, increased search and rescue capabilities, or greater domain awareness. This indecisiveness makes international collaboration challenging (Heather, 2021). Therefore, the adjustment of the Biden administration's Arctic policy has attracted attention. Expectations for the Arctic to be separated from the competition of major powers and to shift to responding actions to climate change promote the sustainable development and cooperation have risen significantly. Many scholars expressed their views that in response to the Arctic climate change and melting ice acceleration, the Biden administration will develop new commitments and implementing new policies on Arctic climate change and the advance scientific research has staked out clear differences with the policy priorities and framework developed by the previous administration, most notably a desire to work more closely with U.S. allies and partners and to tackle climate change and environmental issues head-on (Stronski & Kier, 2021).

Meanwhile, as main actors in Arctic affairs, Russia and the U.S. are both struggling with simultaneously adjusting their economic model and addressing increased climate devastation, the possible climate and environmental cooperation between the U.S. and Russia was once seen as an important driving force for changing political norm in the Arctic. The meeting between top diplomats of the U.S. and Russia in Reykjavik at the Arctic Council Ministerial meeting on May 19, 2021 before the one of President Biden and President Putin in Geneva on June 16, 2021 was regarded by some observers as the beginning of a *thaw* of the relationship and new start of Arctic cooperation (Reuters, 2021).

However, considering the major interaction mode of *sanctions and countermeasures* between the two countries, the return to the relatively benign geopolitical environment in the Arctic that existed there in the 1990s is unlikely. *First*, the general framework of the new normal of confrontation between Washington and Moscow is hard to change. Against the backdrop of a series of events such as *election interference*, cyberattacks, *anti-Putin* sentiments have become a political red line in Washington and part of the U.S. social consensus, the actual benefits of the Biden administration's improvement of relations with Russia are obviously not in proportion to the political costs.

Second, the nature of the structural contradictions between the U.S. and Russia will remain the same. Washington and Moscow still have sharp differences in their views on global order, their own roles, international security, and development. Relevant cognitive differences not only cover the discourse system of political elites and public opinions, but also extend to the behavior patterns of these two leaders. Meanwhile, their geopolitical competition, regarding Ukraine and Belarus, has deepened their bilateral contradictions.

Finally, the overall hostile ties cannot be totally improved. In the aftermath of the U.S. sanctions on Russia since 2013 and the largest-scale mutual expulsion of diplomatic personnel in history, communication between the two countries has fallen into stagnation. And it is inevitable that bilateral ties will continue to hit the bottom points in the coming years, the *Russia threat* still works well for the Biden administration to reshape trans-Atlantic relations. Overall, despite striving to seek common interests, neither Washington nor Moscow is willing to tackle their structural conflicts. Nor do they have the capability or right conditions to do so, synchronization of sanctions and countermeasures, confrontation and dialogue has become the new normal of US-Russian interaction.

Growing Tensions in Arctic Security and Policy Readjustment

The Arctic's growing geostrategic significance is driving an increase in Arctic states attention to the region's security and stability, some Arctic countries are speeding up their military deployments and joint exercises. For example, U.S. troops alongside NATO allies have continued to participate in large-scale exercises such as "Arctic Edge" (NORAD News, 2020) and the Norwegian-led "Cold Response" (Lopez, 2020), both held in early 2020. For the first time since the end of the Cold War, the U.S. Navy and the British RoyalNavy are making regular voyages above the Arctic Circle, with the four-ship patrol sailing in the Barents Sea (Larter, 2020, May 12), and NATO-allied maritime assets also operate in the Arctic. The U.S. Air Force will soon be deploying fifth-generation combat fighters in Alaska to project military power and protect its interests in the Arctic Ocean (NEWS, 2020). The Army Corps of Engineers and the City of Nome, located on the southern coast of the Seward Peninsula facing the Bering Sea, recently have been engaged in a cost-sharing, collaborative port-modification feasibility study and environmental assessment for expanding the Port of Nome. This may be a strategic first step in providing the U.S. with a timely and visible port presence in its maritime Arctic to support its national security and economic interests (Brigham, 2019).

The former Trump administration's Arctic policy had been overwhelmingly military in focus, and attention has centered on catching up with Arctic competitors. The June 2020 White House *Memorandum on Safeguarding U.S. National Interests in the Arctic and Antarctic Regions* called on executive departments to devise a plan to launch three heavy icebreakers by 2029 and establish two domestic and two international support bases (Larter, 2020, June 9). Early signals from the incoming President Joe Biden administration suggest a less aggressive military stance and an increased diplomatic approach to Arctic issues. In *Strategic Competition Act of 2021*, both U.S. Senate and Congress expressed that the militarization of the Arctic poses a serious threat to Arctic peace and stability, and the interests of U.S. allies and partners, calling to enhance the resilience capacities to military activity from Arctic nations and other nations that may result from increased accessibility of the Arctic Region (Strategic Competition Act, 2021).

Meanwhile, Russia is expanding its military facilities and upgrading radar and electronic warfare systems capabilities by deploying the S-400 system to Novaya Zemlya (Melino & Conley, 2020). Russia's military modernization across the Kola Peninsula serves as Northern Fleet headquarters and as the primary home of Russia's sea-based nuclear deterrent, indicating the growing importance of the Arctic to Russia's power projection capability. In June 2020, the first of Russia's fourth-generation Borei-A-class submarines (SSBN) entered service with the Northern Fleet (Starchak, 2020). While others worry about the ongoing Russian military *build-ups*, President Putin's March 2020 announcement of *Basic Principles 2035* portrays Russia's own concerns over the increasing military presence of foreign countries and the related growing conflict potential in the Arctic as challenges for its national security (President of Russia, 2020, March 5). The document states that U.S. activities in the Arctic and North Atlantic pose a direct challenge to Russia's military and maritime doctrines (Klimenko, 2020). In addition, the National Security Council of Russia has established a special commission that promotes Russian national interests in the Arctic, including an analysis of the military-political situation in the region, which is led by former prime minister and acting Deputy Head of the National Security Council Dmitry Medvedev (The Barents Observer, 2020, August 26). As a response to its security concerns, the Russian government has developed rules for the passage of foreign warships on the NSR, requiring that foreign military vessels notify Russia of their plans 45 days in advance and take Russian pilots aboard (Aliyev, 2019), which may escalate the mistrust and suspicion between Russia and NATO, ultimately affecting the commercial development of the NSR. Hence, how to reduce Arctic military and security tensions, to ensure that the Arctic is an exception area for confrontation and competition, and to maintain the peace, stability, and sustainable development in the region have become targets for all stakeholders. An ability to use the climate change as an instrument to restore consensus on Arctic exceptionalism remains as one of the top priorities.

The Changing Expectation on Arctic Cooperation Impacted by the COVID-19 Pandemic

The Covid-19 pandemic has had an impact on relations between major powers, international energy market and global trade, Arctic scientific research, etc. According to the IMF, nearly $90 billion in investments have *flown out* of emerging economies during the outbreak, and more than 90 countries so far have applied for assistance from IMF's funds (CNBC, 2020). The WTO indicates that world GDP could shrink by as much as 8.8% in 2020 and expand by 5.9% in 2021 (Bloomberg, 2020). A sharp decline in domestic consumption, tourism and business travel, spillovers from weaker demand to other sectors and economies, supply-side disruptions to production and trade, and shifts in health care expenditure are some of the channels through which the COVID-19 pandemic has affected the demand side of the global energy market. As a result, greater uncertainty has accrued regarding the future of the Arctic energy and shipping industry.

Although global shipping is not significantly affected by the downturn of energy markets and the total volume of transportation via NSR in 2019 reached a historical record, figures from the Russian Association of Sea Trade Ports show that north Russian seaports and terminals from January to July 2020 handled 10.2% fewer goods than in the same period last year (Staalesen, 2020, August 28). Recently, Novatek, the major user of the NSR, postponed for two years the commissioning of Ob LNG II. This was to be the first stage of the plant, with a planned capacity of 2.5 mln tons of LNG per year that was to be put into service in 2024 (The Arctic, 2020). With this postponement, projections for transportation demand weakened further.

On the other hand, due to the variability of ice conditions, lack of navigation and communication facilities, trans-Arctic shipments still constitute only a minor share of current Arctic shipping. A total of 37 ships carrying around 700,000 tons of cargo conducted trans-Arctic voyages connecting European and Asian markets in 2019 (Staalesen, 2020, February 28). In addition, the Mediterranean Shipping Company (MSC) has joined fellow shipping giants CMA CGM and Hapag-Lloyd in refusing to use the NSR due to concerns about how increased shipping activity in the Arctic could impact the environment (Taylor, 2019). As the major body responsible for the development of NSR, ROSATOM has now officially requested the Ministry of Transport to lower ambitions by 25%, setting up 60 mln tons of cargo as the new shipping target for NSR instead of 80 mln tons by 2024 (РБК, 2020). Even this revised target for Arctic shipping volume may not be met due to new uncertainties, unrealistic expectations, and new forecasts regarding the NSR. According to latest research, international use of the NSR has increased over the past ten years—but not in the way and scope many had expected, transits between the Pacific and the Atlantic have only seen modest growth and Arctic transits have not become a significant component in international shipping (Gunnarsson, 2021). These shifting expectations and projections attracted attention from all potential users, raising concerns about the reliability of long-term planning strategies.

Meanwhile, Arctic research faced unprecedented disruptions due to pandemic, which has brought polar scientific activity to a near-standstill. International Arctic projects on climate change, oceanography, weather, biodiversity, and other topics have been postponed; the scientific community finds Arctic research capabilities severely limited by travel bans; lack in long-time data collection, which is crucial for understanding the evolution of Arctic, may result in plenty of negative effects on food and water security, fisheries, safety and other aspects of human life, etc.; Logistical challenges for the projects at the Arctic seas (MOSAiC mission). The gap year in Arctic research and dialogue will resonate for decades across Arctic science discipline and governance process, through policy decisions, and into economic investments.

CHINA'S PRACTICE AND BASIC CONCEPTION IN ARCTIC COOPERATION

Unfortunately, many of China's moves relating to the Arctic have been met with suspicion in light of its population size and its status as one of the largest consumers of oil and natural gas products. The *China threat* has become a hot topic that is highlighted in the media worldwide, its increased prominence in the region has prompted concerns from Arctic states over its long-term strategic objectives, including possible military deployment (Reuters, 2018, January 26). Although China is still actively engaged in Arctic cooperation with all Arctic countries and related stakeholders, China's funds, markets, and proficiency relating to infrastructure construction and resource exploitation are highly valued by some Arctic countries.

1. *Sino-Russian Arctic cooperation as the best practice*

Among all Arctic cooperation that China has participated in, Sino-Russian Arctic cooperation can be regarded as the best practice. During Russian President Vladimir Putin's state visit to China in June 2018, China and Russia issued a joint statement, which proposed strengthening China–Russia sustainable development cooperation in the Arctic, including supporting cooperation among the relevant departments, institutions, and enterprises in fields such as scientific research, joint implementation of transport infrastructure and energy projects, developing the potential for the Northern Sea Route (NSR), tourism and ecology. For the first time the statement defined *sustainable development* as the overall framework for China-Russia Arctic cooperation, which is the consensus derived from important realistic basis.

First, the consistency and complementarity of interest demands. Promoting the comprehensive social and economic development in the Russian Arctic region, promoting the development of science and technology related to the Arctic, building modern information and communication facilities, protecting the ecological security of the Arctic and border security are main interests of Russia for its international cooperation in the Arctic. These reflect not only the rising value of the Arctic in terms of strategy, economy, scientific research, environmental protection, sea routes, and resources in recent years, but also a strategic orientation made by Russia in the context of the globalization and the coexistence among major powers, aimed for improvement of its importance to global economy and modernization of energy industry. In China's view, issues such as the climate change, environment, scientific research, utilization of shipping routes, resource exploration and exploitation, security, and global governance in the Arctic are "vital to the existence and development of all countries and humanity, and directly affect the interests of non-Arctic States including China" (State Council Information Office of China, 2018), which forms a unity of acknowledging on the significance, goals, and values of Sino-Russian Arctic cooperation. As the largest Arctic country in terms of geography and population, Russia is the most important partner for China in the Arctic affairs, Sino-Russian Arctic cooperation could also be an opportunity for Russia to solve the *bottleneck* problem in terms of funds, technologies, and resources for Arctic development. Participation in Arctic sea routes, infrastructure investment, and energy projects fall within the scope of plans for deepening pragmatic cooperation between China and Russia and the framework of the BRI maritime cooperation, two countries have overlaps and complementary interests for Arctic cooperation.

Second, the feasibility of achieving all-level cooperation. At the political level, the two governments and leaders have reached mutual trust in the Arctic cooperation. For instance, authorities of two countries have held the regular dialogue on Arctic affairs since 2013, and incorporated the contents of Arctic sea routes cooperation in the joint statement. In 2015, leaders signed the *Joint Statement of the People's Republic of China and the Russian Federation on the Construction of the Silk Road Economic Belt and the Construction of the Eurasian Economic Union* in Moscow, officially proposing the goal of *docking cooperation*, and in the same year in the Joint Communiqué of the 20th Regular Meeting between Head of governments, proposed to strengthen the cooperation in the development and utilization of the NSR and carry out research on Arctic shipping (Ministry of Foreign Affairs of China, 2015). From 2017, President Xi Jinping expressed China's willingness to cooperate with Russia on Arctic sea routes and shipping several times. At present, the transportation departments of China and Russia are negotiating the Memorandum of Understanding on Maritime Cooperation between China and Russia in Polar Waters, constantly improving the policy and legal basis for Arctic cooperation between China and Russia (*People's Daily*, 2018).

At the commercial level, China remains major foreign investor and force for LNG and infrastructure projects in Russian Arctic (Кутузова, 2021). For instance, about 70 projects of the NSR will be covered by the $9.5 billion credit agreement signed with the China Development Bank (Staalesen, 2018, June 12). The National Export–Import Bank of China and the China Development Bank have provided $10.7 billion to the Yamal LNG project—one of the largest Arctic energy and infrastructure complex in Russia's Arctic region using the South Tambey Field as a resource base—with an output capacity of around 16.5 mln tons per year by 2019, and expected to have a total investment of $26.9 billion. Silk Road Fund has also provided a $1.2 billion loan for the project (Novatek, 2013). The field's proven and probable reserves are estimated at 926 billion cubic meters, making it the largest Arctic producer of LNG (Yamal LNG, 2021). In addition, NOVATEK signed in April this year with China National Oil and Gas Exploration and Development Company Ltd. (CNOCD, a wholly owned subsidiary of China National Petroleum Corporation) a binding agreement to enter the Arctic LNG 2 project. As part of Saint-Petersburg International Economic Forum 2019, NOVATEK has signed the Share Purchase Agreement with China National Offshore Oil Corporation (CNOOC). Under these agreements, two Chinese companies will each acquire a 10% participation interest in Arctic LNG 2 project. The Arctic LNG 2 project envisages the construction of three LNG trains at 6.6 mln tons per annum each, based on the hydrocarbon resources of the Utrenneye field, which under the

Russian classification reserves totaled 13,835 mln barrels of oil equivalent (Novatek, 2019). With the construction of the Arctic LNG 2 project, the demand for construction and transportation of Arctic LNG projects is expected to continue to increase. It is foreseeable that Chinese shipping companies will continue to be important investors to Arctic LNG projects regarding ship leasing, logistic infrastructure, shipbuilding, etc.

Regarding ports and railways infrastructure, China represents a key partner in the implementation of relevant infrastructure projects, including the construction of the Belkomur railway line and the Arkhangelsk deep-water seaport (The Barents Observer, 2017). In 2015, China Poly Group Corporation as large central state-owned enterprise signed a framework agreement with Russian Interregional JSC Belkomur on the railway integrated project, which included the construction of a new railway 1252 km long, linking Central Russia to Arkhangelsk in the Arctic, and series of ports and resources development projects along the railway. In addition, the Poly Group and COSCO Shipping are considering to invest $550 mln in the construction of the deep-water port of Arkhangelsk (Nilsen, 2016). China Poly Group Corporation is reportedly set to invest $300 mln in port facilities in Russia's Murmansk, a major transportation junction within the Arctic Circle, offering a positive signal that China may be taking a more active role in the development of the NSR from Northern Europe to East Asia via the Arctic.

At the scientific level, China has actively carried out Arctic scientific research cooperation with Russia in the multilateral frameworks such as the International Arctic Science Council and the Arctic Council in recent years, to strengthen scientific exchanges on the understanding of the Arctic. In order to deepening Sino-Russian scientific cooperation in the Arctic, the two countries launched the first Arctic joint expedition—a joint expedition of scientists on the Chukchi Sea and the Eastern Siberian Sea in the Russian Arctic Ocean exclusive economic zone—in August 2016 (*China Daily*, 2018), conducting a comprehensive survey on the Arctic Ocean has become a historic breakthrough in the cooperation between two countries in the Arctic.

Third, the necessity of finding new growth pole for pragmatic cooperation. It is worth noting that although China-Russia pragmatic cooperation has made great achievements in recent years, however, equivalent boost of economic and trade partnership has not been fully stimulated by the high-level political-security mutual trust and cooperation, bilateral trade consists relatively limited share of total foreign trade of

China. With the continuous development of globalization, the world economy and the global trade pattern have undergone significant changes, exploring the new growth pole of Sino-Russian pragmatic cooperation has become an important mission for both sides. From medium and long-term perspective, the demand and pragmatic cooperation between China and Russia are no longer limited to the relationship between energy consumers and producers, the trade structure is no longer confined to traditional manufacturing and energy resources, and the form of trade is not limited to unilateral investments, it requires adaptation to the current global economic situation, and consistency with the regional environment and of domestic agendas of both countries regarding goals, priorities, and capabilities. Promoting Sino-Russian Arctic sustainable development cooperation with the joint effort on transportation infrastructure and energy projects will not only maintain traditional energy cooperation, but through Yamal LNG and other infrastructure projects which practice innovations on investment models, equity structures, profit sharing methods, will formulate common interests from multiple dimensions, develop new model of mutual beneficial cooperation with shared risks, promote "embedded" development model and win–win results.

Fourth, Russia's long-term strategic planning has become a booster for Sino-Russian Arctic sustainable cooperation. In December 2019, Russia published the *Comprehensive plan for infrastructure development of the NSR for the period 2020–2035* (Comprehensive Plan 2035). The document covers 11 topics for development along the NSR, including: port infrastructure and terminals; search and rescue; navigational and hydrographic support; development of icebreaking capabilities; stimulation of cargo traffic and international transit shipment increases; aviation and railway network development; safety and communications network development; electricity generating capacity to support infrastructure; training and skills development; domestic shipbuilding for Arctic shipping; and ecological safety. On March 6, 2020, President Vladimir Putin approved the *Basic Principles of Russian Federation State Policy in the Arctic to 2035* (Basic Principles 2035), which defines Russia's Arctic interests, goals, and mechanisms of implementation (President of Russia, 2020, March 5). On May 7, the Ministry for the Development of the Russian Far East and the Arctic submitted to the Russian Government a draft of the *Arctic Development Strategy until 2035* (Strategy 2035) (Министерство РФ по развитию Дальнего Востока и Арктики, 2020), which determines the main directions and tasks of the development of the Russian Arctic zone, including development of the NSR.

Enhancing the support capability, commercial attractiveness, and the linkage of inland and port infrastructure are priorities for future development of the NSR. According to Comprehensive Plan 2035, Russia is aiming for a three-stage development of the NSR: Firstly, by 2024, the plan envisages accelerated development of year-round extraction, refining, and transportation of raw materials from ports of the Kara Sea to the west, assigning funds to renovate the icebreaker fleet, and modernizing port infrastructure. Secondly, by 2030, Russia plans to build dozens more ice class vessels, including at least 13 heavy icebreakers, nine of which would be nuclear-powered (TACC, 2019), to provide year-round navigation throughout the NSR and increase cargo carried along the NSR to 90 mln tons. Thirdly, by 2035, it anticipates the creation of an international latitudinal transport corridor (Analytical Center for the Government of the Russian Federation, 2019). The abovementioned documents appear to be a response to accumulated criticism and uncertainty related to the NSR, especially in the areas of SAR, navigational safety, communications, ecology, and predicting weather and ice conditions (Middleton, 2020).

To strengthen the domestic consensus on NSR development, Russia seeks to increase the local development dividend to respond to the social demands of local residents with a comprehensive infrastructure system. For instance, the development plan includes a mechanism for streamlining the social infrastructure called the Arctic Social Development Fund. This will make it possible to return up to 50% of taxes derived from new investment projects to the budgets of Arctic territories and to use these sums for building or renovating schools, hospitals, and kindergartens (The Arctic, 2020). Other examples include: construction of the Obusskaya-Sabetta railway transport corridor, which would connect the seaport and LNG terminal in the northern coast of the Yamal peninsula; reconstruction of airports in the Yamalo-Nenets Autonomous Region, the Chukotka Autonomous Region, and the Republic of Sakha Yakutia; and the launch of the Arkhangelsk-Perm of the Belkomur Railway Project to establish a three-dimensional (Air-Land-Sea) transportation network around the NSR.

As one of the major commercial users and investors of the NSR and related energy projects, Chinese COSCO Shipping Specialized Carriers Co., LTD. completed 31 voyages via NSR/Northeast Passage from 2013 to 2019 and continues to boost numbers of regular transits (see Table 1). Sovcomflot and a joint venture of COSCO Shipping Group and Mitsui OSK Lines (MOL) will own and operate twelve ships ordered by

Table 1 Shipping statistics of COSCO shipping via NSR/Northeast Passage from 2013 to 2019

	Voyage number	Total reduced sail voyage (N.M.)	Total reduced sailing time (days)	Total reduced carbon emission (Tons)
2013	1	2500	11.5	841
2015	2	7000	23	1683
2016	6	32,137	108	12,704
2017	5	25,313	81	6288
2018	8	26,400	82	6366
2019	9	31,457	90	7790
Total	31	124,807	395.5	35,673

Source The authors' estimate based on data provided by the COSCO Shipping Specialized Carriers Co., LTD

NOVATEK for Arctic LNG 2 and Ob LNG projects. The implementation of Russia's ambitious NSR infrastructure plan would be unrealistic without further attracting external investments and deepening its cooperation with countries outside the region, primarily with China. Russia is planning to develop transparent rules and intensify international cooperation to meet its national interests listed it its Arctic 2035 strategies (ТАСС, 2020, Июль 22). Although detailed rules of the standard are not yet clear, Russia's policy orientation to expand the scope and content of international cooperation of Arctic development involving Asian partners such as China, Japan, South Korea, Singapore, and India to contribute to the implementation of Comprehensive Plan 2035 has become more obvious.

2. *Jointly building the Polar Silk Road as the public good for Arctic cooperation*

In response to the opportunities and challenges brought about by the Arctic changes, relevant countries have introduced and updated their development strategies, covering various aspects of Arctic shipping. For instance, one of the principles of the Icelandic Arctic Strategy is to make full use of employment opportunities created by changes in the Arctic region (Ministry of Foreign Affairs of Iceland, 2011), especially focusing on opening up new Arctic shipping routes which connect the North

Atlantic, the Arctic Ocean, and the Pacific. Sweden is calling for efficient, multilateral cooperation on the Arctic, aiming to prevent and limit the negative environmental impact potentially caused by the opening up of new shipping routes and sea areas in the Arctic and contribute to safer and greener shipping (Ministry of Foreign Affairs of Sweden, 2011). One of the priorities of the Finland's Arctic strategy is continue to maintain Finland's position as a leading expert in the Arctic maritime industry and shipping and keep Finnish companies closely involved in development projects in Arctic sea areas (Prime Minister's Office of Finland, 2013). Coastal states of the Arctic ocean are more focused on utilization of new shipping routes and update of related transport infrastructures, especially when Russia has defined use of the Northern Sea Route as a national single transport communication of the Russian Federation in the Arctic as one of its national interests in the Arctic (ARCTIS Database, 2008).

In this context, the idea of joint establishment of the Polar Silk Road (PSR) was first appeared in the Chinese government's document on the international cooperation on the Maritime Silk Road (Xinhuanet, 2017, June 20), which gradually developed during the practice of the Belt and Road initiative, and was fully explained in the White Paper on China's Arctic Policy published by Information office of State Department in early 2018. The idea at beginning has been expressed in mixed definition, including the Ice Silk Road (China Plus, 2017), Silk Road on Ice (Xinhuanet, 2017, November 1) when President Xi Jinping met with Russian leader, and Finland (Ministry of Foreign Affairs of China, 2019). Based on abovementioned policy and pragmatic practices, China has formulated its own understanding of the PSR.

The PSR is an international initiative which refers to specific region, involving the cooperation in Arctic's shipping routes and coastal areas. Although there is absence of the official definition, it is generally believed that the PSR refers to a shipping route that pass through the Arctic Circle and connect the three major economic centers of North America, East Asia, and Western Europe. Due to current natural environmental conditions, the development of the PSR focuses mainly on NSR and NEP. It focuses on Arctic's geopolitical, economic, and social connections to the world by joint efforts by Arctic nations, international organizations, and other stakeholders for Arctic governance. According to the conditions for the development and utilization of Arctic shipping routes, the PSR is currently more concentrated in the development of the NEP, connecting East Asian countries with European partners.

374 L. ZHAO

The PSR reflects the common policy orientation of Arctic states and other stakeholders. In particular for commercial opportunities of development of the Arctic sea routes, while countering enormous ecological and environment challenges with the increase of human activities. The possibility of commercial use of Arctic shipping routes may significantly shorten the traditional voyage, further enrich the international shipping network, and promote economic and trade relationship of relevant countries and region as whole.

Hence, many Arctic countries see the PSR also as an opportunity and give positive responses. Finish President Sauli Niinisto believes that "the Polar Silk Road is not only a plan for more roads, railways and shipping routes, but also a vision for promoting understanding among different peoples" (Xinhuanet, 2017, March 7). Iceland's Foreign Minister, Mr. Thordarson underlined that his "government follows carefully and with interest the Belt and Road Initiative, including the 'Silk Road on Ice', which is focused on opening up new shipping routes through the Arctic" (Thordarsson, 2018). Russian President Vladimir Putin has expressed that Russia is consistently upgrading maritime, railway, and road infrastructure, investing significant resources into improvements to the NEP in order for it to "become a global competitive transport artery", and more importantly to calling for "completely reconfigure transportation on the Eurasian continent", by putting "infrastructure projects within the EAEU and the One Belt, One Road initiative in conjunction with the Northeast Passage" (Putin, 2017).

The PSR is not a *exclusive good* of a individual country, but a new platform for policy coordination and science, industrial, social collaboration among various countries. China advocates multilateral cooperation to jointly build the PSR and focus on the forward-looking investments, focusing on the infrastructure construction and green development to achieve a balance between development and protection of the Arctic. China's participation to the PSR is also a proactive response to the expectations of some countries, regarding China's relative advantages in capital, technology, and talent on the development and utilization of the Arctic.

The PSR serves as one of the most pragmatic platforms of bilateral and multilateral cooperation between Arctic and Non-Arctic states. Although China's perception of changes in the Arctic is direct and rapid, as a Non-Arctic coastal state located beyond the Arctic circle, bilateral or multilateral cooperation based on respect of the sovereignty, sovereign rights, and jurisdiction enjoyed by the Arctic States in this region, respect the relevant marine management policies and willingness of Arctic coastal states are important prerequisite for jointly building the PSR. In practice, China attaches great importance to bilateral cooperation with the Arctic countries, conducts bilateral consultations on Arctic affairs with all Arctic countries, and establishes regular dialogue mechanisms with all Arctic states. In addition, China, Japan, South Korea, and other countries have carried out discussions on Arctic shipping issues, promoting the establishment of equal mutual trust and mutually beneficial cooperation among potential shipping route users and investors, China also supports platforms such as *Arctic: Territory of Dialogue*, *Arctic Circle Assembly*, *Arctic Frontiers*, *China-Nordic Arctic Research Center*, in promoting exchanges and cooperation among the stakeholders, to explore a new model of Arctic international cooperation involving multi-stakeholders.

The PSR is an integral part of China's Arctic policy and an extension of the Belt and Road Initiative. As the major global trade partner and a potential user, cooperation on Arctic shipping routes is undoubtedly becoming one of the policy priorities of China. Starting from 2013, Chinese companies have begun to explore the commercial opportunities associated with Arctic shipping routes. This policy orientation has been demonstrated by the Vision for Maritime Cooperation under the Belt and Road Initiative and the Arctic Policy issued by China, where clearly proposed the construction of the "blue economic passage is also envisioned leading up to Europe via the Arctic Ocean" (Xinhuanet, 2017, June 20). The construction of the blue economic passage and eventually the PSR is not only concentrated on maritime interconnection, but also to promote the free flow of marine knowledge, culture, technology, and talents, advocates peaceful, green, innovative, and win–win maritime cooperation, and deepens global significance and humanitarian care of the BRI.

3. *China's policy orientation for Arctic cooperation*

Arctic sustainable cooperation enriches China's diplomatic practices in the new frontiers. Chinese President Xi Jinping holds that guided by the principle of peace, sovereignty, inclusiveness, and shared governance, we should turn the deep sea, the polar regions, the outer space, and the internet into new frontiers for cooperation rather than a wrestling ground for competition (Jinping, 2017). China advocates the observation of relevant international treaties and general international law and full respect for the Arctic countries' sovereignty, sovereign rights, and jurisdiction in the Arctic, and also expects other countries in pursuing their own interests to fully respect China's lawful rights and concerns in the region. China does not pursue equal rights with the Arctic countries when advancing Arctic cooperation, but stresses reasonableness, lawfulness, and taking the interests of all participants into account. China advocates integrating concepts and practices that advanced all countries in Arctic exploration, protection, and development, coordinating the various countries' interests and development needs, and exploring a new model of international cooperation in the Arctic in which all stakeholders participate.

Arctic sustainable cooperation guides the pluralist trend of international governance. China is not an Arctic country, but it has direct and immediate awareness regarding the changes in the Arctic. On a geopolitical level, the competition among Arctic countries reverberates on the entire regional and international order, and the potential militarization of the Arctic would have far-reaching influence on regional peace and stability. On the geoeconomic level, the Arctic development has an increasingly significant impact on fields such as international shipping, biological and non-biological resources, as well as tourism. As a major emerging market economy and trading power, China is naturally a potential user and important participant in above areas. In terms of ecology, the natural environmental system of the Arctic area is closely related to the functioning of China's own ecological system, affecting its stability as well as the agricultural production security. Environmental changes in the Arctic may have a negative effect on China's climate system and ecological security. Therefore, in building Arctic-related global governance mechanisms, China spares no effort in playing a constructive role, actively participating as an observer in the Arctic Council and its relevant working groups. China also takes the initiative in international forums including the Arctic Circle Assembly, the Arctic Frontier, the Arctic—Territory of Dialogue Forum, has established dialogue mechanisms with all Arctic countries, and is proactively exploring the model of China-Nordic Arctic cooperation (CNARC). China's participation in Arctic cooperation has bolstered the transformation of Arctic governance from a regional responsibility to a global mission, and contributed to the creation of a cooperation model featuring complementarity and connectivity. It has expanded consensus of parties concerned to achieve win–win outcomes, and boosted plural Arctic governance characterized by multiple levels, diversity, combination of hard and soft elements, as well as inclusiveness and coordination, instead of being exclusive and dominated by one or several countries, or driven by a single agenda, mechanism or a small group.

Arctic sustainable cooperation expands maritime cooperation along the Belt and Road initiative. For China, the comprehensive opening of the Arctic shipping route in the future would dramatically reduce traditional sailing distance, further enriching international shipping layout and driving economic and trade development of countries and regions along the route. Normalizing the operation of Northeast Passage not only helps China develop its shipping routes, but also contributes to expanding the connotation of the Belt and Road Initiative and enlarging the share of made-in-China products and equipment in the European market. The operation of Northeast Passage plays a prominent role in connecting China's northern ports with Europe economically. Therefore, China has further expanded the scope and connotation of cooperation in developing Arctic passages, and proposed building three key blue economic passages including one leading up to Europe via the Arctic Ocean. With the theme of *sharing a blue space and developing the blue economy* (Xinhuanet, 2017, June 20), China stresses promoting the utilization of Northeast Passage by multilateral participation. However, it should be noted that China is not an Arctic coastal state, and an important premise for cooperation is respecting the relevant maritime management policies and development interests of Russia and other Arctic coastal states.

Arctic sustainable cooperation prioritizes knowledge accumulation and scientific research. The Arctic is no doubt rich in resources, but is also the region that receives the most direct impact of climate change, climate change is causing major changes in the Arctic, threatening the Arctic ecosystem, including changes in species range, permafrost loss, and destruction of the marine food chain, which demands of utilization and development in a sustainable manner are more urgent than other places. Oil and natural gas, fishery resources and other *Arctic Treasure* are stored in a fragile environment and harsh production conditions. Therefore, in addition to the exploration of Arctic resources and new shipping routes, all human activities regarding resource exploration require environmental risk, production safety risk, and ecological sensitivity assessments. In this sense, the PSR should reflect common exploration of humankind for accumulate knowledge, responsible action, and joint response to global challenges, to understand how climate change and human activities pose obstacles to the migration and reproduction of Arctic species, and how environmental pollution such as oil spills can affect fragile marine ecology. The acquisition of knowledge and the response based on scientific researches are necessary for the Arctic development.

Besides conducting research on climate change trends and ecological assessments, innovation in both the natural and social sciences can be promoted by strengthening research on Arctic politics, economics, law, society, history, culture, and the management of human activities. In addition, sustainable development in the Arctic will need to balance development and protection at the international level and catalyze bilateral and multilateral cooperation across various sectors—e.g., the economy, environment, health, and infrastructure. To this end, Arctic states, non-Arctic states, and nonstate actors should coordinate their long-term policies on technical standards and investment.

Arctic sustainable cooperation promotes green technology solutions and humanistic concerns. Technology serves humanity. The exceptionality of the PSR and Arctic region as whole raising the demand of green economy and green solutions require both *economic development* and *green technology* roadmap. Although the economic benefits driven by the opening up of shipping routes will increase the economic development rate, extreme weather conditions such as low temperatures, magnetic storms will pose a threat to equipment and personnel safety. The core area of Arctic technological innovation needs to focus on communications, navigation, infrastructure, and logistics, in particular on various scientific monitoring and detection technologies, engineering techniques suitable for Arctic environment, shipbuilding and navigation, resource utilization technologies in permafrost regions and fragile environments.

China attaches importance to both land-based and marine-based cooperation, promotes the interaction between the inland economy and the marine economy through infrastructure connectivity, also encourages the development of technology and equipment that pays attention to environmental protection capabilities and innovative elements in the construction of Arctic infrastructure, focuses on sustainable energy system, including wind power, ocean tidal energy, geothermal energy, and hydropower, strengthening clean energy cooperation with Arctic countries, exploring the supply and utilization of geothermal and wind energy, achieving low-carbon development.

Promoting interconnectivity of the Arctic is an important indicator for innovative solutions. To achieve a balance between development and protection, China is committed to green solutions of infrastructure construction and digital connection in the region. Norway is actively considering the possibility of greater involvement by Chinese Arctic shipping stakeholders (Youchang & Shuhui, 2018), the Arctic Corridor project—railway project that would connect the city of Rovaniemi in northern Finland with the Norwegian port of Kirkenes—could be well-suited for cooperation under the PSR framework, parties concerned have come to China to discuss the possibility to cooperate with Chinese companies and the project has a brochure in Chinese (Arctic Corridor, 2019). In addition, Chinese government and enterprises are involved in Arctic cooperation in submarine cable construction. The Ministry of Industry and Information Technology of China and China Telecom are working with the Finland on trans-Arctic submarine cable project—a 10,500-km fiber-optic maritime cable link across the Arctic Circle—and will be joined by Russian, Japanese, and Norwegian partners (Buchanan, 2018).

The Arctic is also home to four mln people, including indigenous populations and other residents highly dependent on the Arctic ecosystem. Accelerated ice melting eases access to resources, aiding the economic development of indigenous communities, but increased offshore and onshore commercial activities endanger the traditions and lifestyles of indigenous peoples, who want to preserve the environment and develop it using traditional knowledge. The cooperation needs to focus on the UN 2030 Sustainable Development Goals and elimination of digital gaps, by developing effective and convenient transportation and communication system, accelerating infrastructure and digital network construction, promoting people's well-being and economic development, and helping to meet the Arctic local social development education and health, language, and cultural needs.

The Common Agenda for Arctic Cooperation in the Post-Pandemic Era

Seek the greatest common divisor within the framework of the Arctic Council. With the return of the climate-led Arctic policy orientation of the U.S., the Arctic Council is gradually eliminating the negative shadows of geopolitics and competition between major powers during the Trump administration and returning to its role as the leading intergovernmental forum for Arctic cooperation.

At the 12th Arctic Council Ministerial meeting in Reykjavik, the Arctic States reaffirmed the Council's commitment to maintain a peaceful, prosperous, and sustainable Arctic region, and addressed the importance of immediately addressing climate change in the Arctic. In recognition of the Council's 25th anniversary, the Ministers adopted Council's first-ever *Strategic Plan* that reflects the shared values, goals, and joint aspirations of the Arctic States and Indigenous Permanent Participants (Arctic Council, 2021). Considering that the current competitive situation among major powers is difficult to reverse in the short term, Arctic States and other stakeholders of Arctic affairs could seek for consensus on Arctic Council's 2030 development goals including Arctic Climate; Healthy and Resilient; Arctic Ecosystems; Healthy; Arctic Marine Environment; Sustainable Social Development; Sustainable Economic Development; Knowledge and Communications; Stronger Arctic Council, to ease conflicts by promoting low politics dialogue and coordination.

Mediate the contradiction between accelerated use of *energy dividends* and the demands to *freeze* Arctic resources exploitation. Affected by the anticipated decline in global demand for hydrocarbons, the advancement of the *carbon peak* and *carbon neutrality* targets of China (Reuters, 2020, September 22) and major economies, and the decline in the political attributes of oil and gas products, Russia's *strategic anxiety* on Arctic energy development has risen, may advocate international cooperation in Arctic development, accelerate the realization of Arctic oil and gas *capacity peak* during its Chairmanship of Arctic Council, and to promote domestic strategic optimization and incentive measures. As proposed by the Chairman of the Russian State Duma's Energy Committee, Russia needs to seize the time window when global demand for hydrocarbons is relatively stable before 2040, use new technologies do its utmost to increase the oil and gas production (Ведомости, 2019). For instance, in 2020, Gazprom Neft has maintained the pace of development in the Arctic. Production at fields beyond the Arctic Circle accounted for 31% of the company's total hydrocarbon volume (Gazprom Neft, 2021), which shows that Russia is continuously accelerating the progress of energy extraction in the Arctic at practical level. Meanwhile, initiatives regarding the strengthening of the green standards for Arctic development investment, the implementation of more environmental protection responsibilities and prudent development plans have been echoed by many Arctic countries, including the U.S. President Biden put a hold on oil and gas drilling in the Arctic just hours after being inaugurated, signed an executive order placing a temporary moratorium on all federal activities related to oil and gas leases in the Arctic National Wildlife Refuge (The White House, 2021).

The contradiction between development and protection of the Arctic may be intensified. Unilateral actions by state or nonstate actors could affect the surrounding states and indigenous communities. The core of Arctic sustainable development cooperation is to find the balance between development and protection at the international level (macro-sustainability) and to catalyze bilateral and multilateral cooperation across various sectors (micro-sustainability); in general, to promote sustainability as the guiding principle for cooperation, while balancing protection and utilization.

Accelerate the policy evaluation and strategy update, to formulate the priority list of Arctic cooperation. On the one hand, Arctic research faces unprecedented disruptions due to pandemic. The scientific community finds Arctic research capabilities severely limited by travel bans and its own trepidation of becoming vectors transmitting COVID-19. The consequences of the prolonged gap in field research will resonate for decades across scientific disciplines, through policy decisions, and into economic investments. It is not just an immediate danger for the Arctic, will have lasting effects on communities as the current health, food security, and economic issues become exacerbated.

Relevant countries could coordinate at the multilateral and bilateral levels, to resume scientific cooperation which was interrupted by the pandemic. As the most promising area of Arctic low politics, interested parties should prioritize joint research and data-sharing. This can occur under the frameworks of the International Arctic Science Committee, Arctic Council working groups, the University of the Arctic, and the Agreement on Enhancing International Arctic Scientific Cooperation. Formulating and implementing mandatory environmental standards and technical requirements based on solid scientific basis is essential to understanding, utilizing, and protecting the Arctic. Besides conducting research on climate change trends and ecological impact assessments, innovation in both natural and social sciences can be promoted by strengthening social science research on Arctic politics, economics, law, society, history, culture, and the management of human activities.

On the other hand, a sharp decline in domestic consumption, supply-side disruptions to production and trade has affected the demand side in the global energy, shipping, and trade market. As the result, greater uncertainty has accrued regarding the future of commercial use of the Arctic. In light of the mid- to long-term demand side changes in the global energy, trade, and shipping markets in the post-pandemic era, it is crucial to adjust the expected progress and project planning of the Arctic oil and gas, biological resources, and shipping development cooperation.

Enhance regional security cooperation by reestablishing dialogue platforms. As militarization persists in the Arctic moving forward, a space for constructive dialogue must be established for the region. During the Russian Chairmanship of the Arctic Council from 2021 to 2023, with increased potential for conflict in the Arctic and no established or still functioning institutional framework for dialogue on security issues in the region, should Russia use its position to expand its mandate and include security issues remain as the key question for all stakeholders. However, scholars argue that the Arctic Council is unlikely to be a useful arena for such discussion. The Arctic Council functions best as a tool to maintain the Arctic's status as a low-tension area and to provide space for cooperation and dialogue between states that have a vested interest in mitigating the potentially disastrous impact of climate change (Boone, 2021).

Therefore, a more realistic approach is to restore the function of the existing dialogue mechanism as soon as possible. Notwithstanding geopolitical realities that are incompatible to sustainable development of the Arctic, security concerns reasonably derive from the national interests of all Arctic states, especially the U.S. and Russia. Restarting the Arctic Chiefs of Defense Staff Conference (ACDSC), Arctic Security Forces Roundtable (ASFR), Arctic Coast Guard Forum (ACGF) which have been frozen since 2014 or maintaining dialogue on regional security matters at necessary level could enhance the management of regional security problems.

Strive for a consensus-based decision-making process. The existing multitiered Arctic governance structures should be strengthened. At the global level, international conventions regulate non-geographical or jurisdictional issues, such as the protection of biodiversity and maritime ecosystems. At the regional level, the Arctic Council— comprising eight Arctic states as members, six indigenous organizations as permanent participants, with non-Arctic states, intergovernmental and inter-parliamentary organizations, and nongovernmental organizations

(NGOs) as observers—provides more practical and legally binding agreements, such as on maritime search and rescue (Arctic Council, 2011), marine oil pollution preparedness and response (Arctic Council, 2013), and scientific cooperation (Arctic Council, 2017). The Barents Euro-Arctic Cooperation, Northern Forum, and the Arctic: Territory of Dialogue, as well as other platforms facilitate more opportunities for coordination. At the subregional level, under the Ilulissat Declaration (The Ilulissat Declaration, 2008) governance model, the five Arctic coastal states (Canada, Denmark, Norway, Russia, and the U.S.) discuss Arctic maritime issues exclusively among themselves and seek limited dialogue on issues of common interest with other members of the Arctic Council (Finland, Iceland, and Sweden), non-Arctic states, indigenous peoples, and other parties. Although states are within their rights to act unilaterally on matters of national interest within their own territorial seas, EEZs, and continental shelves, they should collaborate more broadly on matters in the Arctic that qualify as public goods. These include climate change, Arctic wildlife, scientific exploration, potential international shipping corridors, and the preservation of Arctic indigenous peoples' traditions and cultures. Consensus-based policy- and decision-making at intergovernmental levels can improve cooperation on these matters.

Coordinate the desires and capabilities of the Arctic Eight with other stakeholders where possible. Although the Arctic does not conceptually qualify as a global commons, it manifests complex sovereignty issues, as it encompasses areas and resources within and outside national jurisdictions. Therefore, it would be nearly impossible to formulate a unified Arctic treaty system, similar to the one that exists for the Antarctic. Arctic governance should be based on respect for the sovereign rights and jurisdictions of Arctic countries while taking into account the concerns of non-Arctic states and nonstate actors in accordance with relevant international treaties and international law. On the one hand, voices of all relevant parties should be valued while setting the agenda and building institutions for Arctic governance in order to motivate their capacities regarding capital, market, technology, and human resources. On the other hand, international cooperation should be considered as the essential channel for non-Arctic states to participate in resource exploitation and development, which normally reflects national interests of the Arctic Eight. The practice of 5 + 5 model—negotiations between the five Arctic coastal states and China, Japan, Iceland, the

Republic of Korea, and the European Union on the Agreement to Prevent Unregulated High Seas Fisheries in the Central Arctic Ocean—could be a reproducible framework for such coordination.

Increase the interoperability and update the jurisdictions of existing Arctic governance mechanisms. The fragmentation of existing Arctic governance mechanisms makes it difficult to coordinate responses to and effectively manage national, subregional, regional, and global Arctic challenges. For instance, even though UNCLOS applies to the Arctic as well, it does not contain provisions that determine the policies and procedures regarding Arctic scientific research and resource extraction. In addition, the Arctic Council does not have the explicit authority to determine traditional security issues or formulate legally binding rules on disputes. At this time, efforts to establish a comprehensive and legitimate regime governing all aspects of the Arctic region are unlikely to be successful. Therefore, it would be productive to better integrate the various narrowly focused Arctic institutional arrangements into a wider regime complex (Young, 2012), which is a set of functionally specific regimes that together serve as a foundation for efficient governance. This approach better conforms to current geopolitical realities in the Arctic and, to some extent, would avoid the potential race for dominance among existing governance mechanisms. National governments, international institutions, and nonstate actors should establish a cohesive regime complex that integrates new and existing smaller frameworks to tackle the aforementioned challenges.

The future of the Arctic concerns not only Arctic states but also Arctic local communities and non-Arctic parties. Yet, a cohesive approach to Arctic governance does not exist. The rapid effects of climate change as well as technological innovation intensify the need for increased interaction and coordination among existing frameworks rather than the establishment of a comprehensive and unified mechanism. Actors need to build confidence among themselves, acknowledge one another's rights and duties, and adapt to the rapidly changing Arctic ecosystem by cooperating to explore, understand, and utilize the Arctic in a way that benefits them all.

CHALLENGES AND COMMON AGENDA ...   385

REFERENCES

Aliyev, N. (2019, June 25). Russia's military capabilities in the Arctic. *ICDS*. https://icds.ee/en/russias-military-capabilities-in-the-arctic/. Accessed 28 July 2021.

Analytical Center for the Government of the Russian Federation. (2019, December 12). *Northern Sea Route to become year-round transport corridor.* http://www.ac.gov.ru/en/news/page/northern-sea-route-to-become-year-round-transport-corridor-26161. Accessed 28 July 2021.

Arctic Corridor. (2019). Arctic Railway Rovaniemi-Kirkenes. http://arcticcorridor.fi/wp-content/uploads/jkrautatiekiinascr02.pdf. Accessed 28 July 2021.

Arctic Council. (2011, May 12). *Agreement on cooperation on aeronautical and maritime search and rescue in the Arctic.* https://oaarchive.arctic-council.org/handle/11374/531. Accessed 28 July 2021.

Arctic Council. (2013, May 15). *Agreement on cooperation on marine oil pollution preparedness and response in the Arctic.* https://oaarchive.arctic-council.org/handle/11374/529. Accessed 28 July 2021.

Arctic Council. (2017, May 11). *Agreement on enhancing international Arctic scientific cooperation.* https://oaarchive.arctic-council.org/handle/11374/1916. Accessed 28 July 2021.

Arctic Council. (2021, May 20). *Arctic Council foreign ministers sign the Reykjavik declaration, adopt the council's first strategic plan and pass the chairmanship from Iceland to the Russian Federation.* https://arctic-council.org/en/news/arctic-council-foreign-ministers-sign-the-reykjavik-declaration-adopt-councils-first-strategic-plan/. Accessed 28 July 2021.

ARCTIS Database. (2008). *Basics of the state policy of the Russian Federation in the Arctic for the period till 2020 and for a further perspective.* Adopted by the President of the Russian Federation. http://www.arctis-search.com/Russian%2BFederation%2BPolicy%2Bfor%2Bthe%2BArctic%2Bto%2B2020. Accessed 28 July 2021.

Bloomberg. (2020, April 8). *WTO says global trade collapse may be worst in a generation.* https://www.bloomberg.com/news/articles/2020-04-08/wto-says-2020-global-trade-collapse-may-be-worst-in-a-generation. Accessed 28 July 2021.

Boone, C. (2021, June 29). Arctic Council: Should Russia push for including security issues during its chairmanship? *Modern Diplomacy.* https://moderndiplomacy.eu/2021/06/29/arctic-council-should-russia-push-for-including-security-issues-during-its-chairmanship/. Accessed 28 July 2021.

Brigham, L. (2019). The United States needs a deep-water Arctic port. *Proceedings, 410*, 268–6110. U.S. Naval Institute.

Buchanan, E. (2018, February 1). Sea cables in a thawing Arctic. *The Interpreter.* Lowy Institute. https://www.lowyinstitute.org/the-interpreter/sea-cables-thawing-arctic. Accessed 28 July 2021.

China Daily. (2018, October 31). Sino-Russian expedition provides Arctic data. https://www.chinadaily.com.cn/a/201810/31/WS5bd9016fa310eff3 0328591e.html. Accessed 28 July 2021.

China Plus. (2017, July 5). *Xi's visit witnesses stronger China–Russia ties.* http://chinaplus.cri.cn/news/politics/11/20170705/7787.html. Accessed 28 July 2021.

CNBC. (2020, April 3). *Coronavirus pandemic economic fallout 'way worse' than the global financial crisis.* https://www.cnbc.com/2020/04/03/coronavirus-way-worse-than-the-global-financial-crisis-imf-says.html. Accessed 28 July 2021.

Department of Defense. (2019, June). *Report to congress department of defense Arctic strategy.* https://media.defense.gov/2019/Jun/06/2002141657/-1/-1/1/2019-DOD-ARCTIC-STRATEGY.PDF. Accessed 28 July 2021.

Department of the NAVY. (2021, January 5). *A blue Arctic.* https://www.navy.mil/Press-Office/Press-Releases/display-pressreleases/Article/2463000/department-of-the-navy-releases-strategic-blueprint-for-a-blue-arctic/. Accessed 28 July 2021.

Gazprom Neft. (2021, March 18). *Arctic oil accounts for more than 30% of Gazprom Neft's total production.* https://www.gazprom-neft.com/press-center/news/arctic_oil_accounts_for_more_than_30_of_gazprom_neft_s_total_production/. Accessed 28 July 2021.

Gunnarsson, B. (2021). Ten years of international shipping on the Northern Sea Route: Trends and challenges. *Arctic Review on Law and Politics, 12*(2021), 4–30.

Heather, A. (2021, March 31). Conley and Colin Wall. U.S.–Russian Arctic relations: A change in climate. *CSIS.* https://www.csis.org/analysis/us-russian-arctic-relations-change-climate. Accessed 28 July 2021.

IPCC. (2015). Intergovernmental panel on climate change. "Global warming of 1.5 °C". *Special Report of IPCC.* https://www.ipcc.ch/sr15/. Accessed 28 July 2021.

Jinping, X. (2017, January 18). *Work together to build a community of shared future for mankind.* Speech at the United Nations Office at Geneva. http://www.xinhuanet.com/english/2017-01/19/c_135994707.htm. Accessed 28 July 2021.

Kenneth, J. B., et al. (2008). *Circum-Arctic resource appraisal: Estimates of undiscovered oil and gas north of the Arctic Circle.* USGS. Fact Sheet 2008. https://pubs.usgs.gov/fs/2008/3049/. Accessed 28 July 2021.

Klimenko, E. (2020, April 6). Russia's new Arctic policy document signals continuity rather than change. *SIPRI.* https://www.sipri.org/commentary/essay/2020/russias-new-arctic-policy-document-signals-continuity-rather-change. Accessed 28 July 2021.

Larter, D. B. (2020, May 12). The US Navy returns to an increasingly militarized Arctic. *Defense News*. https://www.defensenews.com/naval/2020/05/11/the-us-navy-returns-to-an-increasingly-militarized-arctic/. Accessed 28 July 2021.

Larter, D. B. (2020, June 9). Trump memo demands new fleet of Arctic icebreakers be ready by 2029. *Defense News*. https://www.defensenews.com/naval/2020/06/09/trump-memo-demands-new-fleet-of-arctic-icebreakers-to-be-ready-by-2029/. Accessed 28 July 2021.

Lopez, C. T. (2020, February 19). Joint exercise to test tactical forces in cold-weather environment. *DOD News*. https://www.defense.gov/Explore/News/Article/Article/2087607/joint-exercise-to-test-tactical-forces-in-cold-weather-environment/. Accessed 28 July 2021.

McKay, H. (2019, March 19). Trump team vows ho hit back against Russia and China's 'Polar Silk Road' with Arctic defense strategy. *Fox News*. https://www.foxnews.com/world/trump-team-set-to-hit-back-against-russia-and-chinas-polar-silk-road-with-new-arctic-defense-strategy.print. Accessed 28 July 2021.

Melino, M., &. Conley, H. A. (2020). *The ice curtain: Russia's Arctic military presence*. https://www.csis.org/features/ice-curtain-russias-arctic-military-presence. Accessed 28 July 2021.

Middleton, A. (2020, January 7). Northern sea route: From speculations to reality by 2035. *High North News*. https://www.highnorthnews.com/en/northern-sea-route-speculations-reality-2035. Accessed 28 July 2021.

Ministry of Foreign Affairs of China. (2015). *A joint communique on the results of the 20th regular meeting between the heads of the Russian and Chinese governments*. http://www.mfa.gov.cn/chn//pds/ziliao/1179/t1325537.htm. Accessed 28 July 2021.

Ministry of Foreign Affairs of China. (2019). *China, Finland vow to write new chapter in bilateral ties*. https://www.fmprc.gov.cn/mfa_eng/zxxx_662805/t1629472.shtml. Accessed 28 July 2021.

Ministry of Foreign Affairs of Iceland. (2011). *A parliamentary resolution on Iceland's Arctic policy*. http://library.arcticportal.org/1889/1/A-Parliamentary-Resolution-on-ICE-Arctic-Policy-approved-by-Althingi.pdf. Accessed 28 July 2021.

Ministry of Foreign Affairs of Norway. (2020). *Nordic foreign and security policy 2020*. https://www.regjeringen.no/globalassets/departementene/ud/vedlegg/europapolitikk/norden/nordicreport_2020.pdf. Accessed 28 July 2021.

Ministry of Foreign Affairs of Sweden. (2011). *Sweden's strategy for the Arctic region*. https://www.government.se/49b746/contentassets/85de9103bbbe4373b55eddd7f71608da/swedens-strategy-for-the-arctic-region. Accessed 28 July 2021.

388   L. ZHAO

NEWS. (2020, September 15). *US eyes deploying 150 supersonic combat fighters in Alaska.* https://news.ru/en/usa/us-eyes-to-deploy-150-supersonic-combat-fighters-in-alaska/. Accessed 28 July 2021.

Nilsen, T. (2016, October 21). New mega-port in Arkhangelsk with Chinese investments. *The Barents Observer.* https://thebarentsobserver.com/en/industry-and-energy/2016/10/new-mega-port-arkhangelsk-chinese-invest ments. Accessed 28 July 2021.

NORAD News. (2020, March 6). *Arctic edge 2020.* https://www.norad.mil/Newsroom/Article/2104838/arctic-edge-2020/. Accessed 28 July 2021.

Novatek. (2013, December 18). *Final investment decision made on Yamal LNG project.* http://novatek.ru/en/press/releases/index.php?id_4=812. Accessed 28 July 2021.

Novatek. (2019, June 7). *NOVATEK and CNOOC sign share purchase agreement for Arctic LNG.* http://www.novatek.ru/en/press/releases/index.php?id_4=3245. Accessed 28 July 2021.

People's Daily. (2018, January 28). *The Polar Silk Road attracts the world's attention* (p. 3). Accessed 28 July 2021.

President of Russia. (2020, March 5). *Vladimir Putin approved basic principles of state policy in the Arctic.* http://en.kremlin.ru/acts/news/62947. Accessed 28 July 2021.

Prime Minister's Office of Finland. (2013). *Finlands strategy for the Arctic region.* Government resolution on 23 August 2013. https://vnk.fi/docume nts/10616/334509/Arktinen+strategia+2013+en.pdf/6b6fb723-40ec-4c17-b286-5b5910fbecf4. Accessed 28 July 2021.

Putin, V. (2017, May 14). *Speech at the One Belt, One Road international forum.* http://en.kremlin.ru/events/president/news/54491. Accessed 28 July 2021.

Reuters. (2018, January 26). *China unveils vision for 'Polar Silk Road' across Arctic.* https://www.reuters.com/article/us-china-arctic/china-unveils-vision-for-polar-silk-road-across-arctic-idUSKBN1FF0J8. Accessed 28 July 2021.

Reuters. (2020, September 22). *China pledges to achieve CO_2 emissions peak before 2030, carbon neutrality before 2060—Xi.* https://www.reuters.com/art icle/un-assembly-climatechange-idUSL2N2GJ105. Accessed 28 July 2021.

Reuters. (2021, May 19). *Blinken, Lavrov agree to work together despite differences.* https://www.reuters.com/world/us-russia-hold-arctic-talks-push-summit-2021-05-19/. Accessed 28 July 2021.

Staalesen, A. (2018, June 12). Chinese money for Northern Sea Route. *The Barents Observer.* https://thebarentsobserver.com/en/arctic/2018/06/chinese-money-northern-sea-route. Accessed 28 July 2021.

Staalesen, A. (2020, February 28). *Russian Arctic shipping up 430 percent in three years*. https://thebarentsobserver.com/en/industry-and-energy/2020/02/russian-arctic-shipping-430-percent-three-years. Accessed 28 July 2021.

Staalesen, A. (2020, August 28). After years of big growth comes decline for Russian Arctic seaports. *The Barents Observer*. https://thebarentsobserver.com/en/industry-and-energy/2020/08/after-years-big-growth-comes-decline-russian-arctic-seaports. Accessed 28 July 2021.

Starchak, M. (2020, June 16). *The Borei-A SSBN: How effective is Russia's new nuclear submarine?* Jamestown Foundation. Eurasia Daily Monitor. https://jamestown.org/program/the-borei-a-ssbn-how-effective-is-russias-new-nuclear-submarine/. Accessed 28 July 2021.

State Council Information Office of China. (2018, January 26). *Full text: China's Arctic policy*. http://www.scio.gov.cn/zfbps/32832/Document/1618243/1618243.htm. Accessed 28 July 2021.

Strategic Competition Act. (2021, April 15). *Act of 2021, S.1169 117th Congress*. https://www.foreign.senate.gov/imo/media/doc/DAV21598%20-%20Strategic%20Competition%20Act%20of%202021.pdf. Accessed 28 July 2021.

Stronski, P., & Kier, G. (2021). *A fresh start on U.S. Arctic policy under Biden*. Carnegie Moscow Center. https://carnegie.ru/commentary/84543. Accessed 28 July 2021.

Taylor, I. (2019). *Global: MSC says it will not use the NSR on environmental grounds*. https://www.bunkerspot.com/bunkerspot-news-rss-feed/14-global/49163-global-msc-says-it-will-not-use-the-nsr-on-environmental-grounds. Accessed 28 July 2021.

The Arctic. (2020, September 25). *Ministry for the development of the Russian Far East and Arctic drafts new state Arctic development program until 2024*. https://arctic.ru/economics/20200925/980282.html. Accessed 28 July 2021.

The Barents Observer. (2017, December 28). *Governor Orlov confirms China as key Arctic partner*. https://thebarentsobserver.com/en/industry-and-energy/2017/12/governor-orlov-eyes-china-key-arctic-partner. Accessed 28 July 2021.

The Barents Observer. (2020, August 26). *Security strongmen take on key role in Russian Arctic policy*. https://thebarentsobserver.com/en/2020/08/security-strongmen-take-key-role-russian-arctic-policy. Accessed 28 July 2021.

The Barents Observer. (2021, January 8). *New U.S. Arctic strategy focuses on 'day-to-day competition' with Russia and China*. https://thebarentsobserver.com/en/security/2021/01/new-us-arctic-strategy-focuses-day-day-competition-russia-and-china. Accessed 28 July 2021.

The Ilulissat Declaration. (2008). *Arctic Ocean conference, Ilulissat*. https://web.archive.org/web/20120310172346/http://www.oceanlaw.org/downloads/arctic/Ilulissat_Declaration.pdf. Accessed 28 July 2021.

The White House. (2021, January 20). *Executive order on protecting public health and the environment and restoring science to tackle the climate crisis.* https://www.whitehouse.gov/briefing-room/presidential-actions/2021/01/20/executive-order-protecting-public-health-and-environment-and-restoring-science-to-tackle-climate-crisis/. Accessed 28 Jul 2021

Thordarsson, G. T. (2018, September 6). Iceland–China relations will continue to strengthen. *China Daily.* http://usa.chinadaily.com.cn/a/201809/06/WS5b90702ba31033b4f465477b.html. Accessed 28 July 2021.

United States Coast Guard. (2019, April). *Arctic strategic outlook.* https://media.defense.gov/2019/May/13/2002130713/-1/-1/0/ARCTIC_STRATEGY_BOOK_APR_2019.PDF. Accessed 28 July 2021.

Xinhuanet. (2017, March 7). *China's Arctic policy in line with international law: Finnish president.* http://www.xinhuanet.com/english/2018-03/07/c_137021608.htm. Accessed 28 July 2021.

Xinhuanet. (2017, June 20). *Full text of the vision for maritime cooperation under the Belt and Road Initiative.* http://www.xinhuanet.com/english/2017-06/20/c_136380414.htm. Accessed 28 July 2021.

Xinhuanet. (2017, November 1). *Xi stresses commitment to good China–Russia relations.* http://www.xinhuanet.com/english/2017-11/01/c_136720942.htm. Accessed 28 July 2021.

Yamal LNG. (2021). *Further information on Yamal LNG is available at its official website.* http://yamallng.ru/en/

Youchang, L., & Shuhui, Z. (2018). *Norway's Arctic town envisions gateway on polar Silk Road with link to China. Xinhuanet.* http://www.xinhuanet.com/english/2018-03/10/c_137029993.htm. Accessed 28 July 2021

Young, O. R. (2012). Building an international regime complex for the Arctic: Current status and next steps. *The Polar Journal, 2*(2), 391–407.

Ведомости. (2019, Февраль 25). Председатель комитета Госдумы по энергетике: «Добыть все, что у нас есть, и продать». https://www.vedomosti.ru/business/characters/2019/02/25/795078-dobit-vse-chto-est. Accessed 28 July 2021.

Кутузова, М. (2021). Китай как крупнейший инвестор арктических проектов. *GoArctic.* https://goarctic.ru/work/kitay-kak-krupneyshiy-investor-arkticheskikh-proektov/. Accessed 28 July 2021.

Министерство РФ по развитию Дальнего Востока и Арктики. (2020, Май 7). Проект Стратегии развития Арктики до 2035 года внесен в Правительство РФ. https://minvr.gov.ru/press-center/news/24847/. Accessed 28 July 2021.

РБК. (2020, сентября 10). «Росатом» предложил снизить на 25% прогноз по объему грузов в Арктике Его пришлось пересмотреть из-за изменений планов компаний по поставкам угля и нефти. https://

www.rbc.ru/business/10/09/2020/5f589b189a794752254570fb?from=col umn_9. Accessed 28 July 2021.

ТАСС. (2019, Апрель 9). Новая стратегия развития российской Арктики до 2035 года будет принята в этом году. Форум "Арктика - Территория Диалога". https://tass.ru/ekonomika/6312429. Accessed 28 July 2021.

ТАСС. (2020, Июль 22). Минвостокразвития: Россия обсуждает с Китаем, Индией и Сингапуром сотрудничество в Арктике. https://tass.ru/eko nomika/9020363. Accessed 28 July 2021.

Japan Facing the Arctic and North: Interplay Between the National and Regional Interests

Marina Lomaeva and Juha Saunavaara

INTRODUCTION

Japan's recent engagement with the Arctic may be analyzed both as an evolving phenomenon in international affairs, and in terms of reconceptualization of the Arctic and North. It may also be approached as a case of multi-level governance in the context of cross-border cooperation. In this chapter, we shall review Japan's interaction with the Arctic, drawing on the notion that the region is neither an ahistorical entity nor a given waiting "out there" to be discovered, but a continuously changing political and sociocultural construction. A relational turn in regional studies marked a shift from the perception of the region as a static bounded space defined by its territory to the dynamic (relational and temporary) products of social and political processes and discourses (Allen et al., 1998, p. 2; Paasi, 2020, pp. 4–6, 22–24, 28, 34). Region-building is thus

M. Lomaeva
Arctic Research Center, Hokkaido University, Sapporo, Japan

J. Saunavaara (✉)
Arctic Research Center, Hokkaido University, Sapporo, Japan
e-mail: Juha.saunavaara@arc.hokudai.ac.jp

© The Author(s), under exclusive license to Springer Nature
Singapore Pte Ltd. 2022
A. Likhacheva (ed.), *Arctic Fever*,
https://doi.org/10.1007/978-981-16-9616-9_15

understood as a process whereby different actors and stakeholders determine the criteria that constitute the region and set up institutions and develop practices that produce and reproduce the region. This process can be manifested in discourse or speech acts, such as political statements or policy documents, proposals made by different actors, or details of particular research or business projects. The institutions and governance structures that are created in the process may be based on both the territorial component of proximity and the relational component of connectivity, i.e., one's participation in the networks shaping the region (Väätänen & Zimmerbauer, 2019, pp. 3–5).

This research also derives from the scholarly discussion of the ways to understand and (re)define the concepts of the Arctic and North. Whereas the Global Arctic approach describes the Arctic as a multifaceted region, which has become part and parcel of the globalized world in all its dimensions: ecological, economic, geo-political, and cultural (Finger & Heininen, 2019, p. 1), the term "arcticization" denotes the process of stretching the meaning of the Arctic space in a manner that allows new states (not traditionally included) to become reconstituted as members of the family of states and other actors tightly connected to the Arctic (Väätänen & Zimmerbauer, 2019, pp. 5, 14–15). Our analysis of Japan's Arctic engagement also touches on the Northeast Asian (NEA) actors' role in the circumpolar north and the emergence of new regional concepts such as the Asian or North Pacific Arctic, which were inspired by the regionalization process in the Barents Region.

Although some of the Arctic states relied on the territorial component and territorially based governance when voicing concerns over admitting the East Asian nations as observers to the Arctic Council (AC) (Bennett, 2014, p. 84), the NEA actors also used proximity to the Arctic for justifying their claims. For instance, China positions herself as a "near-Arctic" state (The State Council of the People's Republic of China, 2021) and Japan describes itself as one of the "surrounding states" with respect to the Arctic (Headquarters for Ocean Policy, 2015). On the other hand, they questioned the "territorial" nature of the Arctic issues by stressing the global impact of the changes observed there, for instance, on the climate. The proponents of reconceptualization of the Arctic also point to the economic interconnections between the Arctic and the North Pacific as a result of the improved maritime accessibility due to the declining sea-ice concentration and thickness and expanding trade networks connecting the Arctic to global flows and markets, particularly those in NEA, as the former exports primary products to the latter. This trend is revealed in the increased volume of shipping passing through the Northern Sea Route (NSR) and the ports of the circumpolar and NEA states, which are identified as "gateways", "windows", and "pivots" to Asia and the Arctic, respectively, and may be viewed as nodes of the networked maritime space of the Asian/North Pacific (A/NP) Arctic region. The vision of the A/NP Arctic region thus rests on both territorial proximity and the relational concept of positionality (position in relational space/time within the global economy) (Bennett, 2014, pp. 72–73, 76; O'Loughlin & Van der Wusten, 1990; Sheppard, 2002, p. 307; Väätänen & Zimmerbauer, 2019, p. 14).

In this chapter, we also examine the role of subnational governments (SNGs) and non-state actors (NSAs) in the interaction between the Arctic and non-Arctic in response to the recent calls for such a perspective from the students of the Arctic governance. Knecht and Laubenstein (2020) as well as Tsui (2020) argue that the existing research of international relations and governance in the Arctic is giving too much weight to sovereign states and their activities within the AC framework, leaving the issues of multi-stakeholder collaboration, science diplomacy, relations between indigenous peoples and subnational entities, etc. underexplored. However, the emerging relational networks connecting non-contiguous areas to the Arctic engender new, cross-border, or transnational affinities between the Arctic and non-Arctic states and/or regions and lead to scale-jumping in governance structures (Bennett, 2014, p. 87). Scale-jumping occurs when SNGs and NSAs, bypassing the national level, develop ties with (sub)national governments of other states or seek representation at the global level. Multi-level governance and paradiplomacy literature offer conceptual frameworks for the study of these phenomena, which may be observed in science and technology and business diplomacy pursued by Japanese actors. In our analysis of the role of the Japanese SNGs, we focus on Hokkaido and its projects aimed at forging and strengthening the ties with the Arctic and northern SNGs of other states.

Japan's Arctic Engagement

Japan's history of polar research and exploration started at the South Pole with Nobu Shirase's Antarctic expedition (1910–1912). Turning to the Arctic, although the signing of the Spitsbergen treaty is often mentioned as a starting point of Japan's involvement, earlier manifestations of Japan's interest have been identified, such as Japan's Ministry of Foreign Affairs (MoFA) attention to the Arctic exploration endeavors and territorial claims including the Soviet sector claim. In the 1930–1940s, MoFA was also watching closely the Soviet efforts at developing the NSR shipping. It appears that the imperial Japanese government was mainly concerned about the security dimension of these developments, considering its economic interests in the North Pacific, such as Japan's "northern fisheries" (in particular, the crab and salmon fisheries off the Soviet coasts and in the Bering Sea) (Leonard, 1944, pp. 28–34; Polutov, 2016).

Although the origins of Japan's Arctic engagement may be traced back to the beginning of the twentieth century, the 1990s marked an important watershed in its relations with the circumpolar north (Table 1).

Table 2 takes stock of the key stakeholders in Japan's Arctic (and Northern) engagement, listing Japan's principal actors among the government bodies and agencies, national and private think tanks, and universities, describing their contributions (Hokkaido-based actors apart from HU will be considered in the following section). Some of the key private companies will be mentioned later in comments to Tables 2 and 4, but as compared to the above-mentioned types of actors, the identification of their involvement poses a number of problems due to their transnational nature (whether they should be identified as Japanese actors), a limited amount of information disclosed (due to confidentiality requirements), etc.

Based on the information in Table 2, the following observations may be made about the key actors in Japan's Arctic engagement:

1. Although the Headquarters for Ocean Policy are designated as the coordinating center for Japan's Arctic policy and inter-ministry- and agency collaboration, Japan's Arctic-related governance structure is polycentric, with distinctive roles played by MoFA, MLIT, and MEXT.
2. Apart from the MoFA-affiliated Arctic Task Force, there are several other domestic platforms for coordination of various actors' Arctic-related activities such as the Arctic Liaison Conferences, meetings of ASR Council, and the Parliamentary League of Arctic Frontier Study.

Table 1 Timeline of Japan's Arctic engagement and establishment of the related institutions

Year	Event
1920	Japan signed the Spitsbergen treaty
1973	Japan established the National Institute of Polar Research (NIPR)
1990	Japan joined the International Arctic Science Committee (IASC) and established the Centre for Arctic Research under the National Institute of Polar Research (NIPR)
1991	NIPR established a permanent research station in Ny-Ålesund on Svalbard
1993	The International Northern Sea Route Programme was started by Japan, Russia, and Norway (see Table 4)
2009	Japan submitted an application for the Permanent Observer status to the Arctic Council (AC) and started participating in the International Maritime Organization (IMO) Correspondence Group working on the Polar Code
2010	MoFA established the Arctic Task Force (ATF) for developing a cross-sectoral approach toward the foreign policy on the Arctic including the international legal aspects
2011	Japan Consortium for Arctic Environmental Research (JCAR) was established as a nationwide network-based organization made up of representatives of universities, think tanks, and science-related government agencies. Hokkaido University (HU) joined the UArctic
2013	Japan was granted the Permanent Observer status at the AC and created the position of Ambassador in charge of Arctic affairs (Arctic Ambassador). The second Basic Plan on Ocean Policy was adopted mentioning the Arctic. Annual Liaison Conferences of Relevant Ministries and Agencies for Arctic Issues (Arctic Liaison Conferences) were started, led by the Ministry of Land, Infrastructure, Transport and Tourism (MLIT)
2014	Council of Industry-Academia-Government Collaboration on the Arctic Sea Route (ASR Council) was established with MLIT as the coordinator
2015	Japan announced its first Arctic Policy and hosted the Arctic Science Summit Week. HU established the Arctic Research Center (HU ARC), and the Arctic Challenge for Sustainability (ArCS) project was launched
2018	Japan signed the Agreement to Prevent Unregulated High Seas Fisheries in the Central Arctic Ocean. The Third Basic Plan on Ocean Policy containing a separate section on the Arctic Ocean was adopted
2021	Japan hosted the Third Arctic Science Ministerial Meeting (ASM3)

3. Private think tanks such as OPRI and Japan Institute of International Affairs (JIIA) have played a major role in drawing up Japan's Arctic policy and subsequently the ocean policy comprising Japan's policy on the Arctic Ocean. JIIA carried out the "Arctic Governance and Japan's Diplomatic Strategy" project in 2012, on the basis of which "Recommendations for Japan's Diplomacy" were produced

Table 2 Japan's principal actors involved in the North/Arctic-related projects

Actor	Arctic/North-related activities
Ministry of Foreign Affairs (MoFA)	Conducts Japan's Arctic diplomacy (sending the Arctic Ambassador to the AC ministerial meetings, etc.). Supervises the ATF
Ministry of Education, Culture, Sports, Science and Technology (MEXT)	Allocates budgets for large-scale research projects aimed at developing research networks and research instruments (including vessels), establishing research stations in the Arctic states, data sharing and management, training and supporting researchers, etc. Supervises the activities of NIPR, JAMSTEC, JAXA, and Japan-US International Arctic Research Center (IARC)
Ministry of Land, Infrastructure, Transport and Tourism (MLIT)	In charge of overall ocean policy (including navigation and shipping infrastructure). Dominates the Arctic Liaison Conferences. In charge of organizing meetings of the ASR Council. Supervises JMA (MLIT, 2020)
Ministry of Trade and Industry (METI)	Involved in the Arctic/North-related policies via its Agency for Natural Resources and Energy, Natural Resources and Fuel Department. Provides support to private companies involved in the Arctic/North-related investment projects
Ministry of Agriculture, Forestry and Fisheries (MAFF)	Collaborates with MEXT, MLIT, MoE, JMA in the study of the effects of global environmental issues on Japan, including its agriculture, forestry and fisheries. Collaborates with the Russian Ministry of Agriculture on joint projects to increase the productivity of agriculture and fisheries in the Russian Far East (including the Arctic zone) (MAFF, 2020; MoE et al., 2018)

Actor	Arctic/North-related activities
Ministry of the Environment (MoE)	Collaborates with MEXT, MLIT, MAFF, JMA in the study of the effects of global environmental issues on Japan, in relation to the climate change and biodiversity, including its impact on natural ecosystems, water environment and coastal areas, and developing proposals of adaptation and mitigation measures (MoE et al., 2018)
Ministry of Defense (MoD)	Assesses the impact of the developments in the Arctic region on Japan's national security, including its economic dimension (*e.g.* in the annual "The Defense of Japan")
Headquarters for Ocean Policy, the Cabinet Office	Formulated Japan's Basic Plans on Ocean Policy (2013, 2018) and Arctic Policy (The Headquarters for Ocean Policy, 2015). In charge of inter-ministry- and agency coordination on the Arctic issues
Parliamentary League of Arctic Frontier Study	Presents policy proposals to the government based on the Arctic and ocean policy documents (Parliamentary League of Arctic Frontier Study, 2017)
Ocean Policy Research Institute (OPRI), the Sasakawa Peace Foundation	Since the 1990s has been involved in Japan's several Arctic research projects (domestic and international) related to the NSR and the Arctic governance (see Table 4). In 2010–2011 held the interdisciplinary Arctic Conference Japan. Together with the Nippon Foundation and the National Graduate Institute for Policy Studies (GRIDS) formed a study group focusing on the future of the Arctic, which published a report in 2017 proposing specific steps with respect to Japan's Arctic engagement (OPRI, 2018)
Japan National Oil, Gas and Metals Corporation (JOGMEC)	Provides support (such as equity financing and loan guarantee) to Japanese private companies participating in energy-related projects (see Table 4)

(continued)

Table 2 (continued)

Actor	Arctic/North-related activities
Japan Agency for Marine-Earth Science and Technology (JAMSTEC)	Together with NIPR has engaged in several Arctic research projects (see Table 4). Conducts studies of ocean and climate, marine ecosystems, geochemical cycles and is engaged in observation technology development. Is planning to build Japan's first research vessel with ice-breaking capabilities to explore the Arctic (Ishikura, 2021; JAMSTEC, 2021)
Japan Aerospace Exploration Agency (JAXA)	Cooperates with Japanese Arctic Research community and other stakeholders interested in the NSR such as JAMSTEC on a project calculating the sea-ice extent in the Arctic (JAXA, 2016, 2020)
Japan Meteorological Agency (JMA)	Started observations of the sea ice in 1892 from its stations in Hokkaido (Abashiri, Nemuro). Cooperates with JAXA, US and Canadian agencies in conducting satellite-based observation of the Arctic Ocean ice (JMA, 2021)
Science Council of Japan (SCJ)	Represents Japan in IASC. Co-organized the Arctic Science Summit Week (ASSW) 2015 in Toyama
National Institute of Polar Research (NIPR)	Japan's core institution for Arctic and Antarctic research. Operates observation stations in both polar regions for studies of the atmosphere, ice sheets, the land and ocean ecosystems, the upper atmosphere, the aurora and the Earth's magnetic field, etc. Runs a 5-year doctoral program. Has engaged in MEXT-funded Arctic research projects (see Table 4) (NIPR, 2021)

Actor	Arctic/North-related activities
Hokkaido University (HU)	Has long been involved in interdisciplinary Arctic research via its departments such as the Institute of Low Temperature Science. The only member of the UArctic. In 2015 established the Arctic Research Center (HU ARC) (Hokkaido University, 2021). HU has a program of training specialists on the Far East and the Arctic (RJE3 Program, since 2014), and since 2015 has been involved through HU ARC in ArCS/ArCS II projects (see Table 4)
Kobe University	As a participant of ArCS/ArCS II established the Polar Cooperation Research Centre (PCRC) in 2015 for promoting the Arctic and Antarctic legal and policy studies. PCRC is involved in both government- and privately funded projects focusing on sustainable use of the Arctic resources (Kobe University, 2021)

(JIIA, 2012), contributing to formulating Japan's Arctic Policy in 2015. The Third Basic Plan on Ocean Policy followed the OPRI's recommendations (its 2017 report), including a separate chapter on the Arctic.

4. Apart from close collaboration with national and private think tanks, the government of Japan from the early stage of its Arctic engagement has sought cooperation of private companies (mostly in the shipping and energy sectors), which influence Japan's Arctic policy via such institutions as the ASR Council and provision of funding for the Arctic-related projects (MLIT, 2014).

5. In addition to conducting research across a wide range of disciplines, the universities mentioned in the table have research centers, which also serve as platforms for industry-academia-government collaboration.

6. With respect to the policy areas and goals, our overview corroborates the oft-mentioned reliance on science diplomacy (particularly related to the studies of the global environmental impact of the changes in the Arctic) and focus on the oil and gas development and shipping opportunities (Chuffart et al., 2020, pp. 332–333; Tonami, 2016, p. 49). As will be demonstrated in Table 4 and the following section, other promising areas of cooperation with the Arctic states include technologies developed for cold regions in such spheres as civil engineering, renewable energy, and agriculture.

Next, we shall turn to the Arctic/North-related forums in which some of the actors listed in Table 2 participate.

The forums in Table 3 are also indicative of the role assumed and performed by Japan's Arctic stakeholders:

1. Even prior to obtaining the AC observer status, Japan has participated in almost all Senior Arctic Officials (SAO) meetings and ministerial meetings since 2009. Before the position of the Arctic Ambassador was created, the MoFA officials and diplomats of different embassies represented Japan. Among the six AC Working Groups (WG), Japan has regularly attended the work of AMAP, SDWG, PAME, and CAFF and joined various Experts Groups and Task Forces. The Japanese participants joining the WG meetings used to be officials from the MoFA, MEXT, and MoE, occasionally

Table 3 Japan/Hokkaido's participation in the Arctic/North-related forums

Forum	Japan's actors involved	Status
Arctic Council (AC)	MoFA	Observer
Barents Euro-Arctic Council (BEAC)	MoFA	Observer
Northern Forum (NF)	Hokkaido International Exchange and Cooperation Center (HIECC)	Business partner
World Winter Cities Association of Mayors (WWCAM)	Sapporo City	Member
International Arctic Science Committee (IASC)	SCJ	Member
UArctic	HU	Member

accompanied by experts from NIPR and JAMSTEC. However, since ArCS launched an initiative to dispatch experts to the AC working groups in 2015, scientific experts (mostly from NIPR, JAMSTEC, and HU) became main participants at the WG level (Babin & Lasserre, 2019, pp. 151–154; Chuffart et al., 2020, pp. 337–340; MoFA, 2017a).

2. Although the NF and WWCAM may be past their heyday (in terms of numbers and regions/countries represented by their members), their existence still attests to the high level of Hokkaido and Sapporo's commitment to sub-state cooperation in the Arctic/North, as will be further discussed in the next section.
3. Hokkaido's unique position among Japanese regions with respect to the Arctic is reflected by the fact that HU is still the sole Japanese member of the UArctic.

Meanwhile, the Arctic Economic Council (AEC) is still lacking its first Japanese member, although economic aspirations have often been cited as important drivers of the East Asian actors' interest in the Arctic (Arctic Economic Council, 2020).

In addition to its engagement with the AC, Japan's Arctic Policy attaches importance to "communicating Japan's viewpoint and observation and research results" at such international Arctic conferences as the Iceland-based Arctic Circle and Norway-based Arctic Frontiers (Arctic Policy, 2015, p. 8). It was at the 2015 Arctic Circle Assembly in Reykjavik when Japan's Arctic Ambassador introduced Japan's Arctic Policy (ArCS, 2016). Most recently (May 2021), the Third Arctic Science Ministerial (ASM3) was co-hosted in a hybrid format by the Japanese government together with the Icelandic Ministry of Education, Science and Culture—for the first time in Asia (3rd Arctic Science Ministerial, 2021). ASM3 was originally meant to be organized back-to-back with the Arctic Circle Japan Forum but the latter was further postponed (Arctic Circle, 2021).

Apart from reflecting close cooperative ties between Japan and Iceland in Arctic-related matters, the ASM3 and the Arctic Circle Japan Forum, as well as Japan's participation in the Arctic Circle Assembly in 2018 also show that Japan has followed the model adopted also by China and South Korea and played an active role in the major international Arctic forums that are outside the AC framework, which divides the nations involved into participants and observers (Steinveg, 2020, pp. 39, 140, 146; 2021).

The concluding part of this section will be devoted to Japan's Arctic-related projects, some of which (research and commercial projects with a strong backing of the government agencies) are summarized in Table 4.

1. The areas covered by these projects support our earlier conclusion about Japan's reliance on science diplomacy (particularly related to the studies of the global environmental impact of the changes in the Arctic) and focus on the oil and gas development and shipping opportunities, as stated in its Arctic policy goals.

2. Expansion into new areas (education, agriculture, telecommunications, and renewable energy), has so far occurred in bilateral and mini-lateral configurations, the preference for which among the NEA states has been pointed out (Bennett, 2014, pp. 82, 85). MAFF- and NEDO-supported projects were launched as part of bilateral cooperation with Russia (corresponding to particular areas specified in the 2016 Japan–Russia Economic cooperation plan: energy development, enhancing production capacity, and developing industries and export bases in the Far East [Embassy of Japan, Moscow, 2021]). RJE3 Program is an example of the MEXT-funded Inter-University Exchange Project aimed at developing academic collaboration with particular countries (not limited to the Arctic eight) reflecting Hokkaido's regional interests. The same applies to HU's Finnish-Japanese Arctic Studies Project (2018–2020) (Opetushallitus, 2020; Saunavaara & Ohnishi, 2020).

Table 4 Japan's representative Arctic/North-related projects

Project	Term	Actors	Outline
International Northern Sea Route Programme (INSROP)	Phase 1 (1993–1995), Phase 2 (1997–1999)	MLIT, OPRI, Nippon Foundation + Russian and Norwegian organizations	A large-scale international project including research and experimental voyages was conducted for testing the feasibility of the year-round navigation in the Arctic Ocean (OPRI, 2018)
Japan Northern Sea Route Programme (JANSROP)	Phase I (1993–1999), Phase II (2002–2005)	OPRI	Phase I was carried out simultaneously with INSROP. Phase II aimed at compiling data on energy, mineral, forest, and fishery resources along with topographical data from Far Eastern Russia into the world's first geographic information system (JANSROP-GIS) and proposed a marine area use consistent with environmental protection in the Sea of Okhotsk (OPRI, 2018)

(continued)

Table 4 (continued)

Project	Term	Actors	Outline
Arctic Climate Change Research Project	2011–2016	MEXT, NIPR, JAMSTEC	Conducted multidisciplinary studies as part of the Green Network of Excellence (GRENE) Program with the purpose of: understanding the mechanism of warming amplification in the Arctic; evaluation of the impact of the Arctic change on weather and climate in Japan, marine ecosystems and fisheries; and projections of sea-ice distribution and navigability of the Arctic sea routes in future (NIPR, 2016)

Project	Term	Actors	Outline
Arctic Challenge for Sustainability (ArCS)	Phase I (2015–2019), Phase II (2020–2024)	MEXT, NIPR, JAMSTEC, HU ARC	Launched with the aim to elucidate climate and environmental changes in the Arctic and their effects on society, and provide accurate projections and environmental assessments for domestic and foreign stakeholders, which may be used for making appropriate decisions on the sustainable development of the Arctic and as a basis for legislation and policy thus contributing to the Arctic governance. ArCS II lays more emphasis on this last aim and social sciences, humanities and engineering sciences (ArCS II, 2021; Saunavaara & Ohnishi, 2020)
Kalaallit Nunaat Marine Seismic (KANUMAS) project	1990–1996	JOGMEC (Japan), Statoil (Norway), BP (UK), ExxonMobil, Chevron (US), Shell (UK/Netherlands), NUNAOIL A/S (National Oil Company of Greenland)	Preliminary studies for hydrocarbon potential offshore eastern and western Greenland. Project was funded by six major oil companies who were granted a special preferential position to be activated when a call for tenders for exploration and exploitation licenses was issued (Gautier, 2007; JOGMEC, 2012)

(continued)

Table 4 (continued)

Project	Term	Actors	Outline
Yamal LNG	2014–	NOVATEK (Russia), Total (France), CNPC, Silk Road Fund China, (China) + JGC Corporation, Chiyoda Corporation, Mitsui O.S.K Lines (Japan)	Development of natural gas production, construction of a liquefied natural gas (LNG) plant and realizing new Arctic shipping solutions. Japanese JGC Corporation and Chiyoda Corporation contributed to the LNG plant construction, and Mitsui O.S.K Lines is heavily involved in the Yamal LNG delivery
Arctic LNG 2	2019–	NOVATEK (Russia), Mitsui & Co., Ltd.; JOGMEC (Japan) + French and Chinese companies	Development of a conventional onshore gas field within the Arctic Circle (northern Russia) and construction of natural gas and liquefaction facilities with the aim to deliver the LNG mainly to Asia and Europe via the Northern Sea Route. JOGMEC and Mitsui & Co., Ltd. concluded a long-term purchase agreement and made an investment worth 10% share of the project
Reloading and storage terminals in Kamchatka and Murmansk regions	2019–	Mitsui O.S.K. Lines, Japan Bank for International Cooperation (JBIC), JOGMEC	Building terminals for reloading LNG produced in the Russian Arctic and transported by specially designed LNG carriers to conventional carriers (Kumagai & Yep, 2020)

Project	Term	Actors	Outline
East Russia–Japan Expert Education Program (RJE3 Program)	2014–	MEXT (until 2019), HU	Program for training Japanese and Russian specialists that will "play leading roles in creating a sustainable future in the Far East, the Arctic Circle and Hokkaido", run by HU in collaboration with 5 Russian universities and with the support of RJE3 Consortium comprising Hokkaido and Russian SNGs and private companies. Focuses on the Arctic and Far East environment, cultural diversity, resource development, and disaster prevention (RJE3, 2021)

(continued)

Table 4 (continued)

Project	Term	Actors	Outline
Greenhouse vegetable production in the Sakha Republic	2016–	MAFF, Hokkaido Corporation (Japan), Ministry of Agriculture, Far East and Arctic Development Fund, LLC Sayuri (Russia)	Part of the Joint Japanese-Russian project to increase the productivity of agriculture and fisheries in the Russian Far East. Greenhouse vegetable production (tomatoes, cucumbers) near Yakutsk (MAFF, 2020; The Arctic, 2020)
Arctic Connect	2017–	Cinia (Finland), Megafon (Russia), Sojitz Corporation, Atago Corporation, Optage, Crypton Future Media, Hokkaido Electric Power Company, Sakura Internet (Japan)	Building a trans-Arctic submarine fiber-optic cable connecting East Asia (Japan), Northern Europe and North America through the Northeast Passage. Six Japanese companies joined the project through Cinia Alliance and provided funding for the development phase. Although the first seabed surveys were made in the autumn of 2020, and the Letter of Intent with NORDUnet for a dedicated fiber pair was signed, Megafon announced in May 2021 that it would freeze the project in order to revise its structure and economics (Cinia, 2020, 2021; Qiu, 2021; Saunavaara & Salminen, 2020; Staalesen, 2020)

Project	Term	Actors	Outline
Wind farms in the Sakha Republic	2018–	New Energy and Industrial Technology Development Organization (NEDO), Mitsui & Co., Ltd., Takaoka Toko Co., Ltd., and Komaihaltec Inc. (Japan), Roshydro (Russia)	Installation of cold-resistant wind turbine generators in Tiksi City for the development of a polar microgrid system comprising an energy management system that will collectively manage the electricity provided by the newly-installed wind turbines, existing diesel generators, and storage batteries (NEDO, 2018)

3. The mode of Japanese actors' participation in the Arctic LNG 2 project and the construction of the LNG transhipment hubs marks a significant departure from the former modus operandi. While various Japanese actors have been involved, the role of the state-controlled JOGMEC has grown immensely. JOGMEC's active role and support of Japanese companies owe partially to the revisions of the JOGMEC Act, most recent of which took effect in June 2020. The fact that Mitsui was the only private company joining the Japanese partnership has drawn some attention. Both Marubeni Corporation (which had signed MOUs concerning the Arctic LNG and transhipment hub projects with Rosneft and Novatek), and Mitsubishi (whose possible participation was often rumored), decided not to join the endeavor (Humpert, 2019; Kumagai & Yep, 2020; Marubeni Corporation, 2013, 2017; METI, 2021; MoFA, 2019; Tonami, 2016; Wee, 2018).

4. Japanese actors have been involved in different trans-Arctic submarine fiber-optic cable projects for years. The unmaterialized Russian Optical Trans-Arctic Submarine Cable System (ROTACS) project envisioned a cable system connecting Japan and the UK through the Northeast Passage. The project to connect Japan, Alaska, and the UK through the Northwest Passage was initiated by Canadian Arctic Fibre but developed and implemented by the Alaska-based Quintillion Subsea Holdings. Although the Japanese parties are most closely involved in the international Arctic Connect project, it remains to be seen whether this project makes progress and how it will compete against Polar Express—the new Russian domestic project that has many similarities with the Russian part of the Arctic Connect project (Nilsen, 2021; Pro Arctic, 2021; Saunavaara, 2018a; Saunavaara & Salminen, 2020).

5. The presence of Hokkaido government, academic, and commercial actors is visible in many of these projects—which brings us to the next step in our study: consideration of the role of Hokkaido-based actors in Japan's Arctic engagement.

Hokkaido's Long History with the North and Recent Interest in the Arctic

The word "Hokkaido" literally means "Northern Sea Route" or "Road to the Northern Sea". The Meiji government gave this name to the territory previously known as Ezochi in 1869, incorporating it as an administrative unit of the Empire of Japan. Hokkaido's new "northern" name reflected its geographical position, but also followed the ancient naming tradition emphasizing the importance of the imperial capital to which all regions were connected (Babin & Saunavaara, 2021, p. 4; Saunavaara, 2018b). Thus, from the perspective of paradiplomacy, Hokkaido started from humble beginnings as compared with many other regions, and yet it eventually developed into one of most active Japanese SNGs, turning its extrinsic "northern" identity to its advantage and positioning itself as the key actor in Japan's Arctic and northern engagement (Table 5).

As can be seen from this table, in (re)constructing their northern identities Hokkaido and Sapporo drew on the concepts of *hoppōken*, the "Northern region" (as a unifying concept for separate northern regions), and "winter city" (superseding the "northern city"). It was an inventive way to redefine the criteria of the "northness" to bridge the "latitude gap" between Hokkaido and Sapporo and circumpolar regions and states.

In technical terms, *hoppōken* is defined as an area north of 40° N with the Warmth Index (WI) lower than 45 (see: National Agriculture and Food Research Organization, n.d.). Although no criteria were explicitly stated for the NF membership, researchers have identified demographic, climatic, economic, and political criteria from the past practices of this organization, whose origins can be traced back to the *hoppōken* concept (Hasanat, 2012; Landriault et al., 2019, p. 45).

In the context of WWCAM, a "winter city" is defined as "one that faces harsh winter climatic conditions, including heavy snowfalls and cold temperatures" (WWCAM, 2020b).

These criteria were instrumental in establishing the NF and WWCAM as forums connecting the Arctic states with their NEA neighbors, establishing direct communication channels for interregional cooperation not easily susceptible to the ups and downs in the relations between their central governments. The existence of these channels also lends support to the vision of the Asian/North Pacific Arctic region.

Table 5 Timeline of Hokkaido and Sapporo's Northern/Arctic engagement (Babin & Saunavaara, 2021; Kossa et al., 2020; WWCAM, 2020a)

Year	Event/activity
1869	Ezochi was renamed Hokkaido by Japan's government
1951	Hokkaido Development Bureau was established and the First Hokkaido Comprehensive Development Plan was adopted
1971	The Third Hokkaido Comprehensive Development Plan was adopted, mentioning Hoppōken Kōso (the Northern Regions Plan) policy and envisioning cooperation with other northern regions of the world
1974	The International Conference on the Human Environment in the Northern Regions (the precursor to the NF) was organized in Sapporo
1978	The Northern Regions Center (the precursor to HIECC) was established
1982	The first Northern Intercity Conference of Mayors (the precursor to WWCAM) was convened in Sapporo
1991	The Northern Forum was established (with the active support of the Hokkaido Government)
1995	Hokkaido hosted the Second General Assembly of the NF in Sapporo
2004	The Northern Intercity Conference of Mayors was renamed as the World Winter Cities Association for Mayors (WWCAM) (with the secretariat at Sapporo City international office)
2011	The Hokkaido International Exchange and Cooperation Center (HIECC) was established as the new coordinator of all international exchange and cooperation, including the northern initiatives
2013–2014	Hokkaido Government left the NF, and HIECC joined it as a business partner
2018	The Arctic Economic Council's 3rd Top of the World: Arctic Broadband Summit was organized in Sapporo

The *hoppōken* concept and the related policy thus manifested the regional government's hopes for increased interregional cooperation between Hokkaido and other northern regions, in particular, the resource-rich Russian Far East (Sakhalin, Primorsky Krai and Khabarovsk Krai), Alaska, British Columbia and Alberta, which would boost economic and industrial growth. Although not all these expectations were ultimately fulfilled, Hokkaido's paradiplomatic activities were noticed and occasionally encouraged by the central government, which has consistently portrayed it as a gateway from Asia to the NSR and through it—to the Arctic region, one of the recent instances being the speech of Japanese

Minister of Foreign Affairs at the 2018 Arctic Circle Assembly in Reykjavik, referring to Hokkaido as a gateway from Asia to the NSR (Babin & Saunavaara, 2021, p. 7; Kossa et al., 2020, p. 672). As for the rationale behind the "winter city" concept, it appears from the agenda of the successive conferences that Sapporo City and its counterparts were mainly motivated by search for solutions to the common urban problems caused by low temperatures and heavy snowfalls and developing wintertime recreational activities to attract more tourists. Similar to Hokkaido, Sapporo is continuously expanding its ties with northern cities such as the Russian Magadan and Norilsk, the latter hosting the WWCAM Working-Level Officials Meeting in 2019 (WWCAM, 2019, 2020c).

The emergence of Hokkaido-based actors' interest in the Arctic coincided with Japan's increased involvement in the region and, as pointed out in previous studies (Babin & Saunavaara, 2021; Kossa et al., 2020; Tonami, 2020), is a natural outcome of its long-term cooperation with other northern regions. Many Hokkaido-based actors cherish the idea that the northernmost island of Japan is in an advantageous position in different Arctic-related initiatives due to its proximity to the Bering Strait (when compared to other East Asian ports, for example) (Kossa et al., 2020; Saunavaara, 2017). The most important actors in Hokkaido's Arctic engagement have been the prefectural government, a few local (port) cities and the Hokkaido Committee for Economic Development, a private business organization issuing policy proposals. While the first studies focusing on Hokkaido's prospects vis-à-vis the NSR started in the first half of the 2010s, these activities intensified after 2015 (as evidenced by the increasing number of actors, widening scope of issues, and the growing international impact) (Babin & Saunavaara, 2021; Kossa et al., 2020). The prominent role of Hokkaido University was described in the previous section. In addition to its involvement in the national Arctic projects, HU is actively contributing to Hokkaido and Sapporo's undertakings, for instance, co-hosting the NF and WWCAM side events and developing bilateral ties with various Russian, Nordic, and American universities and research institutes with shared interest in the Arctic matters (HaRP, 2021).

Besides the Sojitz Corporation that leads the team of Japanese companies joining the Arctic Connect project through Cinia Alliance, the group also includes the Hokkaido-based Crypton Future Media and Hokkaido Electric Power Company as well as Sakura Internet, which is not established in Hokkaido but built one of Japan's largest data centers in the city of Ishikari, Hokkaido (Cinia, 2020). Furthermore, Hokkaido was mentioned as a potential Japanese landing site in the Arctic Fibre project as early as in 2014 (Saunavaara, 2017). Hokkaido Corporation's participation in the greenhouse vegetable production near Yakutsk (see Table 4) and its intermediary role in the infrastructure improvement projects in the Sakha Republic (such as the building of the garbage disposal plant and participation in a plan for improvement of Yakutsk airport) may also be mentioned as examples of Hokkaido NSAs' involvement in the Arctic economies (Hokkaido Corporation, 2018, 2019).

Recently, the Hokkaido Government also expanded the scope of its paradiplomatic activities via bilateral channels with Russia to the Sakha Republic (in 2015 the two regions signed an MOU) and St. Petersburg (in 2018 the two regions established the Working group on cooperation development), thereby strengthening the Arctic and northern elements of the agenda set by the 2019 Plan of Promoting Inter-regional Exchanges between Hokkaido and Russia (Hokkaido-Russia Exchanges Plan). Priority areas of the commercial side of Hokkaido's Arctic engagement include construction, agriculture, and manufacturing (materials, [energy-saving] technologies and products developed for the cold areas) offered by its companies, many of which joined the Hokkaido-Russia Inter-regional Cooperation Team established by the prefectural government in 2013 with a hope of exporting their products and expertise to the Russian northern regions (Hokkaido Government, 2019, 2020, 2021).

However, a few trends counter to these Arctic-related developments need to be taken into account:

1. Hokkaido's gravitation toward more institutionalized bilateral formats in its relations with the circumpolar states, as suggested by its leave from (and the reported refusal to return to) the NF and concentrating its efforts on such bilateral platforms as the Hokkaido-Russia Cooperation Platform and the Council on Promotion of Hokkaido-Russia Inter-regional Exchanges launched in 2020 on the basis of the 2019 Hokkaido-Russia Exchanges Plan.
2. During the early years of the Hokkaido comprehensive development plans there were great expectations of cooperation with the North American partners. Hokkaido and Alaska cooperated very closely for years in the NF, and Edmonton, Montreal and Winnipeg contributed to the WWCAM activities hosting the bi-annual conferences in the late 1980s and early 1990s (WWCAM,

2021). However, despite numerous sister-city and sister-region agreements and the intensive academic cooperation with North America, Hokkaido's recent Arctic initiatives related to economy, logistics, and infrastructure have been launched predominantly with the Russian or Nordic partners.

3. Although several organizations in Hokkaido were established specifically for cooperation with the northern partners, the focus of Hokkaido's international cooperation has widened to include East and Southeast Asian partners, as evidenced by the reorganization of the Northern Regions Center into the Hokkaido International Exchange and Cooperation Center (HIECC).

Arctic as a Part of Japan's International Relations

As demonstrated in the previous two sections, Japan's Arctic policy is closely connected to the country's ocean and energy policy (for instance, to the latter's call for further diversifying the supply sources, particularly, of LNG [METI, 2021]) and reflects Japan's foreign policy priorities such as building stable relations with NEA states and Russia, adopting climate change adaptation and mitigation measures, utilizing science and technology for diplomacy, and promoting resource diplomacy along with foreign direct investment for securing a stable supply of energy and mineral resources at reasonable prices and transportation route safety (MoFA, 2020). The presence and relative weight of the Arctic matters in Japan's bilateral relations with the Arctic states varies greatly. As shown above, the Arctic has played an increasingly important role in the relations with Russia, but is not visible in the key documents describing the Japan–US relationship (MoFA, 2020; U.S. Department of State, 2020). This does not, however, diminish the importance of academic cooperation between Japanese and North American (American and Canadian) researchers. Although the word "Arctic" rarely appears in official statements on Japanese-Canadian relations, the two countries' shared interest in the safety and security in the Arctic is manifested in bilateral security cooperation (Government of Canada, 2021; Sevunts, 2017). The Arctic is high on the agenda in Japan's bilateral relations with the Nordic countries (MoFA, 2016; Pollman, 2017), which is not surprising considering the weight that these countries attach to the Arctic as an area of cooperation with the NEA states, including China.

Japan's Arctic engagement may also be viewed in the context of its relations with the non-Arctic neighbors, particularly China and South Korea. Besides sharing similar interests and objectives vis-à-vis the Arctic, they have a limited capacity to influence the Arctic agenda setting and governance due to the restrictions of the observer status at the AC. Japan, China, and South Korea have held the annual Trilateral High-Level Dialogues on the Arctic since 2016, which have received some attention as a mini-lateral cooperation format (Bennett, 2017; Kim & Stenport, 2021; Kossa et al., 2020). However, the actual results of these have been rather modest, and the Joint Statements adopted at the end of each meeting hardly contain any concrete steps to be taken by the parties (MoFA, 2017b; Ministry of Foreign Affairs of the People's Republic of China, 2018; Ministry of Foreign Affairs Republic of Korea, 2019). At the subnational level, the NEA SNGs are cooperating under the auspices of such forums as the Association of North East Asia Regional Governments (NEAR), established as early as in 1996. While the recent NEAR annual reports included a few references to the Arctic, it has not been high on the agenda (NEAR, 2020). The trilateral academic cooperation has taken the form of co-organized events, MOUs between individual institutions and the North Pacific Arctic Research Community (NPARC). In the context of the High-Level Dialogue, NPARC has been described as a consultative mechanism to pursue bilateral and multilateral joint research and to discuss and work together on various Arctic-related issues (Ministry of Foreign Affairs Republic of Korea, 2019). However, the number of the NPARC meeting participants (considering a high number of NEA scholars in the Arctic-related research) and the amount of attention that these events have attracted are low as compared to many other Arctic conferences attracting numerous speakers and participants from the NEA countries.

The North Pacific Arctic Conferences (NPAC), which have been organized by East-West Center in Honolulu and supported by the Korea Maritime Institute for a decade, are another forum for off the record discussions between participants with different backgrounds (East-West Center, 2020). Whereas the NPAC framework has been open and relied on contributions from the NEA participants, their role in the most recent North Pacific and Arctic cooperation initiatives is yet to be seen. For instance, when the creation of the Bering Pacific Arctic Council (BPAC)—modeled on the Barents Euro-Arctic Council and Barents Regional Council—was announced at the meeting of the Russian American Pacific

Partnership (RAPP) in June 2019, it was presented as a bilateral project. Nevertheless, it is understood that some of the stakeholders in this initiative favor minilateralism. However, at this stage it is hard to predict whether Japanese (and other NEA) actors will be allowed to play any role (Krasnopolski, 2020; Voronenko, 2021). At the subnational level, Hokkaido appears as an eligible partner for the Regional Council not only due to its geographical location but also its long history of the North/Arctic engagement and established ties with the northern and Arctic regions (Babin & Saunavaara, 2021).

Although Japan is a unitary state with a strong tradition of centralization, the national government (especially, MoFA)'s capacity to regulate international flows has weakened during the past decades. SNGs have been at the forefront of the sub- and non-state actors' involvement in Japan's foreign policy, despite the lack of clarity in the legal framework regulating their international functions. MoFA has accepted and valued some of these new initiatives rather than dismissing them offhand (Jain, 2012; Kossa et al., 2020). Whereas Hokkaido's engagement with the Arctic has clearly been the most systematic among the Japanese SNGs, other regions, such as Aomori and Niigata, have also either demonstrated interest or have been mentioned in the context of the NSR-related initiatives (Inano et al., 2012; Saunavaara, 2017).

The traditionally strong role of the national bureaucracy as a powerful policy agent, and their tendency to rely on ministerial advisory or policy deliberation councils when external advice is needed, has limited the role of private research institutions and think tanks in Japan (Abb & Köllner, 2015). However, they have formed another channel and group of actors contributing to Japan's international activity even if their role may not be visible from the analysis of national policies and flagship research projects. In Japan's Arctic engagement, OPRI and its precursor have been important actors committed to long-term involvement. The OPRI's dominant position may also explain why other major think tanks, with the exception of JIIA (closely affiliated with MoFA) and National Institute for Defense Studies (a formal government agency under the MoD), have paid less attention to this region. Among the actors more geographically related to this area, the Institute for Russian & NIS Economic Studies (ROTOBO Institute) and Economic Research Institute for Northeast Asia (ERINA) have conducted several projects and organized events related to the Arctic although they may not be easily identified as "Arctic actors" and focus predominantly on Russia (ERINA, 2020; ROTOBO, 2020, 2021).

Conclusions

This chapter, elaborating on Japan's cross-border interactions related to the Arctic, emphasizes both the changing notions of the "Arcticness" and stakeholdership in the Arctic matters. Although often treated as a geographical entity (with various demarcation lines depending on the criteria used), the Arctic is also a political and sociocultural construction, the meaning and content of which is being constantly renegotiated. In conceptualizing their relations with the Arctic, Japanese actors have occasionally referred to the geographical proximity to the Arctic. However, Japan's claims of possessing linkages to and the need to interact with the Arctic have more often been based on the notion of a common concern (particularly with respect to the climate change and other global environmental issues) and networks (trade, logistics, and academic cooperation). These constructions are often supported by the arguments that developments in the Arctic affect Japan and that actions taken by the Japanese actors may have an effect on the sustainable development of the circumpolar north. Furthermore, Japanese actors' increasing interest in the involvement in the Arctic-related matters may be considered as a reflection of the overall attractiveness of this concept: it appears that the "Arctic" may be replacing alternative spatial concepts such as the "North" as a core around which different types of cross-border cooperation initiatives are constructed (Babin & Saunavaara, 2021).

This study intentionally leaves out some issues and actors that deserve a separate analysis. Further research focusing on the past and present interaction and cooperation between the Ainu and the other indigenous peoples of the north, or the history of Japan's conflict and cooperation with the North Pacific states related to the "northern fisheries" dating back to its sealing in the nineteenth century and including recent wildlife protection initiatives, for instance, would complement the general understanding of the relationship between Japan and the Arctic. Our findings corroborate the previously made argument that Japan's Arctic engagement is not dominated or coordinated by a single actor but is rather a chorus of various actors and voices (Chuffart et al., 2020; Tonami & Watters, 2012). However, the question of how other stakeholders view and possibly attempt to use Japan's presence in the Arctic (for instance, balancing against the increasing influence of China) remains to be answered.

References

3rd Arctic Science Ministerial. (2021). *About ASM3*. https://asm3.org/about-asm3/. Accessed 26 July 2021.

Abb, P., & Köllner, P. (2015). Foreign policy think tanks in China and Japan: Characteristics, current profile, and the case of collective self-defense. *International Journal, 70*(4), 539–612. https://doi.org/10.1177/0020702015592119

Allen, J., et al. (1998). *Rethinking the region: Spaces of neo-liberalism*. Routledge.

ArCS. (2016). *Dr. Fukasawa's talk at Arctic Circle attracted other countries' great interest in the Japan's arctic policy strategy and the ArCS project ArCS*. https://www.nipr.ac.jp/arcs/blog/en/2016/02/arctic-circle-general-assembly-2015.html. Accessed 26 July 2021.

ArCS. (2021). *Project overview—About ArCS II*. https://www.nipr.ac.jp/arcs2/e/about/. Accessed 26 July 2021.

Arctic Circle. (2021). *Arctic Circle Japan forum*. www.arcticcircle.org/forums/japan. Accessed 26 July 2021.

Arctic Economic Council. (2020). *Members*. https://arcticeconomiccouncil.com/members/. Accessed 26 July 2021.

Babin, J., & Lasserre, F. (2019). Asian states at the Arctic Council: Perceptions in Western States. *Polar Geography, 42*(3), 145–159. https://doi.org/10.1080/1088937X.2019.1578290

Babin, J., & Saunavaara, J. (2021). Hokkaido: From the "Road to the Northern Sea" to "Japan's gateway to the Arctic". *Asian Geographer (2019)*. https://doi.org/10.1080/10225706.2021.1910525

Bennett, M. (2014). North by Northeast: Toward an Asian-Arctic region. *Eurasian Geography and Economics, 55*(1), 71–93. https://doi.org/10.1080/15387216.2014.936480

Bennet, M. (2017, June 15). China, Japan and South Korea hold their own Arctic dialogue. *Arctic Today*. https://www.arctictoday.com/china-japan-and-south-korea-hold-their-own-arctic-dialogue/. Accessed 26 July 2021.

Cabinet Office of Japan. (2013). *Basic plan on Ocean policy: A provisional translation*. https://www8.cao.go.jp/ocean/english/plan/pdf/plan02_e.pdf. Accessed 26 July 2021.

Cabinet Office of Japan. (2018, May 15). *The basic plan on Ocean policy*. Cabinet Decision, A provisional translation. https://www8.cao.go.jp/ocean/english/plan/pdf/plan03_e.pdf. Accessed 26 July 2021.

Chuffart, R., Hataya, S., Inagaki, O., & Arthur, L. (2020). Assessing Japan's Arctic engagement during the ArCS project (2015–2020). *The Yearbook of Polar Law Online, 12*(1), 328–348. https://doi.org/10.1163/22116427_012010020.

Cinia. (2020, September 28). *The Arctic connect telecom cable project becomes more international*. https://www.cinia.fi/en/news/the-arctic-con

422 M. LOMAEVA AND J. SAUNAVAARA

nect-telecom-cable-project-becomes-more-international. Accessed 26 July 2021.

Cinia. (2021, January 19). *Arctic gateway for research & education.* https://www.cinia.fi/en/news/arctic-gateway-for-research-and-education. Accessed 26 July 2021.

East-West Center. (2020). *North Pacific Arctic conference East-West Center.* https://www.eastwestcenter.org/research/research-projects/north-pacific-arctic-conference. Accessed 26 July 2021.

Embassy of Japan, Moscow. (2021). *Roshia no seikatsu kankyō taikoku, sangyō-keizai no kakushin no tame no kyōryoku puran* [Russia living environment powerhouse, cooperation plan for the sake of the industry-economy reform]. https://www.ru.emb-japan.go.jp/economy/common/file/8-point-plan-jp.pdf. Accessed 26 July 2021.

ERINA. (2020). *Koronaka no Roshia kyokutou keizai to hokkyokukai kōro* [The economy of Far East Russia under corona calamity and the Northern Sea route]. https://www.erina.or.jp/about/news/141495/. Accessed 26 July 2021.

Finger, M., & Heininen, L. (2019). *The GlobalArctic Handbook.* Springer.

Gautier, D. (2007). *Oil and gas resources of Northeast Greenland.* https://assets.geoexpro.com/legacy-files/articles/Oil%20and%20Gas%20Resources%20of%20Northeast%20Greenland.pdf. Accessed 26 July 2021.

Government of Canada. (2021). *Canada–Japan relations.* https://www.canada international.gc.ca/japan-japon/bilateral_relations_bilaterales/index.aspx?lang=eng. Accessed 26 July 2021.

HaRP. (2021). *Reports.* https://russia-platform.oia.hokudai.ac.jp/en/report. Accessed 26 July 2021.

Hasanat, W. (2012). International cooperation in the Northern Forum: Emerging new norms in international law? *Polar Record, 48*(247), 1–15.

Hokkaido Corporation. (2018). *The project for solution of garbage problems in Russia: To all over Russia Exporting garbage disposal plant.* https://hkdc.co.jp/en/project/300/. Accessed 26 July 2021.

Hokkaido Corporation. (2019). *Participation in a plan for improvement of an airport in Yakutsk, Sakha Republic.* https://hkdc.co.jp/en/topics/176/. Accessed 26 July 2021.

Hokkaido Government. (2019). *Kore made no Hokkaidō to Roshia to no chiiki kōryu ni tsuite* [Concerning the exchanges between Hokkaido and Russian regions so far]. https://www.pref.hokkaido.lg.jp/fs/2/2/7/5/4/2/4/_/20191030Doc3.pdf. Accessed 26 July 2021.

Hokkaido Government. (2020). *(Hokkaidō – Roshia kyōryoku purattofoomu) sanka kigyō – tandai no boshū ni tsuite* [Hokkaido-Russia cooperation platform—Concerning the recruitments of participating companies and associations]. https://www.pref.hokkaido.lg.jp/ss/tsk/russia/russia/tiikikankyou ryoku.html. Accessed 26 July 2021.

Hokkaido Government. (2021). *(Hokkaidō – Roshia chiikikan kōryu suishin hōshin (kashō)) nosakutei ni kakaru yūshikisha kaigi* [Expert meeting to decide on the Hokkaido-Russia interregional cooperation promotion plan (temporary name)]. http://www.pref.hokkaido.lg.jp/ss/tsk/russia/russia/expertsmeeting.html. Accessed 26 July 2021.

Hokkaido University. (2021). *Hokkaido University Arctic Research Center*. https://www.arc.hokudai.ac.jp/en/. Accessed 26 July 2021.

Humpert, M. (2019, June 6). Japan's Mitsui and Mitsubishi take 10 percent stake in Novatek's Arctic LNG 2. *High North News*. https://www.highnorthnews.com/en/japans-mitsui-and-mitsubishi-take-10-percent-stake-novateksarctic-lng-2

Inano, M., Mitsuoka, T., & Koya, T. (2012). *Hokkyokukai kōro ni tsuite – Hokkaidō kōwan no kanōsei ni kan suru kentō* [Concerning the Northern Sea route—Study concerning the possibilities of the Hokkaido-based harbors]. *Hokkaidō Kaihatsukyoku Kōwan-Kūkōbu Kōwan Keikakuka*. https://thesis.ceri.go.jp/db/files/GR0003000104.pdf. Accessed 26 July 2021.

Ishikura, T. (2021, April 12). Japan to build new icebreaker for researching Arctic region. *The Asahi Shimbun*. https://www.asahi.com/ajw/articles/14329185. Accessed 26 July 2021.

Jain, P. (2012). *Japan's subnational governments in international affairs*. Sheffield Centre for Japanese Studies/Routledge Series.

JAMSTEC. (2021). *Institute of Arctic climate and environment research*. https://www.jamstec.go.jp/iace/e/. Accessed 26 July 2021.

JAXA. (2016). *Satellites watch over the Northern Sea Route*. https://global.jaxa.jp/article/2015/special/satellite/sagawa.html. Accessed 26 July 2021.

JAXA. (2020). *"Hokkyokukai no kaihyō menseki ga 9 gatsu 13 nichi ni nenkan saishōchi wo kiroku - eisei kansoku shijō 2 banme no chiisasa* [The Arctic Ocean sea ice extent annual minimum recorded on September 13—The second smallest in the history of satellite observation]. https://www.jaxa.jp/press/2020/09/20200923-2_j.html. Accessed 26 July 2021.

JIIA. (2012). *2012 Research project outcome "Arctic Governance and Japan's diplomatic strategy"*. https://www2.jiia.or.jp/en/research/2012_arctic_governance.php. Accessed 26 July 2021.

JMA. (2021). *Kaihyō kaiseki ni riyō shita deeta ni tsuite* [Concerning the data used in the analysis of the sea ice]. https://www.data.jma.go.jp/gmd/kaiyou/db/seaice/knowledge/ice_data.html. Accessed 26 July 2021.

JOGMEC. (2012). JOGMEC provides equity financing for petroleum exploration offshore Greenland. www.jogmec.go.jp/english/news/release/release0086.html. Accessed 26 July 2021.

Kim, E., & Stenport, A. (2021). South Korea's Arctic policy: Political motivations for 21st century global engagements. *The Polar Journal*. https://doi.org/10.1080/2154896X.2021.1917088

Knecht, S., & Laubenstein, P. (2020). Is Arctic governance research in crisis? A pathological diagnosis. *Polar Record*, 56(35). https://doi.org/10.1017/S0032247420000352

Kobe University. (2021). *About Polar cooperation research centre*. www.research.kobe-u.ac.jp/gsics-pcrc/centre.html. Accessed 26 July 2021.

Kossa, M., Lomaeva, M., & Saunavaara, J. (2020). East Asian subnational government involvement in the Arctic: A case for paradiplomacy? *The Pacific Review*, 34(4), 664–695. https://doi.org/10.1080/09512748.2020.1729843

Krasnopolski, B. H. (2020). Bering/Pacific-Arctic Council (BPAC): Russian-American ecological and social-economic cooperation at the junctions of the North Pacific and Arctic Oceans and the Eurasian and North American Continents. *Journal of Economic and Business Studies*, 3(1). https://doi.org/10.36266/JEBS/146

Kumagai, T., & Yep, E. (2020, September 30). Japan eyes participating in Kamchatka LNG reloading terminal: Official. *S&P Global*. https://www.spglobal.com/platts/en/market-insights/latest-news/natural-gas/093020-japan-eyes-participating-in-kamchatka-lng-reloading-terminal-official. Accessed 26 July 2021.

Landriault, M., et al. (2019). *Governing complexity in the Arctic region*. Routledge.

Leonard, L. L. (1944). *International regulation of fisheries*. Carnegie Endowment for International Peace.

MAFF. (2020). *Joint Japanese-Russian project to increase the productivity of agriculture and fisheries in the Russian Far East*. https://www.maff.go.jp/j/press/kokusai/kokkyo/attach/pdf/200129-1.pdf. Accessed 26 July 2021.

Marubeni Corporation. (2013). *Marubeni and Rosneft sign memorandum for strategic partnership*. https://www.marubeni.com/en/news/2013/release/00015.html. Accessed 26 July 2021.

Marubeni Corporation. (2017). *Marubeni, Mitsui O.S.K. Lines and NOVATEK Sign a memorandum of understanding for an LNG transshipment and marketing project in the Kamchatka area*. https://www.marubeni.com/en/news/2017/release/00019.html. Accessed 26 July 2021.

METI. (2021). *Japan's new international resource strategy for enhancing LNG security*. https://www.enecho.meti.go.jp/en/category/special/article/detail_162.html. Accessed 26 July 2021.

Ministry of Foreign Affairs of the People's Republic of China. (2018). *Joint statement the third trilateral high-level dialogue on the Arctic*. https://www.fmprc.

JAPAN FACING THE ARCTIC AND NORTH: INTERPLAY BETWEEN ...   425

gov.cn/mfa_eng/wjdt_665385/2649_665393/t1567103.shtml. Accessed 26 July 2021.

Ministry of Foreign Affairs, Republic of Korea. (2019). *4th ROK-Japan-China trilateral high-level dialogue on Arctic to take place*. http://www.mofa.go.kr/eng/brd/m_5676/view.do?seq=320573. Accessed 26 July 2021.

MoE, MEXT, MAFF, MLIT, Japan Meteorological Agency. (2018). *Synthesis report on observations, projections and impact assessments of climate change, 2018 "Climate Change in Japan and its impacts"*. https://www.env.go.jp/earth/tekiou/pamph2018_full_Eng.pdf. Accessed 26 July 2021.

MLIT. (2014). *'Hokkyokukai kōro ni kakaru sangakukan renkei kyōgikai' no secchi ni tsuite* [Concerning the establishment of the council of industry-academia-government collaboration on the Arctic sea route]. https://www.mlit.go.jp/common/001294221.pdf. Accessed 26 July 2021.

MLIT. (2020). *Hokkyokukai kōro no rikatsuyō suishin* [Promotion of the usage of the Northern Sea Route]. https://www.mlit.go.jp/sogoseisaku/ocean_pol icy/sosei_ocean_tk_000021.html. Accessed 26 July 2021.

MoFA. (2016). *Joint statement on a strategic partnership between Japan and the Republic of Finland as Gateways in Asia and Europe*. https://www.mofa.go.jp/erp/we/fi/page4e_000391.html. Accessed 26 July 2021.

MoFA. (2017a). *Hokkyoku hyōgikai kōkyū hokkyoku jitsumusha kaigō no kaisai* [The Arctic Council's senior Arctic officials meeting]. https://www.mofa.go.jp/mofaj/fp/msp/page22_002888.html. Accessed 26 July 2021.

MoFA. (2017b). Joint statement: The second trilateral high-level dialogue on the Arctic. https://www.mofa.go.jp/files/000263104.pdf. Accessed 26 July 2021.

MoFA. (2020). *Diplomatic bluebook 2020*. https://www.mofa.go.jp/files/100 116875.pdf. Accessed 26 July 2021.

National Agriculture and Food Research Organization. (n.d.). *Warmth index*. www.naro.affrc.go.jp/archive/niaes/topics/g7/wi_e.html. Accessed 26 July 2021.

NEAR. (2020). *Annual activity reports*. www.neargov.org/en/page.jsp?mnu_uid=3099&. Accessed 26 July 2021.

NEDO. (2018). *Three cold-resistant wind turbine generators start operations for Russian far east energy infrastructure demonstration project*. https://www.nedo.go.jp/english/news/AA5en_100397.html. Accessed 26 July 2021.

Nilsen, T. (2021, April 21). Work on trans-Arctic fiber-optic cable starts this spring. *The Barents Observer*. https://thebarentsobserver.com/en/ind ustry-and-energy/2021/04/work-trans-arctic-fiber-optic-cable-starts-may. Accessed 26 July 2021.

NIPR. (2016). *GRENE Arctic climate change research project*. https://www.nipr.ac.jp/grene/e/. Accessed 26 July 2021.

NIPR. (2021). *About our institute.* https://www.nipr.ac.jp/english/outline/summary/activity.html. Accessed 26 July 2021.

O'Loughlin, J., & Van der Wusten, H. (1990). Political geography of panregions. *Geographical Review, 80*(1), 1–20.

Opetushallitus. (2020). *Asia programme, final report for projects 2018–2020.* https://www.oph.fi/sites/default/files/documents/Summary_Finnish-Japanese%20Arctic%20Studies%20Project.pdf. Accessed 26 July 2021.

OPRI. (2018). *Arctic Ocean.* https://www.spf.org/en/opri/projects/arctic.html. Accessed 26 July 2021.

Paasi, A. (2020). Regional geography. *International encyclopedia of human geography* (pp. 309–320). Elsevier.

Parliamentary League of Arctic Frontier Study. (2017). *Hokkyoku furonthia ni tsuite kangaeru giin renmei kara no kinkyū teigen* [Urgent proposal on behalf of the Parliamentary League of Arctic Frontier study]. www.shindo.gr.jp/cms/wp-content/uploads/2017/09/20170905_shiryo_hokyoku.pdf. Accessed 26 July 2021.

Pollman, M. (2017, July 13). Abe's Nordic Tour and Japan's Arctic ambitions. *The Diplomat.* https://thediplomat.com/2017/07/abes-nordic-tour-and-japans-arctic-ambitions/. Accessed 26 July 2021.

Polutov, A. (2016). Japan and Soviet Arctic: Military history aspect (1932—1945). *Russia and the Pacific* (pp. 69–82). Accessed 26 July 2021.

Pro Arctic. (2021). *МТС присоединилась к проекту подводной ВОЛС в Арктике* [MTS joined the submarine fiber-optic cable project in the Arctic]. https://pro-arctic.ru/03/06/2021/news/43751#read. Accessed 26 July 2021.

Qiu, W. (2021). Trans-arctic cable project Arctic connect comes to a suspension. *Submarine Cable Networks.* https://www.submarinenetworks.com/en/systems/asia-europe-africa/arctic-connect/trans-arctic-cable-project-arctic-connect-comes-to-a-suspension. Accessed 26 July 2021.

RJE3. (2021). *Program feature.* https://rje3.oia.hokudai.ac.jp/en/about/overview/. Accessed 26 July 2021.

ROTOBO. (2020). *Roshia NIS chōsa geppō 2020 nen 4 gatsu gō* [Russia NIS survey monthly report 2020 April]. https://www.rotobo.or.jp/publication/monthly/m202004.html. Accessed 26 July 2021.

ROTOBO. (2021). *Roshia NIS chōsa geppō 2021 nen 3 gatsu gō* [Russia NIS survey monthly report 2021 March]. https://www.rotobo.or.jp/publication/monthly/m202103.html. Accessed 26 July 2021.

Saunavaara, J. (2017). The changing Arctic & the development of Hokkaido. In L. Heininen, H. Exner-Pirot, & J. Plouffe (Eds.), *Arctic yearbook 2017* (pp. 326–338). Northern Research Forum.

Saunavaara, J. (2018a). Arctic subsea communication cables and the regional development of Northern peripheries. *Arctic and North, 32,* 51–67.

Saunavaara, J. (2018b). Reconstructing and redefining Hokkaido during the post-war period. *The International Journal of Asia Pacific Studies, 14*(1).

Saunavaara, J., & Ohnishi, F. (2020). Arctic Challenge for Sustainability II: Japan's new Arctic flagship project. *Current Developments in Arctic Law, 8,* 40–43.

Saunavaara, J., & Salminen, M. (2020). Geography of the global submarine fiber-optic cable network: The case for Arctic Ocean solutions. *Geographical Review.* https://doi.org/10.1080/00167428.2020.1773266

Sevunts, L. (2017, September 27). Japan looks to Canada to keep an eye on China's Arctic ambitions: Expert. *Eye on the Arctic.* https://www.rcinet.ca/eye-on-the-arctic/2017/09/27/japan-looks-to-canada-to-keep-an-eye-on-chinas-arctic-ambitions-expert/. Accessed 26 July 2021.

Sheppard, E. (2002). The spaces and times of globalization: Place, scale, networks, and positionality. *Economic Geography, 78*(3), 307–330.

Staalesen, A. (2020, November 11). Developers of trans-Arctic cable draw closer to Nordic coast. *The Barents Observer.* https://thebarentsobserver.com/en/arctic/2020/11/developers-trans-arctic-cable-take-step-towards-nordic-coast. Accessed 26 July 2021.

Steinveg, B. (2020). *Governance by conference? Actors and agendas in Arctic politics.* Ph.D. dissertation. https://munin.uit.no/handle/10037/20490. Accessed 26 July 2021.

Steinveg, B. (2021). The role of conferences within Arctic governance. *Polar Geography, 44*(1), 37–54. https://doi.org/10.1080/1088937X.2020.1798540

The Arctic. (2020). *Yakutia expects a record harvest of cucumbers, tomatoes and greens.* https://arctic.ru/economics/20201013/983497.html. Accessed 26 July 2021.

The Headquarters for Ocean Policy. (2015). *Japan's Arctic policy.* https://www8.cao.go.jp/ocean/english/arctic/pdf/japans_ap_e.pdf. Accessed 26 July 2021.

The State Council of the People's Republic of China. (2021). *China's Arctic policy.* http://english.www.gov.cn/archive/white_paper/2018/01/26/content_281476026660336.htm. Accessed 26 July 2021.

Tonami, A. (2016). *Asian foreign policy in a changing Arctic: The diplomacy of economy and science at new frontiers.* Palgrave.

Tonami, A. (2020). Hikokka akutā ni yoru paradipuromashī to kihan: hokkyokuiki ni tai suru Hokkaidō no torikumi wo rei ni [Paradiplomacy by non-state actors and Norms: An example from Hokkaido's approach towards the Arctic Region]. In T. Oga, R. Nakano, & A. Matsumoto (Eds.), *Kyōsei shakai no saikōchiku III: kokusai kihan no kyōgō to chōwa* [Reconstruction of the inclusive society III: Conflict and coordination of international norms] (pp. 114–130). Hōritsu Bunkasha.

Tonami, A., & Watters, S. (2012). Japan's Arctic policy: The sum of many parts. In L. Heininen, H. Exner-Pirot, & J. Plouffe (Eds.), *The Arctic yearbook 2012* (pp. 93–103). Northern Research Forum.

Tsui, E. (2020). Looking around: Opportunities of using paradiplomacy scholarship in the Arctic policy discussions. In T. S. Axworthy, S. French & E. Tsui (Eds.), *Lessons from the Arctic: The role of regional government in international affairs* (99–105). Mosaic Press.

U.S. Department of State. (2020). *U.S. relations with Japan.* https://www.state.gov/u-s-relations-with-japan/. Accessed 26 July 2021.

Väätänen, V., & Zimmerbauer, K. (2019). Territory–network interplay in the co-constitution of the Arctic and 'to-be' Arctic states. *Territory, Politics, Governance, 8*(3), 372–289.

Voronenko, A. (2021, January 12). *Sustainable development and trans-boundary international cooperation in Eastern (Pacific) Arctic Zone.* Presentation at the Online workshop: Multilevel Governance and Interregional Cooperation: Vol. 1—The Pacific Arctic. https://www.uarctic.org/news/2020/12/online-workshop-multilevel-governance-and-interregional-cooperation-vol-1-the-pacific-arctic/. Accessed 26 July 2021.

Wee, V. (2018, September 14). MOL, Marubeni sign agreement with advisory group for LNG transhipment terminals in Far East. *Sea Trade Marine News.* https://www.seatrade-maritime.com/asia/mol-marubeni-sign-agreement-advisory-group-lng-transhipment-terminals-far-east. Accessed 26 July 2021.

WWCAM. (2019). *2019 Working-level officials meeting in Norilsk.* https://wwcam.org/en/activity/wlom/2019-working-level-officials-meeting. Accessed 26 July 2021.

WWCAM. (2020a). *Historical background.* https://wwcam.org/en/about/history. Accessed 26 July 2021.

WWCAM. (2020b). *What is a "Winter City"?* https://wwcam.org/en/about/definition.

WWCAM. (2020c). *First Mayors conference.* https://wwcam.org/en/activity/mc/first-mayors-conference. Accessed 26 July 2021.

WWCAM. (2021). *Mayors conference.* https://wwcam.org/en/activity/mc. Accessed 26 July 2021.

Cooperative and Multilateral Agenda of the Arctic Region: Despite All Odds. International Law, Institutions and Regimes for the Arctic Region

Institutional Framework for Arctic Governance: Do We Need Reforms?

Pavel Gudev and Dmitriy Tulupov

INTRODUCTION

In May 2021, the baton of the Arctic Council's presidency was passed over to Russia. This move occurs at the peak of fierce competition with the West, which is setting quite an uncertain background of regional development. The biggest concern for those involved in regional affairs is that eventually, global tensions will trigger negative implications locally (in the Arctic). In this regard, it is worth exploring whether the Arctic governance system is resilient enough to withstand such pressure? What are

---

Dmitriy Tulupov—Participation on the basis of the "GEOSEAS" Project—The Geopolitics and Geoeconomics of Maritime Spatial Disputes in the Arctic", The Fridtjof Nansen Institute, Norway.

P. Gudev (✉)
Center for North American Studies, Primakov Institute of World Economy and International Relations Russian Academy of Sciences (IMEMO RAS), Moscow, Russia
e-mail: gudev@imemo.ru

D. Tulupov
St. Petersburg State University, Saint Petersburg, Russia

© The Author(s), under exclusive license to Springer Nature Singapore Pte Ltd. 2022
A. Likhacheva (ed.), *Arctic Fever*,
https://doi.org/10.1007/978-981-16-9616-9_16

future trends for the institutional and legal foundations of Arctic development? Moreover, finally, is it relevant to explore what kind of role the Arctic Council can play in these troublesome times?

The first part of the section considers institutional features of the Arctic region management, the role and place of the Arctic Council in this system; then it shows the differences between the two polar regions—the Arctic and the Antarctic; gives proposals for giving the Arctic Council new powers and competences; studies the expediency of forming new international structures, including coordination of scientific research in the region; in conclusion—it considers in detail the question of whether it is appropriate to include the topic of military security in the region to the Arctic Council.

THE CURRENT STATE OF AFFAIRS IN THE ARCTIC GOVERNANCE

Concerning the Arctic, as, indeed, to many other maritime regions, three levels of governance can be distinguished: a broad international level; a more substantive one, the regional; and, finally, the narrowest one—the national. There is no doubt now that the 1982 UN Convention on the Law of the Sea is fully applicable to the Arctic region and serves as a "legal umbrella" for it, including determining the applicability of lower-level agreements/arrangements. At the regional level, there have been so-called "fracture-specific" regimes in the Arctic: the 1920 Treaty of Paris on Spitsbergen, the 1973 Agreement on the Conservation of Polar Bears, the 1958 Seal Agreement, and a variety of other bilateral and multilateral agreements. At the same time, national legislation of the coastal states continues to play a much more significant role and weight in the Arctic. This is due not only to the fact that there are maritime zones that are subject to their sovereignty, sovereign rights, and jurisdiction but also to the fact that historically many activities here—primarily navigation—were regulated by the Arctic countries (USSR/Russia; Canada) at the national level, by adopting and developing domestic legislation.

The Arctic Council (AC) indeed occupies a place of honor in this hierarchy as a key regional forum. As the authors of the report "The Arctic Council: Status and Activities" (Vylegzhanin et al., 2021) note, it does not have a monopoly on governing the Arctic region, as there are other intergovernmental fora and structures, among them: Nordic Council of Ministers; Barents/Euro-Arctic Council; Arctic Coast Guard Forum; Arctic Economic Council; International Arctic Scientific Committee, etc.

However, one cannot ignore that the AC is at the center of the established legal mechanism for managing the Arctic Ocean. Its permanent members are countries whose territory lies beyond the Arctic Circle, and five of them are directly washed by the waters of the Arctic Ocean. Given that Arctic indigenous peoples are a crucial feature of the Arctic as a whole, it is no coincidence that the six organizations representing their interests have the status of permanent participants of the Arctic Council, giving them the right to participate in decision-making. The Arctic Council serves as a forum for the conclusion of legally binding agreements concerning the management of the Arctic region, among them: Agreement on Cooperation in Aviation and Maritime Search and Rescue in the Arctic (2011); Agreement on Cooperation in Marine Oil Pollution Preparedness and Response in the Arctic (2013); Agreement on Enhancing International Scientific Cooperation in the Arctic (2017). All of this together raises one very pressing question: isn't it time to start the process of transforming the AC into a full-fledged international organization? First of all, in order to make its decisions binding.

On the one hand, such a change of status would help strengthen the AC's authority. However, on the other hand, such a transformation would inevitably raise highly uncomfortable questions, which could ultimately dilute the current exclusive nature of cooperation and collaboration among the Arctic states.

First, it would be reasonable to assume that the formation of the new organization would once again raise the question of the balance between the AC's permanent members and observers (Arctic Council, n.d.). Although this issue is now completely closed and the number of permanent members cannot be expanded, the observer countries may demand a new status under the new international organization. Indeed, such a situation does not meet the Arctic Five's national interests or the Arctic Eight.

Second, the emergence of a new international organization will be met with interest by most of the interested states, including those who now only claim to obtain observer status in the AC. We would like to recall that among them are Turkey, Mongolia, Estonia, and some others. Obviously, "inclusion" in the Arctic race for many of them is a confirmation of their high international status, such as for the ambitious political regime of President R. Erdogan. For some countries, such as inland Mongolia, economic determinants prevail: Mongolia belongs to the states with the so-called "flag of convenience". It is highly beneficial to "secure" its place within the AC for prospective participants in Arctic transportation.

In our view, the interests of the E.U. are already well represented in the Arctic through the membership of Finland and Sweden in the AC and some European observer states. Moreover, there are countries such as Estonia, which see their participation in the AC as an effective way to reduce the influence of the Russian Federation, including through the maximum involvement of NATO in the Arctic, considering Moscow's policy in the region as a security threat. Of course, the participation of such states in both the AC and any new international organization is not in Russias interests. Moreover, even current attempts by such a supra-national structure as the E.U. to obtain observer organization status are unlikely to support the Russian Federation since the introduction and maintenance of the sanction's regime is a declaration of economic war.

Finally, the format of the international organization suggests that the main question that will inevitably come up on the agenda—what model of decision-making will exist within it? Today within the framework of the Arctic Council, all decisions are made by consensus. It means that any decision is reached not by voting but by negotiating, finding compromises, and mutual concessions. It should be taken into account that consensus does not require the agreement of all participants to the proposed decision; it means only their joint agreement and the absence of any official objections. This is the fundamental difference between the consensus method and the principle of unanimity when a decision is considered to be adopted if all the participants have voted for it. Thus, the text of the 1982 United Nations Convention on the Law of the Sea, namely Article 161 (8) (e), provides, however, concerning the activities of the Council of the International Seabed Authority, that consensus "means the absence of any formal objection" (UN, 1982).

For us, there is no doubt that any potential expansion of the number of AC participants, in case of its potential transition from one institutional state to another, will mean that reaching a mutually beneficial decision in the consensus method will be quite problematic due to the mismatch of interests primarily between regional and extra-regional countries. More-over, on the one hand, the consensus decision-making procedure is essential in order to ensure the broadest possible support for the decision being made. On the other hand, the text of consensus decisions can often be unclear, ambiguous because it is based on some compromise. Moreover, an apparent consensus may conceal disagreement with a decision, which then leads to its non-implementation.

That said, it is also clear that with equal rights for permanent members and observers, and with the door open to all interested parties, decision-making based on the majority principle, or a 2/3 qualified majority would not be in the interest of the Arctic states, as other non-Arctic countries would have a preponderance of the vote. Therefore, the only acceptable option would be an analogy to the UN Security Council, with the Arctic states holding the right of veto within the AC. This option would suit the Russian Federation, but it is highly "toxic" to other states, so it is unlikely to be agreed upon. "Toxic" for the simple reason that although the Arctic remains the only maritime region to which all the complexities of relations between Russia and Western countries do not extend, the level of mutual suspicion is still very high. Moreover, the right of veto may allow, for example, the Russian Federation, to block certain decisions within the framework of the Arctic Council. It is unlikely that the U.S. and other Arctic powers are ready to give Russia such additional rights and opportunities.

ARCTIC GOVERNANCE VS. THE ANTARCTIC TREATY SYSTEM

Many experts have long noted that the two polar regions, the Arctic and the Antarctic, have much in common. For example, the consensus decision-making system also operates within the Antarctic Treaty System (ATS), which has some standard features with the emerging Arctic Council System (ACS) (Molenaar, 2012). During the Antarctic Treaty Consultative Meetings (ATCM), decisions are made by the so-called consultative parties, i.e., the countries endowed with the right to participate in the decision-making process because they have proven their interest in the region, including through active scientific research. However, in contrast to the Arctic Council, their number has grown steadily and now numbers 29 states, although initially there were 12.[1] Despite certain parallels between the ATS and ACS, there are much more differences between them than shared features (Berkman, 2012).

---

[1] Initially it was 12 participants of the Antarctic Conference (Australia, Argentina, Belgium, Great Britain, New Zealand, Norway, the USSR, the USA, France, Chile, SAR, Japan). Then other countries received the right of deliberative vote.

First, Antarctica is the continent of Antarctica surrounded by an ocean, while the Arctic is a maritime region surrounded by continents.

Second, there is a fundamental difference between the two in ice conditions. While Antarctic ice is seasonal, predominantly annual, the Arctic ice is perennial and occupies a large part of the Arctic Ocean water area regardless of the season.

Third, the Arctic continental shelf is characterized by highly shallow depths and considerable length, while the Antarctic shelf is one of the deepest on the planet, but it does not differ in length.

Fourth, the territories, washed by the Arctic Ocean waters, were historically inhabited by representatives of the so-called indigenous peoples of the North, while the Antarctic has no indigenous population.

Fifth, in the Arctic, the zones of sovereignty (internal waters, territorial sea, their bottom and subsoil, and the air space above them) and jurisdiction (the contiguous zone, the 200-mile exclusive economic zone, and the continental shelf) of the Arctic states have long been defined. The existing contradictions concern only the definition of the outer limits and delimitation of the continental shelf, i.e., the underwater margin of the continent, beyond the 200-mile zone from the baselines. The situation around the continental shelf of Antarctica is different: the claimant countries addressed the Commission on the Limits of the Continental Shelf with their applications, including the continental shelf of Antarctica, but with a reservation concerning the fact that the Commission has not yet considered their rightful claims in this part. Article 4 of the 1959 Antarctic Treaty does not recognize any claims concerning the territories located in the area of this agreement; respectively, these claims cause legitimate opposition from other participants of the Antarctic Treaty—first of all, the U.S. and the Russian Federation.

Sixth, non-living (mineral) resources are already being developed in the Arctic, while such activity is prohibited concerning Antarctica. The Protocol on Environmental Protection to the Antarctic Treaty of October 4, 1991 (the so-called Madrid Protocol) prohibits any activity related to mineral resources, except scientific research (Article 7).

Seventh, the Arctic has always had and will always have an essential military-strategic significance. Intercontinental ballistic missiles pass through it, which is why critical attention is paid here to the development of aerospace defense capabilities, including the deployment of U.S. missile defense. The presence of the submarine fleet, which regularly patrols the Arctic waters, necessitates anti-submarine activities.

That is why all proposals to demilitarize the Arctic, including creating a nuclear-weapon-free zone within it, cannot be supported by most Arctic states, primarily Russia and the United States. Whereas Antarctica is not only a fully demilitarized region but also has a nuclear-free status.

Eighth, the Convention on the Conservation of Antarctic Marine Living Resources, concluded in Canberra in 1980, was a "pioneer" in applying the so-called ecosystem approach to the conservation of marine natural resources (Ovlashchenko, 2007). At the same time, despite the recognized need for ecosystem and precautionary approaches in the Arctic, no document of a binding nature has documented the need to apply them. The U.N. Convention on the Law of the Sea contains only one article, Article 194, "Measures to prevent, reduce and control pollution of the marine environment," which states that: "The measures taken under this Part shall include those necessary to protect and preserve rare or fragile ecosystems as well as the habitat of depleted, threatened or endangered species and other forms of marine life." Moreover, the ecosystem approach, based on considering any ecosystem in its entirety, i.e., without considering any dividing borders, including state borders, completely contradicts the so-called "zonal approach" on which the entire 1982 Convention is built. In the Arctic, in contrast to the Antarctic, as it was already mentioned above, there are borders of sovereignty and jurisdiction of the five Arctic states, which cannot be regarded as less significant than borders of this or that Arctic ecosystem.

Ninth, the legal regime of the Antarctic is based entirely on the 1959 Treaty system, while a broad legal framework applies to the Arctic (Gudev, 2016). The Ilulissat Declaration, signed by the five Arctic States in May 2008, stated that "a broad international legal framework applies to the Arctic Ocean" and "the law of the sea provides for important rights and obligations concerning the delineation of the outer limits of the continental shelf, the protection of the marine environment, including ice-covered areas, freedom of navigation, marine scientific research, and other uses of the sea. We remain committed to this legal framework and to the orderly settlement of any possible overlapping claims". It was further stated that "this framework provides a solid foundation for responsible management by the five coastal States and other users of this Ocean through national implementation and application of relevant provisions." That is why there is no "no need to develop a new comprehensive international legal regime to govern the Arctic Ocean."

Thus, these fundamental differences between the Arctic and the Antarctic, primarily in terms of the legal regime and regulation model, put an end to the debate about whether the Arctic needs a new international treaty or an agreement along the lines of the Antarctic Treaty of 1959. This development would suit the non-Arctic states and various kinds of supranational international structures. However, it is hardly in the interests of the Arctic states, which have built a model of governance in the Arctic, including through the activities of the Arctic Council and other institutions and legal regimes.

Prospects for the Implementation of Marine Protected Areas Mechanism in the Arctic

It is fundamentally essential that the Commission for the Conservation of Antarctic Marine Living Resources (CCAMLR) has become a pioneer in creating Marine Protected Areas (MPA) on the High Seas.

In the 1970s, MPAs were mainly established in the territorial sea. In the 1980s, this process spread to the exclusive economic zone, then in the 2000s, the expediency of expanding MPAs by their formation in the coastal zones and the high seas was raised.

Thus, in 2009, the first MPA was established on the high seas in the South Orkney Islands (94 thousand km^2), which regulates such activities as scientific research, fishing activities, navigation. Then, at the end of 2016, a 1.57 mln km^2 protected area (initially planned for 2.1 mln km^2) in the Ross Sea was formed at the United States and New Zealand initiative to protect it from commercial fishing. This event marked the creation of the world's first marine protected area of this scale, where strict restrictions are imposed on certain types of marine economic activities. Now on the agenda, there is a discussion of creating an MPA in East Antarctica (with an area of about 1.7 mln km^2), which Australia, France, and the E.U. propose.

It should be noted that the creation of marine protected areas in the waters around the Antarctic is justified from the viewpoint of protection of the marine environment and its biodiversity.

However, creating MPAs in areas of the high seas directly contradicts the norms and provisions of the UNCLOS, as this is creating some "closed" areas in the zone, which cannot belong to any state. This contradiction gives some countries the right to claim that the establishment of an MPA on the high seas violates the provisions of Article 89 of the 1982

U.N. Convention on the Law of the Sea, which speaks of the illegality of claims to sovereignty over the high seas. Moreover, the establishment of MPAs often contradicts basic principles: freedom of navigation, freedom of laying submarine cables and pipelines, freedom of fishing, and freedom of scientific research. Given that the establishment of MPAs in high seas areas may impinge on traditional high seas freedoms, the evidence base for the legitimacy of the formation of MPAs in a particular area is essential. To date, there are no objective criteria for the necessity of establishing an MPA, particularly concerning the scientific knowledge base (Gudev, 2014).

The establishment of an MPA in the CCAMLR area theoretically contradicts the fundamental principle enshrined in the 1982 Convention on the Conservation of Antarctic Marine Living Resources, namely that while "the purpose of this Convention is the conservation of Antarctic marine living resources," nevertheless "for the purposes of this Convention the term 'conservation' includes rational use" (Article II) (CCAMLR, 1982). From the point of view of supporters of the MPA, the prohibition of specific activities (first of all, fishing) does not contradict "rational use" since the latter is more synonymous with "sustainable use". Opponents of MRAs, traditionally interested in marine commercial fisheries, have always insisted otherwise: "sustainable use" directly permits the exploitation of marine resources, and it cannot be prohibited. The position of fisheries science also proceeds from the fact that the expansion of MPAs questions the further development of fisheries for certain valuable species, as bioresources of the Antarctic cease to be publicly available and become isolated within the MPA.

Despite all the controversy surrounding creating MPAs in high seas areas, it is unreasonable to expect the topic to be removed from the international agenda. For example, over the past 15 years, there has been discussion of the need for a legally binding multilateral agreement, complementary to the UNCLOS, to protect marine biodiversity in areas beyond national jurisdiction (UNGA, 2019). It would prioritize the establishment of MPAs on the high seas. In the case of the Antarctic, it is envisaged that a new agreement might give regional fisheries management organizations such as CCAMLR a new mandate to develop science-based plans for comprehensive MPAs, leading to their universal acceptance (Shuvalova, 2019a).

In theory, the Arctic Council could assume responsibility for developing criteria for establishing MPAs in the central Arctic Ocean outside the jurisdiction of the five Arctic states. This is due to several unfavorable circumstances that may inevitably arise with adopting a new binding instrument.

First, such a binding agreement would substantially expand the number of participating states influencing the decision-making process for establishing one or another MPA, including, for example, the high seas enclave in the Arctic.

Secondly, such an agreement would necessarily contradict the norms and provisions of the 1982 Convention in some issues or even contribute to its cardinal revision in favor of imperative "ecologization", which does not correspond to the interests of major maritime powers, including the Russian Federation.

Third, such projects now emphasize applying the concept of the Common Heritage of Mankind (CHM) to marine genetic resources to prioritize the interests of developing countries, which would receive rents from the exploitation of such resources by developed countries (Shuvalova, 2019b). Obviously, in the current international political conditions, the interests of the poorest states in Asia, Africa, and Latin America would be highly burdensome for the Russian Federation.

Fourthly, such an agreement envisages the establishment of a new global body for the management of the open parts of the World Ocean beyond the zones of national jurisdiction, that is, theoretically and concerning the surface waters of the central part of the Arctic Ocean, which is an enclave of the high seas.

It seems that it would be in the interests of the Russian Federation and other Arctic Council member states to "short-circuit" this discussion regarding the formation of MPAs in the Arctic beyond national jurisdiction exclusively to the format of this international forum. Moreover, it could be considered that the regional fisheries management organization, which could be established concerning the central Arctic Ocean as part of the 2018 agreement, be given the authority to form MPAs in the Arctic in the future since it would not only have accumulated experience in protecting and conserving living marine resources and their habitat, but also a broad scientific knowledge base for creating MPAs (Shuvalova, 2019a). Most importantly, it would be the Arctic Council (or another regional format with a limited number of participants in case the Council is unable to assume such functions), without the participation of any other interested parties and states, that would have the competence to establish MPAs in the Arctic Ocean, outside the national jurisdictions of the Arctic states, and that it would develop the legal framework for establishing such protected marine areas.

We should note that there are specific legal grounds for confining the Arctic Council to the problem of the formation of marine protected areas.

The 1982 U.N. Convention on the Law of the Sea contains Article 123 relating to the cooperation of states surrounded by enclosed or semi-enclosed seas. It states, in part, that:

> States bordering an enclosed or semi-enclosed sea should cooperate with each other in the exercise of their rights and in the performance of their duties under this Convention. To this end they shall endeavor, directly or through an appropriate regional organization:
>
> 1. to coordinate the management, conservation, exploration and exploitation of the living resources of the sea;
> 2. to coordinate the implementation of their rights and duties with respect to the protection and preservation of the marine environment;
> 3. to coordinate their scientific research policies and undertake where appropriate joint programmes of scientific research in the area;
> 4. to invite, as appropriate, other interested States or international organizations to cooperate with them in furtherance of the provisions of this article.

In this connection, "enclosed or semi-enclosed sea means a gulf, basin or sea surrounded by two or more States and connected to another sea or the ocean by a narrow outlet or consisting entirely or primarily of the territorial seas and exclusive economic zones of two or more coastal States" (Article 122).

Up to now, the debate over whether or not the Arctic can be equated with enclosed or semi-enclosed seas, along the lines of the Baltic Sea or the Mediterranean, has not been settled. The proposal has both moderate supporters (Fife, 2013) and fierce opponents, primarily among extra-regional countries. However, in recent years, a concept such as the "Arctic Mediterranean" has been revived, which characterizes very well a possible variant of the development of the governance regime in the Arctic, built on the priority consideration of the interests of regional states.

From our perspective, the Arctic Ocean has several characteristics that fundamentally distinguish it from other maritime regions—for example, the Atlantic, Indian, or Pacific Oceans. Among these differences are: the fact that it is surrounded by the coasts of only five Arctic states; its small area; its shallow water nature; the considerable length of its shelf zone; its unique climatic conditions, including the presence of ice; and its particular environmental vulnerability (Berkman, 2012). Given that, except the central part, which can be regarded as a high sea, most of the Arctic Ocean is an area of sovereignty and jurisdiction of the Arctic states, and the passage to the Arctic by extra-regional states is connected with crossing these very waters, it seems possible to extend to this sea region the conventional status of a semi-enclosed sea.

INTERNATIONAL SCIENTIFIC COOPERATION IN THE ARCTIC

Article 123 mentioned above on the need to coordinate scientific research is an essential component of interstate cooperation in the Arctic. In this regard, the U.S. proposal voiced in 2019 by former senior U.S. official D. Bolton to complement such an international forum as the Arctic Council with a new international organization that would coordinate marine scientific research (hereinafter—MSR) in the Arctic, as well as collect and exchange scientific information, and serve as a platform for combating unregulated fishing in the central part of the Arctic Ocean is controversial.

Indeed, the main disadvantage of the Arctic Council is that, while it is not a full-fledged international organization, it has no management functions and no authority to oversee even the implementation of its instructions and recommendations, and its role in implementing various agreements—on search and rescue, oil spill response, and scientific cooperation—is extremely limited. Moreover, it is moving more and more toward environmental and climate issues, paying less and less attention to specific functional areas (shipping, fishing, oil and gas extraction, development of Arctic tourism, etc.) in the Arctic. The increase of the number of observers within the Arctic Council and the acquisition of this status by supranational international structures like the E.U. substantially blurs the exclusive nature of cooperation between the Arctic Five and Arctic Eight states as permanent members of the AC. The Arctic Council's Agreement on Strengthening International Arctic Scientific Cooperation is merely a framework document that requires, at a minimum, the signing of bilateral or multilateral agreements on specific conditions for marine scientific research, especially in areas under the jurisdiction of the Arctic states (Banshchikova, 2018).

The U.S. proposal to create such an organization is in the principle of interest to the Russian Federation. However, several nuances make it necessary to consider this proposal quite critically in the version formulated by the U.S. side (especially considering Washington's emphasis on the binding character of the proposed organization's decisions).

First, the U.S. project stipulates that absolutely all states interested in conducting MSRs in the Arctic can become participants of such an international organization. This provision seems to open a specific "Pandora's Box" again, as it allows the non-Arctic states to get themselves even more involved in the Arctic issues.

Secondly, such an international structure and the decisions made within its framework will be binding for all its participants and thus will stand above the norms and provisions of the national legislation of the Arctic states, including the Russian Federation.

Thirdly, the geographical scope of regulation of the proposed organization is proposed to cover the central part of the Arctic Ocean and areas under the jurisdiction of the Arctic states. The latter circumstance raises specific concerns since the views of the U.S. and the Russian Federation on the mechanism of conducting MSR in such zones are fundamentally different.

Thus, the 1982 Convention enshrines the right of coastal states to demand from other countries consent to conduct such research in marine areas under their jurisdiction (articles 245, 246). Most states, including the Russian Federation, are acting in this way. The United States is an exception since it does not require other states to formally consent to conduct MSR within its EEZ and continental shelf. Moreover, they have repeatedly reproached Russia and continue to do so because it quite often prohibits the conduct of certain MSRs within its jurisdictional zones, including in the Arctic (Roach, 2018).

In addition, the United States believes that the regime of MSR is not fully prescribed in the framework of the 1982 Convention.[2] Therefore, they are inclined to recognize as MSR only those activities

---

[2] The U.S., it should be recalled, not only has not ratified but also has not signed the 1982 UN Convention on the Law of the Sea. At the same time, they were the main initiators of the revision of its provisions relating to the development of deep-water resources of the World Ocean outside areas of national jurisdiction. Nevertheless, the U.S. states that it considers the norms and provisions of the 1982 Convention to be well-established rules of customary international law that are binding on all members of the international community. This is a rather speculative position, which is not shared at

to expand scientific data on the marine environment: oceanographic, biological, fishery, geological, geophysical, and other research conducted exclusively for scientific purposes (Bureau of Oceans and International Environmental and Scientific Affairs, 1994, p. 20). The U.S. side has advocated that all military activities, including military research, i.e., gathering oceanographic, geophysical, chemical, biological, and acoustic information for military purposes, should be excluded from the scope of scientific research (Svininykh, 2011). Actually, all information within the scope of natural and technical sciences can be one way or another of "dual-use." In this regard, it is highly likely that such Western requests as providing access to national (Russia) databases on the Arctic permafrost development (both in offshore and onshore areas) (Bouffard et al., 2021) will be treated by responsible authorities (e.g., the Ministry of Defense) with a high degree of suspicion.

From the U.S. perspective, scientific research cannot include hydrographic surveying; search for and explore natural resources; search for sunken objects and underwater archeology, and meteorological research. Accordingly, any types of hydrographic surveys to obtain information for making navigational charts, as well as any collection of information for military purposes, regardless of whether it is reconnaissance or not, do not fall under the category of MSR, and therefore do not require the prior consent of the coastal state (Wilson & Kraska, 2009).

It is quite possible that the United States under the previous Trump administration was highly skeptical of the AC, including for its preoccupation with the climate/environmental agenda, and the arrival of the new administration has radically changed the attitude both to that issue and to several international structures and institutions. Moreover, the United States may no longer be active lobbyists for the transfer of some of the functions and powers from the AC to the new international organization.

Nevertheless, let us note that attempts to replace the Arctic Council with new formats of cooperation and collaboration in the Arctic will not go anywhere. Such destructive actions are the hallmark of a number of the AC permanent observers who seem dissatisfied with their current status as observer states and claim to expand not only their powers within the AC but also their role and influence on the Arctic agenda, which is often

---

the level of international legal doctrine, but allows the U.S. to insist on the implementation of the Convention norms by those or other countries, primarily non-parties to this international agreement.

formed without taking into account their interests. For example, back in 2010, Poland initiated the Warsaw Format Meetings, where one of the main participants is the EU. There is also a high-level trilateral dialogue between China, Japan, and Korea on the Arctic agenda (Vylegzhanin et al., 2021). It should be noted that China, even in its first official document on the Arctic policy—the White Paper, positions itself as a state, ready to be responsible for the development and improvement of the rules of conduct in the Arctic, moreover—the management system of the Arctic region as a whole. The goal of such a system is highly universalist—to create conditions for the protection, development, and management of the Arctic in the interests of all mankind. To this end, Beijing is ready to cooperate with the Arctic states and all other countries and participants of the world community, including international state and non-state institutions and organizations. This is an ambitious attempt to lead the activation of extra-regional players, a disguised desire to play one of the leading roles in shaping the agenda (Gudev, 2018).

It is worth recalling that the International Maritime Organization (IMO), responsible for ensuring the safety of navigation, has the status of an observer organization within the AC. So, one of the proposals that the AC could support is to launch an initiative to develop an updated version of the International Code for ships operating in polar waters (Polar Code 2.0). The main problem with the current version of the document is that the provisions of the Polar Code do not apply to several categories of ships that are also exempt from the International Convention for the Safety of Life at Sea 1974 (SOLAS). These include warships, cargo ships of less than 500 gross tonnages; ships without mechanical means of propulsion; wooden ships of primitive construction; yachts not engaged in commercial traffic; and fishing vessels (SOLAS Convention, 1988). In addition, the current version of the Polar Code allows single-board vessels without ice class to operate in polar waters (Mednikov, 2016).

The potential possibility of expanding the volume of Arctic tourism, as well as the development and use of aquatic biological resources of the Arctic, makes the solution of this problem extremely urgent, primarily for the Russian Federation, whose sovereignty, sovereign rights, and jurisdiction extend over vast water areas in the region. At the same time, it is necessary to strengthen the understanding that even the updated Code does not cancel the norms of national regulation of navigation in Arctic waters, which are based on the provisions of article 234 "Ice-covered areas" of the 1982 U.N. Convention on the Law of the Sea. From this point of view, national regulation maybe even more strictly regulated than the norms of the Polar Code, as the 1982 Convention itself grants such right (Vylegzhanin et al., 2015).

SECURITY RELATIONS IN THE ARCTIC

The exposure of decades amassing political and psychological misconceptions between Russia and the West, which took place in terms of the Ukrainian crisis, triggered dismal expectations about consequences for the Arctic security. Indeed, several risky trends have been visible in the past few years throughout the region.

The number and the scale of military exercises have gone upwards since 2014. The most prominent example is the "Trident Juncture" in late October—early November 2018, which has become the most significant military exercise beyond the Polar Circle since the Cold War (Masters, 2018). In turn, forces comprising the Joint Strategic Command "North" have been showing muscle in the Arctic to the United States and its allies during the annual "Sever" and "Vostok" exercises (Kruglov & Ramm, 2018). At the same time, it is peculiar that both parties emphasize a defensive character of their military preparations. However, anyway, such a competing demonstration of the ability to seize control over the Arctic inevitably spurs ever-increasing distrust and suspicion between the Russian Federation and the United States/their allies. Under such a climate of relations, unintended military incidents either at sea or in the air become highly likely.

Trying to contribute to mitigating this risk, during the last few years, experts from Russia and other stakeholder-states have been promoting the introduction of confidence-building measures between key military powers, who have a stake in Arctic affairs. Several such initiatives are worth mentioning in this regard. In 2019 a group of British and Russian scholars presented a briefing note, which emphasized the need "to define what constitutes acceptable and legitimate military practice [in the region]" in terms of a non-binding Arctic Military Code of Conduct (AMCC), which can be negotiated under the Russian chairmanship in the AC (Depledge et al., 2019). In 2020, a large group of experts published a report summarizing a set of possible measures on the control of both conventional and strategic arms, which could prevent further deterioration of the strategic stability in Europe (d'Aboville et al., 2020).

Therefore, the logic of confidence-building in regional military affairs literally shows the way to the Russian diplomacy's actions in the High North. But how likely is the implementation of such measures in terms of the Arctic Council, taking into account the exclusion of hard security issues from the forum's mandate?

Firstly, we assume that a binding arrangement on military security relations in the Arctic is not feasible under existing geopolitical strain. It is much more likely that a non-binding solution will satisfy all stakeholders.

Secondly, Russia is highly unlikely to admit the inclusion of military issues into the AC's sphere of competence. Instead, the implementation of confidence-building measures can occur *under the auspices* of the AC, for example, in terms of the Arctic Coast Guards Forum (ACGF).

Thirdly, the process of confidence-building in the Arctic should be coupled with similar steps in other regions of Russia/NATO contact (especially in the Baltic and Black seas). Otherwise, expected improvements will be only of a limited value.

Fourth, an essential prerequisite of the Arctic confidence-building regime's survival will be the mutual Russia and the United States to find a mutually acceptable compromise on the freedom-of-navigation issues about the NSR area. Negotiating this problem requires maximum flexibility by two powers, as it concerns their core national interests—security and prestige. The key to breaking the deadlock could be found even in the rhetorical changes. Particularly, suppose Russian political authorities stop presenting the NSR as a new alternative to the Suez canal and emphasize that Russia has been investing for decades into the NSR's infrastructure predominantly for domestic economic and security reasons. In that case, it can provide a ground for U.S. authorities to reconsider its radical posture on the conditions of naval ships' access to waters along the northern Russian coast.

CONCLUSION

Thus, in answering the question posed at the very beginning, we can only state that, as of today, the current format of the Arctic Councils activities seems to suit most of its member states. The transition to some new institutional level largely depends on the nature of the interaction between the Arctic countries, the general state of relations between Russia and the countries of the West, and, above all, on the nature of Russian-American relations. At present, mutual contradictions and suspicions are not conducive to any qualitative changes. Just as the end of the Cold War gave impetus to cooperation and collaboration in the Arctic, something extraordinary must happen to launch a new stage of cooperation. By the way, this is probably the reason why the Russian presidency does not involve any breakthrough projects but focuses on standard issues related to the climate, ecology, the environment, and the life of indigenous peoples. However, the gradual opening of the Arctic and the arrival here of all interested states, corporations, and institutions may well require more decisive steps to regulate management in the region, that the eye will again be turned to the Arctic Council!

References

Arctic Council. (n.d.). Observers. *Arctic Council*. https://arctic-council.org/en/about/observers/. Accessed 28 July 2021.

Banshchikova, I. (2018, May 24). Что-то большее, чем просто наука? Вступление в силу Соглашения по укреплению международного арктического научного сотрудничества [Something more than just science? Entry into force of the Agreement on Strengthening International Arctic Scientific Cooperation]. *Rossijskij sovet po mezhdunarodnym delam* [Russian Council on International Affairs]. https://russiancouncil.ru/blogs/estoppel/34192/?sphrase_id=31004656. Accessed 28 July 2021.

Berkman, P. A. (2012). *Environmental security in the Arctic Ocean: Promoting co-operation and preventing conflict*. Routledge.

Bouffard, T. J., Uryupova, E., Dodds, K., Romanovsky, V. E., Bennett, A. P., & Streletskiy, D. (2021). Scientific cooperation: Supporting circumpolar permafrost monitoring and data sharing. *Land, 10*(6), 590. https://doi.org/10.3390/land10060590

Bureau of Oceans and International Environmental and Scientific Affairs. (1994). *Limits in the seas*. U.S. Department of State. https://2009-2017.state.gov/documents/organization/58228.pdf. Accessed 28 July 2021.

CCAMLR. (1982). *Convention on the conservation of Antarctic Marine living resources*. https://www.ccamlr.org/en/organisation/camlr-convention-text. Accessed 28 July 2021.

d'Aboville, B., et al. (2020). Recommendations of the participants of the expert dialogue on reducing the risks of military confrontation between Russia and NATO in Europe. *Social Sciences and Modernity, 6*, 178–190.

Depledge, D., Foxall, A., Boulegaue, M., & Tulupov, D. (2019). Why we need to talk about military activity in the Arctic: Towards an Arctic military code of conduct. *Arctic Yearbook*. https://arcticyearbook.com/images/yearbook/2019/Briefing-Notes/4_AY2019_BN_Depledge.pdf. Accessed 28 July 2021.

Fife, R. E. (2013). Cooperation across boundaries in the Arctic Ocean: The legal framework and the development of policies. In P. A. Berkman & A. N. Vylegzhanin (Eds.), *Environmental security in the Arctic Ocean* (pp. 345–358). Springer.

Gudev, P. A. (2014). *The 1982 UN Convention on the Law of the Sea: Problems of regime transformation.* IMEMO RAN.

Gudev, P. A. (2016). Арктика как «Global Commons»? [Arctic as "global commons"?]. *Пути к миру и безопасности* [Ways to Peace and Security], *50*(1), 53–69. https://www.imemo.ru/files/File/magazines/puty_m iru/2016/01/06_Gudev.pdf. Accessed 28 July 2021.

Gudev, P. A. (2018). Арктические амбиции Поднебесной [Arctic ambitions of the Celestial Empire]. *Rossiya v Globalnoy Politike* [Russia in Global Affairs], *5*, 174–184. https://globalaffairs.ru/articles/arkticheskie-ambiczii-podnebesnoj/. Accessed 28 July 2021.

Kruglov, A., & Ramm, A. (2018, October 18). В Арктике будет жарко: войска испытают Крайним Севером [It will be hot in the Arctic: The troops will be tested by the Far North]. // *Izvestia.* https://iz.ru/822691/ aleksandr-kruglov-aleksei-ramm/v-arktike-budet-zharko-voiska-ispytaiut-kra inim-severom. Accessed 28 July 2021.

Masters, J. (2018, October 23). NATO's trident juncture exercises: What to know. *Council on Foreign Relations.* https://www.cfr.org/in-brief/natos-tri dent-juncture-exercises-what-know. Accessed 28 July 2021.

Mednikov, V. A. (2016, October 13). Полярный кодекс. Попытка критического осмысления [Polar code: An attempt of critical reflection]. *Rossijskij sovet po mezhdunarodnym delam* [Russian Council on International Affairs]. https://russiancouncil.ru/common/upload/6_Mednikov.pdf. Accessed 28 July 2021.

Molenaar, E. J. (2012). Current and prospective roles of the Arctic Council system within the context of the Law of the Sea. *The International Journal of Marine and Coastal Law, 27*, 553–595. https://doi.org/10.1163/157 18085-12341234

Ovlashchenko, A. V. (2007). From the history of formation of the international legal regime of Antarctica. *Moskovskij zhurnal mezhdunarodnogo prava* [Moscow Journal of International Law], *4*, 245–259.

Roach, J. A. (2018). CIL guide to Arctic issues for Arctic Council observers. *Centre for International Law.* https://cil.nus.edu.sg/wp-content/uploads/ 2017/07/CIL-Guide-to-Arctic-Issues-for-Arctic-Council-Observers-Nov ember-2018.pdf. Accessed 28 July 2021.

Shuvalova, T. (2019a, June 20). В ООН разрабатывают новый документ по сохранению морского биоразнообразия [The UN is developing a new document to conserve marine biodiversity]. *Rossijskij sovet po mezhdunaro-dnym delam* [Russian Council on International Affairs]. https://russianco

uncil.ru/analytics-and-comments/analytics/v-oon-razrabatyvayut-novyy-dok
ument-po-sokhraneniyu-morskogo-bioraznoobraziya/?sphrase_id=43746422.
Accessed 28 July 2021.

Shuvalova, T. (2019b, April 1). Морское биоразнообразие в поле зрения
ООН: в ожидании новых ответов на старые вопросы [Marine biodiversity in UN sight: Awaiting new answers to old questions]. *Rossijskij sovet po
mezhdunarodnym delam* [Russian Council on International Affairs]. https://
russiancouncil.ru/analytics-and-comments/analytics/morskoe-bioraznoobra
zie-v-pole-zreniya-oon-v-ozhidanii-novykh-otvetov-na-starye-voprosy/?sph
rase_id=30982812. Accessed 28 July 2021.

SOLAS Convention. (1988). *International Convention for the Safety of Life
at Sea 1974 text as amended by its 1988 protocol (SOLAS-74)* (as amended
January 1, 2016) (revision effective January 1, 2017). http://docs.cntd.ru/
document/901765675. Accessed 28 July 2021.

Svininykh, E. (2011). Перспективы присоединения США к конвенции ООН
по морскому праву [Prospects for US accession to the UN Convention
on the Law of the Sea]. *Zarubezhnoe Voennoe Obozrenie* [Foreign Military
Review], 1. http://pentagonus.ru/publ/perspektivy_prisoedinenija_ssha_k_
konvencii_oon_po_morskomu_pravu/19-1-0-1717. Accessed 28 July 2021.

UN. (1982). *1982 UN Convention on the Law of the Sea.* https://www.un.
org/depts/los/convention_agreements/texts/unclos/unclos_e.pdf. Accessed
28 July 2021.

UNGA. (2019). *Draft text of an agreement under the United Nations
Convention on the Law of the Sea on the conservation and sustainable
use of marine biological diversity of areas beyond national jurisdiction.
A/CONF.232/2019/6.* https://digitallibrary.un.org/record/3811328/files/
A_CONF-232_2019_6-EN.pdf. Accessed 28 July 2021.

Vylegzhanin, A. N., Ivanov, G. G., & Dudykina, I. P. (2015). Полярный
кодекс (оценки и комментарии в зарубежных правовых источниках)
[Polar Code (estimates and comments in foreign legal sources)]. *Moskovskij
zhurnal mezhdunarodnogo prava* [Moscow Journal of International Law], *3*,
43–60. https://www.mjil.ru/jour/article/view/114?locale=ru_RU. Accessed
28 July 2021.

Vylegzhanin, A. N., Rostunova, O., Kienko, E., Bunik, I., & Vyakhireva, N.
(2021). Арктический совет: статус и деятельность. Отчёт 67/2021 [The
Arctic council: Status and activity. Report No. 67/2021]. *Rossijskij sovet po
mezhdunarodnym delam* [Russian Council on International Affairs]. https://
russiancouncil.ru/papers/Arctic-Council-Report67-Ru.pdf. Accessed 28 July
2021.

Wilson, B., & Kraska, J. (2009). American security and law of the sea. *Ocean
Development & International Law, 40,* 268–290.

Channeling of Liability: Shall Arctic States Be Liable for Environmental Harm in the Arctic Caused by Navigation or Polluter Pays Principle Should Prevail?

Daria Boklan

INTRODUCTION

The Arctic plays a critical role in sustaining all life on this planet (Schoolmeester et al., 2019). It is recognized that the Arctic is "vital to the functioning of the earth's terrestrial, biological, climate, ocean and atmosphere systems" (Arctic Council, 2009). Arctic ecosystems, both marine and coastal, contain numerous natural resources that are essential for people all around the world (UNEP, n.d.) The Arctic Council[1] (2019) acknowledged that Arctic marine ecosystems are under increasing pressure

---

[1] The Arctic Council is the leading intergovernmental forum promoting coordination, coordination and interaction among Arctic States, Arctic Indigenous peoples and other Arctic inhabitants on common Arctic issues, in particular on issues of sustainable development and environmental protection in the Arctic. It was formally established in 1996.

D. Boklan (✉)
Department of International Law, Faculty of Law, National
Research University Higher School of Economics, Moscow, Russia
e-mail: dboklan@hse.ru

© The Author(s), under exclusive license to Springer Nature
Singapore Pte Ltd. 2022
A. Likhacheva (ed.), *Arctic Fever*,
https://doi.org/10.1007/978-981-16-9616-9_17

from multiple stressors including ocean warming and acidification, long-range pollution, invasive species, and increased human activities. While sea ice declines, people gain a higher level of ice-free access to the Arctic (UNEP, 2013). Consequently, the Northern Sea Route across Arctic states is becoming a more viable route for ships (Berkman et al., 2007), resulting in a higher level of pollution. Moreover, shipping increase the probability of oil spills, threatening the marine environment in the Arctic (Arctic Council, 2017).

The Arctic region is subject to the undisputed jurisdiction of Arctic states[2] and for the most part environmental protection in that area is based on national environmental laws, although these may implement international environmental obligations (Sands et al., 2018, pp. 632–633). Liability for environmental harm coursed to the Arctic ecosystem by navigation is one of such international environmental obligations.

Principle 22 of the 1972 Stockholm Declaration on the Human Environment called on states to "cooperate to develop further the international law regarding liability and compensation for victims of pollution and other environmental damage caused by activities within the jurisdiction or control of such states to areas beyond their jurisdiction." After 20 years 1992 Rio Declaration on environment and development (Rio Declaration) reflected limited progress made since 1972. Principle 13 of the Rio Declaration provides that: "states shall cooperate in more determined manner to develop further international law regarding liability and compensation for adverse effects of environmental damage caused by activities within their jurisdiction or control to areas beyond their jurisdiction."

At the same time, the accidental spill of oil into Arctic waters remains the most significant threat from ships to the Arctic marine environment. For instance, Tanker Exxon Valdez (Alaska, USA) spilled 37,000 tons of crude oil in 1989. The oil affected 2100 km of coastline, of which 320 km were heavily oiled. Immediate effects included the deaths of

---

[2] There are eight Arctic States—members to the Arctic Council. Arctic states have territories within the Arctic and thus carry the role as stewards of the region. Their national jurisdictions and international law govern the lands surrounding the Arctic Ocean and its waters. The Northern provinces of Arctic States offer a home to more than four million people, whose health and well-being is on the top of the Arctic Council's agenda. These states are Canada, The Kingdom of Denmark, Finland, Iceland, Norway, The Russian Federation, Sweden and The United States. It also should be noted that the US is the only Arctic state not party to the UNCLOS.

250,000 seabirds, 2800 sea otters, 300 harbor seals, 247 bald eagles, and an unknown number of salmon and herring. Exxon spent over $2 billion cleaning up the spill and $1 billion to settle related civil and criminal charges (WWF, 2009). Another example could be MV Selendang Ayu oil spill (Alaska, USA) in 2008. More than 1 million liters of thick fuel oil were spilled, immediate effects included the deaths of over 1600 birds and Resulted in more than $112 million in cleanup costs (National Oceanic and Atmospheric Administration, 2008). In 2009, Full City tanker (Norway) spilled around 200 tons of oil, which contaminated 75 km of the Norwegian coastline. Cleanup costs exceeded $300 million and the spill negatively affected the marine wildlife (Wijnen, 2018).

Future vessel traffic in Arctic waters is projected to rise, thus increasing the risk of a spill (IMO, 2017). International Marine Organization decided to support the initiative of the Association of Arctic Expedition Cruise Operators (AECO, 2019) and introduced a ban on the use of heavy fuel by ships plying in the Arctic starting from 2024. However, until 2029, States can make an exception for ships in inland waters. This means that heavy fuel will be actively used over the next decade in the Arctic (High North News, 2020).

This chapter addresses the issue of channeling liability for environmental harm caused by navigation in the Arctic. Specifically, it focuses on the interplay between strict liability of Arctic states and strict liability of the polluter under the polluter pays principle.

The author of this chapter argues that as soon as Article 234 of the 1982 United Nations Convention on the Law of the Sea (UNCLOS) provides Arctic states with special rights to control navigation beyond the limits of their territory (in the exclusive economic zones[3]) in the Arctic Ocean[4] such navigation should be considered as an activity under

---

[3] The exclusive economic zone (EEZ) is an area beyond and adjacent to the territorial sea, subject to the specific legal regime, under which the rights and jurisdiction of the coastal State and the rights and freedoms of other States are governed by the relevant provisions of the UNCLOS (Article 55 of the UNCLOS). Article 58 of the UNCLOS provides for freedom of navigation for non-costal states in the EEZs.

[4] Article 234 of the United Nations Convention on the Law of the Sea (the UNCLOS) is called "Ice-covered Areas." It enshrines the right of Arctic states to adopt and enforce non-discriminatory laws and regulations for the prevention, reduction, and control, of marine pollution from vessels in ice-covered areas within the limits of the exclusive economic zone, where particularly severe climatic conditions and the presence of ice covering such areas for most of the year create obstructions or exceptional hazards to

control or jurisdiction of Arctic states. Consequently, Arctic states should be considered as "states of origin" of such an activity. Further, the author submits that the right of Arctic states to control navigation beyond the limits of their territory should be balanced with strict liability for environmental harm caused by such navigation. Such strict liability of Arctic states should in its turn be balanced with the strict liability of the operator of navigation set forth by the polluter pays principle. This international legal regime is a combination of the right to control navigation on the one hand and strict liability for environmental harm coupled with the polluter pays obligation of the operator on the other hand could provide an appropriate balance between rights and obligations of all actors in the Arctic and effective prevention of environmental harm caused by navigation.

In this chapter, the author first provides a conceptual discussion on the notion of environmental harm. The author then addresses the question of whether navigation in the Arctic could be conceded as hazardous activity. The next section provides the answer to the question on whether Arctic states should be liable for environmental harm caused by navigation in the Arctic. The fifth section focuses on the polluter pays principle with respect to navigation in the Arctic. The last section concludes the discussion on channeling of liability for environmental harm in the Arctic caused by navigation.

What Is Environmental Harm?

The International Court of Justice (ICJ) specifically recognized that "the environment is not an abstraction but represents the living space, the quality of life and the very health of human beings, including generations unborn. The existence of the general obligation of States to ensure that activities within their jurisdiction and control respect the environment of other States or of areas beyond national control is now part of the corpus of international law relating to the environment" (ICJ, 1996).

However, there is no consistency in defining environmental harm neither in the state practice no in the literature. In defining environmental damage, treaties and state practice reflect various approaches.

---

navigation, and pollution of the marine environment could cause major harm to, or irreversible disturbance of, the ecological balance. Such laws and regulations shall have due regard to navigation, and the protection and preservation of the marine environment based on the best available scientific evidence.

A narrow definition of environmental damage is limited to damage to natural resources alone (air, water, soil, fauna, flora, and their interaction). A more extensive approach includes damage to natural resources and property that forms part of the cultural heritage; the most extensive definition includes landscape and environmental amenity (ILC, 2006, pp. 65–66; Sands et al., 2018, p. 741). For instance, the measurement of damage under the 1992 International Convention on Civil Liability for Oil Pollution Damage does not include moral damage and purely environmental damage; only so-called economic damage is taken into account (Caballero & Soto-Oñate, 2017, pp. 213–219). However, the 2010 Nagoya-Kuala Lumpur Supplementary Liability Protocol (Nagoya Protocol)[5] suggests a broader approach. It defines "damage" to mean "an adverse effect on the conservation and sustainable use of biological diversity, taking also into account risks to human health" (Article 2, para. 2(b)).

The notion which is widely used in environmental treaties and can be a helpful guidance in defining environmental damage is the notion of adverse effects. The Nagoya Protocol describes the adverse effect as an effect that is measurable or otherwise observable taking into account, wherever available, scientifically established baselines or is significant when judged in light of factors such as the long-term or permanent change, the extent of qualitative or quantitative changes that adversely affect the components of biodiversity. Thus, the definition of adverse effect may help in determining the threshold beyond which environmental damage might trigger liability (Sands et al., 2018, p. 742).

However, while human activity having adverse effects might give rise to environmental damage, it is unlikely that all environmental damage results in liability. There are no agreed international standards that establish a threshold for environmental damage that triggers liability (Sands et al., 2018, p. 743). Different environmental treaties establish such thresholds for environmental damage as a basis to invoke liability as "serious" or "significant." The International Law Commission (ILC) in its 2006 Draft Principles on the Allocation of Loss for Transboundary Harm (Draft Principles) observed in the commentaries that "the term 'significant' is

---

[5] The 2010 Nagoya-Kuala Lumpur Supplementary Liability Protocol was adopted to supplement. The 2000 Cartagena Protocol on Biosafety. The 2000 Cartagena Protocol on Biosafety was adopted as a supplementary agreement to the 1992 Convention on Biological Diversity.

456   D. BOKLAN

understood to refer to something more than 'detectible' but need not be at the level of 'serious' or 'substantial'. The harm must lead to a real detrimental effect on matters such as, for example, human health, industry, property, environment or agriculture. Such detrimental effects must be susceptible of being measured by factual and objective standards" (ILC, 2006, para. 2). However, as was already mentioned the problem here is that there are no mutually excepted international standards on environmental damage as a basis for state liability. In addition, as Julie Adshead points out there are self-evident problems in putting a value on pure environmental damage, particularly when an environment or species is eliminated and is irreplaceable. In such cases consideration and calculation of intrinsic value are necessary. Even if such a valuation is possible, questions surround who should be the recipient of damages in such cases (Adshead, 2018). Alongside that, the ILC notes in its commentaries that "there is a clear shift towards a greater focus on damage to the environment per se, rather than primarily on damage to persons and to property" (ILC, 2006, para. 15).

Therefore, establishing the appropriate threshold turns on the facts of each case, and may vary according to local or regional circumstances (Sands et al., 2018, p. 744).

The Arctic is home to over 21,000 species of plants, fungi, mammals, birds, fish, insects, and invertebrates. This region is home to one-third of the world's shorebirds, and two-thirds of the global goose population, which breed in the Arctic and sub-Arctic (Schoolmeester et al., 2019). The Arctic Biodiversity Assessment Report, by the Conservation of Arctic Flora and Fauna (CAFF, 2013, pp. 124, 327), and the Red List of the International Union for Conservation of Nature, show the global conservation status of fauna biodiversity in the Arctic, in accordance with nine categories.[6] These data demonstrate that at least twenty Arctic fauna species are threatened, vulnerable, endangered, or critically endangered.[7]

---

[6] The following categories are used: not evaluated (NE), data deficient (DD), least concern (LC), near threatened (NT), vulnerable (VU), endangered (EN), critically endangered (CR), extinct in the wild (EW), extinct (EX). See IUCN (1998, 2012).

[7] European Eel or Anguilla anguilla (CR), Spoonbill Sandpiper or Calidris pygmanaea (CR), Blue whale or Balaenoptera musculus (EN), Pribilof Island Shrew or Sorex pribilofensis (EN), Siberian Sturgeon or Acipenser baerii (EN), Bowhead Whale or Bolena mysticetus (East Greenland-Svalbard-Barents Sea subpopulation) (EN), Polar Bear or Ursus maritimus (VU), Atlantic Puffin or Fratercula arctica (VU), Greenland shark or

Some of them are listed in Appendices to the CITES Convention.[8] Sea ice is highly important for most marine mammals in the Arctic. For example, walruses, some species of seals, and polar bears use it for sunning, mating, and hunting (Johannessen & Miles, 2011, pp. 244–245). When sea ice is melting, marine mammals are forced to rest ashore, which makes them go hungry, lose weight, and even die. Therefore, such species are highly vulnerable to any changes connected to sea ice (Hassol, 2004, p. 59; UNEP, 2013, p. 24).

Moreover, the geographical characteristics, and the cold climate of the Arctic mean that the region functions as a sink for contaminants from around the globe, and many pollutants remain in the Arctic for long periods. These pollutants are present in the air, water, snow, ice, soil, and living organisms. Some can even accumulate throughout the food chain, posing a serious threat to the health of humans and animals (Schoolmeester et al., 2019). It is also worth noting that the presence of special oil-degrading bacteria is a prerequisite for oil degradation (Wegeberg et al., 2018, p. 6), and complete degradation requires a large consortium of indigenous bacteria (Garneau et al., 2016, p. 2). However, the microbial population in the Arctic marine environment is inadequate to appropriately degrade spilled oil. As has been shown by several experiments, sea ice bacteria are able to remove less than 40% of hydrocarbons, compared to sub-ice seawater (Garneau et al., 2016, p. 11).

All these facts show specific regional conditions and circumstances of the Arctic as a rare and fragile ecosystem. Therefore, the evaluation of environmental damage which may trigger the liability of Arctic states should be based on these specific conditions and circumstances. Consequently, harm to the Arctic environment per se should be considered as

---

Somniosus microcephalus (VU), Walrus or Odobenus rosmarus (VU), Short-tailed Albatross or Phoebastria albatrus (VU), Velvet Scoter or Melanitta fusca (VU), Steller's Eider or Polysticta stelleri (VU), Long-tailed Duck or Clangula hyemalis (VU), Fin Whale or Balaenoptera physalus (VU), Black-legged Kittiwake or Rissa tridactyla (VU), Ivory Gull or Pagophila eburnea (NT), Emperor Goose or Anser canagicus (NT), Spectacled Eider or Somateria fischeri (NT), Common Eider or Somateria mollissima (NT).

[8] Walrus or Odobenus rosmarus (Appendix III), Short-tailed Albatross or Phoebastria albatrus (Appendix I), Fin Whale or Balaenoptera physalus (Appendix I), Blue whale or Balaenoptera musculus (Appendix I), European Eel or Anguilla anguilla (Appendix II). CITES (the Convention on International Trade in Endangered Species of Wild Fauna and Flora) is an international agreement between governments. Its aim is to ensure that international trade in specimens of wild animals and plants does not threaten their survival.

environmental harm under international law. Moreover, the threshold of such environmental harm as a basis for liability should be rather high. If Arctic states develop relevant standards on evaluation of environmental harm caused by navigation it would make easier channeling of the strict liability.

Should Navigation in the Arctic Be Conceded as a Hazardous Activity?

In the case of hazardous activities, there is no presently any single international organization or treaty that establishes principles and rules of general application (Sands et al., 2018, p. 570). The ILC defines "hazardous activity" as any activity which involves the risk of causing significant harm through the physical consequences and underlines that different types of activities could be envisaged under this category (ILC, 2001). They are not prohibited by international law (ILC, 2001, p. 62, para. 2). Moreover, the applicability of international regulations with respect to hazardous activities depends upon the nature and characteristics of a particular location where it is being carried out (Sands et al., 2018, p. 570).

The notion of significant harm was discussed in the previous part of this chapter and it could be reasonably inferred from this analysis that navigation in the Arctic should be considered as "hazardous activity" as soon as it leads to a real detrimental effect on the Arctic environment. It is pointed out in the literature that "a significant impact of shipping is marine pollution from vessels, caused by operational discharges from ships, such as cleaning of tanks or deballasting, or from discharges following accidents" (Sands et al., 2018, p. 486). Specifically, with respect to the Arctic, it is underlined by the International Marine Organization (IMO) that ships operating in the Arctic environments are exposed to a number of unique risks. Poor weather conditions and the relative lack of good charts, communication systems, and other navigational aids pose challenges for mariners. The remoteness of the areas makes rescue or cleanup operations difficult and costly. Cold temperatures may reduce the effectiveness of numerous components of the ship, ranging from deck machinery and emergency equipment to sea suctions. When ice is present, it can impose additional loads on the hull, propulsion system, and appendages (IMO, n.d.). The mere fact that after more than twenty years of negotiations the 2014 International Code for Ships Operating in Polar Waters (Polar Code) was adopted covering inter alia environmental protection matters relevant to ships operating in the Arctic[9] also shows that navigation in the Arctic is considered as hazardous activity. The Polar Code is mandatory under both the International Convention for the Safety of Life at Sea (SOLAS) and the International Convention for the Prevention of Pollution from Ships (MARPOL). However, it falls "short on several aspects, failing to cover all vessels (fishing vessels, pleasure craft and offshore drilling units are not regulated) and all sources of pollution (heavy fuel oil in the Arctic and wastewater from ships are not covered)" (Sands et al., 2018, p. 493). Moreover, it is worth noting that Arctic states concluded the 2013 Agreement on Cooperation on Marine Oil Pollution Preparedness and Response in the Arctic (Agreement on Oil Pollution in the Arctic).[10] The preamble of this treaty provides that parties to the Agreement are mindful of the increase in maritime traffic, and other human activities in the Arctic region, are aware of the parties' obligation to protect the Arctic marine ecosystem, and are mindful of the importance of precautionary measures to avoid oil pollution in the first instance. This motive in the Preamble of the Agreement on Oil Pollution in the Arctic shows that Arctic states themselves consider navigation as a hazardous activity within the meaning of ILC Draft Articles.

SHALL ARCTIC STATES BE LIABLE FOR ENVIRONMENTAL HARM IN THE ARCTIC?

Proving fault is notoriously difficult and time-consuming and may lead to problems in the allocation of liability (Adshead, 2018) For instance, the vessel Prestige sank in 2002, and the Spanish Supreme Court pronounced its judgment in 2016. Now, there are new proceedings to enforce this judgment. This process may be lengthy (depending on several circumstances), and 15 years have already passed since the vessel sank (Caballero & Soto-Oñate, 2017, pp. 213–219). The fragile Arctic environment cannot wait for so long.

Moreover, even if the relevant state fully complies with its prevention obligations under international law, accidents or other incidents may

[9] The Polar Code entered into force in 2017.

[10] This Agreement was concluded by Canada, Denmark, Finland, Iceland, Norway, Russia, Sweden, and the USA and entered into force in 2016.

nonetheless occur and cause harm (ILC, 2006, p. 59, para. 2). For instance, environmental harm could occur because of gradually accumulated adverse effects over the period of time (ILC, 2006, p. 63, para. 7) what could be the case for the Arctic environment taking into account its inability to appropriately degrade spilled oil.

As was mentioned in the Introduction to this chapter as soon as Article 234 of UNCLOS provides Arctic states with special rights to control navigation beyond the limits of their territory such navigation should be considered as activity under control or jurisdiction of Arctic states. Arctic states should be considered as "states of origin" of navigation in the Arctic. According to the ILC "state of origin" means the State in the territory or otherwise under jurisdiction or control of which the hazardous activity is carried out (ILC, 2006, p. 70, para. 25). As was shown earlier in this chapter navigation in Arctic should be regarded as "hazardous activity" under Article 234 of the UCLOS is carried out "under jurisdiction or control" of Arctic states.

Therefore, the author of this chapter submits that the right of Arctic states to control navigation (prescribed in Article 234 of the UNCLOS) should be balanced with strict liability (no-fault liability) of Arctic states for environmental harm caused by navigation.

Such approach will be in the same lines with the ILC commentary, according to which "it is equally recognized that such liability need not always be placed on the operator of hazardous or risk-bearing activity and other entities could equally be designated by agreement or by law. The important point is that person or entity concerned is functionally in command or control or directs or exercises overall supervision and hence, as the beneficiary of the activity, may be held liable" (ILC, 2006, p. 60, para. 8).In the environmental field, no single instrument sets forth the generally applicable international rules governing liability (Sands et al., 2018, p. 738).

The Institute de Droit International (IDI) adopted in 1997 a Resolution on responsibility and liability under international law for environmental damage (Vicuña, 1997). Article 1 of this Resolution prescribes that obligation to reestablish the original position or to pay compensation for environmental damage may arise "from a rule of international law providing for strict responsibility on the basis of harm or injury alone, particularly in case of ultra-hazardous activities (responsibility for harm alone)." Therefore, strict liability is obligation to pay compensation for the harm caused regardless of whether the wrongful act took place and it does not require proof of fault.

Various designations are used to describe contemporary doctrine imposing strict liability, among them: "liability without fault," "negligence without fault," "presumed responsibility," "fault per se," "objective liability," or "risk liability" (ILC, 2006, p. 78, para. 12).

Unfortunately, the states even in the form of ILC Draft articles did not assign strict liability for environmental damage. Moreover, specifically regarding liability under UNCLOS, the International Tribunal for the Law of the Sea in its Advisory Opinion on *Responsibilities and Obligations in the Area* noted that liability for damage of the State is out of the application of strict liability (ITLOS, 2011, p. 61, para. 189). Therefore, imposing strict liability on Arctic states should be prescribed in international law as a best possible practice aimed at effective preservation of vulnerable and rare Arctic environment.

There are examples when states were held liable for environmental harm. For instance, the ICJ in *Gabcikovo-Nagymaros* case confirmed that Hungary is entitled to "compensation for the damage sustained as a result of the diversion of the Danube" (ICJ, 1997, p. 78, para. 152). However, it did not specifically indicate that Hungary was entitled to reparation for purely environmental damages. The 1991 UN Security Council Resolution regarding the situation in Kuwait reaffirmed that Iraq was "liable under international law for any direct loss, damage, including environmental damage and the depletion of natural resources, on injury to foreign Governments, nationals and corporations occurring as a result of its unlawful invasion and occupation of Kuwait" (UNSC, 1991, p. 14). We also may make some relevant examples from the state practice, when states voluntarily compensated environmental damage. For instance, in January 1955, the US government paid 2 million USD to Japan for the purposes of compensation for the injuries or damage sustained by Japanese nationals as a result of thermonuclear tests carried out by the US near the Marshall Islands in March 1954 (Margolis, 1955, pp. 638–639). Another example could be the USSR's consent to pay, and Canada agreed to accept 3 million USD for environmental damage following up the crash of Cosmos 954 in January 1958 (ILM, 1979, pp. 899–908).

Imposing of strict liability on Arctic states will also satisfy the purpose indicated in the Preamble of the ILC Draft Principles on the Allocation of Loss in the Case of Transboundary Harm Arising out of Hazardous Activities (Draft Principles) according to which "those who suffer harm or loss as a result of such incidents involving hazardous activities are not left to carry those losses and able to obtain prompt and adequate compensation" (ILC, 2006, p. 59, para. 3). Moreover, state strict liability already exists in international law, for instance in the case of outer space activities.[11] It is also worth noting that following the Cosmos 954 accident Canada claimed that "the principle of absolute liability applies to fields of activity having in common a high degree of risk [...] and has been accepted as a general principle of international law" (Sands et al., 2018, p. 744).

Navigation in the Arctic should be considered as "activity having a high degree of risk" taking into account the fragility and rarity of the Arctic ecosystem together with the low ability to appropriately degrade spilled oil. Consequently, Arctic states, being "state of origin" of navigation (as submitted earlier) should bear strict liability for environmental harm caused by navigation in the Arctic.

However, such strict liability of Arctic states should in its turn be balanced with the obligation of the operator set forth by polluter pays principle. "The State [...] which steps in to undertake response or restoration measures may recover the costs later for such operations from the operator" (ILC, 2006, p. 73, para. 9). ILC Draft Principles do not impose strict liability on states, but rather provide imposition of strict liability on operators under the "polluter pays principle." There is no general definition of the "operator." According to the ILC Draft principles, the "operator" is any person in command or control of the activity at the time incident causing damage occurs (ILC, 2006, p. 64, principle 2, para. (g)).

The next part of this chapter elaborates on the possible application of the "polluter pays principle" aimed at protecting of the Arctic from environmental harm, caused by navigation.

---

[11] See Article II of The Convention on International Liability for Damage Caused by Space Objects (UNOOSA, 1972), which prescribes that: "A launching State shall be absolutely liable to pay compensation for damage caused by its space object on the surface of the earth or to aircraft flight."

How Polluter Pays Principle Should Be Used for Prevention of Environmental Harm in the Arctic?

Although the polluter pays principle has been referred to as a general principle of international law[12] probably does not have customary law status (Adshead, 2018). Polluter pays principle could be found in treaty practice.[13]

The Organization for Economic Co-operation and Development (OECD) was the first to expressly define the polluter pays principle in its 1972 Recommendation of the Council on Guiding Principles Concerning the International Economic Aspects of Environmental Policies (Guiding Principles) (OECD, 1972). The polluter pays principle was listed as one of such guiding principles and defined as a "principle to be used for allocating costs of pollution prevention and control measures to encourage rational use of scarce environmental resources and to avoid distortions in international trade and investment." Further Guiding Principles provide that the polluter pays principle "means that the polluter should bear the expenses of carrying out the above-mentioned measures decided by public authorities to ensure that the environment is in an acceptable state. In other words, the cost of these measures should be reflected in the cost of goods and services which cause pollution in production and/or consumption. Such measures should not be accompanied by subsidies that would create significant distortions in international trade and investment" (OECD, 1972, para. A (4)). Therefore, the polluter pays principle indicates that the costs of pollution should be borne by the person responsible for causing pollution (Sands et al., 2018, p. 240). The polluter pays principle ensures that the parties who produce pollution are liable for it and requires them to bear the costs of the consequent damage. It is a way of making these parties internalize the costs of prevention and reparation (Caballero & Soto-Oñate, 2017, pp. 213–219). The concept of

---

[12] The Polluter Pays Principle ('PPP' or 'the Principle') is now firmly established as a basic principle of international and domestic environmental laws. It is designed to achieve the 'internalization of environmental costs', by ensuring that the costs of pollution control and remediation are borne by those who cause the pollution, and thus reflected in the costs of their goods and services, rather than borne by the community at large. See UKPC (2017).

[13] See, for example: Council of Europe (1993), Economic Commission for Europe (2003).

the "Polluter Pays Principle" falls under the parasol of absolute liability (Barthakur, 2021).

Although its origins lie in the economic theory of externalities, the polluter pays principle has developed to become a key cornerstone of environmental law and policy (Adshead, 2018). Rather than merely focusing on trade distortions, the polluter pays principle began to be linked with incentives for environmental improvements. Its dissuasive value was recognized along with its role as a complement to the principle of prevention (Adshead, 2018). However, the polluter pays principles limit the extent of any obligation that might apply to states. It does not govern relations or responsibilities between states at the international level of pollution (Sands et al., 2018, p. 241). Pollution incidents often involve a complex web of actors responsible for damage and a key question surrounds how the polluter pays principle is satisfied in terms of the division of liability between the responsible parties (Adshead, 2018). In terms of application of the polluter pays principle, at least in the more serious cases of oil pollution damage, the owners of the ship and the owners of the cargo are both treated as polluters and share the cost of pollution damage (Harrison, 2009, pp. 379, 385). For instance, the 1992 International Convention on Civil Liability for Oil Pollution Damage determined the civil liability of the shipowner. The shipowner is responsible under strict liability following the polluter pays principle. However, the shipowner's liability is limited to an amount that is linked to the ship's tonnage. Additionally, according to this convention, no legal action can be taken against any other actor (captain, crew, cargo owner, certifier, civil servants, etc.). The convention also provides a system of compulsory liability insurance for ships carrying more than 2000t of bulk oil as cargo. The 1992 International Convention on the Establishment of an International Fund for Compensation for Oil Pollution Damage determined the liability of such fund, which comprises funds that the oil industry contributes. It operates when the scope of the damage is higher than the shipowner's limitation of liability in accordance with the 1992 International Convention on Civil Liability for Oil Pollution Damage (Caballero & Soto-Oñate, 2017, pp. 213–219).

However, the polluter pays principle, would seem to indicate that there is no place for responsibility outside of the individuals or state directly involved in the incident (Adshead, 2018). Some scholars argue that resolving a dispute arising from actions of a private company through international litigation is "an indirect and cumbersome" (Stephens, 2009,

p. 136). Hence, the allocation of liabilitie among parties largely depends on what the national courts of justice decide (Caballero & Soto-Oñate, 2017, pp. 213–219). Indeed, as it was already mentioned in the introduction to this chapter the most part environmental protection in the Arctic is based on national environmental laws of Arctic states. This can effectively supplement the strict liability of Arctic states for environmental harm caused by navigation in the Arctic but cannot substitute it. Therefore, to make the protection of the Arctic environment from pollution caused by navigation really effective strict liability should be channeled through both "polluters" and Arctic states.

CONCLUSION

The Arctic is a rare and fragile ecosystem, which is a home for threatened, vulnerable, endangered, or critically endangered species with a cold climate and very low ability of self-purification. At the same time, the Arctic plays a critical role in sustaining all life on this planet. These facts should be taken into account as particular circumstances and conditions for evaluation of environmental damage which may trigger the strict liability of Arctic states. Also, these facts signify that harm to the Arctic environment per se should be considered as environmental harm under international law and the threshold of such environmental harm as a basis for strict liability should be rather high. If Arctic states develop relevant standards on evaluation of environmental harm caused by navigation, it would make easier channeling of the strict liability.

Navigation in the Arctic should be considered as "hazardous activity" as soon as it leads to a real detrimental effect on the Arctic environment. Article 234 of UNCLOS provides Arctic states with special rights to control navigation beyond their territory. Therefore, such navigation should be considered as activity under control or jurisdiction of Arctic states and Arctic states should be considered as "states of origin" of navigation in the Arctic in terms of the ILC approach. According to the ILC "state of origin" means the State in the territory or otherwise under jurisdiction or control of which the hazardous activity is carried out.

Being states of origin of navigation, Arctic states should bear strict (no-fault) liability for environmental harm caused by such navigation. Such an approach will be in the same lines as the ILC approach, according to which such liability need not always be placed on the operator of hazardous or risk-bearing activity and other entities could equally be designated by agreement or by law. The important point is that person or entity concerned is functionally in command or control or directs or exercises overall supervision and hence, as the beneficiary of the activity, may be held liable.

Imposing strict liability on Arctic states could be regarded as the best possible practice aimed at preservation of vulnerable and rare Arctic ecosystem. Such strict liability of Arctic states should, in its turn, be balanced with the obligation of the operator set forth by polluter pays principle. Arctic states undertaking strict liability for environmental harm caused by navigation may recover the costs later for such operations from the operator by the way of recourse.

This is one of the most effective ways of channeling the strict liability for environmental harm caused by navigation in the Arctic. This international legal regime being a combination of Arctic states' rights to control navigation on the one hand and strict liability of Arctic states for environmental harm coupled with the polluter pays obligation of the operator, on the other hand, maybe enshrined in an inter-Arctic states' agreement. Such an agreement could provide an appropriate balance between the rights and obligations of all actors in the Arctic and the effective prevention of environmental harm caused by navigation.

References

Adshead, J. (2018). The application and development of the polluter-pays principle across jurisdictions in liability for marine oil pollution: The tales of the 'Erica' and the 'Prestige.' *Journal of Environmental Law, 30*(3), 425–451.

AECO. (2019, November 7). Expedition cruise industry charts course for sustainable Arctic tourism. *AECO*. https://www.aeco.no/2019/11/expedition-cruise-industry-charts-course-for-sustainable-arctic-tourism/. Accessed 26 July 2021.

Arctic Council. (2009). *Preamble of the 2009 Washington ministerial declaration on the international polar year and polar science.* https://www.mofa.go.jp/policy/environment/convention/atac0904.html. Accessed 26 July 2021.

Arctic Council. (2017). *Circumpolar oil spill response viability analysis: Technical report, No. 9.* https://oaarchive.arctic-council.org/handle/11374/1928. Accessed 26 July 2021.

Arctic Council. (2019). *Rovaniemi ministerial statements.* https://oaarchive.arctic-council.org/handle/11374/2418. Accessed 26 July 2021.

Barthakur, A. (2021). Polluter pays principle as the key element to environmental law. *International Journal of Scientific and Research Publications, 11*(3), 274–277.

Berkman, P., et al. (2007). The influence of human activity in the Arctic on climate and climate impacts. *Climatic Change, 82*(1–2), 77–92.

Caballero, G., & Soto-Oñate, D. (2017). Environmental crime and judicial rectification of the Prestige oil spill: The polluter pays. *Marine Policy, 84*, 213–219. https://doi.org/10.1016/j.marpol.2017.07.012

CAFF. (2013). *Arctic biodiversity assessment 2013: Report for policy makers.* https://www.caff.is/assessment-series/arctic-biodiversity-assessment/229-arctic-biodiversity-assessment-2013-report-for-policy-makers-english. Accessed 26 July 2021.

Council of Europe. (1993). *Convention on civil liability for damage resulting from activities dangerous to the environment.* https://rm.coe.int/168007c079. Accessed 26 July 2021.

Economic Commission for Europe. (2003). *The protocol on civil liability and compensation for damage caused by the transboundary effects of industrial accidents on transboundary waters to the 1992 convention on the protection and use of transboundary watercourses and 1992 international lakes and the convention on the transboundary effects of industrial accidents.* https://treaties.un.org/doc/source/docs/ECE_MP.WAT_11-ECE_CP.TEIA_9-E.pdf. Accessed 26 July 2021.

Garneau, M.-E., Michel, C., Meisterhans, G., Fortin, N., King, T. L., Greer, C. W., & Lee, K. (2016). Hydrocarbon biodegradation by Arctic sea-ice microbial communities during microcosm experiments, Northern Passage (Nunavut, Canada). *FEMS Microbiology Ecology, 92*(10).

Harrison, J. (2009). Regime pluralism and the global regulation of oil pollution liability and compensation. *International Journal of Law in Context, 5*(4), 379–391.

Hassol, S. J. (2004). *Impacts of a warming Arctic: Arctic climate impact assessment.* Cambridge University Press.

High North News. (2020, February 24). IMO moves forward with ban of Arctic HFO but exempts some vessels until 2029. *High North News.* https://www.highnorthnews.com/en/imo-moves-forward-ban-arctic-hfo-exempts-some-vessels-until-2029. Accessed 26 July 2021.

ICJ. (1996). *Legality of the threat or use of nuclear weapons.* Advisory Opinion. https://www.icj-cij.org/public/files/case-related/95/095-19960708-ADV-01-00-EN.pdf. Accessed 26 July 2021.

ICJ. (1997). *Gabčikovo-Nagymaros Project (Hungary v. Slovakia).* Judgment of 25 September 1997. https://www.icj-cij.org/public/files/case-related/92/092-19970925-JUD-01-00-EN.pdf. Accessed 26 July 2021.

468 D. BOKLAN

ILC. (2001). *Draft articles on prevention of transboundary harm from hazardous activities, with commentaries.* https://legal.un.org/ilc/texts/instruments/english/commentaries/9_7_2001.pdf. Accessed 26 July 2021.

ILC. (2006). *Draft principles on the allocation of loss in the case of transboundary harm arising out of hazardous activities, with commentaries.* https://legal.un.org/ilc/texts/instruments/english/commentaries/9_10_2006.pdf. Accessed 26 July 2021.

ILM. (1979). Canada, claim against the USSR for damage caused by Soviet Cosmos 954, 23 January 1979. *International Legal Materials, 18*(4), 899–930.

IMO. (2017, March 31). *Measures to reduce risks of use and carriage of heavy fuel as fuel by ships in Arctic waters.* IMO Doc. MEPC 71/14/4.

IMO. (n.d.). *International code for ships operating in polar waters (Polar Code).* https://www.imo.org/en/OurWork/Safety/Pages/polar-code.aspx. Accessed 26 July 2021.

ITLOS. (2011, February 1). *Responsibilities and obligations of States with respect to activities in the Area.* Advisory Opinion. https://www.itlos.org/fileadmin/itlos/documents/cases/case_no_17/17_adv_op_010211_en.pdf. Accessed 26 July 2021.

IUCN. (1998). *IUCN red list of threatened plants.* https://www.biodiversitylibrary.org/item/97383#page/5/mode/1up. Accessed 26 July 2021.

IUCN. (2012). *IUCN red list categories and criteria.* Version 3.1, Second Edition. http://cmsdocs.s3.amazonaws.com/keydocuments/Categories_and_Criteria_en_web%2Bcover%2Bbckcover.pdf. Accessed 26 July 2021.

Johannessen, O. M., & Miles, M. W. (2011). Critical vulnerabilities of marine and sea ice-based ecosystems in the high Arctic. *Regional Environment Change, 11,* 239–248.

Margolis, E. (1955). The hydrogen bomb experiments and international law. *Yale Law Journal, 64*(5), 629–647.

National Oceanic and Atmospheric Administration. (2008). *Preassessment Data Report #2. M/V Selendang Ayu Oil Spill: Surveys of Intertidal, Subtidal, and Anadromous Stream Habitats.* https://www.fws.gov/r7/fisheries/contaminants/spill/pdf/selendang_Ayu/XXX_2_intertidal_report_final_1-30-08.pdf. Accessed 26 July 2021.

OECD. (1972). *Recommendation of the council on guiding principles concerning international economic aspects of environmental policies.* https://legalinstruments.oecd.org/public/doc/4/4.en.pdf. Accessed 26 July 2021.

Sands, P., Peel, J., Fabra, A., & MacKenzie, R. (2018). *Principles of international environmental law.* Cambridge University Press.

Schoolmeester, T., Gjerdi, H. L., Crump, J., Alfthan, B., Fabres, J., Johnsen, K., Puikkonen, L., Kurvits, T., & Baker, E. (2019).

Global linkages—A graphic look at the changing Arctic. UN Environment and GRID-Arendal. https://wedocs.unep.org/bitstream/handle/20. 500.11822/27687/Arctic_Graphics.pdf?sequence=1&isAllowed=y. Accessed 26 July 2021.

Stephens, T. (2009). *International courts and environmental protection.* Cambridge University Press.

UKPC. (2017). *Judgment on the fishermen and friends of the sea (Appellant) v The minister of planning, housing and the environment (Respondent) (Trinidad and Tobago).* UKPC 37. https://www.jcpc.uk/cases/jcpc-2016-0028.html. Accessed 26 July 2021.

UNEP. (2013). *UNEP year book: Emerging issues in our global environment.* United Nations Environment Programme.

UNEP. (n.d.). *Arctic region.* https://www.unenvironment.org/explore-topics/oceans-seas/what-we-do/working-regional-seas/regional-seas-programmes/arctic-region. Accessed 26 July 2021.

UNOOSA. (1972). *2777 (XXVI). The convention on international liability for damage caused by space objects.* https://www.unoosa.org/oosa/en/ourwork/spacelaw/treaties/introliability-convention.html. Accessed 26 July 2021.

UNSC. (1991). *UN Security Council resolution regarding situation on Kuwait.* https://undocs.org/S/RES/687(1991). Accessed 26 July 2021.

Vicuña, F. O. (1997). *Responsibility and liability under international law for environmental damage.* The Institute of International Law. https://www.idi-iil.org/app/uploads/2017/06/1997_str_03_en.pdf. Accessed 26 July 2021.

Wegeberg, S., Johnsen, A., Aamand, J., Lassen, P., Gosewinkel, U., Fritt-Rasmussen, J., Rigét, F., Gustavson, K., & Mosbech, A. (2018). *Arctic marine potential; of microbial oil degradation.* DCE—Danish Centre for Environment and Energy. https://dce2.au.dk/pub/SR271.pdf. Accessed 26 July 2021.

Wijnen, P. (2018, June 24). Oil spill from Norwegian tanker. *Norway Today.* https://norwaytoday.info/news/two-hundred-ton-oil-spilled-norweg ian-tanker/. Accessed 26 July 2021.

WWF. (2009). *Уроки не усвоены* [The lessons are not learned]. https://wwf.ru/upload/iblock/96d/oilspillrus.pdf. Accessed 26 July 2021.

Cooperative and Multilateral Agenda
of the Arctic Region: Despite All
Odds. Development Projects and Initiatives
in the Arctic Region: Infrastructure, Natural
Resources, Research and Innovation

Northern Sea Route as Energy Bridge

Vitaly Yermakov and Ana Yermakova

INTRODUCTION

The Northern Sea Route (NSR) is part of the Northeastern passage connecting the Atlantic and Pacific oceans through the Arctic seas. It is an important Arctic shortcut between Europe and Asia, providing significant distance and shipping time savings compared with the most often used shipping route from the Atlantic to Asia via the Suez Channel and the Indian Ocean. NSR runs along Russia's Arctic coast from its western boundary in the Kara Sea to its eastern boundary in the Bering Strait. The entire route is within Russia's exclusive economic zone (EEZ) and in Arctic waters, introducing the necessity to follow safety and environment protection requirements amid extreme navigation challenges due to ice conditions for most of the year.

The Russian government has recognized the development of NSR as a significant state priority, part of a broad state program on creating

---

V. Yermakov (✉)
Oxford Institute of Energy, Higher School of Economics, Oxford, UK
e-mail: vermakov@hse.ru

A. Yermakova
University of Denver, Denver, CO, USA

© The Author(s), under exclusive license to Springer Nature Singapore Pte Ltd. 2022
A. Likhacheva (ed.), *Arctic Fever*,
https://doi.org/10.1007/978-981-16-9616-9_18

473

infrastructure that would connect Western and Eastern parts of the country.

Undoubtedly, commercial considerations play a major role in promoting NSR. Developing infrastructure along NSR (including ports, trans-shipping facilities, new generation of ice-resistant vessels and powerful nuclear ice-breakers) holds a promise of an important commercial opportunity for cost-efficient delivery of Russian cargos between Russia's western and eastern regions, and to exports, providing Russian shippers with a competitive edge.

But NSR has also become a geo-political priority. In a world of growing global grivalries a Russia-controlled transportation trade route to China and other Asian markets that is beyond the control of the US Navy and is secure from possible sanctions or blockade represents an important strategic asset for Russia.

This article seeks to review Russia's strategy with regards to NSR and to analyze how the specific goals related to NSR may be achieved as a vital part of the country's overall Arctic strategy. It details which projects will be key in achieving Russian corporate goals and how Russia's overall strategy with regards to the NSR is set to develop.

Northern Sea Route—The Arctic Shortcut

Almost 18% of Russia's territory (over three million square kilometers) is in the Arctic. In addition to its tremendous potential for developing hydrocarbons reserves, it plays an important part in Russia's geostrategic calculations. One of the strategic priorities for the Russian government is to develop the Northern Sea Route (NSR)—the Arctic shortcut to Asia— as part of the Northern Sea Corridor with connections via Barents sea and North Sea to Europe and via Sea of Okhotsk and East China sea to China and wider Asia–Pacific. The route offers a significant reduction in transportation distances (and, therefore, costs) compared with the much longer route through the Suez Canal and is free from the risks of piracy often associated with the travel through the strait of Malacca (see Fig. 1).

NSR Boundaries

NSR extends more than 5000 km (the exact length depends on a specific route within NSR water area) off the coast of the Russian Federation from its western boundary along the meridian of Cape Zhelaniya, the eastern

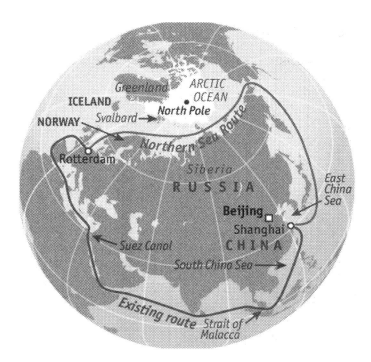

Fig. 1 Northern Sea Corridor and Northern Sea Route (*The Economist*, 2014)

coast of Novaya Zemlya, and the straights of Kara Gate, Matochkin Shar and Yugorskiy Shar to its eastern boundary at Cape Dezhnev (the easternmost point of the Russian mainland) and the demarcation line between the territorial waters of Russia and the US in the Bering strait. It crosses four Arctic seas: Kara Sea, Laptev Sea, East Siberian Sea, and Chukchi Sea within Russia's EEZ. It is noteworthy that the Barents sea is beyond NSR boundaries but is an important western part of the overall route between Europe and Asia.

According to Article 234 of the UN Convention on the Law of the Sea (UNCLOS) of 10 December 1982, the document governing international sea navigation, "coastal states have the right to adopt and enforce non-discriminatory laws and regulations for the prevention, reduction and control of marine pollution from vessels in ice-covered areas within the limits of the exclusive economic zone, where particularly severe climatic conditions and the presence of ice covering such areas for most of the year create obstructions or exceptional hazards to navigation, and pollution of the marine environment could cause major harm to or irreversible disturbance of the ecological balance. Such laws and regulations shall have due regard to navigation and the protection and preservation of the marine environment based on the best available scientific evidence" (UN Division for Ocean Affairs & the Law of the Sea, 1982). Russia's current legislation governing the rules of navigation via NSR has been developed in accordance with the UNCLOS guiding principles.

Russian Legislation on the NSR: The Latest Changes

In 2012 Russia adopted a law on NSR that introduced changes and amendments to the prior legislative acts, eliminating a good deal of the bureaucratic hassle in NSR administration inherited from Soviet times. The 2012 law required the Russian government to introduce the uniform rules for sailing via NSR, to set up a specially designated state entity to administer the rules, to give it authority to organize, permit, and manage navigation along the route. The law also established the key variables (such as a vessel's ice class, navigation period, etc.) for calculation of tariffs for piloting and icebreaker support services in the NSR waters (Government of Russia, 2012).

According to the latest version of the rules for NSR navigation introduced by the Russian Government in 2020 waters (Government of Russia, 2020a), there are 28 different zones within the NSR boundaries; for each, the requirements for ships are set depending on the type of navigation difficulty, based primarily on ice conditions during the passage. The possible routes via NSR involve passage through various combinations of the zones, from the ones closer to shore and usually ice-free for longer periods but at the same time having limited water depth and therefore not suitable for the passage of the larger ships (especially in the western part of East Siberian sea) to the ones further north with no water depth limitations but usually having more challenging ice conditions. For example, the maximum draft in the Sannikov Strait through which a lot of NSR traffic was passing in the past decade is only 12 meters, but the maximum draft along a more northerly route above the Novosibirsk Islands is 20 meters.

The rules set out standardized requirements for the types of ships allowed to travel NSR and outline the requirements for piloting and icebreaker assistance. The ships planning to navigate via NSR must apply in advance, at least two weeks prior to reaching NSR boundaries. The applications to navigate through NSR are considered by Russia's Federal Agency for Maritime and River Transport in coordination with Rosatom, the Russian state nuclear corporation in charge of Atomflot, a state entity running the fleet of Russia's nuclear icebreakers. Rosatom was appointed a single infrastructure operator of NSR in December 2018 (Rosatom, 2018). NSR's Marine Operations Headquarters (MOH) has been formed under the auspices of Rosatom to ensure navigational and environmental safety of passage via NSR. This entity provides navigational and hydrographic support to the ships, monitors ice situation, and coordinates the usage of icebreakers. The approval of passage via NSR is subject to meeting the requirements for the ships traveling in Arctic waters (such as an international Polar ship certificate), ice conditions along the planned route and availability of icebreakers, if and when necessary. During their passage via NSR all ships must follow instructions and navigational orders by MOH. According to the rules, vessels of certain ice class (e.g. Arc-7s) can navigate the entire NSR from July to November without the support of the nuclear icebreakers. For Arc-4 class ships, the option of independent navigation is limited to certain zones within NSR. For lower Arctic-class ships, however, icebreaker assistance is usually required for the entire route, and the associated fees may be significant.

Shipments via NSR to Date: Key Trends

For several centuries, attempts have been made to find the sea passage from the Atlantic to the Pacific through the northern seas and then to commercialize the shipments. The Soviet Union actively developed NSR since the 1930s because it was critical for supplying Russian Arctic cities along the coast and, with the use of Siberian rivers,—further inland.

Soviet success in Arctic shipping was due to creating the fleet of nuclear icebreakers in the 1960–1970s. Their use made possible established navigation in difficult ice conditions through the entire length of NSR. Until today, Russia remains the only Arctic nation with nuclear ice-breakers' capability.

Transportation turnover over NSR (mostly represented by cabotage shipments, the so-called "northern supply" (*severnyi zavoz*) during Soviet times peaked in 1987 at 6.7 million ton, before sharply declining after the collapse of the Soviet Union and overall decline of economic activity in the 1990s. It was not before 2016, however, that transportation turnover through NSR exceeded the Soviet record.

In the past few years a significant boost to shipping via NSR occurred, driven primarily by hydrocarbon shipments directed to exports. Crude oil was primarily represented by shipments from Novoportovskoye project by Gazpromneft and LNG and condensate—from Yamal LNG project by Novatek. The launch of Yamal LNG project in 2018 provided a major boost to NSR shipments which reached 32 million ton in 2020 (see Fig. 2).

In 2020, 86% of total shipments via NSR were represented by hydrocarbons going to export markets, including LNG (18.9 million ton), oil (7.7 million ton), and condensate (1 million of ton). General cargos amounted to 3.5 million ton or about 11% of total shipment volume. Refined products (0.6 million ton) and coal (0.3 million ton) accounted for a relatively minor shares of 2 and 1%, respectively.

It is noteworthy that the bulk of shipments via NSR are performed by vessels of high ice class, capable of independently sailing through relatively thick ice (see Fig. 3).

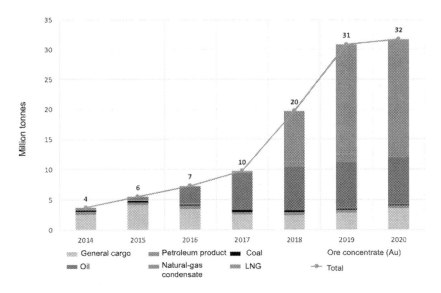

Fig. 2 Volume of shipments via NSR by type of cargo, 2014–2020

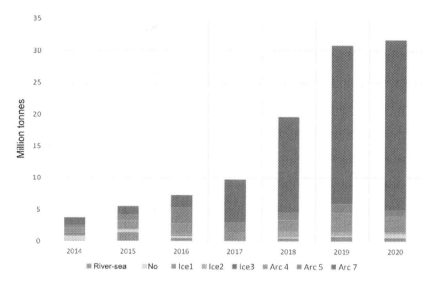

Fig. 3 Shipments via NSR by Arctic class of vessels, 2014–2020

The vessels of high Arctic classes (Arc-4, Arc-5 and Arc-7) represent LNG carriers, and oil and condensate tankers that evacuate hydrocarbons from Russian Arctic projects in the vicinity of Yamal and Gydan peninsulas.

It is evident that Yamal LNG's transportation strategy has been based on creating maximum self-sufficiency using Arc-7 ice-class LNG carriers (Yamal LNG, n.d.). This would allow the Russian Arctic LNG projects to minimize their dependence on the limited number of Rosatomflot's icebreakers and to lower the transportation costs by reducing the payments for icebreakers' support (icebreaker fees can increase overall shipping costs by 30% or more). According to the strategy, the icebreakers would primarily be needed to keep open the channel from the port of Sabetta to the open sea. The current LNG tanker fleet for Yamal LNG comprises fifteen Arc-7s and eleven conventional LNG carriers. The Arc-7s, each with the capacity to hold 170,000 cubic meters of natural gas, are 299 metres long and 50 metres wide. They are powered by 45 MW engines which can be fueled by either marine fuel oil, diesel, or LNG, and can travel at a speed of 19.5 knots in open water and at a reduced speed of 5.5 knots through sea ice up to two meters thick. The Azipod propulsion system allows them to move forward and astern through ice.

The LNG carriers for Yamal LNG have been built in South Korea, following the success of Daewoo Shipbuilding & Marine Engineering Company Ltd. which won a tender in 2013 to build fifteen Arc-7 LNG tankers at a total cost of about US$5 billion (approximately US$333 million per ship). The financing for the construction was organized through third parties including Sovcomflot, Canada's Teekay LNG in a joint venture with China LNG Shipping, and Mitsui OSK Lines in a joint venture with China Shipping Development Company.

For its next big project, Arctic LNG 2, Novatek and its project partners have placed orders for 15 Arc-7 LNG carriers to be built at Zvezda shipyard in Russia and for 6 more Arc-7 LNG carriers—at Korea's Daewoo Shipbuilding & Marine Engineering (DSME) shipyards.

At present, navigation for LNG carriers via the NSR eastwards is possible for six to seven months of the year, depending on the quantity of ice. The new generation of Arc-7 LNG carriers developed for Novatek's projects can travel through two-meter thick ice (although travel speed is significantly reduced), but even Arc-7s require the support of expensive nuclear icebreakers during the winter months. Owing to the width of the LNG carriers, two nuclear icebreakers are currently needed to open up a channel wide enough for the very large LNG tankers, imposing an additional cost on shippers.

As a result of these limitations on eastward shipments to Asia via NSR Yamal LNG's ability to send its liquefied gas westward during the winter season is an absolute must for the project to succeed. When possible, Yamal LNG would like to ship east, with the Northern Sea Route (NSR) serving as an important Arctic shortcut to reach premium Asian markets. However, for the foreseeable future the navigation window is likely to be limited to July–November with June and December as possibilities, depending on the weather). For the rest of the year, Yamal LNG has no other choice but to ship west, to European markets.

The window of opportunity on using NSR has expanded during 2020–21 season, however, as Yamal LNG managed to not only increase the overall number of shipments via the NSR but to start navigation early in May and send its Arc-7 LNG carriers through the NSR in December 2020 and January 2021 without nuclear icebreakers support (see Fig. 4).

These eastward shipments, however, represent only limited share of overall deliveries. For example, in 2020, westward shipments to Europe

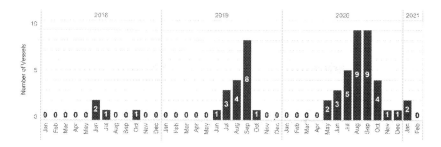

Fig. 4 Number of Yamal LNG carriers navigating NSR per month

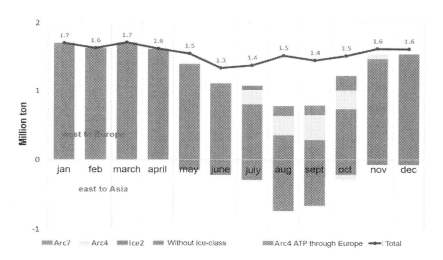

Fig. 5 The split in shipments via NSR between Europe and Asia in 2020

via NSR remained the prime destination for exports of hydrocarbons from the projects in the Russian Arctic with relatively limited volumes later trans-shipped to Asia from the European port via Suez owing to relatively narrow Europe-Asia price differentials in 2020 (see Fig. 5).

Figure 6 shows the volumes and the cargo composition of the international transit via NSR.

These voyages were made possible by the retreat of Arctic Sea ice during the past decade and mostly represent trial shipments by various players who have been testing the possibility of using NSR. The transit

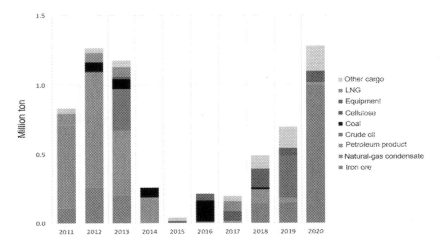

Fig. 6 International transit via NSR

shipping takes place in both directions—from Europe to Asia, and from Asia to Europe. International transit via NSR surged in 2012 and 2013 but then sharply declined, probably reflecting the worries about international sanctions against Russia. In 2020, however, it bounced back to about 1.3 million ton.

The available statistics on the composition of the NSR transit cargo indicate that a large share comprises iron ore and energy products, especially for shipments going eastward. The westward shipments contain petroleum refined products, coal, general cargo, and frozen fish products. However, the transit from Europe to Asia via NSR in the past decade has dwarfed the shipments from Asia to Europe (see Fig. 7).

It appears that the lion's share of transportation turnover via NSR in the foreseeable future will comprise the Russian cargos, mostly hydrocarbons. Expanding the role of NSR as an important transit route for international shipments between Atlantic and Pacific oceans remains a longer-term goal of Russia's strategy.

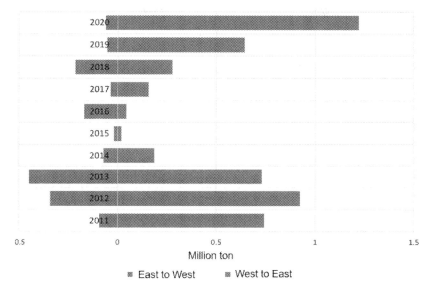

Fig. 7 International transit via NSR by direction of shipment

Russia's Arctic Ambition and the Northern Sea Route

Russian Latest Strategic Documents on Arctic and NSR

NSR takes a prominent place in Russia's Arctic strategy. In 2020 Russia adopted important strategic documents related to its Arctic strategy, outlining the key principles of its policy and specific targets to be achieved during the next fifteen years, and streamlining and codifying its previous regulations:

- *The Foundations of Russia's Arctic State Policy to 2035*—introduced by Presidential Decree #164 of 5 March 2020 (Government of Russia, 2020b).
- *The Strategy for Developing Russia's Arctic and Providing National Security to 2035*—introduced by Presidential Decree #645 of 26 of 26 October 2020 (Government of Russia, 2020c).

These documents characterize the NSR development as Russia's "national interest" and one of key priorities in the Arctic. In order to increase the volume of shipments via NSR and ensure year-round navigation, Russia's strategists propose to develop seaports and railroad links leading to these ports from inland, build new nuclear and diesel-powered icebreakers, and designate the projects that provide cargos for NSR.

The Strategy lists eighteen specific goals to advance the infrastructure development in the Arctic. Some of the goals are organizational or dealing with digitalization and are relatively easy-to-do. Among the ones most relevant to NSR are these: creation of Marine Operations Headquarters for NSR (promptly done in 2021); creation of a digital platform to facilitate the provision of logistical and transportation services in the NSR waters.

More challenging goals relate to the creation of Russia's own system of telecommunications in the Arctic based on a group of Russian space satellites and using Russian equipment and technological solutions and to laying subsea fiber optic cables along the NSR route to ensure fast internet access in all Russian Arctic seaports.

The hard-to-do "big ticket" goals include the construction of the new generation of vessels by 2035 (the Strategy specifically mentions at least five new nuclear icebreakers under the so-called project 22220 and three new nuclear icebreakers "Leader", 16 rescue tugs and support vessels of different sizes, 3 hydrographic vessels, and two pilot ships) and port infrastructure investments, including developing the existing sea ports and building new ones as well as developing the ports on Russian northern rivers (which involves extensive dredging operations).

The Strategy envisions the use of LNG as bunkering fuel in the Arctic, which can drastically reduce harmful emissions of NOx and SOx compared with using low-sulfur marine fuel oil.

NSR's Role in Connecting Russia's Arctic Hydrocarbon Riches with Markets

Russia's Arctic Strategy sets a goal for NSR shipping turnover of 90 million ton per year in 2030 and 130 million ton per year by 2035 (compared with 31.5 million ton in 2019 and 32 million ton in 2020). International transit is expected to represent a small share of the total volume at only 2 million ton in 2030 but rising to 10 million ton by 2035 (compared with 0.7 million ton in 2019).

It is clear that the lion's share of the shipments via NSR would be represented by exports of hydrocarbons, since for many Russian oil and gas projects located in Russia's Arctic sea transportation is a viable alternative to traditional transportation by pipeline or by rail.

Geography has always played a key role in Russia's economics. According to the Arctic Strategy to 2035, Russia's Arctic zone accounts for 80% of natural gas and 17% of crude oil and condensate produced in the country. The Strategy envisions that by 2035 the share of Arctic oil in total Russian output would go up to 26%, and the share of dry natural gas would remain at its present levels. At the same time, the strategy predicts that the amount of LNG produced in the Russian Arctic would reach 91 million ton by 2035 rising four-fold from its present level.

These outlooks are supported by the tremendous resource potential of Arctic hydrocarbons. The estimated mineral reserves for Russia's Arctic continental shelf are estimated to include 85 trillion cubic meters (Tcm) of natural gas and 17 billion ton of crude oil, sufficient to cover domestic and export demand for decades to come. However, the bulk of oil and gas production and most of the reserves are located far from consuming markets at home and abroad. This makes transporting oil and gas from points of production to points of export or domestic sales one of the most significant cost items for Russia's oil and gas producers.

Hydrocarbon projects operating on Russian territory in the vicinity of the NSR are expected to drive a significant increase in shipments via this route by 2035 and beyond and will continue to pioneer Arctic marine transportation solutions, given the need to deliver their output to markets. However, the danger is that the realization of many of the existing and planned oil and gas projects may outpace the infrastructural developments, creating transportation bottlenecks. Russia's Arctic Strategy recognizes this as one of the main risks and challenges to the realization of Russia's ambitious targets.

THE PERSPECTIVES OF YEAR-ROUND SHIPPING VIA NSR

The potential savings from shorter transportation distances associated with the use of NSR are offset by the constraints imposed by difficult ice conditions. Indeed, this has been the most important limiting factor for higher utilization of NSR. But things are starting to change due to climate warming in the Arctic and to the wider use of Arctic-class vessels and ice-breakers. Russia, the only Arctic nation with a fleet of nuclear icebreakers, is planning a major upgrade of its Arctic ships capabilities which could make year-round shipping via NSR a reality in the 2030s.

Climate Change in the Arctic and Its Impact upon Ice-Cover of the NSR

The rise of global temperatures has affected the Arctic region more than other regions of the world. The rise of temperature in the Arctic has been outpacing the growth of average global temperature more than two-fold in the past twenty years. Arctic warming may lead to the reduction of ice-cover in the Arctic seas, opening them for longer periods of navigation. However, it also carries significant dangers related to the melting of permafrost and methane hydrates and release of methane (which is a very potent greenhouse gas) into the atmosphere with a possibility of starting a vicious positive loop of even faster warming.

The temperatures in the vicinity of NSR have been consistently tracked by Russian agencies since the 1950s with the use of 22 meteorological stations located along the entire route. According to Rosgidromet, Russia's Federal Service for Hydrometeorology and Environmental Monitoring (2020), both average winter and summer temperatures increased significantly since 2010. Winter temperatures in the past decade were hovering around minus 20 degrees Celsius compared with about minus 24 degrees Celsius on average during 1970–2000. Summer average temperatures increased from about plus 3 degrees Celsius in 1970–2000 to about 4.5 degrees in 2010–2020 (see Fig. 8).

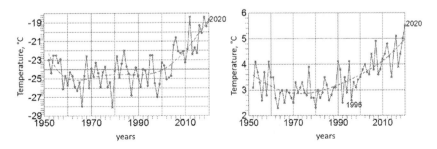

Fig. 8 Average winter (left graph) and summer (right graph) temperatures in the vicinity of the Northern Sea Route

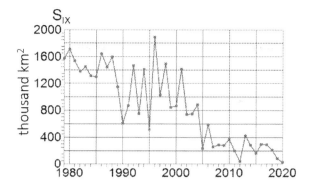

Fig. 9 Extent of minimum ice coverage (recorded in September) of seas along the NSR—Kara sea, Laptev sea, East Siberian sea, Chukchi sea

Warmer temperatures have contributed to the reduction of sea ice coverage in the water area of NSR. In 1979, the year when regular satellite observations of the Arctic began, the minimum ice extent in the NSR water area, which usually occurs in September, was about 1.6 million square km. In contrast, since September 2010 the ice extent in NSR waters declined to around 0.4 million square km, and in September 2012 NSR was ice-free. A new record low for ice extent in the NSR water area was observed in 2020. NSR was completely ice-free again in September 2020. But the extent of ice from year to year remains highly variable (see Fig. 9).

Another striking development has been the reduction of multiyear ice (i.e., ice that has survived at least one summer), which tends to be harder and thicker than first-year ice, posing additional problems for vessels. The overall trend has been for shipments via NSR to increase as ice has receded. Nevertheless, icebreakers' support is an absolute necessity for successful shipping in the Arctic waters. Russia has the capabilities in this area that cannot be matched by any other Arctic nation.

Russia's Plans for a New Generation of Nuclear Icebreakers

Russia is the only country in the world with a nuclear icebreaker fleet, operated by the Rosatomflot subsidiary of Rosatom, Russia's state-owned nuclear energy operator. The history of an outlook for Russia's nuclear icebreaker fleet is presented in Fig. 10.

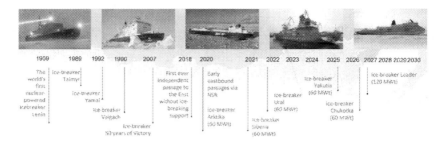

Fig. 10 Chronology of major events in the history of Soviet and Russian nuclear icebreaker fleet

Russia's first nuclear icebreaker "Lenin" started servicing the NSR as early as 1959. Rosatomflot currently provides ice piloting along the NSR and also for other Russian ports which freeze in winter. Russia's nuclear icebreakers are built at the Baltic Shipyard near St. Petersburg. There are five in operation, but three of them ('Taimyr', 'Vaigach', and 'Yamal') were built in 1989–1992 and are approaching the end of their service life. Rosatomflot managed to extend their operations beyond their nominal life spans to cover the period of highest risk in 2020–2021 when the ramp-up of construction activity in the Russian Arctic and rising hydrocarbon production from Russia's Arctic projects is not yet covered by the capabilities of the newly built icebreakers. Another icebreaker, "The 50th Anniversary of Victory", a larger and more powerful nuclear icebreaker was commissioned in 2007 (Rosatom, n.d.). Finally, the fifth nuclear icebreaker on active duty currently is a new "Arctica", the first in the so-called series 22220 that started operations in October 2020.

Two more nuclear icebreakers in the 22220 series, "Sibir" and "Ural" will be commissioned in 2021 and 2022 correspondingly with a reported price tag of about 50 billion rubles (about US$0.75 billion) each. Approximately half of this amount is financed by the Russian budget, with the rest coming from project financing. "Sibir" was put afloat in 2017, and construction is currently in its final phase. "Ural" was put afloat in 2019. The new icebreakers are more powerful (60 MW) and have a better body design which make them able to break through three-meter thick ice. At 34 metres width they can clear the way for a 70,000-dwt tanker (two 30-metre width icebreakers are required to perform this task at present). Another key advantage given the peculiarities of Russian Arctic operations is the dual draft construction that allows the new vessels to enter the river mouth to clear the way to the ports located along the NSR. In theory, this makes the new generation of nuclear icebreakers multi-use and reduces the number of conventional icebreakers required (Ruksha, 2020). For icebreakers under project 22220, however, this capability is expected only for operations in certain Arctic ports, in particular for sailing to the port of Dudinka in the estuary of the Yenisey river (essential for the operations of Norilsky Nickel), and to the oil terminal "Arctic Gate" in the Ob River estuary (essential for Gazpromneft's oil Arctic projects). In 2026–27 Rosatomflot plans to commission two or even three more 60 MW nuclear icebreakers (of the type under project 22220).

But the ultimate goal is to build an even more powerful generation (the LK-110 series) of nuclear icebreakers that would use a 110 MW power propulsion unit to cut through the ice of up to 4.3 meters which is found at higher-latitude routes. Here waters are deeper and could be accessed by larger ships than those navigating the existing NSR route. These icebreakers would have a 48-meter width, which would allow them to cut a channel 50 meters wide for 100,000-dwt tankers. Even more importantly, these icebreakers would maintain a speed of ten knots even while breaking through two-meter thick ice, providing an ultimate solution to cost-efficient year-round transportation via the NSR to Asia. The cost of the 110 MW nuclear icebreaker is currently estimated at about 100 billion rubles (US$1.5 billion). The Russian state budget is going to fully finance the construction of the first vessel in the new series which is projected to be commissioned before 2030 at the Zvezda shipyard in Russia's Far East. The financing sources for the second two are not yet determined at the time of writing.

Main Russian Projects in the Arctic and the Outlook for Future Transportation Turnover via NSR

Russia's Arctic Strategy to 2035 set a goal of increasing the volume of shipments via NSR to 90 million ton by 2030 and to 130 million ton by 2035. This is a difficult-to-achieve target, but it reflects the ambition and priority that Russia's leadership assigns to NSR. The following section reviews the main projects that are expected to generate this transportation turnover.

Novatek's LNG Projects on Yamal and Gydan Peninsulas

The expansion of LNG projects on Yamal and Gydan peninsulas will represent main incremental sources of cargos for the NSR through 2030s. Building on the successful launch of Yamal LNG and good progress with the construction of three trains of Arctic LNG 2 project by 2025 the total output of Novatek's LNG projects is set to reach a level of 38 million tons, and by 2030 it may be as high as 70 million tons, turning the company into an international LNG powerhouse (see Fig. 11).

Novatek and its partners are currently planning the construction of LNG transshipment terminals at both ends of the Northern sea corridor—near Murmansk on the Barents sea and on Kamchatka. The transshipment from Arc-7 LNG carriers to less expensive conventional LNG tankers would reduce the overall transportation costs and increase the efficiency of using the fleet of the Arc-7s by limiting their voyages to Arctic waters, where they are most fit for purpose. This will additional economies to the saving on the number of days of travel compared with other routes. As a result, the comparative disadvantage of Russian LNG projects in high transportation costs relative to their key competitors will be reduced, and their key advantage of extremely low production costs would make them more competitive overall (see Fig. 12).

Crude Oil and Condensate Exports from the Russian Arctic: Vostok Oil Project as Potential Game-Changer

The Vostok Oil project, promoted by Rosneft, is based on the production potential of 13 oil and gas fields on the Taimyr peninsula and in the northern part of Krasnoyarsk kray, some of them already producing like the fields in the Vankor cluster, and some being new developments in the Payakha cluster. Vostok Oil project represents a massive undertaking that is going to lead to significant job creation (the total number of people involved in the work on the project is estimated at 400,000, including 130,000 Rosneft personnel and contractors) and a significant increase in Russia's GDP as a result of both direct and indirect economic effects. This is a flagship project for Rosneft with confirmed oil reserves of 6 billion ton and expected combined hydrocarbons production from the project at 50 million ton by mid-2020s during phase one based on Vankor and Payakha clusters and at up to 100 million ton during phase two, based

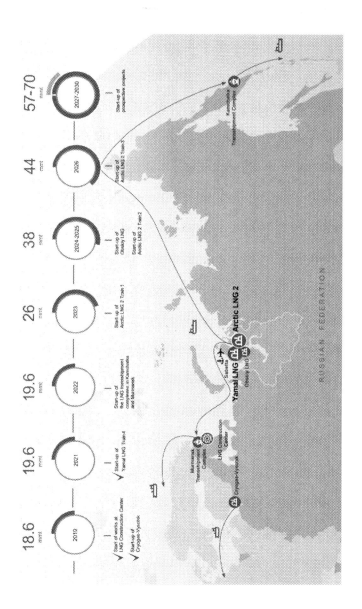

Fig. 11 Novatek's LNG production and evacuation plans

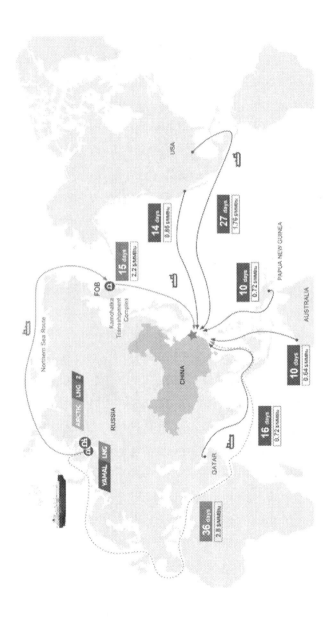

Fig. 12 LNG comparative logistics and costs on shipments to Asia in 2020

on East-Taymyr fields development which is planned by the early 2030s (Rosneft Shareholder, 2021) (see Fig. 13).

Crude from Vostok Oil fields has a uniquely low sulfur content of 0.01–0.04%, making it more valuable and more environmentally friendly (Rosneft Today, 2021). To protect this unique crude quality that would command price premium at the market (Sechin, 2021), Rosneft intends to build a dedicated 770-km pipeline from Vankor to a new seaport in Bay Sever (North) near the existing port of Dixon. Rosneft has pledged to deliver up to 30 million tons of oil to the Northern Sea Route by 2024, and much more in the longer term (President of Russia, 2020).

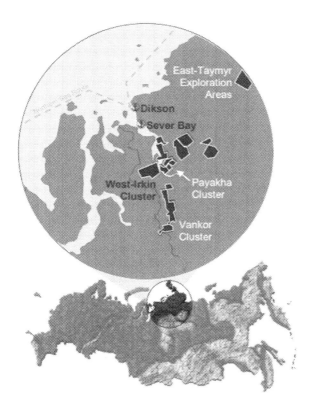

Fig. 13 Vostok oil project

Vostok Oil project indeed may become a game-changer for NSR, ensuring extremely high levels of shipments in the 2030s and beyond.

The project also involves the construction of new ships on a grand scale. In total, 50 vessels of different types, including oil tankers, LNG carriers as well as various support ships are expected to work on the project. The orders for 10 Arc-7 ice-class tankers have been placed at the Zvezda shipyard.

CONCLUSION

It appears that during the past decade the Russian government has taken some important steps to realize its goal of transforming the NSR into a major world trade route between Europe and Asia and managed to clearly formulate its priorities and strategic goals to 2035. These goals suggest that Russia sees NSR (at least initially) as an energy bridge connecting Russia's Arctic resources to the global markets. LNG exports from Yamal and Gydan have emerged as a key driving element behind the expected increase in NSR transportation turnover to 2035.

At the same time, the Russian government seems to recognize that the prospects for a major ramp-up of international NSR transit volumes in the next decade are more doubtful. As a result, the emergence of the NSR as a major Arctic marine shortcut between Europe and Asia that might compete with the Suez route for a significant share of the overall international shipping volumes remains, at best, a distant possibility. Evidently the technological and logistical efficiencies of the well-established international marine trading routes present global shipping companies with sound alternatives, while Russia still has some way to go as it aims to create the logistical infrastructure for NSR almost from scratch.

Nevertheless, it is already clear that Russia has set out on an ambitious course of NSR development supported by domestic industrial development, and although it will have to overcome many practical difficulties in achieving its ambition, it has already taken significant steps forward and appears likely to continue its efforts on putting the NSR traffic on a growth trajectory over the next decade.

NSR has emerged as an important element of Russia's Arctic strategy that now incorporates active development of the hydrocarbon riches in the Russian Arctic, development of the Arctic ports and other infrastructure and relies on expanding domestic capabilities in shipbuilding that involve economic multipliers and are seen as important engines of economic growth and job creation in Russia. From a geo-political standpoint, NSR also provides a new avenue for developing international relations with new and existing customers for Russian hydrocarbons, while also allowing Russia to compete with key rivals in a rapidly globalizing market.

References

Federal Service for Hydrometeorology and Environmental Monitoring of Russia. (2020). Доклад об особенностях климата на территории Российской Федерации за 2020 год [Report on the characteristics of the climate on the territory of the Russian Federation for 2020]. https://www.meteorf.ru/upload/pdf_download/doklad_klimat2020.pdf. Accessed 26 July 2021.

Government of Russia. (2012). Федеральный закон от 28 июля 2012 г. N 132-ФЗ "О внесении изменений в отдельные законодательные акты Российской Федерации в части государственного регулирования торгового мореплавания в акватории Северного морского пути" [Russian Federal Law #132 FZ of 28 July 2012]. http://ivo.garant.ru/#/document/70207760/paragraph/1:0. Accessed 26 July 2021.

Government of Russia. (2020a). Постановление Правительства Российской Федерации от 18.09.2020 № 1487 "Об утверждении Правил плавания в акватории Северного морского пути" [RF Government Resolution #1487 of 18 September 2020 "Rules of navigation in the water area of the Northern Sea"]. http://publication.pravo.gov.ru/Document/View/000120 2009220024. Accessed 26 July 2021.

Government of Russia. (2020b). Указ Президента Российской Федерации от 05.03.2020 г. "Об Основах государственной политики Российской Федерации в Арктике на период до 2035 года" [Decree of the President of Russia "Foundations of the Russian Federation State Policy in the Arctic for the Period up to 2035"]. http://static.kremlin.ru/media/events/files/ru/f8ZpjhpAaQ0WB1zjywN04OgKiI1mAvaM.pdf. Accessed 26 July 2021.

Government of Russia. (2020c). Указ Президента Российской Федерации от 26.10.2020 г. № 645 "О Стратегии развития Арктической зоны Российской Федерации и обеспечения национальной безопасности на период до 2035 года" [Decree of the President of Russia "Strategy for development of Russian Arctic zone up to 2035"]. http://kremlin.ru/acts/bank/45972/page/1. Accessed 26 July 2021.

President of Russia. (2020). Встреча с главой компании «Роснефть» Игорем Сечиным [Minutes of the meeting of Russia's President Vladimir Putin with Rosneft's CEO Igor Sechin on 25 November 2020]. http://kremlin.ru/events/president/news/64493. Accessed 26 July 2021.

Rosatom. (n.d.). Атомный ледокольный флот [Nuclear-powered icebreaker fleet]. https://www.rosatom.ru/production/fleet/. Accessed 26 July 2021.

Rosatom. (2018). Vladimir Putin singed a law on ROSATOM's powers in Northern Sea Route development. https://www.rosatom.ru/en/press-cen tre/news/vladimir-putin-singed-a-law-on-rosatom-s-powers-in-northern-sea-route-development/?sphrase_id=1957495. Accessed 26 July 2021.

Rosneft Shareholder. (2021, June 24). *Rosneft Shareholder*. https://www.ros neft.ru/upload/site1/document_publication/Rosneft_Gazeta2020_RUS.pdf. Accessed 26 July 2021.

Rosneft Today. (2021, June 5). Igor Sechin Presents Keynote Speech at SPIEF's Global Energy Transformation Panel. https://www.rosneft.com/press/today/item/206597/. Accessed 26 July 2021.

Ruksha, V. (2020, December 15). Вячеслав Рукша о новых ледоколах и старых проблемах [Vyacheslav Ruksha about new icebreakers and old problems]. *Kommersant*. https://www.kommersant.ru/doc/4614586. Accessed 26 July 2021.

Sechin, I. (2021). World Energy at the Crossroads. *Rosneft*. https://www.rosneft.com/upload/site2/attach/0/14/02/SPIEF_slides_2021_EN.pdf. Accessed 26 July 2021.

The Economist. (2014). Polar bearings. https://www.economist.com/china/2014/07/12/polar-bearings? Accessed 26 July 2021.

UN Division for Ocean Affairs and the Law of the Sea. (1982). United Nations Convention on the Law of the Sea of 10 December 1982. https://www.un.org/Depts/los/convention_agreements/texts/unclos/UNCLOS-TOC.htm. Accessed 26 July 2021.

Yamal LNG. (n.d.). LNG Shiping. http://yamallng.ru/en/project/tankers/. Accessed 26 July 2021.

Arctic Shelf Projects as a Driver for Social and Economic Development of the High North Territories: International Experience and Potential for Russian Practice

Alexey Fadeev and Marina Fadeeva

INTRODUCTION

In recent years, the most important tendency for states involved in the oil and gas production is to enforce geological exploration and production at the marine hydrocarbon fields.

Many scholars and experts see the key strategic task of the long-term sustainable development of the oil and gas industry in the balanced development of the offshore hydrocarbon potential of the continental shelf

---

A. Fadeev (✉)
G. P. Luzin Institute of Economic Problems of Kola Science Centre, Russian Academy of Science, Apatity, Murmansk region, Russia

Higher School of Industrial Management, Peter the Great
St. Petersburg Polytechnic University, St. Petersburg, Russia

Russian Gas Society, Moscow, Russia

M. Fadeeva
Higher School of Industrial Management, Peter the Great St. Petersburg Polytechnic University, St. Petersburg, Russia

---

© The Author(s), under exclusive license to Springer Nature
Singapore Pte Ltd. 2022
A. Likhacheva (ed.), *Arctic Fever*,
https://doi.org/10.1007/978-981-16-9616-9_19

and the transformation of the Arctic into the largest region of world oil and gas production. In this regard, the state and project operators face completely new organizational and managerial tasks, the solution of which should contribute to the progressive, cost-effective, socially oriented, environmentally balanced and safe development of offshore hydrocarbon fields on the Arctic shelf.

Strategic management of the oil and gas complex in the implementation of offshore projects is a multicomponent process that covers a number of considerable issues in geopolitical, economic, social, environmental dimensions. These problems are solved at the state level and should take into account the interests of coastal regions, related industries and services, the interests of society in terms of compliance with environmental standards and the creation of new jobs. At the same time, it becomes necessary to understand strategic management from the point of view of taking into account the interests of all stakeholders in the preparation and implementation of projects for the development of offshore oil and gas fields.

Taking into account the well-established interaction with oil and gas companies and public environmental organizations, the state should ensure an ecologically balanced model of sustainable nature management, taking into account the special vulnerability of the sensitive Arctic nature and solving the problems of maximizing the preservation of the natural habitat.

Despite the current macroeconomic conditions, the development of the Arctic shelf is still one of the promising areas for the global energy sector. Experts estimate that the Arctic shelf contains up to 25% of all hydrocarbons on the planet.

The Arctic continental shelf of Russia is one of the most attractive and promising areas in terms of hydrocarbon production potential. The resources of the Russian shelf are on average estimated at about 100 billion tons of fuel equivalent (Fadeev et al., 2019). At the same time, it should be taken into account that these estimates are approximate since the shelf study is still far from being ideal.

The Arctic region offers unique prospects for developing energy resources, even though the Arctic is characterized by a harsh climate—with extreme fluctuations in light and temperature, short summers, snowy and icy winters, and vast permafrost areas.

Back in 1970s, several hydrocarbon fields were discovered on the Arctic shelf, some of which are unique. This has largely changed the fuel and energy complex development paradigm: design and technological solutions for hydrocarbon extraction on the Arctic shelf began to be created. As an apogee of these activities, in April 2014, the first batch of arctic oil from the Prirazlomnoye field was shipped, which received its own brand—ARCO (arctic oil).

For Russia, the Arctic zone has always had a strategic character. It is appropriate to recall the expression of the famous Russian naval commander Stepan Osipovich Makarov who said that "Russia is a building with its facade facing the Arctic Ocean". The Arctic has always attracted the attention of explorers. Starting in the eleventh century, the exploration of the Arctic has not ceased, and today, we can state that the Arctic is at the service of humankind (Fig. 1).

Today, the Arctic is an unconditional imperative for the economic strategy of a number of Russian regions. At the end of the last century, deposits classified as unique in terms of reserves were discovered in the Arctic zone. Today, this region is becoming a new oil and gas province, designed to ensure energy security not only for Russia but also for many countries in the world in the long term. Today, the Arctic is a "storehouse of natural resources" capable of guaranteeing the energy security of humanity for decades to come.

At the same time, it is essential to develop a model of ecologically sustainable use of natural resources, which could provide effective and long-term sustainable economic development of coastal areas, as well as

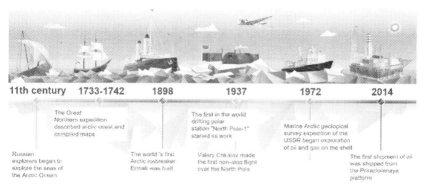

Fig. 1 History of Russian Arctic development (PJSC Gazprom Neft. Access mode: www.gazprom-neft.ru)

provide as possible comfortable living conditions for people in the coastal areas.

The implementation of hydrocarbon production projects in new producing regions can revive the general economic situation in most industries—primarily the heavy industry, construction, and transport sector, which in the regions is represented, as a rule, by small and medium businesses.

This chapter will focus on the role of offshore projects in the social and economic development of territories. The study consistently highlights the role of energy projects as an economic multiplier, foreign experience in implementing projects in the far North, the need to take into account the interests of the indigenous peoples of the North, the importance of preserving the sensitive ecosystem of the Arctic, the formation of an integrated, intersectoral approach to managing the activities of industries in the Arctic and, finally, ensuring the sustainable development of producing areas.

The authors attempt to identify the best international practices in order to project them on modern Russian macroeconomic conditions. The authors are convinced that the leading role of social and economic factors in the development of offshore fields, observed in countries and regions with a dominant role of the hydrocarbon production in the economy (Norway, Russia, Alaska, the northern provinces and territories of Canada), should become an absolute imperative in the implementation of offshore projects in the Russian Arctic.

ARCTIC OFFSHORE PROJECTS AS AN ECONOMIC MULTIPLIER

Oil and gas projects can engage key industries related to other businesses through inter-industry process chains. Obtaining an order by major industries and, consequently, the output is a driving force for the development of related industries, which, in their turn, contribute to the development of domestic suppliers' capabilities, etc. These circumstances lead to the formation of multiplicative effects comparable to the effect of "self-excitation of economic growth". In this case, we are talking about encouraging the unwinding of the upward spiral of production demand, which would indicate investment and consumer demand on its basis. According to research statistics, domestic demand is the most significant and most reliable driver of economic and social growth (PJSC Gazprom Neft. Access mode: www.gazprom-neft.ru).

The multiplication index (multiplier) is a parameter characterizing the degree of particular industries' development. The multiplier value for developed countries is: Australia, 1.8–2.4; USA, 2.1; Norway, 1.6–1.7. According to experts' estimates, the "oil and gas" multiplier for Russia is 1.9, which fully corresponds to the level of multiplication of oil and gas producing countries of the world (Nikitin & Kibitkin, 1999).

It is indicative that according to preliminary calculations carried out by experts at the stage of the feasibility study of the Shtokman gas condensate field development project, the income of the Russian side on the "engineering" (through placing orders with Russian contractors, suppliers of goods and services) could almost double (!) the similar income from gas production and processing. Increased production and subsequently maximum utilization of production capacities of enterprises are going to allow the majority of regional enterprises to equalize the current economic situation, pay off the existing loans and improve their financial situation.

At present, the contribution of small businesses to the country's total GDP does not exceed 20%, while this indicator in several other countries engaged in offshore oil and gas production is about 50–60% (PJSC Gazprom Neft. Access mode: www.gazprom-neft.ru).

The global experience of the leading countries in offshore development, such as Norway, demonstrates that work in the oil and gas complex opens up significant prospects for developing regional enterprises in the regions of operation, creating jobs and improving living standards. In particular, one of the most experienced companies working offshore today is Equinor ASA (formerly Statoil ASA [2009–2018], StatoilHydro [2007–2009])—has been actively involving regional business in the process of implementing large-scale projects for the development of hydrocarbon deposits on the Norwegian continental shelf almost since the start of work on the shelf. This fact is a driver of socio-economic development of the regions where Equinor ASA operates in Norway and beyond (Kutuzova, 2006).

Foreign Experience of Project Implementation in the North

The key positions of the state at all stages of field development is one of the most important features of developing hydrocarbon resources in the Far North of foreign countries. This state participation considers and details the interests of the individual municipalities and provinces affected by oil and gas development.

Among these regions and countries, Norway is the undisputed leader (Dodin, 2007). In 1966, after the demarcation and signing of the relevant agreements on the division of the North Sea bottom with Denmark and Great Britain, oil prospecting drilling on the Norwegian continental shelf has begun. It is interesting to note, that the first drilling rigs in Norway were converted whaling vessels operated by foreign-contracted companies. The Ekofisk field is the first major discovery on the Norwegian continental shelf made by the US company Phillips in 1969.

Norway, having no experience in exploration and development of oil and gas fields and the necessary financial resources, has shown the ability to develop an effective state policy of integrated management of oil and gas resources and attract private capital capable of developing fields at a high technical, technological, and social level (Fadeev et al., 2011). The industrial basis, formed in Norway, made it possible to equip the most advanced oil and gas complex, including the world's largest offshore drilling rig, to organize hydrocarbon production using subsea production complexes, to lay underwater pipes at sea depths of over one thousand meters as well as to build the world's northernmost gas liquefaction plant. Since the start of the oil and gas complex, more than 60 fields have been discovered on the Norwegian continental shelf, and about 3000 production wells have been drilled (Steinar, 2006).

It is noteworthy that the volume of oil produced on the Norwegian continental shelf has begun to exceed the government demand since 1975, which determined, among other things, the specifics of the Norwegian approach to the development of oil and gas resources, including for the future.

Hydrocarbons are a non-renewable national resource—a basic principle underlying the use of Norway's oil and gas resources. For this reason, the development of hydrocarbon resources should be conducted with maximization of possible multiplicative economic effects both for the present generation and taking into account the interests of future generations of

Norway. In the field of oil and gas resources use in Norway the following main objectives of state policy can be outlined (Steinar, 2006):

(a) Ensuring a stable level of welfare and employment while creating the highest possible value of work in the development, exploitation, and production of hydrocarbons;
(b) Internationalization of the Norwegian oil and gas service industry to develop this sector of the economy and at a time of declining production at the fields;
(c) Leadership in energy supply and impeccable environmental standards.

According to the current Norwegian legislation, companies operating on the Norwegian continental shelf have to pay almost 80% tax to the state, which, however, does not prevent them from developing even in times of crisis. Today Norway ranks 10th in the world in terms of daily oil production, and when it comes to supplying gas to Europe, it has become one of the main suppliers, ranking on a par with Russia and Algeria (Steinar, 2006).

It is noteworthy that more than 90% of the hydrocarbons produced by Norway are exported, thus providing almost 70% of the volume of foreign trade (Steinar, 2006). At the same time, the state's domestic energy needs are largely covered by the efficient operation of hydro and wind energy. More than 500 billion kroons a year are received for industrial development and replenishment of the National Stabilisation Fund, which is supposed to ensure stable state development for many years ahead (PJSC Gazprom Neft. Access mode: www.gazprom-neft.ru).

While using international cooperation as an efficient economic and technological development tool, Norwegian companies have taken the lead in almost all areas of oil and gas service, production of equipment for hydrocarbon production, transportation, and processing. To promote Norwegian services technologies abroad, INTSOK was founded. Today it plays a major role in the Norwegian oil and gas sector.

Involvement of the state and increased regulation of the oil and gas industry as a whole has become a major challenge for Norway to strengthen its position through increased domestic presence.

To ensure the long-term socio-economic impact of these resources on the country, the Norwegian government is continuously adjusting policies in the oil and gas sector. To improve efficiency and reduce costs in the oil and gas industry, a new Petroleum Act was adopted in 1996, which is a modernization of the existing regulations in the oil and gas industry and is aimed at addressing many issues, such as the assignment of oil and gas-bearing areas of the shelf.

The greatest source of wealth for the Norwegian economy is the hydrocarbon resources of the country's continental shelf. Today, Norway's oil and gas complex has strong technological links with other sectors of the economy: shipping, finance, information technology, etc. The multiplicative economic effects of the oil and gas complex are very significant for Norway. Thus, the number of people employed in the oil and gas complex in Norway is about 220,000 (all over Norway) (Kutuzova, 2006).

Creating conditions for sustainable development of the territories where hydrocarbon projects are implemented is one of the top priorities of the operating companies operating in Norway. Since the establishment of the Norwegian company "Statoil", there is an active process of involvement of regional business in the implementation of large-scale projects for the development of hydrocarbon resources, which has significantly contributed to the growth of socio-economic development of the territories, which are the regions where "Statoil" is present (Kutuzova, 2006).

Norway has successfully met the strategic challenge of transforming hydrocarbon resources into a technological state superiority, an outcome that was not predetermined. It is interesting that, for example, the experience of the UK in developing the resources of the North Sea, which relied on international technologies instead of developing domestic ones, did not show a similar result. Unlike Norway, which now has a high-tech oil and gas industry, the UK has not achieved a similar result. The Norwegian experience is currently being adopted by other countries: the Chinese oil and gas service market, for example, is developing according to this scenario today.

The experience of projects on the Canadian continental shelf is also useful for Russia in terms of benchmarking. The first major hydrocarbon field being developed in the coastal waters of the Canadian province of Newfoundland is the Habernia project (Steinar, 2006).

The northern coastal conditions require advanced technology that makes the Habernia project unique in terms of technics, policy and enhancement. Implementation of this project at the cost of $7.3 billion (with reserves of 400 million tons) made it possible for Canada to become one of the world's leading countries in offshore oil production. This project, which cost $7.3 billion (with reserves of 400 million tons), made it possible for Canada to become one of the world's leading countries in the field of offshore oil production.

Discovered in 1979, the Habernia field is located on the east coast of Canada. It is important to note that it took more than a decade for agreements between the governments of Canada and the Province of Newfoundland and oil companies to be finalized to allow development to begin.

A general agreement involving joint management of hydrocarbon development was entered into the federal and provincial governments in 1985. The Canadian government, which partially financed the project, hoped to not only recoup its investment in the long term but also to reduce its budget by eliminating its subsidy to the province of Newfoundland. In the opinion of many Canadian experts, the Habernia Project was prioritized over regional development objectives before commercial returns from hydrocarbon production.

In the implementation of the Habernia project, the state was one of the guarantors of compensation for increased risks in the implementation of this project, as well as the role of an arbitrator and guarantor of property rights. To increase investment attractiveness and reduce risks, the Government of Canada was directly involved in the financial support of the project. The main significant forms of support were the following (Dodin, 2007):

(a) 0.25% reimbursement of pre-operational costs to the project operating companies, amounting to $1.05 billion;
(b) 0.40% guarantee of up to USD 1.68 billion of pre-commissioning loans. That is, the operators will transfer to the state the corresponding share in the project in case of impossibility to repay the loans;
(c) an interest-free loan in the event of oil prices falling below $19 per barrel up to $300 million;
(d) if the cost of the pre-commissioning phase exceeds $5.2 billion, additional loan guarantees are provided to cover 40% of the costs.

Increasing the employment and professional competence of the Canadian population was one of the goals of government support for the project. As a result, 66% of the jobs were filled by Canadian nationals, and the combined share of Canadian contractors and suppliers in the implemented project was about 60%. The use of regional labor and local contractors was facilitated by adequate financial support from the state. Analyzing the total costs of the project, it can be stated that $5.8 billion are investments of the operating companies, and $1.5 billion are investments of the state (Dodin, 2007).

In Canada, a special "Habernia Development Act" was enacted to address the pioneering nature of the project. The state was able to resolve the complex issues of work funding and revenue sharing, and a compromise was found to resolve jurisdiction over coastal waters. Thanks to political will and government support, the Habernia project has become one of the largest in the world.

For the Russian Federation, the Norwegian, Canadian, and English experience is very useful in implementing large-scale projects in the public interest, which, in addition to their technological complexity, are also highly capital-intensive.

As foreign experience shows, the implementation of projects solely within the framework of approaches focused on pure commercial efficiency is impossible without considering the social and regional conditions. *None of these projects, implemented in Norway, Greenland, Canada, or the USA, took place in isolation from the solution of socio-economic development problems of the territory*. For example, the launch of the Soviet field development project in the Norwegian sector of the Barents Sea was largely due to potential regional effects.

The previously discussed features of foreign projects implementation imply active participation of the state (both at the federal and regional levels), as well as the application of procedures and approaches based on the program principle.

In the author's opinion, the implementation of Arctic offshore projects should be based on the following:

(a) formation of a unified offshore exploration program;
(b) creation of a common service infrastructure, as well as a coordinated technological scheme for the development and exploitation of closely located sites (cluster of locations);

(c) ensuring sustainable social and economic development of the region of operations;

(d) creation of organizational structures for project implementation, operating companies, as well as a system of state monitoring and support for the implementation of Arctic projects.

When implementing the projects on the development of hydrocarbon resources of the Russian Arctic shelf, the main priorities of state regulation of the oil and gas complex should be aimed at the formation of conditions for "participation" of the fuel and energy complex in solving a wide range of socio-economic problems of the state (Fadeev, 2013; Kryukov & Tokarev, 2007).

Indigenous Minorities of the North and Their Interests in the Implementation of Energy Projects

The Russian Federation is the largest multi-ethnic country in the world. There are 193 nationalities living on the territory of Russia. The legislation of the Russian Federation singles out small peoples as a special group that needs special protection and support. A total of 47 small peoples of the Russian Federation are included in the unified list of small peoples.

According to the definition, small-numbered indigenous peoples include such groups of the population, which live in the territory of the traditional settlement of their ancestors, maintain traditional lifestyles, economy and trades, number less than 50 thousand people in the Russian Federation, and recognize themselves as independent ethnic communities (C3 RF, 1999).

Of the 47 small-numbered peoples in the Unified List, 40 peoples have the status of small-numbered indigenous peoples of the North, Siberia, and the Far East of the Russian Federation (SZ RF, 2006).

The Indigenous Minorities of the North (IMN), Siberia, and the Far East include the Aleuts, Alutorians, Veps, Dolgans, Itelmen, Kamchadals, Kereks, Kets, Koryaks, Kumandins, Mansi, Nanai, Ngansansans, Negidals, Nenets, Nivkhs, Oroks (Ulta), Orochi, Saami, Selkups, Soyots, Tazy, Telengits, Teleuts, Tofalars, Tubalars, Tojin Tuvans, Udegeis, Ulchi, Khanty, Chelkans, Chuvans, Chukchi, Chulymtsy, Shorians, Evenks,

Eveny, Enets, Eskimos, Yukaghirs. These peoples are settled on the territory of 28 subjects of the Russian Federation (the Republics of Altai, Buryatia, Karelia, Komi, Sakha (Yakutia), Tyva, Khakassia; Altai, Transbaikal, Kamchatka, Krasnoyarsk, Primorsky, Khabarovsk territories; Amur, Vologda, Irkutsk, Kemerovo, Leningrad, Magadan, Murmansk, Sakhalin, Sverdlovsk, Tomsk, Tyumen regions; Nenets, Khanty-Mansiysk-Yugra, Chukotka and Yamalo-Nenets Autonomous Areas) (Shtyrova, 2013).

Having centuries-long experience of living in the northern territories, people do not always adapt successfully to the emerging market relations and new forms of socio-economic relations. The current experience in the implementation of natural resource extraction projects has shown that the interests of indigenous minorities have often been neglected, leading to the deterioration of living and working conditions of the indigenous population, disturbance of the balance of territories, alienation of traditional use lands for industrial use, withdrawal of reindeer pastures from circulation, contamination of spawning grounds of valuable fish species.

This approach leads to the loss of traditional livelihoods, cultures, and native languages, negatively impacting the health of people, and creating objective difficulties in employment. These indigenous minorities of the North are among the most vulnerable groups of the population that need maximum care from the state.

It is worth noting that if operations on the Arctic shelf is really a new page in the history of Russian energy companies operations, then operations in the Arctic for Russia is, without a doubt, a traditional and familiar habitat that has already proven its effectiveness. And the indigenous peoples living on the Arctic territory make a significant contribution to ensuring the well-being of the Russian Federation. By engaging in traditional crafts that have developed historically, as well as working on large industrial and energy projects implemented today in the Arctic zone of the Russian Federation, indigenous peoples make a tangible contribution to strengthening the economic well-being of the state.

The industrial presence in the Arctic is constantly increasing. 2/3 of the territory of the Russian Federation are permafrost areas. Not so long ago in Russia, a law was adopted, which officially defined the status of the subjects of the Russian Federation, related to the Arctic. Today the Arctic Zone of the Russian Federation (AZRF) produces up to 15% of the gross domestic product of the country and about 25% of its exports (Fig. 2).

It is important to keep in mind that the Arctic is an area the development of which cannot be determined by the laws of the market economy

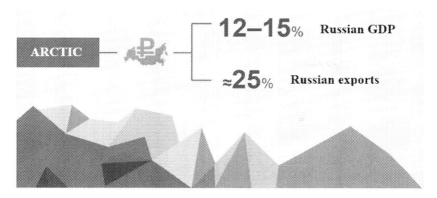

Fig. 2 Contribution of enterprises located in the Arctic zone to GDP and Russian exports

only. Considering the established cooperation with oil and gas companies and public environmental organizations, the state should provide an ecologically balanced model of sustainable nature management, taking into account the special vulnerability of the harsh Arctic nature and solving problems of maximum conservation of the natural habitat.

Ensuring Environmental Safety in Hydrocarbon Extraction and Transportation in the Arctic

Due to the enormous reserves of hydrocarbon resources in the Arctic zone, as well as the increasing role of factors and conditions underlying the political and energy security of the leading industrialized countries of the world, many states now consider the Arctic as a strategic region. Development of the Arctic territories involves the development of transport, extraction of biological resources, and, of course, intensive exploitation of hydrocarbon resources on the shelf. In this connection, the implementation of a rational multiproduct, ecologically balanced model of sustainable nature management, as well as the particular vulnerability of the harsh Arctic nature, make it necessary to study and solve problems of maximum conservation of the natural habitat (including within the framework of international cooperation).

The Arctic ecological system is susceptible to external impacts and has a prolonged recovery rate in negative impacts. The environmental problems of the Arctic zone arouse considerable interest on the part of specialized specialists. Even though the Arctic is characterized by a harsh climate, extreme fluctuations in light and temperature, short summers, snowy and icy winters, and vast areas of permafrost, this is where there are unique prospects for the development of natural resources. Some flora and fauna found in the Arctic have adapted to the harsh conditions of the Arctic zone. Still, this adaptation has, in some cases, made them more susceptible to anthropogenic impact.

The impacts on the environment, ecosystems, and marine organisms in offshore operations begin with the geological and geophysical investigation phase of the seabed. Seismic surveys, based on seismic wave generation and recording of vibrations reflected from the seabed surface, are most commonly used to determine oil and gas-bearing capacity. Such studies allow us to judge the structure and oil and gas content of the sedimentary rocks of the sea shelf.

The effect of a water hammer of up to 150 atm causes damage to organs and tissues of adult fish, fry and even their death. Seismic surveys have the potential to disrupt salmonid fish migration routes in the exploration area. Organizing and conducting seismic surveys generates specific noises that disrupt communication between marine organisms, making it difficult to detect other sounds and, consequently, to find food. Whales are the most afflicted animals in this case. Attracted by unknown sounds, animals can suffer serious, even fatal, injuries from the powerful water shocks.

Some organisms and marine animals are restricted to certain habitats, leading to mortality due to lack of adaptability and subsequent failure to establish themselves in the new environment (Fadeev, 2011).

Seismic activity has been used in the oil and gas industry since the middle of the last century. Since the 1950s, explosives have been used to map the seafloor, causing considerable damage to the ecosystem; twenty years later, air guns were used for this purpose. Seismic surveys have been shown to cause significant damage to fish eggs and larvae that are located in close proximity to the effects of the air gun. It is still a pending issue whether seismic surveys are actually harmful to fish and marine animals impacted within a 2–3 km radius of the vessel. The result of such human activities for fish may be a change in spawning and migratory routes.

Well Drilling and Associated Environmental Risks

The extraction of hydrocarbon resources on the shelf is accompanied by a large amount of emissions of substances into the atmosphere, the marine environment, etc. It is noteworthy that environmental risks remain in the area of the field even after the production of hydrocarbon resources there has been terminated.

If seismic surveys indicate the presence of oil and gas bearing structures, well drilling begins at the exploration stage. The formation of liquid and solid waste accompanies virtually all phases and operations of oil and gas exploration and production. For each passed well, the volume of emissions in the form of the worked-out drilling agents and cuttings (representing the rocks drilled in the borehole) can reach **5000** m^3 (Fadeev, 2011).

Special drilling fluids and acids are used as part of the drilling process. In addition, the drilling process generates liquid wastes containing large amounts of toxic impurities, clayey slurry, and heavy metals that accumulate from rock excavations, which increase water turbidity in the areas of operations. The use of petroleum-based drilling fluids poses the greatest risk. Drilling cuttings impregnated with such a solution act as the main source of the organization's oil contamination and carry out drilling operations.

Discharge of formation water from wells is another significant source of pollution. The composition of such produced water is characterized by abnormal salinity, which is usually higher than sea water salinity, and high content of petroleum hydrocarbons and heavy metals. In the area of formation water discharge this fact may cause disturbance of hydrochemical regime. In addition, when in contact with seawater, natural radionuclides precipitate and form local microscopic deposits. It is worth noting that the volume of produced water increases during the operation of the field. Today, some technologies return produced water to the sea with pretreatment and allow it to be injected back into the wells.

Existing legislation prescribes the accumulation of spent drilling mud as well as other wastes with subsequent transport to shore for further treatment or special treatment. A portion of the waste may be discharged overboard, subject to the presence of contaminants. It is worth noting that the measures prescribed by law are not implemented by all operators and contractors. Moreover, efficient refining technologies for petroleum products in Russia are just being adapted.

According to experts, none of the existing technologies can provide 100% purification of formation water. Therefore, complete prevention of the release of hazardous substances into the marine environment has not been guaranteed to date. The problem of exploitation of old fields containing much more produced water than hydrocarbons directly is topical. As an example, the Tampen area in the North Sea, where the amount of oil produced is half the amount of produced water, is appropriate.

The radius of local impact of drilling waste from a single well extends to a radius of up to 5 km. If the number of wells being drilled is large enough, their negative impact may extend to entire field areas. The ecosystem of the North Sea being that poor, according to the Norwegian Institute of Marine Research, is precisely the result of oil and gas activities.

The Arctic region, with its highly fragile ecosystem, is particularly at risk of anthropogenic interference. Even a small spill of extracted hydrocarbons on the ice-covered shelf for most of the year can cause irreparable environmental damage. In 1989, the wreck of the Exxon Valdez oil tanker in Alaska resulted in one of the largest offshore environmental disasters in history. The result of this catastrophe was a dramatic decline in fish and marine animal populations. According to scientists, it will take at least 30 years to restore some of the Arctic's sensitive habitats. According to the court ruling, Exxon paid a fine of $4.5 billion (Fadeev, 2011).

INCIDENTS AND ACCIDENTS ON OFFSHORE PLATFORMS AND FACILITIES

Rapid development of emergency processes associated with hydrocarbon release and combustion in dense equipment is a distinctive feature of accidents at offshore facilities.

Due to insufficient attention to measures for identifying and mitigating safety hazards, the global history of continental shelf development has been marked by a number of accidents with disastrous consequences. The major incidents and accidents at offshore technical facilities and platforms of various types in recent decades are shown in Table 1.

In April 2010, an even larger environmental disaster occurred in the Gulf of Mexico offshore. The Deepwater Horizon, owned by British Petroleum (BP), sank off the coast of Louisiana after a 36-hour fire following a massive explosion on April 22, 2010. The oil spill caused enormous environmental and economic damage to the states of Alabama,

Arctic Shelf Projects as a Driver for Social and Economic ... 513

Table 1 Major accidents and incidents on offshore platforms and facilities (Fadeev et al., 2019)

Place and date	Accident/Incident	Main causes and brief description	Damage and number of victims
China Sea, November 25, 1979	Platform flooding	The platform was caught in a 10-point storm while being towed offshore. The platform overturned and sank as a result of flooding of the pump room	There were 72 fatalities Damage is the cost of the platform
Red Sea, October 02, 1980	Uncontrolled release of oil	An uncontrolled oil release followed by an explosion on the Ron Tappmayer platform. Oil spill into the sea in the volume of ~150 thousand tons and bags with bulk reagents	There were 19 fatalities Environmental damage—up to $800 thousand
Coast of Canada, October 15, 1982	Platform flooding	The Ocean Ranger jackup rig capsized and sank in stormy conditions. The main reasons are design flaws, unpreparedness and improper actions of the crew, and lack of sufficient rescue equipment	There were 84 fatalities Damage is the cost of the platform
North Sea, March 27, 1983	Explosion, fire, platform collapse	Alexander Kielland platform legs collapse with subsequent explosion and fire in stormy conditions. The main causes of personnel deaths are damage to rescue equipment	There were 123 fatalities Damage is the cost of the platform
Sea of China, October 25, 1983	Platform flooding	The drilling vessel Glomar Java Sea was derailed and capsized during the passage of a tropical typhoon; as a result, the vessel sank	There were 81 fatalities. Damage is the cost of the platform
North Sea, July 06, 1988	Explosion, fire, platform collapse	A series of explosions on the production deck of the Piper Alpha platform during the operation of the gas field, resulting in fire and destruction of the platform	The death toll was 164 people Damage is the cost of the platform

(continued)

514   A. FADEEV AND M. FADEEVA

Table 1   (continued)

Place and date	Accident/Incident	Main causes and brief description	Damage and number of victims
Atlantic Ocean, Brazilian coast, March 15, 2001	Explosion, fire, platform collapse	Damage to one of the base pontoons of a Petrobras oil production platform as a result of a series of powerful explosions. The platform sank and 125,000 tons of oil were released into the ocean	There were 10 fatalities Damage is the cost of the platform
Indian Ocean, July 27, 2005	Ship collision, fire, and platform collapse	A surf wave hit an auxiliary vessel standing next to the platform, resulting in a collision with the platform structure	There were 49 fatalities
Gulf of Mexico, October 23, 2007	A storm collision resulting in a fire	Platform oscillation due to gale force winds resulting in impact with the top of the fountain valve of the adjacent platform. There was an oil and gas leak, with subsequent ignition	21 fatalities
North Sea, May 24, 2008	Oil leak	Oil spill on the Statfjord A oil production platform; some of the oil leaked into the sea	No casualties 156 people were evacuated
Mediterranean Sea, June 15, 2008	Fire on the platform	Fire at the Norwegian oil production platform Oseberg A. The fire was contained	No casualties. Immediately after the fire, four helicopters evacuated 311 oil workers from the platform
Mediterranean Sea, September 17, 2008	Technical failures	Falling on the platform of a pipe that was to be lowered into the sea	There were 3 fatalities
North Sea, October 31, 2008	Oil leak	Oil spill on the Heather Alpha oil production platform	Fifty-six people were evacuated from the platform, a little over thirty stayed on the platform to eliminate the consequences of the accident. There was no fire

(continued)

Table 1 (continued)

Place and date	Accident/Incident	Main causes and brief description	Damage and number of victims
Sakhalin shelf, March 24, 2009	Oil leak	A release of 165 litresof oil onto the ice surrounding the Molikpaq platform as part of the Sakhalin II project, as a result of a malfunction in one of the units	The consequences of the accident were promptly eliminated, and there was no pollution of the sea
Gulf of Guinea, MAy 26, 2009	Platform attack	An attack by Nigerian fighters in a speedboat on a platform. Total oil platform security personnel repelled the attack	No casualties
Timor Sea, November 01, 2009	Fire at a mining platform	Fire at PTT Explo-ration&Production's Thailand oil platform off Australia's northwest coast. The fire broke out during oil spill response operations	No casualties. More than 28,000 barrels of oil spilled into the sea
Gulf of Mexico, April 22, 2010	Fire and platform flooding	The Deepwater Horizon platform belonging to British Petroleum (BP) sank off the coast of Louisiana after a 36-hour fire that followed a powerful explosion	There were 11 fatalities and 17 injured
Pechora Sea, September 18, 2013	Platform attack	Greenpeace activists made a new attempt to enter the Prirazlomnaya platform. Employees of the security service of Gazpromneft's oil platform repelled the attack	No casualties. The activists were detained by officers of the special-purpose unit of the Border Department of the Federal Security Service of Russia
Gulf of Mexico, July 2021	Underwater fire on a gas pipeline at a depth of 80 m	The incident took place off the coast near the town of Ciudad del Carmen (State of Campeche). Due to a gas leak from a 12-inch pipeline at a depth of 78 metres, 150 metres from the Ku-Charly platform	No one was injured in the fire

Mississippi, and Louisiana. The consequences of the accident cost several tens of billions of dollars and nearly bankrupted British Petroleum (Fadeev et al., 2019).

Due to the limited territory and difficulty of evacuation, accidents on offshore drilling platforms are usually accompanied not only by extremely serious environmental consequences, but also by a significant number of human casualties due to thermal impact of fire and toxicity of combustion products.

However, it is worth noting that analysis of statistical data on accidents at oil and gas production platforms shows a decrease in the number of accidents with catastrophic consequences in recent years. This is due to technological and structural improvements to the platforms, the use of modern safety systems, and the timely conduct of exercises.

Uncontrolled (emergency) oil spills. The implementation of hydrocarbon extraction and subsequent transportation projects is accompanied by the risks of oil or chemical spills. Equipment failure, "human factor" (personnel errors), and extreme natural conditions are the most frequent causes of accidents. When accidents occur near shorelines or in areas with delayed water exchange, the environmental consequences of accidental releases are particularly severe.

During drilling operations accidents are characterized by unexpected volley blowouts of liquid and gaseous hydrocarbons from the well in the process of drilling while penetrating zones with abnormally high formation pressure. An accident can have a long-term catastrophic nature with very large pressure differentials. Then it is possible to drill inclined wells to stop the emissions.

"Normal" (regular) accidents can be eliminated within several hours without arranging additional drilling. The danger of such emissions lies in their regularity and a long-term impact on the marine ecosystem.

Oil and petroleum product spills result in serious disturbance of marine life. The deterioration of the chemical composition of water and its physical parameters (transparency, temperature, etc.), forced change of migration routes, molting, nesting, spawning, as well as death of marine living organisms as a result of oil products getting on the surface layer of skin and plumage take place.

Environmental experts estimate that the implementation of oil extraction projects in the Barents Sea poses a risk of water area pollution of up to 100,000 km^2 and can affect the coastline of more than 4000 km in total.

Emissions to the atmosphere. Emissions of pollutants almost always accompany oil operations into the atmosphere. The flaring of associated gas and excess hydrocarbons during well testing and operations is the most common source of such emissions. Environmentalists estimate that up to 30% of flared hydrocarbons are released into the atmosphere, subsequently precipitating onto the sea surface and forming thin films around the drilling platforms.

The introduction of greenhouse gases into the atmosphere. By emitting large quantities of greenhouse gases such as CO_2 and CH_4, oil and gas activities contribute significantly to climate change. The large share of these emissions comes from the flaring of associated gas and from the combustion of oil or gas to produce energy that provides the production platform.

The combustion of associated gas in turbines required for power generation generates NO_X emissions. It is worth emphasizing the local nature of the impact of these emissions, which, however, can cause serious environmental damage to both marine and coastal ecosystems due to the possibility of "acid rains" containing large amounts of this substance.

The World Bank experts' calculations are interesting and revealing. According to them, 100 billion m^3 of associated gas flared annually is equivalent to ¾ of the volume of Russian gas that is exported or comparable to meeting the world's energy needs for 20 days.

nmVOC Emissions. Non-methane volatile organic hydrocarbons are produced due to the evaporation of crude oil during its storage or transshipment to terminals. When nmVOC interacts with NO_X, ozone is formed when exposed to the sun. Concentrations of elevated ozone that collects in the ground layer can be harmful to human health, as well as to vegetation and even buildings.

Increase in the level of seismic hazard. A significant increase in the level of seismological hazard of the region due to subsidence of rocks over vast areas may be observed during the long-term exploitation of hydrocarbon fields. This risk could result in the collapse of the upper layers of rock, leading to potentially high casualties, environmental consequences, and the propagation of a shock wave with possible earthquakes in regions remote from hydrocarbon production operations.

Today, there is no guarantee for monitoring weak earthquakes due to the remoteness of registration centers at 600–900 km from the fields in the Arctic seas. It is necessary to create seismic groups on Novaya Zemlya and Kolguev Island and other islands of the Arctic zone in order to achieve an optimal level of sensitivity and accuracy of the signals received. Kolguev, as well as other islands of the Arctic zone in order to achieve an optimal level of sensitivity and accuracy of the received signals. .

Transportation of hydrocarbons by tankers. The creation of efficient transport and engineering infrastructure capable of operating in extreme natural and climatic conditions is inextricably linked to the development of offshore fields. Obviously, hydrocarbon production and transportation risks on the shelf are much higher than on the mainland. The nature of heat exchange of the ocean surface with the underlying water layers and the atmosphere, the spatial distribution of the Earth's magnetic fields, specific climatic conditions, the duration of daylight hours, as well as the bottom topography, types of shores, and shallow tides significantly reduce the natural self-regulation of the environment. For these reasons, the development of intensive shipping and the creation of offshore production facilities in the Arctic zone requires special attention to environmental safety.

The Rationale for an Integrated (Intersectoral) Management Mechanism for the Development of Arctic Offshore Hydrocarbon Fields

At the moment, there is already a number of economic entities in the Arctic zone, including its sea area. These are, first of all, transport, extraction of biological resources, extraction of aquaculture, and, finally, extraction of mineral and hydrocarbon resources. Taking into account the diversity of economic activities of these economic entities, each of which has its own geography and national–international system of regulation and management, there is often a conflict of interests, which can lead to very negative consequences for both the sensitive ecosystem of the Arctic zone and for the development of individual sectors of the national economy.

In other words, unlike harmoniously created natural ecosystems, human activity on the Arctic seas shelf has no systemic organization, separate industries (transport, bio- and aqua-resources extraction, hydrocarbons extraction, etc.) do not form a single systemic community.

The cumulative set of connections and economic relations at the present time does not have the character of interaction directed on formation of integrally focused useful result. In other words, the complexity of economic activities in the Arctic is not the final result, but a set of parallel processes in the development of sea areas and resources of the Arctic zone. For this reason, such concepts as "oil and gas complex", "fishery complex", "transport complex", "ship repair complex", etc. are present in the economic lexicon (Matishov et al., 2001, 2005; Matishov & Denisov, 2000).

Reasoning from the perspective of the economic postulates of a market economy, a greater number of market participants leads to more competition, which is an obvious advantage, crowding out inefficient participants from the market field. Thinking within the framework of the Arctic zone we are considering the competition between fisheries and hydrocarbon production as an example. There is reason to believe that with obviously lower profits, fisheries will be displaced as well as aquatic biological resources, which are not only the object of industrial fishing, but also an element of biological diversity, which determines, to some extent, the formation of hydrocarbon resources. Thus, the development of the oil and gas industry without the support of fisheries would be profoundly dangerous.

In this regard, *there is a clear need to find a balance between economic efficiency and the possibility of conserving biodiversity.* Finding and ensuring such a balance is the main task of integrated cross-sectoral management.

It is worth noting that in the Russian Federation, the relevance of this problem has only started to be realized; the system of views and methods in this area is at the initial stage of formation, as the development of the Arctic shelf is a relatively new type of activity.

Nevertheless, Russia has accumulated considerable experience in exploiting oil and gas fields located onshore, so it seems promising to apply the management ideas developed for onshore fields to marine activities in the Arctic.

This aspect deals with the adaptation and practical application at sea of the following types of management activities: anticipatory and operational management. The above activities are closely linked and have the common goal of harmonizing management decisions aimed at the efficient and safe development of the Arctic.

Speaking about the mechanism of advanced management, it is worth noting that it is characterized by the composition of several actions performed in a certain sequence: the study of the current state of marine systems with subsequent analysis of human economic activity, modeling the upcoming anthropogenic changes in the system and their assessment, selection of optimal measures to mitigate negative consequences and, finally, implementation of ecological expertise of projects (Matishov et al., 2001, 2005; Matishov & Denisov, 2000).

The concept of integrated intersectoral management of offshore hydrocarbon field development consists of four main components:

1. Within a given water area, water column, bed and banks, all relationships and interdependencies between major ecosystem components (biotic and abiotic) are taken into account for management decisions;
2. The management actions taken should be planned and implemented in the context of the long-term development strategy of the management subjects under consideration;
3. The interrelationships among the various economic actors in the Arctic zone and the socio-environmental values and interests that are interlinked with them must be considered as a whole;
4. To achieve a strategic balance between the economic interests of corporations and the conservation of the sensitive Arctic ecosystem, all emerging territorial/productive conflicts and disagreements in economic issues must be resolved by transforming corporate interests into national ones.

The formation and development of a unified strategy and program of action for all business entities (sectors) is the foundation of integrated management methodology. However, in the case of intersectoral and traditional approaches to governance, the role of the public and the public in the process of development and decision-making is different. In the framework of traditional, branch approach to manage the population and the public are the external environment in relation to the branch. Approaches to sectoral strategic planning consider population as an external constituent, which forms the market and demand for products, or as an internal constituent, which forms the supply of labor. Thus, there is a "consumer" attitude towards society as one of the components of the profit chain. Speaking from the perspective of integrated intersectoral management, the population of the coastal region acts as an equal participant in all the processes taking place in the region. That is why the public and small indigenous peoples of the North should be involved in the procedure of decision planning, implementation, monitoring and control, i.e. to be full participants of the continuous process of interdisciplinary management both in the coastal zone and on the shelf (Matishov et al., 2001, 2005; Matishov & Denisov, 2000).

It is worth mentioning that the object of inter-branch management is a human being.

Thus, we can state that integrated intersectoral management is an impact not on the processes occurring in nature, but on the organization of human activity in order to harmonize with nature.

In cross-sectoral management, environmental principles are the main criterion for evaluating such activities.

Environmental management is undoubtedly one of the foundations of intersectoral management. It is worth noting that the rational use of natural resources within the framework of intersectoral management does not deny the possibility of exploitation of natural resources. Resources can and should be exploited by observing the following basic principles (Matishov et al., 2001, 2005; Matishov & Denisov, 2000):

(a) for renewable resources, the rate of consumption should not exceed the rate of renewal (recovery);
(b) for non-renewable resources, the rate of consumption should not exceed the rate of finding sustainable substitutes;
(c) the volume of pollutants and the intensity of their discharge into the environment during economic activities must not exceed the capacity of the environment to absorb and process these wastes.

The concept of interdisciplinary management of the Arctic offshore hydrocarbon field development differs from the generally accepted management activities in that it is based on taking into account and managing all the factors that are directly or indirectly related to the considered marine ecosystem and coastal zone.

The increasing competition for floor, coastal, aquatic and habitat space resulting from the multiple-use regime of territorial exploitation may make the sharing of ocean resources by different economic sectors incompatible. In order to solve this problem, an integral (comprehensive) assessment of the interests of economic entities, prioritization of their interests, as well as spatial zoning of water areas on a regional scale are envisaged.

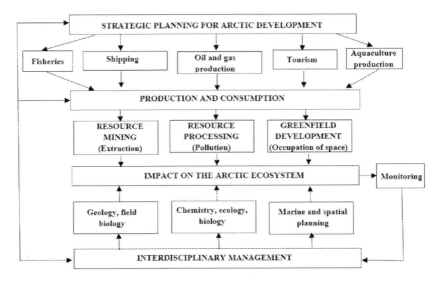

Fig. 3 Inter-sectoral management framework

The schematic diagram of inter-branch management is shown in Fig. 3 (Fadeev et al., 2019).

Sustainable Development of Coastal Regions in the Implementation of Projects on the Arctic Shelf

Sustainable development of the new oil and gas region involves the creation of mechanisms to ensure the necessary development, level of consumption, and social harmony in society, as well as sustainable development of the economy and sustainable functioning of the biosphere. The main direction of the oil and gas complex formation is to create such conditions that would contribute to the convergence of hydrocarbons' realized and potential values. The social value is understood as a set of (direct, indirect, and multiplicative) effects obtained from the development and use of hydrocarbon resources (Kryukov & Tokarev, 2007).

Such effects can be expressed not only in monetary terms but also in the form of indirect and indirect benefits, such as an increase in the value of human capital. Human capital, in this case, is understood as a set of skills embodied in a person, including education, intellect, creativity, work experience, entrepreneurial ability, etc. Thus, during the development of oil and gas resources under the centralized planning and management system conditions, it was often focused primarily on achieving a certain level of production indicators, so the real value (at the regional level) was largely different from its potential level. Ensuring an acceptable level of the social value of hydrocarbon resources is only possible if there is a developed system of modern civil society institutions, as well as an effective specialized institutional system aimed at ensuring socially oriented development of the fields. The economy of oil and gas regions in general is based on the production of hydrocarbon resources and largely depends on the pace of field development. In the process of deployment of economic activity there are significant changes in the living conditions of the population, as well as observed structural shifts in the economy and social sphere of the region, the development of transport systems, changes in the environment, as well as the strengthening of migration influx. Large-scale industrial development of the oil and gas production area, significant changes in the economy and social sphere primarily concern the population living in this territory. At the same time, the process of oil and gas resources development is accompanied by a number of both positive and negative trends, which requires certain targeted impacts from the state to correct these trends. The factor of exhaustibility of hydrocarbon resources requires taking into account not only economic, but also social consequences of resource development and conditions of regional economy functioning at all stages of production.

The specified factors demand the complex approach to an estimation of consequences of oil and gas resources development in the region and full account of both features of oil and gas resources development, and its influence on social and economic system of the region. The experience of the leading oil and gas powers shows that over the past 20–30 years the world has developed and successfully implemented approaches to integrate the development of hydrocarbon resources with a wide range of socio-economic objectives. Such approaches involve a shift in emphasis from projects' solely financial and economic impact to their social and economic outcomes. Analysis of the policy of industrially developed countries, which are simultaneously major subsoil users (Norway, Australia, USA, Great Britain, Germany), shows that the liberal approach towards institutions in the sphere of property relations, related to the use of conventional assets, is supplemented by a branched system of rules, regulations, and procedures in the sphere of use of subsoil resources. These facts provide the state with the protection of its rights as the owner of subsoil resources, as well as form the conditions for the dynamics of the development and use of non-renewable resources effective from the point of view of public interests (Kryukov & Tokarev, 2007).

The balance of interests and minimization of contradictions between the state, oil and gas companies, and the local population largely determine the extractive region's progressive and balanced socio-economic development.

Ignoring or infringing the interests of any of the above entities will inevitably lead to a significant reduction in the so-called synergistic effect based on mutual cooperation. Achieving a balance of interests between business, the state, and the population living in a given territory is one of the key conditions for the sustainable development of regions when developing deposits.

In the development of hydrocarbon deposits, it is customary to distinguish the following macroeconomic effects of their development:

- significant volume of investment attraction;
- modern technologies' transfer;
- budgetary revenues' increase;
- indirect effects related to subcontracting by regional enterprises;
- domestic employment's increase.

Table 2 presents the main positive and negative consequences for the region of the development of oil and gas fields on its territory, affecting the formation of multiplier economic effects (Kryukov & Tokarev, 2007).

All these macroeconomic effects are components of the economic multiplier effect, which expresses the existing dependence between industries. It is customary to distinguish the extractive industry, the so-called "generator" of the investment wave, from which the economic influence is transferred to other related industries. The concept of "multiplier" (from Latin "multiplicator – multiplying") was introduced in economic theory in 1931 by British economist R. Kahn. Reviewing the impact of public works, which the Roosevelt administration organized to combat the economic downturn and unemployment, he noted that government investment in public works produced a "multiplier" employment effect:

Table 2 Objective positive and negative consequences for the region of the development of oil and gas fields on its territory (Kryukov & Tokarev, 2007)

Positives	Negatives
Rapid growth of industrial production in the region	Limiting the economic dynamics to the reserves of the field
Increase in taxable base	Reduced competitiveness of other enterprises in the region due to tax preferences
Improving the profitability of hydrocarbon-related business	Gravitation of the regional economic system to the mono-product type
Rising incomes	Population differentiation by income
Impetus for regional infrastructure development	Dramatic increase in pressure on the ecological system

not only primary but also secondary, tertiary, etc. employment emerged. In other words, the initial investment spending of budget funds led to a multiplication of purchasing power and employment. These notions were soon expressed in the Keynesian theory of the multiplier effect. The multiplier in Keynesian theory refers to the coefficient showing the dependence of changes in output and national income on changes in investment. The multiplier principle is based on the interrelation of different industries or productions in the economy. In general terms it can be formulated as follows: an increase in demand in one industry will automatically cause an increase in demand in other industries, which are technologically related to each other. Thus, the demand for oil and gas equipment causes the growth of demand for metal, components, and electric power. In turn, the metallurgical plant will increase demand for ore, power plants will increase demand for gas, coal, etc. Thus, a number of investment impulses arise, which is very favorable for the economic system (Ilyinsky et al., 2006).

CONCLUSION

An analysis of foreign experience in implementing energy projects in the Far North, including the shelf, shows that none of the projects is being considered and implemented in isolation from solving social and economic problems of the territory development. The principal feature of projects in new areas—the impossibility of solving the problem exclusively within the framework of approaches focused on the pure commercial efficiency of projects for the development of hydrocarbon deposits is no less important.

In the Russian Federation, the development of the Arctic shelf has entered the practical stage. Currently, it is extremely important to transform the rich natural potential of the Arctic into the social and economic well-being of the country inhabitants.

The solution for the most important problems of the state: raising of living standards of the population, the quality and accessibility of healthcare, education, science and culture, while strengthening the statehood, is directly related to improving the economic climate in the country. For a considerable period of time, industry has been a crucial area of strengthening and developing the Russian economy, so it should concentrate the main efforts of all branches of the country's government through the implementation of large-scale offshore projects in the Arctic.

Russia needs to study the accumulated international positive experience in the development of hydrocarbon fields. In this case, an effective modernization of the country's oil and gas complex can be successfully carried out, including the solution of a wide range of social and economic problems.

The development process of hydrocarbon resources of the new regions should have an openly declared socially oriented character. A comprehensive approach to solving the problems of resource territories, taking into account the peculiarities of formation, development, and functioning of the oil and gas sector in the region, is necessary.

Development of the Arctic shelf is a state task. The government's time horizon should be much broader than that of the commercial participants in the investment project. If an investor is concerned with getting back the invested funds as soon as possible without taking high risks, the state, first, is interested in launching a creative economic process to ensure sustainable development of territories.

The strategy of sustainable development of territories in the implementation of offshore projects in the Arctic should be based on the joint use of competitive advantages of the region and the specific project, which should form the basis of the oil and gas complex management strategy in the development of offshore hydrocarbon fields (Quint, 2019).

References

C3 RF. (1999). Federal Law No. 82-FZ of 30 April 1999 'On Guarantees of the Rights of Indigenous Peoples of the Russian Federation'. No. 18. Art. 2208.

Dodin, D. A. (2007). Mineral resources of the Russian Arctic (state, prospects, directions of research). *SPb: Nauka* (766 p.). Science Publishing.

Fadeev, A. M. (2011). General issues of ecological safety of environment. In A. E. Cherepovitsyn, F. D. Larichkin, T. E. Alieva, *Ecology of industrial production: Interindustry scientific and practical journal of domestic and foreign materials FGUP "VIMI"* (Issue 1, pp. 2–11).

Fadeev, A. M. (2013). Actual issues of achieving a balance of interests between the state, oil and gas companies and the local population of the subarctic regions in the development of hydrocarbon resources of the Arctic. *North and Market: The Formation of Economic Order, 6*(37), 80–86.

Fadeev, A. M., Cherepovitsyn, A. E., & Larichkin, F. D. (2011). Foreign experience in the development of hydrocarbon resources of the Arctic continental shelf. *Economic and Social Changes: Facts, Trends, Forecast, 1*(13), 79–89.

Fadeev, A. M., Cherepovitsyn, A. E., & Larichkin, F. D. (2019). *Strategic management of the oil and gas complex in the Arctic* (289 p.). Kola Scientific Center of the Russian Academy of Sciences.

Ilyinsky, A.A., Mnatsakanyan, O. S., & A. E. Cherepovitsyn. (2006). Oil-and-gas complex of the North-West of Russia: Strategic analysis and development concepts (474 p.). Nauka.

Kryukov, V. A., & Tokarev, A. N. (2007). Oil and gas resources in the transforming economy: About the ratio of realized and potential social value of subsoil (theory, practice, analysis and estimations) (588 p.). Nauka-Center

Kutuzova, M. (2006). *In shelf development Statoil relies on local business.* Shelf projects. Special issue of Oil of Russia magazine (52 p.).

Matishov, G. G., & Denisov, V. V. (2000). *Ecosystems and bioresources of the European seas of Russia at the turn of XX and XXI centuries: Prepr* (124 p.). LLC "IPI-999".

Matishov, G. G., Denisov, V. V., Zuev, A. N., & Mishin, V. L. (2005). Methodology and technology of marine EIA. In G. G. Matishov (Ed.), *Modern information and biological technologies in the development of the resources of the shelf seas* (pp. 157–184). Nauka.

Matishov, G. G., Nikitin, B. A., & Sochnee, O. Y. (2001). *Environmental safety and monitoring in the development of hydrocarbon deposits on the Arctic shelf* (232 p.). Gazoil Press.

Nikitin, P. B., & Kibitkin, Y. A. (1999). About methodology of economic evaluation of oil and gas resources of the Russian continental shelf. *MSTU Bulletin, 2*(2), 41–46.

PJSC Gazprom Neft. Access mode: www.gazprom-neft.ru

Quint, V. L. (2019). The concept of strategizing (Vol. I, 132 p.: ill). Series "Library of the strategist". NWIU RANEHS.

Shtyrova, V. A. (Ed.). (2013). Current status and ways of development of small indigenous peoples of the North, Siberia and the Far East of the Russian Federation. Edition / of the Federation Council (2nd edition, revised and supplemented).

Steinar, N. (2006). Management of oil and gas resources of Norway. *Subsoil XXI Century, 1*, 78.

SZ RF. (2006). List of Indigenous Small-numbered Peoples of the North, Siberia and the Far East of the Russian Federation, approved by Order of the Government of the Russian Federation No. 536-r of 17 April 2006. No. 17. Art. 1905.

Innovative Scientific and Educational Projects of the Barents Euro-Arctic Region as a Resource for the Development of Interregional Cooperation in the Arctic

Konstantin S. Zaikov, Lyubov A. Zarubina,
Svetlana V. Popkova, Nikita M. Kuprikov,
Mikhail Yu. Kuprikov, and Denis O. Doronin

INTRODUCTION

The Strategy for Developing the Russian Arctic Zone and Ensuring National Security until 2035[1] defines international relations as one of the priorities for the development of the Arctic territory. The Arctic is a space

---

[1] The official Internet portal of legal information. Collected legislation of the Russian Federation, 02 November 2020, no. 44, art. 6970. Decree of the President of the Russian Federation of October 26, 2020, no. 645 "On the strategy for developing the Arctic Russian zone and ensuring national security until 2035". http://www.pravo.gov.ru. Accessed 25 June 2021.

The chapter is a revised material of a previously published article: Zaikov, K.S., Zarubina, L.A., Popkova, S.V., Kvon, D.A., Ponyaev, L.P. Joint innovative research agenda for the Arctic: Programs, projects, success stories. Sustainability (Switzerland), 2021, 13(21), 11669. https://doi.org/10.3390/su132111669.

K. S. Zaikov (✉)
Department of Regional Studies, International Relations and Political Science, NArFU named after M.V. Lomonosov, Arkhangelsk, Russia
e-mail: k.zaikov@narfu.ru

© The Author(s), under exclusive license to Springer Nature Singapore Pte Ltd. 2022
A. Likhacheva (ed.), *Arctic Fever*,
https://doi.org/10.1007/978-981-16-9616-9_20

for international dialog and cooperation, a zone of coincidence of scientific interests of the Arctic states; and its intellectual development should be carried out in close cooperation with foreign partners. The orientation of the world agenda toward solving problems associated with global challenges leads to the need to strengthen cooperation between participants in scientific and technological processes from different countries of the world.

Cross-border cooperation is an important component of international relations, which stimulates the integrated and sustainable development of regions, creates growth points for innovative projects and is focused on the active development of international economic relations. In 2020, the Government of the Russian Federation approved the Concept of Cross-Border Cooperation in the Russian Federation.[2] Strategic objectives for the modernization and innovative development of the Russian economy in the near future are implemented into the main goals of the concept, including the joint investment projects, the creation of cross-border industrial clusters, the development of international transport corridors, and the infrastructure potential of border areas. As key measures to stimulate the development of cooperation, the concept defines the development

---

[2] The official Internet portal of legal information. Collected legislation of the Russian Federation, 19 October 2020, no. 42 (part III), art. 6650. Order of the Government of the Russian Federation of 07 October 2020 no. 2577-r "On approval of the concept of cross-border cooperation in the Russian Federation". http://www.pravo.gov.ru. Accessed 25 June 2021.

L. A. Zarubina
International Cooperation Department, NArFU named after M.V.
Lomonosov, Arkhangelsk, Russia
e-mail: l.zarubina@narfu.ru

S. V. Popkova
International Cooperation Department, NArFU named after M.V. Lomonosov, Arkhangelsk, Russia
e-mail: s.popkova@narfu.ru

N. M. Kuprikov · M. Yu. Kuprikov
Moscow Aviation Institute, National Research University, Moscow, Russia
e-mail: nkuprikov@yandex.ru

D. O. Doronin
ANO Research Center "Polar Initiative", Moscow, Russia

and participation of regions in programs of cross-border cooperation with foreign states or their associations while ensuring joint funding, including the federal budget of the Russian Federation (see Footnote 2).

In the future, according to the priorities of the Strategy for Developing the Russian Arctic Zone until 2035, the Joint Innovative Research Agenda considers the following measures as trends in international cooperation in science, innovations and technologies, increasing activities for conducting fundamental and applied scientific research in the interests of the Arctic development:

- development of technologies that are critically important, including the creation of new functional and structural materials necessary for carrying out economic activities in Arctic conditions, the development of land vehicles and aviation equipment to work in the natural and climatic conditions of the Arctic, development of technologies for preserving health and increasing in life expectancy of the population of the Arctic zone;
- conducting comprehensive expeditionary research in the Arctic Ocean (including bathymetric and gravimetric work, acoustic profiling), performing hydrographic research to ensure the safety of navigation, as well as long-term hydrographic research, including deep-sea research, in order to study the underwater environment;
- development of a comprehensive plan for international scientific research (including expeditionary ones) of the state of the Arctic ecosystems, global climatic changes and the study of the Arctic (see Footnote 1) (Kudryashova et al., 2019).

International projects are recognized as one of the most effective forms of strengthening international (Arctic) scientific cooperation and a tool for integration into the global space. They contain significant potential for the development of new and support of existing technologies for the development of regions through the network multi-level cooperation (international, cross-country, national, regional, municipal levels), as well as multi-actor cooperation (scientific community, business, government, nonprofit organizations, etc.).

In the context of circumpolar international cooperation within the framework of the Joint Innovative Research Agenda and the implementation of international projects, the development of a systematic approach, it is necessary to use the resources of existing platforms for multi-level mutually beneficial cooperation.

By making the overview of "International cooperation platforms" (Barents Euro-Arctic region as a unique example of international economic interaction; the University of the Arctic as a network project; the Northern Dimension policies) the authors describe the role of northern universities in fostering innovative technologies and as providers of research-based expertise and venues for cooperation. The role of the cross-border cooperation programs in the development of innovations, examples of successful practices aimed at solving common challenges in the Arctic region, spin off effects and innovation component are defined in the part "Success stories: programs and projects". Finally, the authors propose specific recommendations to intensify Arctic research, availability of the support programs to spread technologies and innovations what lead to local growth, economic development, and new models for cooperation.

International Cooperation Platforms

The Barents / Euro-Arctic Region (BEAR) is a unique example of foreign economic interaction, cooperation between parts of the Arctic states, which is a union of regions and countries that are very different in terms of economic and social development, but have a certain commonality, and can be considered as a separate economic and geographical region of the world. BEAR is a territory adjacent to the Barents Sea, which includes the provinces of Norway: Nordland, Troms, Finnmark; the municipalities of Sweden: Västerbotten and Norrbotten; the provinces of Finland: Lapland, Northern Ostrobothnia, and Kainuu; and the regions of Russia: Murmansk and Arkhangelsk oblasts, Republic of Komi and Karelia, Nenets Autonomous Okrug. The territory of the region is 1.75 million km^2, the population is over 5 million people.[3]

The concept of the Barents cooperation was formulated and enshrined by the Kirkenes Declaration of January 11, 1993. The proclaimed goal of the cooperation is to promote the sustainable development of the BEAR, bilateral and multilateral interaction in the field of economy, trade, science and technology, environment, infrastructure, education and

---

[3] The Barentsinfo.org portal. https://www.barentsinfo.org/Barents-region. Accessed 25 June 2021.

culture, tourism, as well as the implementation of projects aimed at improving the situation of the indigenous population of the North.[4]

The core of the Barents cooperation is the relationship between Norway and Russia, and these countries have played a major role in the creation and subsequent development of the Barents Region. The Norwegian Barents Secretariat is one of the institutions that ensured the functioning of the Barents Cooperation.[5] Over the years of partnership, hundreds of joint projects have been implemented, international educational programs have been created and are operating, new partnership formats have been initiated that contribute to the promotion of innovations, action plans, and roadmaps in the Barents Region.

A powerful impetus for the development and internationalization was given by academic exchanges with the northern countries of Europe, which began in the 1990s within the framework of the scientific and educational cooperation in BEAR. Russian universities acted as one of the main subjects of international scientific and technical cooperation and a channel for the knowledge and technology transfer, training of scientific personnel for the technologies of the future (Avdonina et al., 2018; Kudryashova & Zarubina, 2019a).

This is realized through different types of activities: joint educational events, the introduction of innovative technologies in the educational process, scientific expertise of northern universities, and the implementation of joint projects. An important place is given to the development of international English-language programs with BEAR universities in such priority areas as environmental protection and conservation, resource conservation, information and communication technologies, sustainable development of the Arctic circumpolar territories, tourism, and recreation industry in the Arctic.

Examples include the interdisciplinary course "The Changing Arctic" based at the University of Oslo under the project "AwaRE: Arctic Research and Education" and the international project "Arctic Bridge" in cooperation with the University of Nord (Norway), which studied the

---

[4] Official website of the Ministry of Foreign Affairs of the Russian Federation. Barents/Euro-Arctic Region Council Basic Directions of Cooperation (Reference Information). https://www.mid.ru/diverse/-/asset_publisher/zwI2FuDbhJx9/con tent/barencev-regional-nyj-sovet-spravocnaa-informacia-. Accessed 30 June 2021.

[5] The official Internet portal of the Norwegian Barents Secretariat. https://barents.no/ru/o-sekretariate/istoria. Accessed 30 June 2021.

state of postgraduate education in Russia and Norway and harmonization of postgraduate programs (Avdonina et al., 2018; Kudryashova & Zarubina, 2019a). On an annual basis, young scientists actively participate in courses and competitions organized in the largest platforms for discussing the development of the North and the Arctic in Norway, Finland, Iceland, Canada, and other Arctic countries.

The development of skills of work in a research team, interpersonal and intercultural communication, necessary for barrier-free involvement in the international space and the processes of scientific diplomacy is relevant. It is worth mentioning the International Youth Forum "Arctic. Made in Russia", a youth school, held within the framework of the Fourth International Forum "The Arctic – Territory of Dialogue"[6]; Barents Ph.D. School—the International summer school for graduate students of the Barents region[7]; International postgraduate school "Russia in the Arctic Dialogue: local and global context",[8] as well as traditional schools of management of northern territories, energy efficiency in the Arctic, bioresources of the North, business practices on sustainable management, ecology, forestry in the subarctic region.

This training format in the form of short-term educational platforms on topical science subject-matters proves to be a successful practice that meets global trends in ensuring the quality of training of specialists. Thanks to effective cooperation with universities in the Barents region, a critical mass of well-trained specialists with a high level of education, international competencies, flexibility of thinking, and experience of intercultural communication have been formed in the northern regions of Russia. Their further involvement as managers in the industrial and business structures of the region, authorities, universities, and international organizations has contributed significantly to the development of the human resource of the region, and also to the strengthening of mechanisms of regional integration and innovative development of the territory (Kudryashova & Zarubina, 2019a).

---

[6] The International Youth Educational Forum "Arctic. Made in Russia". https://fadm.gov.ru/activity/events/arctic. Accessed 30 June 2021.

[7] Barents Ph.D. summer school. Arkhangelsk, 20–26 August 2017. https://narfu.ru/en/studies/barents_phd/. Accessed 25 June 2021.

[8] Russia in the Arctic dialogue. https://narfu.ru/en/studies/arcticschool-2019. Accessed 25 June 2021.

Over time, the vectors of international cooperation and the geography of academic mobility began to expand significantly and went beyond the BEAR borders, which took place in the context of the country's development and its strategic guidelines for increasing the competitiveness of Russian education at the world level, and export cooperation.

In the context of circumpolar cooperation, it is necessary to highlight the **University of the Arctic**[9] network project, created by the decision of the Arctic Council in 2001 and having the observer status of this international organization. The University of the Arctic is the largest international network of educational and research institutions (more than 200 organizations from the Arctic and non-Arctic states), conducting scientific and educational activities in the North. The main goal of the consortium is the production of knowledge and scientific potential through the resources of international cooperation to ensure sustainable progress in the circumpolar region and favorable conditions for the northern residents.

The topics of cooperation are extensive: development of innovations, protection and preservation of the environment, planning at the local level, climate change and sustainability, security, construction in northern climatic conditions, renewable energy, education in the North, history and current problems of international relations in the Arctic, health and well-being, and many others.

Among the most significant initiatives in the work of the Research Office of the University of the Arctic in Arkhangelsk[10] are the international project "Global Access to Higher Education in the North", aimed at increasing the attractiveness and promotion of northern universities in the global educational market; an international Ph.D. school "From Lomonosov to Nansen and beyond: energy, infrastructure, transport in the Arctic" (November 2011); the Seventh UArctic Rectors' Forum at NArFU with the participation of the Heads of 28 universities from 8 countries (June 2013); an international school "Model Arctic Council" with the participation of undergraduates and postgraduates from the USA, Canada, Norway, Sweden, Great Britain, Russia (February 2014); the Russian-American project "Natural Disasters in the Arctic" and a

---

[9] The official Internet portal of the University of the Arctic (UArctic). https://www.uarctic.org/. Accessed 25 June 2021.

[10] UArctic Research Office in Arkhangelsk. https://narfu.ru/international/university_arctic_research/. Accessed 25 June 2021.

similarly-named educational course; the international project UCCARP / UArctic Community Consultation on Arctic Research Planning (Canada), aimed at studying the request of the northern territories for scientific research and being an integral part of the international initiative ICARP III; a project to study the needs of academic mobility in the North "North-to-North Plus"; a project within the framework of the cross-year of Russia and the UK "Development of the UK – Russia Arctic Research and Collaboration Network" in 2017–2018.

In 2017, with the expert support of the Research Office, reports were translated and published in Russian, containing an analysis of global trends in scientific research in the Arctic using bibliometric and other methods. Digital Science, UberResearch, Altmetric and Elsevier Publishing House, which publishes about a quarter of all scientific journals in the world, are partners of this large-scale project in collaboration with the University of the Arctic.

UArctic in cooperation with universities in Sweden (Stockholm University, Royal Institute of Technology, Umeå University), Japan (University of Tokyo), Russia (Northern (Arctic) Federal University), and the USA (University of New Hampshire) and with the support of the Swedish Foundation for International Cooperation in Research and Higher Education STINT in 2019–2020, implemented the project "Arctic Science Integration Quest / ASIAQ".[11] Project work, including scientific internships, seminars, and joint publications, solved the problem of building a cross-disciplinary scientific partnership at the junction of four areas of knowledge: Arctic engineering, physical sciences, social sciences, medicine, and health care.

In 2020, on the basis of the Research Office, the project "Barents Sea Leadership on Marine Litter" was launched, implemented with the support of GRID-Arendal—the Norwegian Center of Excellence of UNEP (UN Environment Program) and the Ministry of Environment of Norway.[12] An online course on marine litter was launched, targeting specialized federal, regional and local government officials with the aim of networking to bring together stakeholders working on marine litter in the Norwegian and Russian parts of the Barents Region.

---

[11] Official site of the ASIAQ project. https://asiaq.org/. Accessed 25 June 2021.

[12] Project "Barents sea leadership training on marine litter". https://narfu.ru/international/projects/mezdunarodnie_proekti/detail.php?ID=343955. Accessed 27 June 2021.

Also, a unique platform for multi-level mutually beneficial cooperation between Russia, the European Union, Iceland, and Norway is the *Northern Dimension Policy* within the framework of the activities of four partnerships: in the field of environmental protection, transport and logistics, health and welfare and culture; as well the activity of the Parliamentary Forum, the Business Council and the Northern Dimension Institute.

The Northern Dimension Institute (NDI) brings together more than 30 universities and research organizations in the region and is an important expert and information platform for this format of international cooperation in northern Europe.[13]

A special case of effective cooperation is the interdisciplinary research project "Development of Think Tank Functions of the Northern Dimension Institute", which was launched in 2019 (supported by the European Commission).[14] The project involves international teams of experts from Finland, Russia, and Austria: representatives of Aalto University, NArFU, St. Petersburg State University of Economics, University of Oulu, and the International Institute for Applied Systems Analysis. They conduct interdisciplinary research on the development of logistics and ensuring the safety of maritime navigation, environmental protection, cultural innovations, health care, and the quality of life of people in the northern regions.

Within the framework of the project, training and expert seminars are organized, including research methodology and issues of interaction between the academic community and government authorities to take into account the results of scientific expertise in decision-making processes. The results of the joint scientific work form the basis for recommendations for the development of the Northern Dimension partnership policy and are presented at the annual Northern Dimension Future Forum.

Thus, the implementation of projects through the prism of the international dimension is an opportunity to expand horizons for solving the problem not only from the point of view of national approaches, but also through a transnational view of the essence of the problem,

---

[13] The official Internet portal of the Northern Dimension. https://www.northerndimension.info/. Accessed 27 June 2021.

[14] NDI Think Tank Project. https://www.northerndimension.info/projects. Accessed 27 June 2021.

taking into account the best world practices and consolidated resources of international partners.

Success Stories: Programs and Projects

Attention to international projects is due to their key characteristics, such as focus on a specific result achieved over a certain period of time using attracted grant funding; partnership and cooperation, innovation, interculturality. Modern challenges, especially concerning the Arctic region, are transnational in nature (Gorokhov et al., 2018; Kudryashova et al., 2020; Lipina, 2017; Zaykov et al., 2016, 2017, 2018). In this context, international scientific projects are becoming one of the most productive ways to develop scientific partnerships and a unifying platform for solving common challenges in the Arctic.

Projects with powerful spin off effects and an innovative component include projects that are implemented within the framework of cross-border cooperation programs.

Cross-border cooperation is one of the recognized models of cooperation between countries, a sustainable dialog mechanism and a significant research topic. According to the Foreign Policy Concept of the Russian Federation (Official Website of the Ministry of Foreign Affairs of the Russian Federation, 2016), the development of cross-border cooperation between regions is an important component of bilateral relations in the field of trade and economics, ecology, humanitarian and other areas. The concept of cross-border cooperation takes into account the accumulated experience and proceeds from the unity and integrity of the territory and the internal market of the Russian Federation and the coordination of national interests and the interests of the population of the border territory of the Russian Federation (see Footnote 2). The priorities of the programs are linked to the strategic documents of the Russian Federation.

Cross-border cooperation programs for the northern territories of Finland, Sweden, Norway, and the North-West of Russia began to be implemented in 1996 (Barents II A 1996–1999, INTERREG III A North 2000–2004), laying the foundations and principles of work on financing projects. According to the report of the interim working group of the Council of the Barents Euro-Arctic Region on the study of financial mechanisms of cooperation in the BEAR (Financing of Barents Cooperation, 2015), at present, the programs of cross-border cooperation "Kolarctic" and "Karelia", the programs Interreg North, Interreg

Baltic Sea Region Program, Northern Periphery, and Arctic Program are of particular importance for international cooperation projects in the region. *The Kolarctic program of cross-border cooperation between the EU and Russia* is recognized as the most effective instrument of partnership that best meets the priorities and tasks of the region's development and covers the entire territory of the BEAR.

The implementation of the first period of the European Neighborhood and Partnership Instrument "Kolarctic ENPI 2007–2013" program actually started in 2010 with the extension of projects until the end of 2015 and summing up the final results at the level of the program region and, in general, the EU cross-border cooperation programs in 2017.

The Kolarctic ENPI program area is about 2 million km^2 and includes Lapland (Finland), Norbotten (Sweden), Finnmark, Troms and Nordland (Norway), Murmansk Oblast, Arkhangelsk Oblast and the Nenets Autonomous Okrug (Russia), which are the main applicants by projects and recipients of funding. Surrounding areas are Ostrobothnia in Finland, Vesterbotten in Sweden, the Republic of Karelia, the Leningrad Oblast, and the city of St. Petersburg in Russia.

The overall goal of the Kolarctic Program is to reduce the periphery of the partner countries' border regions and related problems, as well as to promote the development of multilateral cross-border cooperation in the Barents Region by strengthening the economic, social and environmental potential of the territories achieved through the implementation of international projects.[15]

As a result of four project competitions, 51 projects received approval and grant support, of which 48 standard projects and 3 large-scale infrastructure projects (Myllylä & Cicero, 2015). In total, 33,420 people from 801 organizations from 12 regions and 202 municipalities of Finland, Norway, Sweden, and Russia took part in the program.

The structure of the program participants is distributed as follows: the largest number of participating organizations is government agencies. Among them, the leading role of universities and research institutions in the initiation and implementation of regional development projects should be highlighted. In total, 36 educational institutions and research organizations from the program and adjacent territory took

---

[15] Joint Operational Programme, ENPI CBC Kolarctic 2007–2013. https://www.kolarcticenpi.info. Accessed 27 June 2021.

part in the projects (including Russia—16 universities and research institutes, Finland—10, Norway—8, Sweden—2) (Kudryashova & Zarubina, 2019b).

Active participation of government bodies of all levels in projects (90 institutions, including 34 institutions from Russia) as applicants and project partners, first of all, indicates the compliance of the program objectives and implemented actions with strategic objectives and road maps for the development of territories and government support for cross-border cooperation. The active involvement of representatives of authorities at different levels is one of the key factors in the success of projects, ensuring the implementation of the achieved results and their further financial and organizational stability, which is confirmed by the results of 3 large-scale projects aimed at the infrastructural development of the Russian program area. The attracted investments totaling about 31.9 million euros made it possible to reconstruct the automobile border crossing point Borisoglebsk in the Murmansk Oblast, the highway connecting Kandalaksha and Alakurtti with the Salla BCP, and to transfer the energy supply system of the Nenets Autonomous Okrug from hydrocarbon fuel to local alternative electric energy sources (Kudryashova & Zarubina, 2018).

The following project initiatives in the field of innovation development, in which partners from the Arkhangelsk Oblast took part, can be cited as successful projects. Within the framework of the project "The Atlantic Salmon in the Barents Region", the Arkhangelsk scientists of the Northern Branch of the Polar Research Institute of Marine Fisheries and Oceanography named after N.M. Knipovich (Research Institute "SevPINRO"), together with scientists from the three countries collected genetic data on the salmon population in the Barents and White Seas, which made it possible to create a unique genetic map of the northern salmon populations and their migration patterns, as well as to develop recommendations on the most rational and scientifically based management of salmon resources in the Barents region (Kudryashova & Zarubina, 2018).

Among the main socio-economic effects of the two implemented transport projects "Safer Roads for Users" and "Barents Freeway" (lead partner—Avtodorkonsulting LLC) is the creation of a risk management model in areas where road accidents are concentrated, assessment of opportunities and proposals for the development of roadside service infrastructure, informing users on providing assistance to victims of road accidents at the direction of the cross-border road (Kudryashova & Zarubina, 2018). In addition to achieving the main goal of the project, mechanisms for long-term interaction between the actors were formed, which made it possible not only to implement further joint initiatives to develop the achieved results, but also to solve systemic problems at the regional, interregional, and interstate levels within the framework of the integrated strategy for the development of the BEAR transport system developed by the partners.

Building intercultural networks and working with information "at the intersection of cultures" created a platform for gaining valuable experience of intercultural interaction. Projects with the participation of the Ministry of Culture of the Arkhangelsk Oblast and the Arkhangelsk Museum of Local Lore brought together regional museums and more than 70 craftsmen from 11 districts of the Arkhangelsk Oblast to analyze the modern development of craft traditions in the region; to find innovative approaches in order to preserve cultural traditions; to improve cultural management and entrepreneurship in the field of creative industries, taking into account the experience of Scandinavian partners (Garcia-Rosell et al., 2013).

The "Barents Cross-Border University (BCBU+) Development Project" (2011–2013)[16] contributed to the development and launch of an integrated master's program "Information Technology in Medicine and Social Sphere", participated in the promotion of university education to meet the needs of the Barents Euro-Arctic region in the training of highly qualified specialists and the development of guidelines for the creation of a virtual cross-border campus in the BCBU network.

The team of the project "CETIA: Coastal Environment, Technology and Innovation in the Arctic" (2011–2014)[17] carried out integrated monitoring of coastal areas in order to create and implement new technological approaches to bioremediation. A joint master's program in Environmental Management in the Arctic was developed, as well as a master's program in Environmental Risk Management in the Arctic.

As a result of the implementation of the project "ArctiChildren InNet ENPI – Empowering School e-Health Model in the Barents Region"

---

[16] BCBU+: development of the Barents cross-border university. https://narfu.ru/intern ational/projects/mezdunarodnie_proekti/detail.php?ID=26127. Accessed 27 June 2021.

[17] CETIA—Coastal Environment, Technology and Innovation in the Arctic. https:// en.uit.no/prosjekter/prosjekt?p_document_id=294447. Accessed 27 June 2021.

(2012–2015), a specialized web platform for monitoring students in pilot schools was created, and research papers on the topic of children's health in the Barents Region were published.[18]

The analysis of participation of the Arkhangelsk Oblast in the Kolarctic program in 2010–2015 showed that international project cooperation with partners from the Barents region brought concrete results, contributing to a more effective solution of economic, transport, and social problems of the region, as well as strengthening international cooperation in the Barents region. The attracted resources made it possible to introduce innovative technologies and methods, improve social infrastructure, continue the transfer of knowledge and develop the knowledge-intensive cluster of the region, expand contacts and mutual understanding between people. Scientific and educational institutions of the region and organizations from various fields of activity demonstrated their readiness for cooperation, as well as a high level of competence in the international project management and communication in a cross-cultural space. As a result of the projects, platforms for network partnership were created through the combination of business, government agencies, NGOs, and authorities both at the local level and at the level of the Northwestern Federal District and BEAR.

Currently, the second period of the European Neighborhood Instrument program *"ENI Kolarctic 2014–2020"* was implemented with a total amount of funding of 66.3 million euros (including 12.4 million euros from the Russian Federation). As a result of competitions, 187 applications were submitted, of which 45 projects were approved for funding.[19]

On the example of projects with the participation of partner organizations of the Arkhangelsk Oblast, a number of technological projects aimed at introducing innovations and transfer of expertise, attracting breakthrough IT technologies (blockchain, artificial intelligence, Internet of things) to the region in order to develop knowledge-intensive clusters and key industries in the region were supported.

Examples of the innovative projects that have united partners of the northern regions in the implementation of digital technologies for the

---

[18] ArctiChildren InNet: Development of an e-health system in schools in the Barents region. https://narfu.ru/international/projects/mezdunarodnie_proekti/detail.php?ID=31455. Accessed 27 June 2021.

[19] Kolarctic CBC program. https://kolarctic.info/. Accessed 27 June 2021.

needs of the regions are "*I2P: From Idea to 3D Printing*", "*Disruptive Information Technologies for Barents Euro-Arctic Region*", "*Ice Operations*".

The project "*I2P: From Idea to Printing of Metal Products*" is being implemented in the period 2019–2022 and is aimed at developing the innovative industry of 3D printing on metal, as well as the potential of small and medium-sized enterprises using the latest additive manufacturing technologies and the scientific and practical capabilities of universities and their laboratories. Universities-partners of the project are Luleå University of Technology (lead partner) (Sweden), NArFU (Russia), University of Oulu (Finland), and University of Tromsø—Arctic University of Norway.[20]

As part of the first year of the project implementation in 2020, an economic assessment of specialized enterprises in the Russian part of the region of the Kolarctic programs (Arkhangelsk Oblasts, Murmansk Oblasts and NAO), potentially interested in the introduction of innovative technologies; mapping the local manufacturing industry; and questioning business companies in the regions was carried out with the aim of further assessment of manufacturing capabilities for the use of 3D printing technologies. International webinars and cyberlabs on additive manufacturing technologies for metal products were held. In October 2020, together with Luleå University of Technology, a "Metal Additive Manufacturing Webinar and Cyberlab" was organized with the participation of about 40 representatives of universities and business companies of Sweden, Finland, Norway, and Russia. A new collaboration platform for cooperation in BEAR in the field of additive technologies in industrial production was created: samples for experiments using a 3D printer were selected, the obtained samples were tested, and production capabilities were assessed. Experts of NArFU and Luleå University of Technology created specialists web portal www.i2metprint.com. Users of this resource will have access to the experience of modern industrial companies.

"*The Disruptive Information Technologies for Barents Euro-Arctic Region (DIT4BEARs)*" project, which is being implemented in the period 2020–2022, involves partners from all four program countries: Luleå University of Technology (lead partner) (Sweden), NArFU, St. Petersburg National Research University of Information Technologies,

---

[20] I2P: From Idea to Printing of Metal Products. https://narfu.ru/international/pro jects/mezdunarodnie_proekti/detail.php?ID=332977. Accessed 27 June 2021.

Mechanics and Optics (Russia), University of Tromsø—Arctic University of Norway, Lapland University of Applied Sciences (Finland), Non-profit Partnership of Software Developers RUSSOFT.[21]

The project implements scientific and technological partnership, technology exchange and develops innovative IT solutions to address common challenges of the Nordic partner countries in the following areas:

- SmartID: development of a system of personal identification of citizens based on blockchain technologies in the state and municipal services.
- SmartWaste: development of a smart waste management system in northern municipalities.
- SmartRoad: solving the problem of winter road maintenance in the Barents region, associated with unstable weather conditions.
- ConnectedDeer: development of IT services in the field of reindeer husbandry (IT monitoring, GPS information, ensuring the safety of keeping animals).

Technology transfer is carried out in a concept created by partners—Living Laboratory, which represents an open international innovation ecosystem focused on representatives of business, municipalities, universities and other stakeholders to take advantage of new opportunities associated with disruptive information technology. The work of the laboratory includes conducting scientific research, organizing hackathons, schools and international expert support of cases at the request of companies.

As an example, we can demonstrate the experience of organizing in 2020 the international online hackathon "Smart Solutions for the North", designed to facilitate the transfer of information technologies. For 36 hours, the hackathon participants solved problems from companies from Russia, Finland, Sweden, and Norway related to electronic identification based on blockchain technology, digital technologies in the forest industry, smart garbage collection, transport security, and reindeer

---

[21] Disruptive Information Technologies for Barents Euro-Arctic Region. http://dit4be ars.org/. Accessed 27 June 2021.

husbandry. 13 teams from various universities took part in the hackathon and presented specific solutions to the requests of business companies.

The IT technologies in ice modeling in the North Seas is used in the research project "*Ice Operations: Ice Management in the Barents Sea*", implemented by an international consortium uniting the large research center SINTEF Narvik A.S. (Norway) (lead partner), NArFU, Luleå University of Technology, Finnish Meteorological Institute, Maritimt Forum Nord and Storvik & Co OY, Sozvezdiye Oil and Gas Suppliers Association.[22] The project has a common goal—to promote the industrial development of the Arctic territories. An international team of scientists from four countries is working on the tasks of accumulating knowledge and collecting data on ice conditions in the northern seas, developing and improving navigable accessibility, and predictive mathematical models of ice conditions to ensure industrial and environmental safety during field development. They are working on recommendations for the oil and gas industry and an expert assessment of specific cases of business companies. The formation of a database on risk assessment in the Barents Sea in the context of the requirements of the Polar Code will improve the safety of maritime transport.

The international project "*DeConcrete / Eco-Efficient Arctic Technologies Cooperation*" solves the problems of international scientific research to develop new technological approaches for the recycling and environmentally friendly use of waste concrete in the Arctic.[23] NArFU is the leading partner and leader of the international research alliance of the University of Tromsø—the Arctic University of Norway, the Norwegian Research Institute SINTEF, the University of Oulu (Finland), and the Norwegian Cluster for Reinforced Concrete, of which 34 Norwegian organizations are members. Project implementation period is 2019–2022. Scientists are solving the problem of finding the most effective way for a number of physical and chemical characteristics of dismantling, separation, and reuse of concrete waste even before the stage of destruction of concrete structures. Sampling of used concrete fractions was carried out in the countries participating in the project; parallel comparative studies are being carried out. To conduct research in NArFU, a unique equipment

---

[22] Ice Operations. http://iceops.eu/. Accessed 27 June 2021.

[23] DeConcrete: eco-efficient arctic technologies cooperation (KO 4068). https://narfu.ru/deconcrete/. Accessed 27 June 2021.

was purchased—a thermal analyzer SDT650+, which allows conducting research of physicochemical and chemical transformations occurring in secondary crushed concrete and screening of concrete crushing, identification of individual minerals, and determination of their quantitative content in concrete, research of mechanisms and speed of changes occurring in concrete. This thermal analyzer, when combined with the already existing Unique Scientific Installation "Physical Chemistry of Surfaces of Nano-Dispersed Systems", made it possible to create the only analytical system in Russia for solving problems of this kind. Laboratory studies were carried out on the use of the smallest fractions (cement-concrete dust), which allowed creating a waste-free production. Possible areas of reuse of concrete structures in the most efficient way are being studied together with regional business, recommendations are being developed. Based on the results of the research carried out in collaboration with foreign scientists, 8 scientific articles were prepared and published. This program became one of 15 projects selected for participation in the international exhibition "Innovations across Borders", demonstrating the potential of international projects and their contribution to business development in the Barents Region (Oulu, September 21–25, 2020) as well as EU cross-border cooperation programs "Kolarctic", "Karelia", cross-border cooperation programs "Interreg. Baltic Sea Region", "Interreg Nord", "Northern Periphery and the Arctic" organized by Russia.

Within the framework of the international project of the Kolarctic Program *"FAMARB: Facility Management of Residential Buildings in the Barents Region"*, energy efficiency and energy saving technologies are investigated and implemented in the interaction of the industrial sector of the Scandinavian countries and the North of Russia.[24]

An international scientific alliance, represented by the University of Tromsø—the Arctic University of Norway, NArFU, the University of Applied Sciences (Oulu), the Swedish Research Institute, is working on the development of models for energy efficient management, operation and maintenance of construction projects. The results of scientific research in Norway, Finland, and Russia are being successfully implemented into practice: using the example of a demo object of NArFU,

---

[24] FAMARB: facility management of residential buildings in Barents region. https://narfu.ru/international/projects/mezdunarodnie_proekti/detail.php?ID=294062. Accessed 27 June 2021.

scientists prove the effectiveness of using the latest technologies for managing camp accommodation facilities in conjunction with the architectural features of buildings. Scandinavian technologies for energy optimization, operation, and maintenance of construction facilities, as well as possible ways to reduce the impact on the environment, have been studied and implemented at the NArFU demo facility. Experts monitor the microclimatic parameters of the premises on an ongoing basis with subsequent technical optimizations to achieve the most favorable microclimate with minimal energy consumption, creating opportunities for international business and cooperation between enterprises.

The issues of efficient use of forest resources of the North, including non-timber resources, were actively addressed within the framework of the project *"AgroFore: Agroforestry in Barents Region"* in cooperation with partners from Finland, Russia, Norway, represented by Lapland University of Applied Sciences, Finnish Institute of Natural Resources, NArFU, Norwegian Institute for Bioeconomic Research. Key thematic blocks of project work included the development of agroforestry in the North through the introduction of agroforestry practices that combined agricultural and forestry technologies and options for the multipurpose use of biological resources.[25]

The experts analyzed the historical and modern aspects of agroforestry in the Barents region, presented forecast calculations of the yield of berries, considered the issues of the economic accessibility of wild plants, analyzed the forest management practice of assessments, and conducted a study of the dynamics of post-agrogenic lands, the possibilities of their use for agroforestry purposes.

Research results on the development of agroforestry practices in Northern Europe were presented at the international Arctic Resilience Forum 2020, organized by the Working Group on Sustainable Development of the Arctic Council, chaired by Iceland.

"The Northern Axis-Barents Link" project contributes to the development of activities to address transport challenges in the region and the implementation of the tasks of the joint transport plan of BEAR, paying special attention to the current priority area—studying the potential of the main transport infrastructure of the border regions in the transport corridor "Northern Axis – Barents Link", in particular, the use of a new

---

[25] AgroFore: Agroforestry in Barents region. https://narfu.ru/international/projects/mezdunarodnie_proekti/detail.php?ID=294063. Accessed 27 June 2021.

direct federal road connection Vartius / Lutta (checkpoint on the border of the EU and the Russian Federation)—Arkhangelsk and the construction of a road between the Nenets Autonomous Okrug (Nes village) and the Arkhangelsk Oblast (Mezen).[26] Technological solutions include increasing the availability and quality of transport infrastructure, taking into account the need to develop energy supply systems and expand the use of renewable energy sources in the North. Experience shows that for some regions of Russia wind energy is the only energy resource for the population of remote areas, but the economic assessment indicates high costs and long payback periods. In this regard, the topical issue of the applicability of wind energy for remote northern territories and the assessment of economic efficiency for the needs of the Northern Sea Route will be separately studied within the framework of the project.

In general, the Kolarctic program gave a new impetus to cooperation in the North and made it possible to organize it at a qualitatively new level, both on an interregional and interstate scale. The contribution of this tool to the development of border areas is obvious and is of particular relevance in the current geopolitical situation, and it has a great potential.

OTHER CASES

It is necessary to note another important support tool aimed at stimulating the development of science and its innovative component on the part of the Russian Federation through the implementation of projects of an interdisciplinary and international nature, uniting scientists of different academic fields from leading Russian and foreign centers: it is the so-called "mega grants".

NArFU became one of the winners of the fifth round of the megagrant competition. As a result, in 2017, a grant from the government of the Russian Federation, received on a competitive basis for state support of scientific research conducted under the guidance of leading scientists in Russian educational institutions of higher professional education was allocated to establish the Arctic Biomonitoring Laboratory at NArFU. The main direction of its scientific research is the development of a methodology for monitoring, assessing, predicting, and preventing

---

[26] Northern Axis-Barents Link. https://narfu.ru/international/projects/mezdunaro dnie_proekti/detail.php?ID=332991. Accessed 27 June 2021.

risks associated with the transfer of highly toxic pollutants by biological pathways that can accumulate in food chains and spread in Arctic ecosystems (Sorokina, 2018). The work in the laboratory is carried out under the scientific supervision of Ingvar Thomassen, professor at the National Institute of Occupational Health in Oslo (Norway). The project, in addition to solving the main research problems, has become a kind of "workshop" for the training of highly qualified specialists in the field of environmental protection and human health in the Arctic. The analysis of the medical and demographic indicators of the indigenous population was carried out based on the results of studies in the central part of the Arctic zone of the Russian Federation; the choice of optimal ways to reduce the content of toxic substances in raw materials from commercial fish species, traditionally consumed by residents of the Russian Arctic, was made; a modern model of predictive assessment of risks associated with harmful effects of persistent toxicants on the human reproductive system was developed. Confirmation of the competence of the accredited person of the Arctic biomonitoring laboratory in the field of the stated research (tests) and measurements was carried out, taking into account the requirements of the interstate standard GOST ISO/IEC 17025-2019.

An innovative project that unites young people and researchers from different countries in order to study the Arctic territories, to conduct international multilateral dialog and partnership in the field of scientific and educational development of the Arctic, to train personnel, is the scientific and educational expeditionary project *"Arctic Floating University"*, implemented by NArFU since 2012 (Avdonina et al., 2019) in the high latitudes of the Russian part of the Arctic with the support of the Ministry of Science and Higher Education of the Russian Federation, the Ministry of Natural Resources of the Russian Federation, the Russian Geographical Society.

The expeditionary project consists of educational and research modules. The educational program includes a series of lectures, seminars, and workshops on a cycle of subjects that form comprehensive knowledge of the flora and fauna of the Arctic region among students and graduate students. The research module includes comprehensive monitoring of the state of the Arctic environment and the study of natural phenomena in the Arctic in the context of global climate change. For eight years of the project, 13 sea expeditions took place, in which more than 600 people took part. In general, about 300 young scientists and students were trained, incl. 90 foreign students from 20 countries of the world (Avdonina et al., 2019).

A significant contribution to the deepening of cooperation is made by the Norwegian Ministry of Foreign Affairs, which supports international projects, gives impetus to the development of new directions and "innovation zones".

One of the priority areas of international cooperation in the Arctic is the collaborative work in the field of response to ES. This is important for all Arctic countries. For example, more than 20 organizations from Norway, Russia, Iceland, Denmark, and Sweden participated in the project "MARPART: Joint Task Force Management in High North Emergency Response" (2014–2019), supported by the Ministry of Foreign Affairs of Norway. For the first time an attempt to create a scientific basis for the coordination of resources for joint actions to respond to emergencies in the Arctic and an assessment of the organizational structure and organization system of emergency response in the Arctic countries, participating in the project, was made (Kuznetsova et al., 2019).

The lead partner of the project was Nord University. A long-term forecast of the development of economic activities in the Arctic seas and a risk analysis were presented; an assessment of the organizational structure, forces, and means that ensure security in the Arctic countries participating in the project was given; an acquaintance with the systems of organizing emergency response in different countries was carried out. At the second stage, the emphasis was placed on the study and analysis of training systems for future rescue specialists in the national educational systems of the Arctic countries, as well as on the development of recommendations for improving the quality and harmonization of training programs (Kuznetsova et al., 2019).

Within the framework of the project, practical exercises and classes were carried out, through which industry professionals improved their knowledge, skills, and competencies. The results of the project have been introduced into educational programs for rescuers and managers on the prevention and elimination of emergencies.

The results of such large international projects also find their application in the planning of the Barents Rescue international exercise. These initiatives are stipulated by the intergovernmental Agreement between the Government of the Russian Federation and the Government of the

Kingdom of Norway on cooperation in the search for missing persons and rescue of people in Distress in the Barents Sea of October 04, 1995.[27]

The importance and necessity of further joint projects in this area, cooperation with emergency services and scientists from the leading Arctic world centers are of great interest, which is also reflected in the strategic document adopted in 2020 "Basic Principles of Russian Federation State Policy in the Arctic to 2035". This document defines one of the main tasks in the development of international cooperation—the assistance in building up efforts of the Arctic states to create a unified regional system of search and rescue, prevent man-made disasters and eliminate their consequences, as well as coordinate rescue forces.

The issues of international Arctic science are also defined in the Agreement on Enhancing International Arctic Scientific Cooperation within the framework of the activities of the Arctic Council, including the exchange of research data, access to facilities, joint monitoring, registration of traditional knowledge of the indigenous peoples of the North, etc.[28]

CONCLUSION

Summing up, the authors can conclude that the "Arctic fever", the intensification of the Arctic scientific partnership through programs to support the introduction of technologies and innovations, scientific stations in the Arctic latitudes directly affect the development of local territories, give an impetus to economic growth and create new models of cooperation.

International project activity, due to its integrity and multiplicity of effects (the so-called phenomenon of "circles on the water", spin-off effect) makes a significant contribution to the development of scientific research and innovation.

In the context of the openness and expansion of the boundaries of the intellectual labor market, internationalization and international scientific

---

[27] Agreement between the Government of the Russian Federation and the Government of the Kingdom of Norway on cooperation in the search for missing persons and rescue of people in Distress in the Barents Sea of October 04, 1995. *Bulletin of International Treaties* 6, June 1996, https://docs.cntd.ru/document/1901171?section=status.

[28] Agreement on Enhancing International Arctic Scientific Cooperation, signed at the Fairbanks Ministerial meeting, 11 May, 2017, https://oaarchive.arctic-council.org/han dle/11374/1916.

and technical cooperation are becoming a decisive factor in the preparation of a new type of labor force and the most demanded instrument in the context of circumpolar international cooperation and the development of a systematic approach through existing platforms of multi-level mutually beneficial partnership.

Leading positions in the development of advanced ecosystems and the implementation of high technologies, including ensuring the training of highly qualified personnel for the Arctic, creating end-to-end digital technologies, transforming priority sectors of the economy and social sphere, are occupied by universities and research institutes as holders of expertise and centers for studying the best world practices, best experience, for startups.

Involvement in the global intellectual space gives young scientists access to the world "frontier" of knowledge and foreign research resources, allows them to gain experience in international cooperation, to develop skills in working in an international research team, thereby contributing to the professional growth of a young scientist.

Assistance and encouragement of the integration of young researchers into the global communication of scientists will contribute to the building of human potential and the formation of qualitatively new labor resources in order to increase the intellectual promise of the country.

Along with the presented effective practices, for the further international scientific cooperation, it is necessary to develop effective measures of state support, new programs and forms of scientific and educational partnership for young personnel, the creation of new mechanisms for the development of exchange programs for young scientists, the formation of institutional and material infrastructure for international research and development.

The regional specificity of cooperation in the Arctic region necessitates the solution of important issues of grant support for scientific cooperation, academic mobility of undergraduates and graduate students to geographically remote northern partner universities and the organization of joint field research and expeditions that require significant financial and organizational resources. The investment in the development of scientific stations in high latitudes for field research and intensification of the Arctic scientific partnership, as well as various formats for involving and collaboration of young scientists in the North is very important.

The integration of young researchers into the global communication of scientists will contribute to the growth of human resources and the formation of qualitatively new labor resources in order to increase the intellectual potential of the country.

REFERENCES

Avdonina, N. S., Kudryashova, E. V., & Zaikov, K. S. (2019). Terrae Novae: The tenth scientific and educational expedition 'Arctic floating university'. *The Polar Journal, 9*(2), 473–475. https://doi.org/10.1080/2154896X.2019.1615202

Avdonina, N. S., Tamitskiy, A. M., & Zaikov, K. S. (2018). The seventh international forum: "The Arctic: Present and future: Perspectives and actions." *The Polar Journal, 8*(1), 213–215. https://doi.org/10.1080/2154896X.2018.1477425

Financing of Barents Cooperation. (2015). *Report of the BEAC Ad Hoc working group on financial mechanism study.* Ministry for Foreign Affairs of Finland. Helsinki. https://www.barentsinfo.fi/beac/docs/LOW_UM_Barents_eJulkaisu_A5.pdf. Accessed 27 June 2021.

Garcia-Rosell, J.-C., Hakkarainen, M., Koskinen, M., Paloniemi, P., Syjala, N., Tekoniemi-Selkala, T., & Vahakuopus, M. (2013). *Barents tourism action plan.* Erweko Oy.

Gorokhov, A. M., Zaikov, K. S., Kondratov, N. A., Kuprikov, M. Y., Kuprikov, N. M., & Tamickij, A. M. (2018). Analysis of scientific and educational space of the Arctic zone of the Russian Federation and its contribution to social and economic development. *European Journal of Contemporary Education, 7*(3), 485–497. https://doi.org/10.13187/ejced.2018.3.485

Kudryashova, E. V., Lipina, S. A., Zaikov, K. S., Bocharova, L. K., Lipina, A. V., Kuprikov, M., & Kuprikov, N. M. (2019). Arctic zone of the Russian Federation: Development problems and new management philosophy. *The Polar Journal, 9*(2), 445–458. https://doi.org/10.1080/2154896X.2019.1685173

Kudryashova, E. V., & Zarubina, L. A. (2018). International projects as a tool of regional development and cooperation enhancement (case of Arkhangelsk region participation in Kolarctic CBC programme). *Vestnik SAFU. Seriya "Gumanitarnyye i sotsialnyye nauki"* [Vestnik of Northern (Arctic) Federal University. Series "Humanitarian and Social Sciences"], *6*, 88–97.

Kudryashova, E. V., & Zarubina, L. A. (2019a). International cooperation as factor of formation of intellectual potential in the North. *Alma Mater (Vestnik vysshey shkoly)* [Alma Mater (Higher School Herald)], *11*, 23–29. https://doi.org/10.20339/AM.11-19.023

Kudryashova, E. V., & Zarubina, L. A. (2019b). Cross-border cooperation programmes as a resource of social and economic development of Barents region (case of ENPI Kolarctic programme). *Sovremenaya Evropa, 4,* 85–96. https://doi.org/10.15211/soveurope420198596

Kudryashova, E. V., Zarubina, L. A., Popkova, S. V., & Baykina, N. V. (2020). Potential of international project activity for university development. *Vysshee obrazovanie v Rossii* [Higher Education in Russia], *29*(7), 125–134. https://doi.org/10.31992/0869-3617-2020-29-7-125-134

Kuznetsova, S. Y., Zaikov, K. S., Zarubina, L. A., & Baikina, N. V. (2019). The international cooperation on emergency preparedness and response in the Arctic seas: The experience of the Northern (Arctic) Federal University named after M.V. Lomonosov. *Arkticheskie vedomosti* [The Arctic Herald], *2*(27), 11–17. http://arctic-herald.ru/?p=707

Lipina, S. A., Zaykov, K. S., & Lipina, S. V. (2017). Introduction of innovation technology as a factor in environmental modernization in Russian Arctic. *Economic and Social Changes: Facts, Trends, Forecast, 10*(2), 164–180. https://doi.org/10.15838/esc/2017.2.50.9

Myllylä, M., & Cicero, V. (2015). *Fiftyone: Information about 51 Kolarctic ENPI CBC Projects.* Lulea Grafiska AB.

Official Website of the Ministry of Foreign Affairs of the Russian Federation. (2016, November 30). Foreign Policy Concept of the Russian Federation. Approved by the President of the Russian Federation V.V. Putin, paragraph 106. http://www.mid.ru/foreign_policy/news/-/asset_publisher/cKNonkJE02Bw/content/id/2542248. Accessed 27 June 2021.

Sorokina, T. Y. (Ed.). (2018, November 26–27). Biomonitoring in the Arctic. In Proceedings of International Conference. Arkhangelsk: NArFU Publ. https://narfu.ru/upload/medialibrary/217/5-Sorokina-T.YU.-Biologicheskiy-monitoring-v-Arktike-kak-mezhdistsiplinarnyy-proekt.pdf. Accessed 27 June 2021.

Zaykov, K. S., Kalinina, M. R., Kondratov, N. A., & Tamitskiy, A. M. (2017). Innovation course of economic development in the Northern and Arctic territories in Russia and in the Nordic countries. *Economic and Social Changes: Facts, Trends, Forecast, 10*(3), 59–77. https://doi.org/10.15838/esc/2017.3.51.3;13

Zaykov, K. S., Kalinina, M. R., Tamitskiy, A. M., Saburov, A. A., & Shepelev, E. A. (2016). Scientific and educational space of the Arctic: Norway. *Arctic and North, 23,* 144–170. https://doi.org/10.17238/issn2221-2698.2016.23.144/

Zaykov, K. S., Maksimov, A. M., Tamitskiy, A. M., & Troshina, T. I. (2018). Ethnosocial situation in Arctic regions of Russia and the State national policy. *Polis (Political Studies), 2,* 57–67. https://doi.org/10.17976/jpps/2018.02.05/

INDEX

A

Abashiri, 400

AggloLab, 184

Air Force, 15, 16, 18, 33, 34, 36–38, 195, 212, 213, 215, 360, 363

Alabama, 512

Alakurtti, 540

Alaska, 15–17, 36, 68, 90, 121, 141, 193, 194, 197, 202, 213–215, 217–222, 295, 321, 359, 363, 412, 414, 416, 452, 500, 512

Alberta, 414

Aleutian chain, 194

Aleutian Islands, 194

Altai, 508

Antarctica, 195, 222, 315, 436–438

Aomori, 419

Arctic Bay, 259

Arctic Circle, 85, 101–103, 194, 206, 213, 216, 220, 277, 278, 280, 281, 295, 314, 359, 363, 369, 373, 375, 376, 379, 380, 403, 404, 408, 409, 415, 433

Arctic coast, 5, 15, 473

Arctic Corridor, 379

Arctic Council, vi, viii, 5, 7, 12, 13, 22–25, 55, 59, 92, 93, 95, 102–104, 195, 201, 203–206, 208, 210, 221, 223, 245, 251, 253, 260, 278, 282, 284, 292, 294, 311–313, 318, 320, 324, 348, 359, 361, 369, 376, 379–382, 384, 394, 397, 403, 418, 431–435, 438–442, 444, 447, 451, 452

Arctic Economic Council, 250, 403, 433

Arctic governance, 5, 7, 12, 19, 27, 93, 104, 306, 311, 318, 347, 358, 373, 376, 382–384, 395, 399, 407, 431

arcticization, 394

Arctic Military Environmental Cooperation (AMEC), 62, 90

Arcticness, 307, 420

Arctic Ocean, 6, 10, 13, 19, 20, 23, 32, 68, 78, 85, 90, 91, 93, 95, 101, 103, 120, 194, 205, 223,

---

© The Editor(s) (if applicable) and The Author(s), under exclusive license to Springer Nature Singapore Pte Ltd. 2022
A. Likhacheva (ed.), *Arctic Fever*,
https://doi.org/10.1007/978-981-16-9616-9

556 INDEX

260, 280, 292, 294, 307, 319, 357, 359, 360, 363, 369, 373, 375, 377, 384, 397, 400, 405, 433, 436, 437, 439–443, 452, 453, 499

Arctic policy, vi, 8, 10–14, 80, 98–100, 102, 127, 129, 196, 243, 248, 253, 254, 266, 279, 283, 286, 287, 294, 295, 306, 307, 309–312, 314, 315, 323–327, 339, 360, 361, 363, 373, 375, 379, 396, 397, 399, 402–404, 417, 445

Arctic powers, 39, 435

Arctic region, v, vi, 5, 8, 9, 23, 39, 48, 61, 69, 80, 86, 87, 89, 91, 92, 99, 100, 102, 104, 108, 125, 142, 246, 282, 305–307, 311–313, 315–317, 320–326, 339, 348, 367, 368, 372, 378, 380, 384, 395, 399, 413, 414, 432, 433, 445, 452, 459, 486, 498, 512

Arctic research, 39, 222, 366, 381, 399–401

Arctic resources, 9, 12, 15, 32, 37, 55, 68, 77, 101, 137, 141, 166, 187, 308, 334, 346, 377, 380, 401, 494

Arctic seas, 21, 77, 80, 122, 212, 366, 473, 475, 486, 517, 518

Arctic shelf, 77, 80, 122, 345, 346, 498, 507, 508, 519, 522, 526

Arctic states, vi, 5–7, 12, 13, 19, 22–26, 39, 55, 60, 85, 88, 91, 92, 94, 98, 99, 102, 106–108, 201, 205, 208, 223, 224, 250, 291, 292, 311, 361, 363, 366, 374, 378, 382–384, 394, 398, 402, 413, 417, 433, 435–438, 440–443, 445, 452–454, 457, 459–462, 465, 466

Arctic Strategy, 4, 15, 16, 21, 26, 37, 39, 287, 360, 372, 484, 485, 489

Arctic triangle, vi

Arkhangelsk, viii, 124–126, 131, 170, 369, 371

ASEAN, 27, 79

Asia, vii, 7, 26, 37, 47, 50, 70, 72, 74, 75, 77–79, 207, 334, 337, 340, 342, 345, 346, 358, 369, 373, 395, 404, 408, 410, 414, 418, 419, 440, 473–475, 480–482, 489, 492, 494

Asian/North Pacific (A/NP), 395

Asian states, 27, 77

Asia-Pacific, 70, 75, 79, 334, 340, 474

Atlantic, 17, 18, 35, 68, 209, 212, 215, 286, 288, 294, 362, 364, 365, 373, 441, 456, 473, 477, 482, 514

Atlantic Fleet, 35

Australia, 334, 335, 435, 438, 501, 515, 523

Austria, 537

AWACS, 36, 40

B

B-1B, 34

Ballistic Missile Early Warning System, 90

Barents Region, 394

Barents Sea, 33, 68, 78, 207, 211, 215, 277, 278, 283, 285, 286, 289, 290, 294, 295, 321, 346, 363, 456, 474, 475, 490, 506, 516

Beaufort, 68, 194, 200, 218, 263

Beijing, 4–8, 20, 25, 26, 39, 194, 201, 205–207, 223, 291, 292, 338, 339, 347, 445

Belkomur, 369, 371

INDEX 557

Belt and Road Initiative, 10, 194, 338, 347, 374, 375, 377
Bennett, Carolyn, 255, 264
Bennett, M., 219, 291, 394, 395, 418
Bering Sea, 208, 363, 396
Bering Strait, 200, 214, 415, 473
Biden, Joe, 24, 46, 196, 197, 202, 203, 212, 222, 223, 291, 343, 350, 361–363, 381
Bodø, 280, 292, 293
Bohai Bay, 17
Bolton, 442
Borisoglebsk, 540
bornite, 219
British Columbia, 414
British Petroleum, 338, 512, 515
Bureau of Indian Affairs, 220
Butte, 177, 178

C
California, 47
Canada, vi, 9, 13, 19, 22, 24–26, 33, 39, 68, 72, 78, 85, 92–94, 98, 100, 101, 106, 108, 121, 195, 201, 205, 211, 215, 241–254, 256–258, 260–266, 285, 294, 307, 311, 312, 321, 348, 358, 383, 417, 432, 452, 459, 461, 462, 480, 500, 505, 506, 513
Catlettsburg, 177
Chilingarov, Artur, 100, 284
China, v, vi, 3–15, 17–27, 37–40, 46, 50, 52, 54, 58, 70–72, 75, 79, 80, 93, 95, 102, 104, 105, 108, 172, 194–197, 201, 203, 205–208, 212, 213, 216, 222–224, 280, 284, 287, 291, 292, 335, 338–340, 342–350, 359–361, 366–369, 372–380, 383, 394, 404, 408, 417, 418, 420, 445, 474, 480, 513
China Development Bank, 368

China Telecom, 379
Chinese COSCO Shipping Specialized Carriers Co., 371
Chinese National Petroleum Corporation, 25
Chinese Navy, 9, 18
Chrétien, Jean, 243–245
Chukchi, 194, 200, 214, 218, 369, 475, 487, 507
Chukotka, 32, 125, 148, 170, 179, 186, 371, 508
climate change, vii, 4, 5, 7, 8, 11, 14, 22, 25, 37, 38, 40, 45–50, 52–55, 57, 58, 60–63, 67–71, 73, 75, 86, 88, 90, 92, 96–98, 102, 107, 108, 118, 120, 121, 123–125, 128, 194, 196, 197, 200–204, 221, 222, 224, 242, 246, 250–252, 254, 257, 259, 307–309, 325, 334, 345, 346, 348–350, 360, 361, 364, 366, 367, 377, 378, 380–384, 399, 417, 420, 517
CO2 emissions, 45, 46
coal, 71–77, 89, 126, 128, 143, 170, 199, 200, 208, 282, 341, 478, 482, 525
Coast Guard, 195, 204, 211–213, 215, 245, 292, 360, 382, 433
Cold Response 2020, 33
Cold War, 31, 35, 49, 57, 87–89, 91, 92, 95, 99, 107, 194, 204, 210, 223, 245, 246, 284–286, 288, 290, 349, 359, 363, 446, 448
Common Fisheries Policy, 307
Convention on the Conservation of Antarctic Marine Living Resources, 437, 439
Copenhagen, 295
corporate social responsibility (CSR), 148

558 INDEX

Council, 8, 10, 12–14, 25, 39, 59, 93, 95, 102, 143, 195, 203, 204, 217–221, 223, 248, 250, 260, 291, 294, 306, 311, 318, 320, 321, 324, 325, 339, 359, 367, 369, 379, 380, 382, 394, 396–398, 400, 402, 414, 416, 418, 432–435, 440, 442, 448, 451, 452, 463
Council of the European Union, 306
COVID-19, 45–47, 49, 61, 71, 76, 80, 265, 343, 360, 364, 365, 381
Czech Republic, 320

D

Danube, 461
d'Arvor, Olivier Poivre, 316, 319
DDG-75, 33
DDG-78, 33
DDG-80, 33
DeHart, James, 203, 204, 207, 222
Denmark, 9, 13, 24, 25, 78, 85, 92–94, 101, 103, 108, 195, 196, 205, 207, 215, 248, 278, 294, 311, 313, 358, 383, 452, 459, 502
Department of the Air Force, 4, 16
Department of the Army, 15, 16, 26, 212, 214
DESRON, 33
Draft Principles on the Allocation of Loss for Transboundary Harm Draft Principles, 455
Duma, 380

E

Eastern Siberian Sea, 369
East Siberian Sea, 475
East-Taymyr, 493
EEZ. *See* exclusive economic zone

Eimskip, 220
Ekofisk, 502
Erdogan, R., 433
Espoo, 177, 178
Estonia, 320, 433, 434
Eurasia, 48, 85, 90, 340, 347
Europe, vii, 4, 7, 8, 15, 26, 34, 37, 47, 49, 71, 74, 77–80, 90, 124, 195, 207, 212, 213, 293, 308, 319, 325, 334, 340–344, 346–348, 358, 369, 373, 375, 377, 408, 410, 446, 463, 473–475, 480–482, 494, 503
European Commission, 71, 105, 306, 308, 310, 311, 343
European Economic Area (EEA), 307
European Parliament, 306, 309
European Union (EU), 13, 24, 54, 71, 72, 75, 105, 283, 284, 292, 293, 305–313, 320, 324, 326, 327, 340–344, 346, 347, 349, 445
exclusive economic zone, 19, 22, 91, 106, 202, 283, 369, 436, 438, 453, 473, 475

F

F/A-18E/F, 36
F-15EX, 36
F-22A, 36
F-35B, 35, 36
Far East, 90, 130, 337, 370, 398, 401, 404, 409, 410, 414, 489, 507
Far North, 127, 144, 180, 252, 502, 525
Faroe, 101, 207, 293, 321
Finland, vii, 9, 24, 33, 85, 92, 101, 107, 195, 207, 290, 307, 311, 313, 358, 373, 379, 383, 410, 434, 452, 459
Finnmark, 280

France, vii, 12, 93, 201, 306, 308, 313–320, 326, 327, 408, 435, 438

Franz Josef Land, 32

G

G7, 46, 47

gas, 11, 12, 25, 38, 46, 50, 68–78, 101, 122, 126, 128, 150, 167, 169, 173, 175, 183, 201, 202, 208, 217–219, 250, 253, 254, 278, 283, 286, 315, 321, 324, 327, 333–342, 344–346, 348, 349, 358, 360, 366, 368, 377, 380, 382, 399, 402, 404, 408, 442, 479, 480, 485, 486, 490, 497–504, 507, 509–517, 519, 522–526

Gazprom, 94, 127, 150, 173, 380

GIUK, 35, 212, 215

Global Arctic, 394

global warming, 10–12, 46–49, 53, 54, 60–63, 86, 121, 199, 202, 246, 309, 314, 345, 348, 357

Great Britain, vii, 12, 35, 102, 435, 502, 523. *See also* United Kingdom

great power, 3–6, 12, 15, 16, 19, 21, 22, 24, 25, 50, 279, 347, 360, 361

Green Deal, 45, 71, 105, 327, 341, 349

Greenland, 9, 69, 95, 101, 103, 108, 121, 195, 196, 205–207, 209, 212, 216, 219, 284, 295, 307, 308, 311, 321, 407, 456, 506

Grøtsund, 34

Guiding Principles Concerning the International Economic Aspects of Environmental Policies Guiding Principles, 463

Gulf of Guinea, 515

Gulf of Mexico, 512, 514, 515

H

Habernia, 504–506

Harper, Stephen, 247–252, 254

Harstad, 280

High Arctic, 88, 280

High North, vi, 26, 35, 85, 87–92, 94–96, 98, 100, 102, 107, 193–195, 197, 200, 203, 204, 208, 209, 217, 219–221, 223, 225, 277–280, 284–288, 291, 292, 294, 295, 306, 447, 453

Hokkaido, vi, 395–397, 400, 401, 403, 404, 409, 410, 412–417, 419

hoppōken, 413, 414

Houston, 173

Hungary, 461

I

Ice-covered areas, 6, 445

Iceland, 8, 9, 13, 25, 33, 38, 85, 92, 95, 98, 101, 107, 195, 203, 206, 212, 217, 220, 292, 293, 307, 311, 321, 358, 372, 374, 383, 403, 404, 452, 459

Ice Silk Road, 373

ICEX, 32

Ilulissat Declaration, 93, 102, 205, 383, 437

India, 12, 13, 27, 52, 54, 58, 59, 79, 93, 95, 201, 372

Indian Ocean, 8, 55, 79, 473, 514

indigenous
native, 5, 13, 25, 69, 86, 92, 121, 123, 124, 128, 130, 131, 139, 144, 197, 200, 220–222, 248, 280, 341, 379, 381–383, 395, 420, 433, 436, 448, 457, 500, 507, 508, 520

560 INDEX

INDOPACOM, 36
International Arctic Forum, 131
International Convention for the Prevention of Pollution from Ships (MARPOL), 459
International Convention for the Safety of Life at Sea (SOLAS), 445, 459
International Court of Justice (ICJ), 454
International Energy Agency (IEA), 71–75, 77, 341
International Law Commission (ILC), 455
International Marine Organization (IMO), 453, 458
International Maritime Organization, 13, 107, 308, 397, 445
International Seabed Authority, 434
Inuit, 103, 220, 248, 249, 251–256, 259, 260, 262, 263
IR, 48, 51–53, 55–57, 59–61, 63
Iraq, 461
Ireland, 63, 320
Irkutsk, 508
Italy, 93, 201, 308, 313, 320–323, 325, 327

J
Japan, vi, 12, 13, 27, 72, 79, 93, 172, 201, 292, 340, 343, 372, 375, 383, 393–400, 402–415, 417–420, 435, 445, 461
JOGMEC, 399, 407, 408, 412
Johannesburg, 177, 178
Joint Strategic Command North, 32, 209

K
Kainuu, 532
Kamchatka, 408, 490, 508
Kandalaksha, 540
Kara Gate, 475
Kara Sea, 68, 126, 371, 473, 475
Karasjok, 280
Karelia, 508
Kemerovo, 508
Kerry, John, 24, 203, 343, 350
Khabarovsk, 414, 508
Khakassia, 508
Khanty-Mansiysk-Yugra, 508
Kinzhal, 210
Kirkenes, 206, 379
Kiruna, 9, 184
Kogalym, 182
Kola Peninsula, 32, 288, 364
Kolarctic, 308
Kolarctic Programme, 308
Komi, 170, 508
Korea, Republic of, 12, 13, 27, 72, 79, 147, 384
Kotelny, 209
Kotzebue, 194
Krasnoyarsk, 125, 173, 176, 180, 490, 508
Kuskokwim, 194, 219
Kuwait, 461

L
Labrador, 254, 256
Lapland, vii
Laptev Sea, 475
Lavrov, Sergei, 203, 285, 289
Leningrad, 508
liquified natural gas (LNG), 9, 25, 32, 75, 77, 146, 167, 175, 206, 224, 334, 335, 337–341, 345, 346, 358, 368, 370, 371, 408, 417, 478–481, 484, 485, 490–492, 494
Little Diomede, 214
Liu Xiaobo, 291

INDEX 561

LKAB, 184
London, 38, 90, 177, 178, 194
Longyearbyen, 282
Louisiana, 512, 515
Lyubertsy, 176

M
Macron, Emmanuel, 315
Madrid, 318, 323–325, 436
Magadan, 125, 148, 415, 508
Maine, 220
Manitoba, 256
Marine Protected Areas (MPA), 438
Maritime Silk Road, 373
Marshall Islands, 461
Martin, Paul, 247
Matochkin Shar, 475
McMurdo Station, 215
Mediterranean, 47, 213, 365, 441, 514
Medvedev, Dmitry, 278, 364
MetLab, 184
Middle East, 8, 47, 50, 279, 338
MiG-31BM, 209
Militarization, vi
Mississippi, 215, 516
Mitsubishi, 345, 412
Mitsui & Co., 345, 408, 411
Monchegorsk, 173, 176
Mongolia, 433
Moscow, 3, 4, 6, 7, 15, 19, 21, 22, 24–26, 38–40, 106, 125, 126, 173, 175, 176, 196, 197, 202, 203, 208–211, 213, 216, 224, 334, 336, 344, 348, 350, 362, 368, 404, 434
Munich, 173, 175
Murmansk, 90, 125, 126, 160, 170, 179, 180, 186, 204, 322, 369, 408, 490, 508
Mussolini, Benito, 321

Mys Kamenny, 127

N
Nagoya Protocol, 455
Nagurskoe, 209
Nanook, 250
NAO. *See* Nenets Autonomous Okrug
Narvik, 34
National Export-Import Bank of China, 368
National Security Strategy, 99, 118, 212
Native, 220
NATO, 4, 13, 14, 16–18, 20, 21, 24–26, 31, 33–35, 37–40, 107, 195, 210, 211, 223, 224, 260, 282, 285, 286, 288, 290, 293, 295, 359, 363, 364, 434, 447
Near-Arctic State, 7, 359
Nemuro, 400
Nenets, 124, 125, 156, 169, 170, 179, 180, 182, 371, 507
Nenets Autonomous Okrug (NAO), 156, 169, 170, 179, 180, 182
Netherlands, 93, 173, 201, 407
New Arctic, v, 86, 87, 92, 93, 95, 96, 98, 222
Newfoundland, 254, 256, 315, 504, 505
New Green Deal, 45
New Hampshire, 536
New North, 249
Niigata, 419
Niinisto, Sauli, 374
Nobile, Umberto, 321
Nome, 219, 363
non-Arctic states, vii, 12, 13, 19, 20, 22, 23, 93, 94, 201, 208, 260, 261, 311, 378, 382, 383, 395, 438, 443
NORAD, 36, 216, 245, 363
Nordland, 280

562 INDEX

Norilsk, 78, 120, 122, 126, 127, 143, 146, 147, 149, 160, 169, 171–173, 176–178, 186, 415
Norilsk Nickel, 120, 127, 147, 149, 160, 169, 171–173, 176, 178, 186
Norrbotten, 532
North America, 37, 47, 49, 74, 75, 85, 195, 220, 245, 246, 261, 289, 373, 410, 417
Northeast Asian (NEA), 394
Northeast Passage (NEP), 358, 359, 371, 372, 374, 377, 410, 412
Northern Dimension, 245, 246, 252
Northern Dimension, partnership, 308
Northern Edge 2021, 36
Northern Fleet, 15, 16, 32, 34, 209, 288, 293, 364
Northern Ostrobothnia, 532
Northern Sea Corridor, 474, 475
Northern Sea Route (NSR), 8, 9, 12, 17, 19–21, 23, 33, 37–39, 68, 78, 79, 100, 106, 125, 128, 129, 158, 202, 205, 206, 208, 209, 211, 215, 324, 334, 335, 339, 340, 358, 364, 365, 367–373, 395–397, 399, 400, 405, 408, 413–415, 419, 447, 452, 473–490, 493, 494
Northern territories, 247
North Pacific, 394, 396, 413, 418, 420
North Pacific Arctic, 394, 413, 418
North Sea, 283, 474, 502, 504, 512–514
Northwest Passage, 39, 106, 201, 215, 245, 246, 359, 412
Northwest Territories, 247, 249, 254, 256, 263
Norway, vi, vii, 8, 9, 13, 24, 25, 32–34, 39, 68, 77, 78, 85, 89,

92–94, 105, 147, 195, 205, 206, 215, 277–295, 307, 311, 321, 325, 326, 358, 361, 379, 383, 397, 403, 407, 431, 435, 452, 453, 459, 500–504, 506, 523
Norwegian Sea, 34, 293
Novaia Zemlia, 209
Novatec, 25
NOVATEK, 127, 368, 372, 408
NovaTEK. See Novatek
Novatek, 171–175, 178, 186, 322, 334, 335, 337, 338, 342, 345, 365, 368, 412, 478, 480, 490, 491
Novaya Zemlya, 32, 364, 475, 517
Novosibirsk, vii, 32, 125, 476
Novosibirsk Islands, 32, 476
nuclear, 74
Nunakput, 250
Nunalivut, 250
Nunangat, 254, 262, 263
Nunavut, 247, 251, 254, 256–258, 262, 263, 265
Nuuk, 219
Ny-Ålesund, 321, 397

O

Obama, Barack, 194, 221, 253
Ob River, 489
oil, 11, 32, 38, 58, 68, 69, 73–79, 94, 101, 122, 126, 150, 156, 166, 168, 169, 183, 200, 202, 208, 217–219, 223, 250, 253, 254, 278, 283, 286, 315, 321, 322, 324, 327, 333–337, 339, 341, 344–346, 348, 358–360, 366, 368, 369, 377, 378, 380, 382, 383, 399, 402, 404, 407, 433, 442, 452, 457, 459, 460, 462, 464, 478, 479, 484, 485, 489, 490, 493, 494, 497–505, 507, 509–517, 519, 522–526

INDEX 563

One Belt—One Road, 46, 374
Ørland, 34
Oslo, 34, 279, 282, 292
Ostrobothnia, 539
Ottawa, 92, 201, 204, 242, 245, 254, 263
Ottawa Declaration, 92, 204
Oulu, 537, 543, 545, 546

P

P-8A, 34, 217
P-8A Poseidon, 217
Paris, vii, 45–47, 50, 70–72, 173, 175, 202, 314–316, 349, 432
Payakha, 490
Pechora Sea, 515
Perm, 371
PLA, 17, 18
PLA Navy, 17
Polar Code, 13, 58, 107, 223, 308, 397, 445, 446, 459
Polar Silk Road, 10, 11, 26, 103, 194, 339, 360, 372–374
political science(s), 48, 53
Pompeo, 14, 195, 203, 206, 208, 291
Porcupine, 194
Portland, Maine, 220
post-Cold War, vii, 91
PRC, 8–11, 18, 26, 39. *See also* China
Primorsky Krai, 414, 508
Prirazlomnoye, 32, 78, 94, 499
Putin, Vladimir, 38, 131, 197, 288, 338, 348, 350, 358, 362, 364, 366, 370, 374

Q

Qatar, 334
Quebec, 177, 178, 254, 256

R

RAZ, 117–120, 122, 123, 125, 126, 128–130
realpolitik, 347, 349
Red Sea, 513
renewable, 74
Reykjavik, 203, 223, 314, 362, 380, 403, 415
Reykjavik Declaration, 203, 223
Rio Declaration, 452
Rocard, Michel, 315, 316, 318
Roland, Floyd, 249
Rome, 320
Rosatom, 335, 477, 487, 488
Rosneft, 127, 170, 412, 490, 493
Ross Sea, 438
Rota, 33
Royal, Ségolène, 315, 316
Russia, v–vii, 3–7, 9, 12–17, 19–27, 31–35, 37–40, 50, 54, 58, 62, 68, 77, 78, 85, 89, 93, 94, 99, 100, 105, 106, 108, 120–125, 127, 129, 131, 137, 142, 145–150, 155, 159, 160, 162, 169, 170, 173, 178, 179, 185–187, 194–197, 202, 203, 205–213, 215–217, 222–224, 243, 246, 250, 261, 278, 280, 282, 284–291, 293, 295, 307, 308, 311, 312, 321, 325, 326, 333–344, 346–350, 358, 360–363, 366–374, 377, 380, 382, 383, 397, 404, 405, 408–411, 416, 417, 419, 431, 432, 434, 435, 437, 443, 444, 446, 447, 459, 473–477, 480, 482–490, 493, 494, 498–501, 503, 504, 507, 508, 511, 515, 519, 526
Russian Arctic, 7, 14–16, 20, 22, 23, 25, 33, 78, 79, 99, 117, 119–129, 131, 142, 147, 151,

564 INDEX

155, 156, 160, 169–172, 179, 181, 185, 187, 206, 209, 337, 339, 345–347, 349, 350, 358, 366–370, 408, 477, 479, 481, 484, 485, 488, 490, 494, 499, 500, 507
Russian coast, 78, 447
Russian Federation, 32, 38, 99, 100, 117–119, 123, 127, 129, 130, 145, 207, 289, 334, 335, 337, 344, 368, 370, 371, 373, 434–436, 440, 443, 445, 446, 452, 474, 506–508, 519, 526
Russian navy, 16

S

Sakha, 180, 371, 410, 411, 416, 508
Sakhalin, 150, 414, 508, 515
Salekhard, 125
Salt Lake City, 177, 178
Sami, 280
Sapporo, 403, 413–415
Sarkozy, Nicolas, 315
Savikataaq, Joe, 265
Sea of China, 513
Sea of Okhotsk, 405, 474
security, 6, 7, 9, 13–16, 19, 21, 24, 26, 31, 37, 38, 49, 51, 54, 57–59, 61–63, 69–71, 86, 87, 89, 93, 96–100, 103, 105, 107, 108, 118, 119, 123, 126–128, 162, 196, 197, 204, 207, 209, 211, 215, 224, 245, 246, 248, 250, 252, 254, 255, 258, 260, 261, 279, 280, 285–290, 292–295, 307, 308, 313, 339, 341, 347, 348, 350, 358–364, 366, 367, 369, 376, 381, 382, 384, 396, 399, 417, 432, 434, 446, 447, 499, 509, 515
Security Council, 435
Sever, 209, 446, 493

Severnaya Zemlya, 32
Severomorsk, 209, 288, 293
Sevmash, 170
Shirase, Nobu, 395
Siberia, 47, 89, 146, 182, 199, 334, 339, 507
Sibir, 488
Silk Road on Ice, 373, 374
Simon, Mary, 97, 248–250, 255, 256, 266
Singapore, 12, 63, 93, 150, 339, 342, 372
Sola, 34
South China Sea, 8, 12, 20, 21, 195, 205, 213, 291
South Pole, 320, 323, 395
South Tambey Field, 368
Soviet Union, 33, 49, 90, 92, 194, 245, 288, 289, 349, 477. *See also* USSR
Spain, 33, 93, 201, 308, 313, 319, 320, 323–327, 340
Spitsbergen, 39, 89, 282, 395, 397, 432
Spitsbergen Treaty, 89
Sredny, 209
START, 90
Stavanger, 34
Stockholm, 49, 308, 452
Stoltenberg, Jens, 283–285
Støre, Jonas Gahr, 277, 280, 284, 285
St. Petersburg, 32, 125, 160, 173, 416, 488
Strait of Malacca, 79, 339, 474
Suez. *See* Suez Canal
Suez Canal, 68, 79, 80, 206, 474
Sustainable Development, 59, 72–75, 140, 141, 150, 379
sustainable growth, 115, 116, 141
sustainable development goals (SDGs), 140, 141

Svalbard, 9, 54, 89, 98, 105, 206, 277, 280, 282, 283, 289, 293, 321, 324, 326, 397, 456. *See also* Spitsbergen
Sverdlovsk, 508
Sweden, 8, 9, 24, 33, 85, 92, 101, 107, 195, 278, 290, 308, 310, 311, 313, 358, 373, 383, 434, 452, 459

T

Taimyr, 120, 170, 488, 490
T-AO-203 Laramie, 33
Tapiriit Kanatami, 249, 255, 263
Tapirisat, 255
terra nullis, 220
Thordarson, 374
Thule, 209, 216
Tiksi, 411
Timor Sea, 515
Tokyo, 90, 173, 177, 178, 222
Tomsk, 508
Transbaikal, 508
Trident Juncture, 33, 211, 446
Troms, 280
Tromsø, 34, 277, 278, 280, 284, 292
Trudeau, Justin, 241, 242, 244, 253–255, 257, 260, 263, 265
Trudeau, Pierre, 243
Trump, Donald, 4, 13, 196, 197, 202, 203, 211, 212, 215, 290, 291, 343, 360, 363, 379, 444
Tsirkon, 210
Tu-160, 209
Turkey, 47, 433
Tyumen, 125, 160, 173, 175, 508
Tyva, 508

U

Ukraine, 17, 33, 195, 208, 252, 284, 286, 312, 362

Ukrainian crisis, 33, 211, 446
UN Conference on the Human Environment, 49
UN Convention on the Law of the Sea (UNCLOS), 6, 7, 9, 19–23, 58, 91, 106, 202, 205, 358, 384, 432, 434, 437–439, 441, 443, 445, 452, 453, 460, 461, 465, 475
United Kingdom (UK), vii, 38, 72, 93, 102, 108, 201, 212, 310, 317, 340, 407, 412, 504
United Nations, 49, 50, 253, 434, 453
United Nations Human Development Programme, 49
United States, 4, 6, 7, 9, 14, 15, 20–23, 25, 31, 33, 35, 50, 71, 78, 85, 90, 92–94, 99, 106, 108, 172, 193–196, 201, 203, 205, 207, 208, 210, 212–216, 218–223, 246, 250, 260, 291, 307, 311, 334, 335, 343, 349, 350, 358, 360, 361, 363, 382, 383, 437, 438, 443, 446, 447, 452. *See also* US
United States Army, 4
UN Millennium Development Goals, 117
UN Security Council, 295, 350, 461
Ural, 143, 488
US, v, vi, 3–7, 14–22, 24–26, 32–37, 46, 62, 68, 245, 254, 280, 282, 290, 291, 293, 309, 343, 345, 346, 350, 360, 362, 398, 400, 407, 417, 447, 452, 461, 474, 475, 480, 488, 489, 502
U.S. Air Force, 37
US Army, 15, 16, 26, 37
US Marine Corps, 35
US Navy, 32, 33, 35–37, 290, 474

566 INDEX

US Special Presidential Envoy for
Climate, 24
USSR, 4, 31, 89, 90, 143, 171, 194,
209, 432, 435, 461

V
Vaigach, 488
Vankor, 490, 493
Verkhoyanks, 47
Vologda, 508
Vostok, 150, 211, 446, 490, 493
V. Pyshma, 177

W
Warren Harding, 194
Washington, 20, 22, 24, 26, 194,
196, 197, 201, 208, 212, 219,
221, 224, 245, 295, 362, 443
White Paper, 8, 10, 373, 445
World Bank, 141, 517
Wrangel, 32, 209
Wrangel Island, 32

WWCAM, 403, 413–416

X
Xi, Jinping, 340, 368, 373, 375

Y
Yakutia, 170, 180, 371, 508. *See also*
Sakha
Yakutsk, 125, 410, 416
Yamal, 9, 25, 32, 77, 127, 146, 167,
169, 180, 182, 224, 322, 334,
337, 338, 340, 345, 358, 368,
370, 371, 408, 478–481, 488,
490, 494
Yamalo-Nenets Autonomous Region,
125, 371
Yekaterinburg, 125, 175, 176, 178
Yellow Sea, 17
Yenisey, 489
Yugorskiy Shar, 475
Yukon, 194, 219, 247, 256

Printed in the United States
by Baker & Taylor Publisher Services